ROUTLEDGE HANDBOOK OF QUALITATIVE RESEARCH IN SPORT AND EXERCISE

The last two decades have witnessed a proliferation of qualitative research in sport and exercise. The *Routledge Handbook of Qualitative Research in Sport and Exercise* is the first book to offer an in-depth survey of established and emerging qualitative methods, from conceptual first principles to practice and process.

Written and edited by a team of world-leading researchers, and some of the best emerging talents, the book introduces a range of research traditions within which qualitative researchers work. It explores the different methods used to collect and analyse data, offering rationales for why each method might be chosen and guidance on how to employ each technique successfully. It also introduces important contemporary debates and goes further than any other book in exploring new methods, concepts and future directions, such as sensory research, digital research, visual methods and how qualitative research can generate impact.

Cutting-edge, timely and comprehensive, the *Routledge Handbook of Qualitative Research in Sport and Exercise* is an essential reference for any student or scholar using qualitative methods in sport and exercise-related research.

Brett Smith, PhD, is Professor of Physical Activity and Health in the School of Sport, Exercise and Rehabilitation Sciences at the University of Birmingham, UK. His research focuses on disability, sport and physical activity. He is also interested in qualitative inquiry and its possibilities for social change. Brett is Associate Editor of *Psychology of Sport and Exercise* and serves actively on seven editorial boards, including the *Sociology of Sport Journal* and *Sport, Exercise and Performance Psychology*. He is co-author of *Qualitative Research in Sport, Exercise and Health: From Process to Product*. He is also co-editor of the Routledge book series on *Qualitative Research in Sport and Physical Activity*. Brett is the founder and former Editor-in-Chief of the international journal *Qualitative Research in Sport, Exercise and Health*.

Andrew C. Sparkes, PhD and professor, is currently with the Institute for Sport, Physical Activity and Leisure, at Leeds Beckett University, UK. His research interests are inspired by a continuing fascination with the ways that people inhabit and experience their bodies differently over time, and in a variety of contexts. To explore such experiences he draws on life history, ethnography, auto-ethnography and ⋯ of *Qualitative Research in Sport, Exercise and Heal⋯ in Biographical Methods: Creative Applications*, bc⋯

ROUTLEDGE HANDBOOK OF QUALITATIVE RESEARCH IN SPORT AND EXERCISE

Edited by Brett Smith and Andrew C. Sparkes

Routledge
Taylor & Francis Group

LONDON AND NEW YORK

First published in paperback 2019

First published 2017
by Routledge
2 Park Square, Milton Park, Abingdon, Oxon OX14 4RN

and by Routledge
711 Third Avenue, New York, NY 10017

Routledge is an imprint of the Taylor & Francis Group, an informa business

British Library Cataloguing-in-Publication Data
A catalogue record for this book is available from the British Library

Library of Congress Cataloging-in-Publication Data
Names: Smith, Brett (Brett M.), editor. | Sparkes, Andrew C., editor.
Title: Routledge handbook of qualitative research in sport and exercise / edited by Brett Smith and Andrew C. Sparkes.
Other titles: Handbook of qualitative research in sport and exercise
Description: Abingdon, Oxon ; New York, NY : Routledge, 2016. | Series: Routledge international handbooks | Includes bibliographical references and index.
Identifiers: LCCN 2016012313| ISBN 9781138792487 (hardback) | ISBN 9781315762012 (ebook)
Subjects: LCSH: Sports sciences--Research--Methodology. | Exercise--Research--Methodology. | Qualitative research--Methodology.
Classification: LCC GV558 .R679 2016 | DDC 796.01/5--dc23
LC record available at https://lccn.loc.gov/2016012313

ISBN: 978-1-138-79248-7 (hbk)
ISBN: 978-1-138-35348-0 (pbk)
ISBN: 978-1-315-76201-2 (ebk)

Typeset in Bembo Std
by Swales & Willis Ltd, Exeter, Devon, UK

CONTENTS

ABOUT THE EDITORS

Brett Smith, PhD, is Professor in Physical Activity and Health in the School of Sport, Exercise and Rehabilitation Sciences at the University of Birmingham, UK. Prior to that, he was Professor in Qualitative Health Research in the School of Sport, Exercise and Health Sciences at Loughborough University. His research focuses on disability, sport and physical activity. He is also a methodologist in qualitative inquiry. Brett's research has been published widely in leading journals, such as *Social Science and Medicine*, *Health Psychology*, *Sociology of Health and Illness* and *Qualitative Research*. His research has also been communicated in numerous invited keynotes and the media, as well as to policymakers, the Houses of Parliament, all-party parliamentary groups, clinical reference groups, The Royal Society of Medicine, sport organisations, disability user groups and health professionals around the world. Brett serves on the Disability Rights UK '*Get Yourself Active*' national steering group, and on seven editorial boards, including the *Sociology of Sport Journal* and *Qualitative Research in Psychology*. He is Associate Editor of both *Psychology of Sport and Exercise* and *Sport, Exercise and Performance Psychology*, co-author (with Andrew Sparkes) of *Qualitative Research in Sport, Exercise and Health: From Process to Product* (2014), and co-editor (with Michael Giardina) of the Routledge book series on *Qualitative Research in Sport and Physical Activity*. Brett is also honoured to be the founder and former Editor-in-Chief of the international journal *Qualitative Research in Sport, Exercise and Health*.

Andrew C. Sparkes, PhD and professor, is currently with the Institute for Sport, Physical Activity and Leisure, at Leeds Beckett University, UK. His research interests revolve around the many ways that people inhabit and experience their bodies differently over time in a variety of contexts. Recent work has focused on interrupted body projects (e.g. spinal-cord injury) and the narrative reconstruction of self; ageing bodies in sport and physical activity contexts; sporting auto/biographies and body-self-culture relationships; and sensual ways of knowing and being in sport, physical activity and leisure. To explore such experiences he draws on autobiographical, life history, ethnography, auto-ethnography and narrative approaches. Andrew is co-author of *Qualitative Research in Sport, Exercise and Health: From Process to Product* (2014), and co-editor of *Advances in Biographical Methods: Creative Applications* (2015), both published by Routledge. He is Editor of the British Sociological Association *Auto/Biography Yearbook*. Andrew feels privileged to serve on the advisory boards of the following journals: *Sport, Education and Society*; *Qualitative Research in Sport, Exercise and Health*; and the *Qualitative Research Journal*. He is on the editorial board of the following journals: *Journal of Aging Studies*; *The Sport Psychologist*; *International Journal of Men's Health*; *European Physical Education Review*; *Methodological Innovations Online*; *Qualitative Research in Education*; and *Agora: Para la Educacion Fisica y el Deporte* (Spain); and *La Revista Educación Física y Deporte* (Colombia, South America).

ILLUSTRATIONS

Figures

Tables

Boxes

CONTRIBUTORS

Jacquelyn Allen-Collinson, PhD, is Reader in the Sociology of Sport, and Director of the Health Advancement Research Team (HART) at the University of Lincoln, UK. Her research interests cohere around the sociology and phenomenology of the body, including sporting bodies and injured bodies, identity and identity work, auto-ethnography and auto-phenomenography.

Michael Atkinson, PhD, is Professor and Vice Dean in the Faculty of Kinesiology and Physical Education at the University of Toronto, Canada. Michael's central research interests pertain to the experience of human suffering in/as physical culture, radical embodiment and the senses, existential phenomenology, and ethnographic research methods. Michael's research efforts include the study of fell runners, greyhound racing and fox-hunting cultures, Ashtanga yoga practitioners, violence in youth sport, epilepsy as physical culture, Parkour and depression among male athletes. He is author/editor of nine books, and his research has appeared in diverse academic journals, including *International Review for the Sociology of Sport, Body & Society, Sex Roles, Field Methods, Youth & Society,* and *Health.* Michael is a past Editor of the *Sociology of Sport Journal* and is co-editor of *Qualitative Research in Sport, Exercise and Health.*

Amy T. Blodgett, PhD, is a researcher in the School of Human Kinetics at Laurentian University, Canada. Her research is conducted in the area of cultural sport psychology (CSP), where sociocultural issues that shape sport/physical activity participation and performance are explored via contextually driven modes of inquiry. Specifically, Amy has worked with an Aboriginal community over the past nine years, engaging in CSP research grounded in praxis. This research has facilitated novel understandings of the cultural issues that are tied to Aboriginal athletes' sport participation, and revealed how their experiences can be enhanced and made more meaningful.

Virginia Braun, PhD, is an associate professor in the School of Psychology at the University of Auckland, New Zealand. A feminist and critical psychologist, her research explores gender, bodies, sex/sexuality and health. She is co-author of *Successful Qualitative Research* (Sage), and numerous other methodological works, including on thematic analysis.

Andrea Bundon, PhD, is an associate professor in the School of Kinesiology at the University of British Columbia (Canada). Her work spans the fields of the sociology of sport and critical disability studies. She is particularly interested in exploring ways that digital methods can be used to carry out community-based, participatory research projects. Her exploration of the Paralympic Games, disability sport and online networks of para-athletes has been published in the *Journal of Sport and Social Issues* and *Disability and Society*.

Shaunna Burke, PhD, is a lecturer in Exercise and Health Psychology at the University of Leeds, UK. Her research focuses on the role of physical activity in health and disease. She is particularly interested in physical activity as a complementary therapy to manage the adverse effects of cancer and improve quality of life across the disease continuum. She is also interested in the advancement of qualitative research methods within clinical and health-services research, evaluations of exercise interventions in public health and strategies to increase activity levels across the lifespan.

Cora Burnett, PhD, is a professor in the Department of Sport and Movement Studies at the University of Johannesburg, South Africa. She holds two doctorates and has published extensively in the field of Sport for Development and Peace – relating specifically to social-impact assessments. Some recent publications include special editions on the significance of sociological studies on sport within the African context. This includes the publication *Sport in Society: Issues and Controversies* (Southern-African edition) with Jay Coakley, *Stories from the Field* (with 45 case studies relating to issues of equality, gender and youth empowerment through sport) and various chapters and articles.

Nick Caddick, PhD, is a post-doctoral research fellow at the Veterans and Families Institute at Anglia Ruskin University, UK. His research explores different forms of mental-health and social-care support for military veterans and their families, particularly including non-medical alternatives such as surfing and other forms of physical activity. He explores this topic primarily through qualitative methodologies, including narrative inquiry, discourse analysis and phenomenology. He is also interested in how, through pluralistic data analysis, different methods can act as tools to explore different facets of a data set or multiple aspects of a research question.

Tania Cassidy, PhD, is an associate professor at the University of Otago, New Zealand. Tania's research interests are informed by interpretive and critical perspectives, and focus on the pedagogy of sports coaching and coach development. She is on the editorial boards of eight international journals, and is the lead author of the third edition of *Understanding Sports Coaching: The Pedagogical, Social, and Cultural Foundations of Coaching Practice*. As a consequence of Tania's community activism she is the President of the Opoho Bowling Club, and in her free time is an active hockey player and lawn bowler.

Kerry Chamberlain, PhD, is Professor of Social and Health Psychology at Massey University, Auckland, New Zealand. He is a critical psychologist whose research focuses on health and the everyday, with specific interests in medications, materiality, mundane ailments, media, food and disadvantage, as well as innovative qualitative research methodologies. He is co-editor of the book series *Critical Approaches to Health* (Routledge; with Antonia Lyons), co-author of *Health Psychology: A Critical Introduction* (Cambridge University Press; with Antonia Lyons), and co-editor of *Qualitative Health Psychology: Theories and Methods* (Sage; with Michael Murray).

Nicola J. Clarke, PhD, is a senior lecturer in sports coaching at Leeds Beckett University, UK. Her research explores parenting in youth sport from a social–psychological perspective. Using a range of phenomenological and discursive methods, she aims to understand the experiences of young sports performers, and how the social context influences parent–child interaction and relationships. Methodologically, she is interested in how pluralism can be used to enhance understanding of how psychological phenomena are experienced, and how these experiences are constructed through interaction with the world. Her teaching activities include applied developmental psychology and qualitative research methods.

Victoria Clarke, PhD, is an associate professor in Sexuality Studies at the University of the West of England, UK. Her research focuses on sexualities – particularly in relation to appearance and embodiment, and relationships and families – and qualitative methods; her books include *Out in Psychology* (Wiley), *LGBTQ Psychology* (Cambridge University Press) and *Successful Qualitative Research* (Sage).

Cheryl Cooky, PhD, is an associate professor of American Studies at Purdue University, USA. She received her PhD in Sociology and Gender Studies from the University of Southern California. Her research has been published in *Communication & Sport, Sex Roles, Feminist Studies, Journal of Sex Research, American Journal of Bioethics, Sociology of Sport Journal, Sociological Perspectives, Journal of Sport and Social Issues*, and in many edited books and anthologies. She is the President of the North American Society for the Sociology of Sport, and serves on the editorial boards of the *Sociology of Sport Journal, Communication & Sport, Qualitative Research on Sport, Exercise & Health* and the *International Review of the Sociology of Sport*.

Suzanne Cosh's (PhD) research interests lie primarily within qualitative sport psychology and critical-health psychology. In particular, she has a strong interest in athletes' mental health, athletic retirement, and body regulation and eating disorders in sport settings. Her research interests also extend to include social psychology, health psychology and mental-health research.

Melissa Day, PhD, is a reader in qualitative sport psychology at the University of Chichester, UK. Her research publications focus on the psychology of injury, trauma and disability, alongside the application of qualitative methods. She has co-authored two books and is on the editorial board for the journal *Qualitative Research in Sport, Exercise and Health*. Melissa is an accredited sport scientist (British Association of Sport and Exercise Sciences), chartered scientist (Science Council) and a registered practitioner psychologist (Health and Care Professions Council).

Nollaig Frost, PhD, is interested in qualitative and pluralistic methodology, which led to the development of the Pluralism in Qualitative Research (PQR) project, to explore the benefits and tensions of combining qualitative methods. The PQR team wrote one of the first books on pluralistic research – *Qualitative Research in Psychology: Combining Core Approaches* (ed. N. A. Frost, Open University Press, 2011) – and the project has now developed into an international network (www.npqr.wordpress.com), providing information, support and resources for researchers interested in pluralistic research. Nollaig's interests in pluralistic research approaches underpin her research in motherhood, mental illness and migration, to which she also seeks to bring feminist perspectives.

Michael D. Giardina, PhD, is Associate Professor of media, politics and cultural studies in the Department of Sport Management at Florida State University, USA, where he also serves as the Associate Director of the FSU Center for Sport, Health, and Equitable Development. He is the author or editor of 17 books, including *Sport, Spectacle, and NASCAR Nation:*

Consumption and the Cultural Politics of Neoliberalism (with Joshua Newman; Palgrave Macmillan, 2011), which received the 2012 Outstanding Book Award from the North American Society for the Sociology of Sport (NASSS), and was named on *CHOICE*'s 'Outstanding Academic Titles' list, *Sporting Pedagogies: Performing Culture & Identity in the Global Arena* (Peter Lang, 2005), which received the 2006 NASSS Outstanding Book Award, and *Qualitative Inquiry—Past, Present, and Future: A Critical Reader* (with Norman K. Denzin; Left Coast Press, 2015). He is the Editor of the *Sociology of Sport Journal*, Special Issues Editor of *Cultural Studies <=> Critical Methodologies*, and Associate Director of the International Congress of Qualitative Inquiry. Michael is also co-editor of the Routledge book series on *Qualitative Research in Sport and Physical Activity*.

Kass Gibson, PhD, is a lecturer in the Faculty of Sport and Health Sciences at the University of St Mark & St John. Plymouth, UK. Kass earned his PhD from the University of Toronto and has taught in schools, colleges and universities in New Zealand, Japan, Canada and the United Kingdom. At the University of St Mark & St John Kass teaches research methods, social theory and pedagogy. He is currently engaged in research related to exercise prescription and exercise as medicine, initial teacher education in Physical Education, constructions and experiences of mental health in elite sporting environments, and free-diving and spearfishing cultures.

Michael Anthony Hart, PhD, is a citizen of Fisher River Cree Nations residing in Winnipeg, Manitoba, Canada. He is the Canada Research Chair in Indigenous Knowledges, Director of Master of Social Work based in Indigenous Knowledges and Associate Professor at the University of Manitoba Faculty of Social Work. His work focuses on a broad range of areas including anti-colonialism, Indigenism and research with, for and by Indigenous peoples.

Ken Hodge, PhD, is a professor in sport and exercise psychology at the School of Physical Education, Sport & Exercise Sciences, University of Otago, New Zealand. His research focuses primarily on the psychosocial effects of participation in sport. In particular, he has investigated issues such as motivational orientations in sport, prosocial and antisocial behaviour in sport, athlete burnout and athlete engagement, life-skill development through sport, and self-esteem and moral development in sport.

Nicholas L. Holt, PhD, is a professor in the Faculty of Physical Education and Recreation at the University of Alberta, Canada, and director of the Child & Adolescent Sport & Activity lab. He conducts applied research to improve the physical and mental well-being of children, adolescents and their families. His diverse research programme examines psychosocial factors associated with youth sport, physical activity, play and paediatric weight management. He has published over 130 peer-reviewed articles and book chapters, and four books. His research is funded by the Canadian Institutes of Health Research and the Social Sciences and Humanities Research Council of Canada.

Tess Kay, PhD, is Professor of Sport and Social Sciences and Theme Leader for *Welfare, Health and Wellbeing* research at the Institute of Environment, Health and Societies at Brunel University, London, UK. She began her research career with her doctoral study of unemployed people's response to sport interventions in the 1980s, and since then has undertaken a wide range of policy-oriented research in the UK and internationally. Her work addresses a broad social-justice agenda, focusing on the experiences of individuals and social groups, especially those vulnerable to disadvantage, poverty and exclusion. Tess has a particular interest in the extent to which UK physical activity research remains isolated from the global health inequalities agenda, and underplays social determinants of health.

Samantha King, PhD, is a professor in the School of Kinesiology and Health Studies at Queen's University, Kingston, Ontario, Canada, where she researches the embodied dimensions of consumer culture. Her essays have appeared in venues such as *Social Text, Racial and Ethnic Studies*, the *Sociology of Sport Journal* and *Health Communication*. Her book, *Pink Ribbons, Inc: Breast Cancer and the Politics of Philanthropy* (Minnesota, 2006), was the inspiration for a 2011 National Film Board documentary by the same name. She is currently working on an interview project in which scholars who work in the field of critical animal studies discuss their personal and political relationships to eating non-human animals.

Camilla J. Knight, PhD, is a senior lecturer in the applied sport, technology, exercise and medicine research centre, in the College of Engineering at Swansea University, UK. Camilla's research examines psychosocial experiences of children in sport, focused particularly upon the influence of parents. Camilla is particularly interested in better understanding the experiences of parents, and how parents can be better supported in the youth sport environment. Camilla has used a range of qualitative methodologies to address these topics and her results have helped to inform policy and practice across a number of sports organizations.

Vikki Krane, PhD, is a professor of Teaching Excellence in the School of Human Movement, Sport, and Leisure Studies at Bowling Green State University, USA. She also is an affiliated faculty member of the American Culture Studies and Women's, Gender, and Sexuality Studies programmes. Krane teaches courses in sport psychology, gender and sport, and research. Her research focuses on gender, sexuality and sport. Krane is a former editor of *The Sport Psychologist* and *Women in Sport and Physical Activity* journals.

Amanda LeCouteur, PhD, is Associate Professor, Psychology, at the University of Adelaide, Australia, where she teaches in the fields of research methods, gender and philosophy of science. Her main areas of research include health, sport and communication. She has had a long-standing interest in social and psychological issues associated with elite performance in sport, and acts as a recruiting and development consultant in the Australian Football League. Her current research involves analysis of real-life interaction in contexts such as help-line, medical, counselling and sport settings.

Antonia C Lyons, PhD, is Professor of Psychology at Massey University, Wellington, New Zealand. She has published widely on the social and cultural contexts of behaviours related to health and their implications for individual subjectivities, gendered identities and embodied experiences. She is a co-editor (with Dr Poul Rohleder) of *Qualitative Research in Clinical and Health Psychology* (Palgrave, 2015). With Kerry Chamberlain she has co-authored *Health Psychology: A Critical Introduction* (Cambridge University Press, 2006) and co-edits the Routledge book series *Critical Approaches to Health*. Antonia is currently a co-editor for the journal *Qualitative Research in Psychology* and an associate editor for *Health Psychology Review*.

Kerry R. McGannon, PhD, is an associate professor in Sport and Exercise Psychology, Laurentian University, Canada. Her work 'bridges' psychology and cultural studies to study self-identities and critical interpretations of sport, exercise and health via interpretive qualitative methodologies. Her scholarship includes over 68 national and international presentations, and over 75 publications in refereed journals and scholarly books. She is co-editor of the books *The Routledge International Handbook of Sport Psychology*, *The Psychology of Subculture in Sport and Physical Activity: Critical Perspectives* and *Community Based Research in Sport, Exercise and Health*. She is Associate Editor of the *Journal of Applied Sport Psychology* and *Psychology of Sport and Exercise,* and Co-Editor-in-Chief of *Qualitative Research in Sport, Exercise and Health*.

Tara-Leigh McHugh, PhD, is an associate professor in the Faculty of Physical Education & Recreation at the University of Alberta, Canada. Her nationally funded programme of research is focused on working collaboratively with community partners and decision-makers to better understand and enhance the physical activity, sport, and body-image experiences of Aboriginal youth. She is currently the lead academic for the University of Alberta's Certificate in Aboriginal Sport and Recreation.

Jenny McMahon, PhD, is a researcher and lecturer at University of Tasmania in Launceston, Australia. Jenny was a former elite swimmer and represented Australia on numerous occasions. Academically, Jenny has a particular interest in Creative Analytical Practices (CAP) research, as well as sport pedagogy, sporting cultures, human rights of athletes in sport and coach education, and has published numerous journal articles and book chapters.

Brad Millington, PhD, is a lecturer in the Department for Health at the University of Bath, UK. His research is focused on physical culture, with a particular focus on sport's relationship with the environment, media production, representation and consumption, and health and fitness technologies. Brad's work appears in a range of scholarly journals. He is also the co-author of the book *The Greening of Golf: Sport, Globalization and the Environment* (with Brian Wilson, Manchester University Press).

Moss E. Norman, PhD, is an assistant professor in the Faculty of Kinesiology and Recreation Management at the University of Manitoba, Canada. He uses a qualitative, community-based research design in examining the relationship of physical culture, masculinity, embodiment and health. He is currently the principal investigator on a Social Science and Humanities Research Council-funded project that explores contemporary and historical Indigenous physical cultural masculinities in Fisher River Cree Nation (Manitoba).

Rebecca Olive, PhD, conducts work that engages with politics of identity and place in recreational sporting cultures. Her research explores representations and lived experiences in the field, as well as on social media, and how these two participatory spaces intersect. She is also interested in feminist methodologies, with a focus on using social media as a space and method for empirical research. Drawing on areas including cultural studies, gender studies, sociology and history, she has published in journals including *International Journal of Cultural Studies*, *Sport, Education & Society*, and *Media International Australia,* as well as writing for mainstream and surf media.

Catherine Palmer, PhD, is Professor of Sociology at the University of Tasmania, Hobart, Australia. Catherine's research principally explores aspects of sport and social policy, and she has published research on sport and alcohol, the commercialization of risk in adventure tourism and lifestyle sports, sport and newly arrived refugee communities, and the Tour de France.

Anthony Papathomas, PhD, is a qualitative researcher and lecturer in Sport and Exercise Psychology within Loughborough University's School of Sport, Exercise and Health Sciences, UK. Based within the National Centre for Sport and Exercise Medicine, his research explores the psychosocial impact of storytelling in clinical populations. Drawing predominantly on narrative inquiry, Anthony has published numerous papers on how personal narratives help people make sense of chronic illness and disability. He is also an advocate for the role of narrative in health-behaviour change.

Cassandra Phoenix, PhD, is a reader in the Department for Health at the University of Bath, UK. Over the last decade, her research has spanned three complementary themes: the embodiment of ageing and physical activity; everyday experiences of chronic illness and impairment; and the use of outdoor spaces to manage and promote well-being. Co-edited books include: *The World of Physical Culture in Sport and Exercise: Visual Methods for Qualitative Research* and *Sport and Physical Activity in Later Life: Critical Perspectives.*

Susanne Ravn, PhD, is Associate Professor at the Department of Sports Science and Biomechanics at the University of Southern Denmark. In her research she critically explores the embodied insights of different movement practices, and deals actively with the interdisciplinary challenges of employing phenomenological thinking into the analysis of these practices. She is the author of several books in Danish and English and has published her research in journals related to phenomenology, qualitative research methods in sport, exercise and health, dance research and sociological analysis of embodied experiences.

Emma Rich, PhD, is a reader in the department for health at the University of Bath, UK. Over the last decade she has been undertaking critical-health research examining the recent changes in policies and practices geared towards tackling the perceived risks associated with obesity, and the impact this has on young people's experiences of their bodies, weight and health practices. Her recent work is focused on digital health and the relationships among learning, technologies and health (e.g. exergaming, mobile health, social media). Her major publications (books) are *The Medicalization of Cyberspace, Education, Disordered Eating and Obesity Discourse: Fat Fabrications,* and *Debating Obesity: Critical Perspectives.*

Robert J. Schinke, Ed.D., is the Canada Research Chair in Multicultural Sport and Physical Activity and a professor in the School of Human Kinetics at Laurentian University in Canada. As a Canadian Sport Psychology Association registered practitioner, Schinke has extensive experience working with national teams and professional athletes worldwide. Robert has authored more than 100 refereed publications and co-edited fifteen textbooks. His research is supported by the Social Sciences and Humanities Research Council of Canada, the Indigenous Health Research Development Program, and the Canadian Foundation for Innovation. In addition, Robert serves as an Associate Editor for *Psychology of Sport and Exercise, The Journal of Sport and Social Issues,* and as Co-Editor for *The International Journal of Sport and Exercise Psychology.* Robert is also the current President of the Association for Applied Sport Psychology, and serves as a member of the Managing Council for the International Society of Sport Psychology.

Lee-Ann Sharp, PhD, is a lecturer in Sport and Exercise Psychology at the School of Sport, Ulster University, Northern Ireland, and is a member of the Sports and Exercise Sciences Research Institute (SESRI). Since completing her PhD in sport psychology at the University of Otago, New Zealand, Lee-Ann has conducted research within the broad area of social–psychological aspects of sport participation. In particular, Lee-Ann has explored the sport psychology consulting relationship, applied sport psychology practice with athletes and coaches, youth athlete development and the psychology of sports coaching.

Rachel L. Shaw, PhD, is a registered Health Psychologist. Her research is focused on relationships, communication and decision-making between patients and their family/carers and health-care professionals. Rachel takes a holistic approach in her research and employs qualitative methods and phenomenological methods of analysis to make sense of the data generated. Rachel has also developed expertise in evidence synthesis of qualitative and mixed methods research, which is fundamental to evidence-based health care. Rachel has published in health psychology and has authored a number of qualitative methodology textbook chapters.

Brett Smith, PhD, is Professor of Physical Activity and Health in the School of Sport, Exercise and Rehabilitation Sciences at the University of Birmingham, UK. His research focuses on disability, sport and physical activity. He is also interested in qualitative inquiry and its possibilities for social change. Brett is Associate Editor of *Psychology of Sport and Exercise* and actively serves on seven editorial boards, including the *Sociology of Sport Journal* and *Sport, Exercise and Performance Psychology*. He is co-author of *Qualitative Research in Sport, Exercise and Health: From Process to Product*, and also co-editor of the Routledge book series on *Qualitative Research in Sport and Physical Activity*. Brett is the founder and former Editor-in-Chief of the international journal *Qualitative Research in Sport, Exercise and Health*.

Jonathan A. Smith, PhD, is Professor of Psychology, Birkbeck University of London. He developed interpretative phenomenological analysis (IPA) and has applied it to a wide range of areas in psychology; for example, the transition to motherhood, clinical genetics, the experience of illness. He has published many journal papers presenting IPA studies and is first author on the major text on the approach: *Interpretative Phenomenological Analysis: Theory, Method, Research* (Smith, Flowers & Larkin, 2009, Sage). He has also edited or co-edited a number of other books, most recently: *Qualitative Psychology: A Practical Guide to Research Methods* (3rd edition, 2015, Sage).

Andrew C. Sparkes, PhD and professor, is currently with the Institute for Sport, Physical Activity and Leisure, at Leeds Beckett University, UK. His research interests are inspired by a continuing fascination with the ways that people inhabit and experience their bodies differently over time and in a variety of contexts. To explore such experiences he draws on life history, ethnography, auto-ethnography and narrative approaches. Andrew is co-author of *Qualitative Research in Sport, Exercise & Health: From Process to Product* (2014), and co-editor of *Advances in biographical methods: Creative applications* (2015), both published by Routledge.

Natalia B. Stambulova, PhD, is a professor in Sport and Exercise Psychology at School of Health and Welfare at Halmstad University, Sweden. Her professional experiences in sport psychology refer to her work for more than three decades as a teacher, researcher and practitioner in the USSR/Russia, and since 2001 in Sweden. Her research and about 200 publications relate mainly to the athlete-career topic, with an emphasis on athletes' career transitions and crises. Dr Stambulova is a member of editorial boards of several international journals, and an associate editor of *Psychology of Sport and Exercise*.

Holly Thorpe, PhD and associate professor, is a sociologist of sport and physical culture at the University of Waikato, New Zealand. Her areas of research expertise include gender, youth culture, social theory, action sports, qualitative methods and sports for development. She is the author of *Snowboarding Bodies in Theory and Practice* (2011) and *Transnational Mobilities in Action Sport Cultures* (2014), and co-editor of the forthcoming *Women in Action Sport Cultures* and *Handbook of Physical Cultural Studies*.

Paul Weate completed his M.Sc. in Sports and Exercise Psychology at the University of the West of England, Bristol. His dissertation was supervised by Victoria Clarke. He is currently completing a PhD in the Department of Psychology at the University of Bath, on the role of social media and new technologies in young people's alcohol consumption.

Toni L. Williams, PhD, is a senior lecturer in Sport and Exercise Psychology at Leeds Beckett University, UK. Her research explores the impact of physical activity in spinal-cord injury rehabilitation on health, well-being and hope. Toni's research interests also include narrative inquiry, disability studies, psychology of injury and rehabilitation, and qualitative meta-synthesis. Her work in this area has been published in leading international journals including *Health Psychology Review* and *International Journal of Qualitative Studies on Health and Well-Being*. She has also published book chapters on the use of qualitative methods to conceptually advance the field of sport and exercise science.

Brian Wilson, PhD, is a sociologist and professor in the School of Kinesiology at The University of British Columbia, Canada. He is author of *The Greening of Golf: Sport, Globalization and the Environment* (2016, with Brad Millington), *Sport & Peace: A Sociological Perspective* (2012), and *Fight, Flight or Chill: Subcultures, Youth and Rave into the Twenty-First Century* (2006), as well as articles on sport, social inequality, environmental issues, media, social movements and youth culture. He currently leads a Social Sciences and Humanities Research Council of Canada-funded project entitled 'Fostering "Sport Journalism for Peace" and a Role for Sociologists of Sport'.

ACKNOWLEDGEMENTS

Thank you to Simon Whitmore, William Bailey and Cecily Davey from Routledge for their support in developing the handbook. Gratitude is extended to Gale Winskill for her editorial skills and hard work. Thank you also to the six proposal reviewers who offered sage advice and backing.

Conversations with numerous colleagues over the years have helped shape the structure and content of the handbook. We also appreciate their encouragement for the project and critical insights offered along the way. Many thanks as well to our students. Over the years they have provided thoughtful questions and insightful comments on qualitative research. They have played a vital role in guiding what should be included in a handbook and what should be left aside for another time.

Brett would like to thank his colleagues at the University of Birmingham. Thanks as well to colleagues at Loughborough University, where the project started. The Swan in Rushes is greatly acknowledged for providing valued space to think about the handbook and develop it. A special thank you to Cassie for your love. Your kindness and patience, especially when I asked myself why I ever got into this project in the first place, helped keep me on track. Thank you also to Edward for enriching my life in many ways. If I could bottle one thing and hold it with me everyday, it would be your laugh on Team Pebble days.

Andrew would like to thank his colleagues in the School of Sport at Leeds Beckett University for their support and tolerance since he joined them. Most of all, he wishes to 'acknowledge' and thank his mum and dad, and Kitty, Jessica and Alexander for everything that they are, and for all that they bring to the world in their wonderfully different ways of being.

The most important role in such a handbook in the end is that of the authors. Without their generosity to accept our invitation to write a chapter, readiness to engage with our visions for the handbook, and energy to deliver chapters in time after reviews and comments, the book would not have ended up as it looks now. Thank you all. We hope the final product meets your expectations.

1

INTRODUCTION

An invitation to qualitative research

Brett Smith and Andrew C. Sparkes

Qualitative research is a craft skill that to master takes time, practice and intellectual engagement (Demuth, 2015). It is, as Denzin and Lincoln (2011) point out, a field of inquiry in its own right that cross-cuts disciplines, fields and subject matter. They note that a complex, interconnected family of concepts and assumptions surround the term, and that qualitative research, as a set of *interpretive* activities, privileges no single methodological practice over another. In her review of twenty-five years of rapid development in qualitative research, Lincoln describes the following situation.

> We are interpretivists, postmodernists, poststructuralists; we are phenomenological, feminist, critical. We choose lenses that are border, racial, ethnic, hybrid, queer, differently abled, Indigenous, margin, center, Other. Fortunately, qualitative research – with or without the signifiers – has been porous, permeable, and highly assimilative . . . Its adherents, and theorists have come from multiple disciplines . . . Consequently, we have acquired richness and elaboration that has both added to our confusion and at the same time, been broad and pliant enough to encompass a variety of claimants.
>
> *(Lincoln, 2010, p. 8)*

Given the open-ended nature of the qualitative research project and its multiplicity, it becomes almost impossible to provide, or impose, a single all-encompassing definition of the field. It means different things to different people at different historical periods of moments. That said, Denzin and Lincoln offer an initial generic definition.

> Qualitative research is a situated activity which locates the observer in the world. Qualitative research consists of a set of interpretive, material practices that make the world visible. These practices transform the world. They turn the world into a series of representations, including fieldnotes, interviews, conversations, photographs, recordings and memos to the self. At this level, qualitative research involves an interpretive, naturalistic approach to the world. This means that qualitative researchers study things in their natural settings, attempting to make sense of or interpret phenomena in terms of the meanings people bring to them.
>
> *(Denzin & Lincoln, 2011, p. 3)*

To interpret phenomena in terms of the *meanings* people bring to them, qualitative researchers draw on a variety of empirical materials that include case study, personal experience, life-story and life-history interviews, participant observation, artifacts, cultural texts and productions, along with observational, historical, interactional and visual texts. Accordingly, as Denzin and Lincoln point out, qualitative researchers deploy a wide range of interconnected interpretive practices, "hoping always to get a better understanding of the subject at hand. It is understood, however, that each practice makes the world visible in a different way" (2011, p. 5).

Qualitative research is a movable and constantly expanding scholarly community of practice and intellectual engagement. For example, in comparing the fourth edition of the *Handbook of Qualitative Research* published in 2011 to the third edition published in 2005, Denzin and Lincoln (2011) state that the latest edition is virtually a new volume with nearly two-thirds of the authors from the third edition being replaced by new contributors. They point out that there are 53 new chapters, authors and/co-authors, with 18 totally new chapter topics. These include contributions on critical social science, Asian epistemologies, disability communities, criteria for assessing interpretive validity, models of representation, varieties of validity, qualitative research and technology, queer theory, performance ethnography, narrative inquiry, arts-based inquiry, the politics and ethics of on-line ethnography, teaching qualitative research, and controversies in mixed-methods research.

In terms of expansion, it is interesting to note that in the 1994 edition of the *Handbook of Qualitative Research* a key chapter by Guba and Lincoln analyzed four paradigms that they considered to be competing for acceptance as the one of choice for informing and guiding qualitative inquiry. These paradigms were those of positivism, postpositivism, critical theory and related ideological positions, and constructionism. Moving on to the 2011 edition of the *Handbook*, the chapter by Lincoln, Lynham and Guba that deals with paradigms and perspectives in contention, includes the four paradigms named previously but adds the participatory paradigm. Likewise, in their introductory chapter to the first edition of the *Handbook*, Denzin and Lincoln (1994) name the following paradigms: positivist/postpositivist, constructionism, feminist, ethnic, Marxist, and cultural studies (see also Chapter 10). All but positivist paradigms can be seen to fall under the umbrella of interpretivism. In the fourth edition Denzin and Lincoln's introductory chapter adds queer theory to this list of interpretive paradigms. Therefore, the number of paradigms that inform qualitative research is not fixed but is flexible and changes over time. Interpretivism has therefore grown into a variety of different paradigms.

Even though the terrain of qualitative research is constantly shifting and characterized by multiplicity, this does not mean that a state of confusion prevails. Certainly, differences exist between the paradigms mentioned above as basic belief systems and worldviews that define for their holder the nature of the world, the individual's place in it, and the range of possible relationships to that world and its parts. However, a sense of purchase can be gained by examining the ways in which proponents of any given paradigm respond to the three fundamental questions posed by Guba and Lincoln (1994), which are interconnected in such a way that the answer given to any one question, taken in order, constrains how the others may be answered.

The three fundamental questions posed by Guba and Lincoln (1994) are as follows (see also Chapters 10, 18, 21, 25, and 29). First, the *ontological* question: What is the form and nature of reality, and, therefore, what is there that can be known about it? Second, is the *epistemological* question: What is the nature of the relationship between the knower and would-be knower and what can be known? How this question is answered is constrained by the answer given to the ontological question; that is, not just *any* relationship can now be postulated. Third, there is the *methodological* question: How can the inquirer (would-be knower) go about finding out whatever they believe can be known? Once again, the answer given to this question is constrained by the answers given to the two previous questions; that is, not just *any* methodology is appropriate.

At a fundamental level, as the work of Demuth (2015), Guba and Lincoln (1994), Krane and Baird (2005), Lincoln, Lynham and Guba (2011), Sparkes (2015), and Sparkes and Smith (2014) illustrate, researchers of different paradigmatic persuasions respond to these questions in different ways (see also Chapters 10, 25, and 29). Thus, in response to the ontology question adherents of positivism call upon naive realism, whereas those that subscribe to postpositivism connect with critical or neo realism. Rather than adhering to a form of realism, many qualitative researchers subscribe to a form of interpretivism, and therefore respond in a different way from positivists to the ontological question. For example, in response to the ontological question about the nature of reality, critical theory and other openly ideological approaches call on historical realism, constructionism on relativism, and participatory research on participative realities. In relation to the epistemological question, positivism adopts a dualist/objectivist position, and postpositivism a modified dualist/objectivist position. In terms of interpretive paradigms, critical theory adopts a transactional/subjectivist position with value mediated findings, constructionists a transactional/subjectivist position but with cocreated findings, while participatory research holds to a critical subjectivity with practical forms of knowing and cocreated findings. The responses to these two questions shape the responses to the methodological question, which for positivism is experimental/manipulative, for postpositivism is modified experimental/manipulative, for critical theory is dialogical/dialectical, for constructionism is hermeneutic/dialectical, and for participatory it is political participation in terms of collaborative or community action inquiry.

How these three questions are answered, as Lincoln, Lynham and Guba (2011) illustrate, has further implications for how each paradigm positions itself on selected practical issues, such as the aims and purpose of inquiry, researcher posture, the role of values in the inquiry, the criteria used to judge the quality of the inquiry, and the nature of "voice" within the inquiry. For example, with regard to inquirer posture, for positivists it is that of the disinterested scientist who should remain distant and detached. In contrast, the constructionist researcher is seen as a coconstructor of knowledge, of understanding and interpretation of the meaning of lived experiences. Different again, is the posture adopted by the critical researcher, which involves being an activist and transformative intellectual.

As Lincoln, Lynham and Guba (2011), and Sparkes and Smith (2014) argue, the differences that exist between paradigms lead researchers working within them to generate different questions, develop different research designs, use different techniques to collect various kinds of data, perform different types of analyses, represent their findings in different ways, and judge the "quality" of their studies using different criteria. For some, these differences are problematic. For us, however, such differences are to be celebrated and valued because they allow us to know and understand the social world, including that of sport and exercise, in diverse and enriched ways.

The proliferation of paradigms, perspectives, traditions, theories, methodologies and methods signaled above, has been mirrored in the rapid growth of, and importance attached to, qualitative research in the domain of sport and exercise. For example, in their review of qualitative research published in three sports psychology journals during 2000–2009, Culver, Gilbert and Sparkes (2012) point to a 68% increase in the percentage of qualitative studies published since the period 1990–1999 (from 17.3% to 29%). They also found that there was a significant increase in the number of authors publishing qualitative research in these journals. Accordingly, not only is more qualitative research being published in sport psychology journals but also, very importantly, more scholars are engaging with and producing qualitative work of different kinds. While similar numerical comparisons are not available in relation to sociological journals, such as the *Sociology of Sport Journal*, the *International Review for the Sociology of Sport*, *Sport, Education and Society*, and *Journal of Sport and Social Issues*, it is self-evident from what is published within them that such journals are favorably inclined towards and supportive of qualitative research of various forms.

A significant marker in the development and legitimation of qualitative research in sport and exercise was the launch, in 2009, of a new journal by Routledge, entitled *Qualitative Research in Sport, Exercise and Health* (twitter @QualiSEH). This journal is dedicated to supporting work produced in different paradigms and encourages innovative methodologies within a multidisciplinary framework. The success of this journal is evidenced by the diverse range of articles that have appeared in it to date, and the international nature of the authors who submit their work there for consideration. For example, yearly this journal receives over 200 manuscripts from over 100 different authors around the globe. In 2012 the journal was also awarded "Gold" by peers for the best special issue published by all Routledge journals (over 50) that year on the Olympics and Paralympics. There is also an ever-growing number of conferences and workshops attempting to address the demand for qualitative research from students, researchers, practitioners, and policymakers. For instance, the *International Qualitative Conference in Sport and Exercise* now occurs every two years, attracting established scholars and newcomers from around the world.

Finally, the rapid growth of interest in qualitative research in sport and exercise is evident in the increasing number of books devoted specifically to this topic. Most recently, these include the following: *Qualitative Research in Physical Activity and the Health Professions* (Pitney & Parker, 2009), *Research Methods for Sport Studies (2nd edition)* (Gratton & Jones, 2010), *Qualitative Research for Physical Culture* (Markula & Silk, 2011), *Qualitative Research in Sport and Physical Activity* (Jones, Brown, & Holloway, 2012), *Qualitative Research on Sport and Physical Culture* (Young & Atkinson, 2012), and *Qualitative Research in Sport, Exercise and Health: From Process to Product* (Sparkes & Smith, 2014). These books are excellent resources for seasoned qualitative researchers, as well as for newcomers to the field. This said, as we know from our own experience of producing one of the books named above, we had to cover a lot of ground within the word limits imposed on us by the publishers. Consequently, we necessarily touched on many issues but were unable to deal with any of those in an appropriate depth. There was also far too much we had to omit about qualitative research. As such, we did the best job we could, but feel and know we could have done better. We are sure the authors of the other books named earlier will validate our experiences.

The *Routledge International Handbook of Qualitative Research in Sport and Exercise*, the first of its kind, allows the shortcomings of any one book as we have described above, to be rectified. Of course, no handbook can cover *everything*, certainly not to all readers' satisfaction. Whereas a handbook can cover much more than a book, handbooks will also always contain gaps, absences, different concerns, and differently organized content. That accepted, this *Handbook* extends what has been written in qualitative books on sport and exercise by offering a highly varied, deep, and detailed menu of qualitative research. Written by leading scholars and some of the best emerging talents, the chapters in the *Handbook* operate collectively to provide a wide-ranging, original, timely, and cutting-edge resource for students, established scholars, and scholars who wish to learn about qualitative research. For example, chapters map in some detail commonly used and more novel ways of collecting, analyzing, and representing data in the sport and exercise sciences. Many chapters also push boundaries by offering an expanded vision of what the future might hold, in terms of both the process and products of inquiry. As such, the contributors to the *Handbook* consolidate what we know, but also ask critical questions and pose challenging dilemmas to disturb taken-for-granted ways of thinking, and guard against any misplaced sense of methodological complacency that might occur.

The *Handbook* contains 38 chapters, with the majority of the 49 contributors coming from the disciplines of the Sociology of Sport, Sport and Exercise Psychology, or Sport Coaching. However, most of these authors here cross discipline boundaries by drawing on work from both inside and outside their disciplinary home to support points, serve as examples, stimulate debate, and so on. Several leading figures from "mainstream" qualitative research also contribute chapters. They not only extend their previous work, but also connect with different disciplines in the sport and exercise sciences. Crossing boundaries is no easy task (Smith & McGannon, 2015; Sparkes & Smith, 2016). We are therefore grateful to all contributors for doing the hard work of moving outside their discipline and engaging with different vocabularies, ways of thinking, and histories. The combination of all these scholars, and the different disciplines within the sport and exercise sciences that are engaged with here, help make the *Handbook* further accessible and relevant for the widest possible audience.

The chapters in the *Handbook* are organized into six parts. We appreciate that certain chapters may seem more protypical of that part than others. Some chapters may fit equally comfortably in two or three parts simultaneously. Therefore, we suggest that readers use the categorization of parts as a guide. The guide might be useful for readers who wish to devour the *Handbook* in its entirety, or to nibble selectively at its chapters, depending on their specific tastes and needs at any given time. Each chapter also suggests related chapters in the handbook to help navigate the content.

Part I presents a range of qualitative traditions, in an effort to represent some of the diversity that helps make up and define the field of qualitative research. No tradition is positioned in the *Handbook* as better or worse than another. Each tradition differently structures and influences, sometimes very subtlety, how we can think about qualitative research, go about doing it, and judging the work that follows. Part II presents a varied and detailed selection of methods to collect qualitative data. These include interviewing, observation, visual methods, media research, material objects, and documents of life, such as diaries and autobiographies. Many of these chapters describe *what* each data collection is, present rationales for *why* each might be used, and offer some practical tips for *how* to go about collecting said data. Conceptual discussions and critical insights are also provided.

Part III focuses on methods of analysis. Out of the many that could have been chosen, attention is given to thematic analysis, phenomenological analysis, interpretive phenomenological analysis, discourse analysis, conversational analysis, narrative analysis, and qualitative meta-synthesis. Together the chapters connect with some traditions (e.g. phenomenology and narrative inquiry) outlined in Part II. The combination provides a flavor of the diverse landscape of analyses available to us, ranging from widely used methods in certain disciplines, like thematic analysis and interpretive phenomenological analysis in sport and exercise psychology, to analytic approaches that have been rarely utilized in all of the sport and exercise sciences, such as conversational analysis and qualitative meta-synthesis. Throughout, rationales for choosing an analysis, practical tips for implementing each, and discussions of major intellectual challenges are offered.

Part IV examines how we might represent qualitative research, evaluate it, and go about doing ethical work. Combined, the chapters present a respectful overview of some traditional, yet still very important issues that qualitative researchers need to grapple with. These include communicating research through realist tales, respecting writing as a form of analysis, engaging carefully in procedural ethics, and reflecting critically on commonly used criteria to judge qualitative research. The chapters also develop understandings by, for example, providing a nuanced account of how realist tales might be understood now, presenting an overview of various creative analytical practices (e.g. different kinds of auto-ethnography and performance social science), thinking of ethics as a process and chain-like, and highlighting contemporary ways to think about "validity" in qualitative research.

Part V is concerned with opening up qualitative research practices (further). This section seeks to open up different and relatively new ways of doing research by focusing on sensory research, Internet research, and pluralistic qualitative analysis. It aims to open up more informed dialogues about integrating qualitative research in mixed-methods research. This part also opens up access further to the role of theory, interpretation, and critical thinking in qualitative work, especially for those new to the field. It makes an exciting opening into a too often neglected topic; that is, teaching qualitative methods and methodologies in "research methods" university courses. The penultimate chapter in the section is an opening into the issue of impact, and how qualitative research can make a difference in society. It provides a resource that gives seasoned researchers from different paradigms and methods, newcomers, policymakers, and organizations a strong rationale for what qualitative research can do, and why it is so valuable. The last chapter in this section turns to Indigenous physical cultures. Complementing several other chapters in other parts of the *Handbook*, such as Chapter 8, that focuses on community-based participatory action research, this final section chapter opens up further dialogue into Indigenous methodologies and insights into why these matter.

Part VI speculates on the future of qualitative research. Authors in this section come mainly from Sociology of Sport or Sport and Exercise Psychology. Each author was invited to write a short chapter on what they perceived to be the future issue(s) in qualitative research. All took a different tack, and each scholar raises differing questions for the future of qualitative research in the Sociology of Sport and/or Sport and Exercise Psychology.

The *Routledge International Handbook of Qualitative Research in Sport and Exercise* is not a final statement. It is a starting point. We hope it is a springboard for new thought and new work. It is hoped that this *Handbook*, with all its strengths and flaws, will contribute to the growing maturity and influence of qualitative research in the sport and exercise sciences. We hope you gain as much from reading it as we have gained from acting as editors, and working with the excellent scholars whose contributions have made it all possible.

References

Culver, D., Gilbert, W., & Sparkes, A. C. (2012). Qualitative research in sport psychology journals: The next decade 2000–2009 and beyond. *The Sport Psychologist, 26*, 261–281.

Demuth, C. (2015). "Slow food" post-qualitative research in psychology: Old craft skills in new disguise? *Integrative Psychological and Behavioral Science, 49*, 207–215.

Denzin, N. & Lincoln, Y. (1994). Introduction: Entering the field of qualitative research. In N. Denzin & Y. Lincoln (Eds.), *Handbook of qualitative research* (pp. 1–17). London: Sage.

Denzin, N. & Lincoln, Y. (2011). Introduction: The discipline and practice of qualitative research. In N. Denzin & Y. Lincoln (Eds.), *Handbook of qualitative research* (pp. 1–19). London: Sage.

Gratton, C. & Jones, I. (2010). *Research methods for sport studies* (2nd ed.). London: Routledge.

Guba, E. & Lincoln, Y. (1994). Competing paradigms in qualitative research. In N. Denzin & Y. Lincoln (Eds.), *Handbook of qualitative research* (pp. 105–117). London: Sage.

Jones, I., Brown, L., & Holloway, I. (2012). *Qualitative research in sport and physical activity*. London: Sage.

Krane, V. & Baird, S. (2005). Using ethnography in applied sport psychology. *Journal of Applied Sport Psychology, 17*, 87–107.

Lincoln, Y. (2010). "What a Long, Strange Trip It's Been . . .": Twenty-five years of qualitative and new paradigm research. *Qualitative Inquiry, 16*, 3–9.

Lincoln, Y., Lynham, S., & Guba, E. (2011). Paradigmatic controversies, contradictions, and emerging confluences revisited. In N. Denzin & Y. Lincoln (Eds.), *Handbook of qualitative research* (pp. 97–128). London: Sage.

Markula, P. & Silk, M. (2011). *Qualitative research for physical culture.* London: Palgrave.

Pitney, W. & Parker, J. (2009). *Qualitative research in physical activity and the health professions.* Champaign, IL: Human Kinetics.

Smith, B. & McGannon, K. (2015). Psychology and sociology in sport studies. In R. Giulianotti (Ed.), *Routledge handbook of the sociology of sport* (pp. 194–203). London: Routledge.

Sparkes, A. C. (2015). Developing mixed methods research in sport and exercise psychology: Critical reflections on five points of controversy. *Psychology of Sport and Exercise, 16,* 49–59.

Sparkes, A. C. & Smith, B. (2014). *Qualitative research methods in sport, exercise and health: From process to product.* London: Routledge.

Sparkes, A. C. & Smith, B. (2016). Interdisciplinary connoisseurship in sport psychology research. In R. Schinke, K. R. McGannon, & B. Smith (Eds.), *Routledge international handbook of sport psychology* (pp. 581–588). London: Routledge

Young, K. & Atkinson, M. (Eds.) (2012). *Qualitative research on sport and physical culture.* Bingley, UK: Emerald.

PART I

Traditions of qualitative research

2

BREATHING IN LIFE

Phenomenological perspectives on sport and exercise

Jacquelyn Allen-Collinson

Some critics have accused philosophical phenomenology of being dry, abstract and 'airy fairy', whereas for many phenomenologists, it is anything but – revealing 'earthy', sweaty, fleshy, sensuous corporealities. The purpose of this chapter is to explore some of the ways in which phenomenology as methodology has challenged, and can be applied to challenge, taken-for-granted assumptions, and to generate rich, evocative and detailed insights into the domain of sport and exercise studies. Although usually termed the phenomenological 'method', this is meant as much more than a particular method, such as interviewing or documentary analysis, and more as a *Weltanschauung*: a whole way of seeing (and otherwise sensing) the world. The chapter addresses: 1) what is phenomenology? - a brief overview for those unfamiliar with the principal tenets; 2) phenomenology as 'method'? - a description of the phenomenological 'method'/methodology; 3) why use phenomenology? – its strengths and weaknesses; and 4) future directions for phenomenology: an example of a new empirical phenomenological form: autophenomenography (Allen-Collinson, 2011).

What is (and is not) phenomenology?

The term phenomenology is derived from the Greek *phainomenon*, taken from the root *phôs*, meaning 'light'. *Phainomenon* refers to something that is placed in the light, made apparent, shown, from which our word *phenomenon* is derived, meaning an appearance, a perceived thing, an observable occurrence. Phenomenology is therefore the study of phenomena; things as they present themselves to, and are perceived in consciousness. *Noumena*, in contrast, are the 'actual' objects 'producing' the phenomena, although any notion of an object's independent existence constitutes the subject of intense debate within philosophy. Schwartz (2002, p. 53), for example, argues that, whilst all existents[1] must be transformed into, and treated as, phenomena (i.e. things as they appear to consciousness), the existence of any 'objective' 'external' world is not denied, only construed as problematic. For phenomenologists, body/consciousness/world are all fundamentally connected, braided, interrelating and mutually influencing. Phenomena are thus not separate from human consciousness and experience, but form part of our incarnate subjectivity; the nexus of mind, body and environment is not optional and discretionary, but, as Francesconi (2009) argues, is necessary and circular.

What is often termed 'modern phenomenology' (Embree & Mohanty, 1997), originated from the ground-breaking work of Edmund Husserl (2002/1913), who set out to remedy what he considered the inadequacies of scientific, purportedly 'objective' investigations of human existence, by developing transcendental or descriptive phenomenology (described below). Husserl sought to question and unsettle scientific 'habits of thought' that left unquestioned and unproblematized fundamental assumptions regarding a phenomenon or phenomena (for example, the experience of one of our hands touching the other). Nowadays, phenomenology encompasses a rich tapestry of multiple strands. One upshot of this is that, as Maurice Merleau-Ponty (2001, p. vii), a leading existential phenomenologist, noted, the question of what phenomenology actually 'is' has not been fully answered. It should then be emphasized that philosophical phenomenology is highly complex, nuanced and contested, and there is scope here for only a schematic portrayal, a taste of its potential. With this caveat in mind, amongst the many more phenomenological traditions, in the following sections I portray three key forms of phenomenology: transcendental/descriptive, existentialist and empirical – the last is often applied within the sociology and psychology of sport and exercise. I would stress, however, that the following are 'tendencies' rather than clear-cut, unambiguously different traditions; they overlap and intertwine, whilst growing from their Husserlian root-stock.

Transcendental, constitutive or descriptive phenomenology

These terms are applied, often interchangeably, to Edmund Husserl's (2002/1913) form of phenomenology, which underwent substantial revision and reworking throughout his lifetime. Embree and Mohanty (1997) note that 'constitutive' phenomenology relates broadly to the notion that we are simultaneously in, and part of, the world; we have an 'idea' of the world and act on this ideational basis; we 'constitute' ourselves and the world. One of Husserl's key insights was the notion that human consciousness is *intentional*, always directed at something. Husserl (2002/1913) considered phenomenology a rigorous human science that aimed to generate detailed descriptions of phenomena, hence the label 'descriptive'. Husserl's notion of the 'phenomenological reduction' lies at the heart of his work, providing a means of 'cutting through' the layers of taken-for-grantedness that envelop a phenomenon, via the *epochē* – sometimes termed 'bracketing' – allowing us to arrive at its *eidos*, its core, 'essential' feature(s). Husserl sought to 'bracket' (i.e. stand aside from) existing beliefs and presuppositions about a phenomenon in order to return 'to the things themselves' (*zu den Sachen selbst*). This phenomenological tradition is also termed 'transcendental', given its aims to transcend individuals' tacit, taken-for-granted assumptions about phenomena, including 'scientific' assumptions. The notion that we can somehow stand outside our own historical, cultural and social-structural 'location' is, of course, highly problematic for those of us working from a sociological or cultural perspective. Indeed, as his writings evolved considerably over time, it is not clear whether Husserl himself believed it truly possible to bracket oneself entirely via the transcendental reduction and thus attain 'pure' transcendental consciousness.

In his later writings, Husserl (1988/1931) shifted his focus towards the relationality of human existence and shared social reality. His notion of the *Lebenswelt*, our common-sense 'lifeworld' of everyday immediate experience, constructed intersubjectively in human interaction, was of analytic interest to sociologists and social psychologists employing a phenomenologically inspired approach; for example, in Schütz's (1972) social phenomenology. Accessing the *Lebenswelt* requires of researchers the application of the phenomenological method to identify and seek to bracket everyday, common-sense assumptions, the 'natural attitude', which envelopes the essential structures or patterns of experience. Schütz's social–phenomenological work in turn inspired the radical thinking of Garfinkel (1984) in developing ethnomethodology: the detailed investigation of the methods social actors use to go about 'doing' everyday life. Taking a different tack, but drawing upon descriptive phenomenological principles, Giorgi (1985) applied this tradition to areas of psychology in a form of empirical phenomenology (addressed below). Within sport and exercise settings, descriptive phenomenology has been used, for example, by Moe (2004) in exploring technical skill acquisition in sport, and in a certain form by Ravn and Christensen (2014), who examine self-consciousness in an elite golfer.

Existentialist phenomenology

This form of phenomenology draws upon existentialist philosophy in addressing questions of ontology and existence, seeking insight into and understanding of what it means to be human. Although developing from Husserl's work, it differs from transcendental/descriptive phenomenology in its strong focus upon embodiment and the corporeal grounding of our lived experience, and also in problematizing the possibility of full *epochē*. Leading existentialist writers such as Simone de Beauvoir and Jean-Paul Sartre worked closely with Maurice Merleau-Ponty, whose work combined existentialist and phenomenological traditions (Ehrich, 1999). Existentialist phenomenology explores the body–world–consciousness nexus, portraying these as fundamentally braided, intertwined and interrelating. Merleau-Ponty (2001), for example, considers the role of our own body (*le corps propre*) as the standpoint of perception, and highlights the ways in which other people and 'things' in the world all form part of our incarnate subjectivity, and way of being-in-the-world (*Dasein*, literally 'there being'). In his later unfinished work, Merleau-Ponty (1969) argues for our existential unity with the *chair* (flesh) of the world, and portrays the experiencing of phenomena at a deeply corporeal, sometimes pre-reflective level. Problematizing any neat distinction between the interior and the exterior world, Merleau-Ponty's (1969) use of the term 'flesh-of-the-world' (the French, *chair*) seeks to convey the continuity of body and world, and to capture its primordial, elemental character (Morley, 2001).

Existentialist phenomenology has proved particularly insightful to researchers in sport and exercise employing an empirical phenomenological approach. Feminist phenomenological analyses of the gendered dimensions of lived sporting experience, for example, often draw upon De Beauvoir's and Merleau-Ponty's work. Young's (1980, 1998) critical analyses of 'throwing like a girl', together with studies of women's involvement in: climbing (Chisholm, 2008), running (Allen-Collinson, 2011), golf (Ravn & Christensen, 2014), and boxing (Allen-Collinson & Owton, 2015) provide examples within this corpus. Similarly, Merleau-Ponty's (1969) focus upon intercorporeality, the ways in which bodies interrelate in shared time and space, has been taken up by researchers in sport and exercise to examine interembodiment and moving bodies in action (for example, Allen-Collinson & Hockey, 2016; Meyer & Van Wedelstaedt, 2016). Such a focus is important as our experience of embodiment is 'always already mediated by our continual interactions with other human and non-human bodies' (Weiss, 1999, p. 5), and intercorporeality often forms a key dimension in our lived experience of sport and exercise.

The sensory dimensions of embodiment (see Chapter 26) are also explored from an existentialist perspective by Merleau-Ponty (1969) and have begun to be examined in studies of sport and exercise (e.g., Hockey & Allen-Collinson, 2007; Sparkes, 2009). In this domain, too, Merleau-Ponty's (2001, p. 93) concept of 'reversibility' is salient, and refers to the ways in which our sensory perceptions are reversible. For example, when we reach out to touch someone, we both touch that person and are ourselves touched. We are thus haptically and inextricably intertwined, and our embodied subjectivity inheres in both our active touch and our tangibility. In the domain of sport and exercise studies, this haptic relationship relates to other participants such as fellow team members and competitors, and to objects such as sports clothing and equipment (Hockey and Allen-Collinson, 2007); for example, hockey sticks, cricket bats and balls, tennis racquets, and so on. Many of these become 'incorporated' as 'body auxiliaries', extensions of the body that are experienced as part of our own body (Merleau-Ponty, 2001).

Empirical phenomenology

In contrast to the above forms of phenomenology (transcendental/descriptive and existentialist), which are grounded strongly in the *philosophical* tradition, in more recent times a form of what some sport philosophers term 'empirical phenomenology' (Martínková & Parry, 2011) has also developed (see, for example, work by Moustakas, 1994; Dale, 1996; Hockey & Allen-Collinson, 2007; Halák, Jirásek & Nesti, 2014). Such use (some would say 'misuse') of the term 'phenomenology' in this work has not been without problematization. For instance, the phenomenological credentials of *some* (by no means all) of this work have been questioned and trenchantly critiqued by philosophical phenomenologists for their lack of engagement with phenomenology and phenomenological writers (see Martínková & Parry, 2011, 2013, and Halák *et al.*, 2014, for good critical reviews). Indeed, as I have noted elsewhere (Allen-Collinson, 2009), sometimes it can be difficult to ascertain just why a sports/exercise study has been described by its authors as 'phenomenological', when there is scant if any reference to phenomenological principles or theorists within the account. Phenomenology is a particular tradition, and most certainly not synonymous with 'qualitative' research or research into concrete, individual, subjective experience, as Martínková and Parry (2011) argue so incisively. To 'qualify' as phenomenological, a study must go far beyond providing a description, however detailed and well-grounded, of the subjective experience of phenomena; this would constitute phenomenalism, and phenomenology is *not* phenomenalism (see Halák *et al.*, 2014). Phenomenology is thus *not* concerned with recounting the immediate, subjective experiences of a particular person(s) as lived in everyday life, but rather about fundamentally problematizing that 'everydayness', 'standing aside' from the everyday flow of subjective experiences and taken-for-granted ways of thinking and being. This requires the disciplined suspending or bracketing of the 'natural attitude' to look anew at, and reflect upon the phenomenon, to identify its *structure* or core essence, the thing without which it would cease to be the phenomenon under study.

To give a flavour of how this form of phenomenology can be employed to investigate *empirically* the domain of sport and exercise, the following are just some examples of research in sport psychology and sport sociology that have adopted a phenomenologically inspired perspective. Rail (1992) provides an interesting phenomenological foray into women's basketball, focusing upon intercorporeality and the experience of physical contact between players. Endurance sports and physical activities such as long-distance walking (Crust, Keegan, Piggott & Swann, 2011), distance running (Allen-Collinson & Hockey, 2011, 2016), and ultramarathons (Simpson, Post, Young & Jensen, 2014) have attracted phenomenological research interest, drawing particularly upon existential insights. The female golfing body and the development of technical skills have been examined by Ravn and Christensen (2014) utilizing a Merleau-Pontian theoretical framework. The intercorporeal development of skilled action (Breivik, 2007) has similarly been examined in a range of different physical cultures, including football/soccer (Hughson and Inglis, 2002; Hemphill, 2005), running (Allen-Collinson & Hockey, 2016), and rowing

(Lund, Ravn & Christensen, 2012). Merleau-Ponty's work has also provided powerful insights when applied to mind-body practices and physical cultures; for example, Morley's (2001) study of yoga practice and breath control, and McDonald's (2007) examination of Kalarippayattu, a southern Indian traditional martial art.

Having provided a brief overview of just three out of the panoply of phenomenological traditions, I now consider the element that perhaps most closely links all these different strands: phenomenology as method/ology.

Phenomenology as 'method'?

One of the key issues relating to the 'phenomenological method' is that it is not really 'method' at all, at least not in terms of the traditional qualitative meaning of a research method, such as semi-structured or unstructured interviewing. The phenomenological 'method' is much more than a specific research technique, but rather embraces a whole way of thinking and being; a whole worldview (*Weltanschauung*). This is known as the phenomenological *attitude*, and is characterised by openness, curiosity and a sense of wonderment; maintaining this attitude requires sustained work, particularly in undertaking the *epochē*. Commensurate with Varela's (1996) and Ravn and Christensen's (2014) position, I argue for phenomenology as a specific type of reflection or attitude about our human capacity for, and mode of, being conscious. Above all, this requires a deep, fundamental challenging of the taken-for-granted, a willingness to identify, question and bracket (as far as possible) existing assumptions and presuppositions regarding a phenomenon, in order to approach it 'fresh', and to identify its essential characteristics.

Whilst the different strands of phenomenology have their own distinctive ethos and principles, there exist four themes or qualities, derived initially from Husserlian phenomenology, that provide cornerstones for researchers undertaking phenomenologically inspired research. This does not mean that all empirical research undertaken with a phenomenological eye or ethos *should* incorporate all four elements, however. In agreement with Gallagher and Zahavi (2008) and with Ravn and Christensen (2014), I consider that phenomenology – or at least a phenomenological sensitivity – can be 'put to work' in reflecting on data generated by a range of different methods (see also Allen-Collinson, 2009) and in providing conceptual clarifications of the phenomena of participants' life worlds. The four cornerstones do, however, provide us with a helpful guiding structure for 'doing' phenomenologically inspired research.

1. **Description** has different connotations within the different phenomenological traditions (some of which were noted above). For qualitative sociological phenomenologists, for example (where the focus is often on interpretation and meaning), there can be no 'pure' description without some degree (at least) of interpretation (see also Chapter 30), and we acknowledge that our social-structural and cultural location, gender, age, and so on, influence how we compile descriptions, and indeed what we even 'see' as being available for description. In contrast, Husserlian transcendental, descriptive phenomenology has as its quest to 'go back to the things themselves', to describe phenomena by suspending – as far as humanly possible – our prior knowledge, assumptions, attitudes and interpretations regarding a phenomenon, by trying to cut through the layers of meaning and interpretation to arrive at its *eidos*, its essential core characteristic(s); the thing(s) without which it ceases to be the 'thing' of study. As can doubtless be surmised, for many phenomenologists who followed in the footsteps of Husserl, including Merleau-Ponty, attaining this level of 'pure' description via the phenomenological reduction, was deemed an impossibility.

2. ***Intentionality*** is a key Husserlian concept highlighting how consciousness is always consciousness of *something*; it is thus intentional, directed towards someone or something, so that intentionality brings an object (or idea) into the frame, somewhat analogous to a photographer framing and focusing their shot. Thus, it is argued, a thing must present itself to us as something recognizable within our schema of the world, in order for it to be perceived and recognised at all. Intentionality helps explain why different people perceive and experience the 'same thing' in radically different ways. Merleau-Ponty (2001) makes a distinction between two forms of intentionality: *intentionality of acts*, when we consciously and actively take up a position; and *operative intentionality*, which is a form of pre-reflective intentionality, a tacit, 'background noise' to our lives, which can only be 'placed in the light' via the phenomenological reduction (see also Reuter, 1999).

3. **Epoché, *bracketing and eidetic reduction***: as noted earlier, *epochē* is a core element in the phenomenological enterprise, derived from the Greek 'to abstain, stop' or 'to keep a distance from'. It involves the suspension or bracketing of the 'natural attitude', our taken-for-granted, everyday assumptions and presuppositions, in order to be able to 'cut through', arrive at and describe the essential characteristics of a phenomenon. When the natural attitude has been suspended via engagement in *epochē*, *eidetic reduction* is undertaken in order to reduce the phenomenon to an exemplar of an essence or an *eidos* (see below). Bracketing techniques used in sports research include researcher triangulation (see also Chapter 29), and bracketing interviews where an interviewer challenges the researcher regarding their presuppositions about the phenomenon to be investigated (see also Allen-Collinson, 2011). For sociological (and other) empirical phenomenologists, however, full *epochē* is acknowledged to be an impossibility, as we can never truly stand outside of culture/social structure, including the constraints of language.

4. ***Essences***: eidetic reduction is used to distil a phenomenon to its *eidos* or core meaning, having sought to identify the tacit, taken-for-granted assumptions enveloping it. For Husserl (1988/1931), a central aim of phenomenology was the discovery of universal essences of experience, in order to create a 'systematic and disciplined methodology for the derivation of knowledge' (cited in Kerry and Armour, 2000, p. 3). An essence is the *sine qua non* of a thing, without which it would cease to be the thing it is. For existential and empirical phenomenologists, however, any universality or existence of 'essences' outside of sociocultural frameworks is highly problematic. For Merleau-Ponty (1963) too, the 'situatedness' of experience is salient. In empirical phenomenology, we therefore seek 'typical' (rather than essential, universal) structures (see also Giorgi, 1985).

These four elements are core within philosophical phenomenology, but for many empirical phenomenologists, any method that can produce rich, in-depth, detailed descriptions of participants' own concrete, lived experiences has the *potential* to generate data to which phenomenologicallyinspired analysis or reflection can be applied. Methods range from semi-structured interviews (e.g., Crust, Swann, Allen-Collinson, Breckon & Weinberg, 2014) through observations (e.g., Ravn & Christensen, 2014), to autoethnography (see Chapter 23) and, to be portrayed shortly, autophenomenographic data (e.g., Allen-Collinson, 2012). Giorgi's (1985, 1997) phenomenological research approach has been utilised widely within empirical phenomenology, deploying a Husserlian-inspired perspective. Giorgi (1985) provides detailed guidelines for undertaking this form of research (see also Chapter 16), which have been used in addressing sporting phenomena (e.g. Allen-Collinson, 2012):

1. The collection of concrete, 'naive' descriptions of the phenomenon from participants.
2. The researcher's adoption of the phenomenological attitude and engagement with the *epochē*.
3. An impressionistic reading of each transcript/description to gain a feel for the whole.
4. An in-depth re-reading of the description to identify 'meaning units'.
5. Identifying and making explicit the significance of each meaning unit.
6. The production of a general description of the structure(s) of the experience.

Moving away from the more Husserlian end of the phenomenological spectrum, Interpretative Phenomenological Analysis (IPA) provides a popular and accessible research technique that has been applied extensively within psychology, including sport and exercise psychology (see Chapter 17). Having identified some of the key elements of phenomenology as a methodological perspective, I now consider why researchers in sport and exercise might consider employing empirical phenomenology.

Phenomenology: its strengths and weaknesses

Why, we might ask, use a phenomenologically inspired approach? For me, the answer lies in the heady (and sometimes headachy) combination of a rich philosophical tradition with highly specific ways of analytically addressing the various life worlds of sports and physical cultures, with the demands and rigour of a 'method' that exhorts the researcher to be open, curious and full of 'naive' wonder before phenomena, taking nothing for granted. The latter can be difficult to sustain, particularly for the 'older', longstanding researcher! I do employ other research approaches, depending upon the ethos of the project I'm undertaking, but whilst phenomenology *is* undoubtedly demanding, there are distinct advantages. Though departing from its original philosophical form, empirical phenomenology provides a powerful theoretical and methodological synthesis that *demands* that researchers fundamentally and systematically challenge taken-for-granted definitions, interpretations and meanings, to an extent, and with a rigour that can leave us exhausted. It does, however, cohere strongly with a sociological enterprise that similarly seeks to contest everyday, 'common-sense' conceptualizations and, for me, this has provided a stimulating theoretical and methodological nexus. Phenomenology draws on a rich and distinctive theoretical tradition of investigating the consciousness–body–world nexus. Existential phenomenology, for example, is particularly well placed to investigate issues of embodiment and our bodily ways of being and knowing. It draws on the work of phenomenologists such as De Beauvoir and Merleau-Ponty, who argued for the importance of our corporeal 'situatedness' in lived experience, and in epistemological grounding.

Empirical phenomenology seeks, via a rigorous, but also adventurous and challenging 'method', new ways of investigating how it feels to be the person in the sporting body/mind. Participants as co-researchers provide the 'expert' accounts of their own experiences and life worlds, and phenomenology requires that as researchers we acknowledge their expertness and proficiency, but also analytically distinguish their *phenomenal*, first-hand, subjective experiences from the 'doing' of phenomenology. This includes fundamentally (and sometimes painfully) challenging our own preconceptions about a phenomenon via the *epochē*. Whilst acknowledging the impossibility of full bracketing, empirical phenomenology nevertheless highlights the need for acute, sustained and thorough-going researcher reflexivity in seeking to identify the everyday assumptions that can cloak the phenomenon, clouding the analysis.

Although phenomenology undoubtedly has strengths in providing a distinctive theoretical and methodological tradition, inevitably, as with all methodologies, it has its limitations.

In relation to philosophical phenomenology, the search for 'universal' experience, and thus the lack of recognition of, and analytic attention to the specificities of lived experience engendered by, for example, gender, 'race', ethnicity, age, dis/ability, are problematic, particularly for sociologists and others, who argue for the huge impact of social-structural forces and location. Empirical phenomenology can address such problems head on, however, by incorporating insights from other disciplines and subject areas. For example, phenomenology can be combined with critical sociology (Hughson and Inglis, 2002) feminist theory (Young, 1980, 1998; Fisher & Embree, 2000; Allen-Collinson, 2012; see also Chapter 7, this volume), or queer theory (e.g. Ahmed, 2007), to give just some 'flavours'. In combination with phenomenology, sociology, for example, incorporates insights into the specifics of socioculturally placed and historically located, socially interacting bodies, rather than positing some kind of gender-neutral, universal 'every-person' experience. In this, it departs radically from the philosophical tradition. In phenomenological sociology, our bodies and lived experiences are acknowledged to be specifically human, but also gendered, 'classed', sexually 'oriented', aged, 'ethnicized', and with differing degrees of dis/ability and corporeal variation. Analogously, psychological phenomenology, such as IPA, eschews any universalist tendencies, focusing upon the idiographic, and analysing the individual's lived experience.

Empirical phenomenological forms such as sociological and psychological phenomenology have encountered criticism, however. The lack of generalizability and universality, as noted above, are certainly problematic from a philosophical phenomenological standpoint, and also from a positivistic one that values statistical generalizability. However much we might wish to identify essential structures of experience, for most empirical phenomenologists, generalizability is generally acknowledged to relate to *analytic generalizability* (Sparkes & Smith, 2014), and not to 'universal essences' of experience. Furthermore, in operationalizing phenomenological principles, researchers can encounter problems when utilizing traditional qualitative approaches such as semi-structured interviews that to some extent 'impose' pre-existing definitions and meanings upon participants. A researcher's assumptions and preconceptions, including theoretically driven ones, may, despite best efforts, filter through – to a greater degree than in unstructured interviews or participant diaries, for example. The use of extant concepts and models, as can be the case with *some* studies within sport and exercise employing IPA (e.g. Shepherd, Lee & Kerr, 2006; Warriner & Lavallee, 2008) can be problematic from some phenomenological perspectives. Whilst all researchers necessarily hold preconceptions about their topic of enquiry, strong adherence to existing theoretical and conceptual frameworks, models and constructs, sits very uneasily with phenomenology's quest to fundamentally challenge existing frameworks and habits of thought. As Willig argues: 'the researcher's choice of label for the phenomenon of interest is not merely a descriptive act but a constitutive one' (2007, p. 216). A further problem with empirical phenomenological research, noted by Gruppetta (2004) and Allen-Collinson (2011), is that many phenomenologically inspired researchers do not actually participate in the life worlds they study, and second-hand accounts can lose something in 'translation'. One means of addressing this is the relatively novel automethodological approach of autophenomenography, which has been signalled as a possible future direction for empirical, phenomenologically inspired research (Allen-Collinson, 2009, 2011).

Future directions for empirical phenomenology: autophenomenography

Whilst the use of 'second-hand' participant accounts is not *necessarily* a weakness of empirical phenomenology, lack of researcher familiarity with the phenomenon/phenomena under investigation can be a limitation. It is thus incumbent upon empirical phenomenologists in sport and exercise, who do not hold 'insider' experiential knowledge of the sporting milieux they examine, to proceed with caution in imposing any second-order constructs upon the accounts of participants. A goal of empirical phenomenology is often to understand and perhaps vicariously to 'experience' phenomena from the standpoint of those studied; to provide a feel for what it is like to be in the shoes (or trainers) of participants, in order to identify the core, essential structures of that experience. Autoethnographic phenomenology or autophenomenography is one possible research avenue that addresses some of the problems of using second-hand accounts of a phenomenon. The term appears to have been coined by Gruppetta (2004) in an educational context. She argues that if the researcher studies a phenomenon rather than a 'cultural place', then the appropriate term should be autophenomenography, rather than autoethnography, as the latter focuses upon an individual's experiences primarily *qua* member of a cultural or subcultural group. We should perhaps remember that the social group (the *ethnós*) is a key component of 'autoethnography'. There are of course overlapping elements between autophenomenography and autoethnography (see Chapter 23), given that our experience of phenomena is conceptualized as culturally (and subculturally) framed, at least for those of working in phenomenological sociology. I should at this juncture explain why I use the term autophenomenography rather than 'autophenomenology'. In relation to the 'graphy' element, this refers to the research process in general, rather than only to the written (or representational) product of that process. In addition, 'autophenomenology' has specific and highly contested meanings within philosophical phenomenology itself (see Drummond, 2007 for an excellent discussion); my use of the term is therefore deliberate, to distinguish it clearly from philosophical phenomenology.

Another criticism sometimes directed against empirical phenomenology is the tendency for some researchers to use highly abstract language in their general statements of phenomena, thereby losing the 'feel', richness, vitality, textures, evocativeness and grounded 'bodyfulness' of the lived experience. Thus, Todres cautions that: 'One could describe the general themes of an experience in such an abstract way that the qualities are devitalised . . .' (2007, p. 9); a tendency fundamentally anathema to the phenomenological project. Autophenomenography can address this devitalising tendency in making sustained efforts to 'bring to life' the essential/typical structures of lived experience, to engage in 'the breathing of meaning' (Van Manen, 1990, p. 36). Analogous to its autoethnographic counterpart, autophenomenography can generate the rich, finely textured descriptions of first-hand experience, central to our quest to bring to life the felt, lived bodily experience. Within the autophenomenographic genre there is scope for a wide spectrum of representational styles, including evocative forms such as poetic representations and performative (see Chapter 23), audience-interactive presentations, already familiar to those working with autoethnographic perspectives.

The autophenomenographic researcher treads a sometimes difficult pathway in seeking to convey, both analytically and descriptively, but also powerfully, evocatively and aesthetically, even poetically, the phenomenon under investigation. Autophenomenography seeks to provide highly textured, in-depth descriptions that locate the structures of individual experience within broader, more general structures of human experience; for example, the lived experience of being a running woman training in public space (Allen-Collinson, 2010). Commensurate with autoethnography, autophenomenographic accounts can generate an empathic *feeling* of understanding in the reader (Todres, 2007, p. 9), thus interlinking, to some degree at least, the embodiment of researcher-author and reader. For researchers in sport and exercise, providing these 'bodyful', 'fleshy', corporeally textured, and sensuously evocative descriptions can help to promote understanding of what it is to be human and to 'do' sport and exercise, and to inhabit particular physical-cultural life worlds. Importantly, though, autophenomenographers must fundamentally question their own taken-for-granted assumptions and presuppositions about the phenomenon or phenomena they study, and in which they participate; this is a deeply challenging – and often exhausting – research proposition (see also, Allen-Collinson, 2011 for the challenges and tensions involved). Autophenomenography seeks to identify the structures or patterns of experiences relating to phenomena, rather than to recount direct phenomenal experiences themselves.

Concluding discussion

This chapter has portrayed how phenomenologically inspired perspectives – both theoretical and methodological – can bring fresh insights to the portrayal and grounded analysis of the lived experience of sport and exercise, requiring us to fundamentally question and challenge taken-for-granted, common-sense, and also scientific 'habits of thought'. Having portrayed some of the key strands of phenomenological thought, and the ways in which empirical phenomenology in particular has been employed to generate both descriptive and analytic insights into researching sport and exercise domains, I have sought to give some idea of the possibilities offered by this particular theoretical and methodological framework. This is not, I should emphasize, to promote phenomenologically inspired approaches above others, but if the purpose of the research is to challenge preconceived notions of the phenomenon, to address it afresh, and generate detailed analytic accounts of the lived experience of a particular sporting or exercising life world, grounded deeply in – but also questioning of – participants' own accounts, then phenomenology provides an excellent avenue. Such descriptions and analyses can engender a critical re/consideration of the 'essences' of sport and exercise experience: corporeal, psychological, emotional and social. They can also promote reflection upon, and empathic understanding of, how it might *feel* to be a sporting/exercising body in a particular life world. Furthermore, for sociological and social-psychological and other empirical phenomenological researchers, these embodied experiences are analysed as deeply contextualised in terms of sociocultural and temporal location (see Chapter 16 on phenomenological analysis).

Of particular interest to those researching the social and interactional aspects of sport and exercise domains, phenomenology can not only generate insights into human sporting and exercising embodiment and experience in general, but also provide a powerful means of examining intersubjectivity and intercorporeality: the ways in which our minds and bodies share the world, interact, socially relate and mutually influence, in particular, sporting and exercise contexts. Currently, there is somewhat of a lacuna in relation to studies of embodied interaction between sports and exercise participants, including the often finely attuned intercorporeality necessary to accomplish sporting enaction (Allen-Collinson & Hockey, 2016; Meyer & Van Wedelstaedt, 2016). A corpus of work is beginning to develop in this field, for instance, in relation to mixed martial arts (Spencer, 2012; Vaittinen, 2016), karate (Masciotra, Ackermann & Roth, 2001), and distance running (Allen-Collinson & Hockey, 2016), but at present, the literature synthesizing the phenomenological and the interactional remains relatively sparse.

Furthermore, phenomenologists such as Merleau-Ponty (2001) have emphasized the role of human–object interaction, highly salient in many sporting and exercise contexts, where participants often become highly skilled in the use of objects, such as tennis racquets, hockey sticks, parallel bars, cricket bats and balls, and so on. The deployment of such skill requires of participants the development of a spectrum of sensory intelligence that is employed to execute skilful, practical action. This knowledge-action synthesis gradually, over time and repeated practice, becomes embodied and incorporated into the self. For as Leder notes: 'A skill is finally and fully learned when something that was extrinsic, grasped only through explicit rules or examples, now comes to pervade my own corporeality' (1990, p. 31). Our sporting skills are not fully learnt once and for all, but require regular and frequent practising and refinement. Furthermore, as phenomenology highlights, although such skilled actions may be repeated hundreds, even thousands of times, their reproduction is never identical. For sports people and exercisers, the environment – both physical and social – is constantly changing, demanding of skilled practitioners ongoing improvisational adjustment and readjustment. Our engagement with objects and equipment, terrain, physical and meteorological conditions, with animals, human and non-human, and with fellow sports people and exercisers, is demanding interactional work. As Ingold notes, skill is not merely 'an isolated ability in a person's body, but is better understood as a meshing of a person's intentions, through their abilities with the environment (including other people), already interrogated by a skilful person for significant information' (2000, p. 353f). Mind, body and world are thus powerfully interconnected and mutually influencing, as phenomenology so vividly portrays.

Note

1 Defined by Schwartz (2002, p. 53) as 'any physical, social, abstract, emotional object – which has content, meaning, characteristics, features – which coheres in our experience as an enduring object, and which somehow presents itself to us as existing'.

References

Ahmed, S. (2007). *Queer phenomenology: Orientations, objects, others*. Durham, NC: Duke University Press.

Allen-Collinson, J. (2009). Sporting embodiment: Sports studies and the (continuing) promise of phenomenology. *Qualitative Research in Sport and Exercise*, 1(3), 279–296.

Allen-Collinson, J. (2010). Running embodiment, power and vulnerability: Notes towards a feminist phenomenology of female running. In E. Kennedy & P. Markula (Eds.), *Women and exercise: The body, health and consumerism* (pp. 280–298). London: Routledge.

Allen-Collinson, J. (2011). Intention and epoché in tension: Autophenomenography, bracketing and a novel approach to researching sporting embodiment. *Qualitative Research in Sport, Exercise & Health*, 3(1), 48–62.

Allen-Collinson, J. (2012). Feminist phenomenology and the woman in the running body. In I. Martínková & J. Parry (Eds.), *Phenomenological approaches to sport* (pp. 113–129). London: Routledge.

Allen-Collinson, J. & Hockey, J. (2011). Feeling the way: Notes toward a haptic phenomenology of scuba diving and distance running. *International Review for the Sociology of Sport*, 46(3), 330–345.

Allen-Collinson, J. & Hockey, J. (2016). Intercorporeal enaction and synthrony: The case of distance-running together. In C. Meyer & U. van Wedelstaedt (Eds.), *Intercorporeal and interkinesthetic enaction in sports*. Amsterdam: John Benjamins.

Allen-Collinson, J. & Owton, H. (2015). Intense embodiment: Senses of heat in women's running and boxing. *Body & Society*, 21(2), 245–268.

Breivik, G. (2007). Skilful coping in everyday life and in sport: A critical examination of the views of Heidegger and Dreyfus. *Journal of the Philosophy of Sport*, 34(2), 116–134.

Chisholm, D. (2008). Climbing like a girl: An exemplary adventure in feminist phenomenology. *Hypatia*, 23(1), 9–40.

Crust, L., Keegan, R., Piggott, D. & Swann, C. (2011). Walking the walk: A phenomenological study of long distance walking. *Journal of Applied Sport Psychology*, 23(3), 243–262.

Crust, L., Swann, C., Allen-Collinson, J., Breckon, J. & Weinberg, R. (2014). A phenomenological exploration of exercise mental toughness: Perceptions of exercise leaders and regular exercisers. *Qualitative Research in Sport, Exercise & Health*, 6(4), 441–461.

Dale, G.A. (1996). Existential phenomenology: Emphasizing the experience of the athlete in sport psychology research. *The Sport Psychologist*, 10, 307–321.

De Beauvoir, S. (1974). *The second sex.* New York: Vintage.

Drummond, J.J. (2007). Phenomenology: Neither auto- nor hetero- be. *Phenomenology and the Cognitive Sciences, 6,* 57–74.

Ehrich, L.C. (1999). Untangling the threads and coils of the web of phenomenology. *Education Research and Perspectives, 26*(2), 19–44.

Embree, L. & Mohanty, J.N. (1997). Introduction. In L. Embree *et al.* (Eds.), *Encyclopedia of phenomenology* (pp. 1–10). Dordrecht: Kluwer Academic.

Fisher, L. & Embree, L. (Eds.) (2000). *Feminist phenomenology.* Dordrecht: Kluwer Academic.

Francesconi, D. (2009). Embodied mind between education and cognitive sciences: Bodily consciousness and meditation training. *The International Journal of Interdisciplinary Social Sciences, 4*(10), 19–27.

Gallagher, S. & Zahavi, D. (2008). *The phenomenological mind.* London: Routledge.

Garfinkel, H. (1984). *Studies in ethnomethodology* (revised ed.). Cambridge: Polity Press/Blackwell.

Giorgi, A. (Ed.) (1985). *Phenomenology and psychological research.* Pittsburgh, PA: Duquesne University Press.

Giorgi, A. (1997). The theory, practice, and evaluation of the phenomenological method as a qualitative research procedure. *Journal of Phenomenological Psychology, 28*(2), 235–260.

Gruppetta, M. (2004). Autophenomenography? Alternative uses of autobiographically based research. In P.L. Jeffery (Ed.), *Association for Active Researchers in Education (AARE) Conference Paper Abstracts, 2004.* Sydney: AARE. Retrieved 29 September, 2014, from: http://www.aare.edu.au/04pap/gru04228.pdf.

Halák, J., Jirásek, I. & Nesti, M.S. (2014). Phenomenology is not phenomenalism. Is there such a thing as phenomenology of sport? *Acta Gymnica, 44*(2), 117–129.

Hemphill, D. (2005). Deeper inside the beautiful game. *Journal of the Philosophy of Sport, XXXII,* 105–115.

Hockey, J. & Allen-Collinson, J. (2007). Grasping the phenomenology of sporting bodies. *International Review for the Sociology of Sport, 42*(2), 115–131.

Hughson, J. & Inglis, D. (2002). Inside the beautiful game: Towards a Merleau-Pontian phenomenology of soccer play. *Journal of the Philosophy of Sport, XXIX,* 1–15.

Husserl, E. (2002/1913). *Ideas: General introduction to pure phenomenology.* London: Routledge. First published 1913, in German, as: *Ideen zu einer reinen Phänomenologie und phänomenologischen Philosophie. Erstes Buch: Allgemeine Einführung in die reine Phänomenologie.*

Husserl, E. (1988/1931). *Cartesian meditations* (trans. D. Cairns). Dordrecht: Kluwer.

Ingold, T. (2000). *The perception of the environment.* London: Routledge.

Kerry, D.S. & Armour, K.M. (2000). Sports sciences and the promise of phenomenology: Philosophy, method, and insight. *Quest, 52*(1), 1–17.

Leder, D. (1990). *The absent body.* Chicago, IL: University of Chicago Press.

Lund, O., Ravn, S. & Christensen, M.K. (2012). Learning by joining the rhythm: Apprenticeship learning in elite double sculls rowing. *Scandinavian Sport Studies Forum, 3,* 167–188.

Martínková, I. & Parry, J. (2011). An introduction to the phenomenological study of sport. *Sport, Ethics and Philosophy, 5*(3), 185–201.

Martínková, I. & Parry, J. (2013). Eichberg's 'phenomenology' of sport: A phenomenal confusion. *Sport, Ethics and Philosophy, 7*(3), 331–341.

Masciotra, D., Ackermann, E. & Roth, W.-M. (2001). 'Maai': The art of distancing in Karate-Do: Mutual attunement in close encounters. *Journal of Adult Development, 8*(2), 119–132.

McDonald, I. (2007). Bodily practice, performance art, competitive sport: A critique of Kalarippayattu, martial art of Kerala. *Contributions to Indian Sociology, 41*(2), 143–168.

Merleau-Ponty, M. (1963). *The structure of behaviour* (trans. A.L. Fisher). Boston, MA: Beacon Press.

Merleau-Ponty, M. (1969). *The visible and the Invisible* (trans. A. Lingis). Evanston, IL: Northwestern University Press.

Merleau-Ponty, M. (2001). *Phenomenology of perception* (trans. C. Smith). London: Routledge & Kegan Paul.

Meyer, C. & Van Wedelstaedt, U. (2016). Intercorporeal and interkinesthetic enaction in sports: A new perspective on moving bodies in interaction. In C. Meyer & U. van Wedelstaedt (Eds.), *Intercorporeal and interkinesthetic enaction in sports.* Amsterdam: John Benjamins.

Moe, V.F. (2004). How to understand skill acquisition in sport. *Bulletin of Science, Technology & Society, 24*(3), 213–224.

Morley, J. (2001). Inspiration and expiration: Yoga practice through Merleau-Ponty's phenomenology of the body. *Philosophy East and West, 51*(1), 73–82.

Moustakas, C. (1994). *Phenomenological research methods.* London: Sage.

Rail, G. (1992). Physical contact in women's basketball: A phenomenological construction and contextualisation. *International Review for the Sociology of Sport*, *27*(1), 1–24.

Ravn, S. & Christensen, M.K. (2014). Listening to the body? How phenomenological insights can be used to explore a golfer's experience of the physicality of her body. *Qualitative Research in Sport, Exercise & Health*, *6*(4), 462–477.

Reuter, M. (1999). Merleau-Ponty's notion of pre-reflective intentionality. *Synthese*, *118*, 69–88.

Schütz, A. (1972). *The phenomenology of the social world*. London: Heinemann.

Schwartz, H. (2002). Phenomenological reductionism: An explanation and a critique. *Ethnographic Studies*, *7*, 53–60.

Shepherd, D.J., Lee, B. & Kerr, J.H. (2006). Reversal theory: A suggested way forward for an improved understanding of interpersonal relationships in sport. *Psychology of Sport and Exercise*, *7*(2), 143–157.

Simpson, D., Post, P.G., Young, G. & Jensen, P.R. (2014). 'It's not about taking the easy road': The experiences of ultramarathon runners. *The Sport Psychologist*, *28*(2), 176–285.

Sparkes, A.C. (2009). Ethnography and the senses: Challenges and possibilities. *Qualitative Research in Sport and Exercise*, *1*(1), 21–35.

Sparkes, A.C. & Smith, B. (2014). *Qualitative research methods in sport, exercise and health. From process to product*. London: Routledge.

Spencer, D.C. (2012). *Ultimate fighting and embodiment*. London: Routledge.

Todres, L. (2007). *Embodied enquiry: Phenomenological touchstones for research, psychotherapy and spirituality*. New York: Palgrave Macmillan.

Vaittinen, A.M. (2016). Intersections of ways of knowing mixed martial arts and visual culture. *Amodern*, 3 (Sport and Visual Culture). 28 October, 2014. Available from: http://amodern.net/issues/amodern-3-sport-visual-culture/.

Van Manen, M. (1990). *Researching lived experience: Human science for an action sensitive pedagogy*. New York: State University of New York Press.

Varela, F. (1996). Neurophenomenology: A methodological remedy for the hard problem. *Journal of Consciousness Studies*, *3*(4), 330–349.

Warriner, K. & Lavallee, D. (2008). The retirement experiences of elite female gymnasts: Self-identity and the physical self. *Journal of Applied Sport Psychology*, *20*, 301–137.

Weiss, G. (1999). *Body images: Embodiment as intercorporeality*. London: Routledge.

Willig, C. (2007). Reflections on the use of a phenomenological method. *Qualitative Research in Psychology*, *4*, 209–225.

Young, I.M. (1980). Throwing like a girl: A phenomenology of feminine body comportment motility and spatiality. *Human Studies*, *3*, 137–156.

Young, I.M. (1998). 'Throwing like a girl': Twenty years later. In D. Welton (Ed.), *Body and flesh: A philosophical reader* (pp. 286–290). Oxford: Blackwell.

3

DOING GROUNDED THEORY IN SPORT AND EXERCISE

Nicholas L. Holt

Grounded theory is a qualitative methodology based on the premise that theory is indispensable for gaining deep knowledge of social phenomena (Glaser & Strauss, 1967). It originated in sociology in the 1960s and has since become one of the most widely used qualitative methodologies, popular across academic disciplines, and used to pursue a range of research questions. With the popularity and growth of grounded theory it has been subjected to review, critique, modification, and some entertaining disputes played out in the academic literature. The literature is vast, vibrant, and reflects different philosophical and methodological perspectives.

Grounded theory arrived in the sport and exercise literature in the 2000s. Although numerous grounded theory studies have been published over the past two-and-a-half decades, the extent to which researchers in sport and exercise have followed "true" grounded theory methodology has been questioned (Holt & Tamminen, 2010a, b; Hutchinson, Johnston, & Breckon, 2011; Weed, 2009, 2010). A major criticism is that sport and exercise researchers have cherry-picked a handful of techniques from grounded theory rather than using the methodology more completely. This chapter is based on the assumption that the most appropriate application of grounded theory is as a "total" methodology (Weed, 2009). Consequently, my aim in this chapter is to encourage and provide direction for the use of grounded theory as a total methodology. To achieve this aim, I address the question "What makes a grounded theory research a grounded theory?"

What is grounded theory?

As the question I posed above perhaps reflects, there are some issues with the nomenclature surrounding grounded theory that need to be understood to access the literature. First, the term "grounded theory" is used to refer to both the *process* of conducting a study (i.e., the methodology) and the *product* (i.e., the theory produced). For instance, a researcher might say "I did grounded theory" to indicate that s/he used grounded theory methodology. Later s/he might say "I created a grounded theory," and in this instance s/he is referring to the theoretical product arising from the research. Rather confusingly, the term grounded theory is often used interchangeably to refer both to the process and the product of the research. In an attempt to clarify the nomenclature, in the remainder of this chapter I use the term "grounded theory methodology" (GTM) when I am referring to the methodology, and the term "grounded theory" when I am referring to the product (i.e., the theory produced).

A second issue is that GTM is an "umbrella term" used to refer to *a range of different methodological approaches* (i.e., variants of GTM), all of which are theory-generating research methodologies. As a result there is no singular definition of GTM. Yet, in the various definitions of GTM that are available it is clear they share some common characteristics. For instance, Bryant and Charmaz suggested most approaches to GTM involve a "systematic, inductive, and comparative approach for conducting inquiry . . . that leads researchers to examine possible theoretical explanations for empirical findings" (2007, p. 1). According to Charmaz GTM is "a systematic, yet flexible methodology for collecting and analyzing qualitative data to construct theories that are grounded in the data themselves" (2006, p. 2). Similarly, Strauss and Corbin wrote that GTM means "theory was derived from data, systematically gathered and analyzed through the research process. In this method, data collection, analysis, and eventual theory stand in close relationship to one another" (1998, p. 12).

As these descriptions and definitions suggest, unlike the content and thematic analysis (see Chapter 15) – approaches used frequently in the sport and exercise literature (for reviews, see Brustad, 2008; Culver, Gilbert, & Sparkes, 2012) – the end product of GTM research should not simply be a set of themes. Rather, when using GTM the aim is to produce a set of "grounded concepts" (i.e., grounded in data collected in the field) integrated around a central or core category, to form a theoretical framework that explains how and why persons, organizations, or communities experience and respond to events, challenges, or problematic situations (Corbin & Holt, 2011). In other words, the point of using GTM is to develop theory that is grounded in the data. Therefore, I would define GTM as a set of methodological approaches that include techniques and strategies designed to develop theory based on, and grounded in, data collected from people and in social settings.

In order to understand GTM it is necessary to have some understanding of theory itself (see also Chapter 30). After all, if the goal of using GTM is to produce a grounded theory, researchers need to have a basic conceptualization of what that theory might be. Theories can take many forms, varying in terms of their sophistication, structure, and modes of derivation (Morse, 1997). Some theories are highly conceptual with broad applicability and scope, whereas others are more parsimonious and narrow. From a GTM perspective, Corbin and Strauss suggested:

> Theory denotes a set of well-developed categories (themes, concepts) that are systematically developed in terms of their properties and dimensions and are interrelated through statements of relationship to form a theoretical framework that explains something about a phenomenon.
>
> *(Corbin & Strauss, 2015, p. 62)*

Clearly theories are constructions. In GTM, theories are constructed from data provided by participants, which researchers interpret, frame, and retell (Charmaz, 2006; Corbin & Strauss, 2008, 2015). Glaser and Strauss (1967) differentiated between substantive (topic-focused) grounded theories, and formal (concept-focused) grounded theories. Substantive grounded theories are more specific to group and place, whereas formal grounded theories are less specific, and can be applied to a wider range of disciplinary concerns and problems. GTM is rarely used to create formal grounded theories in sport and exercise research. Rather, most grounded theories are at the substantive level; they are process-bound and rarely extend beyond the scope of the phenomenon under study, and are only generalizable to other contexts and other participants experiencing similar phenomena (Morse, 1997). Good grounded theories – especially substantive level grounded theories in sport and exercise – should also have practical applications.

A (very) brief history of GTM

Some of the key moments in the history of GTM provide context for the remaining sections of the chapter.[1] The "first generation" of GTM was presented by Barney Glaser and Anselm Strauss. They developed GTM during the course of a research study of people dying in hospitals (Glaser & Strauss, 1965). Then, somewhat as a reaction to the positivistic and deductive approaches to theory development and research that were popular in health sociology at the time, they wrote the seminal book on the methodology, titled *The Discovery of Grounded Theory* (Glaser & Strauss, 1967). Over time, a "split" occurred as Glaser and Strauss began to take fundamental features of GTM in different directions. Corbin and Strauss noted that it was "not that [Strauss] departed from the methodology developed by him and Glaser but that he had his own techniques or ways of thinking about data when doing analysis" (2015, p. 7). As a consequence, two versions of the methodology emerged, which became known as the Glaserian approach and the Straussian approach. Researchers began to side with one or the other of these approaches, as each became more clearly articulated and the differences between the originators became irreconcilable (conceptually and methodologically).

Although there are many subtle differences between Glaserian and Straussian GTM, the main point of contention is what became known as the "emergence versus forcing debate." Glaser (1992) suggested the analytic tools in Strauss' approach "force" the data, and instead argued that theory emerges from the data. Dr. Juliet Corbin (who many consider the cocreator of Straussian GTM) and I argued the notion of emergence implies that "a theory is embedded in the data and it is the task of the analyst to discover what the theory is" (Corbin & Holt, 2005, p. 49). Arguably, the emergence perspective therefore follows the idea there is "one truth" in the data, whereas the Straussian view acknowledges there are multiple realities and multiple ways of interpreting a data set. In other words, Glaser adopted a more realist philosophical perspective, whereas Strauss' approach is based on interactionism and pragmatism (Corbin & Strauss, 2015).

Glaser and Strauss (and Corbin) continued to develop their individual conceptualizations of GTM (e.g. Corbin & Strauss, 2008, 2015; Glaser, 1978, 1992; Strauss & Corbin, 1990, 1998). Over time they shifted their positions on certain points and added others. Meanwhile, a "second generation" of grounded theorists with their own unique perspectives emerged. For example, Bryant and Charmaz's (2007) edited work titled the *Handbook of Grounded Theory* has 27 chapters from 34 contributors, who have all "studied, applied, taught, and/or written about" GTM (p. 11). The breadth of the GTM literature is a sign the methodology is healthy and growing.

As Bryant and Charmaz's (2007) book demonstrated, many perspectives on GTM exist. Nonetheless, it is possible to identify three "main" versions that are used most widely; namely, the Glaserian approach, the Straussian approach, and Charmaz's more recent constructivist approach. Again, there are subtle differences between each version of GTM. As mentioned above, Glaser defined GTM as a method of discovery and treated categories as emergent from the data. Strauss, while agreeing that theories should be traceable to the data, argued that researchers' interaction with data leads to the construction of a grounded theory, rather than a theory emerging from the data. Charmaz (2006) took this "constructivist perspective" a step further. She argued researchers construct a theory through their interactions with the data and, while the theory will be grounded in the participants' experiences, Charmaz suggested it is impossible to create a theory entirely separate from the researcher. Needless to say, as a result of these conceptual differences there are also some notable differences among the Glaser, Strauss, and Charmaz approaches in terms of coding (i.e., specific data analysis techniques), which are discussed later, and detailed in Table 3.1.

Why use GTM?

GTM, like many other qualitative approaches, is not particularly well suited to *testing* existing theories (Holt, Knight, & Tamminen, 2012). The main reason to use GTM is to create *new theories* that explain some kind of social phenomena. Of course the selection of any methodology is partly based on the research question (which is underpinned and shaped by a coherent epistemology and ontology). The research question is the specific query to be addressed in the research that "sets the parameters of the project and suggests the methods to be used for data gathering and analysis" (Corbin & Strauss, 2015, p. 31). Research questions well suited to the use of GTM focus typically on discovering participants' patterns of action/interaction with changes in conditions, either internal or external to the process itself. GTM methodology is particularly useful when there is little pre-existing theory available to explain a certain social process, where theories are underdeveloped for particular populations, or if existing theories are incomplete.

Key features of a grounded theory study

In the following section I list some of what I consider to be the common features of GTM, drawing from principles in the three main approaches described above. This list also draws from previously published works in the sport and exercise literature (Holt & Tamminen, 2010a, b; Holt *et al.*, 2012; Hutchinson *et al.*, 2011; Weed, 2009, 2010). As with any list, it is not definitive. The astute reader will note it is heavily influenced by my own background in the Straussian approach (Corbin & Holt, 2005; 2011). Nonetheless, I hope it provides a fair representation of the features typically associated with most variants of GTM. It also provides a guide for *doing* a good grounded theory study.

Theoretical approach from the start. Grounded theorists should "think theoretically" from the start of a study with the mindset that the goal of the research is to create a grounded theory. It should be clear that initial sampling was dictated by the research question and the goal of developing theory (Hutchinson *et al.*, 2011). For example, in Hutchinson, Johnston, and Breckon's (2013) study of long-term physical-activity behavior change, the research question was "How do people successfully change their PA [physical-activity] habits?" (p. 111). Their goal was to create a context-specific (i.e., substantive) and ecologically valid (i.e., grounded) explanatory model (i.e., theory) of successful processes of change in physical-activity behavior. This study reflected the principle of "thinking theoretically from the start," because the authors clearly decided the best way to answer their research question was by building a theory, which led to the use of GTM. Hence, from the outset the study was designed to develop theory. This is an exemplary way to begin a GTM project.

Iterative process. Data analysis should begin as soon as the first data are collected and there should be interaction between data analysis and data collection (facilitated by theoretical sampling, which is discussed below) throughout the study. This is referred to as the iterative process of data collection and analysis (Corbin & Strauss, 2015). For example, in Holt, Tamminen, Black, Sehn, and Wall's (2008) study of parental involvement in competitive youth soccer settings data were collected through two main phases of fieldwork, allowing for the interaction of data collection and analysis throughout the research. As Holt *et al.* explained, "Data analysis commenced as soon as the first data were collected, and there was a constant interaction between data collection and analysis both *within* and *between* each phase of the study. This iterative process is a fundamental feature of grounded theory" (2008, p. 667; italics added).

Theoretical sampling. Theoretical sampling refers to sampling based on the concepts identified during initial data collection and analysis (Corbin & Strauss, 2008; Strauss & Corbin, 1998). Sampling is flexible as researchers seek new participants in order to help saturate key findings. Often, the *initial sample* can be sampled more purposefully; researchers may initially select a group to interview based on a set of criteria. Then, as the research study progresses, the requirement to sample new people or settings may become apparent as data analysis is used to identify new areas and issues. Researchers may have to go back to the field and broaden their sampling frame, interviewing new people who were not accounted for in the initial purposeful sampling criteria. Theoretical sampling both drives, and is driven by, the interaction of data collection and analysis.

Use of literature. The ways in which literature can be used has been debated among grounded theorists. A good grounded theory is rarely deductively generated based on an existing theory. Glaser (1992) actually argued against conducting a review of literature and using pre-existing theory early in the research process, because it could lead to researchers applying preconceived ideas to the data, rather than letting the data emerge for itself. Although Charmaz (2006) agreed with Glaser that researchers should avoid imposing pre-existing theory onto data, she argued it is impossible to approach research *without* pre-existing ideas. Researchers seldom commence a study with a *tabula rasa* (or "blank slate"), entering the field with no knowledge of the research area (Weed, 2009). Previous research and theory may inform the conceptual context and research questions, may be used at some point during the analysis, or even as late as the discussion/interpretation of the results (Sandelowski, 1993). From my own (Straussian) perspective, a literature review is a valuable and necessary tool to develop research questions, identify whether pre-existing theories exist, and provide justifications for a study (Corbin & Strauss, 2008). I also side with Dey (1999), who suggested GTM researchers should approach their studies with an open mind but not an empty mind. Indeed, from an epistemological perspective it is difficult to imagine theory-free knowledge. Even from a practical perspective it is difficult to imagine a researcher being able to set aside knowledge of the literature while conducting a study. I suggest the literature (i.e., theory and empirical research) should be used sensitively and not rigidly imposed on the data. To use the literature sensitively researchers must therefore have thorough knowledge of the literature in the area they wish to study. This knowledge also provides researchers with a foundation for ensuring their work produces unique insights rather than merely (or unintentionally) replicating previous work.

Coding. Coding refers to a range of analytic techniques used to ask questions of data to identify dimensions of concepts and categories (often referred to as themes in other forms of qualitative research) and relationships therein. By coding data, researchers move from interview transcripts (and other raw data) toward interpretation and the production of a grounded theory. There are some subtle differences in the way coding techniques are described in the three main approaches to GTM (see Table 3.1). The Glaserian (Glaser, 1978, 1992) approach involves *substantive coding* and *theoretical coding*. The Straussian approach (Corbin & Strauss, 2008, Strauss & Corbin, 1998) involves three stages of coding; *open coding*, *axial coding*, and *theoretical integration*. In their most recent work Corbin and Strauss (2015) updated these coding approaches to reflect a more flexible approach, and highlighted the potential use of a range of other analytic tools (see pp. 85–105). Charmaz's (2006) constructivist approach involves *initial coding, focused coding*, and *theoretical integration*. No matter which specific methodology is used, there are at least two shared principles in GTM coding. First, the early stages of coding involve "breaking down" data, whereas the latter stages of coding (i.e., theoretical coding/integration) involve reconstructing the data in theoretically meaningful ways. Second, although these coding techniques are often described in a linear sequence, in fact they are used in an iterative and cyclical manner throughout a study. For example,

Table 3.1 Comparison of coding across different versions of grounded theory

Glaserian (Glaser 1978, 1992)	Straussian (Corbin & Strauss, 2008; Strauss & Corbin, 1998)	Constructivist (Charmaz, 2006)
Two stages of coding to move from substantive codes to a grounded theory: 1. Substantive Coding: through a process of open coding (examination of all the pieces of data) researchers develop substantive codes, which specify the substance or meaning of each segment of data. 2. Theoretical Coding: theoretical codes are applied to the data to allow researchers to integrate substantive codes into a theory. Theoretical codes provide researchers with a means of ordering substantive codes within the social world. Glaser established a list of 18 coding families (groups of theoretical codes) that researchers may use to identify relationships between substantive codes, leading to the development of fully integrated theories.	Three stages of coding to move from description to theory: 1. Open Coding: described as a brainstorming approach, in which researchers fracture the data into its smallest units. Microanalysis, which is the detailed coding of each identified concept, is often a key feature of open coding. 2. Axial Coding: through this process concepts identified during open coding are related to each other. In their original texts Strauss and Corbin (1990, 1998) placed greater emphasis upon axial coding, encouraging researchers to consider their data in terms of conditions, actions, and consequences to identify relationships. In later texts (Corbin & Strauss, 2015) less emphasis is placed on axial coding. 3. Theoretical Integration: the process of linking all the categories together and refining ideas. A core category is created, which is central to the final grounded theory. Note: Corbin and Strauss (2015) updated their discussion of coding to highlight a range of analytic tools that can be used in the coding process.	At least two stages of coding, followed by theoretical integration: 1. Initial Coding: detailed examination of each fragment of data to identify actions. May include word-by-word, line-by-line or incident-to-incident coding. 2. Focused Coding: the process of selecting the most useful codes developed during initial coding and then testing them against further data. Coding of larger segments of data occurs. Through this process codes become more directed and selective. This is a more conceptual step that leads toward theoretical integration. 3. Theoretical Integration: a process through which categories identified in focused coding are integrated. Specific relationships between categories are identified. Charmaz encouraged the use of Glaser's 18 coding families if they fit the data and the previous analysis.

Source: Adapted from Holt, Knight, and Tamminen (2012).

29

if conducting a study that takes three months using the Straussian approach, one does not spend the first month doing open coding, the second month doing axial coding, and the last month doing theoretical integration. Open coding usually comes first, but all three techniques are used iteratively and cyclically from the moment data analysis begins (which, of course, is also the moment data collection begins).

Constant comparison. Constant comparison involves comparing incident with incident in order to classify data. In the words of Corbin and Strauss, constant comparison is "the analytic process of comparing difference pieces of data against each other for similarities and differences" (2015, p. 85). In addition to comparing data with data, data can also be compared with concepts, comparisons can be made between concepts, and with existing theory (Holt & Tamminen, 2010a). By making these comparisons the researcher engages with data in "deep" cognitive ways and works toward the construction of a grounded theory.

Theoretical saturation. Theoretical saturation, a term unique to GTM, is slightly different from the term "data saturation" (which is a term widely used in qualitative research more generally). The differences between these terms are subtle but nonetheless important. Data saturation is taken to mean data should be collected until no new data are generated (O'Reilly & Parker, 2012). In grounded theory, the notion of theoretical saturation does not refer to the point in a research project when no new data are generated, but rather when categories and concepts are fully accounted for (saturated), and relationships between categories and concepts are explained (Green & Thorogood, 2004). Theoretical saturation is "a matter of reaching the point in the research where collecting new data seems counterproductive; the 'new' that is uncovered does not add that much more to the *explanation* at this time" (Strauss & Corbin, 1998, p. 136; italics added). In other words, with theoretical saturation, there are no more emergent patterns in the theory (i.e., the explanation), as opposed to no new data per se. Arguably there will always be new data, but with theoretical saturation those new data do not substantially add to or change the theory being generated.

Theoretical saturation remains a relative concept – a theory is never completely and irrefutably saturated. Rather, researchers should strive to reach an *adequate level* of saturation such that their concepts, categories, and the relationships between these concepts and categories are clearly articulated. Theoretical saturation is therefore a judgment made by the researcher during the process of conducting a study. It is absolutely essential there is interaction between data collection and analysis, because otherwise the researcher cannot make informed judgments about the level of saturation. As such, theoretical saturation is also a principle used to determine a sample size (i.e., when adequate theoretical saturation is obtained the sample size is sufficient).

Whereas theoretical saturation is a vitally important principle, I have learned it is necessary to use additional information to provide sample-size estimates prior to beginning the research (e.g., for grant applications, thesis/dissertation proposals, or research ethics board applications). I use three sources of information to provide a convincing justification for sample-size estimates. First, I explain that the final judgment on sample size will be determined using the principle of theoretical saturation. Second, I estimate a sample size by using the published literature. For instance, if there are similar types of GTM studies that involved 20 and 30 participants, respectively, then I can reasonably estimate my study will require about 25 participants (of course, issues like the level of participant engagement, length, and number of interviews also need to be factored in). Finally, some authors have provided guidelines for sample size in GTM studies (e.g., Mason, 2010; Morse, 2000). Combined, the principle of theoretical saturation, the size and scope of previous similar studies, and published guidelines can create a compelling argument for sample-size estimates.

Potential pitfalls when using GTM

In the introduction I mentioned a major criticism of the use of GTM in sport and exercise has been the cherry-picking of some techniques rather than embracing GTM as a total methodology (Weed, 2009). In other words, some researchers have used a couple of techniques – most often coding techniques – and mistakenly labeled their studies as grounded theories. In Holt and Tamminen's (2010a) review of GTM research in sport and exercise psychology, of the 17 studies they reviewed only 9 presented some kind of grounded theory. In other cases, researchers used techniques from GTM to produce a list of themes and categories rather than a theory. If the point of using GTM is to develop theory, then one would expect a theory to be produced. Thus, it would be wise to avoid the pitfall of cherry-picking a few techniques and rather, no matter which variant of GTM is being used, embrace it as a total methodology. On a related note, it is also wise to avoid trying to somehow amalgamate the different variants of GTM in a particular study because of the important philosophical, conceptual, and procedural differences between the variants.

Another potential pitfall, which has not been discussed extensively in the sport and exercise literature, concerns the use of diagrams and figures to represent the final outcomes of GTM (i.e., the theories themselves). A common mistake I have come across (most often when reviewing papers for journals – many of which sadly never make it through to publication) is the presentation of incredibly complex diagrams and figures as the grounded theory product/output. More often than not these diagrams and figures include a vast number of unidirectional and bidirectional arrows. Presumably arrows are intended to depict some kind of relationship between concepts. However, I am frequently disappointed by the fact that researchers fail to even discuss what the arrows might mean on their diagrams and figures. This is a major oversight because part of the analysis in GTM involves identifying *statements of relationships* between concepts. These statements of relationships should be as well saturated as the concepts and categories they are intended to link. I offer two pieces of advice on this issue. First, if you are going to include arrows, the nature of the relationships must be explained (and, you can document your emerging views on statements of relationships during the coding process by writing memos throughout the analysis). Second, it would be wise to produce parsimonious models with a relatively limited number of arrows/relationships. The more arrows you have, the more difficulties you will face in trying to saturate and explain them.

Drawing further on my personal experience with GTM, another pitfall I have learned to avoid is thinking too descriptively. Over the years I have discussed the evolution of my thinking on this topic in a couple of book chapters (Corbin & Holt, 2005, 2011). It all stems back to my first attempt at GTM research, which was a study of talent development in soccer (Holt & Dunn, 2004). In the early days of this research I thought about the study in very descriptive terms. I concentrated on fully expanding concepts and categories, and paid less attention to how these concepts and categories may be related (the relationships being the key element of a grounded theory of course). In fact, during my PhD, it was only when one of my supervisors (Dr. Juliet Corbin) commented on my "descriptive obsession" that I understood the need to move away from describing the data and toward a more theoretical approach. It was an "aha" moment when I realized the entire point of my research enterprise was to develop a theory, not to write wonderfully detailed accounts of concepts and categories. Of course, researchers need detailed concepts and categories, but not at the expense of theoretical development. Grounded theorists must think theoretically from the very moment they conceptualize and plan their studies.

Armchair walkthrough

A useful tool for planning qualitative studies is the "armchair walkthrough." Originally presented by Morse (1999) and revised by Mayan (2009), the armchair walkthrough has been adapted for GTM studies (Holt & Tamminen, 2010b). An overview of the process of the armchair walkthrough is provided in Table 3.2. The armchair walkthrough is based on the principle of methodological coherence, which means "congruence between your epistemological and ontological viewpoint, your theoretical position/perspective, your research question, and so on" (Mayan, 2009, p. 13). The armchair walkthrough is a heuristic intended to provide a planning framework for the key decisions a researcher may take in planning a GTM study. As Holt and Tamminen (2010b) noted, two caveats must be considered when completing the armchair walkthrough provided in Table 3.2. First, the items are presented in a linear manner, but decisions about methodological coherence are made in a more cyclical, interactive way. For instance, decisions about an appropriate number of participants may change as researchers seek a sample size necessary to achieve theoretical saturation. Second, the armchair walkthrough is not a prescriptive formula, but rather a guide to "help researchers make important research decisions as they plan their grounded theory studies" (Holt & Tamminen, 2010b, p. 420).

Table 3.2 A heuristic for planning methodologically coherent grounded theory studies

Research Decisions	Issues to Consider	Suggested Readings
Ontology, Epistemology	Select philosophical perspective consistent with variant of GTM.	Weed (2009) Weed (2010)
Research Question	Usually focus on examining some form of social process in context, with the goal of creating a grounded theory. GTM is useful for areas/issues where adequate theorizing does not exist.	Refer to original GTM methodological texts.
Selection of GTM Variant	Select variant of GTM consistent with philosophical perspective.	Bryant and Charmaz (2007)
Participants	Identify appropriate population and settings to be sampled. Purposeful sampling may be established to define initial sample.	Refer to original GTM methodological texts.
Sample Size	Use principle of theoretical saturation, make estimates based on previous studies, use guidelines in literature.	Mason (2010), Morse (2000)
Planning for Interaction of Data Collection and Analysis	Engage in analysis as soon as first data are collected.	Bruce (2007)
Data-Collection Methods	Consider interviews, observations, documentary analysis (specific decisions will be based on variant of GTM selected).	Refer to original GTM methodological texts.
Data-Analysis Methods	Use coding techniques and other theory-generating techniques based on variant of GTM selected.	Refer to original GTM methodological texts.
Final Product	Know what type of theory will be created (e.g., substantive or more formal). Diagram possible 'final' theories.	Refer to original GTM methodological texts.

Source: Adapted from Holt and Tamminen (2010b).

Additional tips for planning GTM studies

Building from the armchair walkthrough and incorporating the contributions of Bruce (2007), here I provide some further suggestions for planning GTM studies. These suggestions are far less conceptual and deal with practical issues. They are suggestions that may help to create 'optimal conditions' for conducting GTM studies (Holt & Tamminen, 2010b). Again, like the armchair walkthrough, these are not fixed and prescriptive guidelines, but rather a flexible list that may be useful for students and supervisors alike in the early stages of research design.

Prior to engaging in research (often during the proposal writing, grant writing, or research-design planning stage, depending on the nature of the research), researchers face a number of decisions. Therefore, I first detail some "pre-research" decisions before going on to consider some practical factors to consider during the process of conducting the study.

Pre-research considerations

Ask a research question suited for the use of a GTM approach. The choice of methodology is largely based on the research question. Hence, it stands to reason that the research question(s) posed should logically lead to the choice of a GTM. Questions well suited to the use of GTM include "How do people successfully change their PA [physical activity] habits?" (Hutchinson *et al.*, 2013, p. 111) and "How do talented children become professional adult athletes?" (Holt & Dunn, 2004, p. 199). Note that both these questions refer to some kind of process, and GTM can be quite useful for helping to unravel different components of a process and how they may be related.

Obtain training. Learning GTM is a *craft* that takes time and thoughtful supervision to develop. Morse (1994) described "the menace of minus mentoring," which is when researchers learn methods only from books and end up muddling them. I have found workshops to be an invaluable resource for learning more about research methodologies. These are offered on a regular basis at conferences and in special seminars around the world. A practical tip, therefore, is to attend these workshops. In the ideal world one would attend a workshop based on the variant of GTM to be used, presented by one of the world's leading experts in that variant. This may be unrealistic but, fortunately, with an increasing number of researchers who study, apply, teach, or write about GTM (Bryant & Charmaz, 2007) there are many skilled individuals who frequently present workshops. It is a good idea to take one to begin the journey of developing the craft of practicing GTM research.

Select a variant of GTM. I have mentioned this before, but feel the need to stress the issue. From my perspective, researchers should select the variant of GTM they are going to use and stick with it. Selecting a variant that fits with one's philosophical perspective is a good idea. To be blunt, cherry-picking or taking a "pick and mix" approach (Weed, 2009) is not a good idea.

Consider existing knowledge. As research questions are formulated the broad area of study comes into focus. An important issue to consider is whether there is a great deal of existing theory in the area of study. If there is extensive prior theoretical work, this is red flag to a grounded theorist. Remember that the entire point of using GTM is to create theory. If extensive theory already exists, there is not going to be much room for a new grounded theory. Take, for example, the goal orientations literature in sport psychology. This has been studied extensively for over 30 years, with an exceptionally strong theoretical basis. Researchers may not have a great deal of success creating a new grounded theory of goal orientations. On the other hand, relevant issues that have little theoretical foundation are often ideally suited for the use of GTM. It is wise to ask research questions in areas that are relatively underdeveloped theoretically.

During-research considerations

Interaction between data collection and analysis, driven by theoretical sample, must occur. One of the most critical components of a GTM is the interaction between data collection and analysis. This is not to say other qualitative approaches do not involve interaction between data collection and analysis (e.g., most forms of ethnography require researchers to be engaged in data analysis while they are in the field). In GTM interaction of data collection and analysis is driven by, and drives, theoretical sampling, all with the end goal of developing theory in mind. On a purely anecdotal level I have found that data collection and analysis in GTM takes about twice as long as a graduate student thinks it will take!

Remember to go back to your research ethics board. When I submit a proposal for a GTM study to our institutional research ethics board (see also Chapter 24), I make an educated guess about the sample size *and* who I need to sample. For instance, for a (hypothetical) study of parenting in youth sport, I know I will have to speak with parents and it is quite likely I will also have to speak with their children to gain additional perspectives. Thus, in submitting ethics, I would clearly identify both samples and include interview guides that I will use for parents and children. As a study progresses I may realize that additional theoretical sampling is needed. Perhaps I need to speak to coaches, league administrators, or change my initial sampling criteria to recruit different groups of parents (e.g., those whose children have dropped out of sport). All these changes require amendments to research ethics board approvals. Hence, it is quite typical – and usually necessary – to go back to a research ethics board, sometimes on several occasions, during the process of conducting a GTM study.

Conclusion

The question I posed at the beginning of this chapter was "What makes a grounded theory a grounded theory?" The interaction of data collection and analysis, driving and driven by theoretical sampling, alongside a range of data analysis techniques are all hallmarks of GTM. Just including these techniques, in my opinion, is not enough for a "true" GTM. The production of a grounded theory is really what makes grounded theory a grounded theory. The techniques, thoughtfully applied, should enable the researcher to produce the grounded theory. In this sense, as I mentioned in the introduction, grounded theory is both the process and the product.

As my own career has developed, so too has my understanding of GTM. Certainly not all the studies in which I mentioned GTM would fit my (current) "purist" approach to using the methodology as a total methodology. As I look back at some of my own studies I cringe at the times when I dropped in the occasional reference to GTM when I was not using it as a total methodology. But, as I have argued previously, as thoughtful and self-reflective researchers we must "readily acknowledge the mistakes of the past for fear of simply repeating them. This may mean putting egos aside for a moment for the good of the discipline" (Holt & Tamminen, 2010b, p. 422). My hope is that this chapter enables researchers to understand and let go of mistakes of the past and set new standards for GTM research in sport and exercise.

Note

1 For more complete information on the history and variations in GTM see Bryant and Charmaz (2007).

References

Bruce, C. (2007). Questions arising about emergence, data collection, and its interaction with analysis in a grounded theory study. *International Journal of Qualitative Methods, 6*, 1–12.

Brustad, R. J. (2008). Qualitative research approaches. In T. Horn (Ed.), *Advances in sport psychology* (3rd ed., pp. 21–43). Champaign, IL: Human Kinetics.

Bryant, A. & Charmaz, K. (2007). *The Sage handbook of grounded theory.* Thousand Oaks, CA: Sage.

Charmaz, K. (2006). *Constructing grounded theory: A practical guide through qualitative analysis.* Thousand Oaks, CA: Sage.

Corbin, J. & Holt, N. L. (2005). Grounded theory. In B. Somekh and C. Lewin (Eds.), *Research methods in the social sciences* (pp. 49–55). Thousand Oaks, CA: Sage.

Corbin, J. C. & Holt, N. L. (2011). Grounded theory. In B. Somekh and K. Lewin (Eds.), *Theory and methods in social science research* (2nd ed., pp. 113–120). London: Sage.

Corbin, J. & Strauss, A. L. (2008). *Basics of qualitative research: Techniques and procedures for developing grounded theory* (3rd ed.). Thousand Oaks, CA: Sage.

Corbin, J. & Strauss, A. L. (2015). *Basics of qualitative research: Techniques and procedures for developing grounded theory* (4th ed.). Thousand Oaks, CA: Sage.

Culver, D. M., Gilbert, W., & Sparkes, A. (2012). Qualitative research in sport psychology journals: The next decade 2000–2009 and beyond. *Sport Psychologist, 26*, 261–281.

Dey, I. (1999). *Grounding grounded theory.* San Diego: Academic Press.

Glaser, B. (1978). *Theoretical sensitivity.* Mill Valley, CA: Sociology Press.

Glaser, B. (1992). *Basics of grounded theory analysis: Emerging vs. forcing.* Mill Valley, CA: Sociology Press.

Glaser, B. G. & Strauss, A. L. (1965). Discovery of substantive theory: A basic strategy underlying qualitative research. *American Behavioral Scientist, 8*, 5–12.

Glaser, B. G. & Strauss, A. L. (1967). *The discovery of grounded theory: Strategies for qualitative research.* New York: Aldine.

Green, J. & Thorogood, N. (2004). *Qualitative methods for health research.* London: Sage.

Holt, N. L. & Dunn, J. G. H. (2004). Toward a grounded theory of the psychosocial competencies and environmental conditions associated with soccer success. *Journal of Applied Sport Psychology, 16*, 199–219.

Holt, N. L., Knight, C. J., & Tamminen, K. A. (2012). Grounded theory. In K. Armour & D. MacDonald (Eds.), *Research methods in physical education and youth sport* (pp. 276–294). London: Routledge.

Holt, N. L. & Tamminen, K. A. (2010a). Improving grounded theory research in sport and exercise psychology: Further reflections as a response to Mike Weed. *Psychology of Sport and Exercise, 11*, 405–413.

Holt, N. L. & Tamminen, K. A. (2010b). Moving forward with grounded theory in sport and exercise psychology. *Psychology of Sport and Exercise, 11*, 419–422.

Holt, N. L., Tamminen, K. A., Black, D. E., Sehn, Z. L., & Wall, M. P. (2008). Parental involvement in competitive youth sport settings. *Psychology of Sport and Exercise, 9*, 663–685.

Hutchison, A. J., Johnston, L. H., & Breckon, J. D. (2011). Grounded theory-based research within exercise psychology: A critical review. *Qualitative Research in Psychology, 8*, 247–272.

Hutchinson, A. J., Johnston, L. H., & Breckon, J. D. (2013). A grounded theory of successful long-term physical activity behavior change. *Qualitative Research in Sport, Exercise, and Health, 5*, 109–129.

Mason, M. (2010). Sample size and saturation in PhD studies using qualitative interviews. *Forum: Qualitative Social Research, 11*(3). Available from http://www.qualitative-research.net/index.php/fqs/article/view/1428/3027.

Mayan, M. J. (2009). *Essentials of qualitative inquiry.* Walnut Creek, CA: Left Coast Press.

Morse, J. M. (1994). *Critical issues in qualitative research methods.* Thousand Oaks, CA: Sage.

Morse, J. M. (1995). The significance of saturation. *Qualitative Health Research, 5*, 147–149.

Morse, J. M. (1997). *Completing a qualitative project: Details and dialogue.* Thousand Oaks, CA: Sage.

Morse, J. M. (1999). The armchair walkthrough. *Qualitative Health Research, 9*, 435–436.

Morse, J. M. (2000). Determining sample size. *Qualitative Health Research, 10*, 3–5.

O'Reilly, M. & Parker, N. (2012). "Unsatisfactory saturation": A critical exploration of the notion of saturated sample sizes in qualitative research. *Qualitative Research, 13*, 190–197.

Sandelowski, M. (1993). Theory unmasked: The uses and guises of theory in qualitative research. *Research in Nursing and Health, 16*, 213–218.

Strauss, A. & Corbin, J. (1990). *Basics of qualitative research: Grounded theory procedures and techniques*. London: Sage.

Strauss, A. & Corbin, J. (1998). *Basics of qualitative research: Techniques and procedures for developing grounded theory* (2nd ed.). Newbury Park, CA: Sage.

Weed, M. (2009). Research quality considerations for grounded theory research in sport and exercise psychology. *Psychology of Sport and Exercise, 10*, 502–510.

Weed, M. (2010). A quality debate on grounded theory in sport and exercise psychology? A commentary on potential areas for future debate. *Psychology of Sport and Exercise, 11*, 414–418.

4

NARRATIVE INQUIRY

From cardinal to marginal ... and back?

Anthony Papathomas

This chapter is a story about stories. It is a story about the historical significance of narrative inquiry and its current and future role within qualitative research in sport and exercise. Consistent with the relativist beliefs upheld by most of those who subscribe to narrative forms of knowing, this chapter represents *a* story, not *the* story. In this chapter I do not claim to be objective, definitive, or that most poisonous of chalices, 'right'. Writing to be right – or to be authoritative and comprehensive – enslaves an academic to pre-existing insights and conservative platitudes. The safety of a well-worn path can breed a self-confirming body of knowledge; chapter after chapter, article after article, each indiscernible from the other. In contrast, here, my goal is both more humble and more challenging. I aim to encourage the reader to think differently about the roots of narrative inquiry, to promote a critical awareness of narrative work within sport and exercise and to envisage its diverse innovations and rich potentialities. First, a brief history of narrative is offered. Second, I consider how we might define narrative from a methodological perspective. Third, various examples of narrative inquiry are reviewed and I highlight the types of research questions to which it is most suited. Fourth, innovative practices in narrative-based research are explored.

Philosophical prologue

As a prologue to this *story about stories*, it is important to briefly outline the philosophical foundations that underpin narrative inquiry. Narrative inquiry typically falls within an interpretivist paradigm characterized by ontological relativism and epistemological social constructionism. A relativist perspective asserts that reality outside of the physical world, that is, psychosocial reality, is multiple, malleable and mind-dependent. Social constructionism proffers that knowledge is constructed through cultural auspices and relational interactions rather than something that is *objectively observed*, *discovered* or *found* (Burr, 2015). We are always intimately a part of any understanding we have of what counts as knowledge; there can be no theory-free knowledge (Smith & Deemer, 2000). These assumptions clash with those of the positivist paradigm of the natural sciences which is underpinned by ontological realism and the belief that, with sound methods, we can accurately and unbiasedly discover an objective reality (Angen, 2000).

What does narrative's philosophical backdrop mean for narrative inquiry? First, narrative researchers are interested in personal truth ahead of objective truth, because for them 'objective Truth' does not exist. Narrative scholars therefore seek out personal experience stories not in spite of their subjectivity but *because* of their subjectivity – subjective narrations illuminate the many versions of reality that co-exist. These stories are gleaned through methods that allow the narrator to offer their own world view, such as unstructured or semi-structured life-story interviews. Further, narrative researchers will ask unrehearsed questions and will prompt, react and interact authentically within an interview setting. This is because narrative researchers are unafraid of their own biases owing to a principal belief that all knowledge is theory-laden. Bias then is embraced and acknowledged in both method and analysis, and it becomes integral to the co-constructed knowledge of any given inquiry.

Narrative's rich tapestry

The drive to narrate, the *urge* to story our experience (Myerhoff, 2007), has been with us for at least 40,000 years. Palaeolithic cave art, for example, is imbued with narrative content and can display complex literary features such as composition, juxtaposition, association and scene (Dobrez, 2012). Equivalently, prehistoric Australian rock paintings demonstrate similar storied form, and represent performances of the cultural environments inhabited by hunter-gatherer clans (Layton, 1985). It is argued that the dawn of the oral tradition may even predate these visual artefacts, thereby placing the first examples of narrative as anywhere up to 100,000 years old (Sugiyama, 2001). Historian Yuval Noah Harari (2014), in his international bestseller *Sapiens: A Brief History of Humankind*, argued that our capacity to tell stories, to imagine, to use mythical tales to make sense of the world around us, has been fundamental to the survival of the human species and essential to our rise to the pinnacle of the animal kingdom. *Homo sapiens,* unlike other animals, could tell complex tales that could bond, mobilize, warn and teach. Constructing grand myths about abstract concepts such as gods and spirits promoted cooperation on a grand scale through a shared commitment to a given story or belief. This notion of narrative capacity as an adaptive evolutionary function is an attractive theory and one that Sugiyama also adheres to:

> The universality of narrative suggests that those individuals who were able (or better able) to tell and process stories enjoyed a reproductive advantage over those who were less skilled or incapable of doing so, thereby passing on this ability to subsequent generations. It would appear, then, that storytelling has played an important role in our development as a species.
>
> *(Sugiyama, 2001, p. 235)*

If narrative capacity was central to the survival of early *Homo sapiens,* then, to borrow from MacIntyre (1981), we have truly evolved into 'storytelling animals'. For Nigam, it is a process that continues into the modern world: 'A compelling storyteller would seem to have a survival advantage. Just as now, in a market place full of narratives . . . the better storyteller is likely to out-compete poorer storytellers for resources' (cited in Bochner & Riggs, 2014, p. 569). According to Sugiyama, such evolutionary perspectives may explain why narratives are so inherent to our existence. For example, by the age of three most children can tell a story (Engel, 1995) and this sophisticated narrative competency occurs without formal schooling. In turn, neuroscientists suggest our brains are particularly receptive to stories. Studies deploying functional magnetic resonance imaging (fMRI) of the brain have shown that a process of *neural-coupling* occurs between a storyteller and listener; the brain activity of the latter mirrors that of the former (Stephens, Silbert & Hasson, 2010). In effect, stories may be abstract social constructions, but their impact can be biological.

Narrative as inquiry

Narrative therefore should not be considered some new methodological fad, but rather the most ancient and refined means to knowledge and understanding available to us. Narrative is the cardinal approach to making sense of our worlds. Yet, somewhere along the way, amidst an uprising of the positivist paradigm, narrative became less cardinal and more marginal. So dominant is the positivist ideology that it is often seen as the *received view* and can be considered representative of science as we know it; the search for universal laws that support explanation, prediction and control (Ponterotto, 2005). Emergent in the natural sciences, this hypothetico-deductive approach also prevailed in the social and human sciences. Despite being replete with personal stories, fields such as sociology and psychology have traditionally been studied according to the same scientific principles as fields such as physics and biology. This is to say that, as misguided as it now seems, the same methods used to get to the *Truth* of a cell or an organism have been used to understand cultural attitudes or human emotions. Other ways of knowing, including narrative approaches, were dismissed as soft, unscientific and non-generalizable.

The narrative turn can be loosely conceived as a small but significant eruption of scholarly writings around the mid-1980s that argued for the merits of narrative knowing within the human and social sciences (e.g. Bruner, 1986, 1990; Polkinghorne, 1988; Rosenwald & Ochberg, 1992; Sarbin, 1986). This call to narrative was born out of a fervent dissatisfaction with the capacity for positivist science to address issues that were personally, socially and culturally complex; human issues. Polkinghorne lamented his 'loss of faith in the ability of research in the human disciplines to deliver on their original promise of helping to solve human and social problems' (1988, p. ix). For him, and others within sociology and psychology, the natural science replication project was failing. The positivist emphasis on control and prediction was so dismissive of context, subjectivity and meaning that it ceased to be of any relevance to what happened in people's worlds. Narrative, argued to be a vital means by which human experience can be made meaningful (Polkinghorne, 1988), offered an attractive alternative. For the first time, the study of personal stories was posited as not only a valid form of scientific inquiry but an essential one.

As the acceptance of narrative as a form of scientific investigation increased, so too did the need to consider more closely what characteristics constitute the narrative form. As a result, there is no shortage of definitions for what a narrative is. However, a narrative represents a curious social artefact in that it is so familiar to us – so deeply entrenched in everything we think, feel and do – that it perversely becomes quite difficult to articulate. It is comparable to describing a universal human emotion such as joy or anger; a concise definition often escapes us and those that exist usually feel incomplete, unsatisfactory or astray from our own personal conceptions. Indeed, most concerted attempts to define narrative come with an obligatory disclaimer that what is to be offered is in no way complete or definitive (e.g. Riessman, 2008; Smith & Sparkes, 2009a). For some, including many researchers in sport and exercise (e.g. Jowett & Frost, 2007; Lally, 2007; Lauer, Gould, Roman & Pierce, 2010), a segment of spoken or written text is sufficient to constitute a narrative. Broad, generic definitions of this kind typically view narrative as synonymous with all forms of interview data, rather than as something with specific characteristic features that is tied to a particular genre of research. As such, instances where data are referred to as narrative are not always examples of narrative inquiry.

Where narrative is conceived as both a theoretical and a methodological construct with associated ontological and epistemological underpinnings, definitions are forced to become more specific and more complex. In their well-cited narrative position piece, Smith and Sparkes drew on a range of sources to offer the following:

> . . . a narrative is taken to mean a complex genre that routinely contains a point and characters along with a plot connecting events that unfold sequentially over time and in space to provide an overarching explanation or consequence. It is a constructed form or template which people rely on to tell stories.
>
> *(Smith & Sparkes, 2009a, p. 2)*

In dissecting this layered definition it is possible to tease out three important features that connote the presence of a narrative. Specifically, where there is an identifiable genre, plot and character, there is usually narrative. To illustrate their importance, it is necessary to delve into each of these three interrelated constructs.

First, the notion of a 'genre', or similarly a 'template', tells of the generality of narrative. Narratives represent the overarching thematic structure of a story and there are a finite number of these structures to draw from. Literary theorists have long suggested there may be as few as four very general narrative forms from which we draw on to make sense of the world: comedy, romance, tragedy and irony (see Frye, 1957). Similarly, Gergen and Gergen (1986) regularly refer to progressive, regressive and stability narratives as the three primary story structures that are used to understand life experiences. For them, whether we are recounting significant events of the day or those experiences that define a lifetime, the fundamental template seldom strays from some combination of bad to good (progressive), good to bad (regressive) or stable (unchanged). Other narrative theorists have sought to identify context-specific narrative types. For example, the study of illness narratives has led to numerous theories regarding the often constrained ways that individuals come to understand chronic ill health. For example, Frank (1995) explored narratives of illness and medicine and argued that serious illness is predominately characterized by one of three narrative types; restitution, chaos or quest. The former is deemed to be the most dominant storyline and holds a basic structure of 'yesterday I was healthy, today I'm sick, tomorrow I'll be healthy again' (p. 77). This master narrative is adopted by ill people throughout the Western world irrespective of the intricate details that characterize their own personal story. Whether it's cancer (Simpson, Heath & Wall, 2014) spinal-cord injury (Sparkes & Smith, 2005) or an eating disorder (Papathomas, Smith & Lavallee, 2015), restitution is often the genre of choice. It is the template on which to map personal stories of illness. Indeed, this speaks to the difference, albeit contested, between narrative and story. We can have two different stories (e.g. spinal injury and eating disorders) guided by the same narrative genre (restitution).

The second important feature of narrative is the presence of plot and an associated 'overarching explanation or consequence'. In simple illustrative terms, experience 'A' leads to experience 'B', culminating in experience 'C'. Narratives therefore often involve extended recounting, although the length of articulation by no means determines the existence of plot and thus of narrative. For example, a rich and vivid description of the psychophysiological symptoms of athlete performance anxiety may be useful phenomenologically, but to constitute a narrative there must also be a description of why this anxiety response occurred and/or what the short-term (e.g. choking) and/or long-term (e.g. burnout, dropout) consequences of it were. These details are central to narrative inquiry as they tap into an individual's emplotment work: the act of organising life events into an order that makes explanatory sense and provides meaning to experience

(Ricoeur, 1984). The importance of plot is further underlined by Jarvinen (2001), who has asserted that to describe a life is to explain a life, as each significant event is causally linked to the next, providing the emplotment that gives meaning to who we are.

The third feature – character – identifies both personal and social elements of a good story. All narratives present characters who act, as well as interact, desire, think, feel and move the plot within which they are framed towards resolution or meaning (McAdams, 1993). Narratives do not only contain character, they *reveal* character, or, more specifically, they reveal identity. The athlete who tells of overcoming adversity to succeed – a redemption narrative – constructs an identity based on resilience and heroism. As argued by Ricoeur, it is 'the identity of the story that gives the identity of the character' (1992, p. 148). For McAdams (2001), identity is constructed via a personal myth – an evolving, carefully crafted life story – which serves to integrate the various facets of who we are. This process of identity construction is very much a conscious effort according to McAdams. Although he acknowledges the cultural and relational contributions to a personal myth, personal agency remains at the fore in how we shape the self. We, as the lead characters, craft and refine our personal myth over time, as prompted by biological and psychological developmental needs such as 'puberty' and the 'midlife'.

Others see narratives as predominantly social and interpersonal constructions that occur through and within various 'intersubjective webs of relationality' or 'public narratives' (Somers, 1994, p. 618). Public narratives are conceptualized as dominant stories within institutional networks such as the family, school or church, and it is argued that they hold a primary and immediate influence on the stories we tell as our own (our ontological narratives). Rather than a conscious project across the life-course (McAdams, 1993, 2001), Somers views identity as a more malleable, transient and socially determined construct:

> The narrative identity approach embeds the actor within relationships and stories that shift over time and space. It thus precludes categorical stability in action . . . hence narrative identity is processual and relational . . . *all* identities (male and female) must be analyzed in the context of relational and cultural matrices because they do not 'exist' outside of those complexes.
>
> *(Somers, 1994, p. 621f)*

From this perspective, narrative identity is considered a primarily *interactional accomplishment* (Gubrium & Holstein, 2009). As such, the myriad of characters that are portrayed in a given narrative may be as relevant as the central character of the narrator. These individuals, who at times can seem peripheral, give important clues as to how meaning was constructed.

Narrative inquiry in sport and exercise

Scholars in sport and exercise often refer to narrative inquiry as *alternative* (Tsang, 2000) and *emerging* (Phoenix & Smith, 2011). This is not to say that these scholars are unwitting of narrative's great tradition; as pioneers of narrative inquiry in sport and exercise they actually represent a minority who are fully cognizant of its heritage. Rather, my critique is levelled at the disciplines, whether sport psychology or sport sociology, to which these scholars speak. Disciplines with such reprehensibly narrow methodological repertoires that terms such as alternative and emerging are, in fact, *accurate* descriptions of narrative's role within them. Despite Denzin and Lincoln's claim that 'the narrative turn has been taken' (2000, p. 3), the majority of those researching sport and exercise are only just approaching the junction, with some so stubbornly focused on the road ahead that the turn has been missed with little more than a cursory glance as to where it may have led (e.g. Eklund, Jeffery, Dobersek & Cho, 2011).

Regardless of such pockets of uninformed scepticism, important strides have been made towards narrative forms of knowing within sport and exercise studies. When discussing narrative's progression in the field from embryonic to substantive, the collaborations of Brett Smith and Andrew Sparkes are an obvious and appropriate starting point. Their corpus of work developed in men paralysed through sport (e.g. Smith & Sparkes, 2002, 2004; Sparkes & Smith, 2003, 2005, 2008, 2011), as well as their series of methodological position pieces (e.g. Smith & Sparkes, 2009a, b; Sparkes and Smith, 2009), was instrumental in inspiring a proliferation of narratively framed research. Speaking at the sociology-psychology intersection, these studies awakened scholars to the capacity for narrative inquiry to address issues relating to each respective discipline, as well as narrative's potential to draw connections between the two.

Smith and Sparkes have been effective in showing the power of culture in determining the workings of the mind, but also that such cultural determinism is not absolute and that there is human agency in our narrative constructions. In terms of the former, supported by extended interview extracts, Sparkes and Smith (2005) theorized that spinally injured men made sense of paralysis by adopting pre-existing, culturally available narrative types, and that the type of narrative drawn upon shaped individual thoughts and behaviours. Whether these paralyzed participants experienced hope or crisis, anger or contentment, regret or optimism was determined largely by narratives that are out there circulating in culture. Essentially, our sociocultural worlds impact our psychological worlds. Equally, in other work, the authors have demonstrated that men adapting to sudden paralysis are not empty vessels passively taking on cultural understandings, but instead can have an active role in shaping a story to live by. Specifically, they have highlighted principles of *narrative practice in action* and identified the ways spinally injured men compose their own personal story (Smith & Sparkes, 2002). For example, independently formulating narrative linkages – essentially emplotment work – added nuance to dominant illness and injury narratives, and opened up possibilities for alternative understandings. Personally constructing linkages can lead to *narrative slippage*; the elements of disconnect between the features of a cultural narrative and precisely how an individual *chooses* to integrate that narrative into their lives. For Smith and Sparkes, this means a 'narrator is capable of fashioning diverse themes that are pertinent to his life story and biographical particulars, and through the act of composition he gains a degree of narrative ownership' (2002, p. 160). Here, the psychological impacts the cultural.

Although it cannot be claimed that narrative inquiry has burgeoned since these initial studies, there has been a steady growth of narratively framed constructionist research across sport and exercise. The work of Carless and Douglas (see Douglas & Carless, 2009a, Carless & Douglas, 2009, 2012, 2013) around the performance narrative in elite sport has provided new insights regarding the darker side of competitive sport, as well as the difficulties associated with transitioning out of it. The performance narrative is a culturally determined story of dedication to sporting achievement to the exclusion of other areas of life (Douglas & Carless, 2009a). When an athlete's experience does not align with the performance narrative – such as when sporting achievement is not forthcoming – the authors argue that the consequences can be psychologically devastating and can include issues such as self-harm and depression (see Carless & Douglas, 2009; Douglas & Carless, 2009a). Although narrative inquiry is useful for understanding moments of trauma and difficulty, it can also be used to identify healthier storylines by which to live. Healthier narratives have been identified that broaden how success is conceptualized to incorporate process over outcome, embodied experience and social connectedness (Carless & Douglas, 2012).

Narrative modes of inquiry have also been applied to explore the lives of athletes with eating disorders. Given the aforementioned capacity for narrative to speak to both psychological and sociological issues, narrative inquiry actually presents a very logical choice for the study of eating disorders, which are universally considered to be 'psychosocial' in nature (e.g. Keel & Forney, 2013). In a study that compared male and female runners' experiences of disordered eating, Busanich, McGannon and Schinke (2014) found narrative theory useful for identifying the ways divergent gendered discourses impacted psychological health. The two athletes interviewed both subscribed to a 'success at all costs' storyline, which created a narrative space within which to legitimize dangerous eating behaviours. This was especially important for the male participant who was eager to story his disordered eating as a sporting issue, thereby distinguishing it from the culturally defined 'female disease'. On the other hand, the female participant discussed her eating behaviours openly and frankly, suggesting maladaptive eating can be constructed as a normalized activity amongst female athletes. Busanich and colleagues argue that cultural conceptions of eating disorders as a female disease can infiltrate narrative constructions causing fear, shame and embarrassment amongst male athletes, and leading to an unhealthy sense of inevitability and normality amongst female athletes.

A further athlete eating disorder study explored how the illness is narratively constructed within an athlete's immediate family unit (see Papathomas, Smith & Lavallee, 2015). Drawing on numerous interviews carried out over a 12-month period, this study was the first to incorporate an athlete's parents' stories of family life with an eating disorder alongside the athlete's own personal tale. When family members drew upon the same narrative constructions – namely, restitution and the desire to overcome the illness – relationships were strengthened as they worked towards a joint goal of recovery. Over time however, with the eating disorder persistent and recovery not forthcoming, living by a restitution narrative became burdensome. Explicitly, the authors claim that the 'mismatch between actual experience and preferred experience placed great strain on family relationships' (Papathomas *et al.*, 2015, p. 323). Moreover, although the athlete was able to draw on a different narrative resource – one that placed less emphasis on recovery – in order to realign her story with her experience, her parents remained totally committed to restitution and the promise of a return to health. When family members draw on contrasting illness narratives therefore, frustration, anger and conflict ensue. On a broad level, the study demonstrates that narratives are interactional accomplishments, co-constructions taken on through social relations; but also individual endeavours that can contrast markedly with the narrative constructions of those closest to us, sometimes at great expense.

From an exercise perspective, narrative principles have been used to explore both the health benefits of exercise, as well as the mechanisms underpinning exercise promotion and maintenance. Contrasting traditional exercise and well-being research, which has focused on measuring symptom amelioration, Carless (2008) drew on a range of life-history data sources to narratively explore a man's experiences of running and schizophrenia. In the analysis, it is argued that running provides a narrative thread that could connect the participant's pre-diagnosis and post-diagnosis selves. With his identity plunged into chaos on *becoming* schizophrenic, re-engaging with running enabled identity to be restored and a sense of narrative coherence achieved. When the *story of self* is disrupted, as can often be the case with serious mental illness, passion for exercise can provide a narrative bridge that connects the present with the past when few other connections exist. Exercise is useful then not because it takes schizophrenia away, but because it is 'a personally meaningful activity which permits a recreation of identity and sense of self' (Carless, 2008, p. 246). Running acts as the narrative glue holding a fragmented life together.

In reference to physical activity promotion and maintenance, Papathomas, Williams and Smith (2015) adopted a narrative approach in an effort to address the shortcomings associated with dominant cognitive approaches. The authors explored the types of narratives that underpinned stories told by physically active spinal injured people. A structural narrative analysis revealed three specific narrative types: *exercise is restitution* (cure); *exercise is medicine* (illness prevention/health maintenance); and *exercise is progressive redemption* (growth in adversity). It is argued that subscribing to two or more narrative types may reinforce exercise motivation as it provides a story to fall back on should one be unfulfilled. This may be particularly the case for individuals telling an *exercise is restitution* story as spinally injured people who are active purely as a means to achieve full recovery may withdraw when recovery is not forthcoming. The authors conclude that the stories people tell, the meanings they construct around exercise, may be powerful indicators of exercise motivation and should be considered in exercise-promotion programmes.

Innovating the innovative and future research

Discussing innovative developments within a methodological genre that relatively speaking is itself innovative may seem somewhat tautological. There are however a select number of scholars who have sought to push the boundaries of what narrative inquiry can be in sport and exercise. One innovative strategy is to assume the role of a storyteller, rather than a story analyst (see Chapter 20). Brendan Stone's (2009) auto-ethnographic account of obsessive exercise, anorexia and wider psychosis is perhaps one of the most accomplished examples of storyteller work within sport and exercise. Stone delivers a jolting, fragmented, non-linear piece, which for him better represents the mental-illness experience. At the same time, he acknowledges that 'we who have known madness also must seek refuge in reason and narrative' (p. 68). The conflict between portraying the incoherence of 'madness' while also maintaining a semblance of narrative structure serves as a fascinating and insightful tension throughout the story told. Autoethnographic work (see also Chapter 23) has also opened up the experience of early career-ending injury (Gilbourne, 2002), the dark side of football coaching (Potrac, Jones, Gilbourne & Nelson, 2012), and sporting environmental pressures to be thin (McMahon & Dinan-Thompson, 2008). These storytellers deliver emotive, multi-layered, personal accounts of sensitive, culturally situated experiences.

As well as biographically inspired storytelling, scholars may also choose to represent traditional participant data – such as interview transcripts or participant observation – through various literary forms such as creative non-fiction (see Chapters 20 and 23). There are examples of creative non-fictions in topics such as sexual abuse (Douglas & Carless, 2009b), exercise and mental illness (Carless & Sparkes, 2008), physical activity knowledge translation (Smith, Papathomas, Martin Ginis & Latimer-Cheung, 2013), and becoming disabled through sport (Smith, 2013). Again, the accounts are always engaging, evocative and rich in covert theoretical nuance. The overwhelming majority of creative non-fiction work in sport and exercise, much like narrative inquiry more generally, stems from a small pool of researchers who have been brave enough to challenge the (post)positivist status quo. This bravery has rarely extended to more experimental forms of creative representation such as enthnodrama, poetry or song. With the increasing digitization of publication platforms however, the opportunity to house dynamic outputs like dramatic performances grows increasingly feasible. Whether a rise in more creative representations of data materializes is likely to depend not on technology but on the attitude of empiricists.

Further potential to innovate within narrative inquiry can be found within the visual methods literature. For extended accounts of visual approaches to research (see Chapter 11).

Phoenix (2010) argued that visual methods, such as photographs, diagrams, sketches or maps, can provide a different way of knowing the world to that achieved through the written and spoken word. Visual methods can work in conjunction with traditional methods such as interviews, as participants are asked to interpretively discuss a visual artefact that is either produced by them or provided by the researcher (Enright & O'Sullivan, 2012). From a narrative standpoint, visuals may speak for themselves and tell the whole story or they can be used to prompt a participant to tell their story orally. The latter approach has been used to explore the sporting experiences of Aboriginal communities in north-east Canada (Blodgett *et al.*, 2013). Participants produced mandala drawings – a culturally relevant art form – which were used as the basis for narrative-inducing conversation-like interviews. The authors stated that the 'visual data was understood as being complementary to the narrative data in terms of opening up different ways of knowing that were more aligned with the culture and lives of the Aboriginal participants' (p. 328). In a further study, men with disordered eating were asked to construct a visual collage representing their relationship with the body, food and exercise (Busanich *et al.*, 2016). Within their visual narrative analysis, the authors drew on the participants' and their own interpretations of the story told. Specifically, as images were typically taken from cultural contexts, it was possible to identify the larger cultural narratives participants drew on to construct meaning. This merging of visual methods research with narrative inquiry is encouraging and provides a new dimension to narratively framed research. Where topics are difficult to narrate verbally – for example, sensitive, taboo or complex topics – visual storytelling may serve as an important narrative technique.

The narrative studies discussed throughout this chapter concern what have come to be known as *big stories*; essentially the overarching plots that people use to make sense of life experience and shape identity. Frank's much discussed restitution narrative, for example, is very much a big story. In contrast, emerging on the peripheries of the wider narrative field is the notion of *small stories*. For Georgakopoulou (2006), small stories are snippets of everyday talk that occur in everyday scenarios and, as such, do not represent narratives in text but rather narratives-in-context. She argues that small stories relate mostly to the recently occurred ordinary events of 'this morning' or 'last night', but can nevertheless be experience-shaping and identity-constituting. Bamberg and Georgakopoulou have stated that narratives are 'aspects of situated language use, employed by speakers/narrators to position a display of contextualized identities' (2008, p. 379). Although critics question whether small stories are actually just small talk – devoid of sufficient narrative features to constitute a storying process (Bochner & Riggs, 2014) – they do present a fresh lens with which to do narrative work. Work on grand narratives or big life-stories is compatible with small-story work: the former focuses on the lived and the told; the latter on the messier business of the living and the telling (Bamberg & Georgakopoulou, 2008). Small-story work may suit researchers in sport and exercise, who engage in participant observation or cultural immersion, and who therefore only have access to snippets of talk. Further, when research participants are children, for example, youth sport or physical education studies, extended narrative constructions may be difficult to collect, and so small-story work may prove valuable. Rare examples of big and middle story research within the sport and exercise sciences, as well as 'middle story' work, can be found in Pheonix and Sparkes (2009) and Griffin and Pheonix (2016).

A reflective summary

In closing this story about stories I am mindful that there are numerous stories I have not told and that there is narrative work I have not covered. In every narrative construction, the narrator edits, selects and modifies the resources available to them, in order to tell a coherent and persuasive tale to satisfy themselves and their audience. Focussing the narrative lens on particular facets of a story means that other features remain blurred and so it is with this chapter; to profile one element of narrative inquiry is to disregard another. As such, these closing comments are pitched more as a reflective summary than a definitive conclusion. As stated in the opening lines of this story, my goal is to be provocative not exhaustive.

I have argued here that narrative has been the cardinal means to human understanding since the dawn of mankind, and it is the principal competency associated with the successful evolution of the human race. Narratives give meaning, purpose and motivation to our psychosocial worlds. We are primed to narrate and do so from a young age. Without narrative, without the capacity to construct meaning where there often is none and situate our day-to-day events within an overarching storied form, we would be no different to any other animal on earth – living from moment to moment and acting on instinct and impulse. Narrative gives us meaning and meaning makes us human. Despite all this, sociological and psychological research communities have for a long time, to a greater or lesser degree, turned their backs on this most basic of routes to knowing our world. The dawn of positivism and its associated empiricist beliefs gained credence with advances in the natural sciences and, as a result, the social and human sciences have jumped on for the ride – forgetting that they should have been heading in a different direction. Such is the power of social construction, narrative ceased to resonate as a worthy object of scientific study. Narrative became marginal. As argued by Bruner 'we have been taught to treat such "said" accounts as untrustworthy, even in some odd philosophical way as untrue' (1990, p. 16). Following in the footsteps of scholars in their parent disciplines, sport and exercise sociology and psychology researchers are once again turning to narrative. It's a fraught journey and resistance is strong but the results are insightful and exciting. As boundaries are pushed with innovative methodologies, narrative researchers in sport and exercise threaten to return the social and human sciences to fields that are more social and more human. In doing so, they may also be able take narrative from marginal back to cardinal.

References

Angen, M. J. (2000). Evaluating interpretive inquiry: Reviewing the validity debate and opening the dialogue. *Qualitative Health Research, 10,* 378–395.

Bamberg, M. & Georgakopoulou, A. (2008). Small stories as a new perspective in narrative and identity analysis. *Text & Talk: An Interdisciplinary Journal of Language, Discourse Communication Studies, 28,* 377–396.

Blodgett, A. T., Coholic, D. A., Schinke, R. J., McGannon, K. R., Peltier, D. & Pheasant, C. (2013). Moving beyond words: Exploring the use of an arts-based method in Aboriginal community sport research. *Qualitative Research in Sport, Exercise and Health, 5,* 312–331.

Bochner, A. & Riggs, N. (2014). Practicing narrative inquiry. In P. Levy (Ed.), *The Oxford handbook of qualitative research* (pp. 195–222). New York: Oxford University Press.

Bruner, J. (1986). *Actual minds, possible worlds.* Cambridge, MA: Harvard University Press.

Bruner, J. (1990). *Acts of meaning.* Cambridge, MA: Harvard University Press.

Burr, V. (2015). *Social constructionism.* London: Routledge.

Busanich, R., McGannon, K. R. & Schinke, R. J. (2014). Comparing elite male and female distance runners' experiences of disordered eating through narrative analysis. *Psychology of Sport and Exercise, 15*(6), 705–712.

Busanich, R., McGannon, K. R. & Schinke, R. J. (2016) Exploring disordered eating and embodiment in male distance runners through visual narrative methods. *Qualitative Research in Sport, Exercise and Health, 8,* 95–112.

Carless, D. (2008). Narrative, identity, and recovery from serious mental illness: A life history of a runner. *Qualitative Research in Psychology, 5,* 233–248.

Carless, D. & Douglas, K. (2009). 'We haven't got a seat on the bus for you' or 'all the seats are mine': narratives and career transition in professional golf. *Qualitative Research in Sport and Exercise, 1*, 51–66.

Carless, D. & Douglas, K. (2012). Stories of success: Cultural narratives and personal stories of elite and professional athletes. *Reflective Practice, 13*(3), 387–398.

Carless, D. & Douglas, K. (2013). 'In the boat' but 'selling myself short': Stories, narratives, and identity development in elite sport. *The Sport Psychologist, 27*(27), e39.

Carless, D. & Sparkes, A. C. (2008). The physical activity experiences of men with serious mental illness: Three short stories. *Psychology of Sport and Exercise, 9*(2), 191–210.

Denzin, N. & Lincoln, Y. (2000). *The Sage handbook of qualitative research.* Thousand Oaks, CA: Sage.

Dobrez, L. (2012). Towards a more rigorous definition of terms: Are there scenes in European Palaeolithic art? *Pleistocene Art of the World*, 316–317.

Douglas, K. & Carless, D. (2009a). Abandoning the performance narrative: Two women's stories of transition from professional sport. *Journal of Applied Sport Psychology, 21*, 213–230.

Douglas, K. & Carless, D. (2009b). Exploring taboo issues in professional sport through a fictional approach. *Reflective Practice, 10*(3), 311–323.

Eklund, R. C., Jeffery, K. A., Dobersek, U. & Cho, S. (2011). Reflections on qualitative research in sport psychology. *Qualitative Research in Sport, Exercise and Health, 3*(3), 285–290.

Engel, S. (1995). *The stories children tell: Making sense of the narratives of childhood.* New York: Macmillan.

Enright, E. & O'Sullivan, M. (2012). 'Producing different knowledge and producing knowledge differently': Rethinking physical education research and practice through participatory visual methods. *Sport, Education and Society, 17*(1), 35–55.

Frank, A. W. (1995). *The wounded storyteller: Body, illness and ethics.* Chicago, IL: University of Chicago Press.

Frye, N. (1957). *Anatomy of criticism.* Princeton: University Press.

Georgakopoulou, A. (2006). Thinking big with small stories in narrative and identity analysis. *Narrative Inquiry, 16*, 122–130.

Gergen, K. J. & Gergen, M. M. (1986). Narrative form and the construction of psychological science. In T. R. Sarbin (Ed.), *Narrative psychology: The storied nature of human conduct* (pp. 22–44). New York: Praeger.

Gilbourne, D. (2002). Sports participation, sports injury and altered images of self: An autobiographical narrative of a lifelong legacy. *Reflective Practice, 3*, 71–88.

Griffin M. & Phoenix C (2016). Becoming a runner: Big, middle and small stories about physical activity participation in later life. *Sport, Education and Society, 21*(1), 11–27.

Gubrium, J. F. & Holstein, J. A. (2009). *Analyzing narrative reality.* London: Sage.

Harari, Y. N. (2014). *Sapiens: A brief history of Humankind.* London: Random House.

Jarvinen, M. (2001). Accounting for trouble: Identity negotiations in qualitative interviews with alcoholics. *Symbolic Interaction, 24*, 263–284.

Jowett, S. & Frost, T. (2007). Race/Ethnicity in the all-male coach–athlete relationship: Black footballers' narratives. *International Journal of Sport and Exercise Psychology, 5*(3), 255–269.

Keel, P. K. & Forney, K. J. (2013). Psychosocial risk factors for eating disorders. *International Journal of Eating Disorders, 46*, 433–439.

Lally, P. (2007). Identity and athletic retirement: A prospective study. *Psychology of Sport and Exercise, 8*, 85–99.

Lauer, L., Gould, D., Roman, N. & Pierce, M. (2010). How parents influence junior tennis players' development: Qualitative narratives. *Journal of Clinical Sport Psychology, 4*(1), 69–92.

Layton, R. (1985). The cultural context of hunter–gatherer rock art. *Man, 20*(3), 434–453.

MacIntyre, A. (1981) *After virtue: A study in moral theory.* London: Duckworth.

McAdams, D. (1993). *The stories we live by: Personal myths and the making of the self.* New York: William Morrow.

McAdams, D. (2001). The psychology of life stories. *Review of General Psychology, 5*, 100–122.

McMahon, J. & Dinan-Thompson, M. (2008). A malleable body: Revelations from an Australian elite swimmer. *Healthy Lifestyles Journal, 54*, 1–6.

Myerhoff, B. (2007). Stories as equipment for living. In M. Kaminsky & M. Weiss (Eds.), *Stories as equipment for living: Last talks and tales of Barbara Myerhoff* (pp. 17–27). Ann Arbor, MI: University of Michigan Press.

Papathomas, A., Smith, B. & Lavallee, D. (2015). Family experiences of living with an eating disorder: A narrative analysis. *Journal of Health Psychology, 20*(3), 313–325.

Papathomas, A., Williams, T. L. & Smith, B. (2015). Understanding physical activity participation in spinal cord injured populations: Three narrative types for consideration. *International Journal of Qualitative Studies on Health and Well-being, 10*, 27295.

Phoenix, C. (2010). Seeing the world of physical culture: The potential of visual methods for qualitative research in sport and exercise. *Qualitative Research in Sport and Exercise, 2*(2), 93–108.

Phoenix, C. & Smith, B. (2011). Telling a (good?) counterstory of aging: Natural bodybuilding meets the narrative of decline. *The Journals of Gerontology, Series B: Psychological Sciences and Social Sciences, 66*(5), 628–639.

Phoenix, C. & Sparkes, A. C. (2009). Being Fred: Big stories, small stories and the accomplishment of a positive ageing identity. *Qualitative Research, 9,* 219–236.

Polkinghorne, D. E. (1988). *Narrative knowing and the human sciences.* Albany, NY: SUNY Press.

Ponterotto, J. G. (2005). Qualitative research in counseling psychology: A primer on research paradigms and philosophy of science. *Journal of Counseling Psychology, 52,* 126–136.

Potrac, P., Jones, R. L., Gilbourne, D. & Nelson, L. (2012). 'Handshakes, BBQs, and bullets': Self-interest, shame and regret in football coaching. *Sports Coaching Review, 1,* 79–92.

Ricoeur P. (1984). *Time and narrative, Vol. 1.* Chicago, IL: University of Chicago Press.

Ricoeur, P. (1992). *Oneself as another.* Chicago, IL: University of Chicago Press.

Riessman, C. K. (2008). *Narrative methods for the human sciences.* Thousand Oaks, CA: Sage.

Rosenwald, G. C. & Ochberg, R. L. (1992). *Storied lives: The cultural politics of self-understanding.* Michigan: Yale University Press.

Sarbin, T. (Ed.) (1986). *Narrative psychology: The storied nature of human conduct.* New York: Praeger.

Simpson, J., Heath, J. & Wall, G. (2014). Living with a pituitary tumour: A narrative analysis. *Psychology & Health, 29,* 162–176.

Smith, B. (2013). Sporting spinal cord injuries, social relations, and rehabilitation narratives: An ethnographic creative non-fiction of becoming disabled through sport. *Sociology of Sport Journal, 30,* 132–152.

Smith, B., Papathomas, A., Martin Ginis, K. A. & Latimer-Cheung, A. E. (2013). Understanding physical activity in spinal cord injury rehabilitation: Translating and communicating research through stories. *Disability and Rehabilitation, 35*(24), 2046–2055.

Smith, B. & Sparkes, A. C. (2002). Men, sport, spinal cord injury and the construction of coherence: Narrative practice in action. *Qualitative Research, 2*(2), 143–171.

Smith, B. & Sparkes, A. C. (2004). Men, sport, and spinal cord injury: An analysis of metaphors and narrative types. *Disability & Society, 19*(6), 613–626.

Smith, B. & Sparkes, A. C. (2008). Contrasting perspectives on narrating selves and identities: An invitation to dialogue. *Qualitative Research, 8*(1), 5–35.

Smith, B. & Sparkes, A. C. (2009a). Narrative inquiry in sport and exercise psychology: What can it mean, and why might we do it? *Psychology of Sport and Exercise, 10*(1), 1–11.

Smith, B. & Sparkes, A. C. (2009b). Narrative analysis and sport and exercise psychology: Understanding lives in diverse ways. *Psychology of Sport and Exercise, 10*(2), 279–288.

Smith, J. K. & Deemer, D. (2000). The problem of criteria in the age of relativism. In N. K. Denzin & Y. S. Lincoln (Eds.), *The Sage handbook of qualitative research* (2nd ed., pp. 877–896). London: Sage.

Somers, M. R. (1994). The narrative constitution of identity: A relational and network approach. *Theory and Society, 23,* 605–649.

Sparkes, A. C. & Smith, B. (2003). Men, sport, spinal cord injury and narrative time. *Qualitative Research, 3*(3), 295–320.

Sparkes, A. C. & Smith, B. (2005). When narratives matter: men, sport, and spinal cord injury. *Medical Humanities, 31*(2), 81–88.

Sparkes, A. C. & Smith, B. (2008). Men, spinal cord injury, memories and the narrative performance of pain. *Disability & Society, 23*(7), 679–690.

Sparkes, A. C. & Smith, B. (2009). Judging the quality of qualitative inquiry: Criteriology and relativism in action. *Psychology of Sport and Exercise, 10*(5), 491–497.

Sparkes, A. C. & Smith, B. (2011). Inhabiting different bodies over time: Narrative and pedagogical challenges. *Sport, Education and Society, 16*(3), 357–370.

Stephens, G. J., Silbert, L. J. & Hasson, U. (2010). Speaker–listener neural coupling underlies successful communication. *Proceedings of the National Academy of Sciences, 107,* 14425–14430.

Stone, B. (2009). Running man. *Qualitative Research in Sport and Exercise, 1,* 67–71.

Sugiyama, M. S. (2001). Narrative theory and function: Why evolution matters. *Philosophy and Literature, 25*(2), 233–250.

Tsang, T. (2000). Let me tell you a story: A narrative exploration of identity in high performance sport. *Sociology of Sport Journal, 17,* 44–59.

5

ETHNOGRAPHY

Michael Atkinson

I have spent the better part of the past twenty years entrenched in one ethnographic research setting or another. My lengthy field experiences do not automatically qualify me as an expert on ethnography, as much as they connote my deep commitment to ethnographic epistemologies. From the very moment I learned about ethnography in an undergraduate lecture hall, I could hardly believe a university would actually pay someone to hang around with people as a legitimate vocation. In my undergraduate days, ethnography generally meant participant observation or fieldwork in the anthropological sense; or simply, deep immersion in the everyday life practices of other people as a means of learning, knowing, and representing them accurately.

More recently, and perhaps owing to both the global growth in sport and exercise science programmes and the interpenetration of substantive and methodological interests among sociologists, psychologists, and other social scientists of health, there has been a conceptual and empirical mushrooming and diversification of ethnographic sensibilities. As a direct function of the comingling between disciplinary traditions and foci of inquiry, social-scientific analyses of sport and exercise now take on a full spectrum of ethnographic tacks. In this chapter, I present several traditional means of doing ethnography alongside more recent innovations. I argue that ethnography in its broadest sense collates, crystallizes, integrates and galvanizes seemingly disparate disciplinary interests, and leads to improved conceptualizations of the multifold cultural roles of sport, exercise, and play in society. Given the recent groundswell in ethnographic methods there is good reason to de-emphasize how diverse theories, paradigms, ideologies, ontologies, and levels of analysis separate researchers of sport and exercise, and emphasize core epistemological ties that bind.

Attempting to define ethnography

The term 'ethnography' (from the Greek *ethnos,* meaning people, and *graph*, meaning writing) is often quite loosely applied to *any* qualitative research project where the in-situ observation of, and interaction with others is used to provide an inductive, detailed, in-depth description of cultural practices. This is sometimes haphazardly referred to as the systematic 'thick description' practices (Geertz, 1973), and their relationship to cultural frameworks. An ethnographer believes that in order to understand, translate, and conceptually explain how culture unfolds, and how it provides what Raymond Williams (1977) describes as 'maps of meaning' for people, one needs to become a member of said culture. An ethnographic epistemology generally upholds that theoretical knowledge about cultures is best generated by direct contact and experience with members of a culture over time (Wolcott, 1999). Therefore, the epistemology is straightforward; one becomes a member of a cultural group, does what they do, travels with them, and lives alongside them as a means of achieving an understanding of their cultural (and indeed psychological) realities.

Realist ethnographic methods have been employed quite extensively in studies of sport, exercise, and physical culture over the past thirty years (Atkinson, 2011). Realist ethnography involves direct and long-term immersion in the cultural life worlds of other people, to grasp how they live, interact, and view life. First and foremost, it involves interaction with them in a sport or exercise setting (such as a gym or sports field), or social practice (such as golfing or running), and the establishment of a personal role in the group. Realist ethnographers typically spend months or years conducting their field research, often forming lasting bonds with people there to eventually write journal articles of full-length books that attempt to accurately and 'realistically' present what the culture is actually like for participants. Many undergraduate students, graduate students, and faculty members conduct ethnographies in the communities where they themselves live and work. Gold (1958) describes four principal ways in which people become ethnographically emplaced in a community to conduct realist research. These participatory roles range along a continuum of social immersion, from *complete participant* (one who is fully immersed and participates in the culture), to *participant-as-observer* (one who participates, but not in everything), to *observer-as-participant* (one who participates moderately, but principally watches the culture from the social periphery), to *complete observer* (one who only observes the culture, without ever participating in or interacting among its members).

Realistic ethnographic efforts exist on surfers (Sands, 2001), boxers (Wacquant, 2004), skateboarders (Beal, 1995); roller-derby participants (Donnelly, 2014); snowboarders (Thorpe, 2011), sport participation among refugees (Spaaij, 2013) sport for development volunteer workers (Darnell, 2010), NASCAR fans (Newman and Giardina, 2011), windsurfers (Wheaton, 2000), media-production workers (Silk, 2001), rugby players (Howe, 2001), and bodybuilders (Monaghan, 2001). In my own research, I have employed realist ethnographic methods to articulate the cultures of duathletes and triathletes, traceurs, fell runners, greyhound-racing enthusiasts, Ashtanga yoga practitioners, anorexics in sport, and, most recently, youth sport coaches in Canada. Sport and exercise researchers undertake realist modes of ethnography to address questions pertaining to who participates in sport, how sport is a site for the (re)production of identities (gender, race, class, ethnicity, sexuality, religion), how sport involvement jibes with one's cultural worldview, and how the construction of one's social and cultural networks are reinforced through participation (Atkinson & Young, 2008).

Realist ethnographies involve the close exploration of several sources of data in the field. Long-term engagement in the field setting or place where people in the culture meet and interact daily is essential, and most commonly called participant observation (Wolcott, 1999). The notion of participant observation captures the dual role of the fully immersed ethnographer in that one is both a participant in the culture, but at the same time is an academic observer. Elias (1987) outlines the degree to which a (field) researcher, like any other social scientist, must strive toward maintaining a balance between empirical involvement with subjects (required to gain a sympathetic understanding of others) and cognitive/emotional detachment from them (required to adequately identify the conceptual themes, patterns, and structures – or, generic social processes – organising cultural life). To develop an involved/detached understanding of what it is like to be a member of a culture, the researcher participates in the settings wherein the culture operates, while also maintaining the stance of an observer, someone who can describe the experience with a measure of what we might call professional detachment; this is how one is able, as the method goes, to produce a realist tale of culture.

Realist ethnography has fallen under critique, as a far too naive approach to studying culture (i.e. as the overt and direct study and description of people's immediate behaviours, thoughts, and constructions of the world in the here and now of everyday life). Critics suggest that realist ethnographers cannot simply know culture by being 'around it', or can be able to translate, into an academic text, a clean and perfect representation of the culture for all people who comprise the culture. For example, realist ethnographers should better attend to and theorise the connection between the actions of people in social settings and the social, economic, and political structures within which those actions occur. As such, the uses of ethnography simply to 'tell non-fictional stories' about sport and physical culture, its meaning, its expression, and its participants are only partially valid since we can neither take behavioural observations as simply representative of some given social world nor fully reveal or reconstruct the social through our understanding of actors' meanings and beliefs. Rather, explaining observable events requires a consideration of the social-structural, behavioural, or even cognitive/emotional conditions that enabled these events – enter, *critical realist ethnography*.

Critical realist ethnography holds to the existence of underlying social (or cognitive and emotional) structures and mechanisms that influence life. Human action is thus conceived as both enabled and constrained by social structures, environmental conditions and one's own personal tendencies and (pre)dispositions. Critical realism, growing especially popular in sport and exercise psychology, offers a meta-theoretical paradigm for explaining the underlying generative mechanisms that shape human action, and the social relations or sets of social values that this agency in turn reproduces and transforms. Whilst deep structures and generative mechanisms that help shape people's involvement in the world, their choices, their feelings, and their perspectives are worthy of study, they are not readily apparent, and can be observed and inferred through their effects. For example, Byers's (2013) study of volunteerism in sport clubs, Sassatelli's (2010) research on fitness centres, Cushion and Jones's (2006) ethnographic venture on coaches, and Tamminen and Holt's (2010) analysis of young athletes' coping strategies equally illustrate the rising prominence of critical realism in ethnographic research on sport culture and the structural components of life that shape individual behaviours.

Throughout the twentieth century, the lion's share of ethnographic inquiries on sport and exercise deployed realist or critical realist methodologies. But any number of ethnographic modes of inquiry are at the disposal of a contemporary sport and exercise researcher. Following a progressive scepticism regarding an ethnographer's ability to merely represent the objectively descriptive or invisibly structural aspects of life via straightforward accounts of others (see Denzin, 2003; Gubrium & Holstein, 1997), a panorama of ethnographic forms emerged that privilege polysemic, fractured, and radically contextual constructions of physical-cultural realities in sport and exercise worlds. Newer modes of ethnography include: standpoint, queer, post-structural and postmodern, feminist, institutional, autoethnographic, media, audience, Internet-based, sensory, mobile, visual, blitzkrieg, guerrilla, and others (Atkinson, 2011). It is beyond the scope of this chapter to enumerate differences between all ethnographic modes, but a handful are worth highlighting.

New ethnographic imaginings

A number of research questions pertaining to studies of sport, exercise and physical culture are well suited for the family of innovative ethnographic approaches. By and large, research questions focusing on the ways in which membership of certain social groups or cultures shape one's personal and collective sport and exercise practices are most amenable to ethnographic modes of inquiry. For example, my first fully ethnographic venture homed in on the ticket-scalping subculture in Toronto, Canada (Atkinson, 2000). I wanted to know how the sub-culture is (re)produced, how members are brought in, how tickets are acquired and what this illegal subculture signifies with regard to the broader sports-entertainment complex in Canada. Such is a classic example of a small-scale (sub)*cultural ethnography* influenced in part by critical realist leanings. The purpose of these ethnographies was to learn the inner workings of a very small group/subculture and then explain how and why the culture operates as it does, induc-tively, as a theoretical venture. Ethnographies involving the study of two or more groups/ cultures over time are often called *ethnologies,* whereas historical accounts of a culture arising from a study of it are referred to as *ethnohistories.* Although not a prerequisite of small-scale cultural ethnography, researchers will occasionally strive to connect what is learned in a local cultural setting with broader trends and processes in a society along critical realist lines; that is, a ticket scalper's subculture is important to study as a means of understanding how culture works on, through and between people, but why and how the ticket-scalping subculture emerges at a particular time, place and historical juncture categorized by broad-scale social tendencies is equally important. In my ticket-scalping study, for example, I argued that the scalping subcul-ture itself is partially produced by diffuse market capitalist trends and neo-conservative political trends in larger Canadian society.

Institutional ethnography is an increasingly popular ethnographic approach to empiri-cal inquiry, most frequently associated with the Canadian feminist scholar Dorothy Smith (1987). The approach emphasises connections among the sites and situations of everyday life, professional practice and policymaking. Somewhat dialogical with critical realist ethnogra-phy, institutional ethnography (sometimes called a *standpoint ethnography*) strives to under-stand how people's culture practices are deeply structured by forces and relationships of power working through and within institutions like the family, media, workplaces, schools and sports organizations. It addresses questions of what it is like to experience and be shaped by the cultural practices of social institutions. To date, and quite surprisingly, very few sport, exercise and physical-culture researchers have explored the potential of institutional or stand-point ethnography (though many have engaged a version of institutional ethnography more loosely described as *feminist ethnography*). Institutional ethnographies, whilst not overly popu-lar, have received considerable attention in sport-policy/management studies of how power in sport institutions may be visible through extant policies, hiring practices, or the treatment of identified groups within the setting (Numerato & Baglioni, 2012). The related feminist/ standpoint ethnography has, by contrast, produced a litany of impressive research on the experience of being structurally positioned and located as sexed/gendered women in sport and exercise settings, including sports fandom (Hoeber & Kerwin, 2013), running (Flanagan, 2014), martial arts (Velija, Mierzwinski & Fortune, 2013), rowing (Caudwell, 2011) and cycling (Fullagar, 2012).

More recently, and taking a conceptual 180-degree turn from realist and institutional eth-nographies, *autoethnographic* methods have grown in popularity within the study of sport and exercise (Sparkes & Smith, 2014; McGannon & Smith, 2015). Autoethnography (see Chapter 23), sometimes phenomenologically inspired, is an approach in which the investigator develops a research question pertaining to a particular cultural process, experience, or personal reality in sport or exercise, and then reflexively fashions a description and analysis of their own account of said process or experience or reality. Autoethnography is an attempt to develop an experi-ential understanding of the behaviours and work context under consideration, by casting the investigator as both the informant insider and the analyst outsider. For example, a spate of running autoethnographies has been published within the recent past (Hockey, 2006).

Audience ethnography broadens the scope of ethnographic practice by striving to understand how people actively receive, decode and use very specific mass-mediated sport or physical-cultural texts. In the typical scenario, participants in audience ethnography are asked to collectively or individually watch, read or listen to selected sport or exercise media and then react/respond to its content. A researcher acts as a facilitator in these scenarios, prompting questions among respondents about what the messages or symbols in the media might mean to them, and how they actively decode them from a variety of cultural standpoints (e.g. age, race, sexuality, gender, class). The underpinning logic of doing audience ethnography is that by observing and questioning how people make sense of media data 'live' and in situ, researchers compile a more valid understanding of the process of immediate cultural reception and cognitive processing of media content; that is, how people visually see media *culturally*. Wilson and Sparks (1996), for example, illustrate how African-Canadian teenage boys fashion their own constructions of, and lived experiences with, Black masculinity to interpret mass mediations of 'Blackness' in basketball shoe advertisements. Wilson and Sparks (1996) attest to how the youth selectively take from the commercials what makes sense to them culturally, and how they negate or resist supposedly preferred images and constructions of 'Blackness' in the commercials.

When the ethnographic subject matter itself pertains to visual culture and its reception by audiences, *visual ethnographic* techniques emerge (see also Chapter 11). Visual ethnography is strongly warranted when researchers want subjects to tell their own stories, from their own visual vantage points, as a means of knowing how culture works. 'Photovoice', or what is also known as autophotography, is a very specialist visual ethnographic method by which researchers encourage or ask participants in a project to take pictures of, video-record or draw people, places, events or images which mean something to them. I have conducted research with chronically ill recreational athletes – people living with cancer, liver disease, HIV, and other conditions. At one stage of the research process I asked several participants to take one of my video cameras and film their own mini-documentaries of a week in their lives. By having the subjects highlight what they understand to be the relevant day-to-day structures and meanings of their lives I gained a deeper understanding of how illness and physical-cultural identities must be negotiated daily when practising sport and exercise in incredibly 'healthist' social spaces. Similarly, Gibson *et al.* (2013) pursued an integrated ethnographic use of audio diaries, photography and interviews in research with disabled young men, to gain a better understanding of how one's personal relationship with embodiment is framed along culturally normative lines. These self-produced methods are very clever because the subjects themselves pick and choose the representations to include. Therefore, the produced representations reveal how they wish others to understand their experiences.

Visual methods are increasingly utilised as a means of representing ethnographic data and breaking down barriers between researchers and potential audiences. Pink (2007) produced intellectually and emotionally engaging visual/written accounts of what it is like to simply walk. Through her use of video recorders and cameras, Pink gives visual life to the joys of walking in space and place, through the use of images taken while walking with others (a form of *mobile ethnography*). I tried to push the visual envelope even further in a study of fell running in the UK, through the use of ethnographic infographics (Atkinson, 2010). I borrowed the notion of infographics from street/city sign-making, where a simple symbol on a posted sign provides information for a pedestrian or driver. In an account of the existential thrill of fell running, I tacked a dozen pictures of the practice into an article, with excerpts from my field notes framing each of them. The goal in such a method is to invite readers to see and potentially feel what I have studied, without being influenced by my academic interpretations of the topic.

A relatively new mode of ethnographic inquiry that builds out of visual ethnographies discussed above, called *sensory ethnography*, is described by Pink (2009) as a way of thinking about and doing ethnography that takes, as its starting point, the multisensory (i.e. hearing, seeing, smelling, tasting and touching) essence of human experience, perception, knowing and cultural practice (see also Chapter 26). Pink describes sensory ethnography as an out-cropping of traditional (realist) forms of ethnography, but emphasises the need to account further for how people's experiences with the senses (i.e. soundscapes, tastescapes, touch-scapes, etc.) in the practice of something like sport and exercise is integral. Here, data on how life is sensorially experienced are relevant both to people who make sense of our cultural practices, like a football game or swimming, palpably and in tactile ways (smell of the grasp, sound of a crowd cheering, burning in the legs, feel of the water), and to how ethnographers experience these sensations while collecting data. A number of sport eth-nographers have explored the multisensoriality of physical-cultural life, including De Garis (1999) and Spencer (2014), whose respective works have focused on understanding the sensory/sensuous aspects of professional wrestling and mixed martial arts. Through studies of running, Hockey (2006) and Hockey and Allen-Collinson (2007) have produced the most sustained interrogations of the sensuous/haptic aspects of physical culture and how it shapes meaning for participants. The recent works of Sparkes (2003, 2004, 2009) and Vannini, Waskul and Gottshalk (2012) provide the most cogent and intellectually moving calls for ethnography of, by and through the senses.

Performance (or *performative*) *methodology* is an emerging arts-based method of inquiry and representation that presents a tangible opportunity to bridge the gap between scholarly activ-ity and community teaching and learning (see also Chapter 23). After spending time in the field with a group of (usually marginalized) others the ethnographer, generally in conjunc-tion with key informants from the group under study, writes and produces a dramatic play, vignette or short film representing the culture. By using the theatre or the screen as a place of research representation, performance ethnography transforms the site from a place of enter-tainment to a venue for participatory action research that extends beyond the performance itself (Alexander, 2005; Finley, 2005). As a forum for cultural exchange, the power of perfor-mance-based interpretation lies in its potential for illumination and engagement of involved researchers, participants and audience. Thrift (2007) pushes boundaries even further, suggest-ing that the next stage in the evolution of embodied ethnographic research might very well be 'non-representational', meaning, that representational practices which portray embodied realities must themselves emerge from written texts and evolve into fully embodied and visceral performance pieces.

Finally, *ethnographic film-making and documentary analysis* (closely related to other visual eth-nographic modalities and arts-based methods; see also Chapter 11) is a powerful medium by which engagements with sport and physical culture may be equally produced and disseminated in order to: capture the experience of sport, exercise and physical culture in more vibrant, embodied, gritty, sensual and kinaesthetic forms; to graphically display aspects of the human condition (such as pleasure and suffering) in an array of everyday settings and contexts; be more inclusive of, and empathic with, participants in the research act; illustrate the impor-tance of ethnography in and of the first person; encourage a different aesthetic to the practice of sport and exercise research; and, enhance the moral validity of the ethnographic research act (i.e. with respect to the medium's accessibility and potential empathic connection with audiences). It is important to note, as Rose (2012) does, that the use of the visual and of film in the production of ethnographic research dates back decades (see Crawford & Turton, 1992; Henley, 2000). The mass availability of picture/recording devices, growing legions of students in the social sciences and elsewhere who are interested in more performative and open qualitative methodologies, the opening up of life and the continued demystification of the world in all social spaces, and the ongoing transformation of most Western nations into visual cultures themselves are primary influences.

Data collection and analytics

Ethnographic data analysis is perhaps the most daunting task for the neophyte researcher. What does one observe, record, attend to or process and given the diversity of ethnographic modes outlined above, how do we even begin to standardize data collection? First and fundamentally, it depends on the sort of access, involvement and role one has ethnographically. Ethnographies, in any manifestation, thrive or fizzle out depending on the researcher's ability to gain access to the setting or culture of their choice. Access to the core networks of lifestyle participants in a sport or physical culture is only the beginning. Several weeks or months may pass before one secures a role in the group, or gains enough trust among them to conduct a study with their active support. Why is this important in ethnography? Because one actually becomes what we call the 'instrument of data collection' (i.e. you are the recorder of data every day in the field): how you access the group, what roles you play therein and how other people position you as a person in the group substantially influences the volume and depth of the information you are able to gather over time. Who you are partially determines what you see, what you are told, and what you eventually know.

The next stage of data collection is the long haul in ethnographic projects. This involves the day-to-day collection of empirical data in a huge variety of forms. Empirical data to an ethnographer could be everything and anything one hears, feels, sees and reads in the field. Most of the time, a researcher will only have a vague understanding of what is important at first (i.e. for answering one's initial research question), and so *everything* is noted, recorded and reflected upon until a dominant theoretical idea or set of main conceptual foci emerge in the study. Conversations with others, descriptions of interaction, artefacts gathered in the field and places visited need to be recorded in meticulous detail. Interviews with key informants may be inserted into the ethnographic act to provide focused data on conceptual and substantive curiosities coming to the fore, and the research focus is narrowed further. What generally starts as a broad and overwhelming venture into the sport and exercise dark transforms into a tightly defined research venture. There are no magic templates, tricks, tips or steps one may employ in order to develop conceptual clarity in a project.

The arduous part of any ethnography commences with the processes of data interpretation, since anything and everything in an ethnographic project is data (at least at first), and the process of whittling down one's study into a paper or even a book-length report can be overwhelming. One commences the data-analysis process from day one; reviewing and making interpretive/analytic notes about things one has heard, experienced, videoed, read, witnessed or discovered in the field with others. As time progresses, one learns to connect discoveries to conceptual ideas, and perhaps even, a new theoretical framework. Field notes, observations, interview data and artefacts gathered serve as partial indicators of broader processes and structures. As such, the lion's share of any ethnographic research is interpretive and qualitative in orientation; that is to say, researchers are not so concerned with testing formal hypotheses derived from theory against data, in most cases. So, it is fair to suggest that ethnographic analysis is based more on the use of field data to generate, explore, probe and extend the empirical applicability of particular concepts, axioms or ideas.

Notwithstanding the above, ethnographic analyses form the basis of classic inductive inquiry, and initiate a programme of investigation intended to flesh out a tentative or working understanding (not explanation) of a phenomenon in the study of sport and exercise cultures. Here, one might only have a general theoretical or substantive clue about what is going on with respect to a sport-related phenomenon (no past theories or studies accurately account for it or provide us with direction), and therefore a researcher embarks on a very loosely structured programme of data collection and analysis to arrive at a tentative understanding. Examples of exploratory questions include: 'Is there a relationship between gender and violence in sport?' 'What is it like to be an athlete with an injury?' 'What is it like to experience depression in an elite level athlete culture' 'How do disabled athletes experience barriers to participation in sport?' or, 'How do people construct the joys of physical activity participation?'

Whereas the role of theory in ethnographic research is quite clear (at least historically), the role of theory in innovative ethnographic research is murkier. Ethnographic questions are often described by sport and exercise researchers as undertaken in the pursuit of 'grounded theoretical' conceptualizations of sport and physical culture's meaning to people (Atkinson, 2011, 2012). The ideal, typical grounded theory, in methodological terms, is most accurately described as a technique of question formation, data collection and data analysis, in which the eventual conceptualizations or theoretical understanding of people, small groups or other social formations one discovers is developed from the data, rather than the other way around (see Charmaz, 2003: Glaser, 2001; Strauss and Corbin, 1998; Chapter 3, this volume). Still, we must question, through careful scrutiny of the methods-data-theory link in each study, if sport and exercise research projects flying under the banner of grounded theory are most likely ventures in *concept elaboration* or straight *theory application* (Atkinson, 2012). This is particularly the case with critical realist, institutional, feminist, and audience ethnographies. Here, a researcher commences with preconfigured conceptual or theoretical ideas in mind (or their preferred theoretical explanations of the world) and then expands them or (even uncritically applies) them, in whole, to emergent ethnographic data. Our concepts might be expanded, contracted, tightened or partially redefined through so-called ethnographic inquiry, but rarely are new theoretical systems or sets of interconnected conceptually driven questions produced.

On ethnography, empathy and 'positive' ethnographies of sport and exercise

The social-scientific study sport and exercise drew my awareness as an undergraduate through its relentless focus on the practical, and seemingly banal, matters of everyday physical-cultural life. Although often unwritten as such, ethnography's enduring contribution to the study of the human condition in sport and exercise cultures (or elsewhere) perhaps rests on its foundational interest in unpacking the ways in which people experience embodied life daily within small groups, institutions and highly organized human figurations. In its essence, ethnography's general epistemological and ontological mandate is one in which people's cultural experiences in the world should and must figure up front in theorising what it means to be a person (Wolcott, 1999); stated differently, the most beautiful, engaging, penetrating, moving, enriching and reality congruent ethnography is one in and of the (cultural) *first person*. Ethnographic research on sport and exercise in and of the first person is a humane, morally guided, emotionally sensitive, embodied and deeply interpersonal enterprise, attentive to the striking similarities, rather than mass differences, of the human experience for people immersed in sport, exercise, physical activity and other movement-based leisure pursuits.

Sport and exercise ethnographers might do well in being both physically and affectively close to their fields of study; and quite confident that the very questions they ask, and why, are framed along consequentialist ethical lines (that is, the outcome of the research act should be scrutinized as morally justifiable in the pursuit of a better world). A person-first, radically empathic sport and exercise ethnography is one predicated on a series of practices. First, it requires a researcher to be personally, affectively, cognitively, physically and socially open *with and among* people, in order to understand them in rounded, intersubjective manners. Second, it demands *co-presence* with them in the practice of everyday culture life, wherever possible, to feel how culture binds people together in practice. Third, the practice of ethnography evolves as a concatenated effort to illuminate *the commonalities of lived experience* and the human condition, in the hope of destabilizing conceptual differences between people that are used, so often, as a social tool of exclusion, power, dominance and exploitation. Fourth, it asks researchers to think creatively and simultaneously about how the *pleasurable and not-so-pleasurable aspects of human existence* are apparent in sport and exercise practices (and not only how sport and exercise cultures work against people and their agency). Fifth, such a vision of ethnography asks researchers to *allow themselves to be written*, in a liminal way, by and through the ethnographic research act; in short, to be changed quite deeply. Sixth, and finally, it requires new and innovative ethnographic modes of representing the human condition as learned and deciphered through fieldwork.

I stress the above features of a person-first ethnography because I think it is fair to write that sport and exercise ethnographies have almost universally homed in on the ways in which suffering, injustice, power, inequality and cultural alienation are located and expressed through sport. This is understandable, as Thin (2014) notes, because the social sciences have, for quite some time, been the academic study of the personally, culturally and socially 'pathological'. As a result, remarkably few contributions have been made to the study of culturally positive aspects of sport, exercise and health, including fun, happiness, joy, pleasure and personal satisfaction through physical-cultural participation and experience (Phoenix & Orr, 2014). Stebbins launched a plea for such a positive orientation in ethnographic studies of sport and exercise, drawing explicitly on the inspiration of the positive psychology movement, and defining his proposed ethnographic focus as, 'the study of what people do to organize their lives such that those lives become, in combination, substantially rewarding, satisfying and fulfilling' (2009, xi). Few sport and exercise ethnographers have, save for Pronger (2002), Pringle (2009), Wellard (2012), explored the intricacies of pleasure in everyday leisure, sport, physical activity and exercise practices.

Recent calls to engage more pleasure or happiness-oriented ethnographies of sport, exercise and physical culture are also timely for another set of reasons. Within the past decade, there has been a renewed, and certainly contested, argument that the research act in sport and exercise studies must become much more civically engaged, applied and culturally meaningful to retain any utility. Such an argument (see Atkinson, 2011; Giardina & Newman, 2011; Silk & Andrews, 2011) hinges upon the related premises that not only does theoretically driven ethnographic research on sport and physical culture offer much insight into a spectrum of problems pertaining to personal struggle and social suffering more generally, it also illustrates how life can be deeply pleasurable. Strangely enough, ethnographically accounting for and documenting the pleasurable aspects of the human condition appears to be a radical conceptual task for ethnographers.

Forward thinking, ethnographically based, studies of sport and exercise in and of the first person, may see the possibility of human pleasure through movement as a (if not *the*) core substantive focus. Such an ethnographic enterprise requires researchers of sport, exercise and physical culture to break new ground, transgress disciplinary boundaries, pursue theoretically driven research with much vigour, and research beyond the comfortable subjects we so regularly study. As Game and Metcalfe (1996) contend, such a discipline requires an orientation of passion and humanism in one's ethnographic enterprise. It requires one, at times, to speak truth (and often *many* truths), to make suggestions, to be morally grounded, and attempt to rekindle a sort of (dare we even say) positivism in ethnographic research often decried as non-value neutral, biased or unscientific. It may require, only as a small list of possible topics, an invested and concerted interest in matters of sport, exercise and physical–culture activity for/as social development, personal growth and self-realization, mental-health improvement, sport and exercise for vulnerable or ageing persons, movement cultures as potential solutions to broad gauge social problems like racism and sexism, human rights in sport and leisure contexts, places to promote inclusively healthy notions of the body, visions of democratic humanism across sport and physical cultures, physical-cultural pastimes outside of the sporting realm, post-sport physical cultures, issues in sport and exercise bioethics and technology, youth development through mainstream and non-mainstream physical activities, experiences of health, wellness, varied (dis)abilities, illness as/in sport and exercise, global sport, leisure and recreation management, and the sensual aspects of sport and exercise; all as vehicles for better seeing how pleasure (and suffering) play out through movement in everyday life.

While generally not written explicitly in sport and exercise texts, there is a growing optimism, even if it remains a whisper, that ethnographic research can and likely should be conducted for the moral and civic good of society. Such sport and exercise ethnographies are to be intextuated with different sensibilities regarding the methodological process. They require a slow and meticulous approach to the ethnographic research act (Silk, Francombe & Andrews, 2014), a willingness to live among and like those we study, and as such, become an *emplaced* presence in the practice of cultural life with others (Pink, 2009; Giardina & Newman, 2011). I would add that a person-first, humanistic sport and exercise ethnography is one in which both interpersonal empathy (between researchers and subjects) and moral validity (of the very research process itself) are deeply engrained in and through the emplaced/embodied research act (see Smith, 2008). As Thin (2014) reminds us, if the goal of interpretive methods like ethnography is to grasp the world through intersubjective connections with others and write culture, human empathy is paramount in the research act (see Wolcott, 1999).

The role of ethnographic empathy in achieving a substantive, let alone theoretical understanding, of others in the research act is gaining considerable attention in contemporary qualitative research (Smith, 2008), but has been a central tenet of phenomenological research for quite some time. Heidegger's thoughts (1997), through his philosophical assertion that simply being close to and present in the world with others (what he refers to as 'being-with', or *Mistsein*), are invaluable for achieving empathy-based, intersubjective understandings of them. Co-presence and the close sharing of time and space, to Heidegger, is an important bridge toward mutual recognition and empathic connection. Merleau-Ponty (1996) offers additional inspiration by stressing how an empathic kinship is created when people physically meet and phenomenologically react to/with one another in time and space. Truly understanding the essence or the self of the other is not as important as simply sharing embodied presence and developing *sui generis* constructions of one another. More recently, Ratcliffe (2012) suggests that the most radical phenomenological studies are ones in which (personal and cultural) empathy figures centrally in the research act. Clearly, I would argue, ethnographic empathy is precisely a tipping point in the development of a person-first and positive ethnographic study of sport and exercise. As Ratcliffe reminds us, 'Radical empathy, like empathy more generally, incorporates a stance of openness to others, a willingness to be affected by them, to have one's own experience shaped by them' (2012, p. 488f). I hope this chapter lays some ground for researchers in sport and exercise to not only be open to ethnography, but also to be affected and shaped by this tradition in ways that enhance our research (whatever that might be) and work with cultural members.

References

Alexander, B. (2005). Performance ethnography: The re-enacting and inciting of culture. In N. Denzin & Y. Lincoln (Eds.), *Handbook of qualitative inquiry* (pp. 411–441). Thousand Oaks, CA: Sage.

Atkinson, M. (2000). Brother, can you spare a seat?: Developing recipes of knowledge in the ticket scalping subculture. *Sociology of Sport Journal, 17*, 151–170.

Atkinson, M. (2010). Fell running in post-sport territories. *Qualitative Research in Sport & Exercise, 2*, 109–132.

Atkinson, M. (2011). Physical cultural studies [redux]. *Sociology of Sport Journal, 28*, 135–144.

Atkinson, M. (2012). *Key concepts in sport & exercise research methods*. London: Sage.

Atkinson, M. & Young, K. (2008). *Deviance and social control in sport*. Champaign, IL: Human Kinetics.

Beal, B. (1995). Disqualifying the official: An exploration of social resistance through the subculture of skateboarding. *Sociology of Sport Journal, 12*, 252–26.

Byers, T. (2013). Using critical realism: A new perspective on control of volunteers in sport clubs. *European Sport Management Quarterly, 13*, 5–31.

Caudwell, J. (2011). 'Easy, oar!': Rowing reflections. *Qualitative Research in Sport, Exercise and Health, 3*, 117–129.

Charmaz, K. (2003). *Constructing grounded theory: A practical guide through grounded analysis*. London: Sage.

Crawford, P. & Turton, D. (1992). *Film as ethnography*. Manchester: Manchester University Press.

Cushion C. & Jones, R. (2006). Power, discourse and symbolic violence in professional youth soccer: The case of Albion F.C. *Sociology of Sport Journal, 23*, 142–161.

Darnell, S. (2010). Sport, race and bio-politics: Encounters with difference in 'sport for development and peace' internships. *Journal of Sport and Social Issues, 34*, 396–417.

De Garis, L. (1999). Experiments in pro wrestling: Toward a performative and sensuous sport ethnography. *Sociology of Sport Journal, 16*, 65–67.

Denzin, N. (2003). *Performance ethnography: Critical pedagogy and the politics of culture*. Thousand Oaks, CA: Sage.

Donnelly, M. (2014). Drinking with the derby girls: Exploring the hidden ethnography in research of women's flat track roller derby. *International Review for the Sociology of Sport, 49*, 346–366.

Elias, N. (1987). *Involvement and detachment*. Oxford, UK: Blackwell.

Finley, S. (2005). Arts-based inquiry: Performing revolutionary pedagogy. In N. Denzin & Y. Lincoln (Eds.), *Handbook of qualitative inquiry* (pp. 681–694). Thousand Oaks, CA: Sage.

Flanagan, K. (2014). *Sporting a skort: The biopolitics of materiality. Cultural Studies ↔ Critical Methodologies, 14*, 506–516.

Fullagar, S. (2012). Gendered cultures of slow travel: Women's cycle touring as an alternative hedonism. In S. Fullagar, K. Markwell & E. Wilson (Eds.), *Slow tourism* (pp. 99–112). Bristol: Channel View.

Game, A. & Metcalfe, A. (1996). *Passionate sociology*. London: Sage.

Geertz, C. (1973). *The interpretation of cultures*. New York: Basic Books.

Giardina, M. & Newman, J. (2011). What is the 'physical' in physical cultural studies? *Sociology of Sport Journal, 28*, 36–63.

Gibson, B., Minstry, B., Smith. B., Yoshida, K., Abbott, D., Lindsay, S. & Hamdani, Y. (2013). The integrated use of audio diaries, photography and interviews in research with disabled young men. *International Journal of Qualitative Methods, 12*, 382–402.

Glaser, B. (2001). *The grounded theory perspective: News conceptualisation contrasted with description*. Mill Valley: Sociology Press.

Gold, R. (1958). Roles in sociological field observation. *Social Forces, 36*, 217–223.

Gubrium, J. & Holstein, J. (1997). *The new language of qualitative method*. New York: Oxford University Press.

Heidegger, M. (1997). *Being and time*. Oxford, UK: Blackwell.

Henley, P. (2000). Ethnographic film: technology, practice and anthropological theory. *Visual Anthropology, 13*, 207–26.

Hockey, J. (2006). Sensing the run: Distance running and the senses. *The Senses and Society, 1*, 183–202.

Hockey, J. & Allen-Collinson, J. (2007). Grasping the phenomenology of sporting bodies. *International Review for the Sociology of Sport, 42,* 115–131.

Hoeber, L. & Kerwin, S. (2013). Exploring the experiences of female sport fans: A collaborative self-ethnography. *Sport Management Review, 16,* 326–336.

Howe, P. (2001). An ethnography of pain and injury in professional rugby union: The case of Pontypridd RFC. *International Review for the Sociology of Sport, 36,* 289–303.

McGannon, K.R. & Smith, B. (2015). Centralizing culture in cultural sport psychology research: The potential of narrative inquiry and discursive psychology. *Psychology of Sport and Exercise, 17,* 79–87.

Merleau-Ponty, M. (1996). *Phenomenology of perception.* London: Routledge.

Monaghan, L. (2001). *Bodybuilding, drugs and risk.* London: Routledge.

Newman, J. & Giardina, M. (2011). *Sport, spectacle and NASCAR nation.* London: Palgrave Macmillan.

Numerato, D. & Baglioni, S. (2012). The dark side of social capital: An ethnography of sport governance. *International Review for the Sociology of Sport, 47,* 594–611.

Phoenix, C. & Orr, N. (2014). Pleasure: A forgotten dimension of physical activity in older age. *Social Science and Medicine, 115,* 94–102.

Pink, S. (2007). *Doing visual ethnography: Images, media and representation in research.* London: Sage.

Pink, S. (2009). *Doing sensory ethnography.* London: Sage.

Pringle, R. (2009). Defamiliarizing heavy-contact sports: A critical examination of rugby, discipline and pleasure. *Sociology of Sport Journal, 26,* 211–34.

Pronger, B. (2002). *Body fascism: Salvation in the technology of physical fitness.* Toronto: University of Toronto Press.

Ratcliffe, M. (2012). Phenomenology as a form of empathy. *Inquiry, 55,* 473–495.

Rose, G. (2012). *Visual methodologies: An introduction to interpreting visual materials* (3rd ed.). London: Sage

Sands, R. (2001). *Sport ethnography.* Champaign, IL: Human Kinetics.

Sassatelli, R. (2010). *Fitness culture: Gyms and the commercialisation of discipline and fun.* New York: Palgrave Macmillan.

Silk, M., (2001). The conditions of practice: Television production practices at Kuala Lumpur 98. *Sociology of Sport Journal, 18,* 277–301.

Silk, M. & Andrews, D. (2011). Toward a physical cultural studies. *Sociology of Sport Journal, 28,* 4–35.

Silk, M., Francombe, J. & Andrews, D. (2014). Slowing the social sciences of sport: On the possibilities of physical culture. *Sport in Society, 17,* 1–24.

Smith, B. (2008). Imagining being disabled through playing sport: The body and alterity as limits to imagining others' lives. *Sport, Ethics and Philosophy, 2,* 142–157.

Smith, D. (1987). *The everyday world as problematic: A feminist sociology.* Boston, MA: Northeastern University Press.

Spaaij, R. (2013). Cultural diversity in community sport: An ethnographic inquiry of Somali Australians' experiences. *Sport Management Review, 16,* 29–40.

Sparkes, A. C. (2003). From performance to impairment: a patchwork of embodied memories. In J. Evans, B. Davies & J. Wright (Eds.), *Body knowledge and control* (pp. 157–172). London: Routledge.

Sparkes, A. C. (2004). Reflections on an embodied sport and exercise psychology. In R. Stelter & K. Roessler (Eds.), *New approaches to exercise and sport psychology* (pp. 31–54). Oxford, UK: Meyer & Meyer Sport.

Sparkes, A. C. (2009). Ethnography and the senses: Challenges and possibilities. *Qualitative Research in Sport, Exercise and Health, 1,* 21–35.

Sparkes, A. C. & Smith, B. (2014). *Qualitative research methods in sport, exercise & health. From process to product.* London: Routledge.

Spencer, D. (2014). Sensing violence: An ethnography of mixed martial arts. *Ethnography, 15,* 232–254.

Stebbins, R. (2009). *Personal decisions in the public sphere.* New Brunswick, NJ: Transaction.

Strauss, A. & Corbin, J. (1998). *Basics of qualitative research: Grounded theory, procedures and techniques.* Newbury Park, CA: Sage.

Tamminen, K. & Holt, N. (2010). Female adolescent athletes' coping: A season long investigation. *Journal of Sports Sciences, 28,* 101–114.

Thin, N. (2014). Positive sociology and appreciative empathy: History and prospects. *Sociological Research Online, 19,* 5.

Thorpe, H. (2011). *Snowboarding bodies in theory and practice.* London: Palgrave.

Thrift, N. (2007). *Non-representational theory: Space, politics, affect.* London: Routledge.

Vannini, P., Waskul, D. & Gottschalk, S. (2012). *The senses in self, society, and culture: A sociology of the senses.* London: Routledge.

Velija, P., Mierzwinski, M. & Fortune, L. (2013). It made me feel powerful: Women's gendered embodiment and physical empowerment in the martial arts. *Leisure Studies, 32*, 524–541.

Wacquant, L. (2004). *Body and soul: Ethnographic notebooks of an apprentice-boxer.* New York: Oxford University Press

Wellard, I. (2012). Body reflexive pleasures: Exploring bodily experiences within the context of sport and physical activity. *Sport, Education and Society, 17*, 21–33.

Wheaton, B. (2000). Just do it: Consumption, commitment, and identity in the windsurfing subculture. *Sociology of Sport Journal, 17*, 254–274.

Williams, R. (1977). *Marxism and literature.* Oxford, UK: University of Oxford Press.

Wilson, B. & Sparks, R. (1996). It's gotta be the shoes: Youth, race, and sneaker commercials. *Sociology of Sport Journal, 13*, 398–427.

Wolcott, H. (1999). *Ethnography: A way of seeing.* New York: Altamira.

6

CASE STUDIES

Ken Hodge and Lee-Ann Sharp

Case studies are possibly one of the least understood research options in the qualitative research tradition. In this chapter we attempt to address a number of misunderstandings by defining what case studies are (and what they are not!), the different types of case studies typically used in sport and exercise research, while also providing readers with a clear rationale for considering case studies in their research. In addition, the challenges of employing case studies will be discussed critically, and we conclude the chapter with some recommendations for future directions employing case-study research in sport and exercise.

Case studies: what are they?

Just like other qualitative traditions, such as narrative inquiry, providing a precise definition of case studies is challenging, owing to the term being used in different ways and as a catch-all category for a variety of research methods. There are also variations in types of case study; something we will discuss shortly. While such diversity and difference is acknowledged, a definitional effort can still be offered. According to Schwandt (1997), a case is typically regarded as a 'specific and bounded (in time and place) instance of a phenomenon selected for study' (p. 12). The terms 'case' and 'unit of analysis' are often used inter-changeably in social science research; however, for the qualitative inquirer, the term 'case' means something more than just '*n*'. It is important for readers to appreciate that a case study is about the *boundedness* of the case and not only about an in-depth study of $N = 1$ (Schwandt, 1997). For example, the phenomenon of interest may be a person, group, process, event, community or organization. A case study is expected to catch the complexity of a single bounded case.

The criterion of *boundedness* is the key defining characteristic of a case study (Yin, 2009). To be a case study the phenomenon of research interest must be bounded in one or more of the following ways:

1. Exclusive membership of a bounded 'group/entity' (in-group vs. out-group);
2. A delineated location/place; and/or
3. A delimited time frame.

Furthermore, as Stake (2005) points out, not everything is a case: if we are moved to study it, the case is almost certainly going to be a functioning unit; that is, a specific and unique *bounded system*. Certain features will be recognized as being within the bounded system; that is, within the boundaries of the case, whereas other features will fall outside of it. According to Thomas (2011), a case study must comprise two elements: (1) a 'practical, historical unity', referred to as the *subject* of the case study; and (2) an analytical or theoretical frame, referred to as the *object* of the study.

Simons (2009) concluded that what also unites the various definitions of case study is a commitment to study holistically the complexity that is involved in naturalistic situations and to define a case study other than by the methods of data collection that it employs (see also Creswell, 2013; McLeod, 2010; Wolcott, 1995). Based on these commonalities Simons (2009) offered the following definition: 'Case study is an in-depth exploration from multiple perspectives of the complexity and uniqueness of a particular project, policy, institution, program or system in a "real life" context' (p. 21). The word *particular* is crucial in Simons' (2009) definition; a case study identifies a particular person, group, community, project, policy, institution, programme or system as the subject of the case study. That 'subject' is a bounded existing entity operating in situ, not an issue or target variable created artificially by a researcher as a proxy or symbolic representation of a phenomenon of interest. The *particularity* of a case study highlights that the research focus is on a distinct, discrete, bounded, and somewhat unique research phenomenon (see also Stake, 2005).

Case study has been variously defined as a method (Gomm, Hammersley & Foster, 2000, 2002), a methodology (Baxter & Jack, 2008), and/or a research design (Gerring, 2004). Simons (2009) emphasized that case study should not be seen as a method in and of itself; rather, it is a design frame that may incorporate a number of methods. In a similar vein Stake (2005, p. 443) stated that: 'Case study is not a methodological choice but a choice of what is to be studied' (also see Seawright & Gerring, 2008; VanWynsberghe & Khan, 2007). As Thomas (2011) concluded, analytical eclecticism is the key. A case study then, is an in-depth exploration from multiple perspectives of the complexity and uniqueness of a *particular* person, group, community, project, policy, programme or system in a bounded context (Baxter & Jack, 2008; Becker, 2000; Flyvbjerg, 2006; George & Bennett, 2005; Gerring, 2004; Gomm *et al.*, 2002; Hammersley, 2012; Lloyd-Jones, 2003; Merriam, 1988; Ragin & Becker, 1992; Thomas, 2011; Yin, 2009). While other qualitative methods also focus on in-depth examinations of research phenomena, case studies allow for a greater degree of depth given their *particularity* and *boundedness*. The boundedness criterion sets a limit on the breadth to be examined and thus frees up the researcher to investigate in as much depth as their data-collection methods/sources will allow.

First, the case-study approach is not a method because case-study researchers cannot actually collect data prescriptively using case study (Gerring & McDermott, 2007; Seawright & Gerring, 2008; VanWynsberghe & Khan, 2007). Instead, researchers employ various research methods (e.g. qualitative, quantitative, mixed methods), which act to build or uncover the case. Moreover, despite the existence of many different types of case study (e.g. intrinsic, instrumental, collective, crucial case) none of them require specific data-collection procedures (Stake, 2005; VanWynsberghe & Khan, 2007). Second, case studies have also been referred to as research designs (e.g. Gerring, 2004). However, VanWynsberghe and Khan (2007) argue that because the case-study approach does not offer a prescriptive guide for how to proceed with the business of collecting, analysing and interpreting data, we cannot consider case study as a research design. They contend that a prototype view, while not claiming to be definitive, offers a way of thinking about case study that allows for variability. They outline seven common features in their prototypical case study: (1) small *N*; (2) contextual detail; (3) everyday settings; (4) boundedness; (5) working research questions; (6) multiple data sources; and

(7) extendability (see VanWynsberghe & Khan, 2007 for detail). Consequently a case study is both a *process* of inquiry about the case and the *product* of that inquiry (Stake, 2005). That is, 'I am doing a case study of a chosen phenomenon and I will present my findings in the form of a case study'.

Functional types of case study

Stake (2005) identified three general types of case study: the intrinsic; the instrumental; and the collective case study. Furthermore, Seawright and Gerring (2008) outlined several specific case-study types (i.e. typical, diverse, extreme, deviant, influential, most similar, and most different), whereas VanWynsberghe and Khan (2007) also described many different specific types of case study (e.g. exploratory, explanatory, extreme, multisite, critical, theory confirming, intrinsic, instrumental, ethnographic, longitudinal, and deviant). Each of these specific types of case study can be classified loosely into one or more of Stake's (2005) functional categories of the intrinsic, instrumental and collective case study. In addition, Gerring (2004) offered insight into 'crucial cases'.

Intrinsic case. An intrinsic case study is undertaken because the researcher wants a better understanding of this particular case (Stake, 2005). Here, the study is not undertaken primarily because the case represents other cases, or because it illustrates a particular trait or problem; rather, it is studied because in all its 'particularity and ordinariness', the case is itself of interest. The purpose is not to explain or understand some abstract construct or generic phenomenon, nor is the purpose to engage in theory-building – though at times the researcher may do just that. 'The study is undertaken because of an intrinsic interest in, for example, this particular child, clinic, conference, or curriculum' (Stake, 2005; p. 445). A fascinating intrinsic case-study exemplar was reported in Balish and Côté's (2014) examination of the influence of one small community (town) on athletic development in rural Canada.

Instrumental case. An instrumental case study is where a particular case is examined mainly to provide insight into an issue or to draw a generalization: 'The case is of secondary interest, it plays a supportive role, and it facilitates our understanding of something else' (Stake, 2005; p. 445). The case is still explored in depth and the context(s) of the case are scrutinized, but the focus is on pursuing the external interest of insight and/or generalization. The case may be seen as typical of other cases or not, but the choice of case is made to advance understanding of the issue of interest. A recent example of an instrumental case study in sport and exercise research can be found in the work of Hodge, Henry and Smith (2014), who investigated the motivational climate of the 2011 World Champion New Zealand rugby team. The team was the case, not the individual athletes, and the focus was on the issue of interest (i.e. motivational climate).

Collective cases. As Stake (2005) observed there are no hard-and-fast lines distinguishing intrinsic case study from instrumental, but rather there may be overlapping purposes. On the other hand, when there is less interest in one particular case, a number of cases may be studied concurrently or consecutively, in order to investigate a phenomenon. Stake characterized this as the *multiple* or *collective* case study (also see Lloyd-Jones, 2003; Merriam, 1988; Yin, 2009). Here, the instrumental case study can be extended to several cases that are chosen because the researcher believes that investigating them will lead to a better understanding, and perhaps better theorizing, about a still larger collection of cases. A sport example of a collective case approach can be found in the work of Gustafsson, Kentta, Hassmen, Lundqvist, and Durand-Bush (2007) regarding athlete burnout.

Crucial case. Of all the case study types, perhaps the most controversial is the crucial-case approach (Gerring, 2007). The crucial-case approach has been used in a substantial number of studies across several social science disciplines and, according to Gerring (2007), has come to be recognized as a staple of the case-study approach. Yet the idea of any single case playing a crucial (or critical) role is not widely accepted. How does one defend the explicit/implicit claim that the case(s) under study are indeed 'crucial', or are the most crucial with respect to the phenomenon of interest? Day and Wadey (2016) offered a sport example of a crucial case when they examined the narratives of trauma and recovery for two athletes with disabilities. They characterized their participant-selection process as being influenced because the two participants 'provided an unusual (or deviant) case' (Day & Wadey, 2016; p.132), or as Stake (2005) suggested 'a case from which we can learn the most (p. 451). One can also focus on critical cases of 'life events' for the crucial-case approach (e.g., Kerr, 2007; Sparkes, Pérez-Samaniego & Smith, 2011). An alternative approach sometimes employed in the crucial-case tradition is to identify a *negative* case example of a phenomenon; for example, Gledhill and Harwood (2015) examined career development and retirement for female soccer players who failed to progress to the elite level.

Why bother?

In this section we attempt to make a 'case' for case studies in sport and exercise research. The key rationale for using the case-study tradition/approach is the capacity to develop an in–depth, holistic understanding of a *particular* issue/event/person (Ragin & Becker, 1992; Simons, 2009; Thomas, 2011, 2012). The strengths and advantages of the case-study approach include the features of providing an in–depth, detailed, comprehensive and holistic examination of a *particular* person, group, community, project, policy, institution, programme or system in situ, and the ability to then make naturalistic generalizations (Chenail, 2010; Stake, 2005; Tracy, 2010; VanWynsberghe & Khan, 2007; Yin, 2009). On the other hand, the potential weaknesses and disadvantages of the case-study approach include the unique, idiosyncratic nature of the information gathered, which *potentially* limits the generalizability of the findings, and may also lead to a number of 'misunderstandings' about the worth of the case study approach.

Misunderstandings of case studies. Flyvbjerg (2006) outlined five misunderstandings about case-study research and then systematically refuted each misunderstanding/criticism (see Flyvbjerg, 2006 for detail; VanWynsberghe & Khan, 2007 also addressed these five misunderstandings):

1. General, theoretical knowledge is more valuable than practical knowledge. Flyvbjerg (2006) argued that concrete, context-dependent knowledge can be just as valuable as seeking predictive theories and universal laws.
2. One cannot generalize from an individual case; therefore, the case study cannot contribute to advancing knowledge. Flyvbjerg (2006) countered, that one can generalize on the basis of a single case (naturalistic generalizations, theoretical inference); nevertheless he concluded that 'formal generalization is overvalued as a source of scientific development' (p. 228).
3. Case studies are useful for hypothesis generation, but other methods are necessary for testing hypotheses and theory-building. If we accept that we can generalize from a single case, then the case study is indeed useful for both generating and testing hypotheses, but importantly it is not limited to those research activities.
4. Case studies reflect researcher bias; that is, an inclination to corroborate or verify the researcher's preconceived notions. As Flyvbjerg (2006) asserted, case studies have their own scholarly rigour, and the focus on 'everyday' situations forces researchers to confront their biases as phenomena unfold in practice. Indeed, Flyvbjerg (2006) claimed that being in the

'field' exerts its own 'disciplinary force' (p. 237) on the researcher and their assumptions. In that regard one could argue that the case study contains a greater bias toward falsification of preconceived notions than toward verification.

5. It is difficult to develop general postulates, guiding principles and/or theories on the basis of individual case studies. Summarizing case studies can sometimes be difficult, but the problem of summarizing is often due more to the properties of the complex phenomena being studied, than the case-study method/approach itself. Besides, a forced summary driven by a fetish for neat, tidy 'take-home messages' ignores and devalues the complex reality of many social phenomena.

Perhaps most difficult, is the underlying concern from many researchers that they cannot reliably generalize from the findings/implications of a case study – 'It's just a case study,' they lament, 'so we can't take it seriously to frame policy or practice!' Not surprisingly, a number of authors have attempted to address this issue by referring to concepts such as naturalistic generalizations (Chenail, 2010), transferability (Tracy, 2010), theoretical inference (Hammersley, 2012), and cases as representative exemplars (Holt & Hogg, 2002). Instead of relying on formal generalizations, case studies offer naturalistic generalizations or transferability: 'processes that are performed by the *readers* of the research' (Tracy, 2010, p. 845). According to Tracy (2010), transferability is achieved when readers perceive a substantial degree of overlap with their own situation and then they intuitively transfer the findings/implications to their own contextual actions. From this viewpoint, good case studies provide readers with a vicarious experience and/or a 'virtual reality' (Flyvbjerg, 2006). Finally, Hammersley (2012) contends that case studies can be used either for explaining an issue or phenomenon, or as the basis for theorizing about the issue or phenomenon (i.e. theoretical inference procedures such as process tracing and/or comparative analysis).

Examples of case studies in sport and exercise research

In the following section we present selected examples of the different types of case studies employed in sport and exercise research. **Intrinsic case studies,** those conducted because the researcher wants a better understanding of a particular case (e.g. in-depth, multiple interviews; document analysis), have been employed to investigate a wide variety of topic areas, including: (1) an examination of a flat-water kayak environment (sports high school) in Norway, with a history of producing top-level senior athletes from among its juniors (Henriksen, Stambulova & Roessler, 2011); (2) illustrating the effectiveness of performance profiling on coach/athlete communication and team goal setting (Dale & Wrisberg, 1996); (3) narrative case stories of disordered eating (Busanich, McGannon & Schinke, 2014); (4) an ethnography of climbing Mount Everest (Burke, Sparkes & Allen-Collinson, 2008); and (5) an autobiographical account of sports injury and altered images of self (Gilbourne, 2002).

Instrumental case studies have been utilized to provide contextually broad accounts of the following issues in sport and exercise: (1) environmental factors impacting talent development (Henriksen, Stambulova, Roessler, 2010); (2) professional team cultures (Cruickshank, Collins & Minten, 2013; Hodge *et al.*, 2014); (3) modelling commitment in Masters sport (Rathwell & Young, 2015); and (4) exercise identities in a business/company environment (Rossing & Jones, 2015). Instrumental case studies have also been utilized to provide contextually broad accounts of the following issues in sports coaching: (1) skill learning/development in youth sport (Christensen, Laursen & Sorensen, 2011), and (2) professional 'role frames' for youth sport coaches (Gilbert & Trudel, 2004).

In addition instrumental case studies have been used extensively in Sociology of Sport to investigate a range of sociological phenomenon and social issues. For example:

1. Violence in youth sport (Cushion & Jones, 2006).
2. Sexual harassment and abuse (Fasting & Brackenridge, 2005).
3. Social development in youth sport (Light, 2010).
4. Socialization into sport (McPhail, Gorely & Kirk, 2003).
5. Retirement from elite sport (McKenna & Thomas, 2007).
6. Power and athlete resistance (Purdy, Potrac & Jones, 2008).
7. Body culture (McMahon & Thompson, 2011).
8. Disability (e.g., Smith & Sparkes, 2008).
9. Illness (e.g., Stewart, Smith & Sparkes, 2011).
10. Job loss in professional football (Roderick, 2014).
11. Gendered injury (Theberge, 2006).

Finally, instrumental case studies have been employed to provide detailed insight into a number of issues within physical education and sport pedagogy, with the aim of providing a more comprehensive understanding of the topic areas in question. These areas included physical education teachers': (1) understanding and responses to curriculum reform (Jin, 2013); (2) perceptions of teamwork (Barker & Rossi, 2012); (3) perceptions of sexism and masculine bias in training (Chen & Curtner-Smith, 2013); (4) gendered norms (Wedgwood, 2005); and (5) views of continued professional development (Makopoulou & Armour, 2011).

Collective case studies have been used to examine a number of issues in sport, such as:

1. Coach education imagery interventions (Callow, Roberts, Bringer & Langan, 2010).
2. The role frame components of youth sport coaches (Gilbert & Trudel, 2004).
3. The impact sport scientists have when working with coaches in wheeled sports (Goosey-Tolfrey, 2010).
4. Cultural narratives and personal stories (Callary, Werthner & Trudel, 2012).
5. Multiple case studies of athlete burnout (Dubuc, Schinke, Eys, Battochio & Zaichkowsky, 2010).
6. Mixed-methods case studies of flow in adventure sports (Houge, Hodge & Boyes, 2013).

Collective case studies have also been used to provide insight into physical education teachers': (1) knowledge of health-related physical education (Harris, 2014); (2) career-long professional development (Makopoulou & Armour, 2014); and (3) reflexivity of teaching philosophies (Mordal-Moen & Green, 2014).

Applied issues in sport: case study examples

Case studies have been used to examine a wide range of applied issues in sport:

1. The effectiveness of psychological skills such as imagery (Evans, Jones & Mullen, 2004), self-talk (Johnson, Hrycaiko, Johnson & Halas, 2004), and hypnosis (Barker & Jones, 2008).
2. Self-efficacy (Barker & Jones, 2005).
3. Decision-making (Martindale & Collins, 2012).
4. Motivation and commitment (Rathwell & Young, 2015).
5. Motivational climate (Hodge *et al.*, 2014).

6. Coping with pressure (Hodge & Smith, 2014).
7. Lifeskills development (Camiré, Trudel & Bernard, 2013).
8. Leadership and team-building (Filho, Gershgoren, Basevitch, Schinke & Tenenbaum, 2014).
9. Ethical decision-making (Dzikus, Fisher & Hays, 2012).
10. Flow (Sparkes & Partington, 2002).
11. Athlete burnout (Dubuc *et al.*, 2010).
12. Injury rehabilitation (Carson & Polman, 2008).
13. Disordered eating (Papathomas & Lavallee, 2012).
14. Retirement from professional sport (Douglas & Carless, 2009).
15. Effective sport psychology consulting relationships (Sharp & Hodge, 2013).

How do I use this research approach?

In this section we highlight several issues and procedures to take into account when considering and then employing a case-study approach. While space restrictions do not allow for procedural advice, and like all other qualitative approaches a case study cannot be reduced to a technical exercise, we highlight important issues for the prospective case-study researcher to consider, and recommend relevant sources to consult for procedural detail (i.e. Baxter & Jack, 2008; Simons, 2009; Stake, 2005; Thomas, 2011, 2012; Yin, 2009). Key issues to consider are as follows:

1. Is a case study the best approach to address my research question? (subject vs object; Thomas, 2011).
2. What is the best case-study 'focus/target' (e.g. a specific issue, topic, life event, organisation, community, team, group, dyad, or individual) for my research project?
3. What 'type' of case study is best suited to my research project (i.e. intrinsic, instrumental, collective or crucial-case study)?
4. Should I use a qualitative or a quantitative case study as a stand-alone method or as part of a mixed-methods approach? (e.g. Jackson & Baker, 2001; see also Chapters 28 and 29, this volume).
5. What source(s) of data should I use? (e.g. primary sources such as interview, focus groups, direct observations, participant-observation; and secondary sources such as textual and digital documentation, and archival records; these data sources might be employed in isolation or as multiple data sources which allow for triangulation).
6. How do I select the participant(s) for my case study? (e.g. which specific type of purposeful sampling might I use and why?: criterion sampling (Patton, 2002); significant samples, (Simonton, 1999); information-oriented selection, extreme/deviant cases, maximum variation cases, critical cases, or paradigmatic cases (Flyvbjerg, 2006). As Sparkes and Smith (2014) have highlighted, given the nature of case study research the selection of cases for study is of crucial importance.

Data analysis and scholarly rigour. Data-analysis processes will vary considerably depending upon the type of case study employed and the type(s) of data/information collected and used in the case report (see Chapters 15–20 for detailed information on data-analysis options). There are a number of potential techniques for analysis of case-study data: for example, thematic content analysis, pattern matching, linking data to propositions, explanation building, time-series analysis, logic models, and cross-case synthesis (see Lieblich, Tuval-Mashlach & Zilber, 1998; Riessman, 2008; Smith & Sparkes, 2012; and Yin, 2009 for detail). To ensure scholarly rigour when using the case-study approach researchers need to employ key processes regarding trustworthiness, credibility and goodness criteria (i.e. scholarly rigour; see Sparkes & Smith, 2009; Tracy, 2010), such as: critical friend(s), thick description (procedures and findings), researcher as instrument, peer debriefer, and an audit trail (see Chapter 25).

The future is here now!

One constant with the case-study approach is change (Merriam, 1988; Ragin & Becker, 1992; Simons, 2009; Smith, 1988; Yin, 2009). Here are some musings about possible future (somewhat underutilized to date) directions for case-study research in sport and exercise:

1. *Ethnographic Case Studies:* Ethnographic studies of sport and exercise groups/individuals (e.g. Burke *et al.*, 2008; Henriksen *et al.*, 2011) are a somewhat underutilized source of data for case studies in sport and exercise research. Case studies employing an ethnographic approach, grounded in a constructivist paradigm (Krane & Baird, 2005), allow the researcher to:

   i. develop a rich understanding of a particular individual or group, without pretending to be value-free;
   ii. consider the case as being historically and situationally bound (i.e. it may not be replicable or generalizable); and
   iii. recognize the influence of the researcher(s) on the research process itself (Henriksen *et al.*, 2011).

   Similarly, life narratives/stories (e.g. Day, Bond & Smith, 2013; Jones, Armour & Potrac, 2003; Shilling & Bunsell, 2014) offer another approach to consider when framing the most useful/appropriate focus for a case study (see also Chapters 4 and 20).

2. *Autoethnography* is another innovative research method that might be employed in case study research (e.g. Douglas, 2014; Gilbourne, 2002; McMahon & Thompson, 2011; Mills, 2015; Purdy *et al.*, 2008; Scarfe & Marlow, 2015; see also Chapter 23). Autoethnography in the sport case study context allows the researcher to connect their personal experiences with their social and sporting subculture(s) through sociological self-exploration. Consequently autoethnography is an optimal case-study methodology to allow the researcher to recollect and excavate their own experiences. In that sense, autoethnography is not simply a subjective autobiography or mere stories of a researcher's experiences; rather it includes autobiographical accounts where the researcher's voice is the authoritative voice of self. It also includes rigorous critical reflection and review through an ethnographic lens, and, importantly, an analysis of cultural practices that serves to offer additional breadth and depth to a case study. From a case-study perspective an autoethnography would aim to produce a case study 'story' that has veracity and authenticity, but is also evocative and enlightening (Ellis, 1999).

3. *Autobiographies as Case Studies*: Autobiographies (see Chapter 14) are a largely untapped source of information for *intrinsic* case studies in sport and exercise (e.g. Stewart *et al.*, 2011). Autobiographies offer detailed descriptions of an individual's life and can often provide rich information about psychosocial phenomena (Bjorklund, 1998; Eakin, 2008; Pipkin, 2008). As naturalistic life stories autobiographies provide insights into 'lived experiences' and 'self-understanding' over time, in the sociocultural context unique to the person/subject of the autobiography (Bjorklund, 1998; Stewart *et al.*, 2011).

4. *Applied issues*: As described earlier the case-study approach has been used extensively to examine the effectiveness of a number of applied interventions/programmes/skills.

The case-study approach is especially useful when practical issues of logistics and limited accessibility to potential participants constrain the researcher's ability to design and execute a large-sample, causal-inference study. In addition, when ethical issues such as with-holding access to interventions expected to improve performance (to a control group) arise, the use of an action-research case-study approach can be a useful ethically acceptable alternative (e.g. Rovio, Arvinen-Barrow, Weigand, Eskola & Lintunen, 2012).

Final thoughts and observations

Case studies are hard, difficult, challenging and a little frightening at times, but also incredibly rewarding. Your ideas, thinking, interpretations and writing skills are brutally exposed for examination by the reader; which can generate feelings of vulnerability and stress even for the most experienced researcher! The variety of studies featured in this chapter provide exemplars of what case studies are (i.e. rigorous, in-depth examinations of a *particular* life event, organization, community, team, group, dyad or individual), and what they are not (i.e. unsubstantiated opinions and/or 'war stories' lacking in substance, insight and scholarly rigour).

Typically a good case study, especially a narrative case study, tells a *good story* (Flyvbjerg, 2006); a good story needs to be *well written*. The story-writing skills required for the presentation of a case-study report are often not a core part of an academic's skill set. Bland, matter-of-fact, academic writing styles will typically not suffice for case-study writing. The researcher seeking to employ the case-study approach will need to work on their 'story-writing' skills – a set of skills that is not easily attained for most researchers (we speak from personal experience!).

References

Balish, S. & Côté, J. (2014). The influence of community on athletic development: An integrated case study. *Qualitative Research in Sport, Exercise & Health, 6*, 98–120.

Barker, D. M. & Rossi, A. (2012). The trouble with teamwork: A discursive investigation. *Physical Education & Sport Pedagogy, 17*, 1–19.

Barker, J. B. & Jones, M. V. (2005). Using hypnosis to increase self-efficacy: A case study in elite judo. *Sport & Exercise Psychology Review, 1*, 36–42.

Barker, J. B. & Jones, M. V. (2008). The effects of hypnosis on self-efficacy, positive and negative affect and sport performance: A case study from professional English soccer. *Journal of Clinical Sport Psychology, 2*, 127–147.

Baxter, P. & Jack, S. (2008). Qualitative case study methodology: Study design and implementation for novice researchers. *The Qualitative Report, 13*, 544–559.

Becker, H. S. (2000). Generalizing from case studies. In E. W. Eisner & A. Peshkin (Eds.), *Qualitative inquiry in education: The continuing debate* (pp. 233–242). New York, NY: Teachers College Press.

Bjorklund, D. (1998). *Interpreting the self: Two hundred years of American autobiography*. Chicago, IL: University of Chicago Press.

Burke, S., Sparkes, A. C. & Allen-Collinson, J. (2008). High altitude climbers as ethnomethodologists making sense of cognitive dissonance: Ethnographic insights from an attempt to scale Mt. Everest. *The Sport Psychologist, 22*, 336–355.

Busanich, R., McGannon, K. & Schinke, R. (2014). Comparing male and female distance runners' experiences of disordered eating though narrative analysis. *Psychology of Sport & Exercise, 15*, 705–712.

Callary, B., Werthner, P. & Trudel, P. (2012). How meaningful episodic experiences influence the process of becoming an experienced coach. *Qualitative Research in Sport, Exercise & Health, 3*, 420–438.

Callow, N., Roberts, R., Bringer, J. D. & Langan, E. (2010). Coach education related to the delivery of imagery: Two interventions. *The Sport Psychologist, 24*, 277–299.

Camiré, M., Trudel, P. & Bernard, D. (2013). A case study of a high school sport program designed to teach athletes life skills and values. *The Sport Psychologist, 27,* 188–200.

Carson F. & Polman, R. (2008). ACL injury rehabilitation: A psychological case study of a professional rugby union player. *Journal of Clinical Sport Psychology, 2,* 71–90.

Chen, Y. & Curtner-Smith, M. (2013). Hegemonic masculinity in sport education: Case studies of experienced in-service teachers with teaching orientations. *European Physical Education Review, 19,* 360–380.

Chenail, R. J. (2010). Getting specific about qualitative research generalizability. *Journal of Ethnographic & Qualitative Research, 5,* 1–11.

Christensen, M. K., Laursen, D. N. & Sorensen, J. K. (2011). Situated learning in youth elite football: A Danish case study among talented male under-18 football players. *Physical Education & Sport Pedagogy, 16,* 163–178.

Creswell, J.W. (2013). *Qualitative inquiry and research design: Choosing among five approaches* (3rd ed.). Thousand Oaks, CA: Sage.

Cruickshank, A., Collins, D. & Minten, S. (2013). Culture change in a professional sports team: Shaping environmental contexts and regulating power. *International Journal of Sports Science & Coaching, 8,* 271–290.

Cushion, C. & Jones, R. (2006). Power, discourse, and symbolic violence in professional youth soccer: The case of Albion Football Club. *Sociology of Sport Journal, 23,* 142–161.

Dale, G. & Wrisberg, C. (1996). The use of a Performance Profiling technique in a team setting: Getting the athletes and coach on the 'same page'. *The Sport Psychologist, 10,* 261–277.

Day, M., Bond, K. & Smith, B. (2013). Holding it together: Coping with vicarious trauma in sport. *Psychology of Sport & Exercise, 14,* 1–11.

Day, M. & Wadey, R. (2016). Narratives of trauma, recovery, and growth: The complex role of sport following permanent acquired disability. *Psychology of Sport & Exercise, 22,* 131–138.

Douglas, K. (2014). Challenging interpretive privilege in elite and professional sport: One [athlete's] story, revised, reshaped, reclaimed. *Qualitative Research in Sport, Exercise & Health, 6,* 220–243.

Douglas, K. & Carless, D. (2009). Abandoning the performance narrative: Two women's stories of transition from professional sport. *Journal of Applied Sport Psychology, 21,* 213–230.

Dubuc, N., Schinke, R., Eys, M., Battochio, R. & Zaichkowsky, L. (2010). Experiences of burnout among adolescent female gymnasts: Three case studies. *Journal of Clinical Sport Psychology, 4,* 1–18.

Dzikus, L., Fisher, L. & Hays, K. (2012). Shared responsibility: A case of and for 'real life' ethical decision-making in sport psychology. *The Sport Psychologist, 26,* 519–53.

Eakin, P. (2008). *Living autobiographically: How we create identity in narrative.* Ithaca, NY: Cornell University Press.

Ellis, C. (1999). Heartful autoethnography. *Qualitative Health Research, 9,* 669–683.

Evans, L., Jones, L. & Mullen, R. (2004). An imagery intervention during the competitive season with an elite rugby union player. *The Sport Psychologist, 18,* 252–271.

Fasting, K. & Brackenridge, C. (2005). The grooming process in sport: Case studies of sexual harassment and abuse. *Auto/Biography, 13,* 33–52.

Filho, E., Gershgoren, L., Basevitch, I., Schinke, R. & Tenenbaum, G. (2014). Peer leadership and shared mental models in a college volleyball team: A season long case study. *Journal of Clinical Sport Psychology, 8,* 184–203.

Flyvbjerg, B. (2006). Five misunderstandings about case-study research. *Qualitative Inquiry, 12,* 219–245.

George, A. L. & Bennett, A. (2005). *Case studies and theory development in the social sciences.* Cambridge, MA: MIT Press.

Gerring, J. (2004). What is a case study and what is it good for? *American Political Science Review, 98,* 341–354.

Gerring, J. (2007). Is there a (viable) crucial-case method? *Comparative Political Studies, 40,* 231–253.

Gerring, J. & McDermott, R. (2007). An experimental template for case study research. *American Journal of Political Science, 51,* 688–701.

Gilbert, W. D. & Trudel, P. (2004). Role of the coach: How model youth team sport coaches frame their roles. *The Sport Psychologist, 18,* 21–43.

Gilbourne, D. (2002). Sports participation, sports injury and altered images of self: An autobiographical narrative of a lifelong legacy. *Reflective Practice, 3,* 71–88.

Gledhill, A. & Harwood, C. (2015). A holistic perspective on career development in UK female soccer players: A negative case analysis. *Psychology of Sport & Exercise, 21,* 65–77.

Gomm, R., Hammersley, M. & Foster, P. (2000). *Case study method.* London: Sage.

Gomm, R., Hammersley, M. & Foster, P. (2002). Case study and generalization. In R. Gomm, M. Hammersley & P. Foster (Eds.), *Case study method: Key issues, key texts* (pp. 98–116). London: Sage.

Goosey-Tolfrey, V. (2010). Supporting the Paralympic athlete: Focus on wheeled sports. *Disability & Rehabilitation, 32*, 2237–2243.

Gustafsson, H., Kentta, G., Hassmen, P., Lundqvist, C. & Durand-Bush, N. (2007). The process of burn-out: A multiple case study of three elite endurance athletes. *International Journal of Sport Psychology, 38*, 388–416.

Hammersley, M. (2012). Troubling theory in case study research. *Higher Education Research & Development, 31*, 393–405.

Harris, J. (2014). Physical education teacher education students' knowledge, perceptions and experiences of promoting healthy, active lifestyles in secondary schools. *Physical Education & Sport Pedagogy, 19*, 466–480.

Henriksen, K., Stambulova, N. & Roessler, K. K. (2010). Holistic approach to athletic talent development environments: A successful sailing milieu. *Psychology of Sport & Exercise, 11*, 212–222.

Henriksen, K., Stambulova, N. & Roessler, K. K. (2011). Riding the wave of an expert: A successful talent development environment in kayaking. *The Sport Psychologist, 25*, 341–362.

Hodge, K., Henry, G. & Smith, W. (2014). A case study of excellence in elite sport: Motivational climate in a world champion team. *The Sport Psychologist, 28*, 60–74.

Hodge, K. & Smith, W. (2014). Public expectation, pressure, and 'Avoiding-the-Choke': A case study from elite sport. *The Sport Psychologist, 28*, 375–389.

Holt, N. & Hogg, J. (2002). Perceptions of stress and coping during preparations for the 1999 Women's Soccer World Cup Finals. *The Sport Psychologist, 16*, 251–271.

Houge, S., Hodge, K. & Boyes, M. (2013). The multi-phasic and dynamic nature of flow in adventure experiences. *Journal of Leisure Research, 45*, 214–232.

Jackson, R. & Baker, J. (2001). Routines, rituals, and rugby: Case study of a world-class goal kicker. *The Sport Psychologist, 15*, 48–65.

Jin, A. (2013). Physical education curriculum reform in China: A perspective from physical education teachers. *Physical Education & Sport Pedagogy, 18*, 15–27.

Johnson, J. M., Hrycaiko, D. W., Johnson, V. & Halas, J. M. (2004). Self-talk and female youth soccer performance. *The Sport Psychologist, 18*, 44–59.

Jones, R., Armour, K. & Potrac, P. (2003): Constructing expert knowledge: A case study of a top-level professional soccer coach. *Sport, Education & Society, 8*, 213–229.

Kerr, J. H. (2007). Sudden withdrawal from skydiving: A case study informed by reversal theory's concept of protective frames. *Journal of Applied Sport Psychology, 19*, 337–351.

Krane, V. & Baird, S.M. (2005). Using ethnography in applied sport psychology. *Journal of Applied Sport Psychology, 17*, 87–107.

Lieblich, A., Tuval-Mashlach, R. & Zilber, T. (1998). *Narrative research.* London: Sage.

Light, R.L. (2010). Children's social and personal development through sport: A case study of an Australian swimming club. *Journal of Sport & Social Issues, 34*, 266–282.

Lloyd-Jones, G. (2003). Design and control issues in qualitative case study research. *International Journal of Qualitative Methods, 2*, 33–42.

Makopoulou, K. & Armour, K. M. (2011). Physical education teachers' career-long professional learning: Getting personal. *Sport, Education & Society, 16*, 571–591. doi:10.1080/13573322.2011.601138.

Makopoulou, K. & Armour, K. (2014). Possibilities and challenges in teachers' collegial learning. *Educational Review, 66*, 75–95.

Martindale, A. & Collins, D., (2012). A professional judgment and decision-making case study: Reflection-in-action research. *The Sport Psychologist, 26*, 500–518.

McKenna, J. & Thomas, H. (2007). Enduring injustice: A case study of retirement from professional rugby union. *Sport, Education & Society, 12*, 19–35.

McLeod, J. (2010). *Case study research in counselling and psychotherapy.* London: Sage.

McMahon, J. & Thompson, M. (2011). 'Body work – regulation of a swimmer body': An autoethnography from an Australian elite swimmer. *Sport, Education & Society, 16*, 35–50.

McPhail, A., Gorely, T. & Kirk, D. (2003). Young people's socialisation into sport: A case study of an athletics club. *Sport, Education & Society, 8*, 251–267.

Merriam, S. B. (1988). *Case study research in education: A qualitative approach.* San Francisco, CA: Jossey-Bass.

Mills, J. (2015). An [AUTO]ethnographic account of constructing, deconstructing, and partially reconstructing a coaching identity. *Qualitative Research in Sport, Exercise & Health, 7*, 606–619.

Mordal-Moen, K. & Green, K. (2014). Neither shaking nor stirring: A case study of reflexivity in Norwegian physical education teacher education. *Sport, Education & Society, 19*, 415–434.

Papathomas, A. & Lavallee, D. (2012). Narrative constructions of anorexia and abuse: An athlete's search for meaning in trauma. *Journal of Loss & Trauma, 17*, 293–318.

Patton, M. (2002). *Qualitative research & evaluation methods: Integrating theory and practice.* Thousand Oaks, CA. Sage.

Pipkin, J. (2008). *Sporting lives. Metaphor and myth in American sports autobiographies.* Columbia, MO: University of Missouri Press.

Purdy, L., Potrac, P. & Jones, R. (2008). Power, consent and resistance: An autoethnography of competitive rowing. *Sport, Education & Society, 13*, 319–336.

Ragin, C. C & Becker, H. S. (1992). *What is a case? Exploring the foundations of social inquiry.* Cambridge, UK: Cambridge University Press.

Rathwell, S. & Young, B. W. (2015). Modelling commitment and compensation: A case study of a 52-year-old masters athlete. *Qualitative Research in Sport, Exercise & Health, 7*, 718–738.

Riessman, C.K. (2008). *Narrative methods for the human sciences.* London: Sage.

Roderick, M. (2014). From identification to dis-identification: Case studies of job loss in professional football. *Qualitative Research in Sport, Exercise & Health, 6*, 143–160.

Rossing, H. & Jones, R. (2015). 'Stepping away from the computer and into the sweats': The construction and negotiation of exercise identities in a Norwegian public company. *Qualitative Research in Sport, Exercise & Health, 7*, 37–52.

Rovio, E., Arvinen-Barrow, M., Weigand, D., Eskola, J. & Lintunen, T. (2012). Using team building methods with an ice hockey team: An action research case study. *The Sport Psychologist, 26*, 584–603.

Scarfe, S. & Marlow, C. (2015). Overcoming fear: An autoenthographic narrative of running with epilepsy. *Qualitative Research in Sport, Exercise & Health, 7*, 688–697.

Schwandt, T. A. (1997). *Qualitative inquiry: A dictionary of terms.* Thousand Oaks, CA: Sage.

Seawright, J. & Gerring, J. (2008). Case selection techniques in case study research. *Political Research Quarterly, 61*, 294–308.

Sharp, L. & Hodge K. (2013). Effective sport psychology consulting relationships: Two coach case studies. *The Sport Psychologist, 27*, 313–324.

Shilling, C. & Bunsell, T. (2014). From iron maiden to superwoman: The stochastic art of self-transformation and the deviant female sporting body. *Qualitative Research in Sport, Exercise & Health, 6*, 478–498.

Simons, H. (2009). *Case study research in practice.* London: Sage.

Simonton, D. (1999). Significant samples: The psychological study of eminent individuals. *Psychological Methods, 4*, 425–451.

Smith, B. & Sparkes, A. C. (2008). Changing bodies, changing narratives and the consequences of tellability: A case study of becoming disabled through sport. *Sociology of Health & Illness, 30*, 217–236.

Smith, B. & Sparkes, A. C. (2012). Making sense of words and stories in qualitative research. Some strategies for consideration. In G. Tenenbaum, R. Eklund & A. Kamata (Eds.), *Handbook of Measurement in Sport and Exercise Psychology* (pp. 119–130). Champaign, IL: Human Kinetics.

Smith R.E. (1988). The logic and design of case study research. *The Sport Psychologist, 2*, 1–12.

Sparkes, A. C. & Partington, S. (2002). Narrative practice and its potential contribution to sport psychology: The example of flow. *The Sport Psychologist, 17*, 292– 317.

Sparkes, A. C., Pérez-Samaniego, V. & Smith, B. (2011). Social comparison processes, narrative mapping, and their shaping of the cancer experience: A case study of an elite athlete. *Health, 16*, 467–488.

Sparkes, A. C. & Smith, B. (2009). Judging the quality of qualitative inquiry: Criteriology and relativism in action. *Psychology of Sport & Exercise, 10*, 491–497.

Sparkes, A. C. & Smith, B. (2014). *Qualitative research methods in sport, exercise and health: From process to product.* Abingdon: Routledge.

Stake, R. E. (2005). Qualitative case studies. In N. K. Denzin & Y. S. Lincoln (Eds.), *The handbook of qualitative research* (3rd ed., pp. 443–466). London: Sage.

Stewart, C., Smith, B. & Sparkes, A. C. (2011) Sporting autobiographies of illness and the role of metaphor. *Sport in Society, 14*, 581–597.

Theberge, N. (2006). The gendering of sports injury: A look at 'progress' in women's sport through a case study of the biomedical discourse on the injured athletic body. *Sport in Society, 9*, 634–649.

Thomas, G. (2011). A typology for the case study in social science following a review of definition, discourse, and structure. *Qualitative Inquiry, 17*, 511–521.

Thomas, G. (2012). *How to do your case study: A guide for students and researchers.* London: Sage.

Tracy, S. J. (2010). Qualitative quality: Eight 'big tent' criteria for excellent qualitative research. *Qualitative Inquiry*, *16*, 837–851.

VanWynsberghe, R. & Khan, S. (2007). Redefining case study. *International Journal of Qualitative Methods*, *6*, 80–94.

Wedgwood, N. (2005). Just one of the boys? A life history case study of a male physical education teacher. *Gender & Education*, *17*, 189–201.

Wolcott, H. (1995). *The art of fieldwork*. Oxford: Rowman and Littlefield.

Yin, R. K. (2009). *Case study research: Design and methods* (4th ed.). Thousand Oaks, CA: Sage.

7

FEMINISMS

Cheryl Cooky

It seems appropriate to begin a chapter on "Feminisms" by addressing the following questions: What is feminism? What is feminist qualitative research? What makes research *feminist*? While seemingly straightforward, these questions are complex, varied, and require further exploration, which I provide below. This chapter will navigate the researcher through the diverse landscape of feminist epistemological and methodological considerations. This chapter does not provide an exhaustive overview of feminist research. Indeed, there are a number of useful textbooks and readers on feminist research, feminist methodology, and feminist theory (for example, see Hesse-Biber, 2012; 2014; Jagger, 2013). Rather, this chapter is intended as an entry point into feminist methodology and feminist qualitative research, specifically in the areas of sports sociology/psychology, and to provide important considerations for those who are new to the field of feminist qualitative inquiry. It is informed by my own experience as an American feminist researcher in the field of sociology of sport, and shaped by my role as an instructor of courses on research methods and feminist methodologies. This chapter will draw from those experiences as a researcher/instructor, as well as original research studies in the fields of Sociology of Sports and Sports Psychology to offer the researcher insights into how he/she/they might embark on a qualitative research study utilizing feminist epistemologies. As in my courses, I hope to encourage the researcher to be mindful regarding how it is that feminism as a theoretical, methodological, or epistemological framework will inform their study/inquiry.

What is feminism? What is feminist research?

As stated in the introduction, while the questions appear straightforward, feminist scholars and researchers will know that the response often depends on who is being asked. It is common to see statements such as, "This study is informed by a feminist perspective" or "Using feminist methods, this study will . . ." Unfortunately, these statements offer little insight into the framework and approach of the researcher, and may unintentionally raise questions and critique that could easily be avoided through an explicit discussion of which feminist theory or methodology is being used, or at the very least through the strategic use of citations, although this can be limiting unless the audience is well versed in feminist theories and methodologies. In terms of theoretical framework, scholars can utilize a range of theories, including liberal feminism, radical feminism, socialist feminism, materialist feminism, new materialist feminism, postmodern feminism, post-structuralist feminism, Black feminism, Chicana feminism, eco-feminism, queer theory, intersectionality theory, among others (see Tong, 2013, for an introductory overview of feminist theory). In terms of feminist methodologies, scholars to can utilize a range of epistemological frameworks including feminist empiricism, feminist standpoint, feminist postmodernism/post-structuralism, among others (see Hesse-Biber, 2012, for an introductory overview of feminist research). As feminist sports studies scholar M. Ann Hall observed, "there is no single way to do feminist research" (1996, p. 74).

In addition to the diversity of frameworks and perspectives, part of the challenge in determining what practices, procedures, research questions, and goals constitute feminist research is that feminism is multidimensional and refers to the sociopolitical movements to end gender-based inequality and women's oppression, the academic theoretical frameworks by which gender-based inequality and oppression is explained, analyzed, and interpreted, as well as a praxis. Feminism as a social movement has informed and been informed by feminist academic inquiry into the lives of women, women's issues, voices, and lived experiences (Hesse-Biber, 2014). In this way, feminist research is often informed by the larger political sensibilities of feminist movements and, as such, its goal is to explain and address the origins of women's oppression and/or offer strategies for social change. Therefore, the diversity of feminist thought, theory, and social movements produces a range of responses to the question: "What is feminist research?"

Feminist scholars have identified some commonalities across this diversity; for example, feminist research is inherently political, given its concern with examining power dynamics in order to address women's oppression. Within the fields of sociology of sport and sport psychology, one of the themes of early feminist research was to address the ways in which sports as a male-dominated institution – or, as some feminists note, the last male preserve – contained and constrained women's participation and experiences (see Fisher & Larsen, 2016; Hargreaves, 1994; Messner, 1988; Theberge, 1985). As Bryson (1987) argued, this constraint and containment manifested through the direct control of women's sport (coaching, leadership, and decision-making positions are overwhelmingly held by men), ignoring women's sports (the lack of media coverage of women's sport), and trivializing women's sport (positioning female athletes in stereotypical gender roles – sex object, wife, mother – first, and athlete second); issues that continue to plague women's sports (Cooky & LaVoi, 2012). As a result, feminist research and theorizing on sport, particularly that in sociology of sport, offered strategies for change ranging from liberal feminist, wherein the goal was to adapt and adopt policies so as to increase opportunities (Boutlier & San Giovani, 1994), to radical feminist, wherein the structural foundations of "male sport," such as the primacy of winning, the hierarchy of authority, and the elitism of skill, are challenged and transformed to be more inclusive, less hierarchical, and oriented towards pleasure and joy (Birrell & Richter, 1987), to contemporary postmodern feminist and queer feminist strategies, wherein the gender binary itself as constituted in sports practices and policies is challenged (Cooky & Dworkin, 2013; Sykes, 2006; Travers, 2006), and the elimination of sex/gender as an organizational category in sport is articulated (for a discussion see Travers, 2008). In this way feminist research often stands in contrast to positivist research, which eschews any social or political influences, goals, or objectives in the attainment of knowledge.

Some feminist scholars have noted the difficulty in utilizing feminist epistemologies in the field of sports psychology, in part due to the ways in which logical positivist epistemologies continue to dominate the field (Fisher & Larsen, 2016; Greenleaf & Collins, 2001; Semerjian & Waldron, 2001). This concern is less salient in the sociology of sport as the parent discipline, sociology, has a history of anti-positivism in various theoretical traditions and schools of thought, and thereby there is more acceptance, albeit contested, of a diversity of nonpositivist epistemological approaches in sociology of sport. In their candid discussion of the role of feminism and feminist research in sport psychology, Greenleaf and Collins (2001) raise important considerations regarding the stature of feminist research in the field (see also Fisher & Larsen, 2016). Given the dominance of positivism and the marginalized status of feminist research, they question whether using "feminist" in the title of a journal article or conference abstract limits the readership. Would those who might potentially benefit from a feminist research study's findings see the "f-word" and thus view the research as irrelevant and subsequently ignore it? Indeed, this appears to be an ongoing concern as researchers who identify as feminist academics are publishing research considered by scholars to be feminist in orientation, design, and impact yet avoid or omit the "f-word" in their papers (with some exceptions). This raises important considerations for feminist scholars as the implications of conducting feminist research are significant beyond the specific study. In the absence of identifying it as such, researchers may, on the one hand, expand the audience for their research while benefiting from the professional job requirements of an academic (publishing, presenting at conference, and so on). Yet, on the other hand, this accommodation of the hegemony of positivism and the way "good" research gets narrowly defined only further marginalizes feminist scholarship and reaffirms feminist research's "second-class" status. This is not to fault individual scholars whose agency is certainly constrained by the institutional imperatives of the University. Indeed, while overall, the terrain of academia is fraught with power dynamics, institutional expectations, and externally imposed definitions of "excellence," how these dynamics manifest and are negotiated by feminist scholars varies by the contextual specificities of a discipline, institution, journal, department, and so on (see Greenleaf & Collins, 2001). Researchers in the field of sport studies conducting qualitative research reside at the intersection of multiple vectors of marginalization as we study 1) sport, 2) from a feminist perspective, 3) using qualitative methods; all three of which occupy subordinated statuses.

The challenge of identifying and locating feminist research in positivist-dominated fields contributes to the lack of clarity in determining what constitutes feminist research. Contributing further to this lack of clarity is the conflation of feminist research with research on gender. Simply including gender in the analysis – for example, by treating gender as a variable within a statistical model or measuring gender differences in performance on a given survey instrument or experimental exercise alone – would not constitute feminist research. Moreover, studies that find gender differences without offering a theoretically informed explanation of why those differences come to exist construct knowledges and ways of knowing that reproduce and reinforce women's subordinated status. Thus, research that examines gender in the absence of a feminist framework, neglect or ignore concerns of inequality, power, hierarchy, and oppression.

Academic feminism and feminist epistemology (including feminist empiricism and standpoint theory), in particular, emerged from a critique of the androcentric bias in scientific research, and a desire among feminists to address that bias, as well as to address the exclusion of women and women's perspectives in knowledge building. As such, feminist research is characterized by the recognition of the importance of women's lived experiences and subjugated knowledge; the movement from "margin to center" in the location of epistemic privilege and production of knowledge, and the elimination of boundaries that privilege dominant forms of knowledge construction (Hesse-Biber, 2012).

Feminist researchers are concerned with issues of power, both societal power dynamics that impact and shape women's lives, as well as the power dynamics that exist between researcher and researched, and the ways power informs every stage of the research process. Feminist researchers are also critically cognizant of and interrogate issues of authority (Who can be a knower? What can be known? Who decides?), reflexivity and the role of the researcher, as well as positionality (both of the researcher and those who are researched), and seek out research questions that address subjugated knowledge in order to achieve social change and social transformation (Hesse-Biber, 2012). How feminist researchers address and resolve the above issues and concerns should be informed and shaped by the epistemological and theoretical frameworks. It is for this reason that researchers should be explicit regarding their epistemological approach. Claiming "feminist ethics would suggest . . ." or "because of our feminist approach we decided . . ." without a sufficient discussion, including key citations, of the specific feminist epistemological and theoretical approach employed in the study, offers little insight into the research process.

While there are commonalities by which feminist research can be understood across the diversity of theoretical and methodological frameworks, as feminist researchers note, methods themselves are not inherently feminist (Stacey, 1988). In a classic essay, Sandra Harding (1987) raises an important question: Is there a unique feminist method of inquiry? Her response, and the response of numerous feminist scholars whose work proceeded her essay is a resounding "No"! In response to Stacey (1988), who posed the question "Can there can be a feminist ethnography?" Wheatley (1994) suggests that rather than being concerned about what makes a method feminist, researchers should instead focus on imbuing research methods with a feminist imagination. In other words, qualitative methods are not inherently feminist because they allow a means by which to capture women's voices and lived experiences. Similarly, quantitative methods can offer important forms of knowledge to advance feminist goals such as social justice and gender equality (Sprague, 2005). Therefore, what constitutes a research method as feminist is the epistemological and methodological orientation of the research, the types of research questions asked, and the overall objectives of the project, which often focus on addressing and/or challenging existing power relations to move towards emancipatory goals (see also Chapters 1, 8, 32, and 34). The following section will provide a brief overview of several major feminist epistemological frameworks often utilized in feminist qualitative research, and offer several examples from the fields of sports sociology and sports psychology to illustrate how these frameworks are utilized in specific research studies.

Feminist epistemologies in qualitative research

Epistemology is "the study of the origin, nature and limits of knowledge" (Hall, 1996, p. 69; see also Chapters 1 and 10, this volume). It is a philosophical perspective "concerned with the nature and scope of knowledge, its presuppositions and basis, and the general reliability of claims to knowledge" (Harding, 1987, p. 22). Epistemology addresses questions such as "who can be a knower and what can actually be known, what constitutes and validates knowledge, and what is the relationship between knowing and being" (Stanley & Wise, 1990, 26). For feminist scholars, what has come to be considered knowledge is not that which is based on human experience. Rather, much of our understanding of the social world has come from the perspective and standpoint of men, which then comes to represent the universal understanding of the social world.

Feminist standpoint epistemology

The concerns of both activists within the US-based women's movement of the 1960s and 1970s regarding the absence of women in scientific thought and discovery, as well as those of academic feminists regarding the androcentric bias in research and knowledge production, lead to the positioning of women's lived experiences as central to knowledge production. According to feminist standpoint theory, relative to those in power (men), women's lived experience of subordination provides an epistemically privileged position from which to better understand domination and the world of gender relations and power inequalities (Ramazanoglu & Holland, 2002). Hartsock (1987), in her classic essay, draws upon Marxist historical materialism to argue that knowledge production should originate from the lives of oppressed/subordinated groups and give voice to women, in part to address masculinist truth claims. In opposition to positivist epistemologies (often critiqued by feminists for masculinist bias and upholding dominant power relations), which assert that the context of discovery should not, or does not, influence or impact the attainment of knowledge, feminist standpoint theory (and other feminist epistemologies) recognizes the contextualized and often politicized nature of all research and scientific inquiry. Rather than engage methodological frameworks that neglect context or purport to remove the context of discovery from the process of research inquiry, feminist standpoint starts with the everyday, lived experiences of marginalized groups to critically evaluate not only existing theories (which are partial in that they were derived from androcentric bias), but also the dominant social institutions that are often upheld by the knowledge claims developed through positivist inquiry (Harding, 1987; Hesse-Biber, 2012).

Hartsock (1987), in her development of feminist standpoint theory, was interested in developing a macrolevel epistemology that privileged women's lives as the starting point for knowledge production. Hartsock acknowledged that while there were differences among women in terms of how they were situated relative to subordination/oppression (for example, women of color, lesbian women), yet, given the division of labor in capitalist economies, she asserted all women were similarly situated relative to men, and as members of the subordinated group women had a more complete (or less partial) understanding of the social world. This has led many feminist scholars to critique feminist standpoint theory as essentialist and universalist. As a result, feminist standpoint theory is often viewed as problematic and its relevance in contemporary feminist scholarship is contested. Conversely, other feminist scholars have argued that the epistemological assumptions undergirding feminist standpoint continue to have relevance and can be aligned with contemporary feminist perspectives, including postmodern feminism (Esmonde, Cooky, & Andrews, 2015; Hirschmann, 2004; Krane *et al.*, 2012). For these scholars, feminist standpoint theory is not universalist, nor does it suggest that those whose standpoint is one of oppression have a vision of the world that will illuminate *the* truth. As Hirschmann explains:

> As a way of seeing the world, redefining knowledge, reconceptualizing social relations, and renaming experience, standpoint theory provides a powerful methodology for understanding "reality" as an ongoing process. That is, the adoption of a particular feminist standpoint allows us to gain a "less partial and perverse" understanding of the world; but that does not mean we have achieved "truth."
>
> *(Hirschmann, 2004, p. 322)*

Extending feminist standpoint theory, Patricia Hill Collins (1990) developed a theory that draws upon standpoint epistemology to give epistemic privilege to the subjugated knowledges of Black women who are positioned as "outsiders within," what she called "intersectionality." Collins' theoretical concept of the matrix of domination provides feminist researchers with the conceptual tools to explain and analyze the ways in which gender-based oppression impacts women differently, given ways in which women are situated relative to structures of oppression and privilege within the matrix of domination. Collins explained: "Subjugated knowledges . . . develop in cultural contexts controlled by oppressed groups. Dominant groups aim to replace subjugated knowledges with their own specialized thought because they realize that gaining control over this dimension of subordinate groups' lives amplifies control" (1990, p. 228). At the same time, Collins recognized there are segments of subordinated communities that internalize and perpetuate dominant ideologies. Thus, the processes of domination and oppression are complex. The result is, "African-American women find themselves in a web of cross-cutting relationships, each presenting varying combinations of controlling images and women's self-definitions" (Collins, 1990, p. 96). The concept of intersectionality (Collins, 1990) refers to this "web of crosscutting relationships," taking into account how various forms of oppression (e.g., race, class, gender, sexuality, disablism) interlock with one another. As such, "both/and perspectives," rather than "either/or perspectives" of social locations are used to understand the ways in which individuals (and social institutions) are situated within inter-locking forms of privilege/dominance and oppression/subordination.

Within the field of sports sociology and sports and exercise psychology (among others), feminist standpoint theory and intersectionality have been useful epistemological frameworks in qualitative research, particularly in qualitative interviewing and fieldwork/ethnography. These epistemological frameworks inform research that seeks to "give voice" to girls' and women's experiences and lived realities within sports contexts. Moreover, intersectionality allows a framework by which the racialized and classed experience of gender and identity can be analyzed and explained (Walker & Melton, 2015; Ratna, 2011; Whithycomb, 2011). While many published articles do not provide an explicit or extensive discussion of epistemology or methodology[1] (most focus on a discussion of *methods* – the *tools* used to answer a research question and the *procedures* by which knowledge was collected/attained and analyzed), there is an extensive body of literature using feminist qualitative methods wherein researchers conduct interviews with girls and women so that those lived experiences, which have been marginalized both in sports contexts as well as in research on sports, are given voice. For example, Vikki Krane's research on lesbian coaches and their experiences of heterosexism and homonegativ-ism in sports is an illustrative example of feminist standpoint epistemology (see Krane, 1996, 2001). In a reflective essay published in a special issue on feminism in *The Sports Psychologist*, Krane (2001) notes that the absence of research on lesbians in sport motivated and validated her interest in the topic. In recent research published in the *Journal of Sport* Management, the authors, Walker and Melton (2015) conducted semistructured interviews with LBG (lesbian, bisexual, and gay) athletes, utilizing feminist standpoint theory and intersectionality to exam-ine the intersection of race, gender, and sexual orientation, and the lived experiences and voices of LGB athletes within the context of collegiate sports. Krane and her colleagues have utilized feminist standpoint epistemology in their more recent work on girls' negotiations of media images of female athletes (Krane *et al.*, 2011). They conducted focus groups with girls to provide girls the opportunity to share their perceptions of various images of female athletes. Subsequent research has explored the girls' lived experiences as they articulated the nego-tiations of identities as female athletes during focus-group discussions (Krane, Ross, Sullivan Barak, Lucas-Carr, & Robinson, 2014).

Earlier iterations of feminist qualitative research utilizing standpoint epistemology with the expressed goal of "giving voice" to girls and women who had been silenced or marginalized in research often romanticized this particular epistemological goal. While it is important to recog-nize the need for inclusion of the experiences of women and girls, particularly when feminist inquiry into sport was an emerging field, contemporary iterations of feminist epistemologies offer a necessary critical intervention. The notion that a researcher will enter into a research site and provide women with a voice (see also Chapters 9 and 36), liberating them from silence, neglects the power dynamics inherent in any research endeavor. Feminist qualitative researchers have turned to Foucault's concepts of power/knowledge to recognize that the construction of knowledge through the research process involves the exercise of power and thus, "knowledge claims are intrinsically tied to the politics of identity, power and exclusion" (Wheaton 2002, p. 250). Indeed, Dowling and Flintoff too "share a concern for an over-zealous adoption of the notion of 'giving voice' to the subjects within our interview projects, which in turn can lead to a reification of a singular voice, at a time when our understanding of knowledge construction implicates multiple voices" (2011, p. 68).

While qualitative methods may be better suited to allowing subjects to express themselves and to have their voices heard than quantitative methods, ultimately the researcher has control over the final research product. It is the researcher who decides what framework to use to analyze the data, what questions will be asked during the interview, how the interviews will be edited, and what segments of interviews or observations will be included in the published/public product. Moreover, the process of conducting qualitative interviews is socially constructed in that often researchers wish to create a context by which knowledge is produced in a linear way that is comfortable for both the researcher and the participant and, as such, researchers often avoid the "messiness" of an interview, and contradictions, tensions, or conflict during an interview is rarely explored (Dowling & Flintoff, 2011). Thus, there is much power in "giving voice." Yet, this power is not something that that the researcher (or the participant) *has*, but is produced dynamically in the context of the research. Some feminists assert participants in qualitative research are empowered in that they can decide what to discuss during an interview, which aspects of their experience to share (Wolf, 1996), and have agency to engage in resistive acts by providing "false" information, or no information at all. Yet ultimately, the final product of the representation of the lives of participants is in the hands of the researcher. Concerns regarding "giving voice" as an epistemological empowerment for women is interrogated by feminist ethnographer, Beatriz Pesquera, who asks, "Are we concerned with the empowerment of the women whose voices we will record and analyze, or are we empowering ourselves, our colleagues, and university students through the use of women's voices who are often less privileged than [our]selves?" (cited in Wolf, 1996, p. 25).

Feminist reflexivity

While there are no straightforward responses to questions of power in the research context, feminist epistemologies compel researchers to critically engage and reflect on these questions and to address any potential for exploitation to the extent possible. Recently, feminist sports studies scholars have employed feminist participation action research (F-PAR) as a method to address these concerns regarding power dynamics and the potential to exploit participants (see also Chapters 8, 33, and 35). F-PAR is a qualitative method that allows for the cocreation of knowledges while simultaneously providing an opportunity to address feminist concerns regarding the hierarchical power relations between researcher and researched that have typically shaped the research process. In their research on a sport-for-development program, Kicking AIDS Out Network, Nicholls, Giles and Sethna (2011) used F-PAR in program evaluation to coconstruct knowledge, giving epistemic privilege to the young, African, women's subjugated knowledges with the goal to counter the "lack of evidence" discourse that pervades the sport-for-development field. In other words, participants themselves become an integral component of the research team, helping to shape the focus of the study, research questions, methods used, and interpretation of data. F-PAR can be particularly useful in creating a space for subjugated knowledges to resist truth claims, often espoused by those in power and when the experiences of participants are significantly different from those of privileged researchers (Nicholls *et al.*, 2011).

Feminist practices of reflexivity and considerations of positionality are also methodological approaches feminist researchers employ to address concerns of power in the research process (for an excellent illustration of how gendered power dynamics shape the context of discovery, and how feminist reflexivity offers a strategy to negotiation those dynamics, see Presser, 2005). For example, in the above discussion of Krane and colleagues' research on girls' lived experiences and the representational preferences of collegiate female athletes, the research team engaged in reflexive journaling, critical reflexivity, and questioning the ethics of their methods (Krane *et al.*, 2012). While considerations of hierarchy were discussed primarily within the context of the research team itself, Krane and her colleagues acknowledged the importance of giving the participants the freedom to express their preferences regarding images of female athletes. At the same time, the research team had concerns as to what might be the implications of this freedom – concerns that many feminist researchers encounter. Specifically, the team questioned:

> *What if they wanted to imitate what is seen in popular sport press? What if they wanted to take off some or all of their clothes? Would we be contributing to the objectification of female athletes if we were to include in our research soft-porn or heterosexy images of the athletes?*
> *(Krane* et al., *2012, p. 257; italics in original)*

For feminist researchers, reflexivity is not simply a "methodological tool" but is understood as "an invaluable part of doing embodied, ethical, and political ethnographic research" (Olive & Thorpe, 2011, p. 424). In their ethnography of action-sport cultures, Olive and Thorpe (2011) admittedly did not enter the site with the expressed goal to conduct a "feminist" ethnography in the sense of giving "voice to the voiceless." Rather, when confronted with ethical, methodological, and personal dilemmas (the researchers were both "cultural insiders" of the communities they studied), the researchers relied upon their feminist habitus to confront and negotiate these dilemmas (see also Chapter 10). Similar to Krane *et al.* (2012), Olive and Thorpe also questioned how to negotiate the "messiness" of the research context:

> When is it appropriate to question sexist, racist, or homophobic sentiments expressed by some participants in our fields of inquiry? How can we effectively challenge perpetrators of violent or misogynistic practices observed in the field? Is it our place to do so? Must we bite our "feminist tongue" to collect quality data? If we do "speak up" for ourselves or others in the field, what are the consequences for our research, as well as our own and others' personal safety?
> *(Olive & Thorpe, 2011, p. 426)*

The following also illustrates the dilemmas faced and speaks to the earlier discussion on the challenges of researchers embracing "messiness" that emerges in the interview process:

> During the early phases of our research, we both experienced some unsettling interactions with participants in which our (apolitical) responses surprised, and sometimes disappointed, us. For example, while conducting an interview with a professional female snowboarder, Holly became derailed when confronted with the accusatory remark, "Oh god, you're not one of those feminists are you?" Rather than challenging her

interviewee's stereotypical assumptions of feminism, Holly panicked and tried to side-step the question, promptly redirecting the conversation into "safer" terrain. Listening to the audio-recordings of the interview, Holly became troubled by her response which she identified as a "feminist failing."

(Olive & Thorpe, 2011, p. 427)

To address these questions, Olive and Thorpe (2011) engaged post-structuralist interpretations of Bourdieu's "regulated liberties" to navigate these research dilemmas. While feminist research upholds the importance of reflexivity, Olive and Thorpe (2011) rightly observe there are few published articles wherein researchers discuss reflexivity, and fewer that offer insights or suggestions on how researchers can develop and address reflexivity. Future feminist research should engage explicitly in these questions, and studies that offer insights and suggestions on how to develop and address reflexivity are needed.

Feminist postmodern epistemology

Feminist postmodern epistemologies situate data (field notes, interviews, focus-group discussions, participant observations, oral histories, textual analyses, etc.) as a "series of representations" that are partial, situated, fluid, contextual, and interpretive (Wheatley, 1994). Postmodern epistemologies reject attempts to capture objective "truth" about reality, the human condition, or society. For postmodernists, there are no objective observations of reality since all observations are filtered through the lens of the seer (who is raced, classed, gendered, etc.) and discursively constituted (Haraway, 1988). Rather, feminist postmodern epistemologies seek to capture the representation and interpretation of social behavior, understandings, and actions.

Objectivity derives from the Enlightenment philosophical perspective that posited knowledge of the physical world as separate from those who would come to know it. In other words, there is a distinct separation between what can be known about the physical world and the researcher who would come to know that world through the research process (what Donna Haraway refers to as the "God trick"). From this perspective, one then can objectively come to know the physical world through the practices and procedures we now come to know as the scientific method. However, postmodern epistemologies assert knowledge of the social world is located in the meaning-making processes of social actors, and as such is discursively constituted (see also Chapters 1, 9, 10, 29, and 30). In that sense, knowledge is not separate from knower; rather knowledge is constructed and embedded in an individual's understanding of the social world (Lincoln & Guba, 2003; Sparkes & Smith, 2014). Thus, objectivity and truth are constructed out of experience in the social world (Wheaton, 2002). Participants in research, or individuals, are seldom able to give full explanations of their actions or intentions. They can only offer accounts of stories of what they did and why (Cooky, 2009; Denzin & Lincoln, 2003). The postmodern epistemological perspective emphasizes that social understandings, social experiences, and social structures are all constituted through discourse (Denzin & Lincoln, 2003).

As mentioned at the beginning of this chapter, feminists acknowledge the importance of lived experience in determining what we can know, and the social processes that allow social actors to come to know what we know. While the recognition of the importance of experience has proved invaluable to feminist research, much of the early research conducted from this perspective often left experience to stand on its own without much theorizing. Yet, taking experience in an unproblematic way can lead to research that reproduces the structures of oppression rather than criticizes and challenges those very structures (Olesen, 2003). As Scott (1991) notes, "Experience is at once already an interpretation and in need of interpretation"

(p. 779). Therefore, feminists should provide a theoretical context and understanding for participants' experiences while recognizing that the experiences of participants are already filtered through an individual's own interpretation.

My own research interests developed in part due to the lack of research on girls and the absence of girls' voices and lived experiences in the sport studies literature[2] (see Cooky & McDonald, 2005). This interest in "giving voice" to marginalized groups has informed other research studies (see also Esmonde, Cooky, & Andrews, 2015). Sensitive to the feminist critique voiced by feminist scholars of color (Collins, 1990), and wishing to avoid essentializing or universalizing the experiences of the girls and women we studied, our epistemological and methodological approach recognized the discursive and political construction of experiences. Rather than taking experience as articulated by participants at face value, we assert experiences are the effects of historically produced and lived discursive practices. Joan Scott's classic essay (1991) has informed the epistemological frameworks used in our research. As Scott explains:

> the origin of our explanation, not the authoritative (because seen or felt) evidence that grounds what is known, but rather that which we seek to ex- plain, that about which knowledge is produced. To think about experience in this way is to historicize it, as well as to historicize the identities it produces.
>
> *(Scott, 1991, p. 780)*

Using this approach, then, it is not merely enough to identify and explicate girls and women's experiences. As we argued in our research on girls' experiences in recreational sports, "critical sensibilities offer fresh interpretations that seek to make visible the ways interpretative meanings interact with bodies and historical practices" (Cooky & McDonald, 2005, p. 160).

In our recent research on women sports fans, we found Scott's conceptualization of experience useful for granting epistemic privilege to women's experiences given the marginalization of women in sports contexts, and specifically in sports fandom contexts, since women's experiences are often not considered, and are even silenced, particularly when researchers, as well as other sports fans, construct the *authentic* fan experience (Esmonde *et al.*, 2015). In that study we conducted semi-structured, in-depth interviews with women's sports fans in. Also, informed by Scott, we examined:

> how the experience of sports fandom is not simply evidence of difference between men and women sport fans, rather we seek to understand the processes by which "difference is established, how it operates, how and in what ways it constitutes subjects who see and act in the world."
>
> *(Scott, 1991. p. 777)*

For Scott, "it is not individuals who have experience but subjects who are constituted through experience." (p. 779). Thus, in that study, we argued the subjectivity of being a sports fan for women is constituted by and through the experience of marginalization; a marginalization that is informed by the intersectional social locations women occupy, as well as by the discursive formations of heteronormative femininity.

Conclusion

The goal of this chapter was to introduce readers to feminist qualitative research and the various feminist epistemological frameworks that inform feminist qualitative inquiry. While many researchers will assert that the research questions of a study should inform the epistemological and methodological framework, researchers may wish to consider how one's epistemological framework informs the types of research questions asked (Krane *et al.*, 2012). In other words, how would you, as the researcher, answer critical epistemological questions regarding what can be known, how knowledge is attained, who can be a knower, and what is the relationship between the knower and the known? It is important to consider these questions at the beginning stage of a research endeavor, as the responses will be a necessary component to deciding what to study, how, and from what vantage point. For some feminist researchers this may be an easy and straightforward exercise. For others, these questions expose the "contested terrain" of feminist research. For example, as a feminist researcher, I have struggled with the question of whether one's epistemological framework can shift based on a particular research project. For example, while all the research I have conducted has been informed by feminist theory and praxis, it is quite varied in epistemological assumptions, methodological frameworks, and has drawn from feminist empiricism, standpoint, and postmodern epistemologies. While feminist empiricism is an important epistemology, particularly in developing public policies focused on feminist social justice concerns, the epistemological assumptions of feminist empiricism, regarding what can be known and how knowledge is attained, runs counter to feminist standpoint, intersectional, or feminist postmodern epistemologies. Moreover, the types of studies that utilize feminist postmodern epistemologies do not readily align with and translate to developing feasible public policy, as this research often addresses resistance and transformation rather than accommodation or incorporation. Thus a question is raised regarding whether a researcher's epistemological assumptions can shift from study to study without compromising the integrity of the researcher's body of scholarship. And if so, how might one reconcile these seeming contradictions of the differing tenets of these oppositional epistemological frameworks? How are we as feminist researchers to develop "evidence-based strategies for change," while also acknowledging truth claims as fluid, partial, and discursively constituted?

Some have recognized the contextually specific aspects of feminist research and the fluidity by which researchers may chose theoretical and methodological frameworks (Rosser, 2012), and these questions will become increasingly salient over time. Feminist postmodern and poststructuralist epistemologies are quite prevalent in feminist qualitative research, particularly in the field of sociology of sport. Yet, while positivist epistemologies have been critiqued extensively by feminists, as discussed in this chapter, the institutional realities of higher education, particularly in the United States, often impose constraints upon researchers that utilize nonpositivist methodologies. This is due in part to the decline in Federal and State funding of higher education, and the increased reliance upon external sources of funding to support the research mission of universities. Moreover, the standards of tenure and promotion, particularly in research intensive universities, reward faculty for publications in "high-impact" journals, and often the research valued in those journals is that which is positivist in epistemological orientation. As such, there are very powerful structural dynamics that enable particular types of research, ways of knowing, and thus knowledge production itself while constraining others. Feminist qualitative researchers have and will continue to have to negotiate the realities of neoliberalism in higher education with the goals and orientation of feminist research.

Notes

1 As such, in this chapter I highlight those studies that purport explicitly to utilize feminist epistemologies. Studies that engage feminist theory or feminist critique of sport are not discussed due to space constraints. The use of feminist theory does not necessarily indicate the use of a specific feminist methodology, although ideally epistemology should inform and guide the use of theory and methods (Krane *et al.*, 2012).

2 This was during the mid- to late 1990s when I was embarking on my Masters thesis. However, as Messner & Musto (2014) have found, studies on youth sports, and particularly girls' sports, continues to remain an understudied area in sociology of sport.

References

Birrell, S. & Richter, D. (1987). Is a diamond is forever? Feminist transformations of sport. *Women's Studies International Forum, 10*, 395–409.

Boutlier, M. A. & San Giovanni, L. F. (1994). Politics, public policy, and Title IX: Some limitations of liberal feminism. In S. Birrell & C. L. Cole (Eds.), *Women, sport, and culture* (pp. 97–109). Champaign, IL: Human Kinetics.

Bryson, L. (1987). Sport and the maintenance of masculine hegemony. *Women's Studies International Forum, 10*(4), 349–360.

Collins, P. H. (1990). *Black feminist thought knowledge, consciousness and the politics of empowerment.* New York: Routledge.

Cooky, C. (2009). "Girls just aren't interested": The social construction of interest in girls' sport. *Sociological Perspectives, 52*, 259–284.

Cooky, C. & Dworkin, S. L. (2013). Policing the boundaries of sex: A critical examination of gender verification and the Caster Semenya controversy. *Journal of Sex Research, 50*, 103–111.

Cooky, C. & LaVoi, N. M. (2012). The unfinished revolution in women's sport. *Contexts: Understanding people in their social worlds, 11*, 42–46.

Cooky, C. & McDonald, M. G. (2005). "If you let me play": Young girls' insider-other narratives of sport. *Sociology of Sport Journal, 22*, 158–177.

Denzin, N. K. & Lincoln, Y. S. (2003). *The landscape of qualitative research: Theories and issues* (2nd ed.). Thousand Oaks, CA: Sage.

Dowling, F. & Flintoff, A. (2011). Getting beyond normative interview talk of sameness and celebrating difference. *Qualitative Research in Sport, Exercise and Health, 3*, 63–79.

Esmonde, K., Cooky, C., & Andrews, D. L. (2015). "It's supposed to be about the love of the game, not the love of Aaron Rogers' eyes": Challenging the Exclusions of Women Sports Fans. *Sociology of Sport Journal, 32*, 22–48.

Fisher, L. A. & Larsen, L. K. (2016). Feminism in sport psychology. In R. J. Schinke, K. R. McGannon, & B. Smith (Eds.), *Routledge international handbook of sport psychology* (pp. 260–271). London: Routledge.

Greenleaf, C. & Collins, K. (2001). In search of our place: An experiential look at the struggles of young sport and exercise psychology feminists. *The Sports Psychologist, 15*, 431–437.

Hall, M. A. (1996). *Feminism and sporting bodies: Essays on theory and practice.* Champaign, IL: Human Kinetics.

Haraway, D. (1988). Situated knowledges: The science question in feminism and the privilege of the partial perspective. *Feminist Studies, 14*, 575–599.

Harding, S. (1987). Is there a feminist method? In S. Harding (Ed.), *Feminism and methodology* (pp. 1–14). Bloomington, IN: Indiana University Press.

Hargreaves, J. (1994). *Sporting females: Critical issues in the history and sociology of women's sports.* London: Routledge.

Hartsock, N. (1987). The feminist standpoint: Developing the ground for a specifically feminist historical materialism. In S. Harding (Ed.), *Feminism and methodology* (pp. 157–180). Bloomington, IN: Indiana University Press.

Hesse-Biber, S. (Ed.) (2012). *The handbook of feminist research* (2nd ed.). Los Angeles, CA. Sage.

Hesse-Biber, S. (Ed.) (2014). *Feminist research practice: A primer* (2nd ed.). Los Angeles, CA: Sage.

Hirschmann, N.J. (2004). Feminist standpoint as postmodern strategy. In S. Harding (Ed.), *The feminist standpoint theory reader: Intellectual and political controversies* (pp. 317–332). New York: Routledge.

Jagger, A. (2013). *Just methods: An interdisciplinary feminist reader.* St. Paul, MN: Paradigm.

Krane, V. (1996). Lesbians in sport: Toward acknowledgement, understanding, and theory. *Journal of Sport and Exercise Psychology, 18*, 237–246.

Krane, V. (2001). One lesbian feminist epistemology: Interrogating feminist standpoint, queer theory and feminist cultural studies. *The Sports Psychologist, 15*, 401–411.

Krane, V., Ross, S. R, Miller, M., Ganoe, K., Lucas-Carr, C. B., & Sullivan Barak, K. (2011). "It's cheesy when they smile": What girl athletes prefer in images of female athletes. *Research Quarterly on Exercise and Sport, 82*, 755–768.

Krane, V., Ross, S. R., Sullivan Barak, K., Lucas-Carr, C. B., & Robinson, C. L. (2014). Being a girl athlete. *Qualitative Research in Sport, Exercise and Health, 6*, 77–97.

Krane, V., Ross, S. R., Sullivan Barak, K., Rowse, J. L., & Lucas-Carr, C. B. (2012). Unpacking our academic suitcases: The inner workings of our research group. *Quest, 64*, 249–267.

Lincoln, Y. S. & Guba, E. G. (2003). Paradigmatic controversies, contradictions, and emerging confluences. In N. K. Denzin & Y. S. Lincoln (Eds.), *The landscape of qualitative research: Theories and issues* (pp. 253–291). Thousand Oaks, CA: Sage.

Messner, M. A. (1988). Sports and male domination: The female athlete as contested ideological terrain. *Sociology of Sport Journal, 5*, 197–211.

Messner, M. A. & Musto, M. (2014). Where are the kids? *Sociology of Sport Journal, 31*(1), 102–122.

Nicholls, S. Giles, A. R., & Sethna, C. (2011). Perpetuating the "lack of evidence discourse" in sport for development: Privileged voices, unheard stories and subjugated knowledges. *International Review for the Sociology of Sport, 46*, 249–264.

Olesen, V. L. (2003). Feminisms and qualitative research at and into the millennium. In N. K. Denzin & Y. S. Lincoln (Eds.), *The landscape of qualitative research: Theories and issues* (pp. 332–397). Thousand Oaks, CA: Sage.

Olive, R. & Thorpe, H. (2011). Negotiating the F-word in the field: Doing feminist ethnography in action sports cultures. *Sociology of Sport Journal, 28*, 421–440.

Presser, L. (2005). Negotiating power and narrative in research: Implications for feminist methodology. *Signs: Journal of Women and Culture in Society, 30*, 2067–2090.

Ramazanoglu, C. & Holland, J. (2002). *Feminist methodology: Challenges and choices.* Thousand Oaks, CA: Sage.

Ratna, A. (2011). "Who wants to make *aloo gobi* when you can bend it like Beckham?" British Asian females and their racialised experiences of gender and identity in women's football. *Soccer and Society, 12*, 382–401.

Rosser, S. V. (2012). The link between feminist theory and methods in experimental research. In S. N. Hesse-Biber (Ed.), *The handbook of feminist research: Theory and praxis* (pp. 264–289). Los Angeles, CA: Sage.

Scott, J.W. (1991). The evidence of experience. *Critical Inquiry, 17*, 773–797.

Semerjian, T. Z. & Waldron, J. (2001). The journey through feminism: Theory, research, and dilemmas from the field. *The Sports Psychologist, 15*, 438–444.

Sparkes, A. C. & Smith, B. (2014). *Qualitative research methods in sport, exercise and health. From process to product.* London: Routledge.

Sprague, J. (2005). *Feminist methodology for critical researchers: Bridging differences.* Walnut Creek, CA: Alta Mira Press.

Stacey, J. (1988). Can there be a feminist ethnography? *Women's Studies International Forum, 11*, 21–27.

Stanley, L. & Wise, S. (1990). Method, methodology, and epistemology in feminist research processes. In L. Stanley (Ed.), *Feminist praxis: Research, theory and epistemology in feminist sociology* (pp. 20–59). New York: Routledge.

Sykes, H. (2006). Transsexual and transgender policies in sport. *Women in Sport and Physical Activity Journal, 15*, 3–13.

Theberge, N. (1985). Toward a feminist alternative to sport as a male preserve. *Quest, 37*, 193–202.

Tong, R. (2013). *Feminist thought: A more comprehensive introduction.* Boulder, CO: Westview Press.

Travers, A. (2006). Queering sport: Lesbian softball leagues and the transgender challenge. *International Review for the Sociology of Sport, 41*, 431–446.

Travers, A. (2008). The sport nexus and gender justice. *Studies in Social Justice, 2*, 79–101.

Walker, N. A. & Melton, N. (2015). The tipping point: The intersection of race, gender, and sexual orientation in intercollegiate sports. *Journal of Sports Management, 29*, 257–272.

Wheatley, E. (1994). How can we engender ethnography with a feminist imagination? A rejoinder to Judith Stacey. *Women's Studies International Forum, 17*, 403–416.

Wheaton, B. (2002). Babes on the beach, women in the surf: Researching gender, power and difference in the windsurfing culture. In J. Sugden & A. Tomlinson (Eds.), *Power games: A critical sociology of sport* (pp. 240–266). London: Routledge.

Withycomb, J. L. (2011). Intersecting selves: African American female athletes' experiences of sport. *Sociology of Sport Journal, 28*, 478–493.

Wolf, D. L. (1996). *Feminist dilemmas in fieldwork.* Boulder, CO: Westview Press.

8

EMBARKING ON COMMUNITY-BASED PARTICIPATORY ACTION RESEARCH

A methodology that emerges from (and in) communities

Robert J. Schinke and Amy T. Blodgett

Community-based participatory research (CBPR) is a useful research approach for those seeking to work at a community (local) level, to support positive social change in and through scholarship. CBPR is slow to develop and often takes many years to complete, in part due to the need to understand the norms, values and goals of the community as the research unfurls (Holkup, Tripp-Reimer, Salois & Weinert, 2004; Minkler, 2005). How scholars enter into this broad area of research could be by formal invitation, or by happenstance, while either working on an earlier project or as a result of having forged relationships with a community's members (Schinke *et al.*, 2009). Regardless of which reason serves as a point of entry, scholars come to realize that CBPR serves a role in scholarship that differs greatly from many others methodologies or traditions, such as grounded theory (see Chapter 3) and ethnography (see Chapter 5, this volume; and also Wallerstein & Duran, 2006). McCullagh (1998) differentiated between three levels of research, based on Christina (1989). Level one, also known as basic research, is focused on knowledge generation and no requirement to bridge with application. Level two refers to applied research, whereby scholars begin to consider how to bridge theory with application through recommendations for practice. Level three, where CBPR is situated, is conceived to develop practical solutions to social and community challenges (Israel, Schulz, Parker & Becker, 1998; Minkler, 2005).

This chapter is focused on CBPR for the very reason that there are times when researchers are compelled to extend beyond recommendations from afar, into practical applications and taking knowledge to mean praxis (see also Chapters 33 and 34). There is no single approach to effectively undertake a CBPR project (Schinke, McGannon & Smith, 2013; Wallerstein & Duran, 2006). CBPR is unique in that it is developed in situ, with a highly organic infusion of local culture and local skills (Israel *et al.*, 1998). Given the scope of what should be discussed within a handbook chapter, we seek to provide an overview of this general approach to methodology as locally derived and led. The chapter begins with the authors situating themselves in relation to the topic area. The reason for this strategic decision is that CBPR researchers transport their identities, privileges, and preferences with them into CBPR projects, and these aspects must be known in order to be mindful and position these as secondary to community standpoints (Schinke, Smith & McGannon, 2013). Next we map the landscape of CBPR, taking first a multidisciplinary approach, followed by a focus on CBPR in sport studies. Later, we focus on why and when CBPR approaches are necessary and worthwhile within research contexts, especially in relation to scholarship undertaken in underprivileged communities. Afterward, we propose CBPR dos and don'ts, building upon discussions undertaken in a special issue of *Qualitative Research in Sport, Exercise and Health*, devoted to community research (see Schinke, Smith and McGannon, 2013). We then conclude with final recommendations and conclusions to spur further dialogue and application of this approach within communities seeking social justice, positive social change, and improved living conditions (see also Chapters 33 and 34).

Situating the authors

We embark on this discussion about CBPR by first situating the authors. Reflexivity is a researcher's critical self-awareness of personal values, beliefs, and preferences, where these have originated from, and why (see McGannon & Johnson, 2009; Schinke, McGannon, Parham & Lane, 2012). Within each research project, researchers carry a proverbial knapsack of values and preferences, driven by who they are and where they come from. Though it might suffice to simply identify these for the reader with various methodologies and even attempt to objectify these, within CBPR the focus is entirely on subjectivity. Following from the importance of supporting community capacity, researchers are asked to move beyond engaging with their subjectivity, onward to learning from their community partners about community values and how these must be placed at the centre of the discussion. Though in theory it is easy to agree that each local community should drive its own research, a tension exists (and often arises) when the skills, steeped in the values and beliefs of academic scholars, emerge, either as a result of initial insecurities by community members, or the challenges of academic scholars to relinquish their place as the researcher experts (Jensen, Hoagwood & Trickett, 1999). Within this section we introspect of as to how the co-authors learned to become more reflexive, and in doing so, struggled with tensions caused by who should lead and who should support.

We, Rob and Amy, have conceived this chapter based on more than ten years working together on four successive projects with Canadian Aboriginal sport participants. As the senior author, I (Rob) entered into a partnership with a community by developing a sport-psychology project that helped me consider an applied question that challenged a national team: How to retain Canadian Aboriginal boxers once they enter into the programme. As a result of this initial question I sought a partnership with one local reserve. The Wikwemikong Unceded Indian Reserve, referred to in this chapter as 'Wiky', has worked with me and my colleagues since the initial project and slowly educated my university colleagues and me about local needs (Schinke *et al.*, 2008). Centralization, they proposed, would happen through regular monthly community meetings, roles in each successive stage of a research project, and co-authoring (Schinke *et al.*, 2009). Throughout this process, I slowly began to learn how community partners could centralize a community and how to de-centre my voice and agenda as a formally educated and socially and financially privileged scholar (Schinke, McGannon, Parham & Lane, 2012; see also Wallerstein & Duran, 2006). I am someone who could easily override voices. Wiky does not value this characteristic; in fact, I remember early on when one of the community members told me a story about why people are blessed with two ears, two eyes, and only one mouth. I wished to fill in the silence, but came to realize that this need to fill the void is my problem and not a good practice within Wiky. I now relish these research consultations and the changing of questions on the spur of the moment when something new and better is revealed in a community discussion. CBPR scholars have identified this form of fluidity as important (Israel *et al.*, 1998). Fluidity during CBPR frees the group from constrained thinking and an over-commitment to a fixed perspective, and a pre-set agenda (Schinke *et al.*, 2008).

I (Amy) have been working with the Wiky community as part of my graduate research programme, under Rob's academic supervision. In this local context my thinking about research has continually been challenged. I have become more aware of my academic preference for clearly defined, linear research processes led by academic researchers. At one meeting early on, I had wanted to share the initial stages of a data analysis with the community members and seek their feedback. I stood at the front of the room with a PowerPoint presentation, and proceeded to give a formal, academic overview of the data analysis. I then distributed an agenda, outlining specific questions and discussion points. The community members remained quiet and respectful throughout my presentation, but afterward, seemed disengaged. Several months later, the community members indicated that they often sit back and observe the way researchers work and interact to gain a better sense of their hearts and their intentions, and assess whether they are willing to work *with* the community in meaningful ways (see also Cook, 2009; Kidd & Kral, 2005).

What is CBPR?

CBPR can be defined in many ways. Similar to Cutworth we define CBPR as the following: 'Community-engaged scholarship is scholarly work undertaken in partnership with communities, draws on multiple sources of knowledge, crosses disciplinary lines and is reciprocal and mutually beneficial' (2013, p. 14). CBPR has emerged as an alternative to conventional positivistic and post-positivistic or realist informed research (see also Chapters 1, 10, and 22) that are characterized by researcher-driven processes and expert 'scientific' knowledge, and that perpetuate dynamics of dominance and oppression. CBPR has been taken up by scholars across the social sciences in recognition of the epistemological and political necessity for local people to be involved in research that affects their lives, and the potential to facilitate positive social change (Brydon-Miller, Kral, Maguire, Noffke & Sabhlok, 2011; Frisby, Reid, Miller & Hoeber, 2005; Israel *et al.*, 1998). Most notably, this methodological approach has gained support and visibility in the areas of public health and nursing, where there is emphasis on reducing health disparities in marginalized populations (Israel *et al.*, 1998; Wallerstein & Duran, 2006), as well as in critical community psychology, where there is a general emphasis on enhancing people's well-being and addressing issues of social inequality (Nelson & Evans, 2014; Viljoen, Pistorius & Eskell-Blokland, 2007). Though CBPR has been less commonly used in sport and physical activity, a growing number of scholars have highlighted this methodology as a valuable approach for working with marginalized or underrepresented sport participants (Schinke, McGannon & Smith, 2013).

CBPR methodologies have been used in Aboriginal contexts to explore Aboriginal youths' meanings of sport (McHugh, Coppola & Sinclair, 2013); to examine the relocation and acculturation experiences of Aboriginal athletes who move off reserves to pursue sport in 'mainstream' contexts (Blodgett *et al.*, 2014; Blodgett *et al.*, 2013); and to develop opportunities for Aboriginal youth to participate in sport and physical activity programmes that develop their leadership skills and enhance their cultural identities (Blodgett *et al.*, 2010; Forsyth & Heine, 2010). Beyond the Aboriginal context, CBPR has also been used to conduct feminist sport research (see Chapter 7) that addresses women's exclusion from community recreation programmes (Frisby *et al.*, 2005), to develop and evaluate sports-based after-school programmes for students in low-income areas (Holt *et al.*, 2013), and to explore the perceptions of physical activity among Somali men in the United States (Mohamed, Hassan, Weis, Sia & Wieland, 2013).

Although each and every CBPR initiative is conceptualized and carried out in diverse ways, there is a common emphasis in CBPR projects on: (1) grassroots participation, wherein community members bring forward their experiential knowledge and inform a locally resonant research agenda; and (2) community enhancement, wherein knowledge outcomes are used to instigate positive changes around the sport and physical activity participation of local people, as well as contribute to wider social change efforts, such as the augmenting of research capacity in communities.

Although the historical roots of CBPR are deep and wide, with contributions from many groups of people and many spaces, the starting point for CBPR can be located in the late 1960s (Kidd & Kral, 2005). During this period there was an explicit questioning of positivism within the social sciences, as claims to value-free knowledge production and objectivity were exposed as being untenable (Brydon-Miller *et al.*, 2011; Israel *et al.*, 1998). Feminist critiques that highlighted the social construction of knowledge and that theory-free knowledge is a chimera were particularly influential, bringing awareness to the fact that the identities and positionalities of those involved in knowledge production affect its processes and outcomes (Brydon-Miller *et al.*, 2011). In addition, various social struggles and movements, such as workers' movements, women's movements, and human rights and peace movements, intersected with and informed the development of CBPR as an alternative to traditional researcher-driven processes that marginalize non-dominant groups (Brydon-Miller *et al.*, 2011). Local participation in social science research was increasingly advocated as a means of generating practical benefits for people in diverse community contexts (e.g., women, African Americans, Indigenous peoples, workers) and, moreover, facilitating critical agendas of social justice and change. As the impetus for more politically informed and socially engaged forms of knowledge development continued to grow, early forms of CBPR were spawned.

Another important contribution to the development of CBPR was the writing of Paulo Freire, a Brazilian educationalist, who reconceptualised adult education as an empowering alternative to traditional colonial education. In his influential text *Pedagogy of the Oppressed* (2005; originally published in 1970), Freire championed a philosophy of education aimed at dismantling relationships of dominance and enabling oppressed peoples to overcome their social conditions by participating in their own liberation. He articulated how emancipation can only occur when oppressors and the oppressed (or colonizers and colonized/leadership and people/ researchers and participants) come together to reflect critically on reality and then take collaborative, informed action upon it. Referring to this process as praxis, Freire explained:

> Attempting to liberate the oppressed without their reflective participation in the act of liberation is to treat them as objects which must be saved from a burning building; it is to lead them into the populist pitfall and transform them into masses which can be manipulated.
>
> *(Freire, 2005, p. 65)*

This writing has contributed to the growth of CBPR as a praxis-oriented form of inquiry (see also Chapter 35), aimed at challenging social inequalities through knowledge production processes that encourage community members to actively engage in reflecting and acting upon their realities, while also encouraging researchers to critically examine their roles in oppression and change (Blodgett, Schinke, Smith, Peltier & Pheasant, 2011; Lather, 1987; Singer, 1994).

Researchers are challenged to reconsider the types of knowledge they produce in the academic/theoretical realm by connecting their research efforts more deeply to the lives of marginalized people (Blodgett *et al.*, 2011; Lather, 1987). Through this alignment between academic and applied knowledge production, more critical social change efforts can be opened up.

Why CBPR?

There are various reasons why a research team might consider a CBPR approach to their research. One possible reason is that the research context is in a location where it is simply not enough to understand or describe participants' words and recommend solutions from afar. The very nature of the participants' realities, socially or historically, sometimes necessitates the use of CBPR to also create capacity in the community's structures contributing to the betterment of lives in a concrete way (Forsyth & Heine, 2010; Schinke, McGannon & Smith, 2013). Relating to our own personal experiences, the Aboriginal community members in Wiky were in the midst of a very real concern – that their community youth were experiencing much higher rates of substance abuse, incarceration, type 1 diabetes and suicidal behaviours than the national norm. In fact, during the conception of one of our youth projects, a very talented youth researcher was incarcerated for attempted murder. This jolt to the researchers' realities affirmed the need for youth programming. The community attributed their youth challenges to physical inactivity, caused by poor sport and recreation programming initiatives, leading to poor retention, followed by maladaptive behaviours, such as becoming sedentary or engaging in harm to oneself or another.

A second possible reason to enter into a CBPR project, which overlaps with the reason above, is when a community wishes to answer a research question and is seeking support from academic scholars in order to assist with the organization of the project, lend academic support, and assist with the creation of a research funding proposal. This distribution of power, in relational terms, is quite different from conventional research approaches where academic scholars would typically lead the research process (Jensen, Hoagwood & Trickett, 1999; Minkler, 2005). Sometimes academics can serve as the conduit, or bridge, connecting a community with financial and expertise support, supporting the creation of infrastructure to address the community's question or concern.

A third possible reason why CBPR is facilitated overlaps with the two reasons above: when conventional research practices do not match with the community's customs and norms. Sometimes communities are inclined toward a collective approach in their research, whereby broad-based group engagement in each and every aspect of the project makes sense. Any antithetical approach to such contexts through research would serve to colonize the community (see Ryba & Schinke, 2009). Power in terms of both project ideas and ongoing decision-making reside with the group, affirming a consensus-based approach.

The three reasons for turning to CBPR outlined together connect perhaps to the overarching reason for using CBPR, which is about working with a community to achieve social change. CBPR does not guarantee it will have a major impact on people and communities, but its characteristics (as described earlier and next) do provide a very strong platform and means to make a difference in the long term.

CBPR dos and don'ts

As part of a list of characterizing traits (see Chapter 25), there are various possible criteria for how to go about effectively engaging in CBPR (Schinke, Smith & McGannon, 2013; see also

Baker, Homan, Schonhoff & Kreuter, 1999; Fawcett, 1991). Although on the surface the items listed below might seem obvious and even easy to achieve, there is complexity surrounding the application of each item. The list below is synthesized owing to page restrictions, and is provided sequentially with one aspect then peeling to a deeper layer of process. What follows is a delineation of CBPR 'how to' criteria that layer onto one another.

Ample time commitments. Many a CBPR scholar has commented about the extensive time commitment required to work effectively within a CBPR project (e.g. Flicker, 2008; Frisby *et al.*, 2005; Israel *et al.*, 1998; Kidd & Kral, 2005). The length of these projects often exceeds the time frame permitted by typical research funding agencies, where projects are supported for two or three years (Kidd & Kral, 2005). Within Canada, the Social Sciences and Humanities Research Council of Canada has recently extended its permissible time frame for community-based research funding to five years duration. Reflecting upon what we have learned through a series of such projects over the course of more than ten years, our initial belief was that when the funding term for a project was completed, so too would be our commitment, other than to finalize manuscripts for publication. Early within the term of the first project, where there was a funding term of two years, we were told very clearly that we were not to research and then run from the community. The expectation was that if the people of Wiky were to share their expertise and open their community to a research partnership, in exchange we would have to promise to stay longer (Schinke *et al.*, 2008). The duration for the term was undefined, but the length of the term would be defined by events, not a clock. The experience then proceeded with the first project leading to a more pertinent project proposed by the community, relating to youth sport engagement (Blodgett, Schinke, Fisher *et al.*, 2010; Schinke, Yungblut, Blodgett, Peltier, Ritchie & Recollet-Saikonnen, 2010), which was followed by the implementation of leadership training in a third project (Ritchie *et al.*, 2010), followed by a reflective project where the community members explored their views of the unfolding work of the research team (Blodgett, Schinke, Peltier *et al.*, 2010, 2011; Blodgett, Schinke, Smith, Peltier & Pheasant, 2011). With each project we went deeper into process and implementation until by the end two of the community researchers also graduated with Bachelor's degrees and one completed her Master's degree. These members now run their own research programme and there is no current need for the academic scholars to assist. We have done ourselves out of a job. Nothing has been said one way or another about the academic researchers having completed our term with Wiky, but it certainly seems that we offer nothing that cannot be found in the community. The programming created by the team is self-governed and self-sustaining and the community members are now training the next generation of community scholars through the youth-leadership programmes that were developed over the course of the team's tenure. Hence, the objective is for scholars to partner with community members only so long as the partnership continues to manifest in community capacity building and independence.

Community members first. Scholarship, be it in terms of funding applications or publication, is most often developed within universities. Academic scholars value the aforementioned sources of recognition given that these are basis for promotion, tenure, and merit increments (Jensen *et al.*, 1999). Not only is it important for scholars to build an impressive curriculum vitae, they must also provide notable evidence of leadership. Each generation of scholars is taught this important lesson from the generation before to the point where often it is assumed that one must be at the front of the order within research. Academics often vie for this leading role in authorship, to the point where the *American Psychological Association's* (6th edition) (2010) addresses order of authorship and publishing ethics as part of a more general publication manual. Within conventional research alone, it is often a challenge to navigate order of authorship and proprietary rights. Even within our own experiences, there have been instances where co-authors have disagreed on who should be placed where, to the point where sore feelings result.

CBPR does not seem to fit with standard values regarding who should lead and who should serve in a supporting role, and therefore CBPR projects raise questions with any research ethics standard that affirms academic scholars into positions of privilege (Kidd & Kral, 2005; Minkler, 2004). Consider the words of one community researcher from Wikwemikong as she recounted an earlier experience with a mainstream approach on Reserve lands:

> When researchers from [outside organization] came in they wanted to look at the biological make-up of our Aboriginal people; is there a difference from mainstream people? . . . Our people were looking at it like, 'Holy smokes; they're trying to segregate us again.' That was my fear.
>
> *(Blodgett, Schinke, Peltier* et al., *2010, p. 63)*

Although academic scholars who undertake this methodology need to advance their careers, these people need to also arrive at a deliberate insight: that their roles are meant to be as supporting actors (Schinke, Smith & McGannon, 2013). The people whose wishes and development comes first in these instances are community members. Returning to a recent case in point, one of our authors just completed supervising a graduate student from an Aboriginal community. This student has been involved in CBPR projects with several different faculty members within the same university, including me (Rob). The graduate student initially approached one faculty member to supervise. The supervisor declined stating that it was a conflict of interest, seeing that both were working together on a funded project. The faculty member did not want to confuse her role as co-researcher in what has been, for her, a fertile research environment to cultivate funding and publications. Shortly after this refusal I met the student by sheer coincidence in an airport terminal. We spoke and I asked the community member how she was. She told the story to me, and I immediately offered to supervise, even though she was also a community scholar on a project that I led. The student then completed her graduate programme. No publications have resulted from the project because publishing the project is not an imperative. What has been achieved through the above story is threefold: (1) the unnamed community now has a community member with formal graduate education; (2) a previous CBPR project is being scrutinized and refined by a community member and her peers; and (3) I continue to serve this community long term, with my role continuing to shift away from leading research, onto building capacity from a supportive and sometimes invisible role.

Locally flavoured approaches. When considering CBPR, the approach to undertake such work, as said already, is not clear-cut and preordained (Cook, 2009; Schinke *et al.*, 2008). The reason why is because the local infusion into each CBPR project takes time to surface. CBPR is a fluid and iterative methodology with approaches for collection, analysis, authoring and implementation refining during each successive community meeting. For example, within a Canadian Indigenous CBPR project, researchers might anticipate that the community context requires a data-gathering strategy that is group-oriented in alignment with a cultural context that is collectivist (Schinke *et al.*, 2009). The proposal of undertaking focus groups meets this general mandate. However, there are more culturally appropriate derivatives to focus groups. Within a focus group there is no ordering to who talks and for how long. There is also often a time limit placed on each group interview and also the number of participants to be included. Contrasted with focus groups, some Indigenous communities are traditional in the retention of their customs. The appropriate data-gathering strategy in such instances would be talking circles, where larger groups of people gather and can only speak when they possess a talking stick, stone or pouch of tobacco (contingent on community customs; see Running Wolf & Rickard, 2003). What follows are words from a community leader, as he reflected on the necessity for talking circles when engaging in research within his local community:

> In Wikwemikong, the circle is symbolic of balance, where no one's opinion is greater than another's. Each voice is equal and each person speaking has an opportunity to be heard by all where the group benefits from the shared knowledge.
>
> *(Schinke* et al., *2009, p. 317)*

There is also no time limit on talking circles (Running Wolf & Rickard, 2003). People speak until there is nothing left to be said, which could consume a full 24-hour time period, although for certain the better part of a day or evening. The circles are event-based and not clock-based. Nuanced further, some Indigenous communities move clockwise when engaging participants and others counterclockwise.

Within each and every community there lies an embedded culture. The ideal is to have a cultural guide help mentor any scholars wishing to engage in CBPR whilst being outsiders to the community. Ours were appointed during the first project we undertook with Wiky, and the community members have continued to guide projects and foresee missteps before these ever happen. The suggestion is to immediately seek the guidance of a community leader regarding possible community participants to champion their project, if this is not initially visible (Blodgett, Schinke, Peltier *et al.*, 2011; Israel *et al.*, 1998). Ideally, the community members know in advance of having scholars into their communities who should be the community's point people. Community members are not to be appeased, but rather learned from (Blodgett *et al.*, 2013). One experience we struggled with earlier was the lack of punctuality by community members for meetings after travelling three hours in the early morning to meet with them on community lands. Upon expressing this frustration to the community lead person, he suggested that we clarify that we are seeking to meet by clock-based time and not eventually (perhaps an hour or two later) by event-based time. With this clarification, it became easier to schedule what were six-hour journeys to and from meetings on Aboriginal lands. Though some might find the solution above a simple negotiation, it truly was part of the Indigenous flavour and customs within Wiky. These meetings also took place over meals, to settle things whilst breaking bread. These are precisely the sorts of nuances that are cultural infusions within local community research projects. These practices need to be understood and embraced for researchers to begin to work together within the cultural contours of the community.

Programming that matters. CBPR is in part a methodology, but the goal through the research process is to develop long-lasting solutions to a community shortcoming or challenge. Community members should lead the programming and provide the deliverables. The community, in turn, is regarded as the owner of what has been created in systems and processes. Community members might come and go from leadership roles within programming, but the final and most critical criteria of evaluation is whether the programming becomes self-sustaining, with social justice served.

Slowly but surely, the reader will recognize that the academic scholars have been written out of the project through the correct sequencing of events. This process of having academic scholars step back and then away from the project is correct practice. Academics ought not to stay beyond when they are needed and the point where the project can be sustained independent of outsiders. Academics could agree with this process of autonomy at the conceptual level. However, when it comes time to let go of after many years of involvement, some falter. After all, many a CBPR project has many thumbprints on them, and not all of these are found from within the home community. Perhaps one solution to ease this process is to look at the various forms of ownership that result from a CBPR projects and who values which ones. There is the possibility that stakeholders will covet different things, such as publications, reports, programming, or capacity building so that each member does have gains beyond the intended spirit of giving associated with CBPR.

CBPR in the future

There are presently only a handful of CBPR projects found within the realm of sport, exercise and physical activity. These projects have emerged within contexts where there is a need for social justice and concurrent programming that leads into self-governance. As we have suggested, projects to present have often revealed limitations that are unintentional and only indicative of a lack of understanding of how CBPR should develop and work. There is a bright future ahead for CBPR projects given the current willingness to attempt such work. This promise is supported by the emergence of sport for development and peace projects (SDP), through such agencies as Right to Play, and also through support offered by the International Olympic Committee and through the United Nations via its Millennium Goals. SDP projects are meant to be highly organic and contextually driven. Many of these writings do not position themselves in relation to CBPR. However, the communities that are being written about are often cultural advocates for decolonizing methodologies in the form of CBPR. There is also a vibrant emerging area within sport and exercise psychology referred to as cultural sport psychology (CSP). This emerging area is gaining in credibility as an international movement. The focus within CSP is how to reveal and centralize marginalized identities through critical scholarship, and to encourage these identities forward (McGannon & Smith, 2015; Schinke & McGannon, 2015).

Each and all of the aforementioned areas are physical and social locations where the process of identity centralization, be it at the individual or community level, is an imperative (Schinke, McGannon & Smith, 2013; Schinke & McGannon, 2015). Given these emerging areas, it makes sense to predict and advocate for CBPR. CBPR projects have begun and, to some degree, have crystallized in universities. We hope that the next wave of such work originates within communities, undertaken entirely by community members.

We propose that the way forward with CBPR is to develop projects that not only answer questions, but also belong within a larger plan where communities can fully take up their own causes, with no infringement from scholars that have little to no understanding of what the problem is, its local significance, and how to help ameliorate challenges within the local topography. We ponder what CBPR projects that originate and are fully undertaken in local communities might look like. To this question, little is presently known in sport and physical activity, but we see a horizon where capacity building in one CBPR project might open communities to entire ownership over successive projects with no external resources. These forms of approaches would not only advance CBPR, they could also create solutions to apparently unresolvable problems that tend to be recurring issues, such as health disparities across the life span, physical inactivity also across the life span, disease prevention, and conflict resolution, under the umbrellas of sport for development and peace or cultural sport psychology (Schinke, Stambulova, Lidor, Ryba & Papaioannou, 2015). The only barriers to these advancements are a lack of researcher reflexivity on the part of scholars seeking to support change and also the current infancy of CBPR within our various subdisciplines, and so, a high degree of expertise to understand and support this format of scholarship.

Closing the loop

We end this chapter where we began. There is no single type of CBPR and the suggestions proposed throughout this chapter are as much based on our own experiences as anything we have read (see also Chapters 33 and 34). CBPR is a unique process in many ways. First, there is no pre-set idea of what the research question might be until it is sufficiently narrowed by the community where the project is taking place. Second, there is no clear-cut and linear way of undertaking CBPR. This methodological approach develops in situ as a result of unforeseen twists and turns in project teamwork. Third, CBPR is very different from level-one and level-two research, where scholars lead the research process, either to generate knowledge or to begin to propose possible applications, which are not clearly connected with the project outcome. With CBPR, we speak of level-three projects that offer solutions at the local level for such social imperatives of developing suitable physical activities for an at-risk population, such as youth at risk on an Aboriginal reserve, or for women with no access to physical activity programmes in their own communities. Fourth, CBPR research is meant to create capacity in several ways. Beyond the development of research into practice, the community researchers also develop their capacities as community scholars, able to develop and undertake their own research practices autonomous of academics. Indeed, in Wiky, one of the community researchers from earlier projects gained her graduate education and now leads (and also vets) research in the community where she lives. Whatever the focus, CBPR is much more than a methodology, it is a means to a better life, and it also should be the catalyst to restorative justice within communities that have been harmed through discrimination and marginalization. We leave you with a powerful quote we heard from an Aboriginal community member in the moment when he was stepping forward and donning a leadership role in a CBPR project:

> When researchers come into a community, any cultural community – whether it's a Native Reserve or Chinatown or whatever – they have to come in like this [with hands held out, palms up and open]; with friendship. That says you're coming to learn something about our people, and the community will then embrace you. I think what was the difference in our research group is that we maintained that relationship. We were honest and we were open-minded with each other. That was the big thing, the open-mindedness and explaining our perspectives. That's the sharing, you know? That's so important. Like, I can only take the group so far; [researcher] can only take the group so far; you can only take the group so far. But if we put all our minds together and our hearts and share that common interest, man, we can go somewhere.
>
> *(C. Pheasant, personal communication, 28 August 2008)*

References

American Psychological Association. (2010). *Publication manual of the American Psychological Association* (6th ed.). Washington, DC: American Psychological Association.

Baker, E.A., Homan, S., Schonhoff, R. & Kreuter, M. (1999). Principles of practice for academic/practice/community research partnerships. *American Journal of Preventative Medicine, 16*, 86–93.

Blodgett, A.T., Coholic, D., Schinke, R.J., McGannon, K.R., Peltier, D. & Pheasant, C. (2013). Moving beyond words: Exploring the use of an arts-based method in Aboriginal community sport research. *Qualitative Research in Sport, Exercise and Health, 5*, 312–331.

Blodgett, A.T., Schinke, R.J., Fisher, L.A., Yungblut, H.E., Recollet-Saikkonen, D., Peltier, D., . . . Pickard, P. (2010). Praxis and community-level sport programming strategies in a Canadian Aboriginal Reserve. *International Journal of Sport and Exercise Psychology, 8*, 262–283.

Blodgett, A.T., Schinke, R.J., McGannon, K.R., Coholic, D., Enosse, L., Peltier, D. & Pheasant, C. (2014). Navigating the insider-outsider hyphen: A qualitative exploration of the acculturation challenges of Aboriginal athletes pursuing sport in Euro-Canadian contexts. *Psychology of Sport and Exercise, 15*, 345–355.

Blodgett, A.T., Schinke, R.J., Peltier, D., Fisher, L.A., Watson, J. & Wabano, M.J. (2011). May the circle be unbroken: The research recommendations of Aboriginal community members engaged in participatory action research with university academics. *Journal of Sport and Social Issues, 35*, 264–283.

Blodgett, A.T., Schinke, R.J., Peltier, D., Wabano, M.J., Fisher, L.A., Eys, M.A., . . . Pickard, P. (2010). Naadmaadmi: Reflections of Aboriginal community members engaged in sport psychology co-researching activities with mainstream academics. *Qualitative Research in Sport and Exercise, 2*, 56–76.

Blodgett, A.T., Schinke, R.J., Smith, B., Peltier, D. & Pheasant, C. (2011). In Indigenous words: Exploring vignettes as a narrative strategy for presenting the research voices of Aboriginal community members. *Qualitative Inquiry, 17*, 522–533.

Brydon-Miller, M., Kral, M., Maguire, P., Noffke, S. & Sabhlok, A. (2011). Jazz and the banyan tree: Roots and riffs on participatory action research. In N. K. Denzin & Y.S. Lincoln (Eds.), *The Sage handbook of qualitative research* (4th ed., pp. 387–400). Thousand Oaks, CA: Sage.

Christina, R.W. (1989). Whatever happened to applied research in motor learning? In J. Skinner, C. Corben, J. Landers, P. Martin & C. Wells (Eds.), *Future directions in exercise and sport science research* (pp. 411–422). Champaign, IL: Human Kinetics.

Cook, T. (2009). The purpose of mess in action research: Building rigour through a messy turn. *Educational Action Research, 17*, 277–291.

Cutworth, N. (2013). The journey of a community engaged scholar: An autoethnography. *Quest, 65*, 14–30.

Fawcett, S.B. (1991). Some values guiding community research and action. *Journal of Applied Behavior Analysis, 24*, 621–636.

Flicker, S. (2008). Who benefits from community-based participatory research? A case study of the Positive Youth Project. *Health Education and Behavior, 35*, 70–86.

Forsyth, J. & Heine, M. (2010). Indigenous research and decolonizing methodologies. In T.V. Ryba, R.J. Schinke & G. Tenenbaum, (Eds.), *The cultural turn in sport psychology* (pp. 181–202). Morgantown, WV: Fitness Information Technology.

Freire, P. (2005). *Pedagogy of the oppressed: 30th anniversary edition.* New York: Continuum.

Frisby, W., Reid, C.J., Millar, S. & Hoeber, L. (2005). Putting 'participatory' into participatory forms of action research. *Journal of Sport Management, 19*, 367–386.

Holkup, P.A., Tripp-Reimer, T., Salois, E.M. & Weinert, C. (2004). Community-based participatory research: An approach to intervention with a Native American community. *Advances in Nursing Science, 27*, 162–175.

Holt, N.L., McHugh, T-L.F, Tink, L.N., Kingsley, B.C., Coppola, A.M., Neely, K.C. & McDonald, R. (2013). Developing sport-based after-school programmes using a participatory action research approach. *Qualitative Research in Sport, Exercise, & Health, 5*, 332–355.

Israel, B.A., Schulz, A.J., Parker, E.A. & Becker, E.A. (1998). Review of community-based research: assessing partnership approaches to improve public health. *Annual Review of Public Health, 19*, 173–202.

Jensen, P.A., Hoagwood, M. & Trickett, E.J. (1999). Ivory towers or earthen trenches? Community collaborations to foster real-world research. *Applied Developmental Science, 3*, 206–212.

Kidd, S.A. & Kral, M.J. (2005). Practicing participatory action research. *Journal of Counseling Psychology, 52*, 187–195.

Lather, P. (1987). Research as praxis. In W.R. Shadish Jr. & C.S. Reichardt (Eds.), *Evaluation studies review annual* (pp. 437–457). Thousand Oaks, CA: Sage.

McCullagh, P. (1998). What is applied in applied sport psychology? The role of integration. *Journal of Applied Sport Psychology, 10*, S1–S10.

McGannon, K.R. & Johnson, C.R. (2009). Strategies for reflective cultural sport psychology research. In R.J. Schinke & S.J. Hanrahan (Eds.), *Cultural sport psychology* (pp. 57–75). Champaign, IL: Human Kinetics.

McGannon, K.R. & Smith, B. (2015). Centralizing culture in cultural sport psychology research: The potential of narrative inquiry and discursive psychology. *Psychology of Sport and Exercise, 17*, 79–87.

McHugh, T-L.F., Coppola, A.M. & Sinclair, S. (2013). An exploration of the meanings of sport to urban Aboriginal youth: A photovoice approach. *Qualitative Research in Sport, Exercise, & Health, 5*, 291–311.

Minkler, M. (2004). Ethical challenges for the 'outside' researcher in community-based participatory research. *Health Education and Behavior, 31,* 684–697.

Minkler, M. (2005). Community-based research partnerships: Challenges and opportunities. *Journal of Urban Health, 82* (supp. 2), ii3–ii12.

Mohamed, A.A., Hassan, A.M., Weis, J.A., Sia, I.G. & Wieland, M.L. (2014). Physical activity among Somali men in Minnesota: Barriers, facilitators, and recommendations. *American Journal of Men's Health, 8,* 35–44.

Nelson, G. & Evans, S.D. (2014). Critical community psychology and qualitative research: A conversation. *Qualitative Inquiry, 20,* 158–166.

Ritchie, S.D., Wabano, M.J., Young, N., Schinke, R.J., Peltier, D., Battochio, R.C. & Russell, K. (2010). Developing a culturally relevant outdoor leadership training program for Aboriginal youth. *Journal of Experiential Education, 32,* 300–304.

Running Wolf, P. & Rickard, J.A. (2003). Talking circles: A Native American approach to experiential learning. *Multicultural Counseling and Development, 31,* 39–43.

Ryba, T.V. & Schinke, R.J. (2009). Methodology as a ritualized eurocentrism: Introduction to the special issue [Special Issue]. *International Journal of Sport and Exercise Psychology, 7,* 263–274.

Schinke, R.J., Hanrahan, S.J., Eys, M.A., Blodgett, A., Peltier, D. & Ritchie, S.D. (2008). The development of cross-cultural relations with a Canadian Aboriginal community through sport psychology research. *Quest, 60,* 357–369.

Schinke, R.J. & McGannon, K.R. (2015). Cultural sport psychology and intersecting identities: An introduction to the special section. *Psychology of Sport and Exercise, 17,* 45–47

Schinke, R.J., McGannon, K.R., Parham, W.D. & Lane, A.M. (2012). Toward cultural praxis and cultural sensitivity: Strategies for self-reflexive sport psychology practice. *Quest, 64,* 34–46.

Schinke, R.J., McGannon, K.R. & Smith, B. (2013). Engaging with communities through methodologies: Expanding the sport research landscape. *Qualitative Research in Sport, Exercise, and Health, 5,* 287–290.

Schinke, R.J., Peltier, D., Hanrahan, S.J., Eys, M.A., Recollet-Saikonnen, D., Yungblut, H., . . . Michel, G. (2009). The progressive move toward Indigenous strategies among a Canadian multicultural research team [Special Issue]. *International journal of sport and exercise psychology, 7,* 309–322.

Schinke, R.J., Smith, B. & McGannon, K.R. (2013). Future pathways for community researchers. *Qualitative Research in Sport, Exercise, and Health, 5,* 460–468.

Schinke, R.J., Stambulova, N., Lidor, R., Ryba, T.V. & Papaioannou, A.G. (2015). International Society of Sport Psychology Position Stand: Sport as social missions. *Psychology of Sport and Exercise, 17,* 45–47.

Schinke, R.J., Yungblut, H.E., Blodgett, A.T., Peltier, D., Ritchie, S. & Recollet-Saikonnen, D. (2010). The role of families in youth sport programming within a Canadian Aboriginal community. *Journal of Physical Activity and Health, 3,* 156–166.

Singer, M. (1994). Community-centered praxis: Toward an alternative non–dominant applied anthropology. *Human Organization, 53,* 336–344.

Viljoen, G., Pistorius, A. & Eskell-Blokland, L. (2007). A critical orientation to community psychology. In N. Duncan, B. Bowman, A. Naidoo, J. Pillay & V. Roos (Eds.), *Community psychology: Analysis, context, and action* (pp. 117–134). Cape Town, South Africa: UCT Press.

Wallerstein, N.B. & Duran, B. (2006). Using community-based participatory research to address health disparities. *Health Promotion Practice, 7,* 312–323.

PART II

Collecting qualitative data

9

INTERVIEWS

Qualitative interviewing in the sport and exercise sciences

Brett Smith and Andrew C. Sparkes

The interview is the most widely used method to collect qualitative data in the sport and exercise sciences. As Jachyra, Atkinson and Gibson (2014) put it, if "there is an epistemological *lingua franca* in qualitative research on sport, it is interviewing" (p. 568). Despite being a mainstay method for data collection, as they also make clear, we should not treat interviews as the default option for collecting qualitative data nor regard interviewing as simple. When interviews are treated as the default choice, or regarded as a method that is easy to design and do well, there is the very real danger of creating a launch pad for poor research. Accordingly, in this chapter we first lay some foundations by presenting a definition of an interview, differentiating between types of interview in terms of structure and participant numbers, and outlining specific kinds of interviewing. Building on this, telephone, mobile, and online interviews are described. In order to help make further informed choices, next we attend explicitly to why we might choose to use interviews. Following this, a large range of practical tips for how to "do" interviews is offered. Two common questions are then tackled: "How many people should I interview," and "How do you know your participant is telling the truth?" Finally, we offer some reflections on the problems with qualitative interviewing and indicate some ways these might be overcome.

Foundations of interviewing: what is an interview?

An interview is a social activity where two or more persons actively engage in embodied talk, jointly constructing knowledge about themselves and the social world as they interact with each other over time, in a certain place, and through a range of senses (Sparkes & Smith, 2014). The purpose of the interview in qualitative inquiry is to create a conversation that invites the participant(s) to tell stories, accounts, reports and/or descriptions about their perspectives, insights, experiences, feelings, emotions and/or behaviors in relation to the research question(s). As captured in this working definition and purpose, an interview therefore cannot be a neutral tool, an objective technique, a transparent window into experience, or divorced from time or space, no matter how much one personally tries or what procedures are put in place. Rather, the talk within an interview is *always* and *inescapably* shaped by numerous social factors. These include the motivations, memories, discursive resources, emotions, literacy, history, age, gender, (dis)ability, class, and race of both the participant and researcher, what each say and how in relation to each other in situ, the changing nonverbal interactions between them, and the context of the interview itself, that is, where it is held and the time is happens (Randall & Phoenix, 2009). Understanding interviews in this way has numerous implications. These include how we might respond to the question of "truth" and the need to include the "social" dynamics of interviews in our reporting of data. We return to such implications later. For now it is useful to continue with the foundations of interviewing by outlining a common typology of interviews.

Within the literature four generic forms of interviewing can be commonly distinguished. These differ in terms of structure and the number of participants in each interview. First, at one end of the structure continuum, there is an *individual structured* interview. This is a highly standardized way of interviewing in which the researcher, using an interview schedule, asks a participant a set of identical closed questions in the same order. Qualitative researchers rarely use this form. Second, in *individual semistructured* interviewing the researcher uses a preplanned interview guide to ask a participant relatively focused but open-ended questions about a specific topic. Third, and at the other end of the structure continuum, is the *individual unstructured* interview. This form has little preset structure, although the researcher still uses a few open-ended questions to help facilitate talk about experiences, circumstances, issues and so on. The combination of not much preset structure and a few broad questions means that, in comparison to the previous two forms of interview, the participant in an unstructured interview has a much higher degree of control over what is said and how.

Fourth is the *focus group*. This form of interview is often semistructured to enable a focus. It is different from the three interviews highlighted above in terms of the number of participants in each interview. Rather than interviewing just one person as in individual structured, semistructured or unstructured interviews, focus groups involve multiple participants at the same time. Most focus groups contain between four and ten participants. While there is no general rule concerning the optimal number of groups, when research is very complex or when numerous different types of individuals are of interest, more focus groups will be required (Hennink, 2014; Stewart & Shamdasani, 2015). This noted, a good rule of thumb is to have at least three groups in a study. In addition to having multiple participants in focus groups, another signature characteristic of this style of interviewing, and the prime reason for using it, is the objective to stimulate talk through interactions among group participants. The researcher takes on the role of moderator whose task is to create a supportive atmosphere in which interaction occurs between participants so that the expression of personal, multiple, and sometimes conflicting viewpoints on the topic of focus are elicited.

Qualitative researchers tend to report within the methods section of a journal article, book, or a university thesis the use of one, or a combination of, semistructured interviews, unstructured interviews, and focus-group interviews. However, over the years interviewing has developed. As part of this development, as Brinkmann (2013) notes, a huge variety of different kinds of semistructured interviewing, unstructured interviewing, and focus-group interviewing exist today. Knowing the differing kinds now available is important, he suggests, as each one differently influences the design, conduct, analysis, and reporting of qualitative interviews. Without being exhaustive given space limitations, the qualitative interview landscape now includes grounded-theory semistructured interviewing, phenomenological semistructured interviewing, ethnographic unstructured interviewing, and feminist focus-group interviewing. Two other kinds of interviewing are life-story and life-history interviews.

The *life-story interview*, or what is sometimes called a narrative interview, is concerned with inviting people to share stories of varying length about their life. It largely falls under the umbrella of a semistructured interview (Bold, 2012). We say largely because, as Brinkmann

(2013) cautions, whilst it is worthwhile to distinguish between structured and semistructured interviews, this distinction "should be thought of as a continuum ranging from relatively structured to relatively unstructured formats" (p. 18). For example, during a life-story interview the questions are initially often framed in a semistructured manner. However, as the stories unfold, ebbing and flowing during the process of interviewing, the interview can move back and forth between a semistructured to an unstructured format (as can be the case in many other types of qualitative interviewing). What distinguishes this type of interview from most other types, like a grounded-theory interview, is the focus on actively working to invite stories, not just information, a set of accounts, or list of reports (Chase, 1995; Smith & Sparkes, 2012). To help with this the interviewer orientates themself to the participant as a storyteller, appreciating that their stories are for another just as much as it is for them, and appreciating that what is spoken is a relationship and one is implicated in this. The researcher seeks to stay with the story being told, moving with it, rather than suppressing or interrupting its movement by asking another question off the interview guide. An example of sporting research using life-story interviews can be found in Ryba *et al.*'s (2015) research on the career pathways of transnational athletes.

The *life-history interview*, or what is sometimes called a biographical interview, lies more on the unstructured end of the continuum of interviewing forms. It is similar to a life-story interview in that it is about inviting rather than suppressing stories. The two data-collection methods part company with respect to the broad purpose. The life-history interviewer purposively seeks to locate the life story within its historical context. That is, in contrast to life-story interviews, life histories aim to contextualize stories in the wider life history of our times. Thus, as Coles and Knowles (2001) put it, the life-history interview "goes beyond the individual or the personal and places narrative accounts and interpretations within a broader context. Lives are lived within the influence of contexts as far ranging as cultural, political, familial, educational, and religious spheres just to mention a few" (p. 20). Examples of research within sport and exercise using life-history interviews can be found in Papathomas and Lavallee's (2014) study of athletic disordered eating, and Barker-Ruchti and Schubring's (2016) work on moving into and out of high-performance sport.

Another type of interviewing, as defined by Ellis, Kiesinger, and Tillmann-Healy (1997), is the *interactive interview*. Although this type usually incorporates some semistructured interviewing throughout the process, it falls largely under the umbrella of unstructured interviews. Interactive interviewing refers to an interpretive practice that places emphasis on what can be learned from interaction within the interview setting, as well as on the stories that the researcher and participant bring to the research encounter. It differs from many other forms of interviewing, including life-story and life-history interviews, in that it involves the sharing of personal and social experiences of *both* participants and researchers, "who tell (and sometimes write) their stories in the context of a developing relationship" (Ellis *et al.*, 1997, p. 121). One rare example of interactive interviewing within the field of sport and exercise can be found in the narrative research of Phoenix and Sparkes (2009) on aging well, physical activity, and health.

Telephone interviews, mobile interviews, and online interviews

Often each of the interviews described above are activated and engaged with in a *face-to-face* manner within an *indoor* space chosen by the participant or the researcher (e.g. the participant's home or a university dedicated interview room). There are, however, other mediums and places to conduct interviews. These include telephone interviews, mobile interviews, and online interviews.

The *telephone interview* has increasingly been harnessed to collect qualitative data. In recent years researchers have also examined this method empirically for what it may offer and miss. For example, drawing on field notes and her interviewees' experiences of telephone interviews, Holt (2010) noted that a weakness of this medium can include the absence of visual cues to facilitate rapport and inform the interviewee if the interviewer is listening. Despite this, she concluded that interviewing over the telephone can still produce rich, detailed data. Further, Irvine, Drew, and Sainsbury (2012) compared semistructured interviews conducted by telephone or face to face. Utilizing conversational analysis (see Chapter 19) they found that certain differences between the two interview modes emerged. To paraphrase, the completion or formulation of interviewee talk by the researcher was more frequent in face-to-face interviews; in telephone interviews interviewee requests for clarification were slightly more common; vocalized acknowledgements given by the researcher were less common in interviews done over the telephone; interviewee checks on the adequacy of their responses to the questions posed by researchers were more common in telephone interviews; and telephone interviews were often shorter than face-to-face interviews. In light of such findings, at this stage it would seem that telephone interviews can be useful for collecting qualitative data, but it is vital for researchers to know what they might be missing or gaining when choosing and doing this mode of interview rather than face-to-face interviews. And of course, a researcher does not have to use one or the other; both face-to-face and telephone interviews can be harnessed. For example, a telephone interview "can be a time-efficient way to ask additional questions or clarify points after a face-face interview" (Sparkes & Smith, 2014, p. 88).

The *mobile interview*, or what is also referred to as the go-along or walk-along interview (we personally don't like this latter term as it has overtones of able-ism – the assumption people are able-bodied and what is normal is a body that walks), is a means of interviewing participants as they move through space(s) (Sparkes & Smith, 2014). Rather than two or more people sitting down in one inside space, as is often the case when conducting a face-to-face interview, in mobile interviewing the researcher interviews the participant as they move together through contextually meaningful spaces that either the participant or researcher chooses. Once in the spaces, the participant walks or wheels the researcher through them, and by asking questions and observing, the researcher can examine the participant's practices and interpretations within a place of interest. Mobile interviews have rarely been used within the sport and exercise sciences. Yet, this medium of interviewing has numerous strengths. It can provide embodied and multisensorial data (see Chapter 26). Mobile interviews can also stimulate memories, as well as provide contextual understandings of behavior, emotion, and feeling. For example, Kassavou, French, and Chamberlain (2015) in their study of walking argued "insufficient attention has been given to the influence of context on health-related behavior change" (p. 1328). To re-address this, they conducted mobile interviews with ten leaders of walking groups while these people led their groups. Likewise, in their methodological reflections on physical activity, blue space, and green space research Bell, Phoenix, Lovell, and Wheeler (2015) noted that the "go-along interviews were particularly valuable in providing subtle insights into the social contexts of participants' well-being" (p. 93). For example, insights were gained into how physical places influenced well-being. Temporal insights into well-being were provided too in terms where and why participants lingered, diverted, and changed pace in their local environment. More recently, Palmer (2016) used mobile methods, including a GoPro™ camera, to capture the experiences of participating in a classic running event. She also provided insightful insights on some of the methodological challenges and theoretical conundrums that arose from her involvement as a runner-researcher in a qualitative mobile methods project.

Online interviews refer to interviews conducted using computer-mediated communication. Such interviews, sometimes also referred to as e-interviews, are used primarily to gather data via the Internet (see also Chapter 27). Emerging information and communications technologies (ICTs) offer various ways to gather such data and conduct interviews. For example, conducted in accordance with ethical guidelines, researchers may interview people using text messaging, immersive virtual games or worlds, video conferencing that has the ability to see people, and web conference meeting spaces that allow for text, video conference, and visual interactions with shared applications, documents, and/or whiteboards (Salmons, 2015). Online interviews are typically divided into two main types according to the ability to send, receive, and respond to messages at the same time (i.e. synchronous communication), or at different times (i.e. asynchronous communication). However, to reflect a time–response continuum rather than a simple either/or principle of interviewing at the same time or at a different time, additional refinements have been introduced to how online interviews are understood. As outlined by Salmons (2015) we can now talk of online interviews as moving between synchronicity (i.e. focused real-time dialogue), synchronous (i.e. exchange in real time), near-synchronous (i.e. near-immediate post and response) and asynchronous communication (i.e. time lapses between message and response). She also suggests that when thinking about online interviews we move from virtual to digital approaches. Virtual approaches are those that import traditional data-collection methods into the online milieu. In contrast, digital approaches require the researcher to do more than simply repurpose data-collection methods by taking "advantage of the unique characteristics and capabilities of the Internet for research" (Salmons, 2015, p. xvii).

Whilst people may not have the technology, technological problems can arise, and some forms of online interviews, like Skype messenger interviewing, cannot capture the subtleties of body language and other social cues, online interviewing has various strengths. According to Salmons (2015), this medium may be chosen because participants are geographically dispersed, hard to reach, or located in settings where the physical presence of researcher would not be allowed. She adds that online interviews are a good choice when dealing with sensitive subjects, as the participant may be more willing to discuss personal matters and emotions. Likewise they are useful when participants prefer to communicate in writing or when a researcher wants to understand someone's cyber experience. Online interviewing can also provide a degree of anonymity for participants. Salmons further notes that online "interview may be selected over telephone interviews because researchers want to see the participant or collect visual data" (p. 7). A relatively rare example of research using online qualitative interviewing within sport and exercise can be found in Bundon and Hurd Clarke (2015).

Why choose interviews?

According to Potter and Hepburn (2005), "the choice to do interviews is often taken-for-granted. There is very little explicit justification for the use of interviews and their appropriateness for the relevant object of study" (p. 283f). This remains the case in sport and exercise. A diligent reader need only read through the content of the past few years of journals in the sociology of sport, sport and exercise psychology, and sport coaching to see it is rare that justifications are provided as to why qualitative interviews were used. Why then use interviews?

Although there are many different types of interviews, a common rationale for using any type of interview is that interviewing is an occasion for conversation. As Brinkmann (2013) argues, human beings are conversational creatures, and through our conversations we can get to know other people. Thus, conversations developed in interviews are an indispensable source of rich and new knowledge about social and personal aspects of our lives. The ability to generate such knowledge is further promoted because interviews are flexible. The flexibility allows researchers to ask unplanned questions as conversations unfold and curiosity is stirred, thereby generating in the process novel or additional insights. Interviewing can also be a source of new knowledge as an interview provides space for participants to direct the conversation so that they can share what is personally meaningful to them. In so doing, the participant can take the researcher down avenues of knowing they had not considered before. Put differently, without having imposed on the person a small set of prescribed and tightly closed questions designed by a researcher for a large number of people, unanticipated insights about a research topic can be generated within an interview.

Interviews are particularly valuable sources of knowledge about experience and meaning. When done well qualitative interviews are an effective way for people to describe their experiences in rich and detailed ways, as well to give their perspectives and interpretations of these experiences. But whilst interviews are useful for generating knowledge about experience and the meanings attached to experiences, two caveats need stressing. First, an interview does not provide a transparent window into the interiority of experience or unmediated access to a private realm of meaning (Atkinson, Coffey, & Delamont, 2003; Randall & Phoenix, 2009). One reason for this is that our conversations *constitute* experience, rather than simply reflecting or reproducing what one has experienced. Further, people draw on discourses from society and culture to build and understand conversations, and in turn, these sociocultural discourses are our crucial resources for constituting experience (see also Chapters 4, 17, 18, and 20). What this means for researchers is that interview material captures shared cultural understandings and enactments of the social world, not pristine private experiences or inner cognitive meaning systems. Talk therefore needs treating as socially created, and experience and meaning as inherently shaped by our sociocultural landscape.

Second, interviews are not a privileged or distinctive means of understanding experience, nor how people make sense of experiences happening to them. Whilst the interview is a very useful source for understanding experience and meaning via the ways these are constituted through talk, it is one of a number of qualitative methods for understanding experiences and meanings. For example, observation (see Chapter 10), visual methods such as autophotography (see Chapter 11), and documents of life like diaries (see Chapter 14) can offer understandings into experience and the ways people make meaning. Therefore, when choosing to use interviews we need to seriously consider the other options available to us rather than making the interview the default option. We also need to develop rationales for our choices that go beyond simply claiming that an interview helps understand experience and meaning.

In addition to interviews providing new or rich knowledge, and helping us come to "know" people's experiences and meanings, interviewing can provide detailed and complex insight into people's decisions, values, motivations, beliefs, perceptions, motivations, feelings and emotions. Because our accounts, stories, descriptions, reports, and so on, told in an interview are never truly are formed inside a person but rather are shaped by the discursive resources made available to us by the society and culture we inhabit, interview talk can reveal the sociocultural dynamics of human lives. They can illuminate the ways in which societies and cultures shape personal experience, meaning, decisions, values, motivations, and so on. An interview can also generate insights into the context in which people live. When researching sensitive topics that require a degree of trust, rapport, and empathy between people, and an intimate setting to facilitate all this, interviews can be useful. Although the notion of "giving voice" to people is problematic given, for example, the power relations between participants and the researcher (see Chapters 7 and 36), another reason often given for using interviewing is that this method can capture people's voices and provide an opportunity to put these in dialogue with other voices witnessed in different interviews. Interviews can also provide insights into temporal dimensions of human life, including past events, present actions, and imagined futures. This is especially so when the interview is a narrative occasion; that is, an opportunity for storytelling (see Chapters 4 and 20). Interviews, most notably a focus group, additionally provide a context for interaction between people. These interactions, in turn, become not simply a resource for stimulating different stories about a specific topic. The interview itself can be a topic for the analysis of interaction and talk. This includes an interest in how a researcher and participant converse with each other and the effects of this telling on what is spoken and not said. More will be said about interaction in the concluding section. For now, let us turn to what Josselson (2013) described as a topic that is too often neglected in texts that discuss interviewing.

Doing interviews

Just like qualitative research in general, interviewing is much more than a prescribed set of techniques to follow; it is a craft (Demuth, 2015). As Kvale and Brinkmann (2009) outline in terms of interviewing, craft refers "to mastery of a form of production, which requires practical skills and personal insight acquired through training and extensive practice" (p. 86). Clearly then, if a researcher wishes to both use interviews and produce high-quality qualitative research, they cannot treat interviewing as a simple task or mechanical method that anyone can do well after a few attempts. Rather, they need to spend much time learning the craft of qualitative interviewing. Kvale and Brinkmann suggest that learning the craft can be done through apprenticeship in a community of experienced and competent practitioners, through observation and imitation of examples of best practice, through doing interviewing, through feedback on one's own performances, and through continual practice. Given this, the "tips" for doing qualitative interviews that follow are not a recipe for ensuring successful interviewing. Rather, each may be seen as examples to help prepare for interviewing and enhance the prospects of doing it well, as part of the process of learning the craft of qualitative research interviewing. Also consistent with conceptualizing interviewing as a craft, a researcher may find that some examples are more useful than others at certain points as one learns interviewing by doing it over time.

Drawing from Sparkes and Smith (2014), and expanding here on what was offered in their text by harnessing additional sources (e.g., Brinkmann, 2013; Josselson, 2013; Kvale & Brinkmann, 2009; Salmons, 2015), the following tips are offered. We break these into three parts: before the interview, during the interview, and after the interview.

Before the interview

1. Ask yourself, what are the epistemological and ontological assumptions that underpin how I might go about interviewing? This is vital to engage with as these assumptions shape and frame the entire research process and products that are developed. For example, when we subscribe to a postpositivist or neo-realist worldview (see Chapter 1) we move toward operating as a "miner" in interviewing (Kvale & Brinkmann, 2009). In the miner meta-phor, knowledge is understood as buried, to be dug up, and to be discovered by an inter-viewer. In contrast, when subscribing to a form of interpretivism like constructionism or critical inquiry (see Chapters 1 and 10) the interviewer may be cast as "traveler" who journeys with the participant and constructs knowledge together (Kvale & Brinkmann, 2009). One implication of this change in metaphor is that the researcher as traveler makes no claims as to producing knowledge that is independent of them and objectively found.

Nor do they view this as a limitation to somehow be overcome. Rather, the interpretivist traveler considers interview knowledge to be socially constructed, and they play a part in this construction (Smith, 2010). Our job is to be reflexive about our biases in this constructive process whilst trying to "understand people better – or at least differently – than they understand themselves" (Josselson, 2013, p. 2).

2. Develop an interview guide. In developing an interview guide, the following issues are worthy of consideration:

    a. Drawing on relevant literature and personal experience (if appropriate) generate a list of draft questions that relate to the research topic. Consider questions that address the topic in terms experience, behavior, context, values, senses, and personal background.

    b. Reduce the list of questions. Discard those that don't really address the research topic or are similar to other questions in the list. To assist this process, think about planning the interview around a few big issues.

    c. Use open-ended rather than closed questions. Closed questions elicit "thin" answers and invite a "yes" or "no" response. For example, "Have you ever experienced a serious injury during your playing career?" In contrast open-ended questions are designed to encourage richer descriptions. For example, "Please tell me about your experiences of serious injury during your sporting career."

    d. Refine your questions. Work at phrasing so that the questions are intelligible, clearly worded, and understandable to the participant. Avoid using jargon, abstractions, or academic terminology. Don't flood the guide with social scientific language. Questions shouldn't confuse participants but should rather be an invitation for them to talk freely and happily about something they have experienced. Each question should address one point. Don't produce a question, like in the example that follows, that asks the participant to respond to several points: "What inspires (point 1) and motivates (point 2) you to play sport."

    e. Group questions around similar themes.

    f. Structure questions by funneling them in a way that keeps the interview going and opens up issues as the interview unfolds. It can be useful to begin with "grand-tour" or "ice-breaker" questions. For example, "Can you tell me about your life as an athlete?" Such grand-tour questions can then be followed with the set of "mini-tour" questions.

    g. Place any sensitive questions in the middle or towards the end of the guide.

    h. The final set of questions, what might be termed a "closing tour," invites the participant to fill in any gaps that might not have been covered in the guide. For example, "Is there anything else you'd like to add about your experiences as an athlete that we haven't explored?"

    i. Ensure you've not overloaded the final guide with too many questions. Often, asking less generates more and better quality data.

    j. Whenever possible practice using the interview guide by interviewing a friend or a colleague. After this "pilot interview" or "dry run," ask them to give you feedback on the kinds of questions you have asked. For example, which ones opened up the conversation and which ones closed it down, and which questions were hard to understand or were too vague. Also, listen to the recording of these pilot interviews to check on your own questioning style and where you might have jumped in and interrupted the speaker before they had finished what they wanted to say. Does the interview look like a list of questions and brief responses? Is there a lot of turn taking between you, reducing the interview into question-and-answer format? If so, you need develop your interviewing style so that "the amount of interviewee text vastly overshadows the interviewer's interventions" (Josselson, 2013, p. 121). More will be said about learning from interviews in the section "after the interview."

k. Be mindful that, as the study proceeds, the questions in the interview might evolve. Qualitative research is circular and iterative in the sense that as you learn more about the topic, questions may need to be added, changed, and/or excluded.

3. In addition to the guide, develop "pocket questions" (Josselson, 2013). These are a set of auxiliary questions that may be useful to draw "from your pocket" to give direction to the interview, to help keep a conversation going, and to navigate emotion-laden areas.

4. Contact your participant at least one day before the interview by phone and/or email as a courtesy reminder, or to reschedule, if necessary, in case the participant needs to change the date, time or location.

5. Practice using your digital voice recorder, or computer if using Skype, for example.

6. Because how you appear will influence the interview, think about what you will wear and how you want to appear to the participant. What will they expect you to wear? What assumptions will they make about you? How will they respond to certain kind of dress or appearance?

7. Be well organized on the day. Check again your digital voice recorder is working and you've put fresh batteries in it. Have extra batteries just in case of a problem. Ideally also bring an extra digital voice recorder.

8. If the interview is a second or third follow-up interview, read and analyze the transcripts beforehand to formulate new questions or new topics for exploration suggested by the data and your preliminary analysis.

During the interview

Arrival and introductions

1. The first moments when you meet the participant are vital. Enter the interview in a courteous and respectful manner. Greet your participant appropriately. For example, don't presume to use their personal name – wait to be invited to do so.

2. Try to make the participant feel comfortable and relaxed. Small talk can be useful.

3. If you are asked if you want a cup of tea or coffee, say yes!

4. Think about where you will be seated. For example, is there too much distance between you and the participant? Is there large furniture between you that obscures body language or connotes formality and power relations? Does where you both sit enable the digital tape-recorder to capture all voices clearly?

Introducing the research

1. Before the formal interview, remind the participant about how you have come together (e.g. "As you know, when we discussed over the phone, I am interested in how people deal with retirement from disabled sport").

2. Having explained once again the purpose of the study, explain the interview procedure and ethical issues like anonymity, confidentiality, data storage, and how the information will be recorded. Invite them to ask any questions about ethics. It is important to remember that ethics does not stop here; it is a process, continuing through the research (see also Chapter 24).

3. It can be useful to say to the participant at this stage that there are no right or wrong answers; it is their own views and experiences that matter.

Conducting the interview

1. Once the interview has begun check again that the digital recorder is actually working!
2. Be an "active" listener as listening is active, not passive. Active listening is a process of being attentive, curious, and responsive. It can involve adopting a receptive style of interviewing. For example, show the participant that you are listening through your bodily demeanor and your general attitude. Actively listen too by asking for more information and to elaborate with more detailed stories. Be alert to any disruptions in your relationship, and address these as the conversation unfolds.
3. Active listening can also be enabled by the use of probes (we prefer the term curiosity-driven questions/exploration as, like Josselson, the term "probe" for us conjures "intrusion, penetration, and an absence of mutuality" [2013, p. 66]). Curiosity-driven questions include *detail-oriented explorations* (i.e. a "probe" designed to fill out the picture of whatever it is you are trying to understand – e.g. "What was it like being there?"), *elaboration explorations* (i.e. a "probe" designed to encourage the participant to tell us more about a particular point related to the interview – e.g. "Tell me more about that"), and *clarification explorations* (i.e. a "probe" to clarify any point that was not clear – e.g. "I'm not sure I understand what you mean by 'burnout.' Can you help me understand what that means?").
4. Allow the participant time to reply to a question.
5. As part of listening actively, and allowing time for the participant to reply, appreciate the value of silence. Silence during a conversation can make the researcher uncomfortable, leading them to feel the need to say something from the interview guide. However, silence can be beneficial to elicit additional information. It is crucial also to the creation of meaning during the interview. The participant can use silence in an interview for a period of reflection, allowing them to provide richer and more detailed explanations. Equally, if they remain silent, the researcher can ask, "Were you having some other thoughts about that?" Just as silences should not be too short, silence shouldn't be too long. When silence feels too long the researcher might repeat some aspect of the last narration to indicate you've heard what was said. "Probes" can also be useful. Silences can also be punctuated with an affirming smile and nod or commiserating groan. Assenting sounds such as "Mmm–hmm" can also be useful to help the conversation flow.
6. Don't ask too many questions at once. This can overwhelm the participant. Avoid asking either/or questions. This can set up the participant with limited choices and may inhibit answers.
7. Don't cut people off, interrupt with a premature request for more information, or indicate that they digressing.
8. Don't put the "answers" to your research question(s) in the participant's mouth. For example, "Would you say that having free time and money are the reasons you exercise more now?"
9. Don't use academic jargon when speaking with the participant or expect them to answer the research question(s) easily.
10. Never assume an understanding of what someone means.
11. Seek to establish rapport and empathy, when appropriate. Empathetic responses are useful here. To help with empathic responsiveness, summarize, paraphrase, or mirror what has been said (Josselson, 2013). Responding in the same tone as the participant can be useful

too. Another way to empathetically follow the story is to consider matching the feeling or point expressed with a smile, laugh, groan, or grimace, for example. At the same time, when actively empathizing it is important to respect the difference between you and the participant. For example, it can be tempting to respond to the interviewee with a smile and nod, and then say, "I've felt exactly like that. I totally understand." Such identification and attempt to "step in the shoes of the other," is, however, problematic. The other person is always *other* to you (alterity), and this needs respecting. Failure to do so can detract from the interviewee's sense that you are trying to understand their personal qualities and experiences. It can limit understanding. Thinking that you can identify with them and project yourself into their skin may sometimes also upset the person, producing a form of symbolic violence (Smith, 2008). Thus, on the one hand, when appropriate it can be vital to maintain an empathic stance by resonating with the person. On the other hand, the difference between you needs respecting. The other person is just that – other.

12. Where appropriate, and often only occasionally, consider moving from a receptive style of interviewing to an assertive style of interviewing (Brinkmann, 2013). This latter style is similar to what Roulston (2010) called a transformative conception of interviewing and, in sport and exercise, what Dowling and Flintoff (2011) termed antagonistic interviewing. In contrast to a receptive style, in an assertive style the interviewer seeks to provoke the participant, confront them, and illuminate any contradictions across their talk. The interviewer seeks to challenge not just the participant to think critically about the topic of investigation but themself too. Although this style of interviewing may accentuate ethical issues, and is not always appropriate to adopt, it can allow researchers to tackle the moral justifications participants give to their viewpoints and challenge conflicting views offered. Done in a respectful way, it may also provide a platform to explicitly confront power relations between the researcher and interviewee, as well as in the relationships the participant talks about. Key in this assertive process, suggest Dowling and Flintoff, is the need for interviewers/ees to move their conversation from *doxa* (being opinionated) to *episteme* (being capable of questioning and justifying one's position).

13. Keep reminding yourself of the research questions that inform the interview and the general purposes of the research project. This said, important information can come from spontaneous parts of the interview, where the participant has seemingly wandered "off track." Be flexible in your approach. Josselson (2013) puts it well:

> Your stance as the researcher/interviewer is to be holding firmly to two ropes: one the rope of the conceptual question (what you, as the researcher, are doing the interview for), and the other the rope of engagement with the participant – the human relationship in which the interview unfolds. If there are moments where your handholds on the ropes feel tenuous or in danger, *always* let go of the conceptual question rope and hold on to the rope of your relationship with the interviewee . . . Keep the interview setting as secure as possible, affirm your interest in the interviewee's experience, keep your compassion and concern foregrounded, and follow where the interviewee goes. You can always go back later and pick up the conceptual question rope.
>
> *(Josselson, 2013, p. 78)*

14. To further encourage and support participant talk consider asking the participant to imagine their life as an unfinished book. Ask them to divide their life into its major chapters, and briefly describe each chapter. Each person can be encouraged to give a name to each

chapter and describe the content of each. They can be asked to describe who the characters are in each chapter, what the central theme(s) or message(s) of the book are about, and what future chapters might contain. The researcher may also discuss with the participant what made for a transition from one chapter to the next, and who they would share the book with, hide it from, and say needs to read it.

15. Another possibility to encourage and support talk is to use *elicitation devices*. For example, qualitative researchers may use *material* aids to evoke or focus interview talk. Materials may include prerecorded video unsolicited written diaries, sports equipment, scrap books, t-shirts, letters, and trophies (see Chapters 13 and 14). Participant talk might also be encouraged through the visual aid of *photo-elicitation* (see Chapters 11 and 26). Relational mapping and timelining are two other visual aid options to elicit and support talk. In *relational mapping* participants are asked to draw a map of their relationships. *Timelining* involves a participant and/or researcher drawing a temporal plot about a specific subject in order to visually represent their experience of the subject matter as it unfolded over time. *Video diaries* solicited by the researcher, or footage collected from *head-mounted video cameras* (see Mackenzie & Kerr, 2012), may be used also to help stimulate talk and recall in an interview.

    Other possibilities that use both the technological and visual are *accelerometer* data and a *Global Positioning System* (GPS). For instance, Bell *et al.* (2015) asked participants to wear accelerometers over a week in order to understand activity levels, as well as to carry a small GPS unit to gain insights into the locations of activity. The integrated location/activity data were then mapped with a Geographical Information System (Quantum GIS v.1.8, www.qgis.org) to provide a visual representation of participants' routine place interactions, depicting location and relative levels of physical activity. The personalized map – a geo-narrative – created was then used in interviews (including mobile interviews) to elicit talk and engage participants in the interpretation of their own GPS/accelerometer activity maps. Bell *et al.* noted numerous benefits of using such a geo-narrative map, including how it encouraged detailed accounts of participants' physical activity experiences in their own terms, offering subjective insights into participants' shifting well-being needs and priorities, and the ways in which they sought to meet them through diverse local-place interactions. The maps provided a visual aid to discussion the importance of participants' routine, often prereflective practices.

16. Be aware that in any interview all the senses are used in creating meaning and understanding. Try to be aware of the sensorium in action and make a note of these wherever possible (see Chapter 26).

17. Where appropriate make notes in the interview to record, for example, nonverbal communication or the biographical objects in the room referred to by the participant (e.g. family photographs at sporting events).

18. Watch out for signs of tiredness from yourself and research participant. Suggest a break where appropriate.

19. In rare cases, where the participant seems too upset to continue, you might suggest moving onto something else and perhaps coming back to this later. You might ask the participant, in a compassionate and empathetic manner, if they want to continue. You might alternatively ask if they want to take a break. Again, there is no rule to follow here. The relationship being built, the empathetic attunement to the interviewee, and the emotional needs of the participant, for example, all play a part in how you respond at that moment in time. With practice you get to feel how to better respond to a person in an interview.

Ending the interview

1. About five to ten minutes before the end of the interview signal that the interview is close to ending. For example, "There is one last thing I'd like to discuss before we draw to a close . . ." Although the interview may continue much longer than the five minutes you thought, signaling to the participant the interview is close to ending can revitalize them.
2. Invite the participant to raise anything they feel is pertinent but which has not been discussed.
3. Invite them also to ask you any questions about the interview and project in general. At this point, you may also want to ask how the interview experience has been for them. On occasions you may also share your experiences of the research.
4. If required arrange a follow-up interview.
5. Take time to say goodbye. Thank the participant for being involved, expressing gratitude for the participant's generous sharing of experience. Without overdoing it, if you were particularly touched by the interview you may say so. For example, "I've learned a great from you that will really help the research. I really am thankful for your openness and willingness to share so many of your experiences." Ultimately, say goodbye in human terms.

After the interview

1. Make reflexive field notes as soon as possible after interviewing and try to recall as much details of the interview as possible. For example: What kind of relationship do you feel you developed with the participant? How did you feel and respond to the stories the participant told? How did they react to your questions? Did they appear nervous or open and at ease answering your questions? What was the interview context like, and how did it influence the conversations? Ultimately, adopt a reflexive stance to the interview process and product. Reflexive notes can be harnessed to help with the analysis. They may be incorporated in the final report, PhD thesis, and so on.
2. It is courteous to contact the participant to thank them formally for giving up their time to be interviewed.
3. If you had not done so at the end of the interview, you may also consider contacting the participants in order for them to give you feedback on the experience of the interview process and ways that you might improve it for them. For example, "How was the interview for you?"
4. Sometimes a participant wishes to continue the relationship after the interview. On some occasions, this may happen because they felt that the interview was therapeutic in some way. In such circumstances, you must gently but clearly restate your role as a researcher. You may again provide them with an information sheet containing therapeutic contacts, reminding them gently that you are not a therapist and that you, as a researcher, just have a certain amount of time to devote to each participant.
5. As soon as possible after an interview, transcribe it and start analyzing these data (see Chapters 15–20). Although it is now common practice for researchers to pay a professional transcriber or to delegate transcription to someone else, ideally transcribe the data yourself. This is a lengthy process, and is sometimes thought of as a chore. But, transcription is tremendously important. It *is* a form of analysis. Transcribing material yourself also helps you refamiliarize yourself with the participant. It can help with data interpretation and mistaking phrases/words (e.g. distinguishing "I don't, no" from "I don't know"). Further doing transcription yourself is another opportunity to learn about your interviewing style.

6. Decide on what transcription approach to use. The approach chosen will often depend on the intended use of the transcript. For example, you might choose an extremely detailed conversational analytic approach, like Jefferson transcription, if you seek to capture in great detail not just what people say but also how they say things (see also Chapter 19). In this approach the transcriber captures the subtle interactional dynamics of talk, such as micro pauses between words (marked by (.)); emphasis (underlined sounds are louder, capitals louder still); noticeable pitch rises (marked by the sign ↑); the pace of speech (inwards (<) arrows show faster speech, outward slower (>)) and the nuances of laughter. An alternative approach is orthographic transcription. Here words and sounds are transcribed verbatim (i.e. word for word) to gain a consistent representation of what is said and who is speaking. However, the transcript does not include the very fine details of how people talk, including most paralinguistic information (e.g., nonverbal sounds, stress, pitch, loudness, voice quality, pace, or timing, sighs, audible breaths, coughs, or snorts). This noted, transcribing using an orthographic approach still involves judgments about what level of detail to choose (e.g. noting empathetic responses like "hmm-mmm") and how to represent the verbalization of talk (e.g. "hwarryuhh" or "How are you?"). Whilst there is no correct or universal form of transcription, it is important that your transcripts are thorough and of high quality.

7. To produce the transcript, if possible get a good-quality headphone to listen to the interviews, transcription software (e.g. Express Scribe – free to download) to speed up or slow down the playback pace, and/or a transcription foot peddle to control play. Some people have also experimented with using voice-recognition software (e.g. Dragon) to do transcription (see Perrier & Kirkby, 2013).

How many people should I interview?

This is a commonly asked question. However, as Brinkmann (2013) points out, people "frequently ask this question with a quantitative logic in mind: The more interviews, the more valid and reliable the analysis will be" (p. 58). This though is seldom the case. For Brinkmann, qualitative interviewing distinguishes itself by its ability to get close to people, not by including a large number of participants. A researcher "cannot get close to the lives of 50 or 100 people in an interview study . . . The aim is not statistical representativeness . . . but instead the chance to look in detail at how selected people experience the world" (p. 59). Given this, according to Brinkmann, the logical answer to the "how many people" question is: "It depends. Interview as many people as necessary to find out what you need to know."

Other researchers support and add to this. For example, Sandelowski (1995) argued that there are no computations or power analyses that can be done in qualitative inquiry to determine a priori the minimum number of people to be sampled. The main goal, he suggested, is to ensure that the sample size is small enough to manage the material and large enough to provide "a new and richly textured understanding of experience" (Sandelowski, 1995, p. 183). Thus, sometimes an individual case study might be appropriate. At other times, Sandelowski suggested, a sample of twenty people may need to be interviewed. Drawing on previous research in which fourteen prominent qualitative researchers and five early career academics were asked the question "How many qualitative interviews is enough?", Lichtman (2014) likewise noted the response was "It depends" (p. 251).

What does it depend on though? In addition to seeking new and intimate awareness and understanding about unfamiliar and taken-for-granted aspects of human life, she highlighted that it depends on the epistemological, ontological and methodological assumptions that underpin the research (see Chapter 1). How many people one should interview can also depend on whether the focus of objectives is on commonality, difference, uniqueness, comparison or instances. Lichtman (2014) further pointed out that practical issues need to be taken into account, including the level of degree (e.g. undergraduate or PhD), the time available, policy aspirations, and the judgments of the academic community in which one wishes to be located. The tradition one adopts can also influence how a researcher responds to the question "How many people need to be interviewed?" For example, in a phenomenological study (see Chapters 2, 16 and 17) between four to ten people are often interviewed. In contrast, in a grounded-theory study (see Chapter 3) a higher number of people (e.g. 20) are frequently interviewed in order to achieve theoretical saturation. This form of saturation means that categories are fully accounted for, the variability between them is explained, and the relationships between them are tested and validated, and thus a theory can emerge (see Chapter 3).

Another issue one might consider when thinking about how many people to interview is data saturation. This is very different from theoretical saturation. Data saturation is an iterative process that involves collecting and transcribing initial data, immediately assessing it, and then continuing to collect and assess data until nothing new is generated (O'Reilly & Parker, 2013). For example, when considering how many people to interview in their study of narrative as a way to translate physical activity knowledge, Smith, Tomasone, Latimer-Cheung, and Martin Ginis (2015) used data saturation; that is, when there were no more emergent patterns in the interview data, and data began to repeat itself in interviews and through analysis, they stopped interviewing participants. Thus, if asked at the beginning of the study how many people should be interviewed, Smith *et al.* would have found it hard to offer a definitive answer. Their answer instead lay in the idea of data saturation. The number of people to interview would depend on when the data started to repeat itself and little extra insight could be gained from doing more interviews. This could be truly ascertained only after a certain number of interviews had been conducted and analyzed. In the case of Smith *et al.*, this number was 43. Often, however, data saturation occurs at around 20 people. Of course, whilst data saturation might be useful to inform how many people are to be interviewed, some traditions and types of analysis, like in conversation analysis (see Chapter 19), it becomes redundant. This is because in this analytic approach a preference is for small data sets of naturalistic data. This refers to data that have been generated without the influence of the researcher.

How do you know your participant is telling the truth?

This is another recurrent question. One response is to search for the truth as it really is through a set of methods properly applied. This quest for the single truth is grounded in the logic of quantitative research, postpositivism, neorealism (see Chapter 1). However, for many qualitative researchers to assume that the truth can be truly found independent of the people involved is problematic for many interconnected reasons (see also Chapters 7, 30 and 36). As noted earlier, an interview is unavoidably and inescapably shaped by social factors. For example, through our questions, interactions, history, interests, and motivations we as researchers always have a part to play in creating the "truth." In other words, there can be no theory-free knowledge as who we are is crucial to how we see the world around us.

In light of the impossibility of separating the researcher from the researched, and thus the researcher unavoidably playing a part in creating the truth, one could turn to methods to solve the question. However, a method is not neutral but a social construction (Smith, 2009; Smith & Deemer, 2000). Thus, a method is unable to secure procedural objectivity and provide an objective route to the truth (Smith & Hodkinson, 2009). Likewise, calling on interrater reliability, as some do, will not ensure any claim that the truth as it is really has been got at. Interrater reliability refers to the procedure of bringing two or more researchers together to independently code interview data, to compare these codes, and then together seek a high level of agreement/consensus through discussion. Amongst the numerous problems with interrater reliability that make it untenable, and a myth, is the possibility that coders agree by chance. Other problems include the absence of an agreed-upon threshold for what constitutes a numerically high level of agreement among coders (e.g. 89%, 90%, 95%, or 98% agreement), personal interests, and the power relations between coders that can profoundly shape what is said, what is not said, and how discussions unfold. A further problem is that often the researchers who code are often theoretically homogeneous (i.e. they share the same theoretical background and interests), and therefore can read the data similarly. Quite simply, interrater reliability does not work in terms of ensuring reliable results or that the single truth has been found in an objective way.

Another reason why seeking to find if the participant is telling the truth is problematic is because human memory is not objective or always reliable, but is "by definition a factionalizing faculty" (Randall & Phoenix, 2009, p. 130). Furthermore, a concern with unearthing the truthfulness of people's accounts given in an interview often rests on the picture theory of language. This theory contends that the meaning of a word is the object to which it refers. However, as Smith (2009) reminds us, a descriptive language, cleansed of evaluative terms, is not possible, both abstractly so and practically so. The problem, he notes, "is that our language is irretrievably loaded with terms that are fuzzy when it comes to the question of whether they are descriptive or evaluative" (p. 94). Another problem with this picture theory is that the same word can mean different things at different times and in different contexts. Finally, but by no means least, a concern with finding out if the participant is telling the real truth is problematic because our accounts, stories, and conversations *constitute* experience, rather than reflect it in some pristine form. Our words, like our memories, provide an evolving constructed and constructive interpretation of experiences. The person being interviewed could not then be a transparent reporter of some independent reality, and cannot – even in principle – be a "truthful" witness of a world independent of their interpretations of it.

Having problematized the question and a common response to it, where then does all this leave a qualitative researcher, or those who are called on to judge qualitative research grounded in interview data? First, since our words don't represent, match, or mirror transparently experience, and as there is no way of getting at the truth as it truly is independent of us, we need to accept that the quest for the one single truth is a chimera. We need, as Atkinson *et al.* (2003) advised, to eschew "trying to piece together fragments of evidence, testing the veracity of informants, exposing some of them as liars–all to establish the truth" (p. 139). We need to move beyond the concern with finding out if the participant is telling the truth, the whole truth, and nothing but the truth. Second, such a movement does not mean that anything goes. Not only do we all make judgments, but as noted next, qualitative researchers need to engage in rigorous analyses of data.

Third, and moving productively on from these two points rather than abandoning altogether the issue of "truth," different questions about truth need to be asked. A key starting point is to ask what is now meant by truth in qualitative research. Framed by a contextualist theory of truth, Smith (1989) argues that "truth – or what we come to accept as true in terms of intentions, purposes, and meanings – is the result of socially conditioned agreement, arising from dialogue and reasoned discourse" (p. 171). Or as Atkinson *et al.* (2003) put it, "Truth, credibility, facticity, rationality – these are all *achievements* on the part of social actors. There are various contexts in which they are performed. The interview is one such site" (p. 132).

Complementing this contextualist understanding of truth is a difference between narrative truth and historical truth. The latter is concerned with the accuracy of a history event, such as "Team X beat Team Y by six points in 2016 to win the league," or "I suffered a spinal cord injury whilst playing rugby two years ago." Narrative truth is about people's experiences and meanings of such events, and the ways these are constituted and rendered intelligible through our talk. Thus, in narrative truth "if that is my story, then it is my truth about the event." With these understandings of truth now framing qualitative research, a researcher moves from a concern with whether the participant is telling the truth in any objective way to the analytic opportunities that data offer. These include a rigorous analysis of the complexities of what people say, competing versions of "the same" event, the meanings people attach to experience, how people achieve truth, and what people agree and disagree on in relation to a historical event, why this is the case, and with what effects on behavior and emotions.

Brief reflections: problems and opportunities

In this final part of the chapter we engage with some potential problems that have been leveled at interviewing by qualitative researchers. The problems focused on have rarely been highlighted within sport and exercise science literature. This needs reversing. As we reflect on our experiences of reviewing papers submitted to international journals for many years, we realize how common many of the problems noted below are. Reflecting on our own work we also have been guilty of reproducing some of these problems. The following are by no means the only problems we need to engage with in sport and exercise, but all are possibly relevant for any researcher who wishes to make adequately grounded claims on the basis of an interview study. Moreover, as Potter and Hepburn (2005) argued, engaging with problems like those below is vital as part of doing high-quality qualitative research as, not least, with each problem can come the opportunity to do better interview research.

One common problem within qualitative research in the sport and exercise sciences is that the active role of the interviewer is deleted in research reports (Brinkmann, 2013; Potter & Hepburn, 2005). Frequently in published research the interviewer is absent when data are presented. The extracts used come only from the talk of the interviewee. Yet, as noted earlier, an interview is a social activity in which the interviewee and interviewer actively co-construct knowledge. This core understanding needs to be followed through in research reports. When the interviewer is deleted not only is an asocial account produced, but also talk is taken out of context (Brinkmann, 2013). It is also more difficult for readers to judge the quality of the data and the rigor of the research. To help overcome such problems the active role of the interviewer in coconstructing the data needs presenting. At the minimum, one way to do this is to include the interviewers' question(s) or responses (e.g. agreements or disagreements) that precede and/or follow the interviewee's talk in the report. Here are two instances of including the interactional flow with a question (NC = interviewer) and response (Lewis and Feddie = participants) in a report from work on combat veterans, post-traumatic stress disorder (PTSD), and physical activity in the blue gym by Caddick, Smith, and Phoenix (2015):

NC: So why do you think it maybe took a while to admit to yourself then that things were going wrong?
Lewis: Erm – you' re a bloke and you're stubborn and you got like, male pride. And also the fact that I feel like I was . . . I was very lucky compared to other people out in Iraq. I thought you had to see your mate get blown up or something like that before you had PTSD . . . (p. 101).

Freddie: I'm a bit of a loner, I don't mix with anyone anyway. I don't know if you noticed that while we were there, I was a bit more stand-off-ish. I had the odd word to say, but most of the time I' d just stand back and watch and listen. And apparently, it turned out I were being negative. When they [staff] gave everybody a debrief on the last day, I was told I was being negative.

NC: That's how it was seen maybe, was it?

Freddie: Mmmm – because I didn't stop at the dinner table after I'd eaten my meal and chat like everybody else – I had my meal, and sat there for a little while and then I'd bugger off, go off into my own little world and sit in the bedroom or whatever. I mean that's me, that's the way I am, even now that's the way I am . . . If I wanna be negative, I'll be negative – that is part and parcel of PTSD. But because I voiced my negativity, it didn't go down very well.

(Caddick, Smith, & Phoenix, 2015, p. 104)

Another related problem is the failure to consider interviews as interaction. This is especially so in focus-group research. On the one hand, the highly interactive nature of focus groups is a main reason for choosing this kind of interview. On the other hand, too often the interactions are wiped out in analysis and the reporting of data. Just as the interviewer is often deleted from the data in research reports, there is frequently no trace of the interactions between group participants that helped produce what is presented in the final report. One way to remedy this is to emphasize how the data to be reported (i.e. the extract that shows what was said by one person) was built up. This might be done by including participants' talk, laughs, pauses, vocal emphasis, and/or overlapping speech that helped to shape what another participant said. Taken from the work on parental stressors in professional youth football academies by Harwood, Drew, and Knight (2010), here is a brief example of inserting focus-group interactions between two participants (i.e. P1 and P4) into a research report to show how a core theme was coconstructed.

P1: My concern with it now is my son is going to do his GCSE [British examination at 16 years old] in sport.

P4: Snap.

P1: Is this teacher gonna hold it against them because a lot of the assessment is done by the teacher watching them play sport?

P4: I said to the teacher "is this gonna affect him next year? Because I certainly hope it doesn't." So we have one or two issues with the school, yes.

Researcher taking this perspective looks at the transcriber, as well as the interviewer, as mediating the interaction with the research subjects.

(Harwood, Drew, & Knight, 2010, p. 50)

A further potential problem that arises when using interview data, according to Potter and Hepburn (2005), is the way cognitive and individualist assumptions about human actors are presupposed. Notwithstanding the many problems with cognitivism (the questionable idea that psychological processes uniquely take place in "the mind" of individuals), as Potter and Hepburn argued, the problem here is that there is no way of testing cognitive assumptions and finding cognitions within an individual from most interview research. This is because language is neither referential nor a picture. That is, language does not transparently represent any presupposed inner psychological object of some kind, nor give a pristine picture of any presupposed psychological process inside the individual. As noted earlier, language constitutes. Thus, in interview studies the constitutive nature of language needs stressing and working with analytically. Researchers should also be very cautious about making claims from interview data that a particular psychological concern or object (e.g. flow, stress, resilience, mental toughness) is a cognitive process. Often there is no evidence of this.

Last, but by no means least, much qualitative work in sport and exercise relies on what Chamberlain (2012) termed "drive-by interviews." This refers to the practice of interviewing each participant just once and thinking this is a sufficient means of obtaining rich data for analysis. Let us first be clear. A single interview when done well *can* generate such data. However, one *potential* problem with interviewing a person once is that we can unthinkingly view participants as nothing more than data sources (Chamberlain, 2012). In addition, only so much can be claimed about the knowledge generated. The same goes for claims about rapport, empathy, and trust. It can often take longer than one interview to develop such social relational matters. Given such potential problems, researchers might consider doing more than one interview with each participant. As Josselson (2013) suggested, the "advantages of a second interview are that you and the participant have gotten to know each other; the participant has had time to reflect on what has already been told; and new material is sure to emerge" (p. 53). Another option is to expand the methods used to collect data. For example, researchers might use the single interview in combination with other forms of data, like diaries, observation, autophotography, and material objects (Gibson *et al.*, 2013). Furthermore, we might begin to draw much more on naturalistic data. Indeed, at least for those researchers who see "bias" and "memory recall" as limitations of interview research that need overcoming, such data would be preferable. It would likewise help them to deal with the conceptual "dead social scientists test" – would the data be the same, or be there at all, if the researcher got run over on the way to work?

Interviews are the preeminent data-generation technique in qualitative research within the sport and exercise sciences. It is perhaps not surprising then that so much could be written about interviewing. In this chapter we chose to focus on a range of issues that spanned the definitional (e.g. what is an interview), the traditional (e.g. semistructured interviews), the more novel (e.g. mobile interviews and GPS), the practical (e.g. tips on how to do an interview), common questions (e.g. how do you know the participant is telling the truth?), and interview problems (e.g. data floating in a social vacuum), and how these might be dealt with (e.g. inserting the interviewer in the reported data). Other important issues, like gender, race, (dis)ability, interviewing "elites," and complex ethical issues like anonymity and confidentially, have sadly been neglected for space reasons. We would however encourage readers to engage with such complex issues by crossing boundaries into "mainstream" qualitative research, reading books and articles in such journals as *Qualitative Research*, *Qualitative Inquiry*, and the *International Journal of Qualitative Methods*. We also hope that researchers in the sport and exercise sciences can contribute much more to debates on interviewing. Recent examples of this include Allain's (2014) work on engaging with gatekeepers as a woman and the challenges of conducting interviews as a women with young male ice-hockey players, the research by Jachyra *et al.* (2014) on the relational and performative aspects of gender in the interview space, and Andersen and Ivarsson's (2015) reflections on compassion and transference during researcher–participant encounters.

References

Allain, K. A. (2014). "What happens in the room stays in the room": Conducting research with young men in the Canadian Hockey League. *Qualitative Research in Sport, Exercise and Health, 6*, 205–219.

Andersen, M. & Ivarsson, A. (2015). A methodology of loving kindness: How interpersonal neurobiology, compassion, and transference can inform researcher–participant encounters and storytelling. *Qualitative Research in Sport, Exercise and Health, 8*, 1–20.

Atkinson, P., Coffey, A., & Delamont, S. (2003). *Key themes in qualitative research*. Oxford: Alta Mira Press.

Barker-Ruchti, N., & Schubring, A. (2016). Moving into and out of high-performance sport: The cultural learning of an artistic gymnast. *Physical Education and Sport Pedagogy*, *21*, 69–80.

Bell, S. L., Phoenix, C., Lovell, R., & Wheeler, B. W. (2015). Using GPS and geo-narratives: a methodological approach for understanding and situating everyday green space encounters. *Area*, *47*, 88–96.

Bold, C. (2012). *Using narrative in research*. London: Sage.

Brinkmann, S. (2013). *Qualitative interviewing*. Oxford: Oxford University Press.

Bundon, A. & Hurd Clarke, L. (2015). Honey or vinegar? Athletes with disabilities discuss strategies for advocacy within the Paralympic movement. *Journal of Sport and Social Issues*, *39*, 351–370.

Caddick, N., Smith, B., & Phoenix, C. (2015). Male combat veterans' narratives of PTSD, masculinity, and health. *Sociology of Health and Illness*, *37*, 97–111.

Chamberlain, K. (2012). Do you really need a methodology? *QMiP Bulletin*, *13*, 59–63.

Chase, S. (1995). Taking narrative seriously: Consequences for method and theory in interview studies. In R. Josselson & A. Lieblich (Eds.), *Interpreting experience* (pp. 1–26). London: Sage.

Coles, A. & Knowles, G. (2001). *Lives in context: The art of life history research*. Oxford: Alta Mira Press.

Demuth, C. (2015). "Slow food" post-qualitative research in psychology: Old craft skills in new disguise? *Integrative Psychological and Behavioral Science*, *49*, 207–215.

Dowling, F. & Flintoff, A. (2011). Getting beyond normative interview talk of sameness and celebrating difference. *Qualitative Research in Sport, Exercise and Health*, *3*, 63–79.

Ellis, C., Kiesinger, C., & Tillmann-Healy, L. (1997). Interactive interviewing: Talking about emotional experience. In R. Hertz (Ed.), *Reflexivity and voice* (pp. 119–149). London: Sage.

Gibson, B., Minstry, B., Smith. B., Yoshida, K., Abbott, D., Lindsay, S., & Hamdani, Y. (2013). The integrated use of audio diaries, photography and interviews in research with disabled young men. *International Journal of Qualitative Methods*, *12*, 382–402.

Harwood, C., Drew, A., & Knight, C. (2010). Parental stressors in professional youth football academies: A qualitative investigation of specializing stage parents. *Qualitative Research in Sport, Exercise and Health*, *2*, 39–55.

Hennink, M. M. (2014). *Focus group discussions*. Oxford: Oxford University Press.

Holt, A. (2010). Using the telephone for narrative interviewing: A research note. *Qualitative Research*, *10*, 113–121.

Irvine, A., Drew, P., & Sainsbury, R. (2012). "Am I not answering your questions properly?" Clarification, adequacy and responsiveness in semistructured telephone and face-to-face interviews. *Qualitative Research*, *13*, 87–106.

Jachyra, P., Atkinson, M., & Gibson, B. (2014). Gender performativity during interviews with adolescent boys. *Qualitative Research in Sport, Exercise and Health*, *6*, 568–582.

Josselson, R. (2013). *Interviewing for qualitative inquiry: A relational approach*. London: Guilford Press.

Kassavou, A., French, D. P., & Chamberlain, K. (2015). How do environmental factors influence walking in groups? A walk-along study. *Journal of Health Psychology*, *20*, 1328–1339.

Kvale, S., & Brinkmann, S. (2009). *InterViews* (2nd ed.). London: Sage.

Lichtman, M. (2014). *Qualitative research for the social sciences*. London: Sage.

Mackenzie, S. & Kerr, J. (2012). Head-mounted cameras and stimulated recall in qualitative sport research. *Qualitative Research in Sport, Exercise and Health*, *4*, 51–61.

O'Reilly, M. & Parker, N. (2013). "Unsatisfactory saturation": A critical exploration of the notion of saturated sample sizes in qualitative research. *Qualitative Research*, *13*, 190–197.

Palmer, C. (2016). Research on the run: moving methods and the charity "thon." *Qualitative Research in Sport, Exercise and Health*, *8*(3), 225–236.

Papathomas, A. & Lavallee, D. (2014). Self-starvation and the performance narrative in competitive sport. *Psychology of Sport and Exercise*, *15*, 688–695.

Perrier, M-J., & Kirkby, J. (2013). Taming the "Dragon": Using voice recognition software for transcription in disability research within sport and exercise psychology. *Qualitative Research in Sport, Exercise and Health*, *5*, 103–108.

Phoenix, C. & Sparkes, A. C. (2009). Being Fred: Big stories, small stories and the accomplishment of a positive ageing identity. *Qualitative Research*, *9*, 219–236.

Potter, J. & Hepburn, A. (2005). Qualitative interviews in psychology: Problems and possibilities. *Qualitative Research in Psychology*, *2*, 281–307.

Randall, W. & Phoenix, C. (2009). The problem with truth in qualitative interviews: reflections from a narrative perspective. *Qualitative Research in Sport, Exercise and Health*, *1*, 125–140.

Roulston, K. (2010). Considering quality in qualitative interviewing. *Qualitative Research, 10*, 119–228.

Ryba, T., Stambulova, N., Ronkainen, N., Bundgaard, H., & Selanne (2015). Dual career pathways of transnational athletes. *Psychology of Sport and Exercise, 21*, 125–134.

Salmons, J. (2015). *Qualitative online interviews*. London: Sage.

Sandelowski, M. (1995). Sample size in qualitative research. *Research in Nursing and Health, 18*, 179–183.

Smith, B. (2008). Imagining being disabled through playing sport: The body and alterity as limits to imagining others' lives. *Sport, Ethics and Philosophy, 2*, 142–157.

Smith, B. (2010). Narrative inquiry: Ongoing conversations and questions for sport psychology research. *International Review of Sport Psychology, 3*, 87–107.

Smith, B. & Sparkes, A. C. (2012). Narrative analysis in sport and physical culture. In. K. Young & M. Atkinson (Eds.), *Qualitative research on sport and physical culture* (pp. 81–101). Bingley, UK: Emerald Press.

Smith, B., Tomasone. J., Latimer-Cheung, A., & Martin Ginis, K. (2015). Narrative as a knowledge translation tool for facilitating impact: Translating physical activity knowledge to disabled people and health professionals. *Health Psychology, 34*, 303–313.

Smith, J. (1989). *The nature of social and educational inquiry: Empiricism versus interpretation*. Norwood, NJ: Ablex Publishing Corporation.

Smith, J. (2009). Judging research quality: From certainty to contingency. *Qualitative Research in Sport, Exercise and Health, 1*, 91–100.

Smith, J. & Deemer, D. (2000). The problem of criteria in the age of relativism. In N. Denzin & Y. Lincoln (Eds.), *Handbook of qualitative research* (2nd ed., pp. 877–896). London: Sage.

Smith, J. & Hodkinson, P. (2009). Challenging neorealism: A response to Hammersley. *Qualitative Inquiry, 15*, 30–39.

Sparkes, A. C. & Smith, B. (2014). *Qualitative research methods in sport, exercise and health. From process to product*. London: Routledge.

Stewart, D. W. & Shamdasani, P. N. (2015). *Focus groups* (3rd ed.). London: Sage.

10

CONDUCTING OBSERVATIONS IN SPORT AND EXERCISE SETTINGS

Holly Thorpe and Rebecca Olive

Whether it is a sport scientist watching their participant's responses to an exercise load, a psychologist witnessing a tennis player's reactions to loss, or a sociologist making sense of the ritualistic drinking patterns in a male rugby team, observations are almost always part of the research process. In this chapter we bring observations as a method of data collection centre stage and critically examine the value of observations for sociological and psychological research on human behaviour in sport and exercise settings. We begin with a brief explanation of why sport and exercise researchers should use observations, before highlighting how this method differs depending on the paradigm within which a researcher is working. We then draw upon the literature and our own research experiences to offer suggestions as to how to use observations in sport and exercise settings. All this is vital to making informed decisions about how to use observations to collect data. This is especially so as the practice of observation rarely receives sustained discussion in the methods sections of particular studies, or textbooks on research methods.

Why use observations?

Observations are a method of data collection involving the systematic recording of human behaviour in particular environments. However, there are various approaches to conducting observations. Gold (1958) developed a classification of participant-observer roles to reveal the varying degrees of researcher involvement with members of the social setting, including 'the *complete participant* (a highly subjective stand whose scientific validity is automatically suspect), the *participant-as-observer* (only slightly less problematic), the *observer-as-participant* (more typically associated with anthropologists) and the *complete-unobtrusive-observer*' (Angrosino & Rosenberg, 2011 p. 468). Today, few sport and exercise scholars use the latter uncritically, but the first three approaches are common across sociological and psychological studies of human behaviour in built and natural sport and exercise settings.

Observations can be particularly valuable for critical scholars trying to understand how power works within a sporting culture or context, or to identify inequalities and injustices within sport or exercise settings that participants may not be able or willing to acknowledge, or admit seeing or partaking in. Observations can help researchers identify key themes or tensions that then might be explored in more depth in interviews, media analysis or via other methods, such as surveys. For Tjora (2006), 'interviews and observations are interactive', and the 'interview provides leads for the researcher's observations, while observations suggest probes for interviews' (p. 430). Yet observations are not a purely ethnographic method, and they have much value as an alternative source of data for understanding with and against information gathered through other means (Adler & Adler, 1994). For example, observational and interview data collected by Smith (2013) was underpinned and framed by a narrative approach (see Chapters 4 and 20). He chose participant observation because it allowed insight into the mundane, the typical, and occasionally extraordinary features of everyday life that a participant might not feel worth commenting on in an interview. In terms of a rationale for using observations, Smith further noted that combining observational data with interview data 'enables researchers to understand not just what a participant says they do, but also what they do in everyday life. Thus, the combination of data can act as a resource to generate a more complex understanding of people's lives' (p. 111).

Observations and research paradigms

In this section we consider how our ontological and epistemological assumptions implicitly and explicitly influence our use of observations as a form of data collection. Here we briefly discuss the various paradigmatic approaches to observations to help recognize the diversity of observations as a research method used differently across and within disciplines. Here we focus on: (1) positivist; (2) postpositivist; (3) interpretive; (4) critical; and (5) post-structural/postmodern approaches, to using observations (see Table 10.1; see also Chapter 1). This is by no means a definitive typology. Many scholars work across the paradigms in their research approaches, and some locate themselves and their work in alternative paradigms.

For sport and exercise scientists working in the *positivist paradigm* (see also Chapter 1), observations must strictly follow the 'scientific method' in that they must be highly systematic with a clear set of quantifiable variables structuring observations, typically in laboratory settings (Peshkin, 2001). In contrast, those operating from a *postpositivist paradigm* advocate the value of qualitative data collected out of the laboratory and in more 'natural' settings, such as the classroom, gymnasium, or sports field. Researchers working in the postpositivist paradigm use a variety of methods such as observation, informal interviews and/or textual analysis, with the aim to 'accommodate the influence of natural exercise settings, to include participants' meanings and purposes, and to ground theories more firmly on participants' views' (Markula & Silk, 2011, p. 30). Yet, working in the postpositivist paradigm, many sport and social psychologists still tend to use qualitative methods with similar ontological assumptions as positivists. For example, postpositivist sport researchers using observation tend to do so with the use of scales or grids, a concern for reliability and validity, and with the aim of testing positivist theories (see also Chapter 25).

A particularly significant contribution to the development of observations from an *interpretive perspective* was Geertz's aim for ethnographic observation to provide 'thick description' (Geertz, 1973). In this approach, an ethnographer – through an 'empathy' with participants – includes the meanings specific to the participants, rather than a testing of theories and concepts selected by the researcher (Markula & Silk, 2011). Building upon Geertz's work, many early anthropological studies started out with the general rule to 'enter the field with complete openness' (Glaser, 1978) and 'gather data in a manner that presents the most complete picture of what has happened in the research setting' (Erlandson *et al.*, 1993, p. 432). Over the past two decades, however, the work of many anthropologists has come under heavy criticism, particularly by Indigenous scholars who do not feel their people or communities have been fairly represented via such Western approaches to research (see also Chapters 8, 33, and 34). For example, Tuhiwai-Smith (1999) argues that too often Indigenous people have been marginalized in research through the 'objective' and 'neutral' gaze of scholars working in Western paradigms. She describes this as 'research through imperial eyes' (p. 42), and offers an important reminder of the power of observation and the danger of representations encoded as 'truth'.

Conducting observations within the *critical paradigm* implies that the researcher will have a particular concern with power (including their own). Rather than entering the field with 'complete openness' (Glaser, 1978), the critical scholar tends to approach the field by looking specifically for the operations of power, the reproduction of inequalities, and examples of challenges to existing power structures (see also Chapter 30). Depending on whether the scholar already has a preferred theoretical lens upon entering the field, or if they are adopting a grounded theorizing approach (identifying themes first and then finding or developing a theory that best facilitates the analysis), they will likely be directed towards some practices, interactions, rituals and routines, and perhaps ignore or overlook other behaviours that are not considered relevant to their focus. This is not necessarily a limitation of such scholarship, but rather highlights the importance of researcher reflexivity and awareness of the strengths and limitations of their theoretical perspectives or lenses for informing their data-gathering (Peshkin, 2001), as well as for analysis.

For scholars working in the *post-structural and postmodern paradigms*, understandings of power, culture, social change and the body as a site of multiple forms of power relations and negotiations, have contributed to the use of observations as embodied, reflexive and ethical practices. Research that addresses these kinds of lived, relational complexities has been productive in problematizing observational methods in research about sport and exercise. For example, McLachlan's (2012) postmodern study of swimming pools included multiple field visits to collect 'fragments' related to swimming pools, including her own body moving through pool spaces. For McLachlan, sensual memories were also important and whereas she occasionally took photos and made observational notes, mostly she 'just carried the feel of [her] pool visits', such that the 'fragments' she gathered were 'a mix of tangible and intangible' (McLachlan, 2012, p. 63). This seemingly less systematic and more embodied approach to observations and field notes differs considerably from the positivist and postpositivist paradigms. A key difference is that there is no attempt to search for cultural 'truths' or meta-narratives when conducting observations, or to distinguish the 'objective' observations from the 'subjective' interpretations and experiences of the researcher. Conducting observations from such an approach requires a rethinking of the role and responsibility of the researcher who is not only an observer, but always 'an actor, author, teller and writer' (Coffey, 1996, p. 66). More importantly, observations through the lens of post-structuralism involve the celebration of multiple, sometimes contradictory, fluid and even fleeting, ways of knowing. Clearly, there are multiple ways of conducting observations, and a researcher's ontological and epistemological assumptions will greatly influence how they use this method of data collection.

Doing observations

In the remainder of this chapter a series of key ideas are drawn from the literature, as well as from our own experiences of doing observations of snowboarding and surfing cultures, both individually (see Thorpe, 2011; Olive, 2013a) and collectively (Olive & Thorpe, 2011; Olive, Thorpe et al., in press). We hope that these lessons learned add to the literature and provide others with some help to do 'better' observational data collection.

Table 10.1 Observations and research paradigms

Research paradigm	Aims of the research	Ontological position	Epistemological position	Uses of observations as a research method (typically with other methods)
Positivist Common in the natural science disciplines (e.g. biology, physiology).	To analytically separate distinct variables in an effort to prove causality – cause and effect – and discover generalizable information that illustrates a universal truth (e.g. laws of gravity).	**One reality** **One truth** 'Belief that the meaning of research [is] to understand and detect how things "truly" happen' (Markula & Silk, 2011, p. 27).	**Objective** Researchers are expected to be value-free, neutral and objective.	**Quantitative** Observations often part of laboratory studies, but must follow the scientific method, highly systematic with a clear set of quantifiable variables structuring the observations.
Postpositivist Recognizes limits of positivism, so combines quantitative and qualitative methods.	Main concern is to make a methodological adjustment, not to challenge the basic assumptions of positivist research.	**One reality** **One truth**	**Objective/ subjective**	**Quantitative/qualitative** Observations in natural settings with use of scales to systematically quantify results, and ultimately to test positivist theories. Researcher expected to remain unbiased and objective.
Interpretive	To understand participants' subjective experiences and interpret participants' meanings.	**Relativist ontology** Individuals make multiple meanings of the social world based on their experiences in particular contexts and in relation to others.	**Subjective** Researchers are involved in the production of knowledge, cannot be value-free or neutral.	**Qualitative** Naturalistic observations or participant observations conducted with the aim to better understand human behaviour. Often used in conjunction with other ethnographic methods, such as interviews and/or media or document analysis. Use of systematic note-taking to record observations in the field, often without researcher thoughts, feelings and interpretation.

(continued)

Table 10.1 (continued)

Research paradigm	Aims of the research	Ontological position	Epistemological position	Uses of observations as a research method (typically with other methods)
Critical As research paradigms, both postmodernism and post-structuralism are founded on a critique of humanist qualitative research.	To locate individuals' actions within relations of dominance and subordination. Aim is not only to expose the workings of power, but also to change inequalities.	**Historical realism** Ideological constructions stemming from certain social, political, cultural and economic reality shape identities.	**Subjective** All knowledge is the result of a subjective research process; researcher adopts position of political advocate to fight imbalances of power.	**Qualitative** Observations and participant observations often used in conjunction with other ethnographic methods. Researcher focuses observations on the operations of power within groups or culture (e.g. gender, race, class), and may use a theoretical lens to structure their observations, and possibly their interactions with participants. Systematic approach to field notes that may or may not include researcher reflections.
Post-structural/ postmodern	To understand multiple meanings individuals and groups construct of their social worlds, but interpretations must be interpreted within social and historical context. Aim is to develop more complex understanding of the ways power operates on and through bodies, and to use this knowledge to create change in the world.	**Multiple realities, Multiple truths** Critique of universal meta-narratives: multiple, fractured realities; favour cultural pluralism; social world is in a constant state of flux; no consistent, stable sense of 'self'.	**Subjective** All knowledge is the result of a subjective research process; researcher motivated to create change.	**Qualitative** Observations may be conducted with other ethnographic methods, and/or textual analysis, and narrative. A focus on the body (including that of the researcher), reflexivity, ethics and relationships with participants and communities. An embrace of multi-sensory fieldwork. Problematizes traditional understandings of 'data' and any attempts to identify 'truths'. Celebration of alternative modes of representation to reveal multiple fractured realities, fluid identities, and complex workings of power. No attempt to separate researcher reflections and experiences from field notes, with some opting to embody their observations, interactions and memories.

Source: Adapted from Markula and Silk (2011).

Note: A paradigm is 'an overarching set of beliefs that provides parameters – how researchers understand reality and the nature of truth, how they understand what is knowledge, how they act and the role they undertake, how they understand participants and how they disseminate knowledge – of a given research project' (Markula & Silk, 2011, p. 25).

Spaces, places and length of observations

Early in a research project it is important to delimit the field of study, and to identify spaces and places where observations will (and will not) take place. Of course, such decisions must be informed by the research questions underpinning the project. For example, one researcher might be focused on coach–athlete relationships and thus opt to conduct observations only during the training and competition of a particular team, whereas another researcher may be interested in the team culture more broadly so chooses to include observations in the changing room and various team social functions. For both Holly and Rebecca, understanding the complexities of snowboarding and surfing cultures required observations before, during and after sporting participation. For example, in her study of snowboarding culture, Holly conducted observations in 'natural' settings both on and off the snow, including lift lines, chair lifts, resort lodges, snowboard competitions, prize-giving events, video premiers, bars, cafés, local hangouts and snowboard shops. Similarly, Rebecca conducted observations in the surf, as well as on the beach, in car parks, at bars, festivals, exhibitions, surf shops and cafés.

Another important consideration is how long to spend conducting observations, and what times of the day (or night) will facilitate the most insightful observations for the project (O'Reilly, 2012). Here some preliminary knowledge of the group, team or culture is helpful. Acknowledging that snowboarding and surfing are 'lifestyle sports' in which the cultural practices, performances and interactions of enthusiasts are not limited to their sporting participation, Holly and Rebecca's projects included observations at all times of the day or night, ranging from dawn surfs (Rebecca) to late-night observations in backpackers' and ski-resort bars (Holly). However, Holly and Rebecca's projects differed considerably in their definition of the sporting fields under investigation and the length of time spent in particular locations: Holly set out with the goal of examining the values, practices and interactions of snowboarding bodies within and across local and global contexts, whereas Rebecca's project focused on a local surfing community on the East Coast of Australia in which she had grown up. In contrast to Rebecca's observations, which were conducted in (mostly) familiar spaces in her local community over a three-year period, Holly conducted fifteen 'ethnographic visits' (Sugden & Tomlinson, 2002) – ranging from one week to one month – in an array of snowboarding communities and ski resorts in Canada, France, Italy, New Zealand, Switzerland and the United States, between 2004 and 2010. The key point here is that how a researcher defines their length and field(s) of observation, and the places and spaces where observation will be conducted, must be carefully considered, and always in relation to the research questions being asked.

What to observe

Once a researcher has identified the times and spaces for conducting observations, the next logical question is what to observe in these locations. Denzin suggests that observations should 'describe participants, interactions, routines, rituals, temporal elements, interpretations and social organizations' (cited in Tjora, 2006, p. 432). Researchers have offered various strategies to help structure their observational practices. For example, Wolcott (1981) identifies four strategies in terms of 'what to look for', which are: 'observe and record everything'; 'observe and look for nothing – that is, nothing in particular'; 'look for paradoxes'; and 'look for the key problem confronting the group' (p. 255f). As the researcher gains an in-depth understanding of the broader cultural context, they are then encouraged to continue with more focused observations and detailed descriptions (Tjora, 2006). Adler and Adler (1994) advise following a 'funnel' approach to observations: 'progressively narrowing and directing researchers' attention deeper into the elements of the setting' (p. 381). Similarly, Markula and Silk (2011) identify three stages for observations: descriptive observations – during which the researcher aims to record all the possible details; focused observation – refers to more specific observation that concentrates on more defined activity or location in the field; and selective observations – refers to further specified observation of a more specific aspect of an activity or location (p. 165). Whereas Markula and Silk recognize the value of this systematic approach for 'beginning ethnographers' (p. 165), they also acknowledge that some conduct all three approaches simultaneously. In our studies of snowboarding and surfing cultures, we conducted all three approaches simultaneously – zooming in and out depending on the requirements of the situation – but, along with Markula and Silk (2011), we see value in more structured approaches for novice researchers.

Insider/outsider

Whether a researcher positions themself inside or outside of a group or culture continues to be a contentious discussion among sports researchers (Donnelly, 2006; Labaree, 2002; Pavlidis & Olive, 2014). Past and present cultural commitment is important. Researching from the cultural inside can help the researcher gain access to sources and events, and develop rapport with participants. Yet there are also advantages of being a cultural outsider, particularly as this can give critical distance in observing a field. Moreover, a cultural outsider is perhaps more likely to observe (and perhaps question) practices and behaviours that may be familiar, and thus taken for granted, by an already enculturated researcher. Like a growing number of critical sports scholars, we both approached our fields having already participated in the activity for many years, and with a pre-existing level of physical ability and cultural knowledge such that we could be considered 'cultural insiders' (Evers, 2006; Wheaton, 2002). In the fields of surfing and snowboarding, we negotiated our multiple roles as active participants and researchers (Olive & Thorpe, 2011). Our past and present cultural commitment, physical abilities and social capital within surfing and snowboarding cultures helped us gain access to some cultural spaces and participants and experiences, and gave us a head start in recognizing the significant issues and sensitizing themes and concepts. However, this 'insider knowledge' also carried potential pitfalls and responsibilities. We both found that one of the hardest tasks during the early phases of our research was representing participants' worldviews and subjectivities, while also gaining the 'critical distance' necessary to contextualize those views and actions (Wheaton, 2002, p. 262). This involved not only 'demystifying the familiar' but also 'analyzing respondents' views' (Wheaton, 2002, p. 262), and engaging with them in conversation with the literature. The key here is that whether observing fields from the inside, outside or somewhere in between, each position must be considered in terms of its specific possibilities, challenges and limitations, and always in relation to others in the field who will – despite the best efforts and intentions of the fieldworker – make their own interpretations of their authenticity and trustworthiness as a researcher and cultural member.

Using theory to inform observations

A range of critical social theories (e.g. Marxism, Bourdieu, Foucault, feminism) can be useful to help researchers gain critical distance, structure evidence and look for things that one might not previously have considered significant. For example, Holly approached her fieldwork with the understanding that no matter how sophisticated one's 'techniques of observation and proof', if they are not accompanied by a 'redoubling of theoretical vigilance', they will only 'lead us to see better and better fewer and fewer things' (Bourdieu *et al.*, 1991, p. 88). Thus, Holly used a range of critical social theories to help her gain critical distance, structure her evidence and see 'more and better things' in the field (Thorpe, 2011). In so doing, her approach to observations was unique in that the lenses of critical social theory always explicitly informed her fieldwork.

Adopting an explicitly feminist perspective, sex/gender power relations in recreational surfing culture were the focus of Rebecca's observations. She focused on female surfers' lived and cultural experiences, both in and out of the surf, and their relationships with other female and male surfers. For Rebecca, sex/gender power relations were the focus of her observations, but this focus reminded her of other inequitable issues including sexuality, race/ethnicity, age, dis/ability, etc. When conducting observations, social theory is valuable in that it cannot only help us make meaning of what we do observe, but also prompt us to ask different sets of questions, such as what/who is not there, and what is not being said/done in particular sport or exercise settings.

Recording observations

Another important consideration is how best to record observations for the purposes of research. While 'making good field notes is important in observations studies' (Tjora, 2006, p. 433), the act of recording observations is far from simple. It is unfeasible to expect to record everything observed in the field, and thus researchers must make critical decisions about what is of significance in the field, and what is worth noting. Moreover, the researcher must also decide how and where to include their thoughts, feelings, reactions and initial analyses. Of course, the researcher's epistemological and theoretical lenses are framing these decisions.

According to Babbie (1995), researchers using observations should record both 'what you "know" has happened and what you "think" has happened' (p. 291). The former – 'what you "know" has happened' – is referred to as 'substantive field notes' (Burgess, 1984) or 'running descriptions' (Lofland, 1971) of 'events, people, things heard and overheard, conversations among people, conversations with people and physical setting' (Tjora, 2006, p. 434). During the early stages of the project, the researcher may also draw maps or diagrams to help represent spaces and relationships. The latter, analytic notes – 'what you think has happened' – are 'additional field notes' (Tjora, 2006, p. 434). However, it is often suggested that these ethnography-oriented entries on 'preconceived opinions, and general feelings about certain observed situations' (Berg, 1998, p. 146) – must be 'bracketed and identified to not mix them with actual observations' (Tjora, 2006, p. 433). Some textbooks suggest multiple field diaries, with the researcher's interpretations, reflections and reactions kept separately.

For many sports scholars, making notes in the field can be a difficult task, particularly when one is actively participating in the activity. For Rebecca, working in a beach space raised questions of *how* and *where* she made notes during fieldwork (Hammersley & Atkinson, 2007). Although technology has since developed (Evers, 2016), most practically, the watery nature of the surf break precluded writing and voice-recording devices, but she also felt that visibly writing at the beach or in the car park after surfing was unnecessary and might make people feel uncomfortable about her presence as a researcher. Holly also struggled with making notes in many snowboarding-related spaces. While she was able to carry her notepad in the pocket of her snowboarding gear, and initially tried recording some observations while riding the chairlift alone, she quickly learned that freezing fingers and wet snow complicated this seemingly simple act.

We both understood the importance of writing field notes as soon as possible after being in the field (Emerson *et al.*, 2007), but preferred to wait until we got home (Rebecca), to a hostel or hotel (Holly), or to a café, where writing did not seem culturally strange. Few surfers or snowboarders sit on the beach or on the snow writing notes, and we each received some perplexed looks when we initially experimented with such techniques. Writing notes in the field of observation has some advantages in terms of vividness of memories, but working within an epistemological framework that recognizes knowledge – including memories – as always constructed, we don't believe notes written after leaving the field are any less valid. In fact, we identify advantages in such an approach. Overall, we found the small amount of time that lapsed between the fieldwork and our written accounts and recollections gave us the opportunity to record our observations and experiences in a less frantic and soggy (Rebecca) or chilled (Holly) state. Working within the post-structural paradigm, our field notes and journals were not so much 'jotted notes' as they were 'mental notes', which were recalled and ordered as an 'outpouring of memories, thoughts and words' (Emerson *et al.*, 2007, p. 357f). Ultimately, our field notes acted as both a method of recording observations, as well as a space for reflection and analysis during the research process (Hammersley & Atkinson, 2007; Okley, 2008). In sum, each researcher working within sporting cultures will have unique challenges for recording their observations, and we encourage researcher flexibility and creativity to recording field notes that meet the challenges of the sporting space and physical requirements of the activity.

Home and away

Issues of critical distance are particularly pertinent when researching one's own community. In Rebecca's case, her existing relationships to her home-town surfing community gave her access to a number of people for interviews, and she could continue to surf in the breaks where she was well known by many. However, this access also created difficulties in gaining critical distance in her observations of the research field. For example, it was not until late in her fieldwork that she thought to record observations about the physical geography of the beaches and surf breaks she was researching. Her closeness to her home beaches meant that she took for granted her descriptive knowledge of the places, rather than using them as the beginning of her observational 'funnel' (Adler & Adler, 1994; Markula & Silk, 2011). Another key issue for Rebecca's research was accounting for her established identity as a member of the local community. To facilitate this process, she adopted Elspeth Probyn's (1993) notion of 'thinking the social through the self' (p. 3). Combining observations, interviews and blogging, she developed a process for reflection that explicitly included her own subjectivity, as well as the ways that she was located in the middle of a relational web of exchange and collaboration with her participants and community.

In contrast to Rebecca's project, Holly's fieldwork about transnational snowboarding culture meant her observations were conducted in locations around the world and for much shorter periods of time. Such multi-sited transnational fieldwork, however, raises other issues for the fieldworker. For Holly, each of the locations visited for her project posed different opportunities *and* challenges (e.g. language, localism, cultural access, accommodation, pre-existing contacts in the field, funding). According to Stoller (1997), the key to doing research in complex transnational spaces is 'suppleness of imagination' (p. 91). For example, language barriers in France, Italy, Portugal, Spain and Switzerland, made some aspects of Holly's fieldwork more difficult. In these situations, visual observations became even more important: she found herself paying more attention to the signs and symbols, posturing and interactions of moving bodies in snowy spaces, as well as the tone and inflections of voices.

As part of her fieldwork, Holly also conducted observations at four international snow-sports events (the X Games in France; the Olympics in Canada; the Big Freeze Festival in London; and the Winter Festival in Queenstown, New Zealand). She found her iPhone to be a particularly valuable research tool in such situations, enabling her to take unobtrusive photos of various sights and record sounds as well as her own initial observations. Using the voice-memo application, she was able to capture some of the multi-layered sounds (e.g., commentators, music, helicopters, crowd), thus freeing her to focus on other social and sensual dimensions of the occasion. Listening to these audio recordings and viewing her photos and videos upon returning from the event, was invaluable for evoking her multi-dimensional memories of these socially, physically and sensually loaded phases of fieldwork (see Thorpe, 2011, 2014).

Observations beyond the visual: using the researching body

In light of the recent sensual turn in the social sciences and humanities, scholars have begun to question the bias towards the visual in observational research (see Chapters 11 and 26). Indeed, as suggested above, conducting observations is much more than what one sees in the field, and researchers are increasingly encouraged to draw upon all of the traditionally recognized senses – taste, sound, touch, smell, and sight – as well as non-traditional senses such as kinaesthetic sense, pain, pleasure and other internal senses, and instinctual and embodied forms of knowledge (Stoller, 1997). A number of sport and exercise scholars have embraced such challenges, and are drawing upon all of their senses to conduct more multi-layered observations. Like Evers (2006) and a growing number of others (e.g. Orr & Phoenix, 2015; Sparkes, 2009), our 'researching bodies' not only observed and jotted notes, but also actively participated in the activities of snowboarding and surfing, and in so doing, were 'penetrated by and fe[lt] the field[s]' we were investigating (Evers, 2006, p. 239). Evers was among the first to detail the process of conducting 'research at the embodied level' (p. 239), and such an approach offered us new opportunities for experiencing, observing and sharing the bodily and social pleasures inherent in the practices of snowboarding and surfing. Based on the literature and our own research experiences, we believe that observations can be considerably richer, more memorable and multi-dimensional when a researcher adopts an embodied and multi-sensual approach to data collection.

Reflexive observations

Reflexivity is central to conducting quality observations. Critical scholars challenge the assumption that a researcher can objectively conduct 'pure' observations devoid of any 'possible distortions generated by the researcher's emotions' (Tjora, 2006, p. 434). Rather, the researcher is an integral part of the data-gathering process – their past (in)experience(s) in a particular culture, and their sex, age, nationality, race and/or sexuality, may all play a role in influencing the interactions, relationships and observations they are able to access, and those that are focused on, ignored or not seen at all. The key is to critically reflect upon how the researcher's subjectivities inform all stages of the research process, including the gathering of 'data' from the field. In the words of Angrosino and Rosenberg (2011), if observation is to be useful to the research process, it must be 'as rigorously conducted as it was in the classic period', however 'our social scientific powers of observation must . . . be turned on ourselves and the ways in which our experiences interface with those of others in the same context if we are to come to a full understanding of sociocultural processes' (p. 470). Of course, there are various approaches to reflexivity, some of which will be more productive in conducting observations than others. For example, Denzin (1997) identifies five differing types of reflexivity in use in qualitative research, including methodological, intertextual, standpoint, queer, and feminist reflexivity (also see Pillow, 2003).

Taking inspiration from post-structural feminist theorizing about reflexivity, we have acknowledged the difficulties of developing such reflexivity in the field, and have explored the potential of theoretically informed collaborations for enhancing researcher reflexivity at different stages in the research journey, and particularly for helping scholars access those 'blind spots' in their own identities that may 'never be comprehensively executed by the individual knower' (Pels, 2000, p. 17; see, for example, Olive & Thorpe, 2011; Pavlidis & Olive, 2014; Thorpe, Barbour & Bruce, 2011). Put simply, in both historical and contemporary contexts, reflexivity has had multiple uses and thus we need to critically consider how our ontological and epistemological assumptions, our theoretical frameworks, embodiment and so forth inform our approach to conducting reflexive observations.

Ethics

A particularly important consideration for those conducting observations is whether it is appropriate to adopt a covert research position in which those being observed do not know a researcher is present and gathering information from their activities (see also Chapter 24). As Sands (2008) explains, when or if a researcher 'reveals his/her role as a fieldworker and informs those being observed of the[ir] intent' is a 'matter of ethical concern' (p. 369). For some researchers, an overt positioning in which participants engage in the practice of 'informed consent' (not only knowing that a researcher is collecting data but also have the opportunity to opt out if they do not want their behaviour observed for research purposes) is not only unfeasible but also potentially dangerous, particularly in groupings involving violence, risk-taking or illegal acts. Nonetheless, the covert nature of participant observation raises many ethical issues, in particular the rights of those being observed to know that their behaviour is being recorded for research purposes (Wheaton, 1997). Some researchers conducting covert observations can be accused of 'spying' on participants who do not know they are being observed for research purposes.

With such concerns in mind, upon meeting participants in the field, Holly always tried to be open about her dual roles as a researcher *and* snowboarder, and the purpose of her project. However, in some situations it was not feasible (or, indeed, safe) to declare her researcher identity or ask for informed consent from *all* participants (e.g. observations from the chairlift of unidentifiable snowboarders and skiers interacting on the slopes below; or at a Big Air snowboarding event with thousands of intoxicated spectators). Rather, she negotiated her way through the various social situations differently depending on the dynamics of the interaction and her role in the relations. In so doing, as part of ethics as practice/process (see Chapter 24) she regularly engaged in 'situated ethics'; that is, she made ethical decisions regarding the overt and covert nature of her research based on the dynamics and complexities of the particular social, cultural and/or physical environment (Simons & Usher, 2000; Wheaton, 2002).

Observations in the field can place researchers in other ethical dilemmas. For example, how is the researcher to respond if they happen to observe violence, find themselves in a dangerous situation (see Chapter 24, this volume; Thorpe, 2011), feel threatened by others in the field, or overhear discriminatory comments? The safety of the participants and the researcher must be paramount, and good planning can help us avoid such situations. For researchers working in paradigms with a political focus (i.e. critical, post-structural), however, some of these latter questions take on more weight, particularly as they require the researcher to consider their own roles, responsibilities and ethics, and thus (re)actions in the field. For example, Wheaton (2002) recalled feelings of cultural exclusion when overhearing her male windsurfing buddies making sexist remarks, while Evers (2006) described moments of shame and frustration at the sexism and homophobia he encountered among surfing friends and peers. As O'Reilly (2012) explains, such feelings of discomfort are common when conducting observations, and these moments are important for the researcher to critically unpack as part of their overall project, as well as to facilitate more reflexive research practices.

While many working in less politically motivated paradigms might expect a researcher to adopt a 'fly-on-the-wall' position and not to intervene, in our case, it was our feminist politics that shaped our responses and reactions to some problematic observations and interactions (Olive & Thorpe, 2011). Admittedly, during the early phases of our research, we both experienced some unsettling interactions with participants, which we did not always choose (or know how) to respond to. However, as our projects progressed, we gained our confidence as researchers, and reflected more critically (and collaboratively) on our feminist responsibilities in the field, and thus we became increasingly aware of our participation in the power dynamics in surfing and snowboarding cultures (Olive & Thorpe, 2011). Today, working in the post-structural feminist paradigm, we aim to make ethically informed decisions as to when and how best to respond, question and challenge discrimination or aggressive behaviour in sporting spaces. The key point here is that observations and actions are always mediated by our ontological and epistemological assumptions. Conducting observations with a clear understanding of one's researcher identity, politics and ethics, and relationships to the culture and place of fieldwork, certainly facilitates the process of making ethically informed decisions.

The future of observations: some final thoughts

There are a number of social changes that are influencing the practice and politics of observations as a data-collection method. To conclude, we signpost three important changes with the potential to impact the use of observations in future research on sport and exercise cultures. Firstly, in light of fundamental transformations of space, place and time, scholars are being encouraged to embrace more broad-based research strategies, what some variously refer to as 'globalizing methods' (Stoller, 1997), 'mobile ethnography' (Marcus, 1995), multi-site 'transnational fieldwork' (Knowles, 1999), and 'global ethnography' (Burawoy *et al.*, 2000), in order to understand changes in cultural and social groupings and affiliations. Taking account of the increasing mobility of people, objects and ideas will be increasingly important for those seeking to understand sport and physical cultures within and across local, national and transnational contexts. A growing number of critical sport scholars are taking up this challenge and, in so doing, are adapting research methods, including observations, to better understand sporting cultures within and across borders (e.g. Canniford, 2005; Joseph, 2015; Thorpe, 2014).

Secondly, the 'online, parallel world' (Angrosino & Rosenberg, 2011, p. 477) presents new challenges and opportunities for researchers seeking to understand how groups and cultures interact and make meaning in digital virtual spaces (see also Chapters 11, 12, and 27). Sport and media scholars are certainly embracing such challenges with researchers in sports media (Hutchins & Rowe, 2013; Sanderson, 2014), history (Osmond & Phillips, 2015; Thorpe, 2015), culture (Olive, 2015; Pavlidis & Fullager, 2013), and sociology (Gilchrist & Wheaton, 2013; McKay, 2013; Ruihley & Billings, 2013), conducting more research on online/digital sporting cultures, including fantasy leagues, social media and virtual reality. Some are also exploring the potential of digital/online technologies as participatory observational tools (Francombe, 2013; Olive, 2013b). Of course, the act of conducting observations in online spaces and using digital tools raises some new issues for observational research, including the limits to what one can observe beyond the screen, the anonymity of online media producers and participants, and the covert or overt positioning of the researcher and the ethics of their participation in such spaces. Arguably, many of these digital research challenges are similar to those in offline spaces, and should similarly be seen as potential in encouraging methodological and ethical reflection and reflexivity (see also Chapters 24 and 27). Alongside such developments, new wearable digital technologies (e.g. Go Pro) are enabling new approaches to recording observations. While using such technologies offers exciting opportunities for conducting and recording observations in sporting spaces (particularly when the researcher is adopting a participant-observer role; see Evers, 2016), they also involve a new set of ethical questions regarding informed consent of those being observed and digitally recorded for research purposes (Chalfen, 2014).

Finally, there is increasing awareness of the potential of collaborative approaches to observations. Empirically, collaborations have been used productively to collect data for many years, but it is only recently that researchers are considering the value of multiple subjective perspectives from different positions (e.g. insider and outsider) for more nuanced understandings of sporting cultures (see May & Pattillo-McCoy, 2000; Pavlidis & Olive, 2014; Thorpe *et al.*, 2011). Arguably, collaborative approaches to observation opens new multi-perspective, multi-sensory, multi-subjective ways of observing fields in ways that one person cannot access on their own. Indeed, the various positions and perspectives that different researchers bring to, and occupy within the field can offer various angles on events or interactions, and also encourage productive discussion among researchers, and even highlight researchers' physical and epistemological blind-spots (see Olive, Thorpe *et al.*, forthcoming). In sum, each of these future developments – transnational fields, digital spaces and technologies, collaboration – reflect developments in sport and exercise more broadly, and highlight important new considerations for the use of observations to further enhance our understandings of sport and exercise into the twenty-first century.

References

Adler, P. & Adler, P. (1994). Observational techniques. In N. Denzin & Y. Lincoln (Eds.), *Handbook of qualitative research* (pp. 377–392). Thousand Oaks, CA: Sage.

Angrosino, M. & Rosenberg, J. (2011). Observations on observations: Continuities and challenges. In N. Denzin & Y. Lincoln (Eds.), *The Sage handbook of qualitative research* (4th ed., pp. 467–478). Thousand Oaks, CA: Sage.

Babbie, E. (1995). *The practice of social research* (7th ed.). Belmont, CA: Wadsworth.

Berg, B.L. (1998). *Qualitative research methods for the social sciences* (3rd ed.). Boston, MA: Allyn and Bacon.

Bourdieu, P., Chamboredon, J. & Passeron, J. (1991). *The craft of sociology: Epistemological preliminaries.* Berlin & New York: Walter de Gruyter.

Burawoy, M., Blum, J.A., George, S., Gille, Z., Gowan, T., Haney, L., Klawiter, M., Lopez, S.H., Riain, S.O. & Thayer, M. (Eds.) (2000). *Global ethnography: Forces, connection, and imaginations in a postmodern world.* Berkeley, CA: University of California Press.

Burgess, R.G. (1984). *In the field: An introduction to field research.* London: Allen and Unwin.

Canniford, R. (2005). Moving shadows: Suggestions for ethnography in globalized cultures. *Qualitative Market Research, 8,* 204–218.

Chalfen, R. (2014). 'Your panopticon or mine?' Incorporating wearable technology's Glass and Go Pro into visual social science. *Visual Studies, 29*(3), 299–310.

Coffey, A. (1996). The power or accounts: Authority and authorship in ethnography. *Qualitative Studies in Education, 9*(1), 61–74.

Denzin, N.K. (1997). *Interpretive ethnography: Ethnographic practices for the 21st century.* Thousand Oaks, CA: Sage.

Donnelly, M. (2006). Studying extreme sports: Beyond the core participants. *Journal of Sport and Social Issues, 30*(2), 219–224.

Emerson, R.M., Fretz, R.I. & Shaw, L.L. (2007). Participant observation and fieldnotes. In P. Atkinson, A. Coffey, S. Delamont, J. Lofland & L. Lofland (Eds.), *Handbook of ethnography* (2nd ed., pp. 352–368). London: Sage.

Erlandson, D., Harris, E., Skipper, B. & Allen, S. (1993). *Doing naturalistic inquiry: A guide to methods*. Newbury Park, CA: Sage.

Evers, C. (2006). How to surf. *Journal of Sport and Social Issues*, 30(3), 229–243.

Evers, C. (2016). Researching action sport with a Go Pro camera: An embodied and emotional mobile video talke of the sea, masculinity and men-who-surf. In I. Wellard (Ed.), *Researching embodied sport: Exploring movement cultures* (pp. 145–161). London: Routledge.

Francombe, J. (2013). Methods that move: A physical performative pedagogy of subjectivity. *Sociology of Sport Journal*, 30(3), 256–273.

Geertz, C. (1973). *The interpretation of cultures*. New York: Basic Books.

Gilchrist, P. & Wheaton, B. (2013). New media technologies in lifestyle sport. In B. Hutchins & D. Rowe (Eds.), *Digital media sport: Technology, power and culture in the network society* (pp. 169–185). New York: Routledge.

Glaser, B. (1978). *Theoretical sensitivity*. Mill Valley, CA: The Sociology Press.

Gold, R. (1958). Roles in sociological field observation. *Social Forces*, 36, 217–223.

Hammersley, M. & Atkinson, P. (2007). *Ethnography: Principles in practice* (3rd ed.). Abingdon, UK & New York: Routledge.

Hutchins, B. & Rowe, D. (Eds.) (2013). *Digital media sport: Technology, power & culture in the network society*. New York: Routledge.

Joseph, J. (2015). *Sport in the Black Atlantic: Crossing and making boundaries*. New York: Bloomsbury.

Knowles, C. (1999). Here and there: Doing transnational fieldwork. In V. Amit (Ed.), *Constructing the field: Ethnographic fieldwork in the contemporary world* (pp. 54–70). Florence: Routledge.

Labaree, R. (2002). The risk of 'going observationalist': Negotiating the hidden dilemmas of being an insider participant observer. *Qualitative Research*, 2(1), 97–122.

Lofland, J. (1971). *Analyzing social settings*. Belmont, CA: Wadsworth.

Marcus, G. (1995). Ethnography in/of the world system: The emergence of multi-site ethnography. *Annual Review of Anthropology*, 24, 95–117.

Markula, P. & Silk, M. (2011). *Qualitative research for physical culture*. Basingstoke, UK: Palgrave Macmillan.

May, R. & Pattillo-McCoy, M. (2000). Do you see what I see? Examining a collaborative ethnography. *Qualitative Inquiry*, 6(1), 65–87.

McKay, S. (2013). Skirtboarder net-a-narrative: Young women creating their own skateboarding (re)presentations. *International Review for the Sociology of Sport*, 48(2), 171–195.

McLachlan, F. (2012). Poolspace: A deconstruction and reconfiguration of public swimming pools. Unpublished PhD, University of Otago, New Zealand.

Okley, J. (2008). Knowing without notes. In N. Halstead, E. Hirsch & J. Okley (Eds.), *Knowing how to know: Fieldwork and the ethnographic present* (pp. 55–74). New York: Berghan Books.

Olive, R. (2013a). Blurred lines: Women, subjectivities and surfing. Unpublished doctoral thesis, University of Queensland, Australia,

Olive, R. (2013b). Making friends with the neighbours: Blogging as a research method. *International Journal of Cultural Studies*, 16(1), 71–84.

Olive, R. (2015). Reframing surfing: Physical culture in online spaces. *Media International Australia, Incorporating Culture & Policy*, 155, June, 99–107.

Olive, R. & Thorpe, H. (2011). Negotiating the 'F-Word' in the field: Doing feminist ethnography in action sport cultures. *Sociology of Sport Journal*, 28(4), 421–440.

Olive, R., Thorpe, H., Roy, G., Nemani, M., lisahunter, Wheaton, B. & Humberstone, B. (forthcoming). Surfing together: Exploring the potential of a collaborative ethnographic moment. In H. Thorpe & R. Olive (Eds.), *Women in action sport cultures: Identity, politics and experience*. Basingstoke, UK: Palgrave Macmillan.

O'Reilly, K. (2012). *Ethnographic methods* (2nd ed.). Abingdon, UK: Taylor & Francis.

Orr, N. & Phoenix, C. (2015). Photographing physical activity: Using visual methods to 'grasp at' the sensual experience of the aging body. *Qualitative Research*, 15, 454–472.

Osmond, G. & Phillips, M. (Eds.) (2015). *Sport history in the digital era*. Champaign, IL: University of Illinois Press.

Pavlidis, A. & Fullagar, S. (2013). Becoming roller derby grrrls: Exploring the gendered play of affect in mediated sport cultures. *International Review for the Sociology of Sport*, 48(6), 673–688.

Pavlidis, A. & Olive, R. (2014). On the track/in the bleachers: Authenticity and ethnographic research in sport and physical cultural studies. *Sport in Society: Cultures, Commerce, Media, Politics*, 17(2), 218–232.

Pels, D. (2000). Reflexivity: One step up. *Theory, Culture and Society*, 17(3), 1–25.

Peshkin, A. (2001). Angles of vision: Enhancing perception of qualitative research. *Qualitative Inquiry, 7*(2), 238–253.

Pillow, W.S. (2003). Confession, catharsis, or cure? Rethinking the uses of reflexivity as a methodological power in qualitative research. *Qualitative Studies in Education, 16*(2), 175–196.

Probyn, E. (1993). *Sexing the self: Gendered positions in cultural studies.* London: Routledge.

Ruihley, B.J. & Billings, A.C. (2013). Infiltrating the boys' club: Motivations for women's fantasy sport participation, *International Review for the Sociology of Sport, 48*(4), 435–452.

Sanderson, J. (2014). What do we do with Twitter? *Communication & Sport, 2*(2), 127–131.

Sands, R. (2008). Ethical ethnography: Epistemology and the ethics of good intentions. In M. Atkinson & K. Young (Eds.), *Tribal play: Subcultural journeys through sport* (pp. 353–377). Bingley: JAI Press.

Simons, H. & Usher, R. (Eds.) (2000). *Situated ethics in educational research.* London: Routledge.

Smith, B. (2013). Disability, sport, and men's narratives of health: A qualitative study. *Health Psychology, 32,* 110–119.

Sparkes, A.C. (2009). Ethnography and the senses: Challenges and possibilities. *Qualitative Research in Sport, Exercise and Health, 1*(1), 21–35.

Stoller, P. (1997). *Sensuous scholarship.* Philadelphia, PA: University of Pennsylvania Press.

Sugden, J. & Tomlinson, A. (2002). Theory and method for a critical sociology of sport. In J. Sugden & A. Tomlinson (Eds.), *Power games: Theory and method for a critical sociology of sport* (pp. 240–266). London: Routledge.

Thorpe, H. (2011). *Snowboarding bodies in theory and practice.* Basingstoke, UK: Palgrave Macmillan.

Thorpe, H. (2014). *Transnational mobilities in action sport cultures.* Basingstoke, UK: Palgrave Macmillan.

Thorpe, H. (2015). Death, mourning and cultural memory on the Internet: The virtual memorialization of fallen sports heroes. In G. Osmond & M. Phillips (Eds.), *Sports history and the internet* (pp. 180–200). Champaign, IL: University of Illinois Press.

Thorpe, H., Barbour, K. & Bruce, T. (2011). 'Wandering and wondering': Playing with theory and representation in physical cultural fields. *Sociology of Sport Journal* (Special Issue: Physical Cultural Studies), *28,* 106–134.

Tjora, A. (2006). Writing small discoveries: An exploration of fresh observers' observations. *Qualitative Research, 6*(4), 429–451.

Tuhiwai-Smith, L. (1999). *Decolonizing methodologies: Research and indigenous peoples.* London: Zed Books.

Wheaton, B. (1997). Covert ethnography and the ethics of research. In A. Tomlinson & S. Fleming (Eds.), *Ethics, sport and literature: Crisis and critiques* (pp. 163–172). Aechen: Meyer and Meyer.

Wheaton, B. (2002). Babes on the beach, women in the surf: Researching gender, power and difference in the windsurfing culture. In J. Sugden & A. Tomlinson (Eds.), *Power games: A critical sociology of sport* (pp. 240–266). London and New York: Routledge.

Wolcott, H. (1981). Confessions of a trained observer. In T. Popkewitz & B. Tabachnik (Eds.), *The study of schooling* (pp. 247–263). New York: Praeger.

11

VISUAL RESEARCH METHODS

Cassandra Phoenix and Emma Rich

Introduction

The ability to engage critically with the visual cultures and practices of sport and exercise is an important area of academic study. This is because 'the visual' is central to the cultural construction of social life in contemporary Western societies. Moreover, visual imagery is never innocent, but constructed through various practices, technologies and knowledges (Rose, 2007). This long-standing interest in 'the visual' within the social sciences is reflected by the numerous books (e.g. Banks, 2007; Huggins & O'Mahony, 2012; Margolis & Pauwels, 2011; Pink, 2007; Rose, 2012), scholarly journals (e.g. *Visual Studies, Journal of Visual Culture*) and organizations (e.g. International Visual Sociology Association, British Visual Sociology Group) dedicated to the subject of visual research methods (VRM).

Reflecting this interest, over the last decade scholarly work on the visual cultures of sport and exercise has been gaining increasing attention (see Azzarito & Kirk, 2013; Curry, 2008; Phoenix & Smith, 2011; Stewart & Floyd, 2004). Today, a plethora of topics have been embraced ranging from disordered eating in male distance runners (Busanich, McGannon & Schinke, 2016), to the sensual experiences of physical activity in older age (Orr & Phoenix, 2015), and children's sport coaching (Cope, Harvey & Kirk, 2015). This work has utilized various forms of visual materials including photographs (Mills & Hoeber, 2013), video (Houge Mackenzie & Kerr, 2012) drawings (Gravestock, 2010), 3D body scans (Tarr & Thomas, 2011), collages (Busanich *et al.*, 2016) and the Internet (Miah & Rich, 2008). In doing so, it has demonstrated the value of taking seriously the visual world of the moving body, sport and exercise as a means of enabling researchers to engage with other people's embodied experiences in ways that are empathetic, participatory and aesthetic.

The aim of this chapter is to appraise the extant literature connecting sport and exercise to its wider visual context through the use of visual research methods (VRM). The first section outlines how one might distinguish between different approaches to researching the visual and why they are important. Next, we provide a brief overview of how we might make sense of visual data, before offering a number of cautions of which scholars utilizing VRM within sport and exercise should be mindful. This is followed by a discussion of representation and communication in relation to the production of visual material as part of the 'publicness' of research (Biesta, 2014). Finally, we outline considerations for advancing VRM within the fields of sport and exercise.

Researching the visual

According to Rose (2014), VRM involve visual materials becoming part of the process of creating evidence as a means of exploring research questions. Working with VRM and media is particularly useful to the study of sport and exercise. This is because they can result in new knowledge and understanding of the phenomenon being studied. They can also provide means of communicating research knowledge to diverse audiences within and outside of the academe by 'producing knowledge differently' (Enright & O'Sullivan, 2012). For instance, mixing visual and arts-based methods creatively (see Chapter 23) can generate new ways of interrogating and understanding the social. Additionally, it is argued that VRM can overcome the 'rationalistic' tendencies of text-based approaches (Buckingham, 2009), enabling new ways to explore affect (Georgakis & Light, 2009) and embodied issues in sport and exercise. Given the fundamental part that the aesthetic plays in identity construction, 'the inclusion of non-linguistic dimensions in research, which rely on other expressive possibilities, may allow us to access and represent different levels of experience' (Bagnoli, 2009, p. 547). In this sense, they may provide distinct opportunities for research focused on the body and movement.

Working with VRM is also important owing to the potentially empowering possibilities that they present. These can enable researchers to engage with participants in more empathetic and participatory ways (see Chapters 7, 8, 33, and 34), particularly via respondent-driven methods (see section entitled 'Participant-produced images'). Indeed, in the context of visual leisure, Stewart and Floyd argue that VRM have 'tremendous potential to democratize research through an expanded accessibility of data, an enhanced transparency of argument, and an empowerment of lay people in research-based policy and planning processes' (2004, p. 445). More recently, and referring to young people in particular, Azzarito has argued that new methodological approaches are needed to enable those who participate in research, 'to "speak" meaningfully about their body experiences' (2010, p. 158). In this way, advances in VRM theories and practices have enabled ways of thinking about and with the moving body within sport and exercise cultures that are celebrated for their democratizing potential.

VRM are both multiple and diverse in terms of *what* visual materials are worked with, and the *procedures* undertaken with said materials. Some researchers utilize visual materials that they have produced themselves. Others concern themselves with materials created by the research participants. Working with 'found' visual materials is another strand of VRM.

Researcher-produced images

Qualitative researchers in sport and exercise can create images to document or analyse aspects of social life and social interaction (see Atkinson, 2010; Hockey & Allen-Collinson, 2006). This can include converting the visual perceptions of researchers into sketches and diagrams, signs, words, codes and numbers. That said, photography continues to be the primary means of documenting, representing and analysing within sport and exercise. The prevalence of photography is, perhaps unsurprising, given Prosser and Schwartz's observation that photographs 'may *not* provide us with unbiased, objective documentation of the social and material world, but they can show characteristic attributes of people, objects, and events that often elude even the most skilled wordsmiths' (1998, p. 116). As such, photographs can provide an excellent means to explore relationships that may be subtle or easily overlooked.

These relationships may be between different (groups of) people, or they may be between people and material objects. For example, informed by Callum-Swan and Manning's (1994) conceptualization of the T-shirt as a prime icon of modern life, Pope's (2010a) visual ethno-graphy of the Maadi Cup (New Zealand's major rowing competition) used photography to highlight the significance of the T-shirt within the material culture of this renowned sport-ing event. The 'wearable statements' captured through the lens of the camera connected the T-shirts directly to the context, thereby highlighting the links between sport, youth and material culture in ways that, according to Pope, may not be achieved by textual accounts alone. Indeed, the opportunity to *show* how social context impacts upon and situates people's encounters with sport and exercise cultures is an appealing characteristic of researcher-produced images. Also mindful of context, Jones, Bailey and Santos (2013, p. 657) also empha-sized this focus in their research on how coaches 'care about' and 'care for' athletes through touch (see Chapter 26). By creating images of context-specific actions (e.g. seating/standing arrangements, proximity/distance of bodies, confidence/cautiousness, palpable facial emo-tions and the (non-)touching behaviours), these authors depicted the complexities and micro-realities of learning contexts, in part through the 'depth of emotional engagement displayed by the coaches as they constantly tugged, proposed, judged, patted, scowled at, comforted and occasionally hugged their charges'.

Rather than photographing the interactions that shape the social context of sport and exercise, a slightly different approach is to create visual imagery of the *moving body* as a means to gain insight into 'what it's like' to be/become familiar with a particular state of embodi-ment. Interested in what it *felt like* to be physically active as an older body, yet mindful of the difficulties in accessing sensory knowledge (see, for example, Samudra, 2008), Orr and Phoenix (2015) created images of physically active older adults *doing* their chosen activity. They used the images as an *aide-mémoire* for the participants in a follow-up interview, where they were asked to view and reflect on the images while describing what it was like to *do* their activity. Despite highlighting a number of logistical challenges and unanticipated outcomes that were encountered with this method, Orr and Phoenix concluded that their approach had enabled researcher and participant to 'grasp at' the embodied and sensorial nature of physi-cal activity in older age, beyond what could be achieved in the context of a more standard life-story interview.

Elsewhere, Merchant (2011) also created visual data – this time in the form of underwater videography – as a means of developing a multi-sensuous methodology (see Chapter 26) that 'captured' the embodied moments of tourists 'becoming' divers as they learned to liberate themselves from the endless pull of gravity. What differs in this approach, compared to that of Pope (2010a) and Jones *et al.* (2013) outlined above is the combined use of visual data collection with how audiences experience and respond to visual data 'in the body'. As Merchant explains, this combination can facilitate a mimetic and multi-sensual understanding of the participants' experience through the gaze of the researcher, while also encouraging participants to 're-view, re-sense and bring to cognition non-cognitive ways of knowing, through a sensuously engaged "audience studies" approach' (2011, p. 69).

Participant-produced images

A second strand of visual research revolves around the collection and study of images produced or consumed by the subjects of the research. Here, the power of the image-creating device (be it a camera, a pencil, a paintbrush) is turned over to the research participants to document the images or footage they choose. This is commonly followed by an interview, where they discuss the material that they've produced and the meanings ascribed to it. Working *with* participants in this manner can provide another layer of insight into individual lives by enabling researchers to view the participant's world through their eyes. It can also provide participants with a sense of agency and opportunity to speak for themselves, and subsequently help to erase the traditional power imbalance between researcher and participant (Packard, 2008; Pink 2007). Moreover, participants are able to use their bodies and the space around them to '*show*' rather than just '*tell*' about their lives (Riessman, 2008). For these reasons, this form of data collection has been recognized as especially useful for understanding the experiences of marginalized groups (e.g. see Hill & Azzarito, 2012).

Although this strand of visual research *could* involve researchers in the field spending time with participants as they watch televised sporting events, look through health and fitness magazines, or construct their own videos or photographs of physical cultures, within qualitative research in sport and exercise, to date photovoice in particular (also known as 'autophotography') has been the method of choice (see D'Alonzo & Sharma, 2010; Phoenix, 2010; Chapter 34, this volume). This is perhaps unsurprising given the well-documented advantages to using this method. For example, in their work with Aboriginal youth, McHugh, Coppola and Sinclair (2013) explained how photovoice facilitated an enjoyable, process-orientated and insightful participatory research setting (see Chapter 8) with the Aboriginal youth who were involved in their research into the multiple meanings of sport. Moreover, the activity of discussing participant-produced images enabled specific cultural practices (e.g. offering of tobacco to traditional knowledge keeper) to be observed by the research team.

Elsewhere, reflecting on their participatory-action research with teenage girls (see also Pope, 2010b), Enright and O'Sullivan also make clear the benefits of photovoice, arguing that it enabled them to 'access knowledge which students are often unwilling to share through other methods' (2012, p.45).

More recently, Thorpe (2016, p. 22) sets out a research agenda for action sports and suggests that there are 'valuable opportunities' for sports researchers to include social media and other new technologies (e.g. drones, go-pro cameras) as part of their methods. Given the prevalence of the everyday use of these technologies, she calls 'for more rigorous discussions about how digital environments are being incorporated into our research'; an issue we revisit below. Less common forms of participant-produced visual data within studies of sport and exercise, are those involving arts-based research methods. Like photovoice, arts-based methods are minimally structured, enabling research participants to impose their own forms of organization and expression (see Bagnoli, 2009; Gillies *et al.*, 2005). Many of these methods involve drawing; an activity which provides participants with time to reflect on the issues being explored (Gauntlett, 2007). Drawing *takes* time, but drawing can also *depict* time in ways that may not be possible when producing still images with a camera. Given the significance of temporality within sport, exercise and the lives of those engaging with it (personal bests, training cycles, injury time, match and rehabilitation, athletes' biographical time, and so forth; see Allen-Collinson, 2003; Phoenix, Smith & Sparkes, 2007), there are numerous avenues for theoretical, methodological and empirical development here. Sheridan, Chamberlain and Dupuis's (2011) narrative-based research project on fatness and weight loss provides an example of using arts-based methods in the form of graphical elicitation, or more specifically, 'timelining'. Informed by Gergen and Gergen's theoretical representations of narrative form and 'temporal arrangements of events relevant to goal' (1986, p. 37), timelining has the capacity to provide understandings and interpretations of the past, and how pasts shape presents and futures (Sheridan *et al.*, 2011). Indeed, the focus on temporality is what distinguishes timelining from many of the other visual research methods signposted in this chapter (see also video diaries in Cherrington & Watson, 2010; and Susan Bell's visual narrative/photo diary of breast cancer, in Riessman, 2008).

'Found' visual data

There are various ways in which researchers might work with pre-existing visual representations. Visual material is a ubiquitous part of everyday life, existing in the form of media, art work, data archives, advertising, maps etc., and can be found in many different sport and physical-activity contexts (schools, commercial sector, media, entertainment etc.). These forms of pre-existing data might be explored either by researchers, or by research participants in participatory-action approaches. In either case, although the images are not produced by participants or researchers, there are still aspects of subjective judgement whereby particular visual material is deemed appropriate or relevant and selected for inclusion in the research.

Radical transformations in technology mean that new forms of visual material are constantly being produced and often in more complex and intersecting ways. Moreover, the realization of a digital society (Lupton, 2014) has promoted developments in methodological practices. Reflecting the shift from web 1.0 to web 2.0 over the past decade, masses of visual material are being produced as a result of the expansion of digital practices that permeate people's everyday lives (see Chapter 27). The ubiquitous presence of digital devices means that people now have the opportunity to capture visual material through mobile and wearable technologies (e.g. with GPS) and upload it to platforms such as Flickr, Facebook, Wikis, Apps, YouTube and Instagram. These digital-data practices can be seen 'both as the objects and conduits of enquiry' (Lupton, 2014, p. 46). In this sense, digital technologies provide new ways of undertaking visual methods; first, by producing new forms of visual data; and second, by digital devices and practices being used to visualize social data in particularly engaging and effective ways.

There is a proliferation of research focused specifically on sport and social media addressing a range of issues such as blogging (Bundon & Hurd Clarke, 2015), the use of new media by sports fans (Ozsoy, 2011) and social media for pedagogical change (Goodyear, Casey & Kirk, 2014). Researchers can now explore a range of social issues pertaining to sport and exercise through *material produced* through these platforms and shared publicly. As an example, Quennerstedt, Flintoff and Webb (2013) utilized narrative construction to analyse YouTube clips from 285 Physical Education (PE) lessons from 27 different countries. The data offered insights into embodied experiences of PE practices and provided an opportunity to juxtapose narratives from teachers and students. They argue that using social-media platforms such as YouTube, as forms of visual data 'is one way to get close to social practices and everyday situations of young people' (Quennerstedt *et al.*, 2013, p. 2). To this end, advances in technology have offered new routes into lives and embodied practices of various social groups. Another focus has been to examine the *use of visual material* by sport and exercise companies and organizations, given the growing market in mobile health apps that relate to physical activity and lifestyle. Images are an important aspect of the 'app' and such images might be analysed in relation to their affective/emotional significance (see García, Welford & Smith, 2015). For instance, analysis of the discourses inflected in the images of bodies found in weight-loss and fitness apps and trackers gives insight into contemporary health practices (Rich, forthcoming).

One might also examine how new digital technologies enable different *practices of the production* of visual material, for instance, by examining how they mediate embodiment and the presentation of self in public arenas. It is now well recognized that through participatory applications such as wikis, blogs and social media there exist opportunities for people to be the producers, rather than just the consumers of knowledge. To this end, there are also opportunities to examine how visual cultures can challenge or disrupt dominant sport and exercise practices. The interpretation of images available in social media and other digital platforms can provide insights into various social issues related to identity, embodiment, inequality and power. For example, the rise of the 'selfie' photograph (Rettberg, 2014) and the constitution of digital subjectivities (Warfield, 2015) may provide important insights into how individuals constitute their identities in particular moments within sport or physical cultural sites. Geurin-Eagleman and Burch (2016) for example, examined Olympic athletes' self-presentation on Instagram, revealing how sexually suggestive images were by far the most popular. Similarly, Emmons and Mocarski (2014) used branding theory and content analysis to examine the Facebook profile photos of professional athletes' profile photos, revealing hegemonic gender portrayals.

Making sense of visual data . . . with cautions and caveats

Visual materials can be analysed in a myriad of different ways (see Margolis & Pauwels, 2011; Riessman, 2008; Rose, 2012; Van Leeuwen & Jewitt, 2001). For example, researchers can choose to focus on interpreting the composition (e.g. content, colour, spatial organization, and so forth; see Hardin, Lynn & Walsdorf, 2005) of images ('*compositional interpretation*'), quantifying the characteristics of an image ('*content analysis*', see Delorme & Testard, 2015), examining how images make meaning ('*semiology*', see Osmond & Phillips, 2011), identifying how ideological discourses are articulated through various images ('*discourse analysis*', or '*visual narrative analysis*', see Griffin, 2010; Chapters 18 and 20, this volume), and exploring the ways in which audiences engage with visual materials ('*audience studies*', see Phoenix and Griffin, 2013). Discussing the strengths and weaknesses of these various forms of analysis and outlining how each are employed is beyond the scope of this chapter. This information can be found in the works signposted above. Instead, we focus our attention on a number of cautions and caveats of which qualitative researchers in sport and exercise should be mindful when making sense of visual data via analyses such as those outlined above.

First, although 'how to' texts can be a welcomed provision for anyone about to embark upon VRM within sport and exercise, we maintain the importance of creativity and artfulness that accompanies the interpretation of qualitative data. Analysis is a *craft* that is learned through doing (and indeed feeling), and researchers should be cautious of using what might be offered as *guidelines for approaching analysis* as a rigid and formulaic set of procedures that allow no room for analytic creativity, reflexivity, recognition of the co-produced nature of knowledge and visual material, nor methodological development. This, however, is not to suggest that 'anything goes' when it comes to making sense of images. Researchers must fully justify their interpretation of visual imagery by offering a detailed account of their methodology and methods, regardless of their theoretical stance (Rose, 2012).

Second, despite the varied forms of analyses available to scholars interested in VRM within sport and exercise, the dominance of photovoice and other photo-elicitation studies have resulted in an overreliance on the somewhat descriptive compositional interpretations and subsequent content analysis of associated qualitative interviews. Furthermore, while there is a tendency to focus on the 'depicted' (e.g. 'bodies' in sports advertisements or media), there may be useful insights generated through a focus on the 'representational practices' (Pauwels, 2010), particularly given the rapid developments in digital technologies and opportunities for consumers to now produce their own visual material. The phenomenon of social media, for example, is, after all as much about the 'producers' of visual material as it is about what is being produced. Thus, our analytical interest may do well to extend even further and incorporate the *production* of the visual material. This would involve being attentive to the complex interplay between cultures/contexts, representational practices and power relations through which visual material is mediated, along with the historical, social and cultural contexts of visual production.

Third, the varying ways in which visual materials can be theorized, contextualized and analysed undoubtedly adds to the rich potential of VRM within sport and exercise. Yet the assumption that *all* visual approaches will be mutually compatible and theoretically coherent with each other is a naive one. Rather, while plurality ensures vibrancy within a scholarly area, it can also challenge researchers who seek to understand similar issues from different perspectives (Pink, 2011). Thus, a reflexive sociology of knowledge about the approaches to making sense of visual data is needed. Data analysis is part of the process through which we (co-)produce knowledge, and in this sense and this regard requires degrees of reflexivity.

Rose provides a useful starting point here by encouraging a 'critical visual methodology'. Elaborating further on this, she explains:

> [B]y 'critical' I mean an approach that thinks about the visual in terms of the cultural significance, social practices and power relations in which it is embedded; and that means thinking about the power relations that produce, are articulated through, and can be challenged by, ways of seeing and imagining.
>
> *(Rose, 2012, p. xix)*

These criteria provide the means by which one's chosen method of analysis is then evaluated. Indeed, one of the challenges of working with existing or 'found' visual data is having a sufficient understanding of the technological, sociocultural, historical and political contexts in which the visual material was produced. We urge caution in subscribing to the view that these existing materials provide a simple window into the cultures, bodies or identities they are depicting. The issue of empiricism is a long-standing debate within visual research (see Banks, 2001; Buckingham, 2009; Pink, 2007), with increasing recognition that visual materials are not objective and neutral, but socially constructed and mediated through power relations, and produced in particular historical, sociocultural and political moments.

Our fourth caution relates to both operational and ethical challenges for researchers employing VRM – and there are many! Both of these aspects can impact upon the quality/usability of the data collected and, therefore, any subsequent analysis. For example, with certain groups, the quality/usability of participant-produced data will be dependent on recruitment, photography training and the retrieving of consent forms from those who may be peripheral to a project but captured on film (Novek, Morris-Oswald & Menec, 2012). The rate of production and sheer volume of material enabled by the recent advances in technology can complicate processes of 'selecting' what's deemed (by whom?) to be appropriate data (see Orr & Phoenix, 2015). Moreover, the blurring of private and public spaces (Papacharissi, 2009) in digital environments presents ethical dilemmas arising from the readiness to upload images and videos of seemingly intimate aspects of our lives into public spaces. Increasingly younger people are developing their own social-media sites and utilizing apps such as Tumblr and Pinterest to develop media spaces oriented around issues such as pro-anorexia/orthorexia, overexercising, self-harm, steroid use, extreme body modification and drug use. These social-media platforms work to present a multitude of body images that are available to young people, both normative and resistant to norms and accepted body sizes and health states. Whilst self-presentation online presents a common point of interest for researchers of social-networking sites, the public sharing of information and images about one's body and health will both present unique insights but also a series of ethical challenges. None of this is to forget of course, that the (ethical) challenges inherent to collecting and making sense of visual data often include the very process of gaining ethical approval for the research to take place (see Miller, 2015).

Visual data and publicness

Another aspect of contemporary VRM is the use of visual materials to develop research outputs to represent the research. Although Pink (2007) argued that interventionist-based research has been regarded as a 'hidden' part of VRM history, in recent years, the drive in higher education towards 'Impact' and 'Public Engagement' has meant these elements of visual research are being more recognized as an integral part of the research process. This has drawn attention to the more creative forms of output that develop engagement with various publics.

One such approach is to make public the artwork/visual representations produced by research participants. A rationale for this is that visual practices such as participatory video may have democratizing potential and political implications (Buckingham, 2009). Another is that visual material is multisensory (see also Chapter 26) and can thus stimulate affective responses from those who encounter it through the use of hearing, touching and other senses (Pink, 2006). These aspirations were evident in Azzarito's (2012) visual participatory ethnographic study of physical activity with young people, using digital cameras to create visual diaries entitled *Moving in My World*. Azzarito makes clear that a goal of the research 'was to allow outcomes of the students' work to remain in the research setting' (2012, p. 298). To achieve this, some of the digital photography from the participants' visual diaries was included in exhibitions in community art centres, local museums and schools. In this regard, Azzarito (2012) considers such visual processes to be 'pedagogical tools' that enable students to speak to the public.

Participant-produced visual material is not the only way in which an exhibition or other public event can be created. Rich and O'Connell (2012) describe the process through which Rich's (2010) research on young people's experience of surveillant health policies and practices was the subject of artwork produced by artists for an exhibition entitled *Body Culture*. This involved artists working alongside Rich and O'Connell (curator) to interpret and co-produce an art exhibition that spoke to the research findings. Exhibits included photographs, conceptual sculpture and performance art. In reflecting on this process Rich and O'Connell suggest that the use of visual material to translate and communicate findings, provides an interdiscursive space through which sociocultural meanings of the body and physical activity can be negotiated, resisted and re-imagined in public arenas. However, one of the questions that researchers face in developing more public-facing visual material is the extent to which it is to be contextualized (e.g. through an accompanying text/narrative) or left open to interpretation.

Whatever the visual medium, these approaches attempt to develop what Biesta (2014) describes as *publicness*. With a myriad of tools and processes now available for producing visual material, there is increasing recognition of the importance of the 'representational practices as cultural expressions in relations to what the visuals depict' (Pauwels, 2010, p.11). There is not space to detail the various digital visualizing tools that might be used for (re)presenting social data/research. However, imaginative, creative visualisations of research through digitized imaging technologies (Graham, Laurier, O'Brien & Rouncefield, 2011) play an important role in the relationship between research and 'publicness' (Biesta, 2014).

Moving VRM forward

Having presented a review of some of the existing approaches and challenges of using VRM, we now discuss some of the opportunities for sport and exercise research emerging from the practices and innovations in visual studies more broadly. As Pink (2012) observes, since the turn of the twenty-first century, visual methodologies have continued to develop in innovative, divergent and exciting ways. Whilst there are certainly examples of sport and exercise research drawing on creative visual approaches, we would argue that development of VRM within sport and exercise could be advanced further by a more critical engagement with advances in broader visual studies. In this vein, we would question whether sport and exercise research has kept pace with some of the innovations and debates within contemporary VRM. As an ongoing endeavour, this means engaging with the complexities of a range of issues including, but not limited to: technical expertise; methods; media and modes/types of representation; relationships between theory technology and practice; and ethics.

More specifically, in relation to technical expertise, there has tended to be a focus on camera-based imagery (photographs, videos) within VRM in sport and exercise.

Whilst clearly important, related fields may benefit from an engagement with other visual aspects of sport and exercise as forms of data. Indeed, when appropriate for the research question, and with due consideration given to arising ethical issues (e.g. see Mok, Cornish & Tarr, 2015), we propose that new insights are likely to be derived when researchers draw from the full range of (contemporary) VRM. These might extend to include, for example, citizen media (Rich, 2011), or intersecting more closely with the 'mobilities turn' (Urry, 2007) through the use of mobile methods (Büscher, Urry & Witchger, 2011) such as geo-narratives (Bell, Phoenix, Lovell & Wheeler, 2015) or video telephony (Morel & Licoppe, 2011). The technical expertise of researchers may be a barrier to engaging with more creative and diverse forms of visual material. Whereas professionals (e.g. photographers, artists, technicians) can be involved extremely productively in more challenging technical projects, there may also be occasions where different understandings of the cultural contexts, regarding appropriate forms of (re)presentation, can contrast with those of the academic team (see Rich & O'Connell, 2012). These representational concerns may mean 'balancing the dual researcher roles as artist and messenger'; a task requiring the necessary expertise to deal with these different aspects of the visual process (Galman, 2009, p. 198).

With regards to theoretical grounding, we would urge qualitative researchers in sport and exercise engaging with VRM to go beyond merely 'doing it', and instead, commit to situating their research and findings within the broader literatures of, for example, visual studies, cultural studies, human geography and history, to name but a few. Not only will this help to advance knowledge within our own discipline, it will also allow for more comprehensive and convincing justifications for use that go beyond the all too common 'provide more insight'. In the instance of VRM, we would argue that 'more' is not necessarily better or useful, and researchers should employ caution when lamenting claims of 'value added' (see Jones, Fonseca, De Martin Silva & Davies, 2015). Similarly, the increased accessibility of new technologies that have the capacity to generate novel kinds of data, combined with increasing demands to be ever more 'innovative' in our (funded) research can, in some instances, be nothing more than a distraction. Just because you *can*, does not necessarily mean you *should*. While methodological advancements are a welcome development within VRM in sport and exercise, for their full value to be realised (methodologically, theoretically, empirically), they must – first and foremost – serve the need of the theoretically informed research question.

Sport and exercise VRM could benefit from a more critical theoretical approach to deal with the increasingly complex production and representation of visual material.

This would involve a greater degree of engagement with its political and ethical dimensions, so as to make clear the social relationships, ethical issues, processes of representation and the social contexts in which the research is produced and disseminated. For example, Prins (2010) suggests that while participatory photography projects have potential benefits, cameras can operate as a technology of surveillance and control. Elsewhere, Enright and O'Sullivan (2012) have questioned the point at which co-discussions and analyses of participant-produced images can become nothing other than voyeuristic.

At this juncture we ask how qualitative researchers in sport and exercise will engage visual approaches in order to undertake research within our new technological and digital societies. What advances are necessary to make sense of the emerging, diverse and multimodal/media forms of visual material that are now a feature of contemporary sport and exercise practices (e.g. websites, social-media applications)? How will advances in the digital and technology shape the methodological practices within qualitative research in sport and exercise? The answers to these question lie in the extent to which scholars within the field are prepared to engage with the production, practices and cultural significance of the visual in a more rigorous and complex way; a way that takes seriously the interconnections between disciplines, and between theory and method. In part, this may mean a willingness to become connoisseurs of a broader range of approaches – their strengths *and* limitations – and to avoid supplanting one knowledge form with another; defences may be quick to materialize when particular visual approaches are proclaimed to be *the right* way of doing things. Furthermore, while several authors caution against naive realism, and the assumption that the visual provides a means of 'accessing' some inner truth that can't be articulated through words (e.g. emotions), Buckingham suggests 'this caution has not always extended to the practice of research' (2009, p. 232). Qualitative researchers in sport and exercise must, therefore, be wary of what Piper and Frankham describe as an 'uncritical celebration of representation' (2007, p. 373), and reflexively acknowledge the role of the research and production practices, particularly when working with marginalised groups. VRM have been much celebrated as providing unique insights, but we would argue, however, that the methods themselves *do not* provide access to data that is somehow more 'authentic'.

As these different approaches, theories and practices are debated within Visual Studies alongside reviews of the state of the field and calls for developments (Margolis and Pauwels, 2011), it is a timely opportunity for sport and exercise scholars to contribute to these wider debates. This will lead to pertinent questions about the future of our own disciplinary practices. In this regard, we hope the current chapter provides a useful stepping stone in this endeavour.

References

Allen-Collinson, J. (2003). Running into injury time: Distance running and temporality. *Sociology of Sport Journal*, *20*(4), 331–50.

Atkinson, M. (2010). Fell running in post-sport territories. *Qualitative Research in Sport and Exercise*, *2*(2), 109–132.

Azzarito, L. (2012). Photography as a pedagogical tool for shedding light on 'bodies-at-risk' in physical culture. *Visual Studies*, *27*(3), 295–309.

Azzarito, L. (2010). Ways of seeing the body in kinesiology: A case for visual methods. *Quest*, *62*(2), 155–171.

Azzarito, L. & Kirk, D. (2013). *Pedagogies, physical culture, and visual methods*. London: Routledge.

Bagnoli, A. (2009). Beyond the standard interview: The use of graphic elicitation and arts-based methods. *Qualitative Research*, *9*(5), 547–570.

Banks, M. (2001). *Visual methods in social research*. London: Sage.

Banks, M. (2007). *Using visual data in qualitative research*. London: Sage.

Bell, S.L., Phoenix, C., Lovell, R. & Wheeler, B.W. (2015). Using GPS and geo-narratives: A methodological approach for understanding and situating everyday green space encounters. *Area*, *47*(1), 88–96.

Biesta, G. (2014). Making pedagogy public: For the public, of the public or in the interest of publicness. In J. Burdick, J.A. Sandlin & M.P. O'Malley (Eds.), *Problematizing public pedagogy* (pp. 15–25). New York: Routledge.

Buckingham, D. (2009). 'Creative' visual methods in media research: Possibilities, problems and proposals. In J. Hughes (Ed.), *Sage visual methods* (vol. 31, pp. 227–247). London: Sage.

Bundon, A. & Hurd Clarke, L. (2015). Unless you go online you are on your own: Blogging as a bridge in para-sport. *Disability and Society*, *30*(2), 185–198.

Busanich, R., McGannon, K.R. & Schinke, R.J. (2016). Exploring disordered eating and embodiment in male distance runners through visual narrative methods. *Qualitative Research in Sport, Exercise and Health*, *8*(1), 95–112.

Büscher, M., Urry, J. & Witchger, K. (2011). *Mobile methods*. London: Routledge.

Callum-Swan, B. & Manning, P.K. (1994). What is a T-shirt? Codes, chronotypes and everyday objects. In S.H. Higgins (Ed.), *The socialness of things: Essays on the socio-semiotics of objects* (pp. 415–434). Berlin: Mouton-de-Gruyter.

Cherrington J. & Watson, B. (2010). Shooting a diary, not just a hoop: Using video diaries to explore the embodied everyday contexts of a university basketball team. *Qualitative Research in Sport and Exercise*, *2*, 267–281.

Cope, E., Harvey, S. & Kirk, D. (2015). Reflections on using visual research methods in sports coaching, *Qualitative Research in Sport, Exercise and Health*, *7*(1), 88–108.

Curry, T. (2008). Where the action is: Visual sociology and sport. *Social Psychology Quarterly*, *71*, 107–108.

D'Alonzo, K.T. & Sharma, M. (2010). The influence of marianismo beliefs on physical activity in mid-life immigrant Latinas: A photovoice study. *Qualitative Research in Sport and Exercise*, *10*, 229–249.

Delorme, N. & Testard, N. (2015). Sex equity in French newspaper photographs: A content analysis of 2012 Olympic Games by L'Equipe. *European Journal of Sport Science*. DOI: 10.1080/17461391.2015.1053100.

Emmons, B. & Mocarski, R. (2014). She poses, he performs: A visual content analysis of male and female professional athlete Facebook profile photos. *Visual Communication Quarterly*, *21*, 125–137.

Enright, E. & O'Sullivan, M. (2012). Producing different knowledge and producing knowledge differently: Rethinking physical education research and practice through participatory visual methods. *Sport, Education and Society*, *17*, 35–55.

Galman, S. (2009). The truthful messenger: Visual methods and representation in qualitative research in education. *Qualitative Research*, *9*, 197–217.

García, B., Welford, J. & Smith, B. (2015). Using a smartphone app in qualitative research: The good, the bad and the ugly. *Qualitative Research*, DOI: 10.1177/1468794115593335.

Gauntlett, D. (2007). *Creative explorations: New approaches to identities and audiences*. London: Routledge.

Georgakis, S. & Light, R. (2009). Visual data collection methods for research on the affective dimensions of children's personal experiences of PE. *ACHPER Australia Healthy Lifestyles Journal*, *56*(3/4), 23–28.

Gergen K. & Gergen, M. (1986). Narrative form and the construction of psychological science. In T.R. Sarbin (Ed.), *Narrative psychology: The storied nature of human conduct* (pp. 22–44). New York: Praeger.

Geurin-Eagleman, A. & Burch, L.M. (2016). Communicating via photographs: A gendered analysis of Olympic athletes' visual self-presentation on Instagram. *Sport Management Review*, *19*(2), 133–145.

Gillies, V., Hardeon, A., Johnson, K., Reavey, P., Strange, V. & Willig, C. (2005). Painting pictures of embodied experience: The use of nonverbal data production on the study of embodiment. *Qualitative Research in Psychology*, *2*, 199–212.

Goodyear, V.A., Casey, A. & Kirk, D. (2014). Tweet me, message me, like me: Using social media to facilitate pedagogical change within an emerging community of practice. *Sport, Education and Society*, *19*, 927–943.

Graham, C., Laurier, E., O'Brien., V. & Rouncefield, M. (2011). New visual technologies: Shifting boundaries, shared moments. *Visual Studies*, *26*, 87–91.

Gravestock, H.M. (2010). Embodying understanding: Drawing as research in sport and exercise. *Qualitative Research in Sport and Exercise*, *2*, 196–108.

Griffin, M. (2010). Setting the scene: Hailing women into a running identity. *Qualitative Research in Sport and Exercise*, *2*, 153–174.

Hardin, M., Lynn, S. & Walsdorf, K. (2005). Challenge and conformity on 'contested terrain': Images of women in four women's sport/fitness magazines. *Sex Roles*, *53*, 105–117.

Hill, J. & Azzarito, L. (2012). Representing valued bodies in PE: A visual inquiry with British Asian Girls. *Physical Education and Sport Pedagogy*, *17*, 263–276.

Hockey, J. & Allen-Collinson. J. (2006). Seeing the way: Visual sociology and the distance runner's perspective. *Visual Studies*, *21*, 70–81.

Houge Mackenzie, S. & Kerr, J.H. (2012). Head-mounted cameras and stimulated recall in qualitative sport research. *Qualitative Research in Sport Exercise and Health*, *4*(1), 51–61.

Huggins, M. & O'Mahony (2012). *The visual in sport*. London: Routledge.

Jones, R., Bailey, J. & Santos, S. (2013). Coaching, caring and the politics of touch: A visual exploration. *Sport, Education and Society, 18*, 648–662.

Jones, R.L., Fonseca, J., De Martin Silva, L. & Davies, G. (2015). The promise and problems of video diaries: Building on current research. *Qualitative Research in Sport, Exercise and Health, 7*, 395–410.

Lupton, D. (2014). *Digital sociology*. London and New York: Routledge.

Margolis, E. & Pauwels, L. (Eds.) (2011). *The Sage handbook of visual research methods*. London: Sage.

McHugh, T-L.F., Coppola, A.M. & Sinclair, S. (2013). An exploration of the meanings of sport to urban Aboriginal youth: A photovoice approach. *Qualitative Research in Sport Exercise and Health, 5*, 291–311.

Merchant, S. (2011). The body and the senses: Visual methods, videography and the submarine sensorium. *Body & Society, 17*, 53–72.

Miah, A. & Rich, E. (2008). *The medicalization of cyberspace*. London: Routledge.

Miller, K. (2015). Dear critics: Addressing concerns and justifying the benefits of photography as a research method. *Forum: Qualitative Social Research, 16*, 27.

Mills, C. & Hoeber, L. (2013). Using photo-elicitation to examine artefacts in a sport club: Logistical considerations and strategies throughout the research process. *Qualitative Research in Sport, Exercise and Health, 5*, 1–20.

Mok, T.M., Cornish, F. & Tarr, J. (2015). Too much information: Visual research ethics in the age of wearable cameras. *Integrative, Psychological and Behavioural Science, 49*(2), 309–322.

Morel, J. & Licoppe, C. (2011). Studying mobile video telephony. In M. Büscher, J. Urry & K. Witchger (Eds.), *Mobile methods* (pp. 164–182). London: Routledge.

Novek, S., Morris-Oswald, T. & Menec, V. (2012). Using photovoice with older adults: Some methodological strengths and issues. *Ageing & Society, 32*, 451–470.

Orr, N. & Phoenix, C. (2015). Photographing physical activity: Using visual methods to 'grasp at' the sensual experiences of the ageing body. *Qualitative Research, 15*, 454–472.

Osmond, G. & Phillips, M.G. (2011). Enveloping the past: Sport, visuality and museums. *The International Journal of the History of Sport, 28*(8–9), 1138–1155.

Ozsoy, S. (2011). Use of new media by Turkish fans of in sport communication: Facebook and Twitter. *Journal of Human Kinetics, 28*, 165–76.

Packard, J. (2008). 'I'm gonna show you what it's really like out here': The power and limitation of participatory visual methods. *Visual Studies, 23*, 63–77.

Papacharissi, Z. (2009). The virtual geographies of social networks: A comparative analysis of Facebook, LinkedIn and A Small World. *New Media & Society, 11*, 199–220.

Pauwels, L. (2010). Visual sociology reframed: An analytical synthesis and discussion of visual methods in social and cultural research. *Sociological Methods & Research, 38*, 545–581.

Phoenix, C. (2010). Auto-photography in aging studies: Exploring issues of identity construction in mature bodybuilders. *Journal of Aging Studies, 24*, 167–180.

Phoenix, C. & Griffin, M. (2013). Narratives at work: What can stories of older athletes do? *Ageing and Society, 33*, 243–266.

Phoenix, C. & Smith, B. (Eds.) (2011). *The world of physical culture in sport and exercise: Visual methods for qualitative research*. London: Routledge.

Phoenix, C., Smith, B. & Sparkes, A.C. (2007). Experiences and expectations of biographical time among young athletes: A life course perspective. *Time & Society, 16*(2/3), 231–252.

Pink, S. (2007). *Doing visual ethnography* (2nd ed.). London: Sage.

Pink, S. (2011). Foreword. In C. Phoenix & B. Smith (Eds.), *The world of physical culture in sport and exercise* (pp. x–xi). London: Routledge.

Pink, S. (2012). Advances in visual methodology: An introduction. In S. Pink (Ed.), *Advances in visual methodology* (pp. 3–16). London: Sage.

Piper, H. & J. Frankham (2007). Seeing voices and hearing pictures: Image as discourse and the faming of image-based research. *Discourse: Studies in the Cultural Politics of Education, 28*, 373–87.

Pope, C.C. (2010a). Talking T-shirts: A visual exploration of youth material culture. *Qualitative Research in Sport & Exercise, 2*, 133–152.

Pope, C.C. (2010b). Got the picture? Exploring student sport experiences. Using photography as voice. In M. O'Sullivan & A. MacPhail (Eds.), *Young people's voices in physical education and youth sport* (pp. 186–206). London: Routledge.

Prins, E. (2010). Participatory photography: A tool for empowerment or surveillance? In J. Hughes (Ed.), *Sage visual methods* (vol. 8, pp. v4–221–v4–239). London: Sage.

Prosser, J. & Schwartz, D. (1998). Photographs within the sociological research process. In J. Prosser (Ed.), *Image-based research: A sourcebook for qualitative researchers* (pp. 115–129). London: Falmer Press.

Quennerstedt, M., Flintoff, A. & Webb, L. (2013). Narratives from YouTube: Juxtaposing stories about physical education. *Sage Open, 3*(4), 1–10.

Rettberg, J.W. (2014). *Seeing ourselves through technology: How we use selfies, blogs and wearable devices to see and shape ourselves.* Basingstoke, UK: Palgrave Macmillan.

Rich, E. (2010). Obesity assemblages and surveillance in schools, *International Journal of Qualitative Studies in Education, 23*, 803–821.

Rich, E. (2011). London 2012 and new legacies of learning: Citizen media as public pedagogy. *Culture @ the Olympics, 13*, 27–33.

Rich, E. (forthcoming). Childhood, surveillance and mHealth technologies. In E. Taylor & T. Rooney (Eds.), *Surveillance futures: Social and ethical implications of new technologies for children and young people.* Oxon, UK: Routledge.

Rich, E. & O'Connell, K. (2012). Visual methods in physical culture: Body culture exhibition. In M. Atkinson & K. Young (Eds.), *Qualitative research on sport and physical culture* (pp. 101–127). Bingley, UK: Emerald Press.

Riessman, C.K. (2008). *Narrative methods for the human sciences.* London: Sage.

Rose, G. (2007). *Visual methodologies: An introduction to the interpretation of visual materials.* London: Sage.

Rose, G. (2012). *Visual methodologies: An introduction to researching with visual materials* (3rd ed.). London: Sage.

Rose, G. (2014). On the relation between 'visual research methods' and contemporary visual culture. *The Sociological Review, 62*, 24–46.

Samudra, J.K. (2008). Memory in our body: thick participation and the translation of kinesthetic experience. *American Ethnologist, 35*, 665–681.

Sheridan, J., Chamberlain, K. & Dupuis, A. (2011). Timelining: Visualizing experience. *Qualitative Research, 11*, 552–569.

Stewart, W.P. & Floyd, M.F. (2004). Special issue introduction: Visualizing leisure. *Journal of Leisure Research, 36*, 445–460.

Tarr, J. & Thomas, H. (2011). Mapping embodiment: Methodologies for representing pain and injury. *Qualitative Research, 11*, 141–157.

Thorpe, H. (2016). Action sport, social media and new technologies: Towards a research agenda. *Communication and Sport*, DOI: 10.1177/2167479516638125.

Urry, J. (2007). *Mobilities.* Cambridge, UK: Polity Press.

Van Leeuwen, T. & Jewitt, C. (2001). *Handbook of visual analysis.* London: Sage.

Warfield, K. (2015). Digital subjectivities and selfies: The model, the self-conscious thespian and the #realme. *The International Journal of the Image, 6*, 1–16.

12

MEDIA RESEARCH

From text to context

Brad Millington and Brian Wilson

In this chapter we critically examine the practice of studying sport and exercise media. We do so by first asking *what* (sport) media research is in the first place – an important question in a time of proliferating technologies for representing sporting experience. We then ask *why* one would study sport and exercise media. This is a complex question too, and one that we answer by pointing to the role of media in shaping social norms and impacting on people's sense of identity. Our third question is the 'how' question: *How* do researchers go about studying media once it has been established that this type of work is important? Finally, we conclude this chapter with reflections on the challenges and rich opportunities that lie in the practice of sport and exercise media studies at the current moment in time.

There are two main points that are featured across this analysis. The first is that, whether studying media production, representation and/or consumption, in our view researchers must be attuned to the relationship between media texts and/or media experiences and their surrounding conditions. In other words, media research should be contextualised; media is significant in large part due to the circumstances in which meaning is made. The second point is that both sport psychology and the sociology of sport provide useful 'tools' for the study of sport and exercise media. Not just that, there is much to be gained by strategically bringing these academic disciplines together where possible.

What is media research?

The answer to this first question rests on another, more basic question: what is media? Experience is always *mediated* in some way – even face-to-face communication relies on language to mediate between people. John Fiske's (1990) distinction between *presentational* media (the voice, the face, the body), *representational* media (texts such as books, writing, photographs, and paintings), and *mechanical* media (transmitters of these first two categories, such as radio and television) is therefore instructive (p. 18). Communication scholars have historically been interested in *mass* media: the transmission of meaning from 'one' to 'many' through (mechanical) media well-suited to this purpose (e.g., newspapers). The arrival of *digital* media (see also Chapter 27), however, has complicated media studies. Digital media (sometimes called 'new' media) generally allows for user-generated content, and 'many' to 'many' communication (Creeber & Martin, 2009). Consider, for example, how a social medium like Twitter allows the rapid proliferation of multiple voices around different sport- and exercise-related topics, as opposed to forcing consumers into much slower avenues for self-expression, such as letters to newspaper editors. Digital media also allows for 'convergence': the idea that content can now 'flow' across multiple media platforms (or mechanical media) with ease (Jenkins, 2006, p. 2). It needs to be kept in mind across these terms that media technologies themselves and media experiences are constructed entities. As Lisa Gitelman puts it, media involves '*socially realized* structures of communication' (2008, p. 7; emphasis added).

Media *research*, then, involves the systematic study of media. Typically, media research is focused on at least one of three interconnected elements of a media circuit, or life cycle: media production, representation, or consumption. Production studies are often focused on the activities and aims of media producers themselves. As Clarke and Clarke (1982) long ago surmised, there is an 'invisible apparatus' behind the glitzy shows and films (among other texts) we consume (cf. Silk, 1999). This 'apparatus' involves the production technologies that help in the creation of media texts, as well as the decisions of media producers such as directors and editors. John Hartley (2011) adds that researchers studying production are at times concerned with what is termed the 'political economy' of media, meaning the patterns of media ownership and control that can influence the decisions that media producers actually make. By Silk, Schultz and Bracey's (2008) assessment, the 2004 film *Miracle*, focused on the true story of the American men's ice hockey team's 'miraculous' victory against their high-powered Soviet counterparts in the 1980 Olympics, offered a comforting (or 'sanitized') depiction of historical events (e.g. by emphasising themes such as patriotism and bonding through sport). To Silk, Schultz and Bracey, this was not surprising, as Disney was behind the production of *Miracle*, and Disney is generally inclined towards family-friendly entertainment.

To study representation, meanwhile, is to study the products of media production with an eye towards the meanings or values they privilege – as well as those they omit. The presumption in this case is that media texts like films, once 'delivered' into the world, can be meaningful in ways both intended and unintended by media producers. For example, a text can have *intertextual* significance in the sense that it takes on new or different meaning given the other texts that surround it (Kristeva, 1984; cf. Darnell & Sparks, 2005). The narrative of a film like *Miracle*, while based on true events, is also powerful given its familiarity; it resonates intertextually with other sport films that likewise feature 'impossible' underdog performances (some of which are also produced by Disney). Advertising presents another good example of intertextuality at work. Consider, for example, the strategic placement of television commercials: beer and car adverts might be shown during American football telecasts, and might also emphasise some of the telecast's same themes (e.g. that men should be confident, rugged and 'in control'). Thus, in such cases, there would be a close thematic relationship ('inter') between the adverts and the programmes during which they're shown ('texts') – hence, 'intertextual'.

Finally, consumption studies ask, how do people actually consume media, and what impact does media have on their lives? Researchers studying representation and production are in a way concerned with consumption in that they typically consider *potential* ways in which media texts are consumed. Media consumption studies engage media viewers/consumers directly, asking them what they think about (for example) the themes that seem to be emphasised in a magazine (or series of magazines), where and when they read particular magazines, with whom they partake in such activity (maybe magazine consumption is a vehicle for bonding among friends?), and other questions of this kind. In sport and exercise studies, it is (unfortunately) relatively rare that media researchers actually engage with viewers/users of media. This is perhaps because consumption studies are typically time- and resource-intensive (Plymire, 2005), although this is not a very good excuse! It is also worth noting that, with the proliferation of digital media, the facile divide between media production and consumption – and thus the study of these processes – becomes much blurrier. Consumers are sometimes better understood as 'prosumers' (Ritzer, Dean & Jurgenson, 2012): someone watching a film like *Miracle* today might also tweet about it, write a lengthy Facebook post, and/or contribute to an online fan forum in which they critically reflect on the film with others (Norman, 2014). Said otherwise, people might produce media texts at the same time that they consume them.

Why study media?

If we adopt a wide-angle view in our research, one informed mainly by disciplines like sociology, cultural studies or cultural sport psychology, media is important in affecting what is considered 'normal' within certain sociohistorical conditions. This is the first 'why' of media studies: it is important to study media because media texts make some things (ideas, values, body types, and so on) out to be normal and others, even if by implication, out to be abnormal or deviant. Another way of saying this is that media is about *power*, since making something out to be normal and another thing out to be deviant can have implications for how we understand people and groups. Researchers with differing ontological perspectives on power (meaning, with differing views on the nature of power relations) may differ somewhat in conceptualising these broad implications of media communication. A critical realist perspective on power – which is to say, one that sees power as something that is held by some people and groups through the intentional or direct marginalisation of others – would likely characterise media as *ideologically* potent. This potency lies in the capacity for media texts to subtly or overtly reinforce understandings of particular ideas or practices as being 'normal' compared to others – a process known as hegemony. As Kellner writes, for example, when it comes to politics:

> Media culture produces representations that attempt to induce consent to certain political positions, getting members of the society to see specific ideologies as 'the way things are' (i.e. that too much government is bad, that government deregulation and free markets are good, that protecting the country requires intense militarization and aggressive foreign policy, and so on).
>
> *(Kellner, 2000, p. 59)*

As another example, so common is it for sport media to emphasise a particular ideological view of masculinity that Messner, Dunbar and Hunt (2000) argue that a *de facto* 'Televised Sports Manhood Formula' is at work. This provides 'a remarkably stable and concrete view of masculinity as grounded in bravery, risk taking, violence, bodily strength, and heterosexuality' (p. 392). This 'formula' is produced across texts such as sports highlight shows, American football broadcasts, professional wrestling programmes, beer commercials and other types of adverts. Another way of saying this is that the 'Televised Sports Manhood Formula' is promoted *intertextually*.

In contrast to a critical realist approach, where power is understood as something that is held by some people/groups at the expense of others, a post-structuralist view would see power less as an entity to be held and more an *outcome* that arises through the circulation of 'discourse' (i.e. practices, statements, technologies, ideas, and so on). Think of the difference this way: those adopting a critical realist position tend to see identity as fairly stable, and power as something that operates in a dualistic sense (between empowered business owners and disempowered workers, for example); those adopting a post-structuralist view see identity as much more fragmented (one is not just a worker, but also an athlete, a mother, a daughter, an artist, etc.) and power as something that, accordingly, 'flows' in multiple directions. From the latter point of view, the masculinist character of sport media described by Messner *et al.* (2000) follows from the 'conditions of possibility' that make representing sport and masculinity in rather narrow fashion something that is 'doable' in the first place. These 'conditions' might involve the 'truths' of masculinity that reign at a particular moment in time, the communication infrastructure that allows for the dissemination of knowledge on masculinity, and the gendered organisation of media institutions, among other things. Note that a post-structuralist view does not deny that power relations exist. Quite the opposite: power is everywhere, as is opposition to power. Foucault's axiom that power is necessarily accompanied by resistance has been influential for researchers studying sport in general, and sport media in particular. Marie Hardin (2011) offers one example of this in describing the Women Talk Sports blog network and its critical and pluralist response to the dominant perspectives on gender and sport that stem from mainstream media outlets.

Why study sport and exercise media? A first reason, then, is that media helps in creating or stabilising our sense of what is normal and/or deviant – recognising that one's understanding of this process can vary depending on one's ontological positioning. A second reason pertains to the impacts of media at the 'micro' level, meaning the way media relates to one's sense of self.

As Blackman and Walkerdine (2001) recount, for some time a psychology-influenced 'effects' tradition prevailed in the study of how people engage with media. A key assumption underlying this work is that media can sway individuals directly – especially those who are particularly vulnerable – often by offering distorted images of reality. As Blackman and Walkerdine (2001) write: 'The psychological literature documents a range of "media effects" in relation to the "problem of the vulnerable individual", from behavioural disturbances, increased aggression and arousal, to a range of psychopathological symptoms' (p. 40). Some of the literature on violence in sport media and its effects on young athletes can be situated within this tradition. Young and Smith (1988/89) offered a thorough synopsis of this literature as it pertains to ice hockey, at a time when sport media still centred on print publications and television. While laboratory and field experiments had shown that subjects 'exposed to filmed or televised models displaying aggression tend to exhibit similar behaviour when subsequently given the opportunity' (p. 299), Young and Smith note that results from these controlled environments do not translate perfectly to the 'real world'. More convincing in their assessment is research that suggests young athletes learn about violent sporting behaviour from media representations, without the guarantee that they will follow through on this newfound knowledge (e.g. Young, 1986). Young and Smith also present the argument that sport media violence *legitimises* violence – a point that aligns with the critique of sport-media ideology outlined above. The overall point here is that, for some time, the question 'why study media?' would have been answered by saying 'because media texts have *direct* effects on individuals'.

The effects tradition, however, eventually came under criticism for being too deterministic (as Young and Smith suggest). Blackman and Walkerdine (2001) themselves vouch for an approach to understanding media at a 'micro' level that moves in another direction – in their description, 'a radically different way of approaching the relationship between psychology and the media' (p. 47). This is an approach that sees media experience as an active process of developing a sense of selfhood – and a sense of 'otherness'. Why study media? Not because we are necessarily influenced (or 'brainwashed') by TV shows, films, websites and so on, but because media texts are *resources* in people's lives that can become part of the process of making sense of oneself and others. In saying this, Blackman and Walkerdine (2001) also caution against replacing a vision of consumer passivity and vulnerability with one of unimpeded agency. Their point is that there is no original, autonomous form of personhood that media experience 'affects'; 'We relate to ourselves "as if" we are selves of a particular kind, and representations of the "other" confirm this form of selfhood as ideal, normal and natural' (p. 48). Sonia Livingstone (1998) makes a similar case in characterising television programmes as texts and not stimuli, and in suggesting they provide 'multiple yet *bounded* paths for the reader' (p. 171; emphasis added).

An example of a study that puts to work an understanding of media influences and identity along these lines is the work of McGannon *et al.* (2012) on the magazine *Runner's World* (RW). From McGannon *et al.*'s 'cultural sport psychology' (CSP) perspective, 'identities are complicated, multi-dimensional and fluid, depending upon the broader narrative(s) within which they are formed' (p. 827). This supposition is borne out in these authors' (2012) textual and visual analysis of two issues of *Runner's World* (RW) – both focused on the British long-distance runner Paula Radcliffe. A general 'pregnancy and motherhood as redemption' narrative cuts across the magazine texts with which McGannon and her colleagues are concerned. That is to say, pregnancy and motherhood are depicted in *RW* as crucial to allowing Radcliffe to live a more fulfilling and complete life than elite athlete status (allegedly) allows in itself. From there, *RW* frames two contrasting Radcliffe identities: (1) 'elite athlete and mother as one' (i.e. compatibility between these two roles); and (2) 'primarily a mother, athlete as secondary' (i.e. whereby a mothering role takes precedence). Of course, McGannon *et al.*'s (2012) analysis is focused on representation; we might well presume that consumers of these texts – what with their own unique identities – are likely to be variously swayed by *RW's* messaging.

For these purposes, McGannon *et al.*'s (2012) research is instructive as much for its disciplinary approach as it is for its key findings. While we would not insist that sport media researchers align themselves with these authors' CSP perspective, in general we see their willingness to assemble different disciplinary conventions (in their case, those of cultural studies and psychology) as a productive inclination. Ryba and Wright (2005) similarly vouch for the integration of cultural studies and sport psychology. Once entwined, 'the athlete is considered to be a subject of multiple discourses and various identifications, a member of numerous social and cultural groups, and a part of sport as an institution immersed in a particular sociocultural and historical context' (2005, p. 204). We would add that sport-media producers and consumers are likewise dispersed in their identifications, and can be influenced by the contexts in which they are situated.

How can we study sport media?

The question as to why one would study sport media thus can be answered by pointing to the role of media in influencing the discourses or norms that hold sway in particular contexts and to media's ability to help shape a sense of identity and otherness among individuals (without presuming media will have direct, necessary effects). To move from this response to the question we are concerned with in this section – how can we actually go about studying sport media? – requires consideration of research methods and methodology.

Here we are influenced by Andrews and Giardina's (2008) review of the emergence of research on sport and physical culture, or what is now commonly known as physical cultural studies (PCS) – a scholarly (sub)discipline that, like cultural sports psychology, is influenced to a great extent by the cultural studies research tradition (and particularly its British inflection via the Birmingham Centre for Contemporary Cultural Studies). For Andrews and

Giardina (2008), PCS revolves around a radical form of 'contextualism' – which is to say a heightened emphasis on the role of context in shaping possibilities for human experience. What this means methodologically is that researchers need to pay careful attention to – even begin from – the contexts in which the 'objects' of their research are situated. According to Andrews and Giardina: 'Unearthing the socially and historically contingent matrix of social, economic, political, and technological articulations represents the primary method of contextual cultural studies' (2008, p. 406). Certainly PCS researchers are not the only ones to value contextual analyses of this kind; the Marxist axiom that people make their own histories, but not under conditions of their own choosing, suggests that such a perspective has a lengthy history. Still, the emphasis on context in PCS and cultural studies in general is especially pointed.

From this initial point of assessing social, economic, political and technological contexts, Andrews and Giardina (2008) advocate the use of 'secondary' research methods to analyse 'that which is under scrutiny' (p. 407). Here research methods such as interviews, focus groups and participant observation come to the fore as ways of assessing how objects, ideas and practices emerge within wider circumstances (see Andrews, Mason & Silk, 2005). On this matter, Lawrence Grossberg's view on empiricism is instructive:

> I believe that one can and should use any and every kind of empirical method . . . Use them as rigorously and as suspiciously as you can. . . . I am in favor of anything that helps you gather more and better information, descriptions, resources, and interpretations.
>
> *(Cited in Wright, 2001, p. 145)*

What does this mean for research on sport media? We would not insist that researchers align themselves with a particular research tradition (in this case, physical cultural studies); indeed, the studies highlighted below are not all informed by the PCS literature. But we do see great value in assessing media production, representation and consumption in and of themselves, *and* in relation to the wider circumstances in which they are situated. This is borne out in past research on sport and exercise media.

Take the work of Silk and Amis (2000) on media production and the 1998 Commonwealth Games in Kuala Lumpur, Malaysia, for example. On the one hand, Silk and Amis were interested in contextualizing television coverage of this event, and as such they examined formal documents and policies related to the Games, such as the Malaysian Government's Vision 2020 strategy. The aim of this strategy was to 're-engineer the social, political, and economic climate of Malaysia by the year 2020' (Silk & Amis, 2000, p. 277) – something that, when brought to bear on the host broadcaster, meant pressure to promote 'the best' Malaysia had to offer. Indeed, when Silk and Amis then turned to 'secondary methods', such as interviews with television producers and participant observation of media production as it unfolded, they found that broadcasters in fact felt pressure to emphasise particular images and themes. For instance, and given their understanding of the context surrounding the Games, it made sense to Silk and Amis when a television director shouted at camera operators during a rugby match to 'pick out Malaysians in the crowd' (p. 288). The desire to create a spectacle of nationalism filtered down into specific production practices.

Silk and Amis' (2000) methods and findings are not unlike those from an earlier study by MacNeill (1996) focused on television coverage of ice hockey at the 1988 Winter Olympics. What one might notice in reading either of these studies is how methods for studying media are not always unique to media studies. Both Silk and Amis (2000) and MacNeill (1996) used interviews and participant observation, which can be applied in studies of all kinds. The main difference is that these researchers directed their attention towards 'tools', processes and relation-ships involved in making meaning through media. Consider MacNeill's comments on where she 'looked' in her own research on (sport and exercise) media:

> Ethnographic observations focused on a multitude of factors during the fieldwork, including in-crew relations, interview relations, work routines, organizational struc-tures, the social use of media technology, the decision-making process, struggles and negotiations over meaning and broadcasting practice occurring during production, and the choice of representational codes used to depict hockey.
>
> *(MacNeill, 1996, p. 105)*

As in Silk and Amis' (2000) work, MacNeill (1996) also *contextualized* these observations through historical, archival and document analyses focused on the political and economic context in which the CTV broadcasts were situated.

How can we study sport media? In the case of production, the answer is to employ tradi-tional methods like interviews and focus groups, but direct these towards issues such as how and why media producers make certain decisions. If we shift to consumption, the answer is much the same. Our own research is instructive in this regard (Millington & Wilson, 2010a, b).

What we explored in our sport and exercise media research was how young males under-stand depictions of masculinity in media (including sport and exercise media), and how they understand and experience masculinity in other aspects of their lives – Physical Education in particular. The first part of this research (how young males understand masculinity in media) is quite clearly related to our interest in this chapter (methods for studying media). Our research was built specifically from Messner *et al.*'s (2000) aforementioned study of masculinity on TV, and the finding therein that a 'Televised Sports Manhood Formula' is prominent in texts such as American football broadcasts. Even with this important finding in hand, however, Messner *et al.* (2000) still express caution in assuming that media 'fits' into young people's (and especially young males') lives in direct and predictable fashion. 'It is not possible,' these authors write in conclusion, 'based merely on our textual analysis of sports programs, to explicate precisely what kind of impact these shows, and the Televised Sports Manhood Formula, have on their young male audiences. That sort of question is best approached through direct research with audiences' (Messner *et al.*, 2000, p. 392). Our research took up this call through focus groups with young males, where we asked about their media-viewing habits and their perceptions of the domineering masculinities that Messner *et al.* (2000) found to be so common in media texts.

But what about the second part – exploring how these same participants understand and experience masculinity in other aspects of their lives? Why not just stop after our media-themed focus groups? Above we described how researchers for some time presumed that audiences are quite vulnerable when it comes to media such as television – the idea being that media has direct effects. But, in the 1980s, a 'new generation' or 'new wave' of audience studies arose whereby researchers were much more apt to think of media consumers as *active* in nature: yes they might be swayed by a particular television programme, but so too might they develop an 'oppositional' reading that rejected the ideas that media producers (presumably) hoped they would embrace (see Alasuutari, 1999). This was soon followed by a 'second generation' of studies that went even further; namely, researchers went beyond interviews and focus groups (typical of the 'first generation') by actually situating themselves in contexts where media was consumed. Ann Gray (1992), for example, spent time in family households to better understand the gendered power dynamics that existed around the use of VCR technology for watching video tapes. Then came a 'third generation', whereby the aim was to understand media as part of people's wider experience. As Pertti Alasuutari (1999) writes, 'The third generation resumes an interest in programmes and programming, but not as texts studied in isolation from their usage in everyday life' (p. 34).

We were influenced by this 'third generation' of studies. It was important to us to know how young males understand messages about masculinity in media, given both the Televised Sports Manhood Formula and the still-lingering tendency to assume that youth are vulnerable when it comes to their experiences with media. But we did not want to study media as something completely separate from other aspects of life. We chose to focus on PE (Physical Education) as well since researchers have shown that school-based PE is a discipline that tends to promote similar ideas to media when it comes to masculinity (i.e. that boys should be aggressive and competitive; e.g. see Brown & Evans, 2004). With this in mind, what we added to the study design were focus groups with the same young males on the subject of their PE experiences (taking place well after focus groups on media), participant observation of PE classes and interviews with PE teachers on the topic of masculinities in the school setting. Note once again the use of traditional methods – focus groups, interviews, and observation – in the practice of studying media.

What we found in our first focus groups (on media) was that the young males in our research were in fact quite *critical* of the media depictions of masculinity described by Messner *et al.* (2000). Take this exchange, for example:

Researcher:	Does the media, you find, give you guys real portrayals of men and masculinity?
Allan:	Not often.
R:	No? How so Allan?
A:	Well, you see 'Roid Droids like the Strongman pulling trucks . . .
Cal:	Or like Bowflex ads.
A:	You need the chiseled abs. Yeah, it's good to be healthy and work-out and stuff like that, but I think that [they're not] healthy, [they're strong] . . . [It's] excess in the portrayal of masculinity.
R:	What do you mean by excess?
A:	Like you need 500 girlfriends and all these steroids . . . and a huge mansion and stuff like that to be a man.

(See Millington & Wilson, 2010b, pp. 1676–1677)

This passage followed from a video montage we showed to all of the young male participants in our research with the goal of 'triggering' discussion by showing male characters in different roles (e.g. a mixed martial arts fight, a professional wrestling match, a figure-skating competition). If strong, aggressive, risk-taking masculinities have become hegemonic in media, this is a *counter-hegemonic* inclination on the part of two adolescents, Allan and Cal, as well as other research participants expressing similar views.

At the same time, however, our other methods – focus groups on the topic of PE, interviews with teachers, and participant observation in PE classes – yielded a different finding from that which emerged in discussing media. Namely, hegemonic masculinity was generally *valued* by young males in PE, with 'weaker' boys and female students seen as unsuited for PE's rough and tumble environment. Said otherwise, participants who were in one sense critical of aggressive, domineering male personae in media often *adopted* such a persona when partaking in a PE culture that tends to reward such behaviour (e.g. by privileging violent games). This was quite a contradiction! And while we will not go into full detail here on how we made sense of these findings, the important point for these purposes is that employing multiple methods in the task of understanding media helped deliver a nuanced view of our contemporary media culture. Our findings on media suggest it is indeed problematic to presume that media directly impacts on young males (as might be assumed through the lens of the 'effects' tradition of research), as young people can be critical media consumers. But our findings also suggest that young people do not necessarily act on their critical media skills in other parts of their lives. The PE climate is well suited to aggressive and competitive masculinities, and so it made sense for young males to engage in behaviour that seemingly clashed with their critical media sensibilities when entering this environment.

Two more example studies can help us answer the question, how can we study media? Here we shift from research on media production and consumption to the study of texts themselves – that is, of media representation. Representation studies are, generally speaking, less about examining lived processes and more about bringing analytical 'tools' to bear on texts themselves. Returning to research by McGannon, Cunningham and Schinke (2013), their study of news media reports on ice-hockey star Sydney Crosby's 2011 in-game concussion employed a method of 'ethnographic content analysis' – 'a form of media analysis used to explore how meanings are created and communicated within media via the verification of prior theoretical relationships, while maintaining an openness to the emergence of new concepts' (p. 893; cf. Altheide, 1996). Indeed, in analysing 68 news articles on Crosby's concussion, McGannon *et al.* (2013) relied on a coding process that used themes from the sport psychology and sociology literatures (e.g. 'playing through pain and injury', 'questioning Crosby's masculinity') while also allowing for the possibility that unexpected findings to emerge. With multiple researchers involved in the study, McGannon *et al.* (2013) also allocated space in their coding documents for the research team to comment on how themes identified in the analysis and coding stage were similar to or different from one another.

Thus, data in McGannon *et al.*'s (2013) study involved headlines and direct quotations from the selected news media reports – and not, as in the case of the studies of production and consumption outlined above, data from interviews, focus groups and observation. Note, however, that much like the studies described above, McGannon *et al.* (2013) are attuned to the significance of specific 'things' (in this case, news media reporting on Crosby's concussion) in relation to wider discourses and events. In fact, 'ethnographic content analysis' is *inherently* calibrated towards contextualized analyses, given that data is coded in part with key themes from existing research in mind. For McGannon and her colleagues (2013), the media's framing of Crosby's concussion as a 'cautionary tale' (among other findings) can be understood vis-à-vis the wider ice-hockey culture that has traditionally valorised risk-taking and neglecting pain and injury.

To be sure, 'ethnographic content analysis' is far from the lone method for studying media representation. As Markula and Silk (2011) describe, for example, there are multiple forms of *discourse* analysis that can be deployed to make sense of media texts – all of which are directed towards understanding how meaning 'lives' within texts and how texts resonate within their wider conditions. As one case in point, Markula and Silk (2011) recount how Silk, Schultz, and Bracey (2008) followed a cultural-studies approach to discourse analysis in their aforementioned study of the film *Miracle*. That is to say, Silk *et al.* (2008) began from a 'close reading' of the film (step 1) and identification of its key narratives and structure (step 2). They then outlined how the film privileged certain meanings (step 3), and in doing so noted its depiction of masculinity and nationalism in the face of adversity, among other themes. An intertextual analysis then situated the film in relation to other texts (step 4). The film was then located in a wider context (step 5) in which other key actors (e.g. government officials) were privileging 'us' vs. 'them' messaging and American patriotism. Finally, in asking 'why this text now?' (step 6), Silk *et al.* (2008) understood *Miracle* as a text that made sense given the moment of its release. It was 'part of the 'sanctioned' sporting texts that were mobilised in the affective substantiation of the geo-political trajectories of the Bush Administration' (Markula & Silk, 2008, p. 128).

Conclusion: challenges and possibilities in the study of sport media

What, why and how: the study of sport media generally involves studying production, representation and/or consumption; this is important work in that media holds the ability to shape norms or discursive formations at a broad level, and influence one's sense of self and otherness on a personal level; methodological approaches that investigate production, consumption and representation in and of themselves (e.g. through interviews, observation, or discourse analysis), and their relevance to particular cultural, economic, political and technological conditions are in our view particularly informative. Such studies also hold potential for political engagement. As Carrington (2001) writes:

> Being able to deconstruct the dialogic processes within a Nike commercial is one thing; connecting them to the exploitative economic production of the shoes themselves in Southeast Asia, through to their consumption in the deprived inner-cities of the West, and the meanings this produces, is quite another, and a process too often not addressed.
>
> *(Carrington, 2001, p. 286)*

We by no means intend to romanticize the study of sport and exercise media. This research presents challenges, many of which apply to social sciences research in general. As said above, for example, the study of media production and consumption is time- and resource-intensive. It generally requires approval from gatekeepers, adherence to sound ethical practice for research with human subjects, data collection across multiple sites, and well-formulated data-management strategies inclusive of processes such as data transcription.

Media research also presents challenges of its own. In studying representation, researchers must make strategic decisions on which and how many media texts (newspaper reports, commercials, TV broadcasts, etc.) to study. Markula and Silk provide a sampling typology for guidance in this regard. 'Extreme or deviant text sampling', for example, is where the researcher intentionally chooses information-rich cases for analysis; 'maximum variation sampling' looks across a wide selection of materials from a certain media source and/or over a particular period of time; 'criterion sampling' involves assessing texts that meet an important condition, such as a study of news reports on gold medallist athletes (Markula & Silk, 2011, p. 114).

Moreover, and as noted above, media representation has grown more complex in that consumers are increasingly able and willing to create their own representations – whether through interactive websites, social media, video games, or other digital media. The study of representation, production and consumption blur together when researchers examine media such as fan or consumer discussion forums, or the use of 'active' video games (or 'exergames'). As one case in point, the first author of this chapter recently carried out a study of exergaming in Canadian retirement centres (Millington, 2015) – one situated against a backdrop of government policies on 'active ageing' aimed at encouraging physical activity participation among seniors (see Pike, 2011). Games like *Wii Bowling* present the opportunity for dynamic, interactive consumption experiences in that the user's movements are reflected on screen – acknowledging Livingstone's (1998) aforementioned point that 'pathways' for consumers are still bounded to a great extent. And so the use of participant observation of exergaming sessions in this research, along with interviews, helped in assessing not only perceptions of media experience among participants, but also what representation within games like *Wii Bowling* 'looked like' in the end. The processes of representation, production and consumption are indeed increasingly blurred.

In sum, and while acknowledging the various and complex ways that research on sport-related media can be undertaken, fundamental questions about 'media influence' understandably linger, as claims and concerns about the potential and real impacts of sport-related media are ongoing when it comes to topics like sport-related violence, representations of the body, and portrayals of gender, disability, age, ethnicity and race. Our point is that although we recognize that researchers cannot truly 'know' the precise ways that media experience sways attitudes, perceptions or behaviours among individuals – or how particular discourses become normalized and taken for granted – questions about media influences and the processes that underlie them are unique to research in this area, as are questions about how conventional and more 'media specific' methods can be best utilized to help those interested in studying these topics.

Ultimately, and even with its many challenges, sport media research retains its importance because sport media *itself* retains its importance. As Silk *et al.* (2008) found in studying *Miracle*, media texts – like consumer and producer experiences – are important in their own right and in their contextual articulations.

References

Alasuutari, P. (1999). Introduction: Three phases in reception studies. In P. Alasuutari (Ed.), *Rethinking the media audience: The new agenda* (pp. 1–21). Thousand Oaks, CA: Sage.

Altheide, D.L. (1996). *Qualitative media analysis*. Thousand Oaks, CA: Sage.

Andrews, D.L. & Giardina, M.D. (2008). Sport without guarantees: Toward a cultural studies that matters. *Cultural Studies <=> Critical Methodologies, 8*(4), 395–422.

Andrews, D.L., Mason, D.S. & Silk, M.L. (Eds.) (2005). *Qualitative methods in sports studies*. New York: Berg.

Blackman, L. & Walkerdine, V. (2001). *Mass hysteria: Critical psychology and media studies*. Basingstoke: Palgrave.

Brown, D. & Evans, J. (2004). Reproducing gender? Intergenerational links and the male PE teacher as a cultural conduit in teaching physical education. *Journal of Teaching in Physical Education, 23*, 48–70.

Carrington, B. (2001). Decentering the centre: Cultural studies in Britain and its legacy. In T. Miller (Ed.), *A companion to cultural studies* (pp. 275–297). Oxford, UK: Blackwell.

Clarke, C. & Clarke, J. (1982). Highlights and action replays: Ideology, sport and the media. In J. Hargreaves (Ed.), *Sport, culture and ideology* (pp. 62–87). London: Routledge.

Creeber, G. & Martin, R. (2009). Introduction. In G. Creeber & R. Martin (Eds.), *Digital culture: Understanding new media* (pp. 1–10). New York: Open University Press.

Darnell, S.C. & Sparks, R. (2005). Inside the promotional vortex: Canadian media construction of Sydney Olympic triathlete Simon Whitfield. *International Review for the Sociology of Sport, 40*(3), 357–376.

Fiske, J. (1990). *Introduction to communication studies* (2nd ed.). London: Routledge.

Foucault, M. (2003). 'Truth and power'. In P. Rabinow & N. Rose (Eds.), *The essential Foucault: Selections from the essential works of Foucault, 1954–1984* (pp. 300–318). New York: New Press.

Gitelman, L. (2008). *Always already new media, history, and the data of culture*. Cambridge, MA: MIT Press.

Gray, A. (1992). *Video playtime. The gendering of a leisure technology*. New York: Routledge.

Hardin, M. (2011). The power of a fragmented collective: Radical pluralist feminism and technologies of the self in the sports blogosphere. In A. Billings (Ed.), *Sports media: Transformation, integration, consumption* (pp. 40–60) Milton Park: Routledge.

Hartley, J. (2011). *Communication, cultural and media studies: The key concepts* (4th ed.). Milton Park: Routledge.

Jenkins, H. (2006). *Convergence culture: Where old and new media collide*. New York: New York University Press.

Kellner, D. (2000). *Media culture: Cultural studies, identity, and politics between the modern and the postmodern*. London: Routledge.

Kristeva, J. (1984). *Revolution in poetic language*. New York: Columbia University Press.

Livingstone, S. (1998). *Making sense of television: The psychology of audience interpretation*. London: Routledge.

MacNeill, M. (1996). Networks: Producing Olympic ice hockey for a national television audience. *Sociology of Sport Journal*, *13*(2), 103–124.

Markula, P. & Silk, M. (2011). *Qualitative research for physical culture*. New York: Palgrave Macmillan.

McGannon, K.R., Cunningham, S.M. & Schinke, R.J. (2013). Understanding concussion in socio-cultural context: A media analysis of a National Hockey League star's concussion. *Psychology of Sport and Exercise*, *14*, 891–899.

McGannon, K.R., Curtin, K., Schinke, R.J. & Schweinbenz, A.N. (2012). (De)Constructing Paula Radcliffe: Exploring media representations of elite running, pregnancy and motherhood through cultural sport psychology. *Psychology of Sport and Exercise*, *13*, 820–829.

Messner, M.A., Dunbar, M. & Hunt, D. (2000). The Televised Sports Manhood Formula. *Journal of Sport and Social Issues*, *24*(4), 380–394.

Millington, B. (2015). Exergaming in retirement centres and the integration of media and physical literacies. *Journal of Aging Studies*, *35*, 160–168.

Millington, B. & Wilson, B. (2010a). Media consumption and the contexts of physical culture: Methodological reflections on a 'Third Generation' study of media audiences. *Sociology of Sport Journal*, *27(1)*, 20–53.

Millington, B. & Wilson, B. (2010b). Context masculinities: Media consumption, physical education, and youth identities. *American Behavioral Scientist*, *53*(11), 1669–1688.

Norman, M. (2012). Online community or electronic Tribe? Exploring the social characteristics and spatial production of an internet hockey fan culture. *Journal of Sport & Social Issues*, *38*(5), 395–414.

Pike, E.C.J. (2011). The active aging agenda, old folk devils and a new moral panic. *Sociology of Sport Journal*, *28*, 209–225.

Plymire, D.C. (2005). Qualitative methods in sport/media analysis. In D. Andrews, D.S. Mason & M.L. Silk (Eds.), *Qualitative methods in sport studies* (pp. 139–164). New York: Berg.

Ritzer, G., Dean, P. & Jurgenson, N. (2012). The coming age of the prosumer. *American Behavioral Scientist*, *56*, 379–398.

Ryba, T.V. & Wright, H.K. (2005). From mental game to cultural praxis: A cultural studies model's implications for the future of sport psychology. *Quest*, *57*, 192–212.

Silk, M. (1999). Local/global flows and altered production practices: Narrative constructions at the 1995 Canada Cup of soccer. *International Review for the Sociology of Sport*, *34(2)*, 113–123.

Silk, M. & Amis, J. (2000). Institutional pressures and the production of televised sport. *Journal of Sport Management*, *14*(4), 267–293.

Silk, M., Schultz, J. & Bracey, B. (2008). From mice to men: Miracle, mythology and the 'Magic Kingdom'. *Sport in Society: Cultures, Commerce, Media, Politics*, *11*(2–3), 279–297.

Wright, H.K. (2001). 'What's going on?' Larry Grossberg on the status quo of Cultural Studies: An interview. *Cultural Values*, *5*(2), 133–162.

Young, K.M. (1986). The killing field: Themes in mass media responses to the Heysel Stadium riot. *International Review for the Sociology of Sport*, *21*(2/3), 253–266.

Young, K. & Smith, M. (1988/1989). Mass media treatment of violence in sports and its effects. *Current Psychology: Research & Reviews*, *7*(4), 298–311.

13

USING MATERIAL OBJECTS AND ARTIFACTS IN RESEARCH

Kerry Chamberlain and Antonia C Lyons

We are intimately caught up in a material world, and things of the world surround us at all times. Sometimes these are engaged with, sometimes they demand attention, at other times they are taken for granted, or overlooked. Historically, materiality has been largely disregarded by social science disciplines, except archaeology and anthropology. However, recently there has been increasing interest in material things and material culture, most strongly within sociology and cultural studies (Hicks & Beaudry, 2010; Woodward, 2007). This chapter examines the value of considering materiality and using material objects in qualitative sport and exercise research. We outline the meanings and complexities of materiality in research and some ways different scholars have approached materiality. We examine illustrative sport and exercise research using materiality, and outline some research methods for involving materiality. We conclude with some observations on future directions for involving materiality in sport and exercise research.

Material objects have huge potential for qualitative research inquiry. They may be objects of investigation in their own right, or they may have more indirect involvements, through their potential to invoke memories and to memorialize. They may be investigated for richer meanings, for their symbolic and metonymic functions, their entanglement in subjectivities and social relationships, or more broadly as part of material culture. These delineations are somewhat artificial because in practice they are frequently bound together and difficult to separate.

We illustrate this complexity initially by considering a research project focused on a specific object, to illuminate the "multiple, complex entanglements and disjunctures" (Cook & Harrison, 2007, p. 40) that are engaged by a single object. In this example, Gibson (2012) makes running shoes (and the sports shoe store) a material focus in his autoethnographic account (see Chapter 23) of purchasing a new pair of running shoes. He describes the space of the store, with its large video display and pulsing music, and the large stylized photographic images of shoes and their sporting wearers surrounding the space. These displays are not his specific focus, but research questions about these material displays could readily be posed. Gibson notes how men's and women's shoes are displayed in separate spaces of the store, reflecting some taken-for-granted gendering of the object; interesting research questions could also be posed around this. Gibson notes the array of laptop computers used to order up specific shoes for trying on, and for customizing the desired shoes. Gibson observes the dress, bodily build and deportment of the (male) salesperson, and reflects on his likely area of sporting expertise and potential knowledge of products. Gibson is engaged by the use of a treadmill for gait analysis, and how that material technology is used to discipline Gibson, as customer, into "the prescription of shoes I did not want, but which the system declared my body needed" (p. 357). This leads Gibson to theorize how practices of consumption and spectacle are combined within the store, how bodies are treated and enabled (or not), how bodies may be extended and enhanced (by the correct shoe), how the technologization of shoes shapes sporting practices and constrains agency, and how the store reproduces societal processes of consumption, and constructs particular versions of running to the exclusion of others.

In this example, we see how a focus on a specific material object, the running shoe, and processes surrounding its purchase, can offer interesting and provocative insights into the nature of sport and how it is constructed in a consumerist society. We also gain insight into the nature of the body as a running and enabled body, and how the material technology surrounding a particular sport can shape the embodied sportsperson. We gain a glimpse into the nature of subjectivity as a runner, and how the shoe selected or approved for purchase may shape this. We begin to understand the running shoe store as a space of gendered sporting consumption. We can also grasp how other methodological approaches to this research would lead to different issues being considered and different findings produced about the running shoe as an object of interest.

Approaching materiality

Using materiality in research is a complicated endeavor, as there are differing disciplinary approaches to how materiality is theorized and investigated (see Berger, 2009; Hicks & Beaudry, 2010), and a variety of ways it can be involved. For instance, many objects in our world are unnoticed, and do their work without coming into view. Miller (1987, p. 85) has labeled this as the "humility of things," commenting that:

> objects are important not because they are evident and physically constrain or enable, but often precisely because we do not "see" them. The less we are aware of them, the more powerfully they can determine our expectations by setting the scene and ensuring normative behaviour, without being open to challenge.
>
> *(Miller, 2005, p. 5)*

Hence a focus on material objects can enable researchers to bring them into view, raise questions about what they do, and explore material culture at work.

Other approaches to materiality have value for sport and exercise research. Herman (1992) outlines two distinct but overlapping approaches to the investigation of objects: one *object-centered*, with the research focused on the object itself; the other *object-driven*, where the focus moves to understanding relationships between objects and the people and cultures that make and use them. Halton argued that the "meanings of things are various, and finding out what they are requires a variety of approaches, from simply asking people what their things mean or observing how they use or do not use them, to backtracking their history, or contextualizing them in broader cultural context" (2009, p. x). Humphries and Smith (2014) offer thoughtful distinctions on the ways that objects may be researched. They were interested in the ways that objects (in their case, an early Xerox 914 photocopier machine) can be facilitators of organizational narratives, and proposed three different domains of object research. We discuss these domains below, and comment on their utility for sport research.

Humphries and Smith's (2014) first domain of research is *object biography*. Here objects, like people, are considered to have biographies – in fact, to have multiple biographies – or to have lived a variety of possible lives, with their use and function changing over time and context, and also changing in their relationships to people. Gosden and Marshall (1999) also argue that objects and people have mutual biographies, such that investigation of the multiple biographies of an object will reveal the different ways in which it is entangled with people and social practices over its life course. Humphries and Smith (2014) demonstrate how the Xerox 914 machine has had at least three lives – as an important new flagship product for Xerox; as an innovative technological device for customers; and as an historical artifact or relic for museum visitors – with each invoking different entanglements and stories. Nathan's (2012) discussion of the footballer's jacket is an example of object biography from sport. Nathan examines the life journey of John Unitas's jacket and the people who came in contact with it, showing how the jacket takes on many different meanings for those people connected with it: as a gift of friendship when originally given by the famous footballer to a friend; as both a metonym for "my relationship with my stepfather" (p. 553) and as an heirloom "to maintain and honor familial relationships and memories" (p. 554) for the current owner; as a commodity to be appraised and valued for the expert on *Antiques Roadshow* to whom it was shown; and as a historical loan item in a sports legend museum, where it promotes "reverie and nostalgia in those who experienced the Colts' 1958 win over the Giants" (p. 553).

The second domain of object research is *object materiality*, where researchers let objects speak for themselves (Humphries & Smith, 2014). Here, a close examination of the materiality of the object allows "access to the hidden stories, and significant assemblages of forces and people that interact with and change the object over time" (p. 483). Humphries and Smith's (2014) physical examination of the Xerox 914 photocopier reveals significant wear and tear that "provides an account of the complex of actors – both human and non-human – that engaged with and physically changed the object" (p. 483). They argue that the object changes as a function of its use, that its use is shaped by networks of social, economic, political, and geographical forces, and that such study of materiality can bring "a suite of actors and histories" (p. 485) into view. In the sporting context, we could examine an old wooden tennis racquet or an early carbon-fiber rowing-eight shell to explore how they were used, modified, and changed, and in doing so, similarly reveal the networks of people and forces engaged around and through the object over time.

The third domain of object research is *object practice*. Here, Humphries and Smith (2014) argue that people and objects are enmeshed in shared activities and that these practices involve "a mingling of objects and people" (p. 486). Practices govern the meanings that can be given to an object, but objects reciprocally determine the constitution of possible and potential practices in which they are engaged. The introduction of the Xerox 914 photocopier changed the way that people performed at work, and in turn these new practices informed the meanings of the photocopier as object. Similarly, Tanggaard, Laursen, and Szulevicz (2015) examined the way in which the materiality of the handball has changed the practice of handball as a sport. These authors accomplish this, reinforcing the material agency of the handball, by creatively presenting their findings as a dialogue between two handballs: one natural leather; and one synthetic leather. They use this approach alongside other research forms to demonstrate how the changing manufacture and material composition of the handball has opened new forms of play for the sport.

These three domains identified by Humphries and Smith (2014) can be difficult to separate clearly, and the arguments raised by such distinctions reinforce Pinney's (2005) comment that "any discussion of materiality that starts and ends with the object is doomed to fail. In configuring materiality as objectness, it accidentally champions one half (objects) of a binary whose other half (subjects) it wishes to attack" (p. 257). However, it can be argued that material approaches to research are actively seeking ways to give material objects more prominence in research, and to recognize the power that objects have to shape human action and performance. A similar approach is found in Actor Network Theory (ANT), which argues for a focus on nonhuman actors in interactions, and for consideration of how different actors, both nonhuman and human, interact within fluid networks of connection (Latour, 2005). ANT seeks to extend the focus from the meanings that material objects have for people who use them to include the ways objects (regarded as nonhuman actors) shape the activities and practices of human actors. As Brown states: "From this point of view, there is no stable distinction between people and things, since both make each other" (2011, p. 25). Hence ANT, by regarding objects as actors, offers objects agency within a network of human and nonhuman actors. As we saw earlier, the running shoe can shape the runner and running practice, the handball can shape the practice of the game.

ANT is not without its critics (e.g., Durepos & Mills, 2012; Ingold, 2010). Humphries and Smith, while acknowledging a debt to ANT, argue the value of a focus on objects beyond networks:

> instead of mapping the connections between objects and other actors, we advocate using an object's materiality as an inductive opening into narrative. Subsequent analysis may extend well beyond descriptions of networks and may, for example, uncover unexpected episodes and events, give voice to those excluded from networks, reveal motives for action, expose the means through which power is established and even highlight *what is not occurring*.
>
> *(Humphries & Smith, 2014, p. 484f; italics in original)*

Ingold (2010) pushes this further, disagreeing with the notion of networks, and arguing for meshwork, or enmeshed practices between things and people, reflecting Gosden and Marshall's argument about the biographies of things: "The central idea is that, as people and objects gather time, movement and change, they are constantly transformed, and these transformations of person and object are tied up with each other" (1999, p. 169). Ingold (2010) further maintains that our world is comprised, not of *objects*, but of *things*. He notes that we are surrounded by material objects, but we need these objects in order to do anything. Without ball, boots, uniforms, the pitch, grandstand, scoreboard, whistle, and the prize, competition football could not be played. Without bats, wickets and ball, a cricket game could not occur. Things are essential for all human activities, and are bound up with these activities. Further, Ingold contends that:

> the thing has the character not of an externally bounded entity, set over and against the world, but of a knot whose constituent threads, far from being contained within it, trail beyond, only to become caught with other threads in other knots. Or in a word, things *leak*, forever discharging through the surfaces that form temporarily around them.
>
> *(Ingold, 2010, p. 4)*

Ingold (2010) argues that things and people are seamlessly interconnected in lived experience, and against the duality that surrounds much work on materiality – between a position of 'brute' materiality, where things in the physical world are considered to be there independently of any presence, activity or purpose of humans, and a position where things are caught up in human activities and given significance by these purposes. Ingold contends instead for following the "fluxes and flows of materials" and the pathways and trajectories where "things continually come into being," an enmeshment of things and people: "when I speak of the entanglement of things I mean this literally and precisely: not a network of connections but a meshwork of interwoven lines of growth and movement" (Ingold, 2010, p. 3).

In a different approach, Hardy, Low, and Booth (2009) discuss how the material objects of sport have shaped sporting practices and beliefs over time. As they argue "One cannot hope to understand game rules, league dynamics or heroic performances without embracing the objects below the rhetorical surface" (Hardy *et al.*, 2009, p. 130). To accomplish this, they propose six systems of practice and belief that have existed for long periods of time across multiple sites of sporting contest: *agon*, the contest; *craft*, the skills; *community*, between athletes and spectators; *gambling*, wagering on outcomes; *eros*, of athletic bodies; and *framing*, the spectacle of sport. These systems provide a means for examining the history and enduring appeal of sport. Moving to consider "the artifacts of the arena, the field, and the court," Hardy *et al.* (2009) propose a classification of the material objects of sport: *playing equipment*; *venues*; *training equipment and sport medicine technology*; *sportswear*; *prizes*; *symbolic artifacts* (e.g., team colors, flags, mascots); *performance measurement technology*; *ephemera/detritus* (e.g., discarded tickets, betting slips); and *memorabilia* (such as collections of various kinds). They note this classification is not exclusive, since some artifacts, such as urine or blood, could fit under multiple categories; nor is it exhaustive, as it does not include artifacts created by sport, such as books and films. These classificatory systems provide a framework for their exploration of the role of material objects in sport and the material culture of sport. As they state:

> The history of skis, boards, gloves, clubs, stadiums and helmets yields great insights into the changing and enduring meanings of sport. As forms of evidence and sources of enquiry, material objects are just as important as the minutes of powerful governing bodies, the recollections of hard-driving magnates and ingenious coaches, or the daily reports and scandals conveyed in the sporting press.
>
> *(Hardy* et al., *2009, p. 148)*

These various approaches provide different ways to approach research on materiality, and a variety of theoretical positions about the nature of materiality and the place of things. In researching materiality, one needs to take a position on these issues. This is important because, in any research activity, we need to clarify our own positioning, epistemologically, theoretically, and methodologically, and ensure that our research practice is coherent, and functions to answer the research questions posited.

Researching materiality

Sport provides a rich arena for research involving material objects, given that most sports require the involvement of specific objects in their activities – running shoes, bobsleds, footballs, rugby boots, golf clubs, kayaks, *judogis*, bows and arrows, racing cycles, speed skates, rowing shells, crampons, cricket balls – and sports create a wide range of material artifacts through their practices – uniforms, flags, stadiums, photographs, news reports, prizes, sporting collections (see also Chapter 14). In this section, we discuss sport and exercise research that has utilized materiality to illustrate a variety of approaches, methods, and findings generated. We connect materiality firstly with time, memory, and history, then with the body and gender, and finally with technology and cyberspace. These are somewhat arbitrary choices; many other topics could have been included. Notably, we have not considered research on visual materials, as this is covered in Chapter 11 of this handbook.

Materiality, time, memory, and history. Material objects exert effects over time, invoking memory and nostalgia, and marking histories and transitions. Things have biographies and social lives (Appadurai, 1986), and their meanings and uses are reworked over time. The cup, when first awarded for achievement, evokes celebration and congratulation; the cup displayed in an athlete's collection twenty years later provokes pride, reminiscence, and invocation of a prior identity; the cup kept by the athlete's grandchild in a cupboard evokes memories of a different time and place. Of course the cup may never make this journey, and its life may end with the athlete's, or even earlier if it is not valued. The discarded cup, bought from an auction room, may be later awarded for a drinking contest, and thus start a new life. Objects take and give meaning through their networks, or meshworks, of use, as we saw earlier with John Unitas's jacket (Nathan, 2012). Borish and Phillips (2012) argue that considering materiality in researching sport history "widens the view" that can be gained over using documentary sources alone and can enhance interpretations: "Historians . . . gain new ways of looking at and interpreting the past when material culture serves as a serious resource of evidence" (p. 466).

One approach to this has examined public statuary of sporting figures and achievements. For instance, Stride, Wilson, and Thomas (2013) discuss the recent erection of statues of football personnel (players, managers, club founders) in the UK as important material markings of football history. Such statues provide a branding tool for football clubs, link fans to clubs, provide reference to past successes, and mark the quality and capacity of the club (as such statues are effectively luxury items). These statues invoke nostalgia, reference history, create heritage, and provide commemoration of people and events. The statues also reveal cultural values and, more pragmatically, promote tourism. Similarly, Smith (2011) considers some recently erected statues of sporting figures in the USA to show how they "exemplify the various ways professional teams, universities and communities represent sporting figures as means of honouring and remembering them, as touristic attractions and as sacred spaces for the retelling of myths" (p. 1256).

These considerations can also take us beyond history. Much commentary on objects written from the perspective of history (and museum studies) treats them as passive relics or illustrations of the active lives of the people with whom they were connected. However, as Schamberger, Sear, Wehner, and Wilson have argued: "This diminishes or obscures objects' agency in shaping a life by restricting them to memorial or representational roles, and limiting the range of their effects to impressions on a somewhat disembodied mind, rather than a sensing and perceptual body" (2008, p. 277). Rather, objects and people can be considered as having mutual biographies, and that "Material things are not external supports or measures of an internal life, but rather people and things have mutual biographies which unfold in culturally specific ways" (Gosden & Marshall, 1999, p. 173). Hence the sporting artifact in the museum is always implicated in particular ways in the lives of past users and present viewers.

Moore (2000), in discussing museums and culture, considers the football used in the 1966 FIFA World Cup match, on display in the National Football Museum in Manchester. He stresses the special significance of this ball as an item of material culture: "few objects have such resonance in English post-war history; few are capable of still meaning so much with such little interpretation" (p. 133). In discussing this commentary, Borish and Phillips note that:

> The meanings associated with the ball, however, are multilayered. As a relic of material culture, it stands for a "convergence of marketing, science and sport"; as a venerated object it has authenticity representing "innovation, Englishness and the 1960s" as well as English success, depicting a particular time when England was a powerhouse

in world football; and as a memory device it contains multiple meanings that, for observers, are shaped by personal experiences as well as larger social and interpretative frameworks . . . As an object on display at the National Football Museum, there are additional layers of meaning associated with the decision-making processes by curatorial staff, who create the story space of the display that houses the World Cup ball.

(Borish & Phillips, 2012, p. 472)

Similarly, Stride *et al.* (2013) observe how football statues can create stories that establish connections between generations and illuminate cultural meanings. Taking this in another direction, Huggins explored how the deaths of top British sports performers are culturally marked, using materiality from a variety of sources, including popular and sporting press obituaries, funeral ceremonies, burials, and monuments and tombstones (Huggins, 2008, 2012). He argued that the tombstones of sportspeople are significant material forms publicly displaying and commemorating past sporting lives, and that examining such material things "can stimulate a more critical appreciation of the historical impact of sport" (Huggins, 2012, p. 493).

Here again, we can discern the wide range of research possibilities made available through consideration of material objects, such as the statuary created around sporting achievements. Other material 'residues' of sport are equally valuable for such purposes. Johnes and Mason (2003), for instance, note that media material, both written and broadcast, and other artifacts, such as programs, ticket stubs, and stadiums, can all provide insights into sporting history. Although the research discussed above focuses mainly on materiality in research into historical aspects of sport, this focus can be readily transcended; material objects have great value in investigating issues of sporting identity, memory, and nostalgia, culture, commodification, and consumption, and so on.

Materiality, gender, and the body. Schamberger *et al.* (2008) raise issues of the material body, in the context of their research interests in the materiality of clothing. Both clothing and the body have implications for research on the materiality of sport. For example, Pope (2010) examines the visuality and materiality of T-shirts at a rowing regatta, to show how these are used as official and unofficial uniforms, as communicative devices, and as valued objects to swap, but more fundamentally to impart shared meanings of what it means to be a rower. Considerable research has examined the sporting body, especially the ways the body is experienced in sport (e.g., Allen-Collinson & Owton, 2015), and the commodification of sporting bodies in advertising and marketing (e.g., Godoy-Pressland, 2015). This research extends into an analysis of gender and how material culture is inherently implicated in gender identities, hierarchies, and power relations within sport and exercise (e.g., Waitt, 2008). We discuss examples below.

Flanagan (2014) explores one piece of clothing, the "skort" or running skirt, to highlight "the biopolitics of materiality" (p. 506). She focuses on the skirt in women's sport, and its meanings as a cultural artifact (in terms of length, style and utility), and how these sustain dominant understandings of women, femininity, and sporting abilities. The increasingly popular running skirt is said to enable versatility, comfort, and attractiveness, but as Flanagan notes, some see it as a "fashion crime" and others as a form of empowerment. Her autoethnographic study demonstrates how the skort functions as a cultural representation of (ideal) femininity, which can:

hegemonically reproduce a system of power relations that ultimately oppresses more than it liberates. That is, the emphasis on the skort's ability to be both comfortable and flattering reinforces a certain feminine ideal enacted and (re)inforced by the body under the gaze of the other.

(Flanagan, 2014, p. 510)

As a material symbol, the skort "marks the body as female, active and attractive" (p. 511), thus accomplishing particular identities. Flanagan concludes that the running skirt is a potent cultural artifact, related to power, surveillance, and identities, and linked to the commodification of embodied gendered identities in sport (Flanagan, 2014). Similarly, Gravestock examined how a material form, the ice skate, can become an integral part of the sporting body. She argues that in learning to skate the relationship between the material ice skate and the skater's body is unstable, but "when it is worn and used correctly, the skate can become an indistinguishable part of the figure skater, both visually with the aid of tights and physically, through a united movement made with the body of the skater" (2010, p. 70). The ice skate then becomes more than an extension of the body, it becomes embodied.

Considerable research addresses the embodiment of masculinity in sport, but the limited attention is given to "issues of technology and gender on the sports pitch" (Schyfter, 2008, p. 83). Schyfter uses men's lacrosse as a case for analyzing interactions between a player's body and the technological artifact of the lacrosse stick. He demonstrates how the lacrosse stick plays "a crucial role in the embodiment of skill and subsequently in the successful reproduction of a locally hegemonic masculinity" (p. 83). Material technologies are understood and used within sociocultural frameworks that include norms, expectations, and imperatives around gender (Schyfter, 2008). The material capabilities of the different sticks used in women's lacrosse limit players' ability to physically engage with others, making the game less physically forceful and noncontact, in contrast to the men's game. In men's lacrosse, skilled use of the stick includes employing it to strike at opponents' bodies and sticks, demonstrating skillful play but also enabling male players to embody a privileged masculinity. Schyfter's (2008) analysis demonstrates that the performance of masculinity "cannot be dislocated from the materiality of the technological artifact or the corporeality of the body" (p. 95). Thus the material world both mobilizes and constrains us in articulating and performing gender identities in sport (Schyfter, 2008).

Materiality extends to the physical space around us and the built environment where we live, and Kidder (2013) has explored how young male parkour athletes "transform the urban environment into a structural resource for asserting masculine gender identities" (Kidder, 2013, p. 6). Such gender performances are not simply about doing gender, but also about spatializing gender, perpetuating (not always intentionally) inequalities in sporting worlds (Kidder, 2013). Thus not only is parkour itself gendered, but so are the ways it is enacted by bodies in public spaces.

Sport and materiality in cyberspace. The last two decades have seen an enormous rise in the development of "apps" for touchscreen devices, such as smartphones and tablets. Many of these apps are focused on health and fitness, especially around weight, diet, sleep, and exercise, and many have relevance for sport. The rise of health and fitness apps reflects the contemporary preoccupation with health in Western societies. This "new health consciousness" (Crawford, 2006, p. 408) reflects an ideology that locates health problems and their solutions within the control of individuals. Consequently, health becomes an individual responsibility, framed within "lifestyles," and invoking moral demand and responsibility on individuals to maintain health. This ideological framework sustains neoliberalism, is strongly linked to consumerism, and has led to the commodification of health in the form of various products and services marketed to people to sustain personal health (Fox, 2015).

Today, thousands of people utilize wearable digital devices that self-monitor and track their biometric data, physiological functioning, movement and exercise. Many such devices are "static," merely recording users' activities and exercise, such as steps taken, time taken, or distance covered. However, the newer generation of digital devices are interactive, Internet-connected, and involve GPS technology to track and record movement and performance. Such devices allow for collecting and displaying performance more publicly and for comparisons with other performers. For example, Strava (strava.com) is a bicycling and running app, where athletes can track activities and performances, map routes taken, and record speeds achieved. On completion of a route, data can be uploaded through the app onto the Strava website, for display and comparison with others who have completed the same route. Data can include detailed analysis of the activity, including the specific route traversed, average speed, maximum speed, speed over subsections, and calories burned. The app displays a leader-board ranking performance, and individual users can set and announce challenges for the route or segments of it. The app allows for social networking so users can follow their friends' (or competitors') activities, compare performances, and set challenges, as well as post information about themselves, their sports gear, and even develop a fan base. There are many similar apps, such as Runkeeper (runkeeper.com), Endomondo (endomondo.com), Runtastic (runtastic.com), Digifit (digifit.com) and Garmin Connect (connect.garmin.com) that could be used in research.

These apps are relatively new, as is the "digital playing field" (Smith, 2015) and the "cyber-urban" (Forlano, 2015), but there is a wealth of research examining digital apps for health and fitness. However, most explore issues such as the potentiality for big-data analysis, extent of use, motivation for use, effectiveness in improving health and fitness, health-promotion opportunities, user experience, and personal health (Fox, 2015). Limited research has focused on the materiality of these devices within sport, and how they are shaping sports people and sporting practice. In one example, Smith (2015) examined how cyclists use the communicative facilities of Strava technology to enact sportsmanship and ethical practice, and how their usage can also shape the technology.

There is substantial potential for further research examining digital technologies from a material perspective. As Lupton (2013) notes, "mobile digital devices have their own social lives and histories, as they are taken up and used as part of embodied practices" (p. 400). The detailed self-monitoring that occurs through health and fitness apps has important consequences for how we understand health, embodiment, and identity (Jethani & Raydan, 2015; Lupton, 2013). Millington (2014) offers a critical commentary on personal fitness devices and the "dataveillance" (Clarke, 1988) that comes with them, particularly concerns over privacy and the enhancement of consumption. Both Lupton and Millington note how the widespread adoption of digital health devices aligns with contemporary neoliberal approaches to health and service provision. Within the sporting arena, digital cyborgs and neoliberalism are connected more strongly through the networked sporting body and the discourses of fitness and consumption.

Material methods

Investigations of materiality require methods that involve material objects. This can be achieved in a range of ways. People can produce objects during interviews that illustrate the topics under discussion, such as the tennis racquet used to win the tournament or the photograph of the winning team. Producing objects in this way can be an evocative aid to the interview, reintegrating contexts and facilitating memories. People can also be asked to bring along specific objects to a focus group, where these can be discussed and debated. Encouraging participants to bring things to interviews or focus groups leads these things to prod, focus, and enrich discussions (Collier, 1957). Alternatively, objects can be the primary focus of the interview, be it an interview with a collector about their collection of baseball cards (Nathan, 2012), with an athlete about the display of their trophies, or a visit to a childhood playing field. The go-along interview (Carpiano, 2009), as part of doing mobile research, provides another method. Going with participants to particular places, to the stadium where they played, or the gym where they trained, reintegrates the activities that occurred there and the memories for past events. Alternatively, going along with an athlete as they train enables observation of (possibly unseen or taken-for-granted) material things and contexts, and facilitates discussion about these. Also, as Miller (1987) argues, things have humility; they are often out of view, in boxes and attics, or have been lost, destroyed, or discarded, and cannot be produced for the research. This can provide an opportunity to reflect on absent objects and bring them into the present and the interview (see Hodgetts, Chamberlain, & Radley, 2007).

Sheridan and Chamberlain (2011) contend that involving material objects in research has at least four important functions. First, things can produce more narrative depth and elaboration in interviews (the football jersey with its number reminds the person that they also played in other positions on the field). Second, things can provide "proof" of the past, in that their production can be used to warrant an account or claim (the rowing crew photograph confirms the person was indeed rather small to act as stroke). Third, things can force changes and revisions in narratives when introduced, as they may not confirm the remembered story (the production of the ice skates reveals that they were hockey skates, not speed skates as thought). Fourth, things can alter the research process and the relationships caught up in it; when participants produce treasured objects, such as an exercise diary completed at the height of athletic prowess, they take risks in exposing personally meaningful material, and create potentially empathic situations between the researcher and themselves.

Future potentials

The potential for sport and exercise research focusing on materiality and artifacts is great, and there are many possible directions such research might take. We have discussed many in the sections above, and briefly extend that here. A focus on materiality could facilitate exploration of the meanings of sport and physical activity in marginalized groups, whose lived experiences may not be easily captured by more traditional methods; for example, for children with attention deficit disorder, the use of scrapbooks alongside interviews has provided insight into their experiences of everyday physical activity (Harvey *et al.*, 2012). Analysis of artifacts in combination with other methods has potential to identify the complex processes involved in developing sporting expertise, as Ollis, MacPherson, and Collins (2006) show with Rugby Union refereeing. New media practices are also highly relevant for research as material objects are increasingly transformed into digital objects, prolonging their life and extending their use, mediating between virtual and non-virtual worlds (see also Chapter 27). McManus (2015) explores this with football fans, and the ways their banners are transformed into digital objects (for example, by taking and sharing digital photos on social-networking sites), expanding links within and beyond the fan community. He argues for increased attention to "the materiality of internet media and the sensate dimensions of the fan experience" in sport research (McManus, 2015, p. 1). Research on materiality also has potential in neoliberal society, where athletes have become "commodities to be consumed selectively and self-consciously by sports fans" (Oates, 2009), through commercialized media technologies such as fantasy football and video games. Such entertainments are popular and lucrative, and frame athletes as property that is ultimately disposable in pursuit of hegemonic masculinity. They also have implications in terms of "integrating and expanding corporate reach while constructing masculine athletic subjectivity in ways that addresses deeply felt anxieties in White masculinity" (Oates, 2009, p. 31). Finally, we might also turn our attention to research practice and examine "how research performs objects: how things emerge through research practice" (Hicks & Beaudry, 2010, p. 4).

Closing comments

Throughout this chapter we have argued continually for the potential and value of involving materiality in sport and exercise research, and we hope this chapter has opened ways in which materiality research can be developed and given an increased profile within the discipline.

Involving material objects and artifacts in research and examining material culture brings methodological demands on research practice. It is essential that methods chosen can answer research questions asked; involving materiality in research requires thoughtful consideration to ensure that aims, theoretical framings, methods, analyses, and interpretations are all appropriately aligned. We should be careful not to involve material objects and artifacts simply because they offer something new and different; we should not seek innovation for its own sake (Travers, 2009), but rather be prepared to invoke innovative methods to advance the quality, depth and rigor of our research. As Wiles, Bengry-Howell, Crow and Nind (2013) comment, innovation is important in advancing research, but needs to be approached carefully so that new methods do not become codified and limiting, and restrictive of researcher reflexivity.

Much of the research cited throughout this chapter utilizes multiple qualitative methods and seeks to integrate knowledge across various aspects of our social, physical, and material worlds. Combining consideration of materiality with other research approaches is highly valuable given the multidimensional nature of the sport and exercise realm. Further, much of the discussion around materiality offered above is drawn from disciplines other than sport and exercise. There is considerable value in going beyond one's own field for ideas and inspirations, as this can foster creativity, deepen research practices, and avoid the restraints and "ruts" of our customary disciplinary practices (Smith & Perrier, 2015).

Hence, as Woodward (2015) has argued, we should expand qualitative research in sport and exercise into materiality, embrace interdisciplinarity, utilize multiple methods, and seek to hold the entanglements between our material and social worlds intact.

References

Allen-Collinson, J. & Owton, H. (2015). Intense embodiment: Senses of heat in women's running and boxing. *Body & Society, 21*(2), 2450–268.

Appadurai, A. (Ed.) (1986). *The social life of things: Commodities in cultural perspective.* Cambridge, MA: Cambridge University Press.

Berger, A. (2009). *What objects mean: An introduction to material culture.* Walnut Creek, CA: Left Coast Press.

Borish, L. & Phillips, M. (2012). Sport history as modes of expression: Material culture and cultural spaces in sport and history. *Rethinking History, 16*(4), 465–477.

Brown, S. (2011). Actor-Network Theory (ANT). In M. Tadajewski, P. Maclaran, E. Parsons, & M. Parker (Eds.), *Key concepts in critical management studies* (pp. 24–28). London: Sage.

Carpiano, R. (2009). Come take a walk with me: The "Go-Along" interview as a novel method for studying the implications of place for health and well-being. *Health & Place, 15*(1), 263–272.

Clarke, J. (1988). Information technology and dataveillance. *Communications of the ACM, 31*(5), 498–512.

Collier, J. (1957). Photography in anthropology: A report on two experiments. *American Anthropologist, 59*, 843–859.

Cook, I. & Harrison, M. (2007). Follow the thing: "West Indian Hot Pepper Sauce." *Space and Culture, 10*(1), 40–63.

Crawford, R. (2006). Health as a meaningful social practice. *Health, 10*(4), 401–420.

Durepos, G. & Mills, A. (2012). Actor-Network Theory, ANTi-history and critical organizational historiography. *Organization, 19*, 703–721.

Flanagan, M. (2014). Sporting a skort: The biopolitics of materiality. *Cultural Studies ↔ Critical Methodologies, 14*(5), 506–516.

Forlano, L. (2015). Towards an integrated theory of the cyber-urban: Digital materiality and networked media at multiple scales. *Digital Culture & Society, 1*(1), 73–92.

Fox, N. (2015). Personal health technologies, micropolitics and resistance: A new materialist analysis. *Health*. [Advance online publication] DOI: 10.1177/1363459315590248.

Gibson, K. (2012). Knight's children: Techno-science, consumerism and running shoes. *Qualitative Research in Sport, Exercise and Health*, *4*(3), 341–361.

Godoy-Pressland, A. (2015). "No hint of bulging muscles": The surveillance of sportswomen's bodies in British print media. *Journalism*. [Advance online publication] DOI: 10.1177/1464884915583770.

Gosden, C. & Marshall, Y. (1999). The cultural biography of objects. *World Archaeology*, *31*(2), 169–178.

Gravestock, H. (2013). Drawing on ice: Learning to create performance with and through the blade and boot of a skate. *Performance Research*, *18*(6), 64–70.

Halton, E. (2009). Preface. In P. Vannini (Ed.), *Material culture and technology in everyday life: Ethnographic approaches* (pp. vii–xiii). New York: Peter Lang.

Hardy, S., Low, J., & Booth, D. (2009). The material culture of sport: Toward a typology. *Journal of Sport History*, *36*(1), 1–24.

Harvey, W., Wilkinson, S., Pressé, C., Joober, R., & Grizenko, N. (2012). Scrapbook interviewing and children with attention-deficit hyperactivity disorder. *Qualitative Research in Sport, Exercise and Health*, *4*(1), 62–79.

Herman, B. (1992). *The stolen house*. Charlottesville: University Press of Virginia.

Hicks, D. & Beaudry, M. (2010). Introduction. Material culture studies: A reactionary view. In D. Hicks & M. Beaudry (Eds.), *The Oxford handbook of material culture studies* (pp. 1–21). Oxford: Oxford University Press.

Hodgetts, D., Chamberlain, K., & Radley, A. (2007). Considering photographs never taken during photo-production projects. *Qualitative Research in Psychology*, *4*, 263–280.

Huggins, M. (2008). Death, memorialisation and the Victorian sporting hero. *Local Historian*, *38*, 257–265.

Huggins, M. (2012). Gone but not forgotten: Sporting heroes, heritage and graveyard commemoration. *Rethinking History*, *16*(4), 479–495.

Humphries, C. & Smith, A. (2014). Talking objects: Towards a post-social research framework for exploring object narratives. *Organization*, *21*(4), 477–494.

Ingold, T. (2010). *Bringing things back to life: Creative entanglements in a world of materials*. [Realities Working Paper #15, 14 pages]. Available at http://eprints.ncrm.ac.uk/1306/.

Jethani, S. & Raydan, N. (2015). Forming persona through metrics: Can we think freely in the shadow of our data? *Persona Studies*, *1*(1), 76–93.

Johnes, M. & Mason, R. (2003). Soccer, public history and the National Football Museum. *Sport in History*, *23*, 115–131.

Kidder, J. (2013). Parkour: Adventure, risk, and safety in the urban environment. *Qualitative Sociology*, *36*(3), 231–250.

Latour, B. (2005). *Reassembling the social: An introduction to actor-network-theory*. Oxford, UK: Oxford University Press.

Lupton, D. (2013). Quantifying the body: Monitoring and measuring health in the age of mHealth technologies. *Critical Public Health*, *23*(4), 393–403.

McManus, J. (2015). Driven to distraction: Turkish diaspora football supporters, new media and the politics of place-making. *Sociological Research Online*, *20*(2), 12.

Miller, D. (1987). *Material culture and mass consumption*. Oxford, UK: Blackwell.

Miller, D. (Ed.) (2005). *Materiality*. Durham, NC: Duke University Press.

Millington, B. (2014). Smartphone apps and the mobile privatization of health and fitness. *Critical Studies in Media Communication*, *31*(5), 479–493.

Moore, K. (2000). *Museums and popular culture*. London: Leicester University Press.

Nathan, D. (2012). John Unitas's jacket and other objects of importance. *Rethinking History*, *16*(4), 543–563.

Oates, T. (2009). New media and the repackaging of NFL fandom. *Sociology of Sport Journal*, *26*(1), 31–49.

Ollis, S., MacPherson, A., & Collins, D. (2006). Expertise and talent development in rugby refereeing: An ethnographic enquiry. *Journal of Sports Sciences*, *24*(3), 309–322.

Pinney, C. (2005). Things happen: Or, from which moment does that object come? In D. Miller (Ed.), *Materiality* (pp. 256–272). Durham, NC: Duke University Press.

Pope, C. (2010). Talking T-shirts: A visual exploration of youth material culture. *Qualitative Research in Sport and Exercise*, *2*(2), 133–152.

Schamberger, K., Sear, M., Wehner, K., Wilson, J., & the Australian Journeys Gallery Development Team. (2008). Living in a material world: Object biography and transnational lives. In D. Deacon, P. Russell, &

A. Woollacot (Eds.), *Transnational ties: Australian lives in the world* (pp. 275–297). Canberra: Australian National University e-Press.

Schyfter, P. (2008). Tackling the "body inescapable" in sport: Body-artifact kinesthetics, embodied skill and the community of practice in lacrosse masculinity. *Body & Society, 14*(3), 81–103.

Sheridan, J. & Chamberlain, K. (2011). The power of things. *Qualitative Research in Psychology, 8*(4), 315–332.

Smith, B. & Perrier, M. (2015). Disability, sport, and impaired bodies. In R. Schinke & K. McGannon (Eds.), *The psychology of sub-culture in sport and physical activity: Critical perspectives* (pp. 95–106). London: Routledge.

Smith, M. (2011). Mapping America's sporting landscape: A case study of three statues. *The International Journal of the History of Sport, 28*(8–9), 1252–1268.

Smith, W. (2015). Communication, sportsmanship, and negotiating ethical conduct on the digital playing field. *Communication & Sport.* [Advance online publication] DOI: 10.1177/2167479515600199.

Stride, C., Wilson, J., & Thomas, F. (2013). Honouring heroes by branding in bronze: Theorizing the UK's football statuary. *Sport in Society, 16*(6), 749–771.

Tanggaard, L., Laursen, D., & Szulevicz, T. (2015). The grip on the handball: A qualitative analysis of the influence of materiality on creativity in sport. *Qualitative Research in Sport, Exercise and Health.* [Advance online publication] DOI: 10.1080/2159676X.2015.1012546.

Travers, M. (2009). New methods, old problems: A sceptical view of innovation in qualitative research. *Qualitative Research, 9*, 161–179.

Waitt, G. (2008). "Killing waves": Surfing, space and gender. *Social & Cultural Geography, 9*(1), 75–94.

Wiles, R., Bengry-Howell, A., Crow, G., & Nind, M. (2013). But is it innovation? The development of novel methodological approaches in qualitative research. *Methodological Innovations Online, 8*(1), 18–33.

Woodward, I. (2007). *Understanding material culture.* London: Sage.

Woodward, S. (2015). Object interviews, material imaginings and "unsettling" methods: Interdisciplinary approaches to understanding materials and material culture. *Qualitative Research.* [Advance online publication] DOI: 10.1177/1468794115589647.

14

DOCUMENTS OF LIFE

From diaries to autobiographies to biographical objects

Melissa Day

Introduction

This chapter examines the rich source of data provided by documents of life. First, the nature and broad range of documents of life are discussed, considering the rationale for their use in sport and exercise research. Next, this chapter focuses specifically on two prominent documents of life: autobiographies and diaries. The strengths of each of these documents of life are outlined, as well as considering their current use in sport and exercise research. While each provides a valuable source of information, it is argued that there are also some common misunderstandings. Consequently, the chapter outlines the challenges associated with using diaries and autobiographies and how these challenges may be addressed. Finally, the chapter concludes by considering future research trajectories using documents of life.

What are documents of life?

Historically, documents of life have long been considered to be of major importance by biographers and historians. Yet it is only more recently that their value in allowing us to better understand various phenomena in the social sciences has been recognized. As Plummer described:

> The world is crammed full of personal documents . . . these expressions of personal life are hurled out into the world by the millions and can be of interest to anyone who cares to seek them out. They are all in the broadest sense "documents of life."
>
> *(Plummer, 2004, p. 283)*

Thus documents of life are resources that provide us with accounts of individual experiences. These include both solicited and unsolicited accounts that "reveal the individual's actions as a human agent and as a participant in social life" (Blumer, 1979, p. 20). While the documents of life used by researchers today are still well represented by Blumer's early description, it may be further proposed that the sources that make up these documents of life have become more diverse as researchers have recognized the valuable contribution such documents can make.

Plummer (2001) highlighted that the documents of life available to qualitative researchers can incorporate a wide range of sources, ranging from letters and diaries, to biographies, life histories, self-observations, knowledge, and alternative perspectives. These documents can either stand alone or can be used as a discussion aid, allowing participants to embellish on the personal meaning of the documents in question.

The wide range of documents of life that are available to researchers illustrates their potential value for those seeking understanding about a particular phenomenon. Yet the strength of this method lies not only in its range of sources but also the wide time frame over which data may be collected. Documents of life provide the opportunity to collect data over time or to use data that represents a wide time frame, thereby acknowledging the temporal context in which the work was produced. As Sandelowski (1999) suggested, "temporal concerns are integral to qualitative research" (p. 79). Consequently, documents of life provide an invaluable resource for researchers who are interested in process and change. Further, these sources provide an additional strength in allowing us to learn from the stories and personal experiences selected by the participant. Thus the participant is afforded a high degree of control and choice over the stories that they tell.

Despite the suggested strengths of using documents of life, the social sciences have been slow to recognize the potential of this data source. In 2001 Plummer even proposed, "it [documents of life] remains the 'outsider' of much social science research" (p. 2). Similarly, authors have illustrated the lack of research using specific sources that represent documents of life. For example Stewart, Smith, and Sparkes (2011) suggested that "despite providing a potentially rich source of data within the field of sports-related studies, published autobiographies have, to date, been a neglected resource" (p. 582). Very recently though, there has been a steady emergence of research using documents of life to explore the domain of sport and exercise. In part, the emergence of this method may reflect the parallels that can be drawn between these disciplines and the health sciences. Keleher and Verrinder (2003) highlighted that health diaries have long been used to collect patient data and to record symptoms of both illness and health. Consequently, the value of recording symptoms over time and gaining the perspective of the patient may have contributed to a growing research interest in recorded experiences.

Whilst the sources available to researchers using documents of life are multiple and varied, the use and application of this method mirrors this diversity. Authors have taken a variety of approaches to using documents of life. Consequently, the aim of this chapter is not to provide a prescriptive description of how these methods should be used, but instead to provide suggestions, aids to decision-making, and outline common considerations and resolutions.

Diaries

From the multiple sources available, a prevalent method of data collection using documents of life has been the longitudinal written diary. Diaries may take various forms, including written, audio (Gibson *et al.*, 2013), or video (Jones *et al.*, 2015). They may be solicited by a researcher or unsolicited, that is, "found" without asking a participant to produce one. Diaries offer a promising method of data collection, allowing the researcher to pose key questions to the participant at specified times. Unlike many documents of life, diaries are typically solicited and thereby afford the researcher some control over the direction of the content. Yet this control is often minimal and thus successful data collection relies on the active participation of the diary writer. As suggested by Day and Thatcher (2012), when using this method the researcher must learn to live with uncertainty, discarding any expectations that the data collected will fit neatly into predetermined research questions.

There are two key decisions that should be justified by researchers when using diaries. First, is the phenomenon in question suitable for data collection using diary methods? As McFee (2009) suggested, the questions addressed by research will be reciprocally related to the methods that are used. Thus diaries are well suited to research which aims to study everyday experiences, or explore process and change. Consequently recruitment for diary studies has frequently focused on understanding the everyday experiences of specific populations. For example, this method has proved valuable in illuminating experiences of stress and coping in specific populations such as swimmers (Didymus & Fletcher, 2012), while Tamminen and Holt, 2010) examined coping in female adolescents. Further, this method has also sought to recruit participants who are deemed information-rich because of their current experiences of the phenomenon in question. Examples include the work of Sitch and Day (2014), who recruited judo athletes making weight, Wagstaff, Hanton, and Fletcher (2013), who used participants receiving one to one coaching as part of an intervention to develop emotional abilities and strategies, and Grenier, Horrell, and Genovese (2014), who recruited participants teaching physical education with a disability.

The second key decision faced by researchers using diaries focuses on how frequently and for how long data should be collected. Wheeler and Reis (2001) suggested that a range of schedules can be used to record daily experiences, but primarily these will either be interval-contingent or event-contingent. An interval-contingent approach asks participants to complete handwritten, audio, or electronic recordings at regular, predetermined intervals. These intervals will vary depending on the nature of the research. For example Nicholls, Holt, Polman, and James (2005), and Didymus and Fletcher (2012) used daily diaries, whereas Day and Thatcher (2009) used a weekly interval. On the other hand, an event-contingent approach asks participants to report a defined event every time it occurs (Wheeler & Reis, 2001). This defined event might include recording data on competition days, when experiencing a particular emotion, or when engaging in a particular behavior.

The length of time that data should be collected for can vary in accordance with the requirements of the research, although this is often determined by the likelihood of adherence. Most diary-based research has used a set time frame. For example, Holt, Tamminen, Black, Sehn, and Wall (2008) collected audio-diary data with families over a six-week period during the soccer season. The alternative to this is that the length of data collection is determined by the event and/or topic in question. For example, Sitch and Day (2014) explored the experiences of judo athletes making weight, and collected data for the length of time that each individual athlete required to make weight. This meant that participants varied in the length of time that they were engaged in the research.

These examples demonstrate not only the ability to collect data over time, but also the ability to select specific time frames in accordance with the phenomenon under investigation. This provides us with an initial indication of one of the key strengths of using a written diary to collect data.

Strengths of using a diary

1. Ability to collect longitudinal data

A central theme evident in papers citing the strengths of using diary-based data collection is the ability to collect longitudinal data. Authors such as Lazarus (1999) have suggested that static research strategies, using just a single snapshot of participant experiences, are unlikely to capture rich information. Instead, diaries have allowed researchers to explore fluctuations during performance (Nicholls *et al.*, 2005) or over longer periods of time (Levy, Nicholls, Marchant, & Polman, 2009). In particular, Tamminen and Holt (2010) make a strong case for using a longitudinal diary approach when studying the coping strategies of female adolescents. In doing this they emphasize the necessary link between the theoretical approach (process–orientated models of coping) and the subsequent research design. Thus it is imperative that researchers should consider whether the use of longitudinal diaries is congruent and indeed valuable when studying the phenomenon in question.

2. Data collection in close temporal proximity to events of interest

A second frequently cited rationale for using diaries is that data can be collected as the participant experiences particular events or emotions. Thus the strength of this method lies in the proximity between the event occurrence and the collection of data. For many researchers, the ability to describe experiences soon after they happen is a frequently cited rationale for the use of daily diaries. For example, Almeida (2005) in his study of resilience and vulnerability to daily stressors highlighted that "diary methods alleviate memory distortions that can occur in more traditional questionnaire and interview methods that require participants to recall experiences over longer time frames" (p. 66). Similarly, Fisher and Noble (2004) suggested that diaries provide a representation of participants' current mindset in comparison to other methods such as interviews that rely on retrospective accounts. Didymus and Fletcher (2012) provide further detail on this strength, suggesting that the advantage of collecting data in close proximity to events is the minimization of memory vagueness, retrospective censorship, and reframing. Thus the overall suggestion here is that proximity is advantageous as it reduces the need to recall events and may limit reappraisal. Interestingly, while Didymus and Fletcher aimed to minimize retrospective recall, they also welcomed a small amount of time between the event and data collection, allowing for participant reflection and therefore a "more complete account of the event" (p. 1383).

3. Participant disclosure

Another key strength of using a diary is that diaries have often been considered a way of enabling participants to frame and tell their own stories. Thus the research diary may be suggested to provide a more personal account of the participant's experiences. As Monrouxe (2009) proposed when discussing audio diaries, this method is potentially useful for capturing phenomenon that might otherwise be inaccessible to researchers, specifically capturing private and sensitive experiences that would be difficult to capture with researcher involvement.

When considering disclosure in diary research, the audience to whom the story is told should be an important consideration. As suggested by Day and Thatcher (2012) diary writing will often be directed towards two types of audiences, either real (e.g., the researcher) or imagined (e.g., the coach). The use of imagined audiences may often reveal concerns that the writer feels unable or unwilling to address in person, but is able to convey in written form, thereby illuminating conversations the writer would like to have. As Charmaz (2004) noted, gaining an insider's view of an experience can often be a problematic and arduous task for the researcher. Thus the use of diary methods may provide one way of enhancing our understanding from the participant's perspective.

Interestingly, when using diaries with older adults, Jacelon and Imperio (2005) found that the first few diary entries were often tentative and brief, providing little reflection on the meaning of activities. Yet as diary use progressed participants became more comfortable with their writing and diary entries became more reflective and introspective. In sport, the use of a written diary is intuitively appealing as a tool for data collection, since it is often suggested to be an extension of the natural process that athletes may engage in when recording progress in training or competition. As a consequence, athletes may be well practiced in completing a regular diary.

Challenges of using diaries

1. The relationship between temporal proximity and truth

While the strength of using diaries has often been cited as the ability to collect data over time, the temporal nature of diary writing should be approached with caution. Authors such as Alaszewski (2006) have emphasized that diaries will minimize retrospection bias, allowing participants to report on experiences in close proximity to their occurrence. While this may provide the researcher with valuable and often emotive data, this does not make diaries a more truthful source, nor negate the impact of continual reappraisal and reflection in diary entries. Indeed as Sandelowski (1999) has suggested, retrospection is important given that participants often need time to articulate their experiences and "transform the event-as-experienced into the event-as-told" (p. 82). Consequently it is vital that qualitative researchers avoid applying criteria that devalue retrospective data, or view this as less valuable than prospective data. Instead researchers should embrace the change in language, emotion, content, and style that may evolve as participants write and reflect upon their experiences. In addition, we should not forget that memory is socially constructed and the construction of memories is not something that can be overcome or deemed a problem but is "how it is" for human beings.

2. Writing may prompt greater reflection, changes in behavior, and even therapeutic effects for participants

The second challenge of using diaries is that the extended time period of data collection afforded by using a diary may not only allow the researcher to gain a better understanding of process and change but may also afford the participant the same opportunity. As Crozier and Cassell (2015) highlight, the very act of completing the diary may contribute to changes in the meaning individuals assign to their experiences. In accordance with this suggestion, researchers such as Day and Thatcher (2009) have reported that participants' diary writing often included their own reflections of events, and demonstrated their awareness of their own changes during the diary writing process. Thus diaries not only serve to enhance the knowledge of the researcher but also the self-awareness of the participant, drawing their attention to particular themes and changes that occur over time. Sitch and Day (2014) suggested that such reflection may be perceived as useful by participants, allowing them to make additional changes. For example, participants who recognized their use of ineffective coping strategies through the process of writing about these were able to make changes. Yet these authors also highlight that "this may be problematic for any researcher who aims to capture a static picture of reality, it serves a poignant reminder that human stories will be in a constant state of change" (p. 38). Consequently, Sitch and Day (2014) suggested that "methods capturing data over time need to be flexible and adaptable to account for (and embrace) such changes" (p. 38).

3. High participant dropout rates of diary research

One of the greatest challenges of using diaries is the high participant dropout rates associated with this method. Stone, Shiffman, Schwartz, Broderick, and Hufford (2003) found that when asked to keep pain diaries, participants often forged their compliance. Their study indicated that participants reported completing 90% of their diary entries at the agreed times, yet electronic recordings demonstrated that actual compliance was as low as 11%. Research using athletes as participants has also acknowledged the difficulties of maintaining participant interest. For example, Nicholls *et al.* (2005) reported that having initially recruited 18 participants, only 11 of these submitted complete data sets. Such findings present challenges for researchers looking to collect data from athletes over a period of time.

In order to reduce the high participant dropout rates when using diaries a variety of suggestions have been put forward. Tamminen and Holt (2010) suggested that the presence of the researcher attending games and practices may serve as a reminder to athletes to complete written diaries. In addition to being present at athletic practices, Day and Thatcher (2009) used a short message service (SMS) in order to enhance adherence and maintain contact with participants. Such a suggestion allows for the remote contact of participants and was similarly used by Didymus and Fletcher (2012), who described their process of sending a short message to participants at the same time every evening in order to prompt their diary writing. In accordance with this strategy, Day and Thatcher (2009) suggested that the level of support provided during the data-collection process may impact not only on the likely adherence of participants but also on the quality of the data. They suggested that feeling valued by the researcher often prompted participants to write more in-depth diary entries.

In addition to maintaining contact with participants, a further suggestion to promote adherence has been the use of alternative forms of diaries. James and Büscher (2006) proposed that the use of email could allow participants to send typed diary entries at their own convenience, thereby reducing the stress of needing to record written data immediately. Further, as an alternative to the written diary, researchers have recently begun to endorse the use of other forms of diary entries. For example, Tamminen and Holt (2010) used audio diaries rather than written diaries, which were collected by the researchers every two weeks. While these authors reported some inconsistencies regarding the rate at which diaries were completed, many athletes maintained their interest in completing these audio diaries and were able to submit completed entries on a weekly basis. Similarly, Crozier and Cassell (2015) have advocated the use of audio diaries, suggesting that these are becoming favorable in comparison to their written counterparts because of their convenience, ease of completion, and lower levels of attrition.

Thus far this chapter has demonstrated that the emerging use of diaries as a method of data collection has provided researchers with a valuable source of information, particularly when studying process and change over time. While the ease of data collection may appeal to many researchers it is important to highlight that the need to develop rapport between researcher and participant is often essential. For the diary writer, audience is key; therefore, if the researcher intends to be the audience or listener to the written unpublished story of the participant, they must create a relationship that will foster this role. Indeed, diaries are rarely for one person; the producer often has an intended and/or phantom audience in mind, thereby making diaries not an individual act but a relational one.

Autobiographies

While diaries represent the predominant document of life used in sport and exercise research, autobiographies may provide us with an alternative, unsolicited, and unobtrusive resource for understanding various phenomena in sport. In simple terms, autobiography is used to describe the story of a person's life, told in their words. Yet these stories may appear under a number of guises including autobiography, life story, life memories, narratives, and sporting tales

(Dart, 2008). What is important to highlight here is that unlike biographies, which tell the life story through another person and are typically written in the third person, autobiographies are most often written as first-person accounts.

One of the key decisions for researchers using autobiographies relates to the selection of texts. As Yin (2014) suggested in his discussion of case studies, when deciding on the case in question the researcher must be aware of the questions and propositions of the research, in order to avoid covering everything about the individual in question. Yin's suggestion provides a valuable consideration that is highly applicable to researchers using autobiographies, particularly given that such documents can span a wide time frame and encompass a variety of topics. In particular, when considering documents such as autobiographies, the researcher may be faced with a multitude of choice. A basic search for sporting autobiographies online can reveal over 20,000 published autobiographies (www.amazon.co.uk). Thus it is imperative to consider the criteria by which we select the stories or sources that will be used.

Given the extensive number of writers who have made data publically available, the researcher must question why the autobiographies of particular athletes have been selected. One example of participant selection is provided by Stewart *et al.* (2011), who used purposive sampling to explore illness and the role of metaphor in athlete autobiographies. Their selection of autobiographies included consideration of both the characteristics of the athlete (e.g., sport, gender) and characteristics of the illness (e.g., life-threatening, life-changing). Thus in selecting potential autobiographies one approach may be to summarize the range of available documents and apply specific criteria using the research aims. In summarizing the potential pool of sporting autobiographies that discussed illness, Stewart *et al.* were able to maximize the variation in those autobiographies chosen for analysis. Yet there are also alternative approaches, whereby autobiographies are selected to focus on just one individual. Here it becomes essential that authors illustrate why this particular case is of interest. For example, Butryn and Masucci (2003) suggest that Lance Armstrong was selected as a case given that he "embodies the quintessential American hero, battling against all odds" (p. 124). These two examples demonstrate how participant selection most often involves a choice between presenting a range of experiences, or depicting how a single athlete embodies and presents a particular phenomenon. Finally, researchers also need to consider the range of autobiographical resources available on a particular topic or phenomenon. Researchers such as Dart (2008) have aimed to utilize all available texts or resources on a particular topic. Dart aimed to explore a range of experiences by using, among other sources, autobiographies, memoirs, and fans' accounts of football hooliganism. He demonstrated that for some research questions it is the range of accounts which is of primary importance, and thus a wider range of sources may provide greater insight. For others, however, autobiographical research focuses on just one type of account. Most importantly, as Prior (2003) suggested, the criteria for including or excluding documents should be well justified.

Autobiographies provide us with data sources that can offer profitable historical resources for the researcher (Dart, 2008). Yet despite this potential, they have scarcely been used within sport and exercise research. This reluctance to use autobiographical sources may stem from criticisms regarding the credibility of accounts. Further, authors such as Mykhalovskiy (1996) have suggested that academics may perceive autobiographies as self-indulgent. Yet what is important to note is that autobiographies provide us with a reflection of the social contours of a given time (Berg, 2004). Consequently providing we acknowledge that autobiographies are socially constructed, and analyze them as social constructions rather than pristine accounts offering true insights into the individual mind, then these may present us with a rich source of data for analysis.

Strengths of using autobiographies

1. Provision of a vast number and range of first-person accounts of sporting experiences

Sporting autobiographies provide the general public with a glimpse into the lives of high-profile athletes, most often focusing on the most significant moments of their sporting careers. Such texts have become consumed in increasing numbers, often topping best-seller charts. As a consequence, it is not only the number of autobiographies that has grown, but the range of authors. In present times autobiographies are no longer only written by athletes but by coaches, managers, trainers, administrators, and as Dart (2008) highlights, even by fans. Taylor (2008) reports that first-person accounts of sport most likely represent the most substantial published source on the history of sport.

It is important then to recognize the wealth of information provided by autobiographies. These not only provide us with access (but not unmediated) into the world of high-level athletes (something which may be unobtainable using traditional interviews), but also afford us insight into sensitive issues. While such publications are often framed as stories about high-profile individuals who experience success, many of these stories also include the battle to overcome adversity. For example, Jones (2014) provided a case study of alcoholism and recovery in a former professional footballer, while Howells and Fletcher (2015) explored adversity and growth experiences in Olympic swimming champions. Interestingly, as Murphy (2012) highlighted, some autobiographies can even tell us about relationships between athletes and other sports professionals. For example, the autobiography of Monica Seles describes her work with a sport psychologist after being stabbed on court.

2. Analysis of autobiography can reveal how athletes construct and represent identity

While autobiographies may offer a useful insight into the personal experiences of high-profile athletes, these accounts are not necessarily historically accurate or objectively reliable. Instead they represent subjective expressions of experience and self. As Butryn and Masucci (2003) emphasized, autobiographies represent acts of self-representation. Consequently, autobiographies provide us with a valuable source for looking beyond the content of the stories that are told, and instead considering how these stories are constructed and how they may change over time.

One example exploring how stories have been told in autobiography is Palmer's (2015) work. Palmer (2015) suggests that autobiographies are part of a broader production and presentation of the self. Thus she suggests that these sources "present a side to celebrity that is not always visible yet is crucial to how they understand, present, conceal, and reveal aspects of themselves" (p. 2). Palmer's work highlights that it is the athlete who selects not only what is included, but also what is excluded in the account of the self that is presented. Woolridge (2008) also proposes that "the autobiography is one of the chief written vehicles for the professional footballer to present himself to the public and it should be a key source of evidence for football historians" (p. 620). Further, it may be suggested that our analysis of autobiography can also examine how this identity is constructed and represented over time. Sparkes (2004) explored the identities and selves constructed by Lance Armstrong over time in relation to the specific narrative resources he had access to, and used, in writing his autobiography. Overall these researchers demonstrate that autobiographies can provide us with a valuable understanding, not only through the stories that are told, but also in exploring how these stories are presented and how the self is represented. The recent work by Sparkes and Stewart (2016) provides further support and reasons as to why autobiographies need to be taken seriously as an analytical and pedagogical resource.

Challenges of using autobiographies

Although it has been recognized that autobiographies can afford the researcher a rich insight and understanding of the writer and their social world, there are a number of criticisms of the use of autobiographies in sport and exercise research. These criticisms most often have a central theme, regarding the truthfulness or transparency of autobiographical data. In particular, there are three main criticisms of using autobiographies:

1. Autobiographies are often ghost-written.
2. Autobiographies can be seen as caricatures with predictable storylines.
3. Autobiographies are not historically trustworthy or accurate as the borders between these and fictional texts may be blurred.

When considering these critiques let us first start with suggestions from Mason (2006) who proposed that all documents are constructed in particular contexts, by particular people, for particular purposes, and for certain audiences. As such, it is important to acknowledge that autobiographies are most often written for entertainment (and profit!), and as a consequence, may provide a highly edited version of personal experiences. That is, autobiographies are social constructions and need to be treated as such.

Accordingly, what is important here is the acknowledgment that the stories presented in sources such as autobiographies do not provide us with a historic truth but a subjective expression of experience that is framed and shaped by the social. As Dart's (2008) work on football hooliganism illustrates, stories told in autobiographies can be written through rose-tinted spectacles. Dart describes the common theme among hooligan autobiographies in which "never a fight was lost" (p. 51), noting that the accuracy of the content may be queried given the self-absorption and narcissistic self-indulgence present in many autobiographical accounts of hooliganism. Nevertheless, such accounts may provide us with a partial window of understanding into the experience described, through the use of language, memory, and sense of self, derived from and constructed through the culture of the biographer.

Mason (2006) reminds us that while using unsolicited data may seem as though the researcher is only involved in "unearthing" documents, the task of excavation (rather than construction) is not that simple. She continues that the excavation metaphor implies the retrieval of solid, factual information, which was naturally occurring. Yet the analysis process requires the researcher to consider the purpose, consequence, detail, authenticity, and consequences of the document, much of which is not evident from reading alone. Just as Randall and Phoenix (2009) suggested that "stories are told in particular situations to particular listeners for particular reasons" (p. 126), in a similar vein autobiographies will allow the writer to tell their stories in a particular way (e.g., success story, hero story), to a particular audience (fans, critics), for a particular reason (e.g., therapeutic, entertainment, identity repair). It is therefore imperative that the researcher acknowledges that autobiographies are not a transparent text. While some authors do not include such considerations and unfortunately analyze autobiographies as if they transparently represent experience or a psychological reality a person holds (e.g., Morgan, Fletcher, & Sarkar, 2015), others (e.g., Dart, 2008) demonstrate more appropriately how such considerations are used as a frame of reference when interpreting autobiographical data. In other words, autobiographies should not be analyzed through a representation view of language that assumes what is said in the text provides a researcher access to some inner reality. Rather they need to be treated as a social and cultural creation that provides insight into human lives as socioculturally constructed (see also Chapter 4).

Suggestions for future research

Having outlined the existing uses of documents of life in sporting research it might be considered somewhat surprising that such documents are used so infrequently by researchers in this context. In particular, these documents offer a unique insight into athletic experiences, acknowledging the temporal context and exploring developing plots, themes, and storytelling. Yet all too often, rather than seeking out documents of life, researchers rely on the use of popular data-collection techniques such as semistructured interviews (Culver, Gilbert, & Sparkes, 2012). Having emphasized the value of documents of life this final section of the chapter outlines three novel thoughts for the future use of these documents.

First, as demonstrated in this chapter, there has been minimal use in sport and exercise research of even the most popular documents of life in society. Thus it may be suggested that in order to extend the use of documents of life, researchers should consider the breadth of documents that may be available to them. Despite the wealth of available documents there is some reluctance, even among researchers who are currently using documents of life, to abandon the written word. Thus, researchers should consider the value in using alternative documents such as biographical objects, photographs, pictures, and audio recordings, which may all provide valuable information. As Mason (2006) suggested, some sources sit less comfortably under the heading of "documents" but may be worthy of consideration, including film, video, television, sculptures, visual arts, and diagrams. Where such resources have been used they have been suggested to be highly valuable in enhancing depth of understanding. For example, Goldblatt and Williams (2014) illustrated that objects can be used to enhance our understanding of past events and experiences. Their research focused on the history of the world cup, using 24 objects to illustrate historical changes. Further, authors such as Cherrington and Watson (2010), and Jones *et al.* (2015), have endorsed the use of video diaries as an alternative method of data collection.

Second, in addition to using a wider range of sources, researchers should consider that documents of life extend into the digital (see also Chapters 11 and 27). Researchers should consider the use of technology and the documents of life that may be evident online. With advancements in technology, Sparkes and Smith (2014) suggested that web-based resources such as Twitter, personal blogs, and Facebook can also be used to enhance our understanding of data. Thus a variety of sources surrounding the life of the athlete can be explored using digital sources to provide richness to the analysis.

The final future direction follows and expands on the popular interview-diary-interview method which has attracted the attention of researchers desiring more information than from the use of diaries alone. While such a method has been well used in diary research (e.g., Holt *et al.*, 2008; Sitch & Day, 2014; Tamminen & Holt, 2010) it might be extended to use alternative documents. Thus documents such as autobiographies may be used as a stimulus during interview to understand the responses of readers rather than presenting the interpretations of the researcher.

What remains important is to consider that documents can allow the researcher to weave a web of connections between people, places, experiences, objects, and stories. As researchers continually strive to achieve a rich understanding, it is important to consider the possible range of documents that may help to construct a more holistic perspective of the participant and phenomenon in question, particularly as we enter a digital age. The examples provided in this chapter illustrate the diversity of methods that encompass documents of life. Yet despite their broad possibilities, these remain an underused resource in both the psychological and sociological study of sport. Thus it is important that researchers recognize the valuable contribution that they may bring to our understanding, either as a supplement to more traditional forms of data collection or as a stand-alone method. I hope this chapter acts as a stimulus to consider harnessing the power of documents of life when studying sport and exercise.

References

Alaszewski, A. (2006). *Using diaries for social research*. London: Sage.

Almeida, D. M. (2005). Resilience and vulnerability to daily stressors assessed via diary methods. *Current Directions in Psychological Sciences, 12*, 64–68.

Berg, B. L. (2004). *Qualitative research methods for the social sciences*. Essex: Pearson.

Blumer, H. (1979). *Critiques of research in the social sciences: An appraisal of Thomas and Znaniecki's* The Polish Peasant in Europe and America. New Brunswick, NJ: Transaction Books.

Butryn, T. & Masucci, M. A. (2003). It's not about the book. A cyborg counternarrative of Lance Armstrong. *Journal of Sport and Social Issues, 27*, 124–144.

Charmaz, K. (2004). Premises, principles, and practices in qualitative research: Revisiting the foundations. *Qualitative Health Research, 14*, 976–993.

Cherrington, J. & Watson, B. (2010). Shooting a diary, not just a hoop: Using video diaries to explore the embodied everyday contexts of a university basketball team. *Qualitative Research in Sport and Exercise, 2*, 267–281.

Crozier, S. E. & Cassell, C. M. (2015). Methodological considerations in the use of audio diaries in work psychology: Adding to the qualitative tool kit. *Journal of Occupational and Organizational Psychology*, 1–25.

Culver, D. M., Gilbert, W., & Sparkes, A. (2012). Qualitative research in sport psychology journals: The next decade 2000–2009 and beyond. *The Sport Psychologist, 26*, 261–281.

Dart, J. (2008). Confessional tales from former football hooligans: A nostalgic, narcissistic wallow in football violence. *Soccer and Society, 9*, 42–55.

Day, M. & Thatcher, J. (2009). "I'm really embarrassed that you're going to read this . . .": Reflections on using diaries in qualitative research. *Qualitative Research in Psychology, 6*, 249–259.

Day, M. C. & Thatcher, J. (2012). Reflections on using writing in sport and exercise psychology research and practice. *Qualitative Methods in Psychology Bulletin, 14*, 24–30.

Didymus, F. F. & Fletcher, D. (2012). Getting to the heart of the matter: A diary study of swimmers' appraisals of organizational stressors. *Journal of Sports Sciences, 30*, 1375–1385.

Fisher, C. D. & Noble, C. S. (2004). A with-in person examination of correlates of performance and emotions while working. *Human Performance, 17*, 145–168.

Gibson, B., Minstry, B., Smith. B., Yoshida, K., Abbott, D., Lindsay, S., & Hamdani, Y. (2013). The integrated use of audio diaries, photography and interviews in research with disabled young men. *International Journal of Qualitative Methods, 12*, 382–402.

Goldblatt, D. & Williams, J. (2014). A history of the World Cup in 24 objects. Display at International Centre for Sports History and Culture, De Montfort University, and the National Football Museum.

Grenier, M. A., Horrell, A., & Genovese, B. (2014). Doing things my way: Teaching physical education with a disability. *Adapted Physical Activity Quarterly, 31*, 325–342.

Holt, N. L., Tamminen, K. A., Black, D. E., Sehn, Z. L., & Wall, M. P. (2008). Parental involvement in competitive youth sport settings. *Psychology of Sport and Exercise, 9*, 663–685.

Howells, K. & Fletcher, D. (2015). Sink or swim: Adversity and growth related experiences in Olympic swimming champions. *Psychology of Sport and Exercise, 16*, 37–48.

Jacelon, C. S. & Imperio, K. (2005). Participant diaries as a source of data in research with older adults. *Qualitative Health Research, 15*, 991–997.

James, N. & Büscher, H. (2006). Credibility, authenticity and voice: Dilemmas in web-based interviewing, *Qualitative Research Journal, 6*(3), 403–420.

Jones, C. (2014). Alcoholism and recovery: A case study of a former professional footballer. *International Review for the Sociology of Sport, 49*, 485–505.

Jones, R. L., Fonseca, J., De Martin Silva, L., Davies, G., Morgan, K., & Mesquite, I. (2015). The promise and problems of video diaries: building on current research. *Qualitative Research in Sport, Exercise, and Health, 7,* 395–410.

Keleher, H. M. & Verrinder, G. K., (2003). Health diaries in a rural Australian setting. *Qualitative Health Research, 13,* 435–443.

Lazarus, R. S. (1999). *Stress and emotion: A new synthesis.* New York: Springer.

Levy, A., Nicholls, A., Marchant, D., & Polman, R. (2009). Organizational stressors, coping, and coping effectiveness: A longitudinal study with an elite coach. *International Journal of Sports Science and Coaching, 4,* 31–45.

Mason, J. (2006). *Qualitative researching.* London: Sage.

McFee, G. (2009). The epistemology of qualitative research into sport: Ethical and erotetic? *Qualitative Research in Sport and Exercise, 1,* 297–311.

Monrouxe, L. V. (2009). Solicited audio diaries in longitudinal narrative research: A view from inside. *Qualitative Research, 9,* 81–103.

Morgan, P. B. C., Fletcher, D., & Sarkar, M. (2015). Understanding team resilience in the world's best athletes: A case study of a Rugby Union World Cup winning team. *Psychology of Sport and Exercise, 16,* 91–100.

Murphy, S. (2012). *The Oxford handbook of sport and performance psychology.* New York: Oxford University Press.

Mykhalovskiy, E. (1996). Reconsidering table talk: Critical thoughts on the relationship between sociology, autobiography, and self-indulgence. *Qualitative Sociology, 19,* 131–151.

Nicholls, A. R., Holt, N. L., Polman, R. C. J., & James, D. W. G. (2005). Stress and coping among International adolescent golfers. *Journal of Applied Sport Psychology, 17,* 333–340.

Palmer, C. (2015). Drinking, downfall and redemption: biographies and "athlete addicts." *Celebrity Studies,* 1–13.

Plummer, K. (2001). *Documents of life 2: An invitation to critical humanism.* London: Sage.

Plummer, K. (2004). On the diversity of life documents. In C. Seale (Ed.), *Social research methods* (pp. 282–289). London: Routledge.

Prior, L. (2003). *Using documents in social research.* London: Sage.

Randall, W. L. & Phoenix, C. (2009). The problem with truth in qualitative interviews: Reflections from a narrative perspective. *Qualitative Research in Sport and Exercise, 1,* 125–140.

Sandelowski. (1999). Focus on qualitative methods. Time and qualitative research. *Research in Nursing and Health, 22,* 79–87.

Sitch, M. & Day, M. (2014). Using a daily diary approach to understand the psychological experiences of making weight. *The Sport Psychologist, 29,* 29–40.

Sparkes, A. C. (2004). Bodies, narratives, selves and autobiography. The example of Lance Armstrong. *Journal of Sport and Social Issues, 28*(4), 397–428.

Sparkes, A. C. & Smith, B. (2014). *Qualitative research in sport, exercise and health: From process to product.* London: Routledge.

Sparkes, A. C., & Stewart, C. (2016). Taking sporting autobiographies seriously as an analytical and pedagogical resource in sport, exercise and health. *Qualitative Research in Sport, Exercise and Health, 8,* 113–130.

Stewart, C., Smith, B., & Sparkes, A. C. (2011). Sporting autobiographies of illness and the role of metaphor. *Sport in Society, 14,* 581–597.

Stone, A. A., Shiffman, S., Schwartz, J. E., Broderick, J. E., & Hufford, M. R. (2003). Patient compliance with paper and electronic diaries. *Control Clinical Trials, 24,* 182–199.

Tamminen, K. & Holt, N. L. (2010). Female adolescent athletes' coping: A season-long investigation. *Journal of Sports Sciences, 28,* 101–114.

Taylor, M. (2008). From source to subject: Sport, history, and autobiography. *Journal of Sport History, 35,* 469–491.

Wagstaff, C. R. D., Hanton, S., & Fletcher, D. (2013). Developing emotion abilities and regulation strategies in a sports organization: An action research intervention. *Psychology of Sport and Exercise, 14,* 476–487.

Wheeler, L. & Reis, H. T. (2001). Self-recording of everyday life events: Origins, types and uses. *Journal of Personality, 59,* 339–354.

Woolridge, J. (2008). These sporting lives: Football autobiographies 1945–1980. *Sport in History, 28,* 620–640.

Yin, R. K. (2014). *Case study research.* London: Sage.

PART III

Analysing qualitative data

15

USING THEMATIC ANALYSIS IN SPORT AND EXERCISE RESEARCH

Virginia Braun, Victoria Clarke and Paul Weate

Thematic analysis (TA) is one of a cluster of analytic approaches you can use, if you want to identify *patterns* of meaning across a qualitative dataset. The widely used version of TA we outline in this chapter is fairly unique in the canon of qualitative analytic approaches in that it just offers the researcher analytic tools to make sense of data. It is not *tied to* a particular theoretical framework, and it does not come with methodological stipulations about, for example, how to sample, or collect data. This gives the researcher great flexibility in how they use TA. Alongside the fact that TA is a relatively accessible qualitative analytic technique, these features make it an excellent and robust method for beginner qualitative researchers, for those wishing to do fairly descriptive work, for those working in teams across disciplinary contexts, or with researchers of mixed (qualitative) experience, and for those wanting to produce research for public consumption (e.g., policy- or practice-oriented research). That said TA also provides a tool that offers the potential for nuanced, complex, interpretative analysis. After introducing TA, and explaining *why* and *when* you might use it, we provide a detailed discussion of *how* you do TA, illustrated with examples from Paul's focus-group study exploring women's perspectives on, and experiences of, exercise.

An introduction to thematic analysis

The term "thematic" analysis has been in use as an analytic concept since the 1970s (Christ, 1970), but what it refers to has varied considerably – from quantitative content analysis (Christ, 1970) to something akin to contemporary versions of TA (Benner 1985; Dapkus, 1985). Similarly, qualitative researchers have a long history of describing as "thematic" their approach to analysis – but often without an explicit reference to a developed method called "thematic analysis." More recently, the writings of Patton (2002), Boyatzis (1998) and, latterly ourselves (Braun & Clarke, 2006), among others, have provided a foundation and set of procedures for *thematic analysis*. Since the publication of our original article in 2006, "thematic analysis" has gained hugely in popularity, and entered the "canon" as a recognizable and reputable method of qualitative analysis, evidenced by its inclusion in volumes such as this.

At its most basic, TA offers a method for identifying patterns ("themes") in a dataset, and for describing and interpreting the meaning and importance of those. However, right from its first entry into the method(ological) spectrum, TA has been described in quite different ways.

It is now possible to identify two broad "strands" of TA: (1) a strand tied to a *realist* ontological framework (or what has been termed "small q" qualitative research; Kidder & Fine, 1987); and (2) a strand not anchored in a particular theoretical tradition, which can therefore be applied flexibly across the spectrum of ontological and epistemological positions. This latter strand fits firmly within the "big Q" qualitative approach, the application of qualitative techniques within a qualitative *paradigm* (Kidder & Fine, 1987), and is the approach we have developed (Braun & Clarke, 2006, 2012, 2013) – and the focus of this chapter.

The small q/big Q division has been used to classify qualitative research into that which retains a foothold in more (post)positivist/quantitative research models, and that which fully embraces a "qualitative" perspective (Kidder & Fine, 1987; see also Braun & Clarke, 2013). The "small q" versions of TA (Boyatzis, 1998; Guest, MacQueen & Namey, 2012; Joffe, 2011) are more "rigid" than our version. Authors such as Boyatzis (1998) advocate for the use of coding frames, and for the use of multiple, independent coders in order to generate "inter-rater reliability scores." In so doing, they implicitly (and explicitly) locate TA within a (post) positivist and (naïve) realist research framework, where a truth can be determined through research, and where clear and fixed meanings can be "found" within the data. Researchers who adopt a more qualitative orientation to TA (and research generally), and understand meaning "in" qualitative data as more contextualized and provisional, can find such criteria problematic – especially when they becomes proxies for the quality of *any* qualitative analysis (see Frieze, 2008). We discuss more appropriate quality criteria for big Q TA below (see also Chapter 25).

The "flexible" version of TA we have developed offers the researcher robust processes for identifying patterns, and interpreting them, in a number of different ways, but detaches these from specific, or inbuilt, ontological and epistemological anchors. What this means is the researcher needs to make some *active* choices about how they engage with the data (Braun & Clarke, 2006). These choices include:

1. Do you primarily engage with the data at the level of: a) the obvious meanings expressed; or b) the meanings and frameworks that underpin the things explicitly stated by participants or in textual representations? We refer to the former as a *semantic* focus – this means you're coding and reporting on *explicitly stated* ideas, concepts, meanings, experiences, etc. For instance, if women reporting feeling *ashamed* about not participating in exercise, and you developed a theme around shame, this would be a semantic theme. The latter we refer to as *latent* – where you code and develop analysis around more implicit ideas or concept that underpin what's explicitly expressed. To continue the previous example, women experiencing their nonparticipation in exercise as shameful might suggest that "exercise" sits within a moral framework, so that nonparticipation can be experienced as individually blameworthy. To capture this you might develop a theme around "exercises as moral/good." Latent ideas can be harder to identity when they map onto cultural common sense; the idea of "exercise as moral/good" (rather than, for instance, exercise as a *privilege*) has become a dominant – common sense - assumption.

2. Do you approach your data coding and theme development in a "data-driven," "bottom-up" or inductive way, where the content itself guides the developing analysis? Or do you take a more "top-up" or deductive approach, where your analytic process is informed or driven by theoretical concepts beyond the data?

3. Is your approach grounded in conceptual, epistemological or ontological frameworks like realism, (post)postivism and essentialism (e.g., Kitzinger, 1995), or contextualist/critical realist approaches (e.g., Ussher, 1997), or critical/constructionist orientations (e.g., Burr, 2003)?

These choices combine in numerous ways, and form quite different versions of TA, although some choices *do* tend to cluster together more "naturally": critical/constructionist, deductive, and latent orientations; realist, semantic, and inductive orientations. At the same time, it is a misconception to view the first two of these questions as involving either/or choices (see Robertson *et al.*, 2013); in practice, most thematic analyses include both semantic and latent, and inductive and deductive elements.

When and why to use thematic analysis

The question of when and why to use TA can be a tricky one to answer because TA can be used for many different purposes (as we outline here), more so than other qualitative analytic approaches, and it is not always the case that there is *only* one analytic approach ideally suited to a particular research question or design. So we are *not* suggesting that qualitative analysis starts and ends with TA! There are numerous types of research questions that TA does *not* work well for, such as questions around narrative and stories (Smith & Sparkes, 2009; see Chapters 4 and 20, this volume), or questions focused both on thematic patterning *and* individual narratives (Darker, Larkin, & French, 2007; see also Chapters 4 and 20, this volume), or questions oriented to language practice and discourse (Locke, 2004; see Chapter 18, this volume). Likewise, if your aim is to develop models and theories from data, this task is best achieved with grounded theory (Holt & Tamminen, 2010; see Chapter 3, this volume).

Research questions guide what we want to know, and good research questions are developed in relation to the purpose or intent of our research (e.g., knowledge generation, policy development); they also reflect our epistemological and ontological positions (Demuth & Terkildsen, 2015; see also Chapters 1 and 10, this volume). We can think of qualitative research questions as clustering into different "types" (Braun & Clarke, 2013), and TA suits a wide range of these different types. It can provide analyses of people's experiences in relation to an issue, or the factors and processes that underlie and influence particular phenomena. It can identify patterns in people's (reported) practices or behaviors related to, or their views and perspectives on, a certain issue. Or, in a quite different way, it can determine common ways an issue or topic is represented (e.g., in media), or explore the way(s) it is "constructed" as an object of interest. If (one or more of) these are the sorts of things you are interested in knowing about, and many of these *are* the sorts of things sports and exercise researchers are interested in, TA provides an excellent tool. Table 15.1 provides a list of suitable-for-TA question types, along with applicable theoretical frameworks, and examples from sport and exercise research.

As noted above, the flexibility of TA means it can be used with a wide range of different research designs and data-collection methods, and there is no "ideal" data type in TA. Semistructured interviews, one of the most common methods of data collection in qualitative research, are excellent for gathering in-depth accounts of "personal experience" (e.g., McArdle, McGale, & Gaffney, 2012); focus groups are ideal if you want to explore shared/contested social meanings or perspectives around a topic (e.g., Hall *et al.*, 2012). Such approaches involve the researcher generating data through interaction with people. TA also works really well with textual data, both researcher-generated (e.g., through diaries, story completion, vignettes), and preexisting (e.g., talkback radio or newspapers; see McCreanor *et al.*, 2010), or any combination of these different data types (e.g., Smith, Tomasone, Latimer-Cheung & Martin Ginis, 2015). If your data are audio (or audio-visual), rather than textual, preparation for TA involves the transcription of all the data (see Braun & Clarke, 2013, for transcription notation suitable for use in TA).

Table 15.1 Examples of published thematic analysis studies

Research question type	Example study	Data-collection method and sample	Approach to TA and themes identified	Theoretical frameworks
Experiences	Investigating men's experiences of an integrated exercise/psychosocial mental-health promotion program, "Back of the Net" (McArdle, McGale, & Gaffney 2012)	A focus group with 9 men; semistructured individual (telephone) interviews with 6 men	A combination small q/Big Q TA (B&C approach supplemented with measures to "minimise individual bias," p. 245); inductive and deductive coding and analysis. Two themes (each with two subthemes): "core structural features" and "the impact of a combined exercise/CBT programme on participants' experiences" (p. 245)	Epistemological/ontological stance not explicitly stated, but experiential and broadly *realist* in orientation; some theoretical confusion – concern with minimizing researcher "bias" yet results discussed in relation to *social constructionist* perspectives on masculinity
Views and perspectives	Exploring Welsh rugby fans' thoughts about their commitment to their team (Hall *et al.*, 2012)	Seven focus groups with a total of 45 participants (29 men; 16 women, aged 12–62)	Inductive TA, four themes generated: affective loyalty, involvement, distinctiveness, and individualism	Epistemological/ontological stance not explicitly stated, but experiential and broadly *realist* in orientation; results discussed in relation to social identity theory
Influencing factors and processes	Examining the underlying mechanisms in the success of football-based health interventions for men (Robertson *et al.*, 2013)	Interviews with "16 staff responsible for delivering and/or managing the initiatives" and "58 men who had participated in the initiatives" (p. 421)	Broadly inductive but also informed by existing theories and concepts. Two overarching themes: "Trust (including what processes it was key to and how it was developed/sustained) and Change (including what it was facilitated by and what it impacted on)" (p. 422)	Epistemological/ontological stance not explicitly stated, but broadly *critical realist* in orientation and analysis informed by critical masculinity theory

Practices/ behaviors	Leadership processes at the London 2012 Olympic Games (Slater, Barker, Coffee, & Jones, 2015)	Leaders' communication in 48 media interviews, 16 speeches or team announcements, and three blogs (92 pages of transcribed text), between April 17 and September 11, 2012	Inductive and deductive TA, five themes identified: creation of team identities; team values; team vision; performance consequences; and "we" achieved	Epistemological/ ontological stance not explicitly stated, but experiential and broadly *realist* in orientation, analysis informed by social identity theory
Construction/ representation	Representations of Māori participation and achievement in New Zealand newspapers' sports coverage (McCreanor *et al.*, 2010)	50 articles from 120 newspapers	TA used in combination with discourse analysis, two overarching themes identified: "Māori sport" ("depicted Māori as exotic and marginal to sporting life in Aotearoa/ New Zealand") and "Māori in sport" ("subsumed Māori within monocultural sporting codes," p. 235)	Critical and constructionist; analysis informed by a theoretical framework of "Māori self-determination and decolonization" (p. 235)

There are no strict guidelines around sample constitution and size, and sampling strategy for TA – these design decisions should be informed by your research question, purpose, and method of data collection, among other things. General guidance around sampling and samples in qualitative research apply (Patton, 2002), but the *key* thing to remember is that TA is about identifying patterns *across* a dataset. Therefore, you need to have a sample large enough to identify patterns in a way that is meaningful, and allows you to say something that carries some weight. We have suggested six interviews as a minimum sample size for TA, but this is a general *suggestion* that does not take account of the specifics of particular research questions and designs (some researchers have used TA in case-study research with a small number of participants; see, for example, Cedervall & Åberg, 2010). For publishable research, you may struggle if your interview sample is less than about 15 (some journals seem to automatically reject samples less than 30!), and therefore "purpose" is an important factor to consider as well. In general, the greater the depth and richness of each data item (e.g., an interview) the fewer individual items you will need.

How to do thematic analysis

We describe the process of TA using a six-phase model, and we outline these phases below. This model risks representing the process of TA as akin to walking (not running; qualitative research is not that quick!) up a flight of steps, where your progress from start to finish is clear and direct. Instead, the progression through TA is more like following a hose through long grass, where you cannot clearly see the way ahead, and the path is not direct: sometimes you move forwards; other times you coil back on yourself. Doing TA (well) usually involves a recursive, reflexive process of moving forwards (and sometimes backwards) through data familiarization, coding, theme development, revision, naming, and writing up. It is crucial, though, to remember that your analysis is not *in* the data, waiting for you to discover it; your themes do not simply "emerge." Instead, your analysis is produced through the intersection of your theoretical assumptions, disciplinary knowledge, research skills and experience, and the content of the data themselves. Analysis is an *active* process, and thus, although we describe TA as a *method* – as *a way* to analyze data, rather than a whole framework – these steps must not be followed in robotic repetition, without thought and deliberation; without conscious choices, action, and thinking.

As well as outlining the phases of TA (for more detailed discussion, see Braun & Clarke, 2006, 2012, 2013), we illustrate key aspects of the process using Paul's focus-group study exploring women's past and present experiences of, and participation in, exercise. The purposive sample consisted of 19 women – both currently (N = 11) and not currently (N = 8) engaged in regular exercise – aged between 18 and 78 (mean = 54; two-thirds aged 50 or older). The women participated in one of four focus groups. It is important to note that a key identified advantage of focus-group data collection is that you gain access to social interaction and the way meaning is "negotiated" in context. This means participants' accounts need to be considered in context, but such interaction is often ignored in pattern-based analyses like TA. Anyone using TA with focus-group data needs to be aware of this aspect of the data, and ideally incorporate it somehow (see Braun & Clarke, 2013, for further discussion).

Phases 1–2: Familiarization and coding. The first phase of TA is familiarization – the process of deeply immersing yourself in your data, so that you become intimately familiar with their content. What this *practically* involves is reading and rereading all data items, and making notes as you go about what grabs or interests you. What you want to achieve at this stage is both a sense that you really "know" the dataset, but also to be engaging with the data *as data* rather than *as information*. What do we mean by this? You want to be reading the data *analytically*, looking for ideas and concepts that can help you address your research question, and reading it in a *curious and questioning* way. The following sorts of questions can help facilitate analytic engagement:

1. Why might the participants be making sense of things in *this* way (and not *that* way)?
2. How would *I* feel in this situation?
3. How could the participants' accounts be *different*?
4. What *assumptions* underpin the data?
5. What *worldview* does the account imply or rely on?
6. What *implications* might this account have?

Familiarization involves critical engagement with the data, but is informal in the way you take notes and generate meaning. The next phase – *coding* – turns this into a systematic and thorough process. Familiarization ensures you begin coding with some sense of the sorts of things you will code for, but it doesn't delimit the scope of coding (remember, our version of TA does not advocate the development of a "coding frame" at this point; a practice which does delimit the focus of coding). Coding is a key step in TA, and systematic and rigorous coding builds solid foundations for theme development – don't be tempted to jump straight into theme identification! – and helps move your analysis beyond immediate or obvious meanings.

A code identifies and labels something of interest in the data – at a semantic and/or a latent level – that is of potential relevance to your research question (although it is important to note that in qualitative research, the research question is not fixed; it can evolve and be refined throughout the analytic process). It is a pithy label that you apply to a segment of data, which captures the content and its analytic relevance. We advocate what we call the "remove the data" test for codes: do they clearly "evoke" the data without needing to read them? If so, they're probably good codes. This is important for the next phase of data analysis.

The practical process of coding involves closely reading the data, and "tagging" with a code each piece that has some relevance to your research question. You can do this in various ways (e.g., pen and paper, using a computer program). Text can be tagged with one or more codes, or it can be left untagged if not relevant. You work systematically through each data item and you code each new relevant extract of text you encounter. As coding is flexible and organic, you need to decide if an already-used code applies, or if you need to create a new one. You can tweak existing codes as you work through the data, expanding or contracting them, splitting them into two or more codes, or collapsing similar codes together, to better fit your developing analysis. Keep coding open and inclusive, as you do not yet know what your themes might finally be. Table 15.2 provides an example of a data extract and associated codes from the

Table 15.2 Example of data extract* and associated codes from women and exercise study

Maria:	[The Wii-fit] was good if you couldn't go out. If the weather was poor then you could still do it.	Bad weather is a barrier to exercise. Outside is best.
Jen:	Hmm, well that's why I do the gym. Because my husband thinks I'm mad, you know, he'll say, "Why are you paying to go and walk?" You know, on a treadmill. "Why don't you just go out for a walk?" and I say, "Well, because I need that structure." If I, (if I didnt have it and I looked at home and I cleaned the bathroom), well not cleaned the bathroom, but you know, I'd do something else, where as if I know I'm going there I'll do it.	Bad weather is a barrier to exercise. Inside space facilitates regular exercise. Gym = bad. Structure facilitates regular exercise. There's always something else to do. Difficult to motivate yourself to exercise.
Maria:	It's a bit like swimming, I go swimming straight from work so I take all my things and go straight from work. If I went home to get my stuff and change it would be really a real effort to leave the house again.	Managing motivation. Difficult to motivate yourself to exercise. Being exercise-minded (disciplined).
Jen:	Maria is my role model for swimming ((laughs)) You know, knowing that she, it's something I want to do and I just don't seem to be able to get round to it and I know that you go every Monday night after and I think, "Oh, that's wonderful." One of these days, I'll get round to it ((laughs)).	Social/relational facilitator. Difficult to motivate yourself to exercise.
Maria:	But it's just a, a structure that I've put in place (Focus Group 1).	Structure facilitates regular exercise.

**Note*: transcription conventions have followed those outlined in Braun and Clarke (2013):

- [text in square brackets] has been added to make the referent of the text clear.
- (text in single parentheses) is the transcribers *best guess* as to what was said – they weren't 100% confident about it.
- ((text in double parentheses)) refers to paralinguistic features of the interview that might be analytically relevant.
- "text in quotation marks" indicates the speaker is reporting someone else's direct speech.

women and exercise study. We coded around the research question "How do women make sense of exercise and their participation (or not) in it?"

It is normal for coding to evolve as you get more analytically engaged; we recommend going through the dataset twice when coding, to ensure a systematic, coherent and robust set of codes. A second coding round can also facilitate the development of more latent codes. In the example in Table 15.2, the codes are both semantic and latent (but mainly semantic). The code "bad weather is a barrier to exercise" is an example of a semantic code – it closely captures the manifest content of Maria and Jen's comments. "Being exercise-minded" is a more latent code. It captures the way exercise was often explained in terms of individual psychological differences (some people are "exercise-minded"; some are not). Jen's description of Maria as her "role model," combined with her own reported failure to swim regularly, *implicitly* frames Maria as disciplined and motivated ("exercise-minded") when it comes to swimming, unlike her.

There is no definite "stop" point for coding; no ideal number of codes. What you want is a set of codes that richly and thoroughly captures the analytically relevant aspects of your dataset. You end this phase with your data thoroughly coded, and all your codes, and the data relevant to each code, collated ready for the next phase.

Phases 3–5: Theme development, refinement and naming. These three phases involve the core *analytic* work in TA: organizing codes and coded data into candidate themes, reviewing and revising those candidate themes, and developing a rich analysis of the data represented by the finalized themes. A useful way to think of your TA is as an "answer" to your research question. What you are doing is developing a really robust, detailed, nuanced answer.

The process of theme development is about clustering codes to identify "higher-level" patterns – by which we generally refer to meanings which are broader and capture more than one very specific idea – you want your themes to have layers. Imagine your analysis is like a short guidebook to a city: your themes are akin to the *chapters* – there might be one for four to five different neighborhoods; your codes are akin to the different neighborhood *features* described in each chapter. Together, the features of the neighborhood (codes) cluster together to give you a coherent sense of each distinct neighborhood (theme). This is what we mean by "higher level" – moving beyond the very specific, which is what codes often capture. Your themes generally want to have texture and nuance, to capture some rich diversity, rather than just a single idea, which would be akin to a chapter that simply described one restaurant (this analogy only works so far, but it should give you a general picture). Another key aspect of higher-level analysis is that is moves your analytic narrative beyond simply summarizing and describing your themes to providing some kind of commentary on their implications and importance.

It is crucial to understand that a "theme" is more than just some coherent, patterned meaning across a dataset – it also has to tell you something important about the data, relevant to your research question. Start the theme-development process first with just the codes. This active process involves you identifying ways you can cluster your codes together around some (bigger) meaning or concept they all share. Not all codes need to be included in these clusters; some inevitably will not fit. That is fine – your analysis is never the *complete* story of what was in the data (that is the raw data themselves!). Once you have some provisional or candidate themes (there is no right or wrong number, but you generally want more than one, and probably less than six, in a 10–15,000-word report), you start a process of review.

Reviewing involves working first with the coded data, and then going back to the whole dataset. The process is about checking two things: first, whether your analysis "fits well" (or well enough) with the data and you are not misrepresenting them, inadvertently, through poor coding; and second, whether the story you're telling is a compelling and coherent way of addressing your research question. We generally do not subscribe to the view that there is only one way of analyzing qualitative data, or only one analysis "in" a qualitative dataset, so this also comes back to the *purpose* of the analysis: what is your aim with the research, and does your analysis enable you to fulfill that?

Revision can range from minor tweaks to a complete restart of the analysis – you have to be open to the possibility that you need to "let go" of some or all of your analysis if the review raises problems. In reviewing your developing analysis, there are a number of factors to consider:

1. Does each theme have a *central organizing concept* so that all the data and codes cohere around a single key analytic point?
2. Is the central organizing concept of each theme distinct?
3. What are the relationships, interconnections, and boundaries between the themes?
4. Do the themes together tell a coherent and compelling story of the data that addresses your research question?

These latter questions highlight the importance of considering the analysis as an *overall* story: when we say "story," we mean a coherent account that is necessarily partial and perspectival, that tells the reader something about the data. The use of visual tools like thematic maps (see Figure 15.1) can be really useful in the process of developing and then reviewing the analysis, and for exploring and revising the relationships between candidate themes (they can change dramatically; see the maps in Braun & Clarke, 2006). These relationships can be hierarchical as well as lateral. We recommend, in general, no more than three theme levels (Braun & Clarke 2013):

1. *Overarching themes* – which tend to organize and structure an analysis; they capture an idea underpinning a number of themes, but are rarely analyzed themselves in any depth, and are not a necessary feature of a TA.
2. *Themes* – which report in detail on meaning related to a central organizing concept.
3. *Subthemes* – which capture and develop an important facet of the central organizing concept of a theme. They are not a necessity, but can highlight an important aspect of a theme, or be used to identify notable distinct patterns *within* a theme.

In the women and exercise example study, the revision process helped Paul to settle on a structure of one *central* theme, which underpins all the other themes ("Exercise is boring and unpleasant"), and three distinct themes related to exercise "motivation." Figure 15.1 maps out these four themes, and the relationships between them. Before revision, Paul was undecided about whether "exercise motivation" should be a single (albeit *huge*) theme; review helped him to identify that "exercise motivation" codes and data clearly clustered around three distinct topics: (1) whether or not people possessed the personal attributes required to exercise regularly; (2) social-structural factors that meant access to exercise was not a level playing field (and hence not solely shaped by individual characteristics); and (3) the central importance of social relationships in exercise participation. Interestingly, the participants often vacillated between explaining exercise motivation in terms of individual differences and social-structural factors. This illustrates an important point – themes can express contradictory ideas, and TA can thus capture tensions and contradictions in the data.

Once you are confident that your TA captures the data content well, addresses the research question, and is mapped out in a way you'll probably not change drastically, you move on to defining the themes, clarifying and refining the scope and focus of each, and building a rich analytic narrative. Analytic narrative refers to the descriptive and *interpretative* commentary you present to the reader, which provides the context of quoted data, tells them about what is

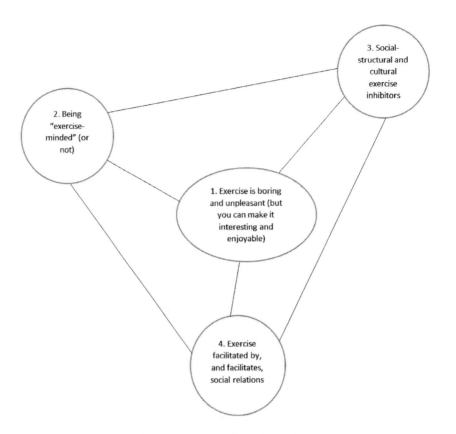

Figure 15.1 Final thematic map from the women and exercise study.

analytically important, and how this addresses the research question. So here you are building *depth* and *detail* into the analysis.

A useful exercise at this point, which can help clarify the "essence" of the analysis, is writing "theme definitions." A theme definition is a brief description (a paragraph or two), which succinctly captures the "essence" of each theme (its central organizing concept), and its scope and boundaries. Writing theme definitions can help to sharpen your analytic focus. Box 15.1 provides (brief) theme definitions for the themes from the women and exercise study.

You also have to decide what you are going to call each theme. Theme names can range from the prosaic to the creative – to some extent, how creative you can be will depend on the *purpose* of the research. Ultimately, you want a name that captures the essence of the theme, but beyond this, it is up to you. Compelling data quotations can work well as part of a theme name, accompanied by explanatory text if necessary (the theme title "Being 'exercise-minded' (or not)" includes a short data quotation that captured precisely the essence of the theme).

Phase 6: Writing up. By this point, you will already have written a lot – "writing" is something you do from early in the analytic process in TA, as in many other qualitative approaches, as you cannot *do* qualitative analysis without writing. So although we call Phase 6 "writing up," we do not think of writing up as a separate phase you start *after* you have completed your analysis – and nor should you. It is an *integral* part of the analytic process. What this phase of TA involves is compiling, developing, and editing *existing* analytic writing, and

---

Box 15.1   Theme definitions from women and exercise study

1. *Exercise is boring and unpleasant (but you can make it interesting and enjoyable)*: although some partici-
    pants described themselves as loving exercise, on the whole exercise was explicitly and implicitly
    framed as something inherently negative – particularly as boring and unpleasant – and this framing
    was strongly connected to the notion that some or all people are "naturally" lazy. Exercise was
    perceived as something separate from everyday life and something that requires "extra" or "spe-
    cial" motivation. However, the participants discussed various ways in which exercise could be
    made interesting and enjoyable, and enjoyment in particular was viewed as the key to regular par-
    ticipation (and, as discussed in theme 4, social relationships were in turn the key to enjoyment).
2. *Being "exercise-minded" (or not)*: the participants often implicitly and explicitly individualized
    exercise motivation and participation, framing it in terms of individual differences in "nature"
    or personality. Sometimes whether or not an individual was "exercise-minded" was presented
    as a "fluke" and at other times, this concept had a moralizing aspect, with people who were
    "exercise-minded" being viewed as having the self-discipline required to overcome the natural
    laziness of human beings (whereas the nonexercise-minded succumbed to this vice).
3. *Social-structural and cultural exercise inhibitors*: Participants also described participation in regular (and
    particular types of) exercise as shaped by a range of social-structural and cultural factors, such as
    gender and social class. For example, women's greater responsibilities for housework, childcare,
    and care of eldery relatives, often alongside paid employment, could result in a lack of time for
    exercise, and concerns about personal safety could shape when, where, and with whom women
    chose to exercise. Likewise, social class could limit women's access to particular kinds of exercise.
4. *Exercise is facilitated by, and facilitates, social relations*: social interaction and relationships were the
    primary exercise facilitators for many of the women; the absence of social interaction was
    likewise a barrier to participation. Women also identified social interaction and relations as
    a benefit of *doing* exercise. Social relationships provided entry to new forms of exercise and
    encouraged continued participation. Ideal forms of exercise were sustained by, and organized
    around, social relationships; in such instances, socializing (and enjoyment) came to the fore, and
    the physical activity was secondary.

---

situating it within an overall report (which generally contains an introduction, method section,
results, discussion – often combined with the results in TA reporting, as in other qualitative
research – and some kind of conclusion; see Braun & Clarke, 2013, for further guidance).
However, writing in TA also involves some important choices. The two elements in your
analysis are data extracts and analytic commentary, and you need to determine a good balance
between the two – too much data, and your analysis is likely to be thin and confined to the
most obvious observations. A 50:50 ratio works for fairly descriptive analyses; more critical/
conceptual analyses often have a greater proportion of analytic narrative. Your narrative will
also be proportionally greater if you combine the results and discussion.

Good data extracts are ones that clearly and compellingly demonstrate the relevant analytic
point or feature. Throughout the analysis, extracts should be selected from across the dataset,
to demonstrate the spread of your themes. There are two broad ways data extracts are used in
TA, which we refer to as "illustratively" and "analytically" (Braun & Clarke, 2013). In the
former, the extract(s) presented serves as an *example* of the analytic claim you are making.

For example, to *illustrate* the notion that exercise in its "pure" form – "deliberate exercise" as Heather (FG2) called it – is an activity separate and distinct from everyday life, either or both of the following two (short) extracts could be used:

Extract 1 (Focus Group 2)
Lindsay: To me exercise is going to the gym or gonna go play squash or tennis – that's exercise.
Heather: Doing sport.

Extract 2 (Focus Group 1)
Maria: I think of exercise, of exercise as something out of your everyday life. Yeah, so we talk about housework and stuff like that, but it's something that you actually make the concerted effort to go out and do, like swimming or dancing or something like that.

The analytic narrative would still make sense if you used either Extract 1 or Extract 2 (Extract 2 *does* provide a richer, more compelling example), or switched one for the other; it would also still make sense if you removed the data extract(s). This illustrative use is common in more descriptive/realist versions of TA, but don't think that just because it is common that this means you can then avoid *interpretation* and simply summarize ... You are still telling an interpretative story about the data and what they mean. In contrast, an *analytic* use of data involves actually discussing specific features of a particular extract. This means you could *not* remove an extract – or replace it with another – and have the narrative still make sense. An example (related to Extract 2) would be:

by creating two separate categories – "housework and stuff like that" versus purposive, "outside the house" activities like "swimming or dancing" – Maria compartmentalizes exercise as something that happens outside the everyday, and therefore something that, implicitly, requires deliberate thought and effort to engage in.

An *analytic* approach is more common in interpretative/critical versions of TA, but in practice, TA research reports often combine both or some aspects of both.

Ensuring quality in thematic analysis

Quality has been a thorny issue in relation to qualitative research, and still is (e.g., Frieze, 2008). The development of "qualitative" quality criteria (e.g., Elliott, Fischer, & Rennie, 1999) has not always been treated with enthusiasm (see, for example, Reicher's, 2000, critique of Elliott *et al.*, 1999), but completely qualitatively oriented quality criterion do now exist (Tracy, 2010; Yardley, 2008). We advise familiarity with these, and the assumptions they rely on – and criteria for judging qualitative research are an ongoing discussion so keep reading (see also Braun & Clarke, 2013; Schinke, Smith, & McGannon, 2013; Sparkes & Smith, 2009)! While we certainly don't advocate "methodolatry" – the privileging of methodological concerns at the expense of others (Reicher, 2000) – we *do* advocate for a rigorous, *deliberative* and reflexive process for doing TA, that keeps "quality" as a foregrounded concern. The "checklist" we developed (see Table 15.3) provides a summary of the points at which TA can fall short in relation to quality. They are the sorts of things we assess research on when supervising, examining or reviewing. Note, this shouldn't be read as the start and end point of quality judgment, but rather a guideline for where you can "fall down" in your analysis. Our "checklist" guidelines promote a thorough and systematic process, and highlight the importance of the active role of the researcher. Keeping a research journal, in which you both record and reflect on the process and practice of your research, can be useful for ensuring a robust qualitative practice (Braun & Clarke, 2013).

Unfortunately TA is not always done well; there are far too many examples of poor TA out there! And the theoretical flexibility of TA can lead to epistemological confusion – the McArdle *et al.* (2012) paper in Table 15.1 provides an example of an epistemologically confused TA – or a failure to explicitly situate TA in relation to theory (or, indeed, to specify how exactly TA has been implemented). We often read papers where the authors cite two very different approaches to TA (e.g., those taken by Boyatzis, 1998 or Braun & Clarke, 2006), without explaining how these two approaches were combined. Furthermore, TA is frequently limited to descriptive – realist/essentialist – analyses, with limited or no engagement with the interpretative potential of TA. Weak TA is one of the reasons why we emphasize the importance of quality. Going forward, we hope to see many more examples of high-quality TA, in which the tools of TA have been used by researchers flexibly and reflexively to produce analyses that "go beyond the obvious," and capture the messy, contradictory, and complex nature of psychological and social meanings.

Table 15.3 15-point "checklist" for a good TA (Braun & Clarke, 2006, p. 96)

Process	No.	Criteria
Transcription	1	Data have been transcribed to an appropriate level of detail, and the transcripts have been checked against the tapes for "accuracy."
Coding	2	Each data item has been given equal attention in the coding process.
	3	Themes have not been generated from a few vivid examples (an anecdotal approach), but instead the coding process has been thorough, inclusive and comprehensive.
	4	All relevant extracts for all each theme have been collated.
	5	Themes have been checked against each other and back to the original dataset.
	6	Themes are internally coherent, consistent, and distinctive.
Analysis	7	Data have been analyzed – interpreted, made sense of – rather than just paraphrased or described.
	8	Analysis and data match each other – the extracts illustrate the analytic claims.
	9	Analysis tells a convincing and well-organized story about the data and topic.
	10	A good balance between analytic narrative and illustrative extracts is provided.
Overall	11	Enough time has been allocated to complete all phases of the analysis adequately, without rushing a phase or giving it a light once-over.
Written report	12	The assumptions about, and specific approach to, thematic analysis are clearly explicated.
	13	There is a good fit between what you claim you do, and what you show. you have done – i.e. described method and reported analysis are consistent.
	14	The language and concepts used in the report are consistent with the epistemological position of the analysis.
	15	The researcher is positioned as *active* in the research process; themes do not just "emerge."

References

Benner, P. (1985). Quality of life: A phenomenological perspective on explanation, prediction, and understanding in nursing science. *Advances in Nursing Science, 8,* 1–14.

Boyatzis, R. E. (1998). *Transforming qualitative information: Thematic analysis and code development.* Thousand Oaks, CA: Sage.

Braun, V., & Clarke, V. (2006). Using thematic analysis in psychology. *Qualitative Research in Psychology, 3,* 77–101.

Braun, V., & Clarke, V. (2012) Thematic analysis. In H. Cooper, P. M. Camic, D. L. Long, A. T. Panter, D. Rindskopf, & K. J. Sher (Eds.), *APA handbook of research methods in psychology, Vol. 2: Research designs: Quantitative, qualitative, neuropsychological, and biological* (pp. 57–71). Washington, DC: American Psychological Association.

Braun, V., & Clarke, V. (2013). *Successful qualitative research: A practical guide for beginners.* London: Sage.

Burr, V. (2003). *Social constructionism* (2nd ed.). London: Psychology Press.

Cedervall, Y. & Åberg, A. C. (2010). Physical activity and implications on well-being in mild Alzheimer's disease: A qualitative case study on two men with dementia and their spouses. *Physiotherapy Theory and Practice, 26,* 226–239.

Christ, T. (1970). A thematic analysis of the American business creed. *Social Forces, 49,* 239–245.

Dapkus, M. A. (1985). A thematic analysis of the experience of time. *Personality Processes and Individual Differences, 49,* 408–419.

Darker, C. D., Larkin, M., & French, D. P. (2007). An exploration of walking behaviour: An interpretative phenomenological approach. *Social Science & Medicine, 65,* 2172–2183.

Demuth, C. & Terkildsen, T. (2015). The future of qualitative research in psychology: A discussion with Svend Brinkman, Günter Mey, Luca Tateo, and Anete Strand. *Integrative Psychological & Behavioral Science, 49,* 135–161.

Elliott, R., Fischer, C. T., & Rennie, D. L. (1999). Evolving guidelines for publication of qualitative research studies in psychology and related fields. *British Journal of Clinical Psychology, 38,* 215–229.

Frieze, I. H. (2008). Publishing qualitative research in sex roles. *Sex Roles, 58,* 1–2.

Guest, G., MacQueen, K. M., & Namey, E. E. (2012). *Applied thematic analysis.* Thousand Oaks, CA: Sage.

Hall, G., Shearer, D., Thomson, R., Roderique-Davies, G., Mayer, P., & Hall, R. (2012). Conceptualising commitment: A thematic analysis of fans of Welsh rugby. *Qualitative Research in Sport, Exercise and Health, 4,* 138–153.

Holt, N. L., & Tamminen, K. A. (2010). Moving forward with grounded theory in sport and exercise psychology. *Psychology of Sport and Exercise, 11,* 419–422.

Joffe, H. (2011). Thematic analysis. In D. Harper & A. R. Thompson (Eds.), *Qualitative methods in mental health and psychotherapy: A guide for students and practitioners* (pp. 209–223). Chichester: Wiley.

Kidder, L. H., & Fine, M. (1987). Qualitative and quantitative methods: When stories converge. In M. M. Mark & L. Shotland (Eds.), *New directions in program evaluation* (pp. 57–75). San Francisco, CA: Jossey-Bass.

Kitzinger, C. (1995). Social constructionism: Implications for lesbian and gay psychology. In A. R. D'Augelli & C. J. Patterson (Eds.), *Lesbian, gay, and bisexual identities over the lifespan: Psychological perspectives* (pp. 136–161). New York: Oxford University Press.

Locke, A. (2004). Accounting for success and failure: A discursive psychological approach to sport talk. *Quest, 56,* 302–320.

McArdle, S., McGale, N., & Gaffney, P. (2012). A qualitative exploration of men's experiences of an integrated exercise/CBT mental health promotion programme. *International Journal of Men's Health, 11*(3), 240–257. doi. 10.3149/jmh.1103.240.

McCreanor, T., Rankine, J., Barnes, A. M., Borell, B., Nairn, R., Gregory, M., & Kaiwai, H. (2010). Māori sport and Māori in sport. *AlterNative: An International Journal of Indigenous Peoples, 6*(3), 235–247.

Patton, M. Q. (2002). *Qualitative evaluation and research methods* (3rd ed.). Thousand Oaks, CA: Sage.

Reicher, S. (2000). Against methodolatry: Some comments on Elliott, Fischer, and Rennie. *British Journal of Clinical Psychology, 39,* 1–6.

Robertson, S., Zwolinsky, S., Pringle, A., McKenna, J., Daly-Smith, A., & White, A. (2013). "It is fun, fitness and football really": A process evaluation of a football-based health intervention for men. *Qualitative Research in Sport, Exercise and Health, 5,* 419–439.

Schinke, R. J., Smith, B., & McGannon, K. R. (2013). Pathways for community research in sport and physical activity: Criteria for consideration. *Qualitative Research in Sport, Exercise and Health, 5,* 460–468.

Slater, M. J., Barker, J. B., Coffee, P., & Jones, M. V. (2015). Leading for gold: Social identity leadership processes at the London 2012 Olympic Games. *Qualitative Research in Sport, Exercise and Health*, 7, 192–209.

Smith, B. & Sparkes, A. C. (2009). Narrative analysis and sport and exercise psychology: Understanding lives in diverse ways. *Psychology of Sport and Exercise*, 10, 279–288.

Smith, B., Tomasone, J. R., Latimer-Cheung, A. E. & Martin Ginis, K. A. (2015). Narrative as a knowledge translation tool for facilitating impact: Translating physical activity knowledge to disabled people and health professionals. *Health Psychology*, *34*, 303–313.

Sparkes, A. C. & Smith, B. (2009). Judging the quality of qualitative inquiry: Criteriology and relativism in action. *Psychology of Sport and Exercise*, 10, 491–497.

Tracy, S. J. (2010). Qualitative quality: Eight "big-tent" criteria for excellent qualitative research. *Qualitative Inquiry*, *16*, 837–851.

Ussher, J. (Ed.) (1997). *Body talk: The material and discursive regulation of sexuality, madness and reproduction.* London: Routledge.

Yardley, L. (2008). Demonstrating validity in qualitative psychology. In J. A. Smith (Ed.), *Qualitative psychology: A practical guide to research methods* (pp. 235–251). London: Sage.

16

PHENOMENOLOGICAL ANALYSIS IN SPORT AND EXERCISE

Susanne Ravn

Phenomenology is "a specific type of reflection or attitude about our human capacity for being conscious" (Varela, 1996, p. 336; see also Chapter 2, this volume). To involve yourself in this kind of reflection, you must find a way to fundamentally problematize your "everydayness" and taken-for-granted ways of thinking *and* constructively draw on prior as well as current phenomenological descriptions. It is my experience that many qualitative researchers new to the domain of phenomenology are a bit overwhelmed by the seemingly double challenge of how to apply relevant methods to "put" this type of reflection "to work" and how to find a way to deal with the very rich and nonhomogeneous philosophical tradition of phenomenology. My purpose in this chapter is to describe how you can deal with both of these challenges. I will do that by providing an overall guide for what to consider, as well as specific advice and examples of how a phenomenological analysis can be done. I will also touch on how different choices might lead the analysis towards different interpretations of why qualitative researchers should choose to incorporate phenomenology into their research. With explicit references to Chapter 2, the first section of this chapter deals with how phenomenological analyses are construed. In the succeeding two sections, how to perform a phenomenological analysis is specified by presenting considerations and tools to employ in the processes of generating and analyzing rich descriptions of practitioners' experience. It should, of course, be noted that the process of generating rich descriptions of experiences already involves an implicit form of analysis, as one chooses to describe something over something else. Thereafter follows an example of how a phenomenological analysis can be performed in the case of elite sports dancers, before I end the chapter with some additional considerations.

What is phenomenological analysis?

In a phenomenological analysis, the first-person perspective is an inevitable premise. However, describing a first-person perspective of experience is *not* per se a phenomenological analysis. As emphasized by Gallagher and Zahavi (2008, p. 19), phenomenology concerns *an account of subjective experience* which should not be misunderstood as a *subjective account* of experience. In other words, phenomenology is *not* concerned with recounting immediate, subjective experiences. No matter how thorough, immediate, or present to the situation the description is claimed to be, such descriptions do *not* per se define a study as phenomenological (see also Chapter 2).

To reflect on our human capacity for being conscious requests that you stand aside from the attitude you "normally" have to your experience by involving a disciplined suspending or bracketing of this "natural attitude." In the philosophical domain, phenomenologists will refer to this disciplined suspension of the natural attitude as the *epoché,* and closely relate it to the processes of reduction, intersubjective corroboration, and eidetic variation. In qualitative studies, the *epoché* is often presented as a first step to take when generating descriptions of practices and experiences. Sometimes the *epoché* is related explicitly to the act of performing a certain shift in attention towards the practice unfolding. However, from a phenomenological perspective, it is important to emphasize that the *epoché* is a never finished process (Merleau-Ponty, 1988/1962, Preface). It might, no doubt, be constructive to shift your attention in certain phases of your observations of the practice, but a shift of attention is generally to be considered a shift in how you deliberately change sensorial preferences and thereby orchestrate your perceptual presence differently (Ravn, 2010; Ravn & Hansen, 2013). To suspend the taken-for-granted ways of being with things and others is a constant challenge to be carried out *throughout* the analysis (Gallagher & Zahavi, 2008; Schmicking, 2010).

In Chapter 2, Allen-Collinson presented the notion of *empirical* phenomenology to characterize studies in which phenomenology is applied within the sociology and psychology of sport and exercise. However, this notion should not give reason to mistakenly think that phenomenologists, like Merleau-Ponty, Sartre, or Zahavi, do not relate to, or involve, empirical data in their reflections. Quite the contrary. Furthermore, one should be aware that, since the 1990s, the interdisciplinary cooperation between phenomenology and the academic domains of neuroscience, cognitive sciences, and psychiatry has constantly grown. For example, a large part of Gallagher's (2005) phenomenological description of the body schema and body image is based on analyses involving experimental testing of a person who has lost his proprioception (the Ian Waterman case), testing of newborn infants' imitation capabilities, and laboratory setups testing the sense of ownership versus agency of hand movements. Besides, one should be aware that when Sartre (2009/1958) turns to the incident of peeping through a keyhole, when Merleau-Ponty (1998/1962) analyses how we experience a mountain as a 'big mountain', even when we are far away and it actually appears small, and when Zahavi (2015) draws on the experience of seeing a hedgehog together with his son to explore how an experience can be shared, these philosophers turn to everyday recognizable incidents as a kind of empirical "data" to support and contribute to their phenomenological analysis. Philosophers, though, often have another interest in involving data than qualitative researchers related to the domains of sports psychology and sociology. In brief, the qualitative researchers tend to employ phenomenology to investigate empirically the domain of sport and exercise, whereas philosophers employ empirical data to participate in explorations within the domain of current phenomenological discussions. The first kind of analysis aims at promoting reflection upon an empathic understanding of how it might feel to be a sporting and/or exercising body in a particular kind of lifeworld, and to present lived experiences of a certain phenomenon of this kind of practice as, for example, the haptic experiences of running and scuba diving (Allen-Collinson and Hockey, 2010), the bodily and interactive experiences of parkour and free running (Clegg & Butryn, 2012), and the essential features of experience in community sports coaching (Cronin & Armour, 2015). The second kind of analysis aims at addressing and contributing to conceptual descriptions and clarifications within the domain of current phenomenological research. The analysis might, for example, clarify the notion of "bodily knowledge" in physical training (Parviainen & Aromaa, 2015), how one is to understand the connection between action and thinking in expertise (Montero, 2013; Høffding, 2014) and the different "ways" in which the physicality of the body can be present to one's experience – where "ways" refers to phenomenological descriptions of how the subject's self-consciousness unfolds in different dimensions (Legrand & Ravn, 2009; Ravn & Christensen, 2014).

Before focusing on how to perform an analysis, it should be made clear that to combine qualitative research methodologies and phenomenology can, basically, be performed by following (at least) two strands of methodological choices, and that each of the strands relates to slightly different kinds of aims for the analysis:

a. *Employing phenomenology in the analysis of qualitative data*: descriptions of lived experience are analyzed to generate rich descriptions of how meanings and sensations are structured within the lifeworld of practitioners.
b. *Employing qualitative data in phenomenological analysis*: descriptions of lived experiences are analyzed to constructively modify, develop, or challenge phenomenological conceptual clarifications.

It should, of course, be emphasized that both strands of methodological choices take off from a process of generating descriptions of lived experiences. Furthermore, the two strands are connected and spill into each other, as will become clear later in this chapter.

How to generate rich descriptions for a phenomenological analysis

The descriptions of lived experiences – your data – are to be as closely related to the way these experiences unfold and take shape in contextualized and "truly lived" situations. In other words, the methods used should give you the opportunity to produce rich, in-depth, detailed descriptions related to participants' concrete, lived experiences on the principles of the athletic practice – a practice which is socially situated and culturally embedded (Allen-Collinson, 2009). Accordingly, the design of the study will – if possible – involve combinations of participant observations and interviews (informal as well as formal).

Participant observations

Participant observation might unfold as relatively passive observing on the sideline, as actively participating in the training yourself, or as observing, in which your own experiences and practices are at the center (see also Chapter 10). No matter how you involve yourself in the practice of observation, your own first-person perspective of experience has importance in relation to what is noticed in the practice unfolding at the site, and how you come to understand the practitioner's description from their point of view. In accordance with ethnographical (see Chapter 5) methodological considerations, the participant observer is herself "the research instrument par excellence" in the process of generating data (Hammersley & Atkinson, 2007, p. 17). Bear in mind that, by definition, you do not have direct access to another person's first-person perspective of experience. Rather, you constructively generate the data by shifting between a second-person and a third-person perspective in relation to the practitioner's experiences (Ravn & Hansen, 2013).

Bear in mind also that your observational notes for a phenomenological analysis should generally pay specific attention to the *what* and *how* of the practice and that you should, accordingly, avoid dwelling on explanations of *why* the practice unfolds as it does. Furthermore, be sure to pay special attention to actual body movements and the different kinds of embodied interaction throughout your observation. The following list of questions can help guide your observations:

1. How is the practice organized by the practitioners? Describe the different kinds of practices within the practice. Aim at being specifically aware of the differences, similarities and connections between these kinds of practices within the practice when it comes to the movement that can be seen and felt.
2. How do the practitioners use their attention and (maybe) change their awareness in the different kinds of practices within the practice? Which kinds of sensations seem to be of importance or special interest to them?
3. Which kinds of sayings, words, and concepts are used by the practitioners? How and when do they communicate, and how is the communication timed in relation to or as part of movements and interactions?
4. How can the sensory involvement related to the practice be described? Prepare certain tasks for yourself to enable you to strategically use a shift in your own perceptual mode of awareness when observing. For example, use 10 minutes three times during the training session to specifically note the sounds of the practice, the smells, the temperature and so on (see also Pink, 2009; Sparkes, 2009; Chapter 26, this volume).

Using observations for a formal interview

During interviews – informal, as well as formal – the overall task is to be specifically aware of distinguishing between what are descriptions and what are considered presentations of the interviewee's opinions (e.g., Gallagher & Fransesconi, 2012). The latter concerns what the interviewee thinks about the phenomena in focus, whereas the former presents descriptions of what experiences are like. These descriptions constitute the valuable data for which you are to aim throughout the different kinds of interview situations. From a phenomenological perspective, however, there is a lot more to be said about the kinds of data which can be generated in an interview.

Like any other formalized interview situation, the interview is an instance of communication. The way the experience is thought of by the practitioner and the way it becomes described will take shape according to the interview situation. In other words, the practitioner's lived experience is not something that is to be revealed through the guidance of the interviewer. Experience is neither a "thing," nor a specific kind of stockpile hidden inside the head or the body and we cannot return to it retrospectively in a straightforward manner. Rather, experience is embodied and enacted in the world, together with other experiencing subjects (Merleau-Ponty, 1988/1962; Zahavi, 2015). During the interview, the practitioner *recalls* the experience according to the principles of the interview situation. As recently emphasized in Høffding and Martiny's (2015) thorough phenomenological analysis of the interview situation, in the encounter, experience becomes an unfolding process that constitutes loops of memory, reflection, description, and questioning.

Participant observations can be used to contextualize the interview situation in several ways. Firstly, sharing experiences from the practice often facilitates the process of making the practitioners feel comfortable about sharing their experiences – sometimes thinking out loud when, for example, figuring out the best way to describe which kind of sensations characterize their performance of a specific skill. Secondly, it familiarizes you with the context of the practitioner's lived experience, including the words and sayings that are part of the actual practice, and thereby gives you the possibility to actively draw on different kinds of situations of the practitioner's practice during the interview. Sharing experiences from the practice thereby offers you the opportunity to prepare follow-up questions with references to specific situations of the practice to elicit further descriptions of what it feels like to perform a specific part of the practice. In this sense, participant observations are used as qualified opportunities to follow the practitioner's descriptions *on the premises* of the practitioner's lived experience. Accordingly, it is important to be aware that using observational notes in this way in interview settings does not present a kind of triangulation of methods, but is to be understood as a combination of methods, where one spills into the other to generate still richer and possibly more varied descriptions of what the practitioner's experiences can be like (Ravn & Hansen, 2013).

Observational descriptions of how the participants structure their sporting or exercise activities often present a relevant outline for how you can structure the interview into different sections. To prepare a relatively open interview guide, begin by reviewing all your notes to get an overall impression of what is fundamental for this kind of practice and, if possible, perform a preliminary round of analysis of your fieldwork data to get a first idea of what might become central "meaning units" and possible themes in the subsequent phases of the analysis. During this first review of your notes, you should also be aware of the ways words, metaphors, and sayings are used. In the interview situation, you should generally take care primarily to use the words, metaphors, and sayings as these are used in the practices observed. The meaning of words and sayings are deeply connected to the practice and the way the ongoing actions involve intersubjectivity (Merleau-Ponty, 1968). There is no prelinguistic kind of pure being opening a direct contact to the world, just as the intertwining of world and subject are not a nonspeaking relation. Rather, as Merleau-Ponty formulates it, "what is lived is lived-spoken" (1968, p. 126). As illustrated by one professional dancer's description in an interview focused on his embodied techniques, the challenge of communicating about movement is not so much the different languages which might be at play. Instead, and as the dancer emphasized with direct relation to a recent process of creating and finishing a choreography with two other dancers (having Swedish, Spanish and English, respectively, as their mother tongues), "it's just as much about sensing how they, like, think as it is about being able to talk and understand each other in a common language. [. . .] It's more like, about *how* you talk" (Ravn, 2009, p. 133).

Prepare a very open interview guide so that you can let the practitioners' experiences – as these experiences are important to them – direct the interview while you take on the role of attentive listener. To be able to be this attentive listener, you should be aware that the experiences of practitioners might be different from what you expected, based on your observations and/or what you have experienced yourself by participating in the same kind of practice. It is part of being an attentive listener that you are able to open (yourself to) the space of possibilities of what the practice can be like. What has been referred to as a nondirective form of interviewing in ethnography presents relevant exemplifications of how the researcher can aim at letting the interviewee's experiences structure the interview (e.g. Hammersley & Atkinson, 2007; Thorpe, 2012).

Here is some advice on how to invite and elicit further descriptions:

1.   Along with open questions, prepare brief sketches of situations that appeared central to the practices you observed. Use the descriptions as an opener to invite the athlete to take over and describe the situation in the way they find relevant.
2.   Even though you think you know what words and sayings mean in relation to the practice, you might get valuable information and descriptions by also asking specifically what certain words and sayings mean in relation to the actual practice during the interview.
3.   Prepare small bits of your own experiences from, for example, participating in the practices, so that you can use these as a kind of follow-up questions to elicit further descriptions related to the experiences just described by the practitioner.

4. Ask the practitioner to recall the same kind of experience, but from another day of training. When relevant, ask the practitioner to describe "the opposite" of a certain kind of experience. For example, in a study where I observed and interviewed an elite golfer (Ravn & Christensen, 2014), the golfer stated that she would only change from one kind of training to another when she had finished with "a good feeling in her body." Obviously, the first question then is to ask if she can describe the good feeling, and, second, if she can describe what "a 'bad' feeling" is like.

Photos, video recordings, drawings, and so on can, in different ways, be used strategically as elicitation techniques in the interview setting. So if you, for example, want the practitioner to engage thoroughly in describing a specific kind of learning situation, video recordings can be used to indicate which kind of situations they are specifically describing their experience of. Or more specifically video recordings of the practices of certain kinds of movement can thus be relevant when exploring how a dancer "combines" the externalized sensations of what her movements look like and her internalized sensation of the movement in the process of being able to imitate the choreographer's way of performing a sequence of a choreography (Ehrenberg, 2012). Using combinations of video recordings and drawings related to practice has also proved valuable when interviewing children in the second grade about their experiences of how dance is different from sports activities (Nielsen, 2009).

If possible and reasonable in relation to the overall design of your project, I suggest that you aim for performing more than one interview with the practitioner. First of all, this will give you the opportunity to begin a preliminary analysis of the first interview before performing the second, and thereby the chance to discover if there are certain aspects of the practice that you need the practitioner to describe more thoroughly. Furthermore, it will open up the possibility of letting the practitioner read a transcription of the first interview and comment on or add to this, if they, for example, feel that there is more to say in relation to what it feels like to be in this specific situation of practice.

Subsequent analysis

In the subsequent analysis, the two strands of methodological choices presented in the beginning of this chapter differ more clearly, as does the researcher's interest in engaging in a phenomenological analysis. It should be remembered here that phenomenology aims at *accounting* for subjective experiences and that phenomenological descriptions, accordingly, are to explore the *structure of experience* in preference to the content of experience (Gallagher & Zahavi, 2008). What should be noted from here on is that the two strands of methodological choices emerge in relation to *which kind of structures* are of interest to the researcher. Studies focused on presenting descriptions of how it might feel to be an exercising body in a particular kind of lifeworld, and presenting lived experiences of a certain phenomenon of this kind of practice, aim to explore the *structure of meanings* as these meanings are of relevance within the academic domain of the researcher. For example, from the domain of psychological research, Giorgi (2008) emphasizes that, in a phenomenological analysis, "the researcher transforms the participant's natural attitude of expressions into expressions that more adequately convey the *psychological meanings* contained in the natural attitude expressions" (Giorgi, 2008, p. 39; my italics). And – from the domain of sociology – Allen-Collinson and Hockey (2010) emphasize the importance of employing insights from phenomenology to challenge, for example, the "hegemony of sight," in sociological descriptions of the sporting body. In this latter example, the structure of meaning relates specifically to descriptions of how heat and pressure are key structures of haptic experience.

Following the other strand of methodological choices, studies will aim to address and contribute to descriptions and conceptual clarifications as related to current phenomenological discussions. The analysis will, accordingly, focus on describing the structure of experience in a transcendental sense. In this kind of analysis, you are thus expected to try to reach *beyond* what the experience of something *means* for the involved subject(s), to attempt to modify, adjust, and change descriptions of the experiential structures of consciousness. For example, recent studies have taken off from the practice-based experiences of batting in cricket (Sutton, 2007), ballet dancing (Montero, 2013), and playing the violin (Høffding, 2014) on internationally recognized levels of expertise. The analyses in these three studies have combined to change Dreyfus's (2014/1997) phenomenological description of expertise. That is, based on explorations of experts' experiences, the studies in each their way contribute to indicating that mindedness is not the enemy of coping, as is claimed in Dreyfus's description (2014/1997). When turning to analyze the experts' actual experiences, it becomes clear that not all reflection or detached observation necessarily degrades skilled coping. Rather, skilled coping is not "one" distinct phenomenon, but a series of connected mental phenomena that spans reflective stances along with trance-like states of absorption (Høffding, 2014).

The latter kind of analysis might at first glance appear to belong to an abstract philosophical level reserved for discussions between philosophers themselves and with little, if any, relevance to the domain of qualitative research in sport, exercise, and health. However, first, the field of phenomenological thinking of today should be neither misunderstood, nor misinterpreted as being limited to philosophers debating and discussing how phenomenological themes of some key philosopher's writings from the last century are to be unpacked and repackaged. Phenomenology is an active field of philosophical studies, which includes continuous discussions of how our sense of self, others, and the world is constituted (Zahavi, 2012). Second, such conceptual clarifications serve to form foundational theoretical grounds for further empirical research. As indicated at the beginning of this chapter, until recently, the interdisciplinary practices of phenomenological analysis have taken place primarily in relation to the framework of the science-based methodologies, like the cognitive sciences, neuroscience, and psychiatry (Gallagher & Zahavi, 2008). Accordingly, the conceptual clarifications in focus have importance in relation to, for example, how schizophrenia is diagnosed (Sass & Parnas, 2003), and how the specific challenges of embodiment in disability, such as cerebral paresis, are to be dealt with in the future (Martiny, 2015). In recent years, phenomenologists have urged the domain of qualitative research to contribute to phenomenological descriptions. From the point of view of qualitative research, I find that one ought to recognize that it will indeed be of importance to future studies of sport, exercise, and health-related activities *how* we, for example, think of the connection between thinking and action in expertise performance (Sutton, 2007; Montero, 2013; Høffding, 2014). Similarly, it will be important to make phenomenologists aware that thorough analysis of sporting bodies can contribute to phenomenological descriptions of our "capacity to be conscious".

Before outlining more specific advice on what and how to continue the analysis, I will sketch the different phases related to the two strands of methodological choices:

1. *Employing phenomenology in the analysis of qualitative data:*
    -   generating rich descriptions of lived experience;
    -   performing an explorative analysis of data, and transforming descriptions into "meanings contained in the expression";
    -   relating the identified "meanings" to themes of relevance within the scientific domain of the researcher.

2. *Employing qualitative research in phenomenological analysis*:
   - generating rich descriptions of lived experience;
   - performing an explorative analysis of data while actively engaging in recent phenomenological discussions;
   - using the analysis of data as "*factual variation*" in the further analysis of phenomenological descriptions.

With reference to Giorgi's guidelines on how to undertake a phenomenological analysis, the explorative phase, which is to be performed in both strands of methodological choices, will standardly involve the steps listed below (see also Chapter 2). In accordance with Schmicking's (2010) recent phenomenological discussion, I propose that you think of these steps as tools belonging to a toolbox in preference to presenting a fixed order of steps to take. As Schmicking notices: "often several of the tools are used simultaneously; different combinations and orders are possible and customary too" (2010, p. 44).

The explorative phase of phenomenological analysis:

1. *Read through to get an overall sense of your data.* Make notes of your immediate understanding of what "this is about." It is often of value to return to this kind of reading through all the notes and transcriptions later on in the analysis, to constantly question if the way you move descriptions further on is coherent with the way expressions are contextualized.
2. *Identify "meaning units."* Remember that these meaning units are "coherent but arbitrary parts" of descriptions, and determined by using criteria that are consistent with the scientific discipline of the researcher (Giorgi, 2008, p. 43).
3. *Organize these meaning units into groups which appear to concern the same aspect of the practitioners' experience.* Read critically through each group of meaning units and re-question if they belong in the same group, as well as how the meaning units within the group differ.

(a) Employing phenomenology in the analysis of qualitative data

Following the strand of (a) employing phenomenology in the analysis of qualitative data (p. 208), you continue by relating the meanings you have identified in the explorative phase to the themes and possible subthemes of analytical relevance within the scientific domain of the researcher (Van Manen, 1990, 2007; Giorgi, 1975, 1997, 2008; Dale, 1996). You can find a very good and illustrative example of how themes can be dealt with in the study of parkour and free running by Clegg and Butryn (2012).

You should be aware that, when aiming to present rich descriptions of lived experiences, you may be requested to distinguish if the way you employ phenomenology in your analysis relates to a *descriptive* or an *interpretative and hermeneutic* phenomenology. Giorgi (1997) argues strongly for aiming at "pure descriptions"; that is, to generate as detailed descriptions of the subject's experience and actions as faithful(ly) as possible compared to what happened as experienced by the subject. Van Manen (1990) argues for constructing "a full interpretative description of some aspects of the lifeworld" (p. 18). Drawing on Gadamer's discussion of hermeneutics, he emphasizes that "interpretation" can be understood as pointing to something, and not necessarily refer to pointing out the meaning of something. Accordingly, one should understand the hermeneutic phenomenological approach as "a revealing of what the thing itself already points out" (Van Manen, 1990, p. 26). So, when focusing on what is actually "done" in what is claimed to be a descriptive versus a hermeneutic analysis, it can be difficult to identify the markers of difference between these two ways of applying phenomenology in the analysis. Following the psychologist Finlay's (2009) considerations, it might be constructive to think of the division between descriptive and interpretative variants of these kinds of phenomenological analysis as part of a continuum.

Furthermore, researchers distinguish between if the analysis is idiographic or aiming for general descriptions. The differentiation corresponds to if the study is aimed at describing the lived experience of "being anxious," or at reaching a more general description of, for example, "feeling anxious" (Finlay, 2009, p. 9). Following Giorgi's recommendations and argumentation, there is no clear division between these two kinds of analysis and an idiographic analysis may form the beginning of a study in which the researcher aims for more generalized descriptions later on (Giorgi, 1997; 2008).

Cronin and Armour (2015) present a study of how an idiographic analysis – or a single case study – can be dealt with. In their exploration of the lifeworld of a coach engaged in community sports, they succeed in making us aware of a dichotomy characterizing the lifeworld of the coach. Accordingly, the coach engaged in community sports is to juggle between a largely unknown, private mode, used predominantly for planning and organizing, and a mode visible in the public arena, focused on delivering fun-based activities, interacting with parents, teachers, and so on. Clegg and Butryn's study on parkour (2012) and Allen-Collinson and Owton's (2014) description of the lived experience of asthma in nonelite sports participants present good examples of how generalized descriptions can be aimed for. The former study illustrates the many aspects of parkour that deviate from other comparable sport experiences. Clegg and Butryn do so by describing the structure of meaning in relation to central structures of importance for "bodily experience" and "interactive experience," respectively. In the latter study, descriptions are focused especially on the aural dimensions of experience. Allen-Collinsion and Owton indicate specifically how asthmatic participants draw on fine distinctions in their auditory attunement when engaging in sporting activities. At the same, time their analysis also contributes to examining sociocultural and historical specificities of sensory experience.

(b) Employing qualitative research in phenomenological analysis

When you aim for an analysis of your data that is relevant to phenomenology, you will obviously be expected to specify which kind of phenomenological concepts your study aims to bring into further analysis. So, in direct relation to the explorative phase, you involve yourself in specifying how the themes of the meaning units can be described, in accordance with phenenological descriptions of related themes and concepts. From there, the phenomenologically related descriptions of observations and interviews can be used as factual variations for phenomenological thinking.

In classical phenomenology, *eidetic variation* (Chapter 2) is about "using our imagination to strip away the unessential properties of things" (Gallagher & Zahavi, 2008, p. 30). As Høffding and Martiny (2015) make us aware, the eidetic variation can be understood as a genre of the classical philosophical thought experiment since it relies on imagination. However, if we want to shake our ingrained assumptions to force us to refine, revise, or even abandon our habitual ways of thinking, "real-life deviations," as presented in different academic domains, present rich sources of challenging material (Zahavi, 2005, p. 141f). Following Gallagher's discussions (2012), one might label the use of empirical data for phenomenological variation as *factual variation* (Høffding & Martiny, 2015). Comparable to the strength of what the case study (see also Chapter 6) can add to current theories (Stake, 1995), the factual variation can be compared to using a phenomenologically specified way to test phenomenological descriptions as your "theory" (Ravn & Christensen, 2014).

Phenomenological analysis of the embodied interaction in elite sports dance: an example of how qualitative data can be employed in phenomenological analysis

In the following, the embodied interaction in sports dance is used to describe further how this kind of expertise interaction can contribute to and modify phenomenological descriptions of how perception-action cycles are not to be reduced to a process of an individualized body-sub-ject. The data and analysis presented are extracts from a study involving two couples of elite sports dancers and several dancers dancing Argentinean tango on a recreational basis (Ravn, 2016).

The example is focused on the data related to the dancers Michelle Abildtrup and Martino Zanibellato. At the time of observations and interviews in 2010, the couple was ranked in the top five in the world of Latin dances (Rumba, Paso doble, Cha-cha-cha, Samba and Jive). They turned professional in 2013 and won the world championship in 2013 and 2014.

As part of the explorative phase of the analysis it turned out that the dancers' sense of connection unfolded in different but interconnected ways: if they feel their own movement is connected, if they feel their partner is connected in his or her movement, and if they feel a connection between their bodies moving is somehow closely linked and closely related. The following quotes from the interviews exemplify "meaning units" that are related to the theme of connection: *feeling connected* and *being part of connection*.

> *Michelle:* And I think what we have learned to understand through the connection, is that a lot of time when you work on connection, you think about push or pull or the arm. But I think that through the years we have learned, that it's actually more about his body and my body, and then the connection should happen a little bit by itself so if I'm right connected, and he is connected, then we should be connected.

At another time during one of the interviews, Michelle explains how her sense of movement extends so that she feels also the movement of his body: "but . . . yeah of course my arm would end in the connection. My body would end in the connecting arm, but I can still feel his hip for example."

> *Martino:* For me it's very important that she feels all the bodyweight that I'm using. Because then she feels how much I want to get out of the step. And that's what I always ask her, to make me feel where she is, at all times. So I can tune in with her own bodyweight.
>
> *He continues:* Now from here, she's telling me that she wants to stay and she put the bodyweight there, and I receive the bodyweight. I can do this without connection, so I make it look like there is a connection, but there is not. She is doing it by herself.

Taking the themes of the explorative analysis into a phenomenological analysis

These descriptions of being connected and each, in their own way, being part of the connection addresses how they feel the lines and flow of movement proceed through different body parts, and continue to form part of their partner's movement. In this sense, the lines and flow of movement of one dancer extends and leads into the movement of their partner. Accordingly, the theme describing their experiences relates to the phenomenological theme of how the interaction between two bodies involves descriptions of "bodies extending."

Turning to recent phenomenological discussions, De Jaegher and Di Paolo (2007) and Fuchs and De Jaegher (2009) have suggested ways in which one might think of perception-action loops extending beyond an individualized subject. They argued that extended perception-action loops also take form in the prereflective dimensions of the subjects' experiences. The subjects incorporate a certain timing and directedness of their movement through micro levels of interaction in underlying levels of perception. Fuchs and De Jaegher (2009) relate their phenomenological exploration of interaction to data obtained from the dyad between mother and infant, as well as to the everyday experiences of stepping aside when passing another person in a narrow corridor. Despite also referring to a tennis player's movement while playing a match, Fuchs and De Jaegher do not consider how their description of interaction relates to the practices of elite athletes – who are also *deliberately* involved in making the interaction work. As elite athletes, the two sports dancers aim for the sublime performance of interaction to achieve the highest score. On the one hand, in their practice, they exemplify the phenomenological description of these extended perception-action loops. On the other hand, they also demonstrate that they shift *strategically* between focusing on their movements as extended and as individualized. The dancers thereby indicate that the experience of the body as extended and shared is not something that just "happens," but is something that can be worked on strategically on the premise of reciprocity of interaction. Furthermore, it is worth noticing that the coordination of movement unfolds in a continuous flux of receptivity and activity of the involved subjects. Thus, the intentionality of the movements fluctuates and does not only belong to an individualized subject, but can vibrate in a decentered way in between, in this case, the two dancers (Ravn, 2016).

Conclusion

Let me begin these concluding remarks by indicating that the contribution that phenomenology can offer to the interdisciplinary domains of academic research is conceptual clarification. In this chapter, I have introduced you to the considerations and choices you should relate to *when* you perform a phenomenological analysis, taking advantage of phenomenological insights. It has been important to me to present the analytical steps as tools in a toolbox. Different kinds of studies will challenge the analytical process in slightly different ways. There is no beaten path to follow and there is no GPS device to lead you the direct way towards "the results." You will have to find and qualify your choices, while paying attention that you also make the path you take transparent to the reader.

The considerations and advice I have presented have generally been related to the challenges of how to generate and analyze descriptions of somebody else's experience. The focus has been on how to familiarize yourself with another practitioner's experience. If the practitioner is also the researcher performing the phenomenological analysis – that is, if you are generating data based on your own experiences – you should be aware that you are still in a process of generating data. Here, the challenge is not as much about familiarizing yourself with the lived experience of another practitioner, but rather about managing to make it transparent and clear to an intersubjective realm, how the descriptions have been generated.

As presented in the introduction, the two strands of methodological choices relate to different interpretations of why qualitative researchers should choose to engage in phenomenological thinking in the analysis. Following the (a) strand of methodological choices, the researcher deals with rich descriptions of how meanings and sensations are structured within the lifeworld of practitioners, to bring to light the carnal realities of sporting bodies, and confront analyses that tend to reduce the body to a mere representation of a discursive practice. Following the (b) strand of methodological choices, the researcher aims at constructively modifying, developing, or challenging phenomenological descriptions. I am well aware that, for many qualitative researchers, the rich descriptions of how meanings and sensations are structured appear of immediate relevance to the environments of sport and exercise. The continuous exploration of how we are to understand fundamental structures of our lifeworld, such as intentionality, the relation between thinking and action, and processes of interaction are central to future analyses. This kind of phenomenological analysis brings to light how practice-based insight can change current theories of consciousness, movement, and embodiment. It brings to the fore that sporting bodies are not only a theme of specific interest but also present cases of importance to contribute to phenomenology.

Acknowledgment

I wish to thank Simon Høffding for his constructive comments on an earlier draft of this chapter.

References

Allen-Collinson, J. (2009). Sporting embodiment: Sports studies and the (continuing) promise of phenomenology. *Qualitative Research in Sport and Exercise*, 1, 279–296.

Allen-Collinson, J. & Hockey, J. (2010). Feeling the way: Notes toward a haptic phenomenology of distance running and scuba diving. *International Review for the Sociology of Sport*, 46, 330–345.

Allen-Collinson, J. & Owton, H. (2014). Take a deep breath: Asthma, sporting embodiment, the senses and "auditory work." *International Review for the Sociology of Sport*, 49, 592–608.

Clegg, J. F. & Butryn, T. (2012). An existential phenomenological examination of parkour and free running. *Qualitative Research in Sport, Exercise and Health*, 4, 320–340.

Cronin, C. & Armour, K. (2015). Lived experience and community sport coaching: A phenomenological investigation. *Sport, Education and Society*, 20, 959–975.

Dale, G. A. (1996). Existential phenomenology: Emphasizing the experience of the athlete in sport psychology research. *The Sport Psychologist*, 10, 307–321.

De Jaegher, H. & Di Paolo, E. (2007). Participatory sense-making: An enactive approach to social cognition. *Phenomenology and the Cognitive Sciences*, 6, 485–507.

Dreyfus, H. (2014/1997). Intuitive, deliberative and calculative models of expert performance. In C. E. Zsambok & G. Klein (Eds.), *Naturalistic decision making* (pp. 3–16). New York: Psychology Press.

Ehrenberg, S. (2012). A contemporary dancer's kinaesthetic experiences with dancing self-images. In S. Ravn & L. Rouhiainen (Eds.), *Dance spaces: Practices of movement* (pp. 193–216). Odense: University Press of Southern Denmark.

Finlay, L. (2009). Debating phenomenological research methods. *Phenomenology and Practice*, 3, 6–25.

Fuchs, T. & De Jaegher, H. (2009). Enactive intersubjectivity: Participatory sense making and mutual incorporation. *Phenomenology and the Cognitive Sciences*, 8, 465–486.

Gallagher, S. (2012). Taking stock of phenomenology futures. *The Southern Journal of Philosophy*, 50, 304–318.

Gallagher, S. (2005). *How the body shapes the mind*. New York, NY: Oxford University Press.

Gallagher, S. & Francesconi, D. (2012). Teaching phenomenology to qualitative researchers, cognitive scientists, and phenomenologists. *The Indo-Pacific Journal of Phenomenology*, 12, 1–10.

Gallagher, S. & Zahavi, D. (2008). *The phenomenological mind*. London: Routledge.

Giorgi, A. (2008). Concerning a serious misunderstanding of the essence of the phenomenological method in psychology. *Journal of Phenomenological Psychology*, 39, 33–58.

Giorgi, A. (1997). The theory, practice and evaluation of the phenomenological method as a qualitative research. *Journal of Phenomenological Psychology*, 28, 235–261.

Giorgi, A. (1975). An application of phenomenological method in psychology. In A. Giorgi, C. Fischer, & E. Murray (Eds.), *Duquesne studies in phenomenological psychology* (vol. 2, pp. 82–103). Pittsburgh, PA: Duquesne University Press.

Hammersley, M. & Atkinson, P. (2007). *Ethnography: Principles in practice* (3rd ed.). London & New York: Routledge.

Høffding, S. (2014). What is skilled coping? Experts on Expertise. *Journal of Consciousness Studies, 21,* 49–73.

Høffding, S. & Martiny, K. (2015). Framing a phenomenological interview: What, why and how. *Phenomenology and the Cognitive Sciences.* DOI: 10.1007/s11097-015-9433-z.

Legrand, D. & Ravn, S. (2009). Perceiving subjectivity in bodily movement: the case of dancers. *Phenomenology and Cognitive Science, 8,* 389–408.

Martiny, K. M. (2015). How to develop a phenomenological model of disability. *Medicine, Health Care and Philosophy, 18,* 553–565.

Merleau-Ponty, M. (1998/1962). *The phenomenology of perception.* London: Routledge.

Merleau-Ponty, M. (1968). *The visible and the invisible.* Illinois: Northwestern University Press.

Montero, B. (2013). A dancer reflects. In K. Shear (Ed.), *Mind, reason, and being-in-the-world* (pp. 303–319). London and New York: Routledge.

Nielsen, C. S. (2009). Children's embodied voices: Approaching children's experiences through multi-modal interviewing. *Phenomenology & Practice, 3,* 80–93.

Parviainen, J. & Aromaa, J. (2015). Bodily knowledge beyond motor skills and physical fitness: A phenomenological description of knowledge formation in physical training. *Sport, Education and Society.* DOI: 10.1080/13573322.2015.1054273.

Pink, S. (2009). *Doing sensory ethnography.* London: Sage.

Ravn, S. (2016). Embodying interaction in Argentinean tango and sports dance. In T. F. DeFrantz & P. Rothfield (Eds.), *RELAY: Theories in motion.* London: Palgrave MacMillan.

Ravn, S. (2010). Sensing weight in movement. *Journal of Dance and Somatic Practices, 2,* 21–34.

Ravn, S. (2009). *Sensing movement, living spaces: An investigation of movement based on the lived experience of 13 professional dancers.* Saarbrücken: VDM, Dr. Müller.

Ravn, S. & Christensen, M. K. (2014). Listening to the body? How phenomenological insight can be used to explore a golfer's experience of the physicality of her body. *Qualitative Research in Sport, Exercise and Health, 6,* 462–477.

Ravn, S. & Hansen, H. P. (2013). How to explore dancers' sense experiences? A study of how multi-sited fieldwork and phenomenology can be combined. *Qualitative Research in Sport, Exercise and Health, 5,* 196–213.

Sartre, J. (2009/1958). *Being and nothingness.* London and New York: Routledge.

Sass, L. A. & Parnas, J. (2003). Schizophrenia, consciousness, and the self. *Schizophrenia Bulletin, 29,* 427–444.

Schmicking, D. (2010). A toolbox of phenomenological methods. In S. Gallagher & D. Schmicking (Eds.), *Handbook of phenomenology and cognitive science.* The Netherlands: Springer.

Sparkes, A. C. (2009). Ethnography and the senses: Challenges and possibilities. *Qualitative Research in Sport and Exercise, 1,* 21–35.

Stake, R. E. (1995). *The art of case study research.* London and New Delhi: Sage.

Sutton, J. (2007). Batting, habit and memory: The embodied mind and the nature of skill. *Sport in Society, 10,* 783–786.

Thorpe, H. (2012). The ethnographic (i)nterview in the sports field: Towards a postmodern sensibility. In K. Young & M. Atkinson (Eds.), *Qualitative research on sport and physical culture* (pp. 51–78). Bingley, UK: Emerald.

Van Manen, M. (2007). Phenomenology of practice. *Phenomenology & Practice, 1,* 11–30.

Van Manen, M. (1990). *Researching lived experience.* New York: State University of New York Press.

Varela, F. (1996). Neurophenomenology: A methodological remedy for the hard problem. *Journal of Consciousness Studies, 3,* 330–349.

Zahavi, D. (2015). You, me, and we – the sharing of emotional experience. *Journal of Consciousness Studies, 22,* 84–101.

Zahavi, D. (Ed.) (2012). *The Oxford handbook of contemporary phenomenology.* Oxford, UK: Oxford University Press.

Zahavi, D. (2005). *Subjectivity and selfhood: Investigating the first-person perspective.* Cambridge, MA: MIT Press.

17

INTERPRETATIVE PHENOMENOLOGICAL ANALYSIS IN SPORT AND EXERCISE

Getting at experience

Jonathan A. Smith

What is interpretative phenomenological analysis?

Interpretative phenomenological analysis (IPA) is a qualitative approach concerned with examining personal lived experience. It was developed in the 1990s to complement the quantitative experimental paradigm of mainstream psychology. An explicit part of the impetus for articulating IPA, however, was also to show continuity with an important but neglected tradition within the disciplines concerned with the examination of personal experience and personal accounts (James, 1890; Allport, 1951). A complete guide to IPA is available, covering its theoretical underpinnings and methodological practice and providing worked examples (see Smith, Flowers, & Larkin, 2009).

IPA has three primary theoretical touchstones. First, it draws from phenomenology, the philosophical position initially espoused by Husserl to examine how experience is recorded in consciousness (see also Chapters 2 and 16). For Husserl (2001/1900) the task for phenomenology is to go 'back to the things themselves' (p. 168); that is, to explore how objects and events are experienced subjectively, untrammelled, as far as possible, by the predilections of researchers or the assumptions of natural science. Following Heidegger, for IPA this is unashamedly an interpretative endeavour. Humans are sense-making creatures; they attempt to make sense of the things that are happening to them. The job for the researcher then is to make sense of the participant making sense of x; this is described as engaging in a double hermeneutic.

Finally, a distinctive hallmark of IPA is its idiography. IPA is concerned with understanding the case, the experience of each participant, in detail. This means sample sizes in IPA studies are small. The process of analysis is one of moving slowly from case to case and only cautiously making claims for the group as a whole. In practice, a good piece of IPA attempts to show how experiential themes are made manifest in the sample through a nuanced analysis of convergence and divergence – showing how participants may share overriding concerns, but highlighting the particular ways in which those concerns reveal themselves for particular individuals.

IPA was first articulated within health psychology (Smith, 1996), and most of the early work was within that discipline. However, it has since been taken up by researchers in a range of disciplines and is now employed in many fields, for example, management, music, education. A growing corpus of work has emerged in sport and exercise and this is now a fertile field for the approach. A similar trend can be seen geographically. While IPA developed and was originally used in the UK, it has now taken off internationally and research using IPA is now done across the world.

Growth of IPA research in sport and exercise

What does the trend of research using IPA in sport and exercise look like? Web of Science is a search engine for papers in journals given an impact factor to reflect their esteem in the field. The number of papers appearing in Web of Science therefore offers a conservative trend of mainstream progress. I searched for the number of papers displaying the search terms *interpretative phenomenological analysis and (sport or exercise)*. And, unsurprisingly, this shows a modest development for IPA in sport and exercise with something of a surge for 2014 reflecting very recent rise in publications (see Table 17.1).

Google Scholar, in contrast, offers a very inclusive search strategy which includes all journals and also books and PhD theses. Its deliberately open search strategy means that figures have to be treated cautiously, because non-relevant items can be included, but a search still shows a relevant trend. I did a search for *interpretative phenomenological analysis and sport* because the word 'exercise' has other usages. The graph in Figure 17.1 shows a dramatic increase in research in sport using IPA in the last 5 years. If one adds 'exercise' in the search the overall trend is similar to this. The Google Scholar results are more in line with my own sense of what has been happening. It is clearly the case that there has been growing interest in and usage of IPA in sport and exercise, and this trend does appear to have accelerated in the last five years. Of course, it will take longer for this to break through into a marked increase in papers published in more mainstream journals but one can expect to see this trend also continue over the next few years.

Why is this growth of IPA in sport and exercise happening?

Why is this expansion happening? I am not primarily a sport and exercise researcher so I am speculating here. It is very interesting to see this rise in research and actually I am not especially surprised. Different research methodologies are useful for different research questions. IPA is a useful approach for research projects focused on understanding the lived experience of their participants. Sport and exercise, like any discipline, have a number of different concerns. I can see that some sport and exercise researchers will be concerned primarily with physiological mechanisms and changes associated with physical activity. Others will emphasize the importance of

Table 17.1 Numbers of IPA papers on sport and exercise recorded by Web of Science

2004	2
2006	2
2008	4
2010	5
2012	3
2014	14

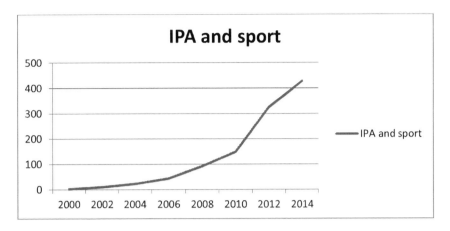

Figure 17.1 Trend in Google Scholar hits for IPA and sport.

interventions to enhance performance. However, it seems to me that one key concern for the discipline will be experience, both in its own terms and as it relates to those two previous concerns. Engaging in sport and exercise is an experience and IPA is well placed to explore the multifarious aspects of that experiential component. Here are just some of the types of research questions that come to mind:

1. Why do individuals do sport and exercise? What motivates them?
2. What leads up to their starting and what sustains them?
3. What is doing sport and exercise like? How do individuals describe the experience?
4. What links do they perceive between mind and body? What metaphors do they use?
5. What is the relationship between participation in sport and exercise and well-being?
6. Can personal accounts of this relationship inform interventions to enhance well-being?
7. How do people feel about competition and how integral is it to the experience of sport?

These type of questions seem to me to be at the heart of sport and exercise, and IPA's foundational position as an experiential approach to inquiry means it is extremely well placed to help ask and answer these and other questions like them.

The growth of work in sport and exercise will also have been facilitated by the existence of accessible step-by-step guides to conducting IPA. I have felt it important at this stage in the development of IPA to offer resources which will encourage newcomers to have a go at using the approach. I come back to this point and discuss it more fully later in the chapter. Finally, I suspect another reason for the growth of IPA in sport and exercise is structural. It is a relatively new discipline and therefore able to be innovative in its approach. IPA as a youngish but now well-established research approach can therefore become part of the portfolio for a discipline working out how best to ask the questions it wishes and needs to ask.

How do you do IPA?

This section will give a brief overview of the main stages in conducting an IPA research study. There are a number of fuller guides available (Smith, Flowers, & Larkin, 2009; Smith & Osborn, 2015), and I suggest the interested reader refers to one of them for fuller information.

The scope of the study will depend partly on what its purpose is. An undergraduate final-year project should be simpler and on a smaller scale than a research project funded by a grant-awarding body and conducted by a post-doctoral researcher. In my experience, novice researchers often try to produce designs which are too complicated, involving too many participants and asking too complicated a set of questions. At this stage in the development of an experiential research paradigm, it is often most valuable to ask a simple phenomenological question – *what is this thing like?* – rather than, for example, *what is this thing like and what do we think caused it?* The latter type of research question may be appropriate for a project conducted by a more experienced researcher.

As the aim is to gain a detailed and personalized understanding of the psychological experience of a phenomenon, IPA analysis involves a close examination of each case. For this reason sample sizes are usually small. For example, many students on postgraduate training courses in clinical psychology now employ IPA for their empirical research project and typical sample sizes are 6–8 (Thompson, Larkin & Smith, 2011). On a broader level, many IPA research studies have sample sizes of 10 or fewer.

IPA advocates purposive homogeneous sampling. If one is looking in detail at the psychological experience of a small sample of participants, it makes sense for that sample to be uniform, as far as is possible, in terms of obvious variables, commonly: age, gender, level of experience. A good IPA analysis usually points to a mixture of convergence and divergence in participants' accounts. If demographic factors can be held reasonably constant then the differences one sees in participants' experiences can more readily be seen as reflecting individual psychological differences between participants.

Most IPA studies obtain data through semi-structured interviews. An interview schedule is constructed but this is intended merely as a stimulus to help get the participant talking, and the schedule is used very flexibly in the interview. Thus participants are probed on important areas that come up and much of this probing will be spontaneous in that the researcher cannot predict exactly what the participant will say.

Good interviewing draws on a number of qualities in the researcher: you need to be attentive and engaged, but also relaxed and flexible; you need to have thought carefully about a plan for the interview in advance, but then you need to be ready to think on your feet during the interview itself. This form of in-depth interviewing needs particular skill and it may involve considerable training and practice before the researcher achieves competence.

It is probably the case that the demands of this part of the research process have been less well articulated than analysis, yet good data collection is crucial. It sets a cap on what can be achieved in the project as a whole. A good interview offers the potential for an excellent analysis; a mediocre interview already prescribes what can be achieved in analysis. The interview participants in an IPA study are a precious commodity. Therefore one should spend a lot of time honing interview skills in advance and this can, for example, include asking friends or colleagues to role-play potential participants as you try out your questions and gain more competence and confidence in the process.

There is not a single right way to do IPA analysis. However, this part of the research cycle can seem particularly intimidating to the novice. It is for this reason that I have written a number of guides to doing analysis. My advice to newcomers is to follow this guide in the first study you do. It has worked for me and many students I have worked with and it will enable you to produce an acceptable analysis. After you have done it once you will be in a better position to appreciate the underlying sensibility of the approach and adapt it appropriately in your next study. As a colleague once said to me, 'It is only because I have followed the rules in this first study, Jonathan, that I now know that I don't need to follow the rules!' I think he got it.

Consistent with IPA's idiographic commitment, each interview transcript is analysed as a case in its own right. You begin with the first transcript and read it a number of times to develop deep familiarity with the content. As you read, use one margin to make notes in response to the text. These initial notes can be pointers to important content, attempts to unravel complications, pointers to metaphors and other linguistic devices used, early interpretative commentary.

After having done this for the whole transcript, you return to the beginning and carefully examine the initial notes made in sequence. The next task is to translate those initial notes into emergent experiential grounded themes which are recorded in the other margin. The aim here is to construct thematic statements which are both specific, dynamic and grounded in what the respondent has said at that point in the interview, but which are also moved to a more distilled and abstracted level. Poor IPA stays too descriptive or moves too abstractedly. The knack is getting the middle level right and, just as with interviewing, this is a difficult skill which can take considerable practice. It is worth lingering on a first case for some time, working and reworking the themes, checking them with your supervisor before you attempt to implement the same process in the second case.

Having documented the emergent experiential themes for the whole transcript, one then needs to examine the corpus of themes and establish a set of coherent inductive clusters from them. Which themes go with which? Do some themes act as a magnet pulling others towards them? For the newcomer, I still recommend the old-fashioned way of doing this. Make a photocopy of the transcript and then put the original to one side. Cut up the themes on the copy so each theme is on a separate piece of paper. Place all the pieces of paper on the floor or on a large table and then spend two hours formulating clusters of themes. Do this when you are mentally alert to give it your best shot. This should be a creative and inspiring part of the process and there is not a single best set of clusters which will emerge.

Once you have a set of clusters, which you feel happy convey the important experiential features of the participant, record the clusters on the computer. Give each cluster a title – this becomes a superordinate theme title – and under each title record the themes which comprise it. Alongside each theme provide a few key words from the participant's own words as a reminder of what was said which generated the theme and, for completion, give the page and line number for the extract.

You then do the same thing for each transcript in turn. Having completed this exercise look closely at the table from each case and use this to generate group themes which go across the set of participants. While some of the group experiential themes will transpire fairly straightforwardly, this stage often generates considerable conceptual work. Confronted with cases which seem to be doing different things forces you, as the reader, to check for ways in which those apparently different things are actually illustrations of the same underlying or transcendent property. As I said earlier, good IPA articulates the co-existence of convergence and divergence in a corpus. So there will be a patterning of similarity and difference in the way the group table maps onto the participants. One might expect all participants to manifest each superordinate theme, but this may be manifest in different participants aligned to different themes within that superordinate construct.

Doing IPA is both linear and iterative. Revisit material in the light of analysis that is conducted, check previous interpretations in the light of new analytic commentary. This also operates at a range of levels. Having completed the overall thematic analysis as described above it is a good idea to look again at sections of the corpus in the light of it. Thus the whole understanding has developed out of analysis of the parts; some of those parts are now looked at again in the light of the whole. This is described as engaging in the hermeneutic circle (Smith *et al.*, 2009). This way the analysis is deepened, the interpretation strengthened.

The usual way IPA is written up is in the form of a narrative presentation of the superordinate experiential themes, introducing each theme in turn and then giving indicative quotes from participants to illustrate the theme. Quotes are followed by interpretative commentary providing the reader with the researcher's analysis of why this is important and interesting, and how it connects to the unfolding experiential account. Analysis continues into writing. As one writes the narrative new ideas emerge and interpretations are filled out and strengthened or modified.

Good IPA research in sport and exercise

I was already familiar with some of the literature in sport and exercise, but as part of preparation for writing this chapter I also looked at a sample of other papers. Given the huge growth of work this is, of course, only a small sample and I am not claiming it is representative. What I have done, however, is to select a set of IPA papers which I think are both good and interesting and which cover topics in the main areas of sport and exercise. In the following sections, I give brief summaries of the papers and point to the particular features which make them good.

Sport and performance

Nicholls, Holt and Polman (2005) explore coping strategies in young international golfers. The paper presents a very thorough description of its methodology. Telephone interviews were conducted with 18 male Irish international golfers aged 14–21 years about stressors they had encountered in their golf careers, and strategies they employed to cope. The paper presents vivid data from participants to illustrate successful and unsuccessful strategies. The idiographic instances illustrate participants selecting their own repertoire of successful strategies, drawing on behavioural and cognitive techniques. Instances of unsuccessful coping are also provided and include, for example, trying too hard, and the use of an inappropriate technical change. This is an interesting and useful paper, and the authors point to how in future work they could look in even more detail at how particular individuals manage stressful situations.

Hefferon and Ollis (2006) present a very clear and thorough analysis of flow experience in professional dancers. They begin with a useful summary of the concept and its importance in performance. Whereas this study is about the experience of professional dancers it is relevant to high-level physical performance more generally, and the paper makes regular links to flow in elite sports personnel. The authors interviewed nine professional dancers about their experience of flow. They then present a clear analysis of the experience itself and the factors which can influence it. All statements are well supported with extracts from the interviews. Key features of the experience itself are confidence in self and skills, and absorption in the task:

> Expressing how you feel right at that moment. I couldn't say that I am conscious of my thoughts. I am just enjoying the purity of the movement and how it felt for me. That's how I am sensitive towards that; you are completely comfortable with yourself and relaxed and open to your body and how you approach the movement, then I find that I get to that place.
>
> Respondent D *(Hefferon & Ollis, 2006, p. 150f)*

Among key factors facilitating flow are: confidence, pre-performance routine, good relationships with others involved.

Warner and Dixon (2015) explore the role of gender in perceptions of competition. The paper looks at the views on competition of male and female athletes who are: 1) currently active (focus groups); and 2) who have retired from sport (individual interviews). They have an unusually large sample for an IPA study, with a total of 76 participants, but descriptive statistics of prevalence of themes are offered at various points. Overall the paper shows a trend, with males feeling positive about competition, females being more mixed. However, the authors are careful to point out that one should avoid over-generalizing; there are exceptions and these are also illustrated. And the picture in the females is interesting. They see the value of external intergroup competition, but find internal competition within the team problematic. By contrast, in general the men see competition at all levels as beneficial. Participants and authors speak of this in biological and social-role terms. The paper draws on a number of interesting theoretical perspectives, including social identity theory, and discusses the various implications, for example, the value of sports programmes that encourage cooperation. It is a thorough, interesting and thought-provoking paper.

Caron, Bloom, Johnston and Sabiston (2013) look at the long-term consequences of multiple concussions on retired ice-hockey players. This is a well-written paper with a good rationale for its approach. The researchers interviewed five former national hockey-league players who had suffered multiple concussions during their career. It has a good clear analysis with powerful data. Participants are still suffering symptoms years later: e.g. vision impairment, inability to concentrate. They also describe serious mental distress: stress, anxiety and suicidal ideation. The paper is also interesting on the reactions of others and the men's transitions from being professional sports players:

> My identity became the hockey player. You're signing autographs, you're on TV and in the print, and your identity gets wrapped up in that. And I don't think it's necessarily an ego thing. It's more how you're identified with people. My identity was stripped from me when I retired and I had to reinvent myself.
>
> Paul *(Caron et al., 2013, p. 175)*

Turner, Barlow and Ilbery (2002) report a study of twelve ex-professional footballers who have subsequently suffered from osteoarthritis. The interview data is strong and the claims made in the paper are well evidenced with extracts from those interviews. The men reflect on how features of the professional game are likely to have affected their current situation. The paper movingly shows how restricted mobility has had a powerful impact on these men, whose identity was so entwined with excellence in their chosen sport. It is also the case that the men show a wide range of coping strategies: for example, upward social comparison with those doing well; downward comparison with some who are having greater difficulties. The paper is very well written and the narrative is persuasive.

Health, exercise and recreation

Sebire, Standage, Gillison and Vansteenkiste (2013) interviewed eleven regular exercisers about their motivations and experiences. Themes are well supported with extracts from participants, and the reader develops a useful cumulative picture of their experience. The authors demonstrate the participants' complex range of responses to observing others in the gym; for example, for some, upward social comparison can act as a motivator, whereas others turn away from such comparisons to concentrate on intrinsic motivation. Participants show a range of attitudes in relation to their ability to achieve their goals, and demonstrate varied ways of marking progress towards those goals

McDonough, Sabiston and Ullrich-French (2011) report a study of dragon-boating and breast-cancer survivors. This is an impressive paper. The researchers recruited seventeen breast-cancer survivors who were part of a dragon-boating activity and interviewed each woman five times over the course of two years. As a result of the analysis, women are placed into four profile groups reflecting their experience of the process. Each profile is well illustrated with extracts to show the process occurring over time. For example, Group 1 is 'developing a feisty spirit of survivorship' and clearly illustrates the development of a communal identity for the women, along with the consequent personal growth which ensued. The third profile group emphasized the importance of the physical activity and this was captured in Samantha's comment: 'It's not about the pink, it's about the paddling' (McDonough *et al.*, 2011, p. 641), which was then used as the title for this group profile. The paper is well written, well framed in relation to extant literature and the authors carefully evaluate their work against the criteria established for IPA (Smith, 2011a).

Borkoles, Nicholls, Bell, Butterly and Polman (2008) report a study of how people diagnosed with multiple sclerosis experience exercise. Participants commented on how their physical ability to exercise was restricted, and some reported fatigue as a particular problem. Respondents also discussed practical problems in using leisure and sports facilities. The paper has a clear focus and is generally well evidenced, resulting in a coherent and persuasive account.

Cassidy, Reynolds, Naylor and De Souza (2011) provide a very useful and accessible overview of IPA written by a group of researchers in physiotherapy and rehabilitation. I would therefore expect researchers in sport and exercise to find the paper resonant and written from a perspective they share. The first part of the paper outlines the primary theoretical touchstones of IPA and the primary steps in doing it. The paper then gives an illustrated example of IPA from the authors' work in physiotherapy. That study is a detailed examination of the lived experience of cerebellar ataxia. The paper carefully and powerfully describes the difficulties affecting the mobility of the participants. This account helps point to clear factors to help interventions in this condition. The example should also help professionals working with other conditions to see how IPA research can help illuminate personal lived experience, and inform therapeutic practice.

Professionals and trainers

Winter and Collins (2015) conducted interviews with nine UK-based applied sports psychologists on what guides their practice. This is an interesting study on the differing perceptions and experiences of academics in the field. Each theme is well evidenced and the paper points clearly to differences of views and tensions; for example, in the theoretical orientation adopted, and the relative weightings of evidence versus experience.

Miller, Cronin and Baker (2015) report a study on talent spotters in elite English youth sport. They interviewed seven talent spotters about the process of talent identification. This is a good, well-conceptualized paper. It clearly demonstrates how talent spotters define their role and the contingencies in which they operate. It is an interesting, nicely written piece.

Callary, Rathwell and Young (2015) offer useful insights into using IPA in sport and exercise. In this paper the authors report on the process involved in working as newcomers to IPA as a team on an IPA project. The paper is well written and informative. It is a really valuable piece for researchers in sport and exercise as it describes in detail the process of conducting IPA by members of their community. The authors do indeed offer valuable insights into what they recognise as a distinctive and demanding approach to research. In addition, the paper is usefully framed in terms of the position of IPA in relation to other research methodology, and offers a contextualization in terms of other recent IPA work in sport and exercise.

Tawse, Bloom, Sabiston and Reid (2012) discuss the development of wheelchair rugby from a recreational pursuit to an elite sport. They interviewed four elite wheelchair-rugby coaches. The paper gives a useful insight into the experience of coaches working in this field. Among the themes found were the importance of a participant-led approach, coupled with having and transmitting strong expectations to the participants.

How do you do good IPA?

There is now a large corpus of research using IPA. This is true both generally and, for example, in sport and exercise in particular. My view is that, in the first stage of developing an experiential qualitative approach, it has been important that researchers are given every encouragement to put the approach into practice. Now we have the fruits of that first phase it is possible to take stock, learn lessons and think of where to go next. And in the next phase my expectation is that there can be greater concentration not just on doing IPA but on doing high-quality IPA. Of course, historically, researchers have had to overcome a series of obstacles to doing this: IPA is hard; time given to it on undergraduate degree programmes has been limited; and there have been far fewer trainers and supervisors available compared to the number of students wanting to use it.

But the situation is changing. In 2011, I conducted a formal assessment of a carefully demarcated corpus of IPA papers (Smith, 2011a, 2011b). Those two papers offer detailed guidance on evaluating IPA research, as well as another set of examples of good work. In that case, the examples were taken from research on the experience of illness, but it is important to remember that the key features of good IPA transcend disciplinary boundaries and subject areas. The IPA researcher from one subject discipline can gain a lot from looking at good examples of IPA from a different field.

So there are now a range of resources available to help people do IPA: papers to help assess the quality of studies; and lists of good examples of IPA papers. In addition, there are now far more academic staff either experienced at using IPA or at least able to supervise it. There are also regional support groups in the UK and international contacts for many countries around the world. Regular training courses are available, and an IPA website points people to these and other useful resources: http://www.ipa.bbk.ac.uk/. Thus there is now an infrastructure to support the production of good IPA studies and my expectation is that the next five years will witness an increase in the proportion of work which is of excellent quality. As part of that process, I offer here a series of suggestions which I think will help researchers do good IPA:

1. Think about how you can maximize your chances of acquiring strong data. Various things that can help this happen are: have a simple, clear, concrete research question; ask participants about an experience which is alive for them, either because it is about something happening now, or because an event from the past is still causing concern.
2. Do all you can to become a proficient interviewer. Some people have a more natural inclination to this than others, but with good training, practice and effort most people can improve and achieve a reasonable level of competence. Acquiring good data is a prerequisite for doing good IPA.
3. Make sure your analysis is interpretative. Go beyond a mere description, push your analysis deeper. This needs courage and creativity. Ask yourself questions of your data. Look at the language the participant is using; what does it tell you about their experience?

4. Be idiographic. Do detailed analysis of particular cases and particular segments of cases. And then try to see how this particularity shines light on the project as a whole. This is one illustration of engaging in the hermeneutic circle. As part of this, look for *gems* in your data: small utterances whose potency is disproportionate to their size and which are extremely illuminatory, both of the case and of the phenomenon as a whole. See Smith (2011c) for a detailed presentation on the power and type of gems in IPA.
5. Be systematic. IPA is scientific as well as creative. Think about what you are doing and document it. Be persistent and thorough; make sure you have done justice to the whole corpus of data you collected. Engage in a process of critical reflection to check this. Ask yourself questions about what you are doing to help the process be explicit.
6. Pay attention to your writing. Qualitative research is a writerly activity. You need to present a persuasive, rigorous, evidenced account to the reader. Make sure your narrative framework is coherent. It is fine to present an account of a phenomenon which is elliptical, ambiguous and contradictory, but your job is to be as clear as you can in your account of that phenomenon rather than to mirror its ambiguity.

Acknowledgement

I would like to express my thanks to Brett Smith for his support and assistance in the preparation of this chapter.

References

Allport, G. W. (1951). *The use of personal documents in psychological science.* Bulletin No. 49. New York: Social Science Research Council.

Borkoles, E., Nicholls, A. R., Bell, K., Butterly, R., & Polman, R. C. J. (2008). The lived experiences of people diagnosed with multiple sclerosis in relation to exercise. *Psychology & Health, 23*, 427–441.

Callary, B., Rathwell, S., & Young, B. W. (2015). Insights on the process of using interpretive phenomenological analysis in a sport coaching research project. *The Qualitative Report, 20*(2), 63–75.

Caron, J. G., Bloom, G. A., Johnston, K. M., & Sabiston, C. M. (2013). Effects of multiple concussions on retired National Hockey League players. *Journal of Sport & Exercise Psychology, 35*, 168–179.

Cassidy, E., Reynolds, F., Naylor, S., & De Souza, L. (2011). Using interpretative phenomenological analysis to inform physiotherapy practice: An introduction with reference to the lived experience of cerebellar ataxia. *Physiotherapy Theory and Practice, 27*, 263–277.

Hefferon, K. M. & Ollis, S. (2006). "Just clicks": An interpretative phenomenological analysis of professional dancers' experience of flow. *Research in Dance Education, 7*, 141–159.

Husserl, E. (2001/1900). *Logical investigations,* Volume I (2nd ed.). D. Moran (Ed.), J. N. Findlay (trans). London: Routledge.

James, W. (1890). *Principles of psychology* (2 vols.). London: Macmillan.

McDonough, M. H., Sabiston, C. M., & Ullrich-French, S. (2011). The development of social relationships, social support, and posttraumatic growth in a dragon boating team for breast cancer survivors. *Journal of Sport & Exercise Psychology, 33*, 627–648.

Miller, P. K., Cronin, C., & Baker, G. (2015). Nurture, nature and some very dubious social skills: An interpretative phenomenological analysis of talent identification practices in elite English youth soccer. *Qualitative Research in Sport, Exercise and Health, 7*(5), 642–662.

Nicholls, A. R., Holt, N. L., & Polman, R. C. J. (2005). A phenomenological analysis of coping effectiveness in golf. *The Sport Psychologist, 19*, 111–130.

Sebire, S. J., Standage, M., Gillison, F. B., & Vansteenkiste M. (2013). "Coveting thy neighbour's legs": A qualitative study of exercisers' experiences of intrinsic and extrinsic goal pursuit. *Journal of Sport & Exercise Psychology, 35*, 308–321

Smith, J. A. (1996). Beyond the divide between cognition and discourse: Using interpretative phenomenological analysis in health psychology. *Psychology & Health, 11*, 261–271.

Smith, J. A. (2011a). Evaluating the contribution of interpretative phenomenological analysis. *Health Psychology Review, 5,* 9–27.

Smith, J. A. (2011b). Evaluating the contribution of interpretative phenomenological analysis: A reply to the commentaries and further development of criteria. *Health Psychology Review, 5,* 55–61.

Smith, J. A. (2011c). "We could be diving for pearls": The value of the gem in experiential qualitative psychology. *Qualitative Methods in Psychology Bulletin, 12,* 6–15.

Smith, J. A., Flowers, P., & Larkin, M. (2009). *Interpretative phenomenological analysis: Theory, method, research.* London: Sage.

Smith, J. A. & Osborn, M. (2015). Interpretative phenomenological analysis. In J. A. Smith (Ed.), *Qualitative Psychology: A practical guide to methods* (3rd ed., pp. 25–52). London: Sage.

Tawse, H., Bloom, G. A., Sabiston, C. M., & Reid, G. (2012). The role of coaches of wheelchair rugby in the development of athletes with a spinal cord injury. *Qualitative Research in Sport, Exercise and Health, 4,* 206–225.

Thompson, A., Larkin, M., & Smith, J. A. (2011). Interpretative phenomenological analysis and clinical psychology training: Results from a survey of the group of trainers in clinical psychology. *Clinical Psychology Forum, 222,* 15–19.

Turner, A., Barlow, J., & Ilbery, B. (2002). Play hurt, live hurt: Living with and managing osteoarthritis from the perspective of ex-professional footballers. *Journal of Health Psychology, 7,* 285–301.

Warner, S. & Dixon, M. A. (2015). Competition, gender and the sport experience: An exploration among college athletes. *Sport, Education and Society, 20,* 527–545.

Winter, S. & Collins, D. (2015). Why do we do what we do? *Journal of Applied Sport Psychology, 27,* 35–51.

18

CRITICAL DISCOURSE ANALYSIS IN SPORT AND EXERCISE

What, why and how

Kerry R. McGannon

Discourse analysis is a name given to a variety of approaches that study texts, talk and language in use or discourse, via different epistemological and theoretical traditions (e.g. social constructionism, post-structuralism) and within different disciplines (Fairclough, 1992; Wetherell, Taylor & Yates, 2001). Critical discourse analysis (CDA) is a specific, though still broad, form of discourse analysis which began developing in the late 1980s as a 'problem–oriented interdisciplinary research programme, subsuming a variety of approaches, each drawing on different epistemological assumptions, with different theoretical models, research methods and agenda' (Wodak, 2013, p. xx), to examine the social and political context of discourses. Despite CDA being firmly established within the social sciences, owing to such diversity, there is no one prescribed method, singular or 'best' approach to CDA (Wetherell *et al.*, 2001).

Research methods books within the sport and exercise realm have outlined discourse analysis in terms of what, why and how, drawing distinct parameters between what constitutes discursive discourse analysis, Foucauldian discourse analysis and CDA (see Markula & Silk, 2011; Sparkes & Smith, 2014). Such parameters were, in part, drawn in light of the different kinds of topics or questions discourse researchers within the sport and exercise realm might be interested in exploring. Discourse analysts might be interested in naturally occurring (i.e. naturalistic data) forms of talk in everyday interactions within a particular sport team, and how that structures relations and experiences of coaches and athletes. CDA or Foucauldian researchers might be interested in how certain forms of femininity are 'constructed' within media discourses and sport institutions which favour men, all of which limit women's access to power and status in sport. The demarcation of particular discourse analysis approaches to each topic was also due to a concern for the nuanced ways that discourse functions to structure social action(s) within the context of power issues. This was particularly the case concerning Foucauldian discourse analysis, within which power is conceptualized as fluid and relational, vs. CDA, which locates power in concrete institutions or dominant groups.

My own journey using CDA began in 1998 during my PhD studies and early publications on *discursive psychology* (McGannon & Mauws, 2000) and *ethnomethodology* and *post-structuralist* views of discourse (McGannon & Mauws, 2002) to study exercise participation. Since my early journey and to the present day, for me, the boundaries between the aforementioned forms of discourse analysis are more blurred (McGannon & Schinke, 2013; McGannon & Spence, 2012). Within this chapter the what, why and how of a 'blended' approach to CDA will be outlined. CDA will be positioned as a synthetic/eclectic approach to discourse (Wetherell, 1998), which focuses on discursive practices (e.g. how discourse is used to perform specific functions, with effects) and discursive resources (e.g. how texts and talk are informed by broader cultural practices and discourses) (Wetherell, 1998; Willig, 2000). Whereas some scholars have suggested that these approaches to discourse cannot be combined because they subscribe to different epistemological assumptions, others have argued effectively for combining them to study exercise (McGannon & Mauwsn, 2002) and health behaviour (Willig, 2000), After introducing CDA, why and when CDA might be used in sport and exercise research will be outlined, followed by a discussion of how one might do CDA, illustrated with examples from a study of one woman's struggle to integrate exercise into her life. I conclude with some future directions for CDA in sport and exercise research.

Critical discourse analysis: three central tenets

To clarify the 'what' of CDA it is useful to outline three assumptions/central tenets. These tenets convey the epistemological and theoretical orientations of a synthetic/eclectic approach, which has implications for why, when and how CDA is used in sport and exercise research. Should readers be interested in more detailed explanations, these tenets have been discussed in depth in relation to CDA and exercise elsewhere (e.g. McGannon & Mauws, 2000, 2002; McGannon & Spence, 2010, 2012; McGannon & Schinke, 2013; McGannon & Smith, 2015).

Tenet One: discourse and language are constructed and constituted

The first central tenet of CDA relies on a view of language that prioritizes the *process* and *outcome* of language, as opposed to the content (the 'whats' of talk), focusing on *how* language is tied to discursive and social practices. This point means that discourse is viewed as *the* primary medium of social action – we 'do things' with words (e.g. blame, justify, make sense of who we are or who others are, decide how we might behave; see also Chapters 4 and 20) because words have associated meanings, actions and consequences depending on people's access to discourses, which are circulated at institutional levels (McGannon & Mauws, 2000; Potter & Wiggins, 2008). While it is beyond the scope of this chapter to detail the various strands of thought from which this view of language stems, the synthetic/eclectic approach to CDA discussed here draws heavily from developments within *discursive psychology* (e.g. Edwards, 1997; Harré & Gillett, 1994). The origins of discursive psychology can be traced to Potter and Wetherell's (1987) form of discourse analysis and Edwards and Potter's (1992) work. These writings inspired a reworking of the 'subject matter' of psychology (i.e. cognitions and mental states) by reconceptualizing and studying psychological phenomena as 'worked' up and given meaning in micro talk and discourse, rather than within the mind.

While still on the margins of sport and exercise scholarship, a growing body of work grounded in discursive psychology within sport aligns closely with the conversation analytic traditions (e.g. Cosh, Crabb & Tully, 2015; Cosh & Tully, 2014; Locke, 2008), outlined in Chapter 19 within the present handbook. This fine-grained analytic approach to action-oriented talk and discourse (i.e. conversation analysis) will not be discussed within the present chapter. Instead, the focus is on discursive psychological approaches concerned with broader discourses, subjectivity and power, grounded in social constructionism and post-structuralism (Wetherell, 1998, 2008).

Tenet Two: self-identity is a discursive construction

The view of discourse and language practices as forms of social action that constitute and shape meanings is grounded in social constructionism. Social constructionists believe 'that all knowledge, and therefore all meaningful reality as such, is contingent upon human practices, being constructed in and out of interaction between human beings and their world, and developed and transmitted within an essentially social context' (Crotty, 1998, p. 42). This socially constructed view of knowledge and reality brings forward the next tenet, which is that self-identity is theorized as the product of individual, social and cultural discourses, which interact to create particular meanings and associated behaviours related to identities (McGannon & Spence, 2010, 2012; Wetherell, 2008). Stated differently, self-identity is a *discursive accomplishment* because it is in discourse that people acquire the resources with which to render their sense of self visible, understood and 'real' (McGannon & Mauws, 2000).

The term 'discourse' is grounded in Foucault's (1978) post-structuralist concept of discourse to understand the relationship between socially constructed forms of truth, power and the implications for self-related knowledge and behavioural practices. For Foucault, language is always located in discourse, which refers to an interrelated 'system of statements that cohere around common meanings and values . . . (that) are a product of social factors, of powers and practices *rather than an individual's set of ideas*' (Hollway, 1983, p. 131; emphasis added). Further, discourse is a broad concept referring to different ways of constituting meaning specific to particular groups, cultures and historical context (Hollway, 1983; Markula & Pringle, 2006).

In order to make the connection between identity, language, discourse and behaviour more explicit, the concept of a 'subject position' is useful to outline. Discourses – be they personal, social or cultural – offer competing and contradictory ways of giving meaning to the world and how we view ourselves. Known as 'subject positions' for individuals to take up (Davies & Harré, 1990; Wetherell, 1998), these positions are conditions of possibility for constituting subjectivity (i.e. identities, understandings of the world) and vary in terms of the power and opportunity they afford (Weedon, 1997). While people may be constituted in one position or another, individuals are not passive as they can (re)negotiate new subject positions by refusing the ones articulated by taking up alternatives within new and different discourses (Weedon 1997, Wetherell 1998). The concept of a subject position suggests the potential for choice, resistance and personal and social change by increasing one's access to, and availability of, discursive resources (McGannon & Schinke, 2013).

Tenet Three: discourses are (re)produced in social practices and institutions

Despite the possibility for agency and change of self-related views and behaviour(s) by taking up new or different subject positions in discourse, discursive resources are not always characterized by infinite possibility. Discourses limit self-identity construction and behaviour because in addition to situating ourselves within discourse, our conversations and everyday talk situate others within discourse (Cosh, Crabb, Kettler, LeCouteur & Tully, 2015; McGannon & Schinke, 2013). The social network (e.g. peers, teammates, coaches, parents, partners, children) within which people are situated is particularly important because identities are *co-constructed* through self-views, as well as others' views of us and themselves, within discourses (Gergen, 1994; McGannon & Mauws, 2002). If people within one's social network construct one's identity by drawing upon old (and more limiting) discourses, it can be difficult to accomplish and maintain a new or expanded discursive identity (and implicitly have new psychological experiences and different behaviours; McGannon & Schinke, 2013).

Another aspect of this central tenet concerning the reproduction of discourse is that discursive resources may be further limited because while local practices (i.e. talk about one's self in relation to sport or exercise) are chosen, these choices are made within a web of discourses held in place by institutional practices of which people are often unaware or cannot always access (McGannon & Spence, 2010; Weedon, 1997). Important in this process is the role of ideology (i.e. expected behaviours based on cultural values and norms), which may perpetuate some discourses as factual and the way 'things were meant to be'. When certain discourses and social and institutional practices are more prevalent and dominant, expansion of discursive resources becomes more difficult (McGannon & Schinke, 2013). In turn, some identities are subverted or marginalized, thus discursive practices have ideological effects which (re)produce unequal power relations (Fairclough & Wodak, 1997).

Speaking of criticality

The preceding tenets discussed culminate in 'criticality' or the 'C' in CDA. Criticality allows us to illuminate and understand the constructive and concrete effects that (often) taken-for-granted discourses have on people's identities and lives, and where we might open up avenues of resistance and/or social change (Wodak, 2013). The 'what' and gist of a synthetic/eclectic CDA in light of these aspects of criticality and the three tenets is summarized nicely by Fairclough:

> Critical approaches differ from non-critical approaches in *not just describing* discursive practices, but *also showing how* discourse is shaped by relations of power and ideologies, and the constructive effects discourse has upon social identities, social relations and systems of knowledge and belief, neither of which is normally apparent to discourse participants.
>
> *(Fairclough, 1992, p. 12; emphasis added)*

Taken in conjunction with the three tenets outlined earlier, the implication of the above quote is that in order to understand and show the links among discourse, sport and exercise within a sociocultural context, it is advantageous to focus on conversations and everyday talk in relation to identity construction, the identities that others or various social agents construct of individuals via conversations/talk, and the taken-for-granted discourses (which are perpetuated by ideologies and institutions) within which our identities are formed and framed (McGannon & Mauws, 2000; McGannon & Schinke, 2013).

Why and when to use critical discourse analysis

Given the above points regarding criticality, CDA would be used by sport and exercise researchers to identify discourses in sport and exercise contexts and then, to be more critical, those discourses would be explored in terms of what discourse 'does' or can do (i.e. the performative implications of talk and discourse within the context of power issues). Ultimately, because a central tenet of CDA is that discourse is constitutive – of identities, social practices, power issues, taken-for-granted ways of thinking, feeling and behaving – sport and exercise researchers might use CDA to understand and 'capture' a socially constructed, nuanced analysis of culture, identity and experience (McGannon & Smith, 2015).

Another reason to use CDA to is that identifying the taken-for-granted discourses at individual and intuitional levels (e.g. sport organizations, various forms of media) to construct discursive self-identities with social and behavioural practices, allows for marginalized or disenfranchised identities within the context of social justice and power issues to be highlighted. By focusing on conversations and micro talk as 'entry points' of analysis within the context of discourses and identity, the 'why' of CDA, and indeed the 'so what' of CDA, is that it can serve to reveal concrete entry points of personal-level intervention and change to address health and well-being issues (McGannon & Schinke, 2013; Smith, Papathomas, Martin Ginis & Latimer-Cheung, 2013).

Following from why and when one might use CDA, is the question of what sorts of 'data' would be drawn upon and collected to study identity-related talk or representations in discourse and the effects/implications (e.g. psychological, social, ideological, power issues). As CDA takes talk and text as the focus, 'any written (e.g. newspapers, magazines, drama, text messages, Internet websites, blogs, emails), visual (e.g. film, photographs, television broadcasts, visual art), audible (e.g. lyrics, conversations) or combination of these texts can be chosen as sources of analysis' (Markula & Silk, 2011, p. 113). There are no strict guidelines as to how much textual 'data' should be gathered for CDA. As with all forms of qualitative research, such decisions should be informed by research aim(s) and question(s), method of data collection and underlying epistemology (Sparkes & Smith, 2014). However, because CDA is about identifying nuanced, specific details and features of talk and text, one needs to be mindful of not collecting too much, but just enough data to be able to describe the detailed aspects of discourses and the various effects of the 'language in use'. While time and space prohibit an in-depth review of studies exemplifying the various tenets of CDA, there are multiple examples of studies within sport and exercise psychology and sociology of sport employing CDA. A handful of these studies will be discussed next to highlight further why and when one might use CDA.

One specific example of CDA in sport psychology comes from Cosh *et al.* (2013), who studied Australian newspaper representations of athletes' comebacks in sport and their retirements, with attention paid to the role of language in the ways in which retirements were depicted in media accounts, and the implications for athletes' identities and lives. Results revealed that athletes were positioned as 'naturally' playing sport for as long as they were physically able, regardless of desires and motivations, with accounts worked up within the media discourses as driven by emotion rather than reason. These discursive constructions of athletic identities were shown to have wider implications for decisions to compete in sport, downplaying alternate reasons for (returning to) competing as inappropriate and, thus compromising athlete well-being. Another study in sport psychology by Kavoura, Ryba and Chroni (2015) used CDA to identify the discourses through which female Greek judokas (i.e. judo athletes) make sense of experiences, and the implications for subjectivity/identity through the negotiation of sociocultural beliefs and gender stereotypes circulated within sport and Greek culture. CDA identified four concepts – biology, gender, femininity, and judo/sport – that centralized the discursive resources through which judokas constructed identities. Athletes were shown to have some agency in negotiating multiple identities in discourse, which allowed them to resist gender stereotypes in sport, but also at times perpetuated gender stereotypes that oppress women in sport.

Two examples of studies from the cultural studies of sport literature using CDA, are work on snowboarding mothers (Spowart, Hughson & Shaw, 2008) and mothers who surf (Spowart, Burrows & Shaw, 2010). Spowart *et al.*'s work is interesting to highlight as the discourses of snowboarding and surfing tend to represent freedom, hedonism and practices associated with irresponsibility, in contrast to meanings associated with traditional gender ideologies and good-mother ideals. CDA was used to explore taken-for-granted truths and power issues surrounding motherhood and sport. Five New Zealand snowboarding mothers were interviewed and CDA showed that through snowboarding these women resisted good-mother ideals that constrain women's identities and behavioural practices as mothers. Such resistance was possible through snowboarding, along with support from family, which resulted in the women's happiness in both family and sporting spheres. Similarly Spowart *et al.* (2010) also interviewed six surfing mothers in New Zealand to explore the discourses drawn upon to construct athlete mother identities and the implications. As with the snowboarding study, through CDA it was found that surfing served as a way to gain agency and to resist and reconfigure motherhood ideologies and status quo concerning what is 'acceptable' regarding motherhood and sport. The women in both of these studies were aware of good-mother ideals circulated by particular discourses and wanted to live up to them. CDA allowed researchers to reveal that sporting women have agency to resist those ideals by drawing upon different discourses.

Readers interested in additional examples of CDA 'in action' within sport and exercise research beyond the ones discussed above can consult studies listed in Table 18.1. This list is meant to offer an additional 'flavour' of some of the sport and exercise work using CDA.

Table 18.1 Additional examples of CDA studies in sport and exercise research

Study	Purpose	Data Source
Exploring news media representations of women's exercise and subjectivity through critical discourse analysis (McGannon & Spence 2012)	Explore news media construction of exercise and taken-for-granted assumptions about exercise, and implications for subjectivity and health promotion	40 stories and accompanying images in women's health section in Midwestern USA newspaper
A champion out of the pool? A discursive exploration of two Australian Olympic swimmers' transition from elite sport to retirement (Cosh, Crabb & Tully, 2015)	Explore retirement and transition in Australian news media and implications for identity and psychological well-being	121 articles reporting on retirement of two elite swimmers seven and five years into retirement
Speaking of the self and physical-activity participation: What discursive psychology can tell us about an old problem (McGannon & Spence, 2010)	Show discursive psychology 'in use' to theorize physical self-identity as a collection of conversations within discourse and power implications	5 interviews with 35-year-old woman over 16 weeks of trying to integrate exercise into her life
Fit for two? A critical discourse analysis of *Oxygen Magazine* (Jette, 2006)	Use Foucault's notions of disciplinary power and biopower to examine representations of pregnancy, fitness and health in fitness magazine discourses	'Fit for two' advice columns for new and expectant mothers in *Oxygen Magazine*
Reproducing, resisting and transcending discourses of femininity: a discourse analytic approach to the study of women's leisure (Lafrance, 2011)	Examine women's accounts of leisure practices to identify ways for women to negotiate hegemonic discourses and position themselves to promote emancipation and health	Interviews with 14 Canadian women ages 18–65 years about physical activity and leisure practices

How to do critical discourse analysis

In terms of how to conduct CDA, it is important to remember that analytic choices are not rigid or 'set-in-stone' steps or rules, particularly given that CDA is a broad field rather than a singular method (Wodak, 2013). Despite this characterization of CDA, it is still possible to outline some guiding principles that align with the central tenets and goals of CDA. Because a synthetic/eclectic CDA approach focuses on the constitutive level of taken-for-granted talk and the effects, as well as on the discourses that frame identity-related talk and views of subjectivity (Wetherell, 1998), in what follows, the process of CDA is described using Parker's (1992) critical approach to discourse analysis. This approach is intended to be viewed as a set of overarching criteria that work together in a back-and-forth manner, rather than as fixed, sequential, linear principles to follow. It should also be stressed that Parker's approach is but *one* analytic choice one might use to carry out CDA (see Markula & Silk, 2011, or Sparkes & Smith, 2014, for additional analytic tools and steps to CDA).

Contextualizing 'how': research example background

In conjunction with outlining Parker's approach, some 'hows' of the criteria will be illustrated by drawing upon examples from my published CDA study, which theorized mother identities as subject positions constructed within discourse(s), and explored the implications for one woman's exercise participation (see McGannon & Schinke, 2013). The following research questions guiding the study further show how one orients to language and discourse as constitutive of identity, meaning and effects before data collection and analysis even begin:

1. How is motherhood identity constructed by one's self and others within discourse(s) and what are the associated meanings?
2. What are the implications (e.g. psychological, behavioural) of a discursively produced mother identity for one woman's exercise participation?

To answer the research questions, a newly active 35-year-old woman ('Joan') with two children aged one and four, her significant other, and her activity partner, were interviewed over 16 weeks. Joan was 35 years old, worked 40 hours a week and was married to Joe, 38 years old, who worked 45 hours per week. She was the children's primary caregiver (e.g. feeding them, putting them to bed, dropping them off at day care). Joan was reintroducing exercise into her life for the first time in 4 years by running 3–5 times per week on a treadmill at work, for 30–40 minutes per session. Joan planned to run with her co-worker, Ray, who was also 35 years of age and married with two boys, ages two and four. Ray was equally responsible for childcare duties, and this was the first time in four years that he had incorporated regular exercise into his life. A total of 9 in-depth, semi-structured interviews were conducted: 5 for Joan over 16 weeks (4 interviews conducted over 12 weeks and a follow-up interview 4 weeks later); and 2 for Joe and 2 for Ray (one at the beginning of Joan's programme, and one during the twelfth week). Significant others were interviewed in this CDA study to align with the central tenet regarding self-identities and discursive resources being reproduced by one's social network.

Parker's critical approach: three criteria

Parker's (1992) criteria for making discourse analysis socially and politically useful is drawn from Foucault's (1972, 1978) insights into discourse to help identify broader discursive repertoires, the implications for subjectivity/identity construction and experiences, and the role of power. Three of these criteria are outlined in terms of how they might be used to direct analysis, steps and questions to consider in the process, along with specific examples from the above study to further illustrate and clarify aspects of the criteria and steps.

Criteria one and two: 1. a discourse is about objects; 2. a discourse is also about subjects; sites of subjectivity/positioning within the discourses must be identified

When performing CDA, a good place to begin is to remind ourselves of what a discourse 'is' and what it 'does' (or can potentially do), and read texts with those points foremost in mind. As mentioned within the central tenets section, a discourse can be regarded as 'a system of statements which construct an object' (Parker, 1992, p. 5), which has associated meanings and practices. In the case of the preceding study about exercise participation outlined, the objects being sought to study were those that related to the identity construction of Joan (e.g. 'good mother', 'exerciser'), each of which has particular meanings depending on how it is used in conversations, talk or text. Thus, one seeks to identify what the discursive objects are within a particular text, and what meanings are being 'worked up' in and through the text. To accomplish these goals one might ask 'what objects were being referred to?' and more specifically, 'what words, concepts and metaphors are being used to discuss such objects?'

After reading transcripts/documents with these questions in mind, the specific words, concepts and phrases can be highlighted, written down and/or recorded in a database. Doing this step of writing and recording allows the researcher to keep track of what is said, how it is said and what the 'objects of talk' are in detail. In addition to identifying and describing 'objects', notes should also be made about how objects are being *used* within the conversations/talk, and the social and behavioural effects, particularly as these relate to the specific aim of the study. In the case of my study, Joan's exercise and non-exercise behaviours were of interest, so when identifying various objects (e.g. 'good mother') and associated meanings (e.g. good mothers put children's needs before their own need to exercise), I would also note in detail how such meanings were encouraging or discouraging exercise behaviour (e.g. by striving to meet needs of children and be a good mother, if one puts one's own leisure pursuits above family well-being, one is selfish or feels guilty. It is thus not worth it or permissible to exercise unless the family's needs are taken care of first). Parker refers to all of the foregoing steps as 'talking about the talk as if it were an object or discourse' (Parker, 1992, p. 9), and it is a process which also contributes toward identifying specific discourses that frame the objects – and subjects – of talk. In the case of my CDA study, the specific statements, words and phrases that constructed a 'good mother' were identified as being worked up within a patriarchal discourse of the family, which positioned what it means to be a mother and a father in a particular way. More will be said about this discourse shortly.

Turning to the 'subjects' of talk and discourse, as noted when outlining the central tenets of CDA, discourses also construct subject positions. These subject positions form and frame certain identities, which encourage particular ways of thinking, speaking and behaving (McGannon & Spence, 2010, 2012). In this way, we might think of a discourse as shouting 'Hey, you there, listen up! I'm speaking to you, with a particular message about what you might think and do!' In order to identify subject positions and identity implications, one might ask what role was the speaker having to adopt within the discourse, and at the same time, what ways and rights of speaking (e.g. particular narratives) did those positions confer within a discourse? (Parker, 1992). The identification of positioning in discourse can be further accomplished by specifying the types of persons talked about, some of whom may have already been identified as objects, as in the case of my study that might include 'good mother' and 'father'. From this identification it can be speculated further as to what someone is afforded to say (e.g. attending to what concepts and terms within a particular conversational account were used by the speaker); 'what rights (does one have) to speak in that way of speaking' (Parker, 1992, p. 10), when speaking from these socially constructed subject positions.

Research example: To further illustrate some aspects of the identification of objects and subject positions in discourse, consider the following extracts from two different interviews; one from Joan during the eighth week of the study when discussing why exercising was difficult; and the other from her partner/husband Joe, who elaborated on why he thought it was difficult for Joan to exercise. In the first extract Joan tells a story about how her youngest son Stephen's lack of sleep had been affecting her when making sense of her exercise:

> On Thursday I was tired. When I'm tired I kind of do different things, change my work a little bit, just to keep awake. But when I get really tired I guess my senses are – I'll either feel nauseous of I'll start getting stomach pains or stressed and I can't exercise. So I thought, *I gotta get him on a schedule cause this is nuts! I can't operate on five hours of sleep every night, I can't do that.* So I didn't even give my exercise a thought because I was too tired and stressed.

When interviewed about her exercise, Joe also concluded that Joan could not exercise because she was too tired due to the children naturally wanting to be with her all the time.

> When Stephen's tired, he wants to be cuddled and it's gotta be Joan. When he's tired he starts getting whiny and you can't console him, I can't do anything. The only one that can console him is her. So in the evenings it's Joan and that's basically her that puts him to sleep and she'll do whatever it takes until he falls asleep. Once she's got him down then David needs to be taken care of. And David's the same way when he gets cranky he wants to be with mum. So it makes it really tough for her to have time alone. Like I said our kids don't go to bed until 11 o'clock. By then, she's exhausted, so she can't exercise.

In both extracts particular terms, concepts and statements were used to form the object and subject of a patriarchal discourse of the family – in this case 'good mother'. Within Joan's story, she talked about the childcare practices that she performed and how she felt about these and, in turn, she tended to draw upon particular terms such as being 'tired' and 'stressed', saying that she 'felt responsible' for getting her son into a proper sleeping routine. She also performed related actions to this, which had the effect of creating and maintaining guilt and anxiety as she attempted to integrate exercise into her life. Speaking in these ways and using terms such as 'tired' and 'stressed' also had the effect of allowing Joan to work up and maintain the subject positions of a 'good mother', who strives to place her children's well-being within a patriarchal discourse of the family. Additionally, because this situation was the product of this discourse, subject positions and connected behavioural practices (e.g. caring for Stephen, being up at night and not sleeping), Joe also used this notion of Joan being 'tired' to position Joan as a 'good mother' who upheld good-mother ideals through sacrifice. Because Joe constructed his own subjectivity as a 'father' in particular way (i.e. as a provider not well-suited to childcare), he did not discuss his own role in this situation, instead concluding that Joan's exercise was not doable because of her natural duties as a 'good mother'.

These two extracts also exemplify the identification made by the researcher of the link between words, language, subject positions and the effects. In the case of the above example, it was noted that Joan was doing particular behaviours that reinforced her 'naturally suitability' as a 'good mother' (e.g. consoling the children until they are asleep, prioritizing the children over exercise). Joe was also not doing particular behaviours because within a patriarchal discourse of the family, the subject position of a 'father' suggests that men are not as well suited to such behaviours (e.g. 'when he's tired he starts getting whiny and you can't console him; I can't do anything') and women are suited to mothering behaviours (e.g. 'The only one that can console him is her'). This discourse and the subject positions of 'good mother' and 'father' have the further effect of (re)producing a situation that is not conducive to exercise. Joan is too tired from caring for the children, Joe is not offering to take them, and neither of them resist the situation because it has been rendered as natural and fixed through their micro talk and behavioural practices, which are constructed within a patriarchal discourse of the family.

Criterion three: consider the discourses as coherent systems of meaning, then refine and name the discourses

What should be clear from the above examples and from the various aspects of criteria one and two outlined, is that none of these criteria operates and/or is used in an isolated, linear manner when doing CDA. Identification and refinement of discourses is an iterative process of moving within and between the texts and also the different discourses discussed in the literature. This process can be achieved by turning to the grouped statements, words and concepts that construct objects of discourse and subject positions identified through criteria one and two into a specific discourse, and then naming that discourse in terms of key meanings and implications of said discourse(s). Facilitation of refining and naming the discourse(s) can also be achieved by employing the theoretical and cultural understandings alluded to earlier as to what a topic or theme consisted of (e.g. a patriarchal discourse of the family constructed the subject position of 'good mother'; this same discourse constructed the identity of 'father'). This process involves mapping out a possible worldview or 'picture' that the discourse paints. In the case of the research example of Joan, a patriarchal discourse of the family maps out a worldview that men are the head of the family and not well suited to helping with childcare, and that women are the primary caregivers and nurturers who must maintain harmony within the family. Table 18.2 exemplifies this step for the patriarchal discourse of the family identified within the study of Joan and the extracts discussed above (see McGannon & Schinke, 2013, for a more in-depth discussion of additional discourses).

In the refining and naming of discourses via the consideration of subject positions and the potential effects (e.g. social, ideological, psychological, behavioural) one should be aware that various terms, concepts and ways of speaking about identity are *always* (in theory) available for use by drawing upon other discourses/discursive resources. This means that a speaker can have space to find another voice available within another discourse, with other behaviours and social practices being encouraged. This point relates to subject positions taken up in discourse, and being aware of the power these afford (or do not afford) people, and has implications for behaviour change and identifying potential areas of resistance and change (see McGannon & Smith, 2015).

Related to the above points concerning power and subjectivity, is the fact that the discourses identified and named should be connected to power and ideology in order to be

Table 18.2 Key features of discourse used to construct and make sense of Joan's subjectivity

Discourse	Key Features, Meanings and World View
Patriarchal discourse of the family	– Roles and duties suited to men vis-à-vis women; these roles structure the so-called 'natural order' of the sexual division of labour within the family.
	– The family is viewed as the natural and basic unit of the social order which meets individual emotional, sexual and practical needs differently if one is a man or a woman.
	– The family has primary responsibility for reproduction, well-being and socialization of children; women primarily take this responsibility on within the family.
	– Statements construct what constitutes 'husband', 'wife' and 'fatherly' and 'motherly' behaviour.
	– Men are best suited to work outside the home, providing for the family; women are best suited to domestic labour and childcare.
	– 'Mothers' are supposed to meet all needs of children and experience self-fulfilment and enjoy sacrifice for the family – this is women's 'true' and 'natural' calling.
	– When women become mothers, motherhood is a central part of selfhood; mothers are 'naturally' nurturing, patient and understanding; mothers can (and should) effortlessly take on morning-to-night practices of childcare with minimal complaint.

critical (Fairclough, 1992; Parker, 1992). This can be done when one is identifying subject positions by noting who is afforded to speak and behave in particular ways, as well as at the level of theoretical and cultural understanding. In this regard, as transcripts are read and reread, various texts can also be drawn upon to make sense of the discourses and the behavioural, psychological and emotional effects. In the case of Joan this process is shown in the difficulties she had with integrating exercise into her life, due to drawing upon a patriarchal discourse of the family, which resulted in distress and fatigue. Such understanding was facilitated by employing readings about women's place and subjectivity in the family, workforce and within the context of motherhood. Feminist texts/readings, particularly those from a post-structuralist perspective, were also useful in providing the identification of discourses and subject positions, as well as elucidating theoretical implications (see McGannon & Schinke, 2013). This final step of theoretical integration allows for a nuanced and critical interpretation of the data with a continuous orientation toward subjectivity as socially constructed within the context of power issues (Wetherell, 2008; Willig, 2000).

Conclusions

As the landscape of qualitative research within sport and exercise research continues to grow, develop and change, researchers have a range of methodological tools grounded in various epistemologies (e.g. postpositivism, social constructionism, post-structuralism) from which to choose to explore research questions and topics of interest. For those interested in understanding sociocultural issues and topics in sport and exercise within the context of power issues, an eclectic approach to CDA has much to offer toward understanding 'the taken for granted' which can (re)produce identities, experience and behaviour. As noted earlier, the particular approach to CDA put forward within the present chapter is but one approach that may be used to investigate the role of discourse, identity and power issues in sport and exercise. Future research employing different forms of CDA from those discussed herein (e.g. those rooted in conversation analysis, Foucauldian discourse analysis, Fairclough's social orientation to discourse) are thus encouraged, to continue to expand understandings of sport and exercise topics and the sociocultural construction of identity and implications.

Given that the use of CDA in sport and exercise psychology and sociology of sport is still relatively novel and growing, the research topics and textual data sources for CDA are wide open. Examples of texts and topics for analysis in CDA research to consider in sport and exercise might focus on the role of others' (e.g. coaches, consultants, training staff, teammates, significant others) talk and conversations in the (re)production of nuanced and taken-for-granted ways of speaking that form cultural identities (e.g. athlete roles within a team, limited forms of masculine and feminine identities for athletes), and their impact on one another (i.e. how some identity talk may be limiting or facilitating of psychological experiences and sport behaviour). A CDA of 'new' media texts (e.g. social media such as blogs, Twitter, Facebook and Instagram representations of sport and exercise communities or incidents, high-profile sport celebrities – see also Chapters 11, 12 and 27) and how these construct certain identities and the practices linked to them, would also be useful windows into understanding the taken-for-granted discourses that frame and form cultural identities (e.g. gay and lesbian athletes, elite athlete mothers or fathers, immigrant athletes, mother-exercisers, racial minorities) and the psychological and behavioural implications. Finally, the role of sport organizations (e.g. National Collegiate Athletics Association in the USA, International Olympic Committee, International Association of Athletics Federations) – including practices, norms and regulations – could also be a useful focal point in future CDA investigations, since discourses that frame identities, experiences and behaviours are powerfully connected to institutions and the taken-for-granted norms, ideologies and practices they circulate.

References

Cosh, S., Crabb, S., Kettler, L., LeCouteur, A. & Tully, P. J. (2015). The normalisation of body regulation and monitoring practices in elite sport: A discursive analysis of news delivery sequences during skinfold testing. *Qualitative Research in Sport, Exercise and Health*, 7, 338–360.

Cosh, S., Crabb, S. & Tully, P.J. (2015). A champion out of the pool? A discursive exploration of two Australian Olympic swimmers' transition from elite sport to retirement. *Psychology of Sport and Exercise*, 19, 33–41.

Cosh, S., LeCouteur, A., Crabb, S. & Kettler, L. (2013). Career transitions and identity: A discursive psychological approach to exploring athlete identity in retirement and the transition back into elite sport. *Qualitative Research in Sport, Exercise and Health*, 5, 21–42.

Cosh, S. & Tully, P.J. (2014). 'All I have to do is pass': A discursive analysis of student athletes' talk about prioritising sport to the detriment of education to overcome stressors encountered in combining elite sport and tertiary education. *Psychology of Sport and Exercise*, 15, 180–189.

Crotty, M. (1998). *The foundations of social research: Meaning and perspective in the research process*. London: Sage.

Davies, B. & Harré, R. (1990). Positioning: The discursive production of selves. *Journal for the Theory of Social Behaviour*, 20, 43–63.

Edwards, D. (1997). *Discourse and cognition*. London: Sage.

Edwards, D. & Potter, J. (1992). *Discursive psychology*. London: Sage.

Fairclough, N. (1992). *Discourse and social change*. Cambridge, UK: Polity Press.

Fairclough, N. & Wodak, R. (1997). Critical discourse analysis. In T.A. van Dijk (Ed.), *Discourse as social interaction* (pp. 258–284). London: Sage.

Foucault, M. (1972). *The archaeology of knowledge and discourse on language*. New York: Pantheon.

Foucault, M. (1978). *The history of sexuality, volume 1: An introduction*. London: Penguin.

Gergen, K.J. (1994). *Realities and relationships: Soundings in social construction.* Cambridge, MA: Harvard University Press.

Harré, R. & Gillett, G. (1994). *The discursive mind.* Thousand Oaks, CA: Sage.

Hollway, W. (1983). Heterosexual sex: Power and desire for the other. In S. Cartledge & J. Ryan (Eds.), *Sex and love: New thoughts on old contradictions* (pp. 124–140). London: Women's Press.

Jette, S. (2006). Fit for two? A critical discourse analysis of *Oxygen Magazine. Sociology of Sport Journal, 23,* 331–351.

Kavoura, A., Ryba, T.V. & Chroni, S. (2015). Negotiating female judoka identities in Greece: A Foucauldian discourse analysis. *Psychology of Sport and Exercise, 17,* 88–98.

Lafrance, M.N. (2011). Reproducing, resisting, and transcending discourses of femininity: A discourse analytic approach to the study of women's leisure. *Qualitative Research in Sport, Exercise, and Health, 3,* 80–98.

Locke, A. (2008). Managing agency for athletic performance: A discursive approach to the zone. *Qualitative Research in Psychology, 5,* 103–126.

Markula, P. & Pringle, R. (2006). *Foucault, sport and exercise: Power, knowledge and transforming the self.* Madison Avenue, NY: Routledge.

Markula, P. & Silk, M. (2011). *Qualitative research for physical culture.* New York, NY: Palgrave MacMillan.

McGannon, K.R. & Mauws, M.K. (2000). Discursive psychology: An alternative approach for studying adherence to exercise and physical activity. *Quest, 52,* 148–165.

McGannon, K.R. & Mauws, M.K. (2002). Exploring the exercise adherence problem: An integration of ethnomethodological and poststructuralist perspectives. *Sociology of Sport Journal, 19,* 67–89.

McGannon, K.R. & Schinke, R.J. (2013). 'My first choice is to work out at work; then I don't feel bad about my kids': A discursive psychological analysis of motherhood and physical activity participation. *Psychology of Sport and Exercise, 14,* 179–188.

McGannon, K.R. & Smith, B. (2015). Centralizing culture in cultural sport psychology research: The potential of narrative inquiry and discursive psychology. *Psychology of Sport and Exercise, 17,* 79–87.

McGannon, K.R. & Spence, J.C. (2010). Speaking of the self and physical activity participation: What discursive psychology can tell us about an old problem. *Qualitative Research in Sport and Exercise, 2,* 17–38.

McGannon, K.R. & Spence, J.C. (2012). Exploring news media representations of women's exercise and subjectivity through critical discourse analysis. *Qualitative Research in Sport, Exercise and Health, 4,* 32–50.

Parker, I. (1992). *Discourse dynamics: Critical analysis for social and individual psychology.* London: Routledge.

Potter, J. & Wetherell, M. (1987). *Discourse and social psychology: Beyond attitudes and behavior.* London: Sage.

Potter, J. & Wiggins, S. (2008). Discursive psychology. In C. Willig & W. Stainton-Rogers (Eds.), *Handbook of qualitative research in psychology* (pp. 73–90). London: Sage.

Smith, B., Papathomas, A., Martin Ginis, K.A. & Latimer-Cheung, A.E. (2013). Understanding physical activity in spinal cord injury rehabilitation: Translating and communicating research through stories. *Disability and Rehabilitation, 35,* 2044–2055.

Sparkes, A. C. & Smith, B. (2014). *Qualitative research methods in sport, exercise and health. From process to product.* London: Routledge.

Spowart, L., Burrows, L. & Shaw, S. (2010). I just eat, sleep and dream of surfing: When surfing meets motherhood. *Sport in Society, 13,* 1186–1203.

Spowart, L., Hughson, J. & Shaw, S. (2008). Snowboarding mums carve out fresh tracks: Resisting traditional motherhood discourse? *Annals of Leisure Research, 11,* 187–204.

Weedon, C. (1997). *Feminist practice and post-structuralist theory* (2nd ed.). Malden, MA: Blackwell.

Wetherell, M. (1998). Positioning and interpretive repertoires: Conversation analysis and post-structuralism in dialogue. *Discourse and Society, 9,* 387–412.

Wetherell, M. (2008). Subjectivity or psycho-discursive practices? Investigating complex, intersectional identities. *Subjectivity, 22,* 73–81.

Wetherell, M., Taylor, S. & Yates, S.J. (2001). *Discourse as data: A guide for analysis.* London: Sage.

Willig, C. (2000). A discourse-dynamic approach to the study of subjectivity in health psychology. *Theory and Psychology, 10,* 547–570.

Wodak, R. (2013). Critical discourse analysis: Challenges and perspectives. In R. Wodak (Ed.), *Critical discourse analysis: Four volumes* (pp. xx–xxliii). London: Sage.

19

CONVERSATION ANALYSIS IN SPORT AND EXERCISE

Amanda LeCouteur and Suzanne Cosh

```
Exercise Physiologist (EP) to Athlete (A), skinfold
testing session:
1 EP:   So. last t↑ime what were your results?
2 A:    I don't remember
3 EP:   Oh↓ Sarah Sarah Sarah=
4 A:    =And [I've been
5 EP:        [Seventeen point two for tricep
6 A:    And I've been really sick as [well
7 EP:   Have you?
```

The above exchange occurred during routine body composition testing at an elite sports institute. The recording was made for a study investigating the suggestion that constant surveillance of athletes' bodies in elite sports environments leaves them vulnerable to developing eating disorders (Cosh, Crabb, LeCouteur, & Kettler, 2011). But what can be done with such conversational data in all its rawness? How might everyday practices in sport and exercise – here, in the form of news delivery around a tricep measurement – be used in analysis? In this chapter, we answer the question by turning to a relatively unexplored approach within sport and exercise: conversation analysis (CA). We first describe what CA is. Next, some reasons for using CA are offered. How to do CA is then described. Finally, we describe some studies that have used CA in sport and exercise settings, and make some suggestions for future application of the method.

Conversation analysis (CA) is an approach to the study of naturally occurring (i.e., nonexperimenter-derived) talk and interaction that grew out of Ethnomethodology, a perspective in Sociology that examines how people make sense of their everyday world. Developed in the 1960s by Harvey Sacks, with contributions from Emmanuel Schegloff and Gail Jefferson,[1] CA focuses on talk and its accompanying nonverbal features of interaction as a central activity in social life. It looks at how interaction is coordinated and talk is organized. Conversation analysts are interested in both ordinary conversation (e.g., informal talk on the telephone or at the dinner table) and talk in institutional settings (e.g., meetings, courtrooms, medical consultations), arguing that examination of such materials allows us to discover how some of the most basic aspects of human social life are accomplished. It is an approach to analysis that has been described as having "unique methodological features," by which researchers have produced "a mass of insights into the detailed procedural foundations of everyday life" (ten Have, 1990: 23). As a result, CA has been taken up in a range of disciplines, including Psychology, Anthropology, Sociology, Linguistics, and Organizational Studies. Recently, CA has been applied within sport and exercise settings (e.g., Groom, Cushion, & Nelson, 2012; LeCouteur & Feo, 2011; Okada, 2013; Poizat, Bourbousson, Saury, & Sève, 2012), but it is still an approach that remains underused.

In general terms, the aim of CA is to "produce descriptions of recurrent patterns of social interaction and language use" (Peräkylä, 1997, p. 202). More specifically, Heritage described the approach as follows:

> [Conversation analysts] describe how people take turns at talk in ordinary conversation and negotiate overlaps and interruptions; how various kinds of basic action sequences are organized and different options are activated inside those sequences, how various kinds of failures in interaction – for example, of hearing and understanding – are dealt with; how conversations are opened and closed; how gaze and body posture are related to talk; how laughter is organized; how grammatical form and discourse particles are related to turn-taking and other interactional issues, and so on.
>
> *(Heritage, 1997, p. 161)*

Methodological features of CA

Naturally occurring talk and interaction as data

One of the defining features of CA is the close examination of recordings of real-life interaction. No data that are created as a result of input by the researcher, such as interviews, surveys, scenarios, role-plays, or experimental methods, are used.[2] These kinds of data are seen as "too much a product of the researcher's or informant's manipulation, selection, or reconstruction, based on preconceived notions of what is probable or important" (Heritage & Atkinson, 1984, p. 2). This insistence on naturally occurring or "naturalistic" data that "derive from situations which exist independently of the researcher's intervention" (Silverman, 2006, p. 201) is unique in the social sciences according to ten Have (2007). The feature stems from CA's beginnings as a sociological enterprise that focused on understanding people's everyday methods for accomplishing successful interaction. Evidence pertaining to this sort of inquiry comes from close attention to recordings of actual human interaction. Antaki described the process using an apt analogy:

> Repeated playing of a recording of a given social scene had the same effect as Eadweard Muybridge's slow-motion photographs had on the science of movement: to reveal a level of subtle organization that demanded a new set of concepts, and a new vocabulary to express them in.
>
> *(Antaki, 2011, p. 2)*

This vocabulary, focusing analytic attention on the basic turn-taking organization of conversation, and the significance of sequences of interaction to participants' understanding, involves features such as "turns-at-talk," "turn construction units," "adjacency pairs," and "preference organization." These basic elements of the CA approach are described below. What we want to highlight here is that a fundamental principle of CA involves the assumption that naturally occurring talk is systematically organized, both serially (that is, in turns) and also in terms of sequences (sequentiality). The sequentiality of conversation refers to the way in which "an utterance is constructed to display its relation to the utterances that precede it and to make expectable a certain type of utterance in the following turn" (Wilkinson, 1999, p. 327). Such conversational organization has been shown to be a central resource for participants in achieving mutual understanding. The primary job of CA is to identify and describe these organizational principles, and the systematic resources that participants use to accomplish them in different settings. For example, the work of Groom *et al.* (2012) examining performance feedback sessions in an English Premier League Academy highlighted how players' contributions were routinely constrained to answering questions and responding to invitations to speak – features which served to reinforce the "social basis of [coach's] power" (p. 452) in this setting.

As described above, data used by conversation analysts involve audio- or video-recordings of naturally occurring interaction that have been transcribed using a conventional form of notation – Jeffersonian transcript (Jefferson, 2004) – some basic features of which are displayed in Table 19.1 below. Increasingly, CA studies also attend to nonverbal features of interaction, aspects like gaze direction, body posture, gesture, use of objects and technology, and spatial positioning – all of which are crucial elements for those interested in analysis of sport performance and exercise. This attention in CA studies to how interaction is done in real life – how things are said, how they are receipted, and what interactants are doing – is represented in the fine detail of transcription. All of the *ums* and *ahs*, false starts, intonation, tempo and

Table 19.1 Transcription symbols used in conversation analysis based on the system developed by Gail Jefferson (see, for example, Jefferson, 2004)

(0.4)	A timed pause, in tenths of a second.
(.)	A just-noticeable pause, less than 0.2s.
word [word] [word]	Square brackets between adjacent lines of speech show the onset and completion of overlapping talk.
word = = word	The equals sign shows 'latching' (no discernable pause or gap) between turns at talk.
.hh, hh	In-breath (denoted by the preceding full stop) and out-breath; more 'h's indicates longer breath.
wo(h)rd	The use of (h) indicates that the word has aspiration (usually laughter) within it.
wor-	A dash indicates a sharp cutoff in the preceding word.
wo:rd	Colons indicate that the preceding sound has been stretched by the speaker.
↓word ↑word	Up and down arrows indicate marked falling or rising shifts in intonation.
word	Underlined sounds indicate speaker emphasis (increasing loudness).
WORD	Capitals indicate that the words/talk is much louder than surrounding speech.
°word°	Degree signs indicate that the talk is quieter than the surrounding talk.
>word word<	Inwards arrows indicate speech that is produced faster than the surrounding talk.
<word word>	Outwards arrows indicate slower speech.
→	An arrow in the left-hand margin signals the analyst's interest in a specific part of an extract under discussion.
( )	Empty brackets indicate the presence of talk that is unclear.
(word)	Words within a single bracket indicate the transcriber's best guess at unclear talk.
((snort))	Words in double brackets indicate the transcriber's attempt to represent sounds that are difficult to represent phonetically.

Note: A detailed description of how to use this system can be found in Liddicoat (2011).

volume changes, the drawing in and out of breath, pauses, interruptions and overlaps, all of the ungrammaticality of ordinary talk is included in the process of transcription. Transcription conventions also record laughter, crying, and nonverbal features such as direction of gaze and hand movements.[3] What analysis of such detailed transcripts has revealed over the half-decade of application of CA research to date, is the minutely organized nature of talk and interaction. Importantly too, such details are shown to be routinely oriented to in interaction. In this sense, they cannot be ignored or treated as insignificant by analysts: "researchers cannot, a priori, assume that interaction is idiosyncratic or that any order of interactional detail is disorderly, accidental, or irrelevant (Robinson, 2007, p. 66). So, although transcription in CA is recognized as a time-consuming process,[4] and is a skill that takes considerable time and effort to develop,[5] it is an aspect of the approach that cannot be scrimped or short-circuited.

Analytic focus on action and activity

CA is primarily concerned with establishing how social activities are accomplished; the analytic focus is on identifying the underlying organization of particular actions in context. Nevile and Rendle-Short put it like this:

> people talk to each other to construct and order the affairs of their ordinary social activities, to act in social identities and roles, to form and maintain social relationships and group memberships, or formal and recognizable organisations and institutions, or to collaborate for work. As Austin (1962) put it, we do things with words. We might ask or answer a question, agree, disagree, tell, explain, announce or acknowledge, assess, doubt, request, offer, demand, complain, invite, accept, decline, compliment, criticize, acknowledge, thank, apologize, greet, joke, praise, insult, notice, ignore, or anything else, and we do so in the course of jointly participating with others to manage the processes of interaction itself.
>
> *(Nevile & Rendle-Short, 2007, p. 30.2)*

More broadly too, what CA identifies is how various types of institutional interaction get done. The focus here is on "interaction between professionals and clients or among professionals" (Peräkylä, 1997, p. 202). For example, how callers formulate their reasons for telephoning, how doctors take patient histories or break bad news, how sport therapists deal with client resistance, how coaches deliver player evaluations, or how netballers communicate on court. Thus, in CA, talk is not treated as involving primarily the exchange of information, but as a highly organized means of accomplishing social actions. The business of analysis is identifying and describing this organization at a level of fine detail. In this way, light is shed on the basic mechanisms of social interaction. Outputs from CA research can also be applied. As Stokoe (2014, p. 256) has demonstrated with the Conversation Analytic Role-Play Method (CARM) used for training practitioners in a number of areas (e.g., mediation, nursing, police, and the law), CA provides actual evidence of "the sorts of problems and roadblocks [that] can occur in interaction, as well as the techniques and strategies that best resolve and overcome them." Such applied potential also extends to sport and exercise. Craig's analysis of game-day interaction in a coaches' box (2008), and coach-player performance feedback sessions (2011), are two instances where CA evidence was used to improve the quality and effectiveness of interaction – both for the interactants and for those seeking training in best practice. LeCouteur and Feo's (2011) analysis of on-court interaction in netball represents another instance where sports coaches and administrators were eager for findings based on real data, in order to improve performance.

The analytic significance of context and sequence

The activity focus of CA research involves analytic concern with how talk unfolds from moment to moment, and how speakers display their understanding in the local interaction. As a result, as mentioned above, the focus is not on individual sentences or utterances, but on larger units that are conceptualized as "sequences of activity and their component unit turns as turns-within-sequences" (Drew & Heritage, 1992, p. 18). A basic assumption of CA is that speakers understand an utterance by reference to this "turn-within-sequence character" (Heritage & Atkinson, 1984, p. 7); that is, by reference to its position within a particular sequence of action. Because turns of talk are organized into sequences, whenever speakers respond, they are displaying an understanding of the preceding turn as a particular type of action. A granting, for example, displays orientation to the previous turn as a request (as does a denial); an acceptance (or refusal) orients to a previous offer, and so on. This aspect of the sequentiality of interaction is considered a central resource both for interactants making sense of what is going on, as well as for "overhearing" analysts. Hutchby and Wooffitt labeled this the *next-turn proof procedure*, describing it as "the most basic tool used in CA to ensure that analyses explicate the orderly properties of talk as oriented-to accomplishments of participants, rather than being based merely on the assumptions of the analyst" (2008, p. 14). Thus in CA, analytic claims are required to be "grounded by reference to the participants' demonstrable orientations" (Wooffitt, 2005, p. 202). Without such grounding in the data, descriptions of what is occurring in interaction are not accepted as valid. As Peräkylä (1997, p. 203) explained, this is one key difference between CA and some forms of Discourse Analysis (see Chapter 18) that emphasize the "openness of any language use to different interpretations and hence underline more the active contribution of the researcher in 'constructing' the descriptions that he or she produces about language use." It is also the case that CA is not concerned analytically with what a section of talk reveals about a speaker's motives, beliefs, or cognitions, in the way that is traditional in mainstream social psychology, as well as in sport and exercise psychology. Instead, the focus in CA is on what is available in the data; namely, what speakers are orienting to and achieving in the interaction, in a turn-by-turn sense, and how such interactional sequences are routinely carried off or accomplished (Hutchby & Wooffitt, 2008). As Edwards put it: "intentions, goals, mental contents and their intersubjective sharing are analysed as kinds of business that talk attends to, rather than being the analyst's stock assumption concerning what is actually going on" (1997, p. 96).

CA has been used to study social interaction and language use in a variety of institutional domains but as Drew and Heritage pointed out, the institutionality of an interaction is not dependent upon its setting: "Rather, interaction is institutional insofar as participants' institutional or professional identities are somehow made relevant to the work activities in which they are engaged" (1992, p. 3). It is in this sense that we can apply CA to the study of interaction in sport and exercise. To the extent that we are interested in considering how particular identities are being worked up in interaction and made relevant to the day-to-day activities of sport/exercise, then we have an appropriate institutional setting in which to investigate how people conduct themselves. A CA study of this kind of institutional talk is concerned with the same issues that drive CA studies of other institutional orders: "how these institutional realities are evoked, manipulated and even transformed in interaction" (Heritage, 1997, p. 162). Following a description of some additional key methodological concepts of CA, we will illustrate the approach with some recent examples of its use in sport settings.

Turn-taking

One of the fundamental organizing principles of talk-in-interaction from a CA perspective is turn-taking. Turn-taking refers to the ways talk is organized so that there are minimal gaps and overlaps between speakers (Schegloff, 2007). The skinfold testing interaction at the beginning of this chapter illustrates this, showing instances (signaled by the square bracket ([) notation) where the sports physiologist's and athlete's talk occasionally overlaps briefly). A fundamental principle guiding turn-taking organization is that only one person should talk at a time (Hutchby & Wooffitt, 2008). Discrete units of talk, known as turns-at-talk, are built out of what are referred to as "turn-constructional units" or TCUs. A TCU is a recognizable action such as a request, acceptance, greeting, or offer (Sacks, Schegloff, & Jefferson, 1974), and can be fashioned out of a sentence, a phrase, or word. The completion of a TCU provides the opportunity for speaker transition. In CA, the span between the completion of one TCU and the commencement of another is referred to as a "transition-relevance place" (TRP). In addition to turn-taking, talk is also organized in terms of sequence; that is, in terms of the ways in which turns-at-talk, and the actions that they implement, are linked to one another (Arminen, 2006). The next section provides an outline of this feature.

Sequence organization

The most basic sequence through which an action can be accomplished is the adjacency pair: two adjacently placed turns-at-talk that are produced by two different speakers (in the skinfold testing extract on p. 243, for example, a question from the physiologist [line 1] is followed by an answer from the athlete [line 2]). The two turns that make up an adjacency pair are said to be "relatively ordered" (Schegloff, 2007, p. 13), in that they consist of a first pair part (FPP) that initiates a particular action (e.g., a question), and a second pair part (SPP) that responds to that action (e.g., an answer). The regular occurrence of such paired actions is explained in terms of the property of "conditional relevance." A particular FPP is said to make relevant and expectable a particular SPP response (Maynard & Clayman, 2003). Specifically, greetings are normatively followed by greetings, questions by answers, and so on. It is through adjacency pair sequences that participants in a conversation can be seen to display their understanding of the ongoing interaction. Although the adjacency pair is seen as constituting the basis of sequence organization, sequences are not always made up of simple two-turn sequences. Adjacency pairs can be expanded at a number of points, leading to the production of long stretches of talk that are centered on an adjacency pair (see Schegloff, 2007).

Preference organization

Although a range of potential SPPs can be made relevant following a FPP, not all responses are of equal value. Some responses are said to be "preferred," whereas some are "dispreferred." The concept of preference, here, does not relate to a speaker's psychological state, but to the action that a FPP is designed to achieve. That is, preferred responses work to further the action trajectory of a FPP, aligning with the stance exhibited in a prior speaker's turn (Schegloff, 2005). For instance, acceptance of an invitation works to advance the trajectory of an invitation sequence, therefore constituting a "preferred" response. By contrast, refusal or rejection hinders the accomplishment of an invitation, and is said to constitute a "dispreferred" response. Preferred and dispreferred responses are typically designed in ways that demonstrate their status. Preferred responses are produced with little delay or accompanying talk. In contrast, dispreferred responses are typically delayed relative to the FPP, and are accompanied by accounts, excuses, or disclaimers (Schegloff, 2007). Common devices for delaying production of a dispreferred SPP include silences, prepausals (e.g., *um, uh*), in-breaths, hedges (e.g., *I don't know*), discourse markers (e.g., *well*), palliatives (e.g., appreciative tokens and apologies that mitigate the negative valence of a dispreferred response), and pro-forma agreements (i.e., agreement followed by disagreement, the canonical form of which is *yes, but . . .*) (see Schegloff, 2007; Sidnell, 2010).

Description of CA method

Heritage (1997) described six basic points of entry that analysts can use to begin examination of institutional interaction using CA. We will describe these features briefly, as they form a useful framework for summarizing how to approach the CA study of naturally occurring interaction.

1. *Turn-taking organization*: Although all interactions involve some kind of turn-taking organization (Sacks *et al.*, 1974), some institutional interactions (e.g., those involving meetings, ceremonies, classrooms, courtrooms), involve very specific and sanctionable turn-taking procedures. A first thing to consider, according to Heritage, is whether the interaction you are studying involves the use of such a special turn-taking organization that, for example, defines and limits topics, forms of speech, or participants' opportunities for involvement.
2. *Overall structural organization*: A second step in dealing with data/recordings is to "build an overall 'map' of the interaction in terms of its typical 'phases' or 'sections'" (Heritage, 1997, p. 166). In the following example, we use a brief extract from a weekly coach–player performance feedback session in a professional sports work setting (Craig, 2011), to illustrate how the interaction can be divided into sections of activity (shown on the right-hand side).

```
Performance Feedback Session: Senior Coach(SC)-Player 3 (P3)
                                              Activity

 1  SC:  Where did you sit in your (.) in our      Request    for
                                                   Information
 2       um (0.3) assessment of leadership (.)     Sequence
 3       what category?
 4  P3:  Three
 5  SC:  And by definition, what was three?
 6  P3:  Follower
 7  SC:  Mmm (1.1) he doesn't cause any problems.  N e g a t i v e
                                                   Assessment
 8  P3:  Yep                                       Sequence
 9  SC:  Big fella
10  P3:  Yep
11  SC:  He doesn't cause any problems.
12       (0.4) a:h he sits there (.)
13       listens (1.2) goes along with things (1.0) but
14       he doesn't influence anyone.
15       (1.6)
16  P3:  Yep
17  SC:  Okay? he's a follower
18       bhh::a::a (0.3) you know what that is?
19  P3:  A sheep
20  SC:  A little sheep (.) one runs through (0.4) fucking
21       others follow, that's you.
22  P3:  Yep
23  SC:  Jump in the air ((SC makes sound of jumping))
24       over the fence (.) follower.
25       you've asked the question (1.0) what else can I do  A d v i c e -
                                                             giving
26       to (.) improve the group or influence the group    Sequence
27       (1.1)
28       I'm suggesting you need to start to ah (2.0) care
29       and influence about some of your teammates.
30  P3:  Yep
```

In this extract, the first section (lines 1–24) might be characterized broadly as the assessment phase of the interaction. The coach initiates this activity by making requests for information from the player (lines 1–6) in the form of *wh*-questions – a common question type that typically seeks a particular piece of information using *who, where, when,* or *what* (Sidnell & Stivers, 2013, p. 420). The player responds on both occasions with a one-word answer ("Three," "Follower"). Following these request/answer adjacency pairs, the coach delivers a sequence of descriptive assessments of the player ("He doesn't cause any problems," "Big fella," and so on, lines 7–24). Each of these assessments is receipted by the player with the single word "Yep." And then, at line 25, we see what might be described as the next phase of the interaction: the coach initiating the activity of advice-giving. He frames his advice as something the player has already asked for, using directly reported speech ("You've asked the question (1.0) what else can I do . . ."). Identifying broad sections of the interaction in this way allows analysts to "examine how the parties progressively develop (or not) a joint sense of the talk . . . and look at the roles each party plays in this process" (Heritage, 1997, p. 168).

3. *Sequence organization*: In analyzing sequences, the focus is on the way in which particular actions are initiated and developed. In the extract above, for example, we might focus on the question/answer sequence commencing on line 1 that initiates the activity of the coach's face-to-face negative assessment of the player. In this question/answer sequence, the coach's interrogative questions are receipted by the player with brief, unadorned, and unmitigated answers. The player does not attempt to provide an account of his previous leadership categorization, nor give a reason or explanatory context for his negative evaluation as a "follower." We might also look at the assessment sequence that follows, focusing on the way it unfolds across numerous turns (lines 7–24). The advice-giving that follows on from this assessment at lines 25–30 can also be examined as a particular type of activity. In terms of the unfolding of sequences in the interaction, we can see how initial focusing inquiries from the coach, followed by specific negative assessment of performance, worked to topicalize particular measures for solution of the player's problem. Further analysis would involve looking across a corpus of such data (e.g., involving performance feedback) to identify recurring interactional patterns in sequences of assessment and advice-giving.

4. *Turn design*: As discussed above, talk is designed to perform actions, and identifying this aspect of talk is a key element of the CA approach. However, analysis is also concerned with describing the specific means selected to perform particular actions, such as how a coach delivers performance feedback, and how this is receipted by a player. Specifically, as Heritage puts it, this is achieved by "looking at the details of a turn's component features, and by determining their interactional purpose or significance" (1997, p. 172). In the above extract, we might look at an interesting feature of the coach's assessment (lines 7–9) in this regard. This feature involves the use of a series of descriptors that work, in part, by way of contrast ("big fella," "little sheep") to denigrate the player's dispositional style. In this instance, too, there is little in the way of qualification or hedging of the negative assessment, presumably due to the institutional authority of the coach, in a professional sporting environment, to deliver critical evaluations of performance. Likewise, a notable feature of the advice-giving turn at the end of this extract is the use of personal perspectival framing ("I'm suggesting. . . .") rather than, for example, alternative forms of delivery that might have been used, such as direct imperatives like, "Start showing some care. . . .," or "You need to start . . ."). What analysts can build up, by way of such focus on turn design, is a catalogue of information about how things are routinely done or (more or less effectively) accomplished in a variety of local interactional settings.

5. *Lexical choice*: An example of the way in which lexical selection can shape the unfolding of an interaction can be seen at line 18 above, where the coach uses a sound ("bhh::a::") to elicit the player's self-description as "a sheep." Rather than simply stating that the player acts like a sheep, the coach uses the baa-ing sound as a preface to a question: "you know what that is?" The upshot of this delivery is that the player is the one who selects the derogatory term to describe himself. The coach is then afforded the opportunity to upgrade the negative description in his next turn, in this case, adding "little" to the phrase.

6. *Interactional asymmetries*: In institutional settings, specific roles and tasks often shape the nature of the interaction that takes place. Institutional representatives – doctors, coaches, exercise physiologists, for example – are often more active in shaping what gets discussed and who gets to speak. They may also draw on specialized knowledge that imparts particular authority. Likewise, there are commonly differences in perspective between routine institutional "knowhow" regarding standard practice or objectives on the part of the professional, and what Heritage (1997, p. 176) referred to as the "singular experience" of the lay participant (involving, e.g., the personal and particular circumstances of their troubles, illnesses, claims). Finally, there are often asymmetries to do with rights of access to knowledge. Obvious examples in the sporting context concern knowledge about who will be selected to play in a particular game, whose contract will be extended at the end of the year, and so on. Such asymmetries provide another point of entry that analysts can use to examine sports interaction using CA.

The CA approach to analysis is generally associated with qualitative research. That said, it is possible to combine CA with some sort of quantification of the data (e.g., Robinson, 2007, p. 65). For example, statistical evidence can be used to substantiate claims about practices of action – what interactants are routinely doing with their talk-in-interaction – via the reporting both of the number of supporting and disconfirmatory cases in a data set. Those interested in more detailed introductions to the application of CA might use the following sources as a starting point: Drew and Heritage (1992, 2006); Hutchby and Wooffitt (2008); Nevile, Haddington, Heinemann and Rauniomaa (2014); Richards and Seedhouse (2005); Schegloff (2007); Sidnell and Stivers (2013); ten Have (2007).

Some criticisms of conversation analysis

Although CA is a well-established approach, criticisms have emerged. Some have questioned CA's stringent requirement of empirical grounding for analytic claims, arguing that just because something is not mentioned in the data does not mean that it is inconsequential (Paltridge, 2012). For instance, contextual factors like class, gender, power, disability are argued, by some, to be overlooked by CA's focus on sequences of interaction alone (ten Have, 1990). Response to such criticism has been that CA avoids the risk of bias involved in imposing researchers' categories and opinions (Wooffitt, 2005), thus enhancing the validity of its findings. Schegloff summarized the CA stance as follows:

> showing that some orientation to context is demonstrably relevant to the participants is important . . . in order to ensure that what informs the analysis is what is relevant to *the participants in its target event*, and not what is relevant in the first instance to its academic analysts by virtue of the set of analytic and theoretical commitments which they bring to their work.
>
> *(Schegloff, 1997, p. 196)*

It has also been pointed out that unlike many forms of quantitative research, in CA the raw data on which analysts' claims are based are present in the report. Such claims are therefore open to testing by readers, thus adding to the reliability of the approach (Hutchby & Wooffitt, 2008).

Another problem that is sometimes raised concerns the risk, in CA research, of overlooking longer-term temporal processes. Typically, CA uses recordings of temporally limited interactions, but Peräkylä (1997) highlighted instances where professionals manage the chronically ill, or where multiple agents and sites of negotiation are involved, as being worthy of study too. Longitudinal study designs can be employed in CA research to examine the way progressive change occurs through repeated interactions (see, e.g., O'Neill & LeCouteur's (2014) analysis of family therapy sessions). Likewise, where people are routinely moving about in particular settings, or where interaction occurs at multiple sites via telephone or computer, static recording methods (either audio-recording or single video camera) may be inadequate to capture what is going on. In such circumstances CA researchers have used multiple cameras to record the nature of interactions (e.g., LeCouteur & Feo's 2011 analysis of on-court talk between netballers; Goodwin & Goodwin's (1996) study of the activities of air-traffic controllers).

Conversation analysis and other qualitative methods: similarities and differences

Although other qualitative approaches, such as Discourse Analysis (DA) and narrative inquiry also focus on language, CA is notably different in its insistence on the use of naturally occurring interactional data (see Smith & Sparkes, 2005; 2009a, b). The focus of narrative inquiry that utilizes data sources such as stories, autobiographies, letters, interviews, as well as conversation, is on how meaning is created over time and how individuals construct versions of their lives. Such a focus is inherently broader and often more cognitively oriented than that of CA, which is concerned not with the overarching stories and narratives that people construct, but with the specific ways in which interactions take place. Where narratives are examined in CA studies, the focus is on the turns that are used routinely to tell stories, and on the organization of narrative sequences (Hutchby & Wooffitt, 2008).

DA and Discursive Psychology (DP) likewise have a focus on language, and both can also be concerned with institutional and mundane interaction as a means through which to explore the social world. CA differs from DA with respect to the types of data that are studied (for an in-depth discussion see Wooffitt, 2005). CA focuses on understanding social action through analysis of the local detail of turn-by-turn management in real-world interactions, whereas DA and DP are focused on broader sets of language practices (such as cultural discourses and/or interpretative repertoires), and how these are invoked in talk to achieve particular social ends and to construct the reality of the world and its phenomena (see also Chapter 18). However, Wetherell (1998) argued that CA can complement and add to discursive analyses, advocating what she termed a "synthetic approach," in which attention is paid both to the microlevel detail of how interactions unfold, as well as to the broader cultural practices being worked up (see also Potter, 1996, 2012, for discussion of combined use of DP/CA).

Using CA in sport and exercise research

Social interaction is the primordial means through which the business of the social world is transacted, the identities of its participants are affirmed or denied, and its cultures are transmitted, renewed, and modified. Through processes of social interaction, shared meaning, mutual understanding, and the coordination of human conduct are achieved.

(Goodwin & Heritage, 1990, p. 283)

This statement by Goodwin and Heritage in an early introduction to CA summarizes aspects of the approach of particular significance to anthropologists. The ongoing relevance of the method to those working in the psychology and sociology of sport remains obvious. Sport is a primary activity through which the contemporary social world is transacted; through which identities (of players, coaches, administrators, and fans) are affirmed or denied, and cultures (national, local, club, team, and any number of subgroupings) are constructed, transmitted and modified. In what follows we provide an overview of recent applications of CA to the field.

Two studies are recognized as having introduced CA as a methodology offering potential for sport and exercise research. Jimerson (2001) used the principles of CA to re-analyse data from an earlier study of athletes' locker-room talk at an American university (Curry, 1991). Although not, strictly, making use of naturally occurring talk – the original data were written down by the researcher "as spoken" in one setting and recalled "as overheard" by an athlete-informant in another – Jimerson showed how close sequential analysis cast doubt on the original conclusion that sexism and homophobia were not publically challenged in the locker room. He cited evidence of dissent involving conversationalists' responses that were "adversarial, ambiguous, ambivalent, or absent" (2001, p. 335). Around the same time, Faulkner and Finlay (2002) demonstrated how CA could be applied to taped telephone interviews with clinicians discussing their perceptions of exercise as an antidepressant, and the role of mental-health professionals in the promotion of physical activity. Focusing on instances of disagreement between interviewer and respondent over the effectiveness of exercise as an adjunct treatment, the researchers aimed to show how CA was an ideal method for investigating interaction, more generally, between "sport psychologist and athlete, coach and athlete(s), physical education teacher and pupil(s), or exercise counsellor and patient(s)" (2002, p. 62). They also highlighted the opportunity afforded by CA for studies that combined examination of conversation and body movement.

This line of investigation was taken up by LeCouteur and Feo (2011), who applied CA to the study of real-time competitive performance in a netball match involving elite players. Responding to a request from coaches, the researchers focused on the nature of on-court communication during defensive play. Players wore recording devices, and video cameras were used to capture images of play. Recordings were coded for frequency of different types of communication and analyzed for evidence of recurring verbal and nonverbal patterns. Descriptive statistics indicated higher frequencies of communication between defenders when opposition players obtained shots on goal. CA provided an opportunity to unpack this finding by examining the interactional consequences of particular verbal and nonverbal communications. Uptake of communication was demonstrated to be crucially dependent upon speakers' taking account, in their verbal and nonverbal conduct, of both their team-mate's current orientation, and visual access to the defensive problem. The researchers highlighted a pattern in which players routinely failed to reference key specific details of a defensive problem in their talk, thereby leading to miscommunication and unsuccessful defensive play. By way of close analysis of actual interaction, the researchers were able to extend previous research findings suggesting that it is a lack of verbal communication that results in poor defense. Using CA to examine the data demonstrated, instead, that it was not the *amount* of talk that was problematic, but the lack of mutual orientation between players, that was key.

A similar study of team coordination in doubles table-tennis matches analyzed the detail of spoken and bodily conduct between points (Poizat, Bourbousson, Saury, & Sève, 2012). Findings reinforced the importance of "public" behaviors like "looks, positioning and movements in the playing space" (2012, p. 636), for the establishment and maintenance of mutual orientation in team sports. The researchers concluded that video analysis of interaction allowed them to take into account practices that are rarely described and commented on by athletes: "behaviors that had become almost 'invisible' to the players because of their embodiment"(2012, p. 636), but that had a particular role in the processes of team coordination. Another study to make use of video analysis, this time in boxing, focused on the process of learning a specific skill. Okada (2013) analyzed how a coach and boxer coordinated their "talk, body, eye-gaze, gesture, and material objects" to accomplish the activity of teaching and learning an effective punch. The following example from this analysis illustrates one way of combining verbal and nonverbal transcriptions of interaction (as well as illustrating how translated speech may be rendered). In the original extract, Okada also transcribes the coparticipants' head and hand movements, as well as the body orientations, that correspond with particular aspects of the talk.

TALK Coach: *sono*   *naka ni:* (.) *e*(.)   [*soo da na,* (0.5)   [*sutoreeto*   *to ka*

that   within   uh   I was wondering   straight   such as

"Within that, uh, I was wondering, (if you can include punches) such as a straight punch or"

Osamu: [*Hai.*]

yes

"Yes"

GAZE Coach: looks at Osamu------------------[looks away------------[looks at Osamu------------------

Osamu looks at Coach---

(Okada, 2013, p. 394)

Although not specifically about sport, work by Keevallik (2010) using video data to investigate how sequences of teaching in a dance class were organized is also relevant here. By combining verbal descriptions with bodily demonstration (body "quotation"), Keevallik showed how teachers corrected or adjusted students' performances via a process of inviting them to coparticipate in examination of problematic behaviors. The organization of such body quotes, their understanding and uptake as a corrective teaching activity, was shown to result in "heightened participation," making them "useful pedagogical devices" (2010, p. 424).

Another area that has been a focus of analysis by CA researchers interested in sport concerns performance analysis and feedback. The social organization of power within an English Premier League Academy was explored by Groom *et al.* (2012), who focused on how a coach used video-based technology to provide performance feedback. They demonstrated how the coach "exercised control over the sequential organization of the sessions, via asymmetrical turn-taking allocations . . . and the use of questioning to select speakers to take turns to talk" (2012, p. 439). As is often the case with CA research, the researchers made recommendations for practice based on their findings, concluding that coaches might be trained in the likely impact, on athlete learning, of specific interactional practices. In research on the same topic, Craig (2011) investigated recurrent strategies in delivery and receipt of performance feedback in a professional Australian Rules Football setting. This study examined the routine practices through which coaches and players exchanged assessments of each other's performance as part of a standardized program of post-game analysis. Delivery of positive feedback was observed to be relatively direct and straightforward, regardless of whether coaches were assessing players, or vice versa. However, whereas coach-to-player negative assessments were regularly delivered relatively directly, the same was not the case for negative feedback delivered by players to coaches. In these cases, negative assessments were marked by pauses, qualifiers, hedges and repairs, demonstrating that even in an institutional environment where critical evaluation of one's coparticipants was a regular, mandated (and trained) activity, negative assessment was performed as a dispreferred action. Craig (2008) also analyzed the organization of talk-in-interaction in an Australian Rules coaching box on game day, focusing on typical activities of information elicitation and provision. In this setting, requests for advice were produced predominantly by the Senior Coach, typically directly, and were regularly accompanied by candidate solutions framed as tag questions (*So what's gonna happen there, boys? Damo will go to Harbison, yeah?*). Such turn designs were argued to allow Senior Coach to make requests for advice while maintaining a demeanor of competence, and promoting a sense of collaboration and inclusivity with Assistant Coaches. Analysis of receipt-of-advice turns demonstrated that speakers' provision of accompanying justification played a key role in determining whether proffered advice resulted in uptake/non-uptake and acceptance/misunderstanding.

A handful of other studies of interaction between sports professionals have also been carried out. Cosh *et al.* (2011, 2015) applied CA-inspired discursive psychology to study interactions within a sports institute. Looking at regular sessions of skinfold testing, they showed how broader discourses of self-regulation and self-surveillance were reproduced in the micro detail of interactions between sport scientists and athletes, and highlighted the specific ways in which athletes were routinely made accountable for failures of such regulation. In an ethnographic study of social identities, Zucc-hermaglio (2005) recorded interactions between members of a professional soccer team in three different settings (pregame, after a victory, and after a defeat). Although not strictly CA, the combination of descriptive statistics and Jeffersonian transcription demonstrated how different identity categories ("a plurality of groups"; Zuccermaglio & Alby, 2011, p. 204) were drawn on by team members in different interactional settings. Zuccermaglio and Alby re-analyzed these data in a subsequent study of situated moment-by-moment construction of identity, concluding that the "'embeddedness' of identity negotiation practices in the characteristic and meaningful activities of a sport group (rather than its existence as a cognitive and individual phenomenon) is visible only if we adopt a sequential analysis of interactive data" (2011, p. 208). Zuccermaglio and Alby (2012) subsequently analyzed their recordings for evidence of how coaches enacted leadership in different contexts of interaction, and also examined how activities, such as planning future matches or analyzing past defeats and victories, were shared during team meetings. These studies were used to show how "classic themes of sport psychology, such as leadership or a team's cohesion, can be studied not as cognitive and individual phenomena, but as interactional constructions that can be empirically observed." (2012, p. 459).

CA has also been used to examine sports talk – specifically between the host of an American television financial program and callers seeking advice about stocks (Dori-Hacohen & White, 2013). The researchers noted that a common structure to calls involved initiation of sports talk by the host in his second turn at talk, before the introduction of the reason for call. They argued that this interactional feature was integral to the creation of hegemonic masculinity in this setting. Two recent reviews have also emphasized CA as a method that has much to offer sport, exercise, and coaching research (Groom *et al.*, 2014; Locke, 2012), highlighting the centrality of interactions between athletes and coaches to the success of sports outcomes.

A new approach to sport and exercise research

CA allows sport and exercise researchers to get out of the laboratory, to ditch the old standards of questionnaire and interview methods, and to focus on a different way of collecting data. It directs us to observe actual performance and interaction, and focus analytic attention on the fine details in all their complexity. As researchers, we are no longer constrained to analyze what people *say* they do in a given circumstance when questioned by a social scientist, nor what they *might* do in response to a hypothetical or role-play scenario. Using CA, we can observe what people *actually do* when they interact; we can make use of participants' own orientations, in their turns-at-talk, to ground our analytic claims. These "unique methodological features" of CA that ten Have (1990, p. 23) described as having produced "a mass of insights" into everyday life, await application to any number of sport and exercise settings. In his commentary on the "promise" of Discursive Psychology (DP) for research into sports coaching, Potter (2012) framed DP as drawing heavily on the insights of CA and its body of findings. His suggested areas for future research are instructive for those contemplating using CA, for example: the salience of bodies and sensation in interaction; and the interactional organization of particular institutional practices in sport. Applied CA – where researchers work collaboratively with sport and exercise professionals to solve practical problems and design interventions – can also be of great value. Topics such as these have already been the subject of a small number of interesting studies. There is potential now for a greater contribution from researchers who choose to make use of a methodology that, in its ability to investigate multimodality in real-life interaction, is uniquely valuable for advancing knowledge in the field of sport and exercise.

We hope, in this brief overview of CA, to have made a positive case for the method's application to the analysis of interaction in sport and exercise. The importance of sport and exercise in contemporary society, and the interest and excitement generated by such activities worldwide, make detailed examination of how these activities are conducted – in real-life settings and using naturally occurring data – a significant issue for social researchers.

Notes

1 Sacks, H. (1992) *Lectures on Conversation*. Volumes 1 & 2, edited by Gail Jefferson with an introduction by Emmanuel A. Schegloff, Oxford: Blackwell. See also Sacks, H., Schegloff, E.A., & Jefferson, G. (1974). A simplest systematics for the organization of turn taking for conversation. *Language*, *50*, 696–735.

2 This is not to say that CA cannot be applied to the study of talk generated in interviews. However, in such cases, conversation analysts would be investigating such talk as a product of the process of interview – studying the interview as an interaction – rather than treating what was said as a means for understanding the beliefs or attitudes of interviewees. Hutchby and Wooffitt (2008) devote a chapter to the application of CA to interview data in their book, *Conversation Analysis*.

3 Examples of how to represent nonverbal features of interaction can be found in Goodwin (2000), Heath (1986, 1997), Hindmarsh and Heath (2000), Jones and LeBaron (2002), Nevile (2002), Parry (2005), Sidnell (2006), and Stivers and Sidnell (2005). Video stills, diagrams and drawings are also frequently used to illustrate nonverbal features.

4 Roberts and Robinson (2004) estimate a transcription-to-recording ratio of one hour per minute as a general rule of thumb.

5 Peräkylä (1997) suggested that those new to CA might find it useful to have their transcripts checked by more experienced researchers, pointing out that this process is useful for anyone working on transcripts. His advice highlights what has become standard practice for those working in the field of CA: work is usually done in collaboration and via workshops where researchers come together to discuss and analyze data extracts in both recorded and transcribed form, and sharing of corpuses is not unusual. Those contemplating adopting CA might find it useful to join online forums and groups of like-minded researchers such as the following: the Ethnomethodology & CA wiki (EMCA Wiki) at http://emcawiki.

net/Main_Page and the *Australasian Institute for Ethnomethodology and Conversation Analysis* (AIEMCA) at http://aiemca.net.

References

Antaki, C. (Ed.) (2011). *Applied conversation analysis: Intervention and change in institutional talk*. Basingstoke: Palgrave Macmillan.

Arminen, I. (2006). Ethnomethodology and conversation analysis. In C. Bryant & D. Peck (Eds.), *The handbook of the 21st century sociology* (pp. 8–16, 437f, 444f). Thousand Oaks, CA: Sage.

Cosh, S., Crabb, S., LeCouteur, A., & Kettler, L. (2011). Accountability, monitoring and surveillance: Body regulation in elite sport. *Journal of Health Psychology, 17*(4), 610–622.

Cosh, S., Crabb, S., Kettler, L., LeCouteur, A., & Tully, P. J. (2015). The normalisation of body regulation and monitoring practices in elite sport: A discursive analysis of news delivery sequences during skinfold testing. *Qualitative Research in Sport, Exercise and Health, 7*(3), 338–360.

Craig, P. (2008). *Communication in the coaching box: An analysis of the elicitation, provision and receipt of advice*. Unpublished Honour's thesis. University of Adelaide, Australia.

Craig, P. (2011). *Performance feedback: Analysis of positive and negative assessment practices in a professional sport setting*. Unpublished Master's thesis, University of Adelaide, Australia.

Curry, T.J. (1991). Fraternal bonding in the locker room: A profeminist analysis of talk about competition and women. *Sociology of Sport Journal, 8*, 119–135.

Dori-Hacohen, G. & White, T. (2013). "Booyah Jim": The construction of hegemonic masculinity in CNBC "Mad Money" phone-in interactions. *Discourse, Context & Media, 2*, 175–183.

Drew, P. & Heritage, J. (Eds.) (1992). *Talk at work: Interaction in institutional settings*. Cambridge, UK: Cambridge University Press.

Drew, P. & Heritage, J. (Eds.) (2006). *Conversation analysis*. Four Volumes. London: Sage.

Edwards, D. (1997). *Discourse and cognition*. Sage: London.

Faulkner, G. & Finlay, S-J. (2002). It's not what you say, it's the way you say it: Conversation analysis: A discursive methodology for sport, exercise and physical education. *Quest, 54*, 49–56.

Goodwin, C. (2000). Action and embodiment within situated human interaction. *Journal of Pragmatics, 32*, 1489–1522.

Goodwin, C. & Goodwin, M.H. (1996). Seeing as a situated activity: Formulating planes. In Y. Engeström & D. Middleton (Eds.), *Cognition and communication at work* (pp. 61–95). Cambridge, UK: Cambridge University Press.

Goodwin, C. & Heritage, J. (1990). Conversation analysis. *Annual Review of Anthropology, 19*, 283–307.

Groom, R., Cushion, C. J., & Nelson, L. J. (2012). Analysing coach–athlete "talk in interaction" within the delivery of video-based performance feedback in elite youth soccer. *Qualitative Research in Sport, Exercise and Health, 4*, 439–458.

Groom, R., Nelson, L., Potrac, P., & Cushion, C.J. (2014). Conversation analysis. In L. Nelson, R. Groom, & P. Potrac (Eds.), *Research methods in sports coaching* (pp. 227–238). Abingdon, UK: Routledge.

Heath, C. (1986). *Body movement and speech in medical interaction*. Cambridge, UK: Cambridge University Press.

Heath, C. (1997). The analysis of activities in face to face interaction using video. In D. Silverman (Ed.), *Qualitative research: Theory, method and practice* (pp. 183–200). London: Sage.

Heritage, J. (1997). Conversation analysis and institutional talk: Analysing data. In D. Silverman (Ed.), *Qualitative research: Theory, method and practice* (pp. 161–182). London: Sage.

Heritage J.M. & Atkinson, J.C. (1984). Introduction. In J.M. Atkinson & J.C. Heritage (Eds.), *Structures of social action: Studies in conversation analysis* (pp. 1–15). Cambridge, UK: Cambridge University Press.

Hindmarsh, J. & Heath, C. (2000). Embodied reference: A study of deixis in work-place interaction. *Journal of Pragmatics, 32*, 1855–1878.

Hutchby, I. & Wooffitt, R. (2008). *Conversation analysis* (2nd ed.). Cambridge, UK: Polity Press.

Jefferson, G. (2004). Glossary of transcript symbols with an introduction. In G. H. Lerner (Ed.), *Conversation analysis: Studies from the first generation* (pp. 13–23). Amsterdam: John Benjamins.

Jimerson, J.B. (2001). A conversation (re)analysis of fraternal bonding in the locker room. *Sociology of Sport Journal, 18*, 317–338.

Jones, S.E & LeBaron, C.D. (2002). Research on the relationship between verbal and nonverbal communication: Emerging integrations. *Journal of Communication, 52*(3), 499–521.

Keevallik, L. (2010). Bodily quoting in dance correction. *Research on Language and Social Interaction, 43*(4), 401–426.

LeCouteur, A. & Feo, R. (2011). Real-time communication during play: An analysis of team-mates' talk and interaction. *Psychology of Sport and Exercise, 12*(2), 124–134.

Liddicoat, A. J. (2011). *An introduction to conversation analysis.* London: Continuum.

Locke, A. (2012). Commentary: Qualitative research in sports and exercise psychology: A timely comment. *Qualitative Methods in Psychology Section Bulletin, 14,* 71–74.

Maynard, D. W. & Clayman, S.E (2003). Ethnomethodology and conversation analysis. In L. T. Reynolds & N. J. Herman-Kinney (Eds.), *The handbook of symbolic interactionism* (pp. 173–202). Walnut Creek, CA: Altamira Press.

Nevile, M. (2002). Co-ordinating talk and non-talk activity in the airline cockpit. *Australian Review of Applied Linguistics, 25,* 131–146.

Nevile, M. & Rendle-Short, J. (2007). Language as action. *Australian Review of Applied Linguistics, 30*(3), 30.1–30.13.

Nevile, M., Haddington, P., Heinemann, T., & Rauniomaa, M. (2014). *Interacting with objects: Language, materiality and social activity.* Amsterdam: John Benjamins.

Okada, M. (2013). Embodied interactional competence in boxing practice: Co-participants' joint accomplishment of a teaching and learning activity. *Language & Communication, 33,* 390–403.

O'Neill, K. & LeCouteur, A. (2014). Naming the problem: A membership categorization analysis study of family therapy. *Journal of Family Therapy, 36,* 268–286.

Paltridge, B. (2012). *Discourse Analysis: An introduction.* London: Bloomsbury.

Parry, R. (2005). A video analysis of how physiotherapists communicate with patients about errors of performance: Insights for practice and policy. *Physiotherapy, 91,* 204–214.

Peräkylä, A. (1997). Reliability and validity in research based on tapes and transcripts. In D. Silverman (Ed.), *Qualitative research: Theory, method and practice* (pp. 201–220). London: Sage.

Poizat, G., Bourbousson, J., Saury, J., & Sève, C. (2012). Understanding team coordination in doubles table tennis: Joint analysis of first- and third-person data. *Psychology of Sport and Exercise, 13,* 630–639.

Potter, J. (1996). *Representing reality: Discourse, rhetoric and social construction.* London: Sage.

Potter, J. (2012). Arsène didn't see it: Coaching, research and the promise of a discursive psychology. A commentary. *International Journal of Sports Science & Coaching, 7*(4), 629–633.

Richards, K. & Seedhouse, P. (Eds.) (2005). *Applying conversation analysis.* Basingstoke, UK: Palgrave Macmillan.

Roberts, F. & Robinson, J.D. (2004). Interobserver agreement on first-stage conversation analytic transcription. *Human Communication Research, 30,* 376–410.

Robinson, J. D. (2007). The role of numbers and statistics within conversation analysis. *Communication Methods and Measures, 1*(1), 65–75.

Sacks, H. (1992). *Lectures on conversation.* Oxford: Blackwell.

Sacks, H., Schegloff, E.A., & Jefferson, G. (1974). A simplest systematics for the organisation of turn-taking for conversation. *Language, 50,* 696–735.

Schegloff, E.A. (1997). In another context. In A. Duranti and C. Goodwin (Eds.), *Rethinking context: Language as an interactive phenomenon* (pp. 191–228). Cambridge, UK: Cambridge University Press.

Schegloff, E. A. (2005). On complainability. *Social Problems, 52,* 449–476.

Schegloff, E. A. (2007). *Sequence organization in interaction: A primer in conversation analysis.* Vol 1. Cambridge, UK: Cambridge University Press.

Sidnell, J. (2006). Coordinating gesture, talk and gaze in re-enactments. *Research on Language and Social Interaction, 39,* 377–409.

Sidnell, J. (2010). *Conversation analysis: An introduction.* Chichester: Wiley-Blackwell.

Sidnell, J. & Stivers, T. (2013). *The handbook of conversation analysis.* Malden, MA: Wiley-Blackwell.

Silverman, D. (2006). *Interpreting qualitative data* (3rd ed.). Thousand Oaks, CA: Sage.

Smith, B. & Sparkes, A. C. (2005). Analyzing talk in qualitative inquiry: Exploring possibilities, problems, and tensions. *Quest, 57,* 213–242.

Smith, B. & Sparkes, A. C. (2009a). Narrative analysis and sport and exercise psychology: Understanding lives in diverse ways. *Psychology of Sport and Exercise, 10,* 279–288.

Smith, B. & Sparkes, A. C. (2009b). Narrative inquiry in sport and exercise psychology: What can it mean, and why might we do it? *Psychology of Sport and Exercise, 10,* 1–11.

Stivers, T. & Sidnell, J. (2005). Multi-modal interaction. *Semiotica, 156,* 1–20.

Stokoe, E. (2014). The Conversation Analytic Role-play Method (CARM): A method for training communication skills as an alternative to simulated role-play. *Research on Language and Social Interaction*, *47*(3), 255–265.

ten Have. P. (1990). Methodological issues in conversation analysis. *Bulletin de Méthodologie Sociologique*, *27*, 23–51.

ten Have, P. (2007). *Doing conversation analysis: A practical guide* (2nd ed.). London: Sage.

Wetherell, M. (1998). Positioning and interpretative repertoires: Conversation analysis and post-structuralism in dialogue. *Discourse & Society*, *9*, 387–412.

Wilkinson, R. (1999). Sequentiality as a problem and resource for intersubjectivity in aphasic conversation: Analysis and implications for therapy. *Aphasiology*, *13*(4–5), 327–343.

Wooffitt, R. (2005). *Conversation analysis and discourse analysis: A comparative and critical introduction*. London: Sage.

Zucchermaglio, C. (2005). Who wins and who loses: The rhetorical manipulation of social identities in a soccer team. *Group Dynamics: Theory, Research and Practice*, *9*, 219–238.

Zucchermaglio, C. & Alby, F. (2011). Identity in sport teams. *Psychology*, *2*(3), 202–209.

Zucchermaglio, C. & Alby, F. (2012). Coach leadership during technical meetings in an Italian soccer team. *Rassegna di Psicologia*, *2*, 91–105.

20

NARRATIVE ANALYSIS IN SPORT AND EXERCISE

How can it be done?

Brett Smith

It would be wrong to say that there is a gigantic swell of sport and exercise researchers turning to a narrative analysis. However, this way of making sense of material has been steadily promoted and productively used within the sport and exercise science qualitative community in recent years. For example, there is work promoting what a narrative analysis "is" and why it might be used (e.g., Dowling, Garrett, lisahunter, & Wrench, 2013; Markula & Denison, 2005; McGannon & Smith, 2015; Smith & Sparkes, 2009a, b; see also Chapter 4, this volume). There is also a growing empirical body of sport and exercise research that has utilized a narrative analysis (e.g., Busanich, McGannon, & Schinke, 2014; Carless & Douglas, 2009; Day & Wadey, 2016; Fasting & Sand, 2015; Griffin & Phoenix, 2014, 2016; Knowles, Niven, & Fawkner, 2014; lisahunter & Emerald, 2016; McMahon & Penney, 2011; Papathomas, Lavellee, & Smith, 2015; Papathomas, Williams, & Smith, 2015; Phoenix & Orr, 2014; Sparkes, Pérez-Samaniego, & Smith, 2012). But one key issue largely absent in the sport and exercise literature is, "how might one go about doing a narrative analysis?" The main purpose of this chapter is to offer some responses to this "how" question. Prior to this a brief contextual backdrop is offered.

Contextual backdrop: what is a narrative analysis and why use it?

To understand what a narrative analysis "is" it is first vital to appreciate the paradigmatic and theoretical assumptions that underpin it. This is of importance because, as Holstein and Gubrium (2012) noted, narrative analyses extend out of, and are informed by, particular epistemological, ontological, and theoretical sensibilities. For example, as several authors have highlighted in reviews of the field (e.g., Schiff, 2013; Sparkes & Smith, 2008), postpositivism, realism, and constructivism have been used to inform how narrative analysis is practiced (e.g., McAdams, 2013). Largely, however, narrative analyses have been underpinned and informed by interpretive epistemologies and ontologies, such as constructionism, post structuralism, or critical inquiry (see Kim, 2016; Sparkes & Smith, 2008; see also Chapters 1, 4, 10, and 21, this volume). Narrative analysis is often also underpinned by a psychosocial approach that emphasizes human beings as meaning-makers who, in order to interpret, direct, and intelligibly communicate life, configure and constitute their experience and sense of who they are using narratives that their social and cultural world have passed down. A complementary core premise of narrative work is that narratives shape human emotion and conduct; narratives can do things for humans and, as actors, narratives can do things on, in, and with us, affecting emotional life and "what people are able to see as real, as possible, and as worth doing or best avoided" (Frank, 2010, p. 3).

Underpinned and informed by these assumptions, narrative analysis refers to a family of methods that have in common a focus on stories (Riessman, 2008). It can be described as an approach that seeks to describe and interpret the ways in which people perceive reality, make sense of their worlds and perform social actions (Griffin & Phoenix, 2016). To add some nuance to this definition effort, following Smith and Sparkes (2009b) and Bochner and Riggs (2014), the family of narrative analytical methods can be sorted into two different standpoints toward stories. These are known as the storyanalyst and storyteller.

A *storyanalyst* places narratives *under* analysis and communicates results via a *realist tale* (see Chapter 22), to produce an analytical account *of* narratives (Bochner & Riggs, 2014). The research conducted then is *on* narratives, where narratives are the object of study and placed under scrutiny by utilizing a specific type of narrative analysis and producing an abstract tale *about* stories. Examples of the types of narrative analysis that a researcher might use when operating as a storyanalyst are as follows:

1. *Thematic narrative analysis* (see below).
2. *Structural narrative analyses* (see below).
3. *Categorical-form narrative analysis* (see below).
4. *Personal narrative analysis*. With a focus on the *whats* of stories, the purpose is to examine the internalized and evolving life stories of individuals (see McAdams, 2013).
5. *Grounded theory narrative analysis*: With a focus largely on the *whats* of stories, the purpose is to develop categories and produce a theory grounded in data while being sensitive to narratives by looking at the ways narrativity can be integrated conceptually and used systematically for shaping the way in which coding, category development and the representation of results in study proceed (see Ruppel & Mey, 2015).
6. *Rhetorical narrative analysis*: With a focus on the *hows* of stories, the purpose is to identify the oppositions (e.g., good and bad therapy) and enthymemes (e.g., incomplete or probable arguments) that make up stories (see Feldman Skoldberg, Brown, & Horner, 2004).
7. *Interactional narrative analysis*: With a focus on the *hows* of stories, and borrowing ideas and techniques from conversational analysis (see Chapter 19), the purpose is to examine the interactional activity through which stories are constructed (see Gubrium & Holstein, 2009; Bamberg, 2012).
8. *Dialogical narrative analysis*: With an interest in the *whats* and *hows* of stories, the purpose is to examine what is told in the story, how it is told, and what happens as a result of telling that story – its effects (see Caddick, Phoenix, & Smith, 2015; Frank, 2010; Smith, 2016).
9. *Visual narrative analysis*: With a focus on the *whats* or *hows*, the purpose is to examine how and when visual material was made, and who created it; what is included (and excluded) in the image itself, how component parts are arranged, and use of color and technologies; and ideally people's responses to an image (see Griffin, 2010; Riessman, 2008; Chapter 11, this volume).
10. *Sensorial narrative analysis*: With a focus on moving between the *whats* and *hows*, the purpose is to examine what senses are used and how for making sense of human life and social actions (see lisahunter & Emerald, 2016; Sparkes & Smith, 2012a; Chapter 26, this volume).

In contrast to a storyanalyst, when operating as a *storyteller* analysis *is* the story and a tale *as a* story is produced via a *creative analytical practice* (CAP) (see Chapter 23). To say that analysis *is* the story is to emphasize that rather than putting a story under analysis and doing research on narratives as a storyanalyst would do, the story in its own right is analytical and theoretical; it does the job of analysis as analysis happens *in* a story (Bochner & Riggs, 2014; Ellis, 2004). Given this, and what producing a tale *as* a story means, data is recast to produce a story and the story is a theory. That is, rather than produce an abstract tale of stories, a story itself is produced. To help keep stories as stories and the analysis in them, a CAP is used. Examples of the types of creative analytical practices that a researcher might use when operating as a storyteller are highlighted below (see also Chapter 23):

1. *Autoethnography*: The focus is on creating stories about the researchers lived experience, relating the personal to the cultural (see McMahon & McGannon, 2016; McGannon & Smith, 2015; Zehntner & McMahon, 2014).
2. *Creative nonfiction*: The focus is on creating a story that is grounded in research findings and composed using the techniques of fiction (see Smith, McGannon, & Williams, 2015).
3. *Messy texts:* The focus is on showing and telling a story in a manner that is characterized by a continuous movement throughout among description, interpretation, and voice (see Griffin & Phoenix, 2014).
4. *Digital stories*: The focus is on using the internet (e.g., Facebook or blogs) to construct and communicate a digital story (see Chapters 11 and 27).
5. *Ethnodrama*: The focus is on producing a written play script based on stories collected and interpreted (see Cassidy, Kidman, & Dudfield, 2015).
6. *Poetic representation*: The focus is on transforming data into a poem-like composition (see e.g., McMahon & McGannon, 2016; Richardson, 2000; Sparkes & Smith, 2014).
7. *Ethnotheatre*: The focus is on turning a written play script into an actual theatrical production. The play becomes another layer of analysis (see Sparkes & Smith, 2014).
8. *Musical performance*: The focus is on using music as way of analyzing data and communicating findings (see Sparkes & Smith, 2014).

A storyanalyst and storyteller are very different, but neither one is better than the other. Researchers may, for certain purposes, choose to operate as one or the other. Or they might move from one standpoint to another within a project, utilizing both rather than pledging allegiance to one standpoint only (e.g., storyteller) and seeing the other (e.g., storyanalyst) as a family enemy. Examples of researchers moving back and forth between standpoints, operating in some instances as storyanalyst and then at other times as storyteller to thicken understandings of a specific topic, can be found in the work of Carless (2014) and Carless, Sparkes, Douglas, and Cooke (2014) on inclusive adventurous training and adapted sport, as well as Smith (2013a, b) and Sparkes and Smith (2011, 2012b) on spinal cord injury, sport, and physical activity. The work of Griffin and Phoenix (2014, 2016) on women and running is another example of researchers moving from a storyanalyst to a storyteller.

There are various reasons why someone might use a narrative analysis. For example, whilst a narrative analysis cannot do everything, it can help us understand the *relational* and *cultural* fabric of *human lives in* and *across time* (Frank, 2010). An analysis of the stories a person uses to communicate their everyday realities and life as lived can provide insight into *personal experiences, emotions, senses of self, actions,* and *meanings* (Bochner, 2014). Further, because people are capable of shaping reality through storytelling (i.e., storytelling actors) and are also shaped by narratives that circulate within culture (i.e., narratives as actors/performative), narrative analyses can help us understand *human conduct* in ways that respect both *agency* and *structure*. An analysis can reveal not just what narratives are about, but also what narratives *do* on, for, and with people

(Frank, 2010). When operating particularly as a storyteller, a narrative analysis can moreover produce research that is *accessible* to wide audiences and, in turn, be highly effective as part of the *knowledge translation* process (Griffin & Phoenix, 2014; Smith, Papathomas, Martin Ginis, & Latimer-Cheung, 2013; Smith, Tomasone, Latimer-Cheung, & Martin Ginis, 2015).

Doing a narrative analysis as a storyanalyst

As highlighted, there are multiple types of narrative analysis that fall under the umbrella of a storyanalyst. For space reasons, three analyses are focused on. These are a thematic narrative analysis, a holistic-form analysis, and a categorical-form analysis. In each section a *guide* for how each analysis might be done is offered rather than a prescribed procedure to follow rigidly. There are good reasons for this. Instead of functioning to "prevent thought from *moving*" (Frank, 2010, p. 73) and shackling "the imagination" (Gubrium & Holstein, 2014, p. 35), thereby risking leading researchers "to produce what the method suggests they should" (Chamberlain, 2011, p. 50), a guide encourages these intellectual resources. As Frank (2010) argued, guides can help thought to move and "interpretive thought that is moving is more likely to allow and recognize movement in the thought being interpreted" (p. 73). Movement of thought can likewise stimulate a complementary resource, that is, imagination. In so doing, as Gubrium and Holstein suggested, the analysts' intellectual curiosity can be stirred, interpretations thickened, and unexpected insights generated into "what can be seen, heard, described, and reported" (2014, p. 47). To help with all this, each guide offers various analytical strategies. Harnessing the power of treating analysis as also a *method of questioning* (see Frank, 2010), many of the strategies include particular questions. Questions can be useful to keep thought moving and stir the imagination whilst equally helping the researcher orientate to a specific analytical concern of storytelling (e.g., what is the story about and what might this content do for the teller) and avoid drifting too far away from the purpose.

Thematic narrative analysis

When operating as a storyanalyst, the most commonly used type of narrative analysis within sport and exercise is a *narrative thematic analysis* (Riessman, 2008). This analysis, which has also been termed a categorical-content analysis (Lieblich, Tuval-Mashiach, & Zilber, 1998), focuses on the *whats* of stories (i.e., the content). It is different from other types of analysis that focus on patterns (e.g., a thematic analysis; see Chapter 15) and interpretative phenomenological analysis (see Chapter 17), in that the purpose is to identify central themes (i.e. patterns) and relationships among these within one specific form of discourse; that is, stories. In other words, the focus on themes in stories, rather than all or any talk, is what distinguishes a narrative thematic analysis from other analyses.

Drawing on Lieblich *et al.* (1998) and Riessman (2008), as well as personal experiences of using a narrative thematic analysis, here is a guide for how this kind of analysis might be done. Like in all other narrative analyses presented here, the guide should be viewed as cyclical and iterative as opposed to linear and fixed. For example, the researcher might move forward through each strategy outlined in each guide, but can move back and forth between each, circling backward and forward sometimes, even jumping between strategies, as well as appreciating that some will have different utility with respect to different stories.

1. *Write*: It may seem strange to start with writing. Yet, this is warranted because analysis happens in the process of writing (Richardson, 2000; Sparkes, 2002). As such, rather than

relegating writing to something that is done at the end of the project when one "writes up the results," researchers need to write continuously and obsessively throughout the research. They should start writing early and revise, edit, and revise their research report along the way. But, writing has to start somewhere. To get analysis moving, to open it up, a thematic narrative analysis can proceed further as follows.

2. *Transcribe data*: If collecting stories from interviews, for instance, transcribe data verbatim as soon as possible after collecting it. Because during transcription analytical thoughts can emerge, percolate, and move, transcribing *is* an analytical process, not just an exercise in getting down on paper, word for word, what someone has said in an interview or naturalistic setting. Given this, write any pertinent thoughts down during the transcription process.

3. *Organize data*: Create and organize files for data.

4. *Narrative indwelling*: This is similar to familiarization or immersion in other types of analysis, like a thematic analysis or interpretative phenomenological analysis, as it involves reading the data (e.g. interview transcript) several times whilst, if possible, listening to any recording and memo-ing by writing initial impressions in the margins or in a notebook of what is being said. It is subtly different though in that the researcher explicitly seeks to think *with* not just *about* stories (Frank, 1995).

5. *Identify narrative themes and thematic relationships*: A narrative theme is a pattern that runs through a story or set of stories. To search for and identify themes in a manner that keeps the story(s) intact, look for patterns within the stories told by closely reading these discourses several times. To help with identifying patterns, ask yourself, "What is the common theme(s) or thread(s) in each story?" and "What occurs repeatedly within the whole story?" Write notes that capture responses. Another way to help develop themes is to highlight in different colors key sentences, underline key phrases, and/or circle keywords within a story. In addition, write extended phrases (e.g., in 4 or 5 words) in the margins of the transcript, field notes and so on that summarize the manifest (apparent) and latent (underlying) meanings of data. It is vital though not to "overcode" as this can fragment the story rather keeping it intact.

6. *Describe and interpret*: Name each theme and then, working back and forth between the data and notes, describe each theme identified in detail. To ensure the analysis remains distinctly narrative, and not simply thematic, it is important to describe the theme or themes of the story. That is, the researcher writes a description of each theme that captures the specific content of a story, and therefore what the story is about. Relationships between themes can also be described. Researchers do not however just describe. They need to offer interpretations (see also Chapter 30) of the thematic content identified too. Interpretations can be enriched by insights from theory and/or other research. Engaging critically with the stories and existing theory can further enhance interpretations. Throughout the process of interpreting continue to write, revise, and edit, interpretations.

7. *Represent results*: Produce a realist tale (see Chapter 22, this volume; Sparkes, 2002) that communicates the themes of the stories in an engaging and insightful manner. Because of the conjunction of analysis and writing, take time to produce multiple iterations of a realist tale until you feel satisfied you've captured the key content of people's stories. This, however, does not mean that the last word is given. Narrative researchers avoid finalizing stories as people can change and tell different tales. As such, any ending of a narrative analysis as represented in a realist tale is necessarily provisional; that is, no final word is claimed (Frank, 2010). Examples from sport and exercise that have used a thematic narrative analysis can be found in Fasting and Sand (2015) and Sparkes and Smith (2011).

Holistic-form structural analysis

Rather than focusing on *what* is said in talk, analyses of structure focus on the *hows* of storytelling by examining the differing ways it is put together. Because there are different ways to think about how stories are structured, several kinds of structural analyses have been developed. Two examples include a *Labovian structural analysis* (see Riessman, 2008) and a *poetic structural analysis* of narratives (see Gee, 1991). These have rarely been used in sport and exercise, despite the potential each holds for understanding human lives. A third example, and one that has been well used by sport and exercise researchers, is a *holistic-form structural analysis* (Lieblich *et al.*, 1998). This specific kind of structural analysis focuses on the formal plot and organization of the story to tease out the distinct structures that hold it together with a view to identifying a particular narrative type. A rationale for using this analysis is that identifying types of narrative is important because narratives are resources, supplied by culture, which people need in order to shape their personal stories and what becomes experience. In other words, narrative types are essential templates that act as resources, like scaffold, for people to structure their story and make sense of their experiences.

In terms of how to do a holistic-form structural analysis, the following guide is offered.

1. *Write*; *Transcribe data*; *Organize data*; and *Narrative indwelling* (see the section on thematic narrative analysis for details).
2. *Identify the narrative type(s)*: To do this, read the data for clues about how the story is shaped. Annotate transcripts or field notes with conceptual comments concerning the presence of particular plots that sequentially connect life events. The aim here is to begin to identify a clear and persuasive narrative line; that is, a story that has a coherent narrative structure that is repeated in different forms throughout the participant's storytelling, and that is related to the issue of interest (e.g., sporting injury). To help with this, read the stories gathered closely several times, asking yourself "what type of narrative is being used here?" Put impressions from this kind of reading into a written form, noting the different types of story being told. To further help with identifying narrative types consider:

   a. the direction(s) of the story (e.g., decline and then progress) and depicting this in a graph;
   b. use of terms (e.g., crossroads);
   c. participant's reflections on specific phases/chapters in their life ("it was then that I realized I had to fight to recover from my injury");
   d. use of evaluative comments ("my life has gone downhill since I retired from sport");
   e. tone and changes in tone of the story (e.g., pessimistic and later optimistic);
   f. the *objectives* or wants of the *characters* involved (e.g., after a serious sporting injury Edward wants to make a comeback with the help of his physiotherapist); the *conflicts* or obstacles they face as they try to achieve their objectives (e.g., doctors say that medicine has not yet found a cure for the injury); *tactics* or strategies they employ to reach their objectives (e.g., seeking experimental surgery at a new clinic); their *attitudes* toward others and given circumstances (e.g., optimistic about returning to sport); the particular *emotions* they experience throughout (e.g., sadness, anxiety); and/or their *subtexts* or underlying and unspoken thoughts (e.g., scared about not returning to sport and having to retire without anything to fall back on).

   Put the impressions developed by asking such questions into a written form, drafting a response to the question "what type of narrative is being drawn on here?"
3. *Build a typology*: Write a description of each narrative type both in detail and concisely by using the notes written from earlier analytical moves (e.g., narrative indwelling and identifying

narrative types) and bringing these together – clustering these – into a set of narratives (ideal types). To help with this process create time to think about what type of story is told, tell the story slowly to oneself, wait and listen to it, and reflect some more without rushing thinking along. Also structure writing around each type, revising and editing along the way to help "discover" further the types of narratives used. It can also be useful to reengage with the literature. Ask if the narrative is one that circulates in wider society and has been noted before? For example, work in sport has identified numerous types of narrative including, chaos and quest narratives (see Sparkes & Smith, 2011), performance, discovery and relational narratives (see Douglas & Carless, 2015), and exercise is restitution, exercise is medicine, and exercise is progressive redemption narratives (see Papathomas *et al.*, 2015). After identifying the types of stories people tell, name each in a way that captures the essence of each narrative. It can be useful after this to revisit the data to ensure the typology being built is grounded in the stories collected. The researcher may then need to revise the typology and names of the narratives.

4. *Interpretation*: Having identified the types of narratives used by the people in the sample, ask about how dominant the type is in culture and where it circulates. Also ask about the performative functions of the types of narratives too. For example, who benefits from narrative, and who does it connect and disconnect (Frank, 2010)? How do the cultural narratives shape what people do and avoid doing? How do these narratives influence how people see the present and future, and what affects might this have on them and other people? To help with this, it can be useful to draw on theory and develop critical insights about what the narratives might do on, for, and with people.

5. *Represent the results*: Structure the results around the typology and produce a compelling realist tale that captures the different narratives types identified (see also thematic narrative analysis for more details). Examples from sport and exercise that have focused on narrative form can be found in Busanich *et al.* (2014), Carless and Douglas (2009), Knowles *et al.* (2014), Papathomas, Williams, and Smith (2015), and Sparkes and Smith (2011).

Categorical-form analysis

Another way to examine the *hows* of stories is to apply a categorical-form analysis, as described by Lieblich *et al.* (1998). Rather than focusing on the type of narrative being used, this narrative analysis focuses on defined linguistic characteristics of the story that offer emphasis and style in retelling the story. Such characteristics or features might include adverbs (e.g., suddenly), mental verbs (e.g., I thought), denotations of time and place, past/present/future forms of verbs, passive and active verbs, intensifiers (e.g., really, very), disruptions of chronological and causal progression, repetitions, and metaphors. For example, the analysis might focus on metaphors because this linguistic characteristic of stories helps guide human conduct and is frequently used to help make stories meaningful (Smith & Sparkes, 2004). With this rationale, the researcher can then utilize a categorical-form analysis to examine what kind of metaphors the storyteller is using, how frequent these are in the stories that people tell, and how they might operate for different people. In terms of how to do this type of analysis, the following guide is offered.

1. *Write*; *Transcribe data*; *organize data*; and *narrative indwelling* (see section on thematic narrative analysis for details).

2. *Select characteristics*: Based on a strong rationale, choose a linguistic characteristic(s) for analysis (e.g., metaphors).

3. *Identify metaphors*: Conduct a word-for-word analysis of the transcribed stories by identifying the stories told and then within each story circle, highlight or underline all metaphors.

Extract the metaphors and gather them into categories/groups. Following this, identify within the stories the salient metaphors and the relationships between them.

4. *Narrative connection and interpretation*: Having identified the salient metaphors used by the people in the sample, and any additional ones that are less frequent but of interest for what they can reveal, connect the metaphors to the stories people tell. To do this think about how the metaphors help form the story being composed and make the story meaningful. To develop interpretations, ask about the cultural construction of the metaphors. For example, which cultures and subcultures supply the metaphors used (e.g., sport cultures often supply the mechanistic metaphors of the "body is a machine that needs fixing following injury"), and how do these metaphors work to support or contest a broad cultural narrative (e.g., the cultural expectation in sport is for people to battle injury, to make a comeback, and to continue living the performance narrative)? Also ask about the performative functions of metaphors by thinking about what the metaphors might do for and on the person telling the story, what actions might they guide, and what affects they might have on listeners. To help with this, it can be useful to draw on theory and develop critical insights about the metaphors and what they might do.

5. *Represent results*: (see thematic narrative analysis for details). A rare example from sport and exercise using a categorical-form analysis to examine metaphors can be found in Smith and Sparkes (2004).

Analytical bracketing

Having highlighted three types of analytical strategies, it needs noting that there is no "best" or "superior" analysis. Each analysis examines stories from different angles as each serves certain purposes. For example, if as in the research by Knowles *et al.* (2014), one wishes to focus on how certain types of stories circulating within physical education culture shape understanding of physical activity behavior, researchers might choose to use a holistic-form analysis. If, however, they had chosen to examine simply what is in the stories of physical activity a thematic narrative analysis would have been a viable option. Furthermore, researchers might need to use two or more narrative analyses when they aim to examine different features or facets of a story in one study. This is especially so when they wish to attend to both the *whats* and *hows* of stories.

However, one cannot focus on both the *whats* and *hows* at the same time, or engage in doing two or more analyses at once. Analytically this is just too demanding, and ultimately unproductive. A technique to help researchers focus on both *what* is and *hows*, and manage more than one narrative analysis in a study, is *analytical bracketing* (Gubrium & Holstein, 2009). This is the process of analytically moving back and forth between certain features of stories that take into account the *whats* and *hows* of narrativity. As analysis proceeds, the researcher alternatively orientates to the different aspects of stories and storytelling. For example, at one stage the researcher might use a thematic narrative analysis to focus their attention on *what* the story is about, temporarily being more or less indifferent to the *hows*. In the next analytical move, they bracket the *whats* and use another type of narrative analysis, such as a holistic-form analysis or categorical-form analysis to attend to the *hows* of stories. The analytic goal is to shift the focus to capture the interplay between the *whats* and the *hows* of narratives. This maneuvering allows the research to alternatively give analytic primacy to one component of the story or the other, giving equal attention to the *whats* and *hows* of narrativity. Thus, the combined result of narrative analyses developed in tandem can be a multilayered panorama of talk. When combined in a thesis, publication, or book it could provide insights in the formal structures of the story being told and how this frames or provides a scaffold for the content of this talk, and how this shapes the meanings given to an experience.

Doing a narrative analysis as a storyteller

When operating as storyteller, there are various creative analytical practices that can be used to make sense of and communicate stories. Most of these kinds of CAP emphasize the reflexive interplay between the *whats* and *hows* of storytelling, showing throughout a text or performance both what is in a story and how it is organized, shaped by narrative environments, and performed in relation to other bodies.

But how might one craft a CAP and show both the *whats* and *hows* of stories? Drawing from Barone and Eisner (2012), Bochner (2014), Ellis (2004) and Ellingson (2009), and as also articulated in Smith, McGannon, and Williams (2015), the following are some guiding tips. The tips are not applicable to all creative analytical practices. They might, however, be useful for certain kinds of CAP, including autoethnography and creative nonfiction. Further, like the guides offered for doing a narrative analysis when operating as a storyanalyst, the set of tips should not be seen as a recipe or set of prescriptive techniques. Rather, it is hoped that some are useful as a guide for helping to transform stories carefully gathered into an autoethnography or creative nonfiction, for example:

1. *Epistemological and ontological awareness*: Throughout writing be attentive to how, as a researcher, one's epistemology and ontology informs the story. Also consider the stories told, characters in the story and how these are inseparable from the narratives that circulate in culture and the social world.

2. *Ethical awareness*: There can be many ethical dilemmas, which are often unique to producing a CAP. This includes issues around consent, anonymity, and vulnerability. It is important then to be not only well versed in the different ethical positions like relational ethics (see Chapter 24, this volume; Sparkes & Smith, 2014), but also in the numerous dilemmas that can arise when operating as a storyteller, and how one might respond to these. To help navigate ethical issues various guides are available (see e.g., Ellis, 2004; Smith, forthcoming).

3. *A purpose*: A story needs to have and communicate an important point. This helps enable stories to succeed not only as artful literary pieces, but as human science research, too. Make sure the purpose is clear to readers.

4. *Analysis*: Some researchers opt first to operate as storyanalyst by conducting a formal analysis of the data (e.g., a narrative thematic analysis) and interpreting the results theoretically. The results of the analysis, along with theoretical interpretations of these, are then gathered together and used to help assemble the story in terms of what the content of the story is about (e.g., what characters say, enact, and don't say), and how the story unfolds in relation to people (e.g., how people say things in interaction with other people). For an example of this see Griffin and Phoenix (2014). Researchers may also add findings from other research to their story. This can help create a more complex picture and show tensions, contradictions, and connections between research. Collating all analytic results in a table can sometimes be useful; it condenses points to be made, is easily accessible, and can help jog the memory about ideas to be included when crafting the story. No matter what, it is important that the story is crafted from and delivers a thick and rich analysis.

5. *Theory*: Ensure that stories show theory. In relation to the stories collected, ask yourself "what theories am I aiming to show and how?" Are these theories shown through the

story? This can be difficult to really know because we cannot control how people interpret a story; stories are always out of control (Frank, 2010). This said, for stories to be called research it is vital that theory is present. Some researchers for certain purposes choose to simply show theory through stories. For other purposes, however, a researcher might offer an explicit theoretical account of stories – a theoretical autopsy (Ellis & Bochner, 2006). For example, a researcher might layer theory in obvious ways throughout the text, or present a theoretical discussion of the story after presenting it. No matter though what choices a researcher makes they need to ensure that theory is used and shown.

6. *Scribble, gestate, and start to write formally*: Scribble notes in a diary or notebook, for example. Scribbling can be a messy process, but it can stimulate ideas and help develop a story. Ideas and stories can take time to arrive at. A period of gestation, or what might be considered *percolation*, is often needed to let these breathe and develop. Scribble new ideas and continue to sketch the story. At some point the computer needs to be turned on, and writing needs to formally start. This is often not easy. But remember no one will see your drafts and judge these. Let your thoughts flow whilst not straying too far from your purpose – but the purpose can be revised as the story is edited and revised as new meanings are discovered in the process of writing.

7. *Verisimilitude*: Seek truthfulness, not "the Truth." The story needs to demonstrate how true to an experience a narrative can be and with that, the evocation of emotion and feeling from the reader(s). This might include, as in the work of Carless *et al.* (2014), trying to create an account that feels close to the participant's own telling, attempting to be faithful to the experiences and emotions described, the meanings they inscribed, and their own styles of speech.

8. *Think with your body*: Draw on your senses (see Chapter 26), listen to the many voices you've heard in your heart and head, feel these stories pulsating through your body, and tell them as if they were your own whilst respecting the fact you can never truly know the other.

9. *Select and develop characters*: Consider who the characters will be and become, how many people are needed to tell the story, how will they drive the story along, what stories will each tell, and how will they interact with each other. Make characters complex, not simply all good or all bad. Consider intersectionality; that is, the intersection of identities grounded in gender, sex, ethnicity, religion, disability and ability, and so on.

10. *Show rather than tell*: Showing is about delivering a rich, vivid description that aims to create images and conjure up emotions within a reader. Telling catalogues actions and emotional life concisely. Here is an example of telling, provided by Gearity (2014): "It was hot outside and my coach yelled at us" (p. 212). In contrast, here is showing: "Sand kicked up as the gruff coach, hoarse from a long afternoon of berating me and twenty-five of my teammates to sprint again and again, stomped his worn cowboy boots across the heat scorn Mississippi field. Beads of sweat poured steadily" (p. 212).

11. *Use dialogue*: Show what has happened, the point of the story, emotions, and so on, through conversations where appropriate.

12. *Embodiment*: Evoke a sense of the character's body in motion and being still. Show bodies being emotionally expressive (or not) and enacting on, within and against stories. Let the characters act out the story in relation to other people and reveal things about themselves to others through these interactions.

13. *Write evocatively and engagingly*: As well as showing through dialogue, use different senses (e.g., smell, sound, taste) to evoke emotions, create suspension, and engage the readers viscerally as well as cognitively. It can also be useful to use flashback, metaphor, and dramatic evocation.

14. *Develop a plot*: A plot can't always contain tension, as everyday life is not like that, but a story needs some dramatic tension. It needs to connect points across time, be cohesive, and have a consequence(s). A story needs a beginning, middle, and "end" (not the final word), but not always told in that order. To help drive the plot along also consider the characters, what obstacles along the story they will face, what they care about, and how they might change, even if only very subtly.

15. *Scene setting*: Think about the contexts, including where (e.g., places) and when (e.g., morning breakfast) to locate people and their conversations (including internal dialogues with phantom others). Ask yourself about the back and front stages people behave in, as well as how many scenes readers are willing to move in and out of.

16. *Selectivity*: No can tell the "whole" story of a research topic. Don't try to pack it all in. Select what needs to be told in this paper, to meet a certain purpose, and to communicate an important point for a particular audience.

17. *Take a break and polish*: Leave your story alone for a while. Come back to it after a break and work through the story. Revise your work – editing, revising, editing more, and revising again – over a period of time until you're satisfied it has met various criteria you and others might judge it by, like insightfulness, coherence, and evocation (see Chapter 25, this volume; Smith, McGannon, & Williams, 2015; Sparkes & Smith, 2014). Make every word count. Don't make the story too long.

A closing

Before offering some modest thoughts about future directions that narrative analyses might travel, several points need emphasizing. First, by ignoring data collection the chapter might give the impression that data collection and analysis occur separately during the research process. However, as in most qualitative research, data collection and analysis proceed concurrently; that is, in an *iterative* fashion, with each informing the other.

Second, without a prescriptive set of formulaic steps to easily follow, it can feel daunting to start a narrative analysis and, once underway as I've also found on many occasions, can sometimes provoke anxiety. Feelings like this are not uncommon, especially so for those new to qualitative research. This said, as suggested earlier, there are very good reasons for promoting a guide rather than a prescribed procedure in terms of narrative analysis. A prescriptive procedure that one must follow, reflecting what Chamberlain (2011) termed the "codification of method" and, similarly, what Brinkmann (2015) called the "McDonaldization of qualitative research," is useful for certain purposes. But, it can function to stifle movement of thought (Frank, 2010) and imagination (Gubrium & Holstein, 2014). These two analytical resources can, however, be opened and thickened when analysis is developed through a guide. At the same time, guidelines allow analytical competence to be worked on rigorously, enabling researchers to orientate to key concerns so that they do not end up drifting too far from data and research questions when thought is moving and imagination stirred. Thus, there are many virtues that go with a narrative analysis.

Third, as noted, a storyteller is not superior to a storyanalyst (or vice versa). Indeed, when based on informed choices, it is fine to operate as one or the other. Equally, both standpoints may be drawn on for certain purposes over the course of a specific project. Drawing on both could have the benefit of developing an engagement with a methodology of *crystallization*. Building on the work of Richardson (2000), Ellingson (2009) described crystallization as a methodology in which multiple forms of analysis and multiple genres of representation are combined in one of two ways. *Integrated crystallization* brings together different analyses and forms of representation to produce a single text. In contrast, *dendritic crystallization* refers to the ongoing and dispersed process of making meaning of the same topic through multiple forms of analysis and forms of representation to produce series of related texts.

Among the numerous directions researchers might travel in the future (see also Smith, forthcoming), is a focus on *digital storytelling* (see Chapters 11 and 27). As part of this, an analysis of *naturalistic data* would be useful. This kind of data refers to a record of human activities that are neither elicited by nor affected by the actions of researchers. Because naturalistic data is very different from most data collected and analyzed within sport and exercise, a sustained analysis of it could reveal new insights into human activities. Joining Demuth (2015), a return to an understanding of qualitative methods as a *craft skill* that takes time to both master and do well would be welcomed. This is especially so in light of the "fast-food" approach (see Brinkmann, 2015) to qualitative inquiry, and narrative work in particular, that is unfortunately developing at pace.

Resonating with a rich array of existing ideas, such as praxis (see also Chapters 8, 18, 33, and 34), another possible direction to travel is to adopt what Gergen (2014) described as a *future-forming* orientation to research. For him, the essence of such an orientation would be to move from simply seeking to establish "what *is* the case," with the intent to illuminate, understand, report on, or furnish insight into given states of affairs, to asking, "what *ought* to be" and "what kind of world *could* we create?" Narrative inquiry can play a role here given that narratives fertilize visionary potentials through their power to *do* things, including creating possible futures worlds. It could place *ought* and *could* at the forefront of our endeavors by asking what narratives of sport and exercise *ought* and *could* do, as part the process of actively creating "better" future worlds with people. Such a vision, coupled with the excellent narrative work being produced, leads me to believe that there is much to be optimistic about narrative analyses in sport and exercise research.

References

Bamberg, M. (2012). Narrative analysis. In H. Cooper (Ed.), *APA handbook of research methods in psychology: Vol 2. Quantitative, qualitative, neuropsychological, and biological* (pp. 85–102). Washington: American Psychological Association Press.

Barone, T. & Eisner, E. W. (2012). *Arts based research*. London: Sage.

Bochner, A. (2014). *Coming to narrative*. Walnut Creek, CA: Lefty Coast Press.

Bochner, A. & Riggs, N. (2014). Practicing narrative inquiry. In P. Levy (Ed.), *Oxford handbook of qualitative research* (pp. 195–222). Oxford: Oxford University Press.

Brinkmann, S. (2015). Perils and potentials in qualitative psychology. *Integrative Psychological and Behavioral Science, 49*, 162–173.

Busanich, R., McGannon, K., & Schinke, R. (2014). Comparing elite male and female distance runners' experiences of disordered eating through narrative analysis. *Psychology of Sport and Exercise, 15*, 705–712.

Caddick, N., Phoenix, C., & Smith, B. (2015). Collective stories and well-being: Using a dialogical narrative approach to understand peer relationships among combat veterans experiencing post-traumatic stress disorder. *Journal of Health Psychology, 20*, 286–299.

Carless, D. (2014). Narrative transformation among military personnel on an adventurous training and sport course. *Qualitative Health Research, 24*, 1440–1450.

Carless, D. & Douglas, K. (2009). We haven't got a seat on the bus for you or All the seats are mine: Narratives and career transitions in professional golf. *Qualitative Research in Sport and Exercise, 1*, 51–66.

Carless, D., Sparkes, A. C., Douglas, K., & Cooke, C. (2014). Disability, inclusive adventurous training and adapted sport: Two soldiers' stories of involvement. *Psychology of Sport and Exercise, 15*, 124–131.

Chamberlain, K. (2011). Commentary: Troubling methodology. *Health Psychology Review, 5*, 48–54.

Day, M. & Wadey, R. (2016). Narratives of trauma, recovery, and growth: The complex role of sport following permanent acquired disability. *Psychology of Sport and Exercise, 22*, 131–138.

Demuth, C. (2015). "Slow food" post-qualitative research in psychology: Old craft skills in new disguise? *Integrative Psychological and Behavioral Science, 49*, 207–215.

Dowling, F., Garrett, R., lisahunter, L., & Wrench, A. (2013). Narrative inquiry in physical education research: The story so far and its future promise. *Sport, Education, and Society, 20*, 924–940.

Ellingson, L. (2009). *Engaging crystallization in qualitative research.* London: Sage.

Ellis, C. (2004). *The ethnographic I.* Walnut Creek, CA: Altamira Press.

Ellis, C. & Bochner, A. (2006). Analyzing analytic autoethnography: An autopsy. *Journal of Contemporary Ethnography, 35*, 429–449.

Fasting, K. & Sand, T. S. (2015). Narratives of sexual harassment experiences in sport. *Qualitative Research in Sport, Exercise and Health, 5*, 573–588.

Feldman, M., Skoldberg, K., Brown, R., & Horner, D. (2004). Making sense of stories: A rhetorical approach to narrative analysis. *Journal of Public Administration Research and Theory, 14*, 147–170.

Frank, A. W. (1995). *The wounded storyteller.* Chicago, IL: The University of Chicago Press.

Frank, A. W. (2010). *Letting stories breathe.* Chicago, IL: The University of Chicago Press.

Gearity, B. T. (2014). Autoethnography. In L. Nelson, R. Groom, & P. Potrac (Eds.), *Research methods in sport coaching* (pp. 205–216). London: Routledge.

Gee, J. P. (1991). A linguistic approach to narrative. *Journal of Narrative and Life History/Narrative Inquiry, 1*, 15–39.

Gergen, K. J. (2014). From mirroring to world-making: Research as future forming. *Journal for the Theory of Social Behavior.* Article first published online: Nov 14, 2014, doi:10.1111/jtsb.12075.

Griffin, M. (2010). Setting the scene: Hailing women into a running identity. *Qualitative Research in Sport and Exercise, 2*, 153–174.

Griffin, M. & Phoenix, C. (2014). Learning to run from narrative foreclosure: One woman's story of ageing and physical activity. *Journal of Aging and Physical Activity, 22*, 393–404.

Griffin, M. & Phoenix, C. (2016). Becoming a runner: Big, middle and small stories about physical activity participation in later life. *Sport, Education and Society, 21*(1), 11–27.

Gubrium, J. & Holstein, J. (2009). *Analyzing narrative reality.* London: Sage.

Gubrium, J. & Holstein, J. (2014). Analytic inspiration in ethnographic fieldwork. In U. Flick (Ed.), *The Sage handbook of qualitative data analysis* (pp. 35–48). London: Sage.

Holstein, J. & Gubrium, J. (2012). Introduction. In J. Holstein and J. Gubrium (Eds.), *Varieties of narrative analysis* (pp. 1–11). London: Sage.

Kim, J-H. (2016). *Understanding narrative inquiry: The crafting and analysis of stories as research.* London: Sage.

Knowles, A. M., Niven, A.G., & Fawkner, S.G. (2014). Once upon a time I used to be active: Adopting a narrative approach to understanding physical activity behavior in adolescent girls. *Qualitative Research in Sport, Exercise and Health, 6*, 62–76.

Lieblich, A., Tuval-Mashiach, R., & Zilber, T. (1998). *Narrative research: Reading, analysis and interpretation.* London: Sage.

lisahunter & Emerald, E. (2016). Sensory narratives: Capturing embodiment in narratives of movement, sport, leisure and health. *Sport, Education and Society, 21*(1), 28–46,

Markula, P. & Denison, J. (2005). Sport and the personal narrative. In D. Andrews, D. Mason, & M. Silk (Eds.), *Qualitative methods in sport studies* (pp. 165–184). Oxford: Berg.

McAdams, D. (2013). *The redemptive self* (2nd ed.). Oxford: Oxford University Press.

McGannon, K.R. & Smith, B. (2015). Centralizing culture in cultural sport psychology research: The potential of narrative inquiry and discursive psychology. *Psychology of Sport and Exercise, 17*, 79–87.

McMahon, J. & Penney, D. (2011). Narrative ethnography and autoethnography: Empowering athletes and their bodies in and through research. *Qualitative Research in Sport, Exercise and Health, 3*, 130–151.

Papathomas, A., Lavellee, D., & Smith, B. (2015). Family experiences of living with an eating disorder: A narrative analysis. *Journal of Health & Psychology, 20*, 313–325.

Papathomas, A., Williams, T.L., & Smith, B. (2015). Understanding physical activity, health and rehabilitation in spinal cord injured population. Shifting the landscape through methodological innovation. *International Journal of Qualitative Studies on Health and Well-being, 10*, 27295.

Phoenix, C. & Orr, N. (2014). Pleasure: A forgotten dimension of ageing and physical activity. *Social Science and Medicine, 115*, 94–102.

Richardson, L. (2000). Writing: A method of inquiry. In N. Denzin & Y. Lincoln (Eds.), *Handbook of qualitative research* (2nd ed., pp. 923–948). London: Sage.

Riessman, K. (2008). *Narrative methods for the human sciences.* London: Sage.

Ruppel, P.S. & Mey, G. (2015). Grounded Theory Methodology: Narrativity revisited. *Integrative Psychological and Behavioral Science, 49*, 174–186.

Schiff, B. (2013). Fractured narratives: Psychology's fragmented narrative psychology. In M. Hyvärinen, M., Hatavara, & L. C. Hydén, L.C. (Eds.), *The travelling concept of narrative* (pp. 245–264). Amsterdam: John Benjamins.

Smith, B. (2013a). Sporting spinal cord injuries, social relations, and rehabilitation narratives: An ethnographic creative non-fiction of becoming disabled through sport. *Sociology of Sport Journal, 30*, 132–152.

Smith, B. (2013b). Disability, sport, and men's narratives of health: A qualitative study. *Health Psychology, 32*, 110–119.

Smith, B. (2016). Narrative analysis. In E. Lyons & A. Coyle (Eds.), *Analyzing qualitative data in psychology* (2nd ed., pp. 202–221). London: Sage.

Smith, B. (forthcoming). Narrative inquiry and autoethnography. In M. Silk, D. Andrews, & H. Thorpe (Eds.), *Routledge handbook of physical cultural studies*. London: Routledge.

Smith, B. & Sparkes, A. C. (2004). Men, sport, and spinal cord injury: An analysis of metaphors and narrative types. *Disability and Society, 19*, 509–612.

Smith, B. & Sparkes, A. C. (2009a). Narrative inquiry in sport and exercise psychology: What is it, and why might we do it? *Psychology of Sport and Exercise, 10*, 1–11.

Smith, B. & Sparkes, A. C. (2009b). Narrative analysis in sport and exercise psychology: Understanding lives in diverse ways. *Psychology of Sport and Exercise, 10*, 279–288.

Smith, B., McGannon, K.R., & Williams, T. (2015). Ethnographic creative non-fiction: Exploring the what's, why's and how's. In L. Purdy & G. Molner (Eds.), *Ethnographies in sport and exercise* (pp. 59–73). London: Routledge.

Smith, B., Papathomas, A., Martin Ginis, K. A., & Latimer-Cheung, A. E. (2013). Understanding physical activity in spinal cord injury rehabilitation: Translating and communicating research through stories. *Disability and Rehabilitation, 35*, 2044–2055.

Smith, B., Tomasone. J., Latimer-Cheung, A., & Martin Ginis, K. (2015). Narrative as a knowledge translation tool for facilitating impact: Translating physical activity knowledge to disabled people and health professionals. *Health Psychology, 34*, 303–313.

Sparkes, A.C. (2002). *Telling tales in sport and physical activity: A qualitative journey*. Champaign, IL: Human Kinetics Press.

Sparkes, A. C., Pérez-Samaniego, V., & Smith, B. (2012). Social comparison processes, narrative mapping, and their shaping of the cancer experience: A case study of an elite athlete. *Health: An Interdisciplinary Journal for the Social Study of Health, Illness & Medicine, 16*, 467–488.

Sparkes, A. C. & Smith, B. (2008). Narrative constructionist inquiry. In J. Holstein & J. Gubrium (Eds.), *Handbook of constructionist research* (pp. 295–314). London: Guilford.

Sparkes, A. C. & Smith, B. (2011). Inhabiting different bodies over time: Narrative and pedagogical challenges. *Sport, Education and Society, 16*, 357–370.

Sparkes, A. C. & Smith, B. (2012a). Embodied research methodologies and seeking senses in sport and physical culture: A fleshing out of problems and possibilities. In K. Young & M. Atkinson (Eds.), *Qualitative research on sport and physical culture* (pp. 169–192). Bingley, UK: Emerald Press.

Sparkes, A. C. & Smith, B. (2012b). Narrative analysis as an embodied engagement with the lives of others. In J. Holstein & J. Gubrium (Eds.), *Varieties of narrative analysis* (pp. 53–73). London: Sage.

Sparkes, A. C. & Smith, B. (2014). *Qualitative research methods in sport, exercise and health. From process to product*. London: Routledge.

Zehntner, C. & McMahon, J. A. (2014). Mentoring in coaching: The means of correct training? An autoethnographic exploration of one Australian swimming coach's experiences. *Qualitative research in Sport, Exercise and Health, 18*, 1–21.

21

SYNTHESIZING QUALITATIVE RESEARCH

Meta-synthesis in sport and exercise

Toni L. Williams and Rachel L. Shaw

A meta-synthesis of qualitative evidence is comparable to a meta-analysis of randomized controlled trials; both methods involve the systematic review of literature and secondary analysis of original data. The meta-synthesis of qualitative research has grown in popularity within health and social sciences over the past 25 years. Despite the growth of primary qualitative research within sport and exercise sciences, the use of meta-synthesis methods is few and far between. The field of sport and exercise sciences has yet to embrace the possibilities to conceptually advance knowledge and influence policy and practice through the systematic review and synthesis of qualitative research evidence. In this chapter, first we explore *what* a meta-synthesis is and *why* a meta-synthesis might be conducted. We then provide some examples of meta-syntheses within sport and exercise sciences to illustrate their potential use in this field. Next, to understand *how* to conduct a meta-synthesis, we outline one type of meta-synthesis – *thematic synthesis* – and provide working examples and critical reflections of the decisions made at each stage in the process.

What is a meta-synthesis of qualitative research and why conduct one?

A meta-synthesis involves the systematic review and synthesis of qualitative research to reveal new knowledge concerning a specific research topic. As Hammell explains, a meta-synthesis is "a rigorous and explicit research method that aims to locate, critically appraise and synthesize the findings of multiple studies pertaining to a specific research question" (2007, p. 125). The aim of a meta-synthesis is to translate the findings from qualitative research into themes, concepts, categories, or theories that *go beyond* the findings in primary studies to reach new or enhanced understandings regarding the phenomenon under review (Paterson, 2012; Ludvigsen *et al.*, 2016). This notion of going beyond the primary research is a defining characteristic of a meta-synthesis and what distinguishes it from a narrative review. A *narrative review* critically evaluates the specific topic under investigation. In contrast, a meta-synthesis is a secondary analysis of primary qualitative research that can reveal more powerful explanations than a narrative review can provide (Paterson, 2012).

Systematically reviewing and synthesizing qualitative research evolved through the need to accommodate other types of research within evidence-based policy and practice (Finfgeld-Connett, 2014; Shaw *et al.*, 2014). The systematic review and meta-analysis of quantitative research contributed multiple benefits to health care through the assessment of empirical evidence and the generation of theory (Paterson, 2012). However, since the eruption of primary qualitative research in the 1980s and 1990s, health-care practitioners and policymakers recognized the contribution that reviewing qualitative research could have to their field. For example, the systematic review and meta-synthesis of qualitative research can provide evidence to support policy and practice, complement or contrast findings of quantitative systematic reviews and meta-analyses, identify gaps and areas of ambiguity in the research, thus identifying directions for future research and informing primary research questions (Walsh & Downe, 2005; Paterson, 2012; Finfgeld-Connett, 2014; Shaw *et al.*, 2014).

With the growing utilization of meta-synthesis within health and social sciences, academics and practitioners have adapted the methods used to synthesize qualitative research. These adaptations were based upon many factors, including the purpose of the review and the underlying epistemological assumptions of the review team. As a result, there are now multiple types of meta-syntheses and many terms used to describe the synthesis of qualitative research. This complex web of terminology and meta-syntheses can "mask some of the basic similarities in approach that the different methods share, and also lead to some confusion regarding which method is most appropriate in a given situation" (Barnett-Page & Thomas, 2009, p. 1). To address this confusion, the different types of meta-syntheses can be distinguished into two broad camps: integrative syntheses and interpretative syntheses (Barnett-Page & Thomas, 2009; Shaw, 2011; Gough *et al.*, 2012).

To some degree, the differences between integrative and interpretation syntheses can be explained by their underpinning philosophical assumptions (ontology and epistemology) and the research question which dictates the approach and output of the synthesis (see also Chapters 1 and 10). For example, interpretative approaches are more exploratory when the authors are not seeking to find one final answer to their research question. Rather, the authors are seeking concepts through new ways of understanding to provide enlightenment and generate new theory (Dixon-Woods *et al.*, 2005). These meta-syntheses offer a more complex and contextual synthesis output. On the other hand, the focus of integrative approaches is to seek evidence whereby the output of the synthesis aims to inform policymakers of practical recommendations for specific interventions (Gough *et al.*, 2012). However, rather than thinking of two distinct types of meta-synthesis, it is useful to view these approaches on a continuum, with some being largely integrative and others being largely interpretative. Some of the defining characteristics and examples of interpretative and integrative meta-syntheses are illustrated in Table 21.1 (for further reading on types of review please see: Weed, 2006; Barnett-Page & Thomas, 2009; Grant & Booth, 2009; Gough *et al.*, 2012; Paterson, 2012).

In practice, many meta-syntheses include elements of both integration and interpretation. For instance, integrative reviews include interpretation "before inspection of the studies to develop criteria for including studies, and after synthesis of the findings to develop implications for policy, practice, and further research" (Gough *et al.*, 2012, p. 5). However, the distinction between interpretative and integrative is useful to consider when deciding upon which meta-synthesis method is most suited to the review. First and foremost, the choice of meta-synthesis should depend upon the research question and purpose of the review. As Shaw explains, if the research question:

> involves making a judgement about and developing a theoretical understanding of the current knowledge base, then an interpretative synthesis will be necessary. By comparison, if the objective is to identify and describe current evidence, then an integrative synthesis will be most appropriate.
>
> *(Shaw, 2011, p. 15)*

Table 21.1 Interpretative and integrative approaches to synthesizing qualitative research

Approach	Interpretative	<---------------------------------->	Integrative
Philosophy	Relativist/Idealist		Realist
Purpose	Explore		Answer
Synthetic product	Complex – enlightenment		Instrumental – clear for policymakers and practitioners
Relation to theory	Generate	Explore	Test
Iteration	More iterative approach to searching and review		Less iteration
Quality assessment	Less clear, less a priori; quality of content rather than method		Clear and a priori
Problematizing the literature	Yes		No
Heterogeneity	Lots		Little
Example meta-syntheses	Meta–narrative Meta–study Meta–ethnography Meta–interpretation	Thematic synthesis Textual narrative synthesis Framework synthesis	Ecological triangulation

Source: Barnett-Page and Thomas (2009), Shaw (2011), Gough *et al.* (2012).

Meta-syntheses in sport and exercise science

As highlighted, the use of meta–synthesis methods within sports and exercise science is sparse. There are far more examples of reviews that combine quantitative and qualitative data than syntheses of qualitative data alone, which is unusual in other areas of health and social sciences, where meta–syntheses of purely qualitative data are more popular. For instance, Caddick and Smith (2014) conducted a systematic review and narrative synthesis to explore the potential impact of sport and physical activity (PA) upon the well-being of combat veterans in the aftermath of physical or psychological combat trauma. This narrative synthesis constituted an "interpretive and integrative process of constructing a textual summary to explain the findings of multiple studies" (Caddick & Smith, 2014, p. 10). The authors drew upon both quantitative and qualitative data to evaluate the role of sport and PA in supporting the well-being of combat veterans. Additionally, the review extended previous knowledge on PA and health and well-being by highlighting the specific consequences (both positive and negative) of veterans engaging in these activities. Notwithstanding the value of a systematic review and narrative synthesis of evidence, a meta–synthesis can offer more than a systematic search and textual summary of multiple studies. As indicated above, the defining characteristic of a meta–synthesis is the ability to *go beyond* the findings of primary studies, and construct new concepts and enhanced understandings of the phenomenon under review.

Whilst rare, there is evidence of the use of meta–syntheses in some sport and exercise related disciplines. For example, there are meta–syntheses that overlap between the field of sport and exercise and the field of health and social sciences. In this instance qualitative research concerning sport and exercise has been synthesized to inform future PA interventions for a given population. For instance, Soundy *et al.* (2014) conducted a systematic review and *meta-ethnography* of the experiences and challenges of PA participation in people with schizophrenia and the healthcare professionals (HCPs) working with these individuals. Noblit and Hare (1988) developed meta–ethnography as the first method to synthesize qualitative research. Meta–ethnography was originally designed for the synthesis of ethnographic research which was comparable in topic and method. However, meta-ethnography evolved to successfully synthesize nonethnographic studies and became a model for the development of the range of meta-synthesis methods used currently to synthesize qualitative research.

Within meta-ethnography there are three different methods of synthesis which reflect the ways in which studies relate to each other: *reciprocal translational synthesis* involves directly comparing similar studies and translating concepts from one study to another; *refutational synthesis* seeks to explore and explain contradictions within studies when studies refute each other; and *lines-of-argument synthesis* involves taking the studies together to build a "line of argument" and develop a greater picture and overarching interpretation of the whole phenomenon under investigation (e.g., culture or organization) (Noblit & Hare, 1988; Barnett-Page & Thomas, 2009). There were several important implications generated by the meta-ethnography for Soundy *et al.* (2014). These included identifying less traditional benefits of PA, the important consideration of how patients with schizophrenia are introduced to PA environments, and the need for HCPs to consider the value of autonomy in PA preferences.

Furthermore, in sport psychology Tamminen and Holt (2010) conducted a *meta-study* of qualitative research examining stressor appraisals and coping among adolescents in sport. The meta-study method developed by Paterson *et al.* (2001) involves three components of analysis that are undertaken before synthesis. These are *meta-data analysis* (analysis of findings), *meta-method* (analysis of methods), and *meta-theory* (analysis of theory). This approach takes into account the social, historical, and ideological context of the primary studies to explain differences in research findings. The meta-study was designed by Tamminen and Holt to create a "synthesis of the qualitative literature to establish 'what is known', and create a conceptual model depicting the state of knowledge about adolescent coping in sport" (2010, p. 1563). This meta-study provided useful direction for future studies by identifying the need to examine social networks and the ways in which adolescent athletes acquired coping skills. Furthermore, the authors noted a lack of variety in the range of qualitative methods and analysis used within sport psychology, and called for a greater diversity of qualitative research methodologies and methods with this discipline.

How to conduct and evaluate a meta-synthesis of qualitative research

As highlighted, the type of meta-synthesis undertaken should be driven by the research question and purpose of the review. We have chosen to draw upon *thematic synthesis* as opposed to any other type of synthesis due to the flexibility of this method to address a range of different research questions (Gough *et al.*, 2012). Thomas and Harden (2008) coined the term "thematic synthesis" for an approach to synthesizing qualitative research that combines and adapts aspects of both meta-ethnography and grounded theory. They developed the method "out of a need to conduct reviews that addressed questions relating to intervention need, appropriateness and acceptability – as well as those relating to effectiveness – without compromising on key principles developed in systematic reviews" (2008, p. 3). The thematic synthesis offers a structured integrative and interpretative method to organize the literature and *go beyond* the original studies to identify analytical themes. The approach to thematic synthesis can be data-driven or theory-driven, and this diversity of approaches to synthesis means it could be utilized across the different disciplines within sport and exercise sciences.

In terms of doing a meta-synthesis, there are five stages. These stages will be illustrated with worked examples and critical reflections throughout (Figure 21.1). The first three stages relate to the purpose of the review, a systematic search and screen of papers, and the appraisal of qualitative research. The fourth and fifth stages involve the synthesis of the selected studies and in this example draw upon the method of *thematic synthesis*.

Stage 1: developing a research question

The first stage of a meta-synthesis is to develop a focused research question (Shaw, 2011). The research question will then guide the search strategy used to locate the relevant literature in the second stage. For example, in a meta-synthesis of barriers, benefits, and facilitators of leisure time physical activity (LTPA) for people with spinal-cord injury (SCI) (Williams *et al.*, 2014), the rationale to conduct the review was justified through an identified need to gain a deeper understanding of the factors that impacted LTPA participation in people with SCI. This information could then be utilized by HCPs, governing bodies, rehabilitation centers, and community organizations to further support and promote people with SCI to be physically active for life. As a result, the purpose of the review was to: (a) systematically search and appraise the qualitative research on LTPA for people with SCI; (b) synthesize knowledge from existing qualitative research regarding the barriers, benefits, and facilitators to being physically active; and c) based on the results, propose improvements to LTPA promotion in SCI for HCPs. The following review question was established: "What does the published qualitative literature contribute to our empirical knowledge of the barriers, benefits and facilitators of LTPA after SCI?" (Williams *et al.*, 2014, p. 405).

Stage 2: identifying relevant papers

The next stage is to identify published papers and determine their relevance to the research question. Some argue that a systematic search to locate all of the relevant literature on a topic is not necessary in a meta-synthesis. For example, in more conceptual and interpretative syntheses, it is reasoned that the results "will not change if ten rather than five studies contain the same concept, but will depend on the range of concepts found in the studies, their context, and whether they are in agreement or not" (Thomas & Harden, 2008, p. 3). The aim of the search would therefore be for *conceptual saturation,* whereby additional studies which may act as negative cases are deliberately sought to increase maximum variability (for further information on seeking the disconfirming case see Booth *et al.*, 2014).

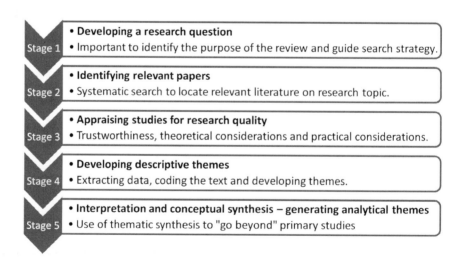

Figure 21.1 Stages of a meta-synthesis.

However, if the purpose of a meta-synthesis is to systematically review current evidence to inform policy and practice, then a systematic search is necessary. In practice most meta-synthesis methods do use a comprehensive systematic search to locate relevant papers and gray literature not located in electronic databases (Walsh & Downe, 2005; Thomas & Harden, 2008; Shaw, 2011). This is achieved through hand-searching relevant journals and papers (and in some instances policy documents, professional guidelines etc.) identified through reference lists, bibliographies, citation searching, and contact with experts. Moreover, a systematic search strategy further distinguishes meta-syntheses from narrative reviews that lack clear and accountable methods (Gough *et al.*, 2012).

To develop a search strategy it is useful to create a mind map of all the relevant terms, keywords, and synonyms related to the review question. A mind map is a visual representation of key concepts with links to connecting meanings and words. These words will form the basis of the search strategy and may be edited and refined throughout the search process to increase the effectiveness of identifying relevant papers (Shaw, 2011). To help identify these words, Shaw (2010) designed the CHIP tool to break a question down into its key components (Context of the study; How it was conducted; the Issues investigated; and the Population involved). Table 21.2 illustrates how the CHIP tool could have been used in the example by Williams *et al.* (2014) to locate papers related to qualitative research, LTPA and SCI.

To conduct a thorough and systematic literature search these terms were entered into bibliographical databases with interdisciplinary coverage (such as Medline and Web of Knowledge), as well as more specific disciplined focused databases (including PsychINFO and SPORTSDiscus). Each database has developed its own subject headings and thesaurus terms for indexing journal articles by topic and methodology. To increase effectiveness it is recommended to adjust the search strategy and employ the subject headings and thesaurus terms used by each database. For a comprehensive account of how to search databases using subject heading and thesaurus terms see Shaw (2011). There are, however, limitations when searching qualitative methodology subject headings in databases. It has been shown that searching the broad terms "findings," "interview★," and "qualitative" are just as effective in locating qualitative studies in comparison to using detailed terms for qualitative research, as illustrated in Table 21.2 (Shaw *et al.*, 2004). Including the specific key terms used to retrieve primary qualitative research studies is an important step in ensuring the transparency of the procedures used (Hannes & Macaitis, 2012).

Table 21.2 CHIP tool to inform search strategy

Context	Barriers, benefits and facilitators
How	*Qualitative methods:* "qualitative research" OR "focus group*" OR interview* OR ethnograph* OR "participant observation*" OR interpret* OR "life world*" OR "lived experience*" OR "grounded theory" OR "content analysis" OR "discourse analysis" OR "thematic analysis" OR "constant comparative" OR "narrative analysis" OR "conversation analysis" OR hermeneutic* OR phenomenology **AND**
Issues	*LTPA:* "leisure time physical activity" OR "physical activit*" OR "physically active" OR exercise OR sport* OR fitness OR "active living" OR training OR leisure **AND**
Population	*SCI:* "spinal cord injur*" OR paraplegi* OR tetraplegi* OR quadraplegi*

Note: The use of * broadens the utility of the search term. For example "spinal cord injur* would retrieve articles including spinal cord injury, spinal cord injuries and spinal cord injured.

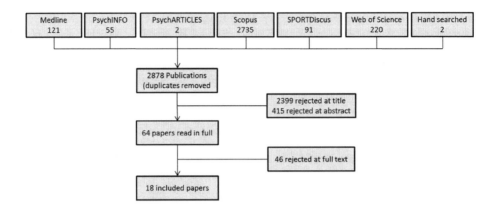

Figure 21.2   Systematic literature search and exclusion of papers.
Source: Williams *et al.* (2014).

The next process is to screen the papers retrieved for relevance to the review question, which can be an onerous task (Shaw, 2011). Using electronic databases means that searches can be saved, downloaded to a reference manager software package, and screened electronically which speeds up the process. The papers should first be screened based on the relevance of the title to the research question. Once those irrelevant papers are removed the abstracts of the remaining papers should be accepted or rejected based on: (1) relevance to the review question; (2) qualitative methodology; and (3) inclusion/exclusion criteria. Where the abstract suggests potential relevance to the review question, or does not provide enough information to apply the inclusion/exclusion criteria, the full text of the article should be read. At this stage it is important to be overinclusive when screening papers for relevance (Shaw, 2011). The final papers will need to be obtained and read in full to justify their inclusion or exclusion in the meta-synthesis.

To ensure transparency of this process it is important to keep a record of the decision-making process in the form of a PRISMA (Preferred Reporting Items for Systematic Reviews and Meta-Analyses) flowchart (Moher *et al.*, 2009). A PRISMA flowchart of the screening process for our example is illustrated above in Figure 21.2. It is also necessary to keep a detailed report on the decisions to exclude individual papers read in full. This information may be requested for supplementary material for some journals.

Box 21.1   Critical reflections on identifying relevant papers

A limitation here of all systematic reviews and meta-syntheses is that even with an exhaustive search strategy it is impossible to ensure that every relevant study that is related to the review question can be found. Using a theoretical sampling technique obviously negates the need to locate all relevant papers. However, if the researchers are not overly familiar with the literature it can be a daunting process to be confident in identifying the initial studies. Using a systematic search strategy on the other hand is time-consuming, but a more established and accepted method to locate literature for a meta-synthesis and a requirement for institutions such as Cochrane and the Joanna Briggs Institute. It is also essential to keep an "audit trail" and document the reason why each study was excluded to "evidence" the decision-making process at this stage. This is particularly useful if a team of researchers is responsible for identifying relevant papers.

Another point for consideration is whether papers are excluded based on the relevance of their research question to the review question and purpose of the synthesis. For example, the review question of the meta-synthesis by Williams *et al.* (2014) focused on factors that impacted LTPA participation. However (as mentioned above), it became apparent through the inclusion/exclusion process that LTPA was included in some studies even when sport and exercise were not the focus of their research question. These references were brief in places, but they were included in the meta-synthesis because they added to the knowledge on the barriers, benefits, and facilitators to LTPA.

Stage 3: appraising studies for research quality

The third stage of a meta-synthesis involves appraising the research quality of the final studies selected for synthesis. Appraising the quality of these studies has been proposed as a vital stage in the process to avoid drawing unreliable or misleading conclusions from studies with perceived methodological deficiencies (Hammell, 2007; Thomas & Harden, 2008; Gough *et al.*, 2012; Hannes & Macaitis, 2012). However, studies perceived to be of a poor quality are not necessarily excluded from the meta-synthesis. Rather, their contribution to the synthesis output can be checked in Stage 5 to ensure that the final concepts are not guided by research judged to be poorly conducted (Thomas & Harden, 2008).

Conversely, judging the quality of qualitative research is not a straightforward task. There is no one agreed method by which to make this assessment for quality and rigor which is reflective of the larger issue around judging qualitative research in general (see Chapter 25). Many meta-syntheses use a predetermined list of criteria to appraise quality. These predetermined lists can be potentially problematic if the criteria do not take into account the different philosophical positions and epistemological assumptions underlying different qualitative research methodologies (Sparkes & Smith, 2009). Further criticism has been offered under the assumption that quality appraisal results in the exclusion of studies, for example:

> Firstly, studies including important and robust findings may often utilize unorthodox yet perfectly valid methods. Such studies would be excluded from many systematic reviews. Secondly, some studies, whilst perhaps being methodologically flawed in part, or with overall findings that do not appear important or relevant, may still be able to offer important insights into phenomena, or may contain important findings in part, whilst not doing so as a whole.
>
> *(Weed, 2006, p. 130)*

To overcome issues of philosophical differences, some have argued that a range of alternative criteria should be used to enable judgments to be made based upon criteria that are appropriate to the specific form of inquiry (Sparkes & Smith, 2009). These criteria are not universal or static in nature, but are lists of characterizing traits that can change over time and in different contexts (see also Chapter 25). This can, however, present a challenge when some authors do not make explicit reference to their theoretical framework and form of inquiry. To compensate for differences in methodology, Garside (2014) recommends that papers in qualitative meta-syntheses should be appraised based on criteria of *trustworthiness* (epistemological aspects), *theoretical considerations,* and *practical considerations* (technical aspects). Garside suggests that rather than using one checklist, this method allows for "careful consideration of the study within its own terms" (2014, p. 11). As part of an ongoing list of criteria, examples of considerations include:

1. *Trustworthiness* – Are the design and execution appropriate to the research question? Are alternative interpretations, theories, etc. explored? How well supported by the data are any conclusions?
2. *Theoretical considerations* – Does the report connect to a wider body of knowledge or existing theoretical framework? If so, is this appropriate? Does the paper develop explanatory concepts for the findings?
3. *Practical considerations* – Does the study usefully contribute to the policy question? Does this study provide evidence relevant to the policy setting? Does this study usefully contribute to the review?

In the example by Williams *et al.* (2014), the authors considered the quality of each paper by addressing the trustworthiness, theoretical, and practical considerations as outlined by Garside (2014). Firstly, trustworthiness was assessed using the above criteria and in all cases each paper had a design appropriate to the research question and used data to supported their concluding statements. Secondly, theoretical considerations were difficult to judge in instances where the papers were exceptionally short in length. In this instance it was decided that the studies should not be rejected based on the word limits imposed by the journal. Thirdly, for practical considerations, it was found that ultimately all papers usefully contributed to the review. Using these guidelines no papers were rejected in the appraisal process.

Box 21.2   Critical reflections on judging quality

Judging the quality of the original papers can be tricky when some of the studies do not include the details that are required to make these judgements. For example, in the Williams *et al.* (2014) study, difficulties arose when judging the quality of the research papers for various reasons. Some papers were very short in length which meant that they didn't include all of the information needed to answer Garside's (2014) questions regarding trustworthiness, theoretical, and practical considerations. Furthermore, some studies did not explicitly identify their conceptual/theoretical framework, form of inquiry, or name their method of analysis. This is common when, often due to restrictions in word lengths in journals, qualitative papers focus on the research findings at the expense of detailing their methodology. Ultimately there is a lack of consensus in the qualitative research community over the methodological detail required for a research article.

By ignoring the methodological detail of the research, the researchers are not providing the transparency or reflexivity that is required to reflect on such issues as the strengths and weaknesses of their chosen qualitative methodology (see Sparkes & Smith, 2014). It would be of benefit for future meta-syntheses – and qualitative research in general – if qualitative researchers included all details of their methodology and the conduct of their work. This is because "without a picture of what was done, it is difficult to make any judgement about whether this is likely to produce meaningful, trustworthy findings" (Garside, 2014, p. 76). If any of the original papers are considered to be of extremely poor quality, then the researchers have to decide whether or not to exclude the study from the synthesis. As detailed above, rather than exclude studies perceived to be of poor quality, it is common practice to check their contribution against the final results of the synthesis.

Stage 4: developing descriptive themes

The next two stages relate specifically to a *thematic synthesis* and will therefore differ from other forms of meta-synthesis. This stage of the synthesis involves extracting data, coding the text and developing themes. One issue in this process is deciding *what counts as data?* Deciding what data to extract from a qualitative study is difficult and some meta-syntheses do differ in what they count as "raw data" and therefore what they are extracting for synthesis (Thomas & Harden, 2008). For example, in the method of meta-ethnography and meta-interpretation it is only the interpretations of data that are extracted for synthesis (Weed, 2006). The rationale for this is that interpretations are always included in the published articles whereas the "raw data" from interviews and observations etc. is not published in full. Furthermore, the interpretations from the original study convey *meaning in context* that participant quotations and observational notes may not illustrate (Weed, 2006). However, extracting raw data in the form of quotations from participants can be easier compared to identifying key concepts of findings, especially if some studies have undertaken a simple analysis limited to describing and summarizing data (Thomas & Harden, 2008). To resolve this issue Thomas and Harden (2008) propose that all text labeled "results" or "findings," including that within the abstract or discussion, should be extracted for coding in a thematic synthesis.

The next step of this phase is to code the text line by line according to both its meaning and content. Coding the data allows for *translation* which, in this context, refers to the "process of taking concepts from one study and recognizing the same concepts in another study, though they may not be expressed using identical words" (Thomas & Harden, 2008, p. 3). Once the data have been coded, the next step is to look for similarities and differences in the codes to group them together into descriptive themes. This phase of generating codes and defining themes is representative of the primary thematic analysis method described by Braun and Clarke (2006). Extracting both participant quotations and themes identified by the researcher has another benefit; it allows for factors highlighted by participants, which were not conceptualized in the original studies, to be included in the synthesis. This point is important because it allows for the construction of new concepts that may not have been identified in one original study to be identified by developing descriptive themes across studies (Hammell, 2007). In the example by Williams *et al.* (2014) the data were extracted only if they were related to the review question. This was because some of the final studies included in the synthesis did not directly address the factors (barriers, benefits, facilitators) that impacted participation in LTPA. For example, some studies were concerned with other aspects of living with SCI, whereby PA was just one component under investigation. Once the data relating to LTPA had been extracted, they were initially grouped into barriers, benefits, and facilitators. The data within each of these groups were coded and descriptive themes within each group were created as described above.

Box 21.3   Critical reflections on extracting data and developing themes

The reason the data were coded and themed within groups at this stage, rather than coding the whole data set as one, like in other thematic syntheses (e.g., Thomas & Harden, 2008), was to make sure the differentiation between a benefit and a facilitator was preserved. The benefits included the positive responses and any perceived advantages from participation in

(continued)

(continued)

LTPA. Facilitators were recorded as factors that allowed people to participate in LTPA, or the motivational reasons as to why they started and continued participation in LTPA. The difference between a benefit and facilitator was important because although perceived health benefits could facilitate continued exercise, they wanted to identify what factors also facilitated initial engagement in LTPA.

There were, however, limitations that arose when extracting data due to the presentation of results and findings in the original papers. In cases where there were other participants included in the study (caregivers, therapists etc.) only quotations or themes that were from individuals with SCI were included. But this distinction amongst participant quotes was not always that obvious. Studies that included other disabilities outside of SCI had to be excluded because the results did not always identify the participants' quotations with their disability. In addition, some original data points were not included in the data-extraction process because the authors did not explicitly relate participant quotes to LTPA. Therefore, there could be other benefits, barriers, and facilitators to LTPA that were not able to be identified. These limitations can only be addressed if researchers are clearer when presenting their research findings.

Stage 5: interpretation and conceptual synthesis – generating analytical themes

The final stage of the thematic synthesis is to generate analytical themes through interpretation and conceptual synthesis. Up until this point in the thematic synthesis the descriptive themes are very close to the findings of the original studies. A key feature of thematic synthesis is its clear differentiation between generating "data-driven" descriptive themes in stage 4 (similar to a thematic analysis) and generating "theory-driven" analytical themes in stage 5. It is in this final stage that the defining characteristic of a meta-synthesis is achieved. This characteristic is the notion of *going beyond* the findings of the original studies to generate additional concepts and analytical themes (Thomas & Harden, 2008). This interpretative stage in the meta-synthesis focuses on answering the review question.

These analytical themes are conceptually equivalent to the development of third-order constructs in meta-ethnography. Both analytical themes and third-order interpretations have explicit mechanisms to offer a transparent process of going beyond the primary studies. However, the difference between them is again down to the purpose of the review. For example, in a meta-ethnography third-order interpretations bring together the implications of translating studies into one another. This method of meta-synthesis can therefore be used when the phenomenon under review is being explored with broad and emergent review questions (Thomas & Harden, 2008). On the other hand, analytical themes constructed through a thematic synthesis are the result of "interrogating a descriptive synthesis by placing it within an external theoretical framework (review question and sub-questions)" (Thomas & Harden, 2008, p. 9). Therefore analytical themes may be more appropriate when a specific review question is being addressed, such as when informing policy and practice.

The production of analytical themes (later referred to as "overarching concepts") in the example of Williams *et al.* (2014) was an iterative process whereby the descriptive themes from the barriers, benefits and facilitators of LTPA were examined again to construct analytical themes. The final stage is therefore also similar to primary analysis methods such as grounded theory (see Chapter 3), as the new analytical themes are developed using a *constant comparison method* (Barnett-Page & Thomas, 2009). This method involves the continuous comparison of codes and themes to check that the analytical themes are grounded in data from the original studies. This process was repeated until the analytical themes encompassed all of the descriptive themes across the barriers, benefits, and facilitators. The results revealed eight overarching concepts that acted as barriers, benefits, or facilitators of LTPA participation in people with SCI. These were: (1) well-being; (2) environmental influences; (3) physical body; (4) body–self relationship; (5) physically active identity; (6) knowledge on LTPA; (7) restitution narrative; and (8) perceived absences (Figure 21.3).

Some of these analytic themes such as well-being and environmental influences were identified in the original studies. However, analytic themes such as the restitution narrative and perceived absences were not identified in the original studies. Although the end of this stage results in overarching analytical themes, there is an opportunity within the discussion to compare and explain any similarities or differences between primary studies. This is achieved in a thematic synthesis by exploring the characteristics and context of the studies and the demographics of participants, as well as checking the relative contribution of each study to the final synthesis against their perceived quality (Thomas & Harden, 2008).

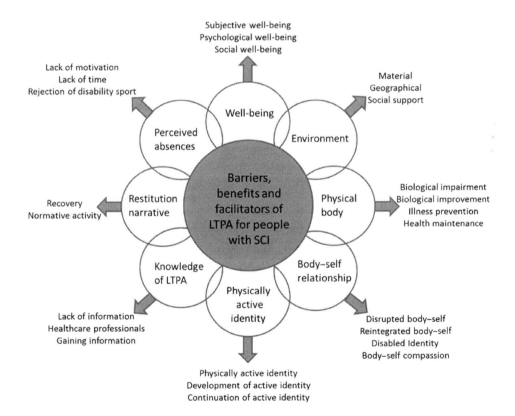

Figure 21.3 Final synthesis of barriers, benefits, and facilitators of LTPA for people with SCI.

Source: Adapted from Williams *et al.* (2014).

> **Box 21.4 Critical reflections on interpretation and conceptual synthesis: judging quality**
>
> As many authors have noted, this final stage of the synthesis is hard to describe. To complicate the matter further, as Hannes and Macaitis point out, there can be a "black box between what people claim to use as a synthesis approach and what is actually done in practice" (2012, p. 434). To be more transparent throughout, it is important to keep a detailed reflexive journal of the decision-making process in each of the five stages. A highly developed reflexive ability is required when conducting a meta-synthesis (Walsh & Downe, 2005) to enable the researchers to apply the same standards of quality to their work as they expect of the papers they are synthesizing. When judging the quality of the synthetic product a clear and transparent "audit trail" of decisions and interpretations ensures the trustworthiness of any meta-synthesis (Dixon-Woods *et al.*, 2005; Weed, 2006; Shaw, 2011). This is because including detailed information about the process and decisions made can enhance the credibility of the research process and support the accuracy of the findings.
>
> One aspect Williams *et al.* (2014) were asked to reflect on was the ease of which they were able to compare and synthesize data sets between different qualitative methodologies. This task was not easy. However, they aimed to preserve the meaning from the original text in the form of raw data as far as possible, to ensure the individual differentiation in each study was not lost in the synthesis. As the "raw data" for a thematic synthesis are publically available it opens up the potential for public scrutiny far greater than the majority of qualitative research (Weed, 2006). Furthermore, including a table of details about each original study (aim, sample, country, data collection, design/analysis) ensures further judgments about research quality can be made. It means that readers of the thematic synthesis can judge for themselves whether the emerging analytical themes are transferable across different study contexts (Thomas & Harden, 2008).

Conclusion

In this chapter, we have presented a meta-synthesis of qualitative research as one avenue to conceptually advance knowledge and inform policy and practice within sport and exercise sciences. We have drawn attention to the different types of meta-syntheses and touched upon some of the central debates within the meta-synthesis literature. Whilst we have provided an example of a thematic synthesis for use within sport and exercise science, it is important to note that the purpose of the review is the driving factor behind deciding which meta-synthesis method should be undertaken. As illustrated in our examples and critical reflections, the purpose of the review and type of meta-synthesis will then inform decisions regarding the searching, appraisal, extraction, and synthesis. We hope that this chapter stimulates further use and critical debate of the use of synthesizing qualitative research within the sport and exercise sciences.

References

Barnett-Page, E. & Thomas, J. (2009). Methods for the synthesis of qualitative research: A critical review. *BMC Medical Research Methodology, 9,* 59.

Booth, A., Carroll, C., Ilott, I., Low, L. L., & Cooper, K. (2014). Desperately seeking dissonance: Identifying the disconfirming case in qualitative evidence synthesis. *Qualitative Health Research, 23*(1), 126–141.

Braun, V. & Clarke, V. (2006). Using thematic analysis in psychology. *Qualitative Research in Psychology*, *3*(2), 77–10.

Caddick, N. & Smith, B. (2014). The impact of sport and physical activity on the well-being of combat veterans: A systematic review. *Psychology of Sport and Exercise*, *15*(1), 9–18.

Cassidy, T., Kidman, L., & Dudfield, O. (2015). Insights into the process of creating a coach development programme: The opportunities and challenges of ethnodrama. *Qualitative Research in Sport, Exercise and Health*, 7, 589–605. doi: 10.1080/2159676X.2015.1012545.

Dixon-Woods, M., Agarwal, S., Jones, D., Young, B., & Sutton, A. (2005). Synthesising qualitative and quantitative evidence: A review of possible methods. *Journal of Health Services Research & Policy*, *10*(1), 45–53.

Douglas, K. & Carless, D. (2015). *Life story research in sport: A narrative approach to understanding the experiences of elite and professional athletes*. London: Routledge.

Finfgeld-Connett, D. (2014). Metasynthesis findings: Potential versus reality. *Qualitative Health Research*, *24*(11), 1581–1591.

Garside, R. (2014). Should we appraise the quality of qualitative research reports for systematic reviews, and if so, how? *Innovation: The European Journal of Social Science Research*, *27*(1), 67–79.

Gough, D., Thomas, J., & Oliver, S. (2012). Clarifying differences between review designs and methods. *Systematic Reviews*, 1, 28.

Grant, M. J. & Booth, A. (2009). A typology of reviews: An analysis of 14 review types and associated methodologies. *Health Information and Libraries Journal*, *26*(2), 91–108.

Hammell, K. W. (2007). Quality of life after spinal cord injury: A meta-synthesis of qualitative findings. *Spinal Cord*, *45*(2), 124–139.

Hannes, K. & Macaitis, K. (2012). A move to more systematic and transparent approaches in qualitative evidence synthesis: Update on a review of published papers. *Qualitative Research*, *12*(4), 402–442.

Ludvigsen, M. S., Hall., E. O. C., Meyer, G., Fegran, L., Aagaard, H., & Uhrenfeldt, L. (2016). Using Sandelowski and Barroso's metasynthesis method in advancing qualitative evidence. *Qualitative Health Research*, *26*(3), 320–329.

McMahon, J. & McGannon K.R. (2016). Whose stories matter? Re-vising, reflecting and rediscovering a researcher's embodied experience as a narrative inquirer. *Sport Education and Society*, *21*, 96–113.

Moher, D., Liberati, A., Tetzlaff, J., & Altman, D. G. (2009). The PRISMA Group: Preferred reporting items for systematic reviews and meta-analyses: The PRISMA Statement. *PLoS Medicine*, 6, 6.

Noblit, G. W. & Hare, R. D. (1988). *Meta-ethnography: Synthesizing qualitative studies*. London: Sage.

Paterson, B. L. (2012). "It looks great but how do I know if it fits?": An introduction to meta-synthesis research. In K. Hannes & C. Lockwood (Eds.), *Synthesising qualitative research: Choosing the right approach* (pp. 1–21). Chichester: John Wiley.

Paterson, B. L., Thorne, S. E., Canam, C., & Jillings, C. (2001). *Meta-study of qualitative health research. A practical guide to meta-analysis and meta-synthesis*. Thousand Oaks, CA: Sage.

Shaw, R. L. (2010). Conducting literature reviews. In M. Forrester (Ed.), *Doing qualitative research in psychology: A practical guide* (pp. 39–52). London: Sage.

Shaw, R. L. (2011). Identifying and synthesising qualitative literature. In D. Harper & A. Thompson (Eds.), *Qualitative research methods in mental health and psychotherapy: An introduction for students and practitioners* (pp. 9–22). Chichester: Wiley Blackwell.

Shaw, R. L., Booth, A., Sutton, A. J., Miller, T., Smith, J. A., Young, B., Jones, D. R., & Dixon-Woods, M. (2004). Finding qualitative research: An evaluation of search strategies. *BMC Medical Research Methodology*, *4*(5).

Shaw, R. L., Larkin, M., & Flowers, P. (2014). Expanding the evidence within evidence-based healthcare: Thinking about the context, acceptability and feasibility of interventions. *BMJ Evidence Based Medicine*, *19*(6), 201–203.

Soundy, A., Freeman, P., Stubbs, B., Probst, M., Coffee, P., & Vancampfort, D. (2014). The transcending benefits of physical activity for individuals with schizophrenia: A systematic review and meta-ethnography. *Psychiatry Research*, *2*(20), 11–19.

Sparkes, A. C. & Smith, B. (2009). Judging the quality of qualitative inquiry: Criteriology and relativism in action. *Psychology of Sport and Exercise*, 10, 491–497.

Sparkes, A. C. & Smith, B. (2014). *Qualitative research methods in sport, exercise & health. From process to product*. London: Routledge.

Tamminen, K. A. & Holt, N. L. (2010). A meta-study of qualitative research examining stressor appraisals and coping among adolescents in sport. *Journal of Sports Sciences*, *28*(14), 1563–1580.

Thomas, J. & Harden, A. (2008). Methods for the thematic synthesis of qualitative research in systematic reviews. *BMC Medical Research Methodology*, 8, 45.

Walsh, D. & Downe, S. (2005). Meta-synthesis method for qualitative research: A literature review. *Journal of Advanced Nursing, 50*(2), 204–211.

Weed, M. (2006). Interpretive qualitative synthesis in the sport & exercise sciences: The meta-interpretation approach. *European Journal of Sport Science, 6*(2), 127–139.

Williams, T. L., Smith, B., & Papathomas, A. (2014). The barriers, benefits and facilitators of leisure time physical activity among people with spinal cord injury: A meta-synthesis of qualitative findings. *Health Psychology Review, 8*(4), 404–425.

PART IV

Representation, evaluation and ethics

22

IN DEFENCE OF REALIST TALES

Samantha King

When the editors of this book first approached me about writing this chapter, I balked. I saw myself neither as an expert in realist tales, nor an advocate for this approach to research. Moreover, the prospect of figuring out how to synthesize the massive and diffuse literature on realism – a concept and practice with multiple meanings dispersed across a range of scholarly disciplines and aesthetic genres – seemed frankly overwhelming. With some reflection and a gentle reminder that I had actually written briefly about realist tales in the past, however, I decided to accept the invitation. A methodological pluralist at heart (see also Chapter 28), in that earlier piece I had argued that such tales – conventionally defined by the almost complete absence of the researcher from the finished text and the presentation of an extensive set of closely edited data contextualized within a tight theoretical account – were as useful as any other approach to communicating research, as long as they were engaging, provocative, and written with due political and ethical care (King, 2009). The realist tale is also the most frequently used mode for communicating qualitative research and thus demands to be both taken seriously and subject to critical attention. In this spirit, this chapter offers less a dogmatic defence of realist tales writ large and more a deliberation on the changing character of the realist genre in the context of the enhanced attention to reflexivity exercised by contemporary authors and readers. The chapter is comprised of three parts. It begins with a discussion of the definition of a realist tale, moves back in time to reflect on why such tales came to be subject to widespread critique, and, finally, seeks to 'work the ruins' (Lather, 2001) of realism by exploring where, how, and with what outcomes this approach appears in current research in sport, exercise, and health.

Realism in brief

To provide a sense of the scope of the realist umbrella Wikipedia offers no less than fifteen separate pages describing topics ranging from realism in international relations to realism in the arts. It also features an entry on ethnographic realism – 'a writing style that narrates the author's anthropological observations as if they were first-hand' – and another on philosophical realism – 'belief that reality exists independently of observers'. These two definitions represent the dual starting points for this chapter. The discussion that follows will encompass more than ethnography (see Chapter 5), or writing based on fieldwork, but it is through debates within the field of anthropology that many sport studies scholars, myself included, were introduced to the promises and pitfalls of realist methodologies. I thus use anthropological literature, with some additional insights from sociology and the philosophy of social science, to ground my analysis. My ideas are shaped by a broadly feminist-postcolonial epistemology (see also Chapters 7, 33, and 34) that is particularly attuned to the gendered and colonial character of knowledge–power relations.

Although the aforementioned encyclopedic definitions seem appropriately simple and straightforward, even the briefest excursion into the humanities and social science literature on realism will reveal that its definition and operationalization, even within disciplines, is variable and contested. Maxwell (2012), for instance, identifies eight approaches within the category of 'critical realism' alone in his textbook on the subject. For the purposes of this chapter, I do not spend time finessing finely gradated, esoteric distinctions between types of realism, but instead simply note that such attempts at categorization do exist should readers be interested in pursuing these approaches in more depth (Maxwell, 2012). It also seems important to acknowledge that while realist tales continue to dominate the qualitative research paradigm, it is widely understood among qualitative researchers that their work is mediated, subjective, and largely severed from its realist legacies. This structuring paradox – that most contemporary scholars do not purport to subscribe to realism even as they adhere to the realist tale – haunts the discussion that follows and makes any general claim about realism in qualitative research hard to sustain.

What is a realist tale?

The realist tale has been much discussed in the sport studies literature, most prominently by Andrew Sparkes (1995, 2002), who in turn draws on John Van Maanen's (2011) widely taught text, *Tales of the Field: On Writing Ethnography*, which is itself heavily reliant on George Marcus and Dick Cushman's 1982 essay, 'Ethnographies as Texts'. Representing one of the earliest efforts to describe and analyse approaches to 'writing culture' (Clifford & Marcus, 1986), Van Maanen's book, first published in 1988, became a must-read for the new anthropologist seeking to conduct and report engaging, self-reflexive, and ethical fieldwork. Clearly influenced by what were, at the time of writing, recent critiques of the realist mode, Van Maanen's tone in his chapter on the subject is sceptical, if not disdainful, as he describes the strategies that realist narratives employ to appear scientific, objective, and true-to-life. While Van Maanen is clearly not an advocate for realism, his work does offer a useful sketch of the typical – or perhaps, stereotypical – realist tale.

Realist conventions, according to Van Maanen (2011), are first and foremost characterized by the absence of the narrator from the text. The focus is on what the subjects of the research who are being observed or interviewed, say, do, and think with the author posing 'as an impersonal conduit . . . who passes on more-or-less objective data in a measured intellectual style that is uncontaminated by personal bias, political goals, or moral judgments' (p. 47). Such 'studied neutrality' (Van Maanen, 2011, p. 47) is accomplished in a variety of ways: Like their counterparts in the natural sciences, ethnographers may use passive voice in order to create distance between themselves and their research participants, or they may appear only in certain sections of the text, often the methods or footnotes. Moreover, realist narratives rely frequently on carefully selected and edited quotes from interviewees, which help to suggest that the reported findings are authentic representations of the people being studied and accurately convey their perspectives, rather than the author's interpretations of the participants and their perspectives (Sparkes, 1995; Van Maanen, 2011). In the words of Marcus and Cushman, in realist narratives, 'the collective and authoritative third person ("the X do this") replaces the more fallible first person ("I saw the X do this"), and the relationship between what the researcher knows and how she came to know it is severed' (1982, p. 32).

While giving voice to the researched was not a priority in early ethnographic work, especially non-feminist work, it has become particularly important in the wake of debates about what counts as the participant's point of view and how to render it in writing. While a traditional realist tale would not usually acknowledge or explore such epistemological issues, it would be hard to find an ethnographic text today, realist or otherwise, that entirely excludes the (assumed) standpoint of the participant.

The presentation of extensive and intricate detail is another characteristic of the realist tale. The ability to 'represent a world as only one who has known it first-hand can', Marcus and Cushman (1982) claim, is 'what gives the ethnographer authority and the text a pervasive sense of concrete reality' (p. 29). Paradoxically, it is the researcher's presentation of a world that is authentic and resonant, which also reveals the intimate link between the act of research and the mode of communicating it. In other words, while realist writing may appear as an unmanipulated reflection of reality, it is in fact 'a complex effect, achieved through writing and dependent on the strategic choice and construction of available detail' (Marcus & Cushman, 1982, p. 29).

Such complexity is not usually visible in a standard realist tale. Van Maanen (2011) uses the term 'interpretive omnipotence' to describe the ways in which realist ethnographic work is presented as the final word on culture – the 'god-trick', as feminist science studies scholar Donna Haraway (1988, p. 582) calls it. Contemporary researchers would no longer dream of writing, as did the founder of functionalist anthropology, Bronislaw Malinowski (1967), that, 'It is I who will describe them or create them' (p. 140), but realist researchers still rarely ask explicitly if they got their account right or if an alternative story is possible. In other words, the self-reflection, equivocation, doubt and polyvocality that characterizes some contemporary research in the social sciences and humanities is not typically found in a realist tale.

Critiques of realism/crises of representation

While, in retrospect, realism represented the dominant approach to anthropological research for much of the twentieth century, it was not until the publication of Marcus and Cushman's (1982) essay, written with the aim of describing a growing anti- or post-realist experimentalism in the field, that this approach to scholarship was named as such. In contrast to traditional ethnographic writing, in which the author disappears from view with little explanation of how they reached or constructed their interpretations of the people they were studying, the emerging experimentalism that Marcus and Cushman highlight was characterized by an explicit epistemological consciousness in which authors actively reflected upon their role in producing and shaping knowledge, often making their reflections a central part of the ethnographic narrative. This new way of writing emerged in part as a response to what Marcus and Fischer (1986) called the 'crisis of representation', in which uncertainty about how to adequately and responsibly describe social reality threatened to undermine the very foundation of the discipline of anthropology.

The movement towards self-reflexivity dovetailed with a series of other paradigm-shifting debates and interventions, both within and outside anthropology, that together challenged the colonial and racializing tropes, and grids of power, upon which much writing about 'the other' was built (Clifford & Marcus, 1986; Geertz, 1988; Mohanty, 1986; Moraga & Anzaldúa, 1981; Said, 1979). Within feminist anthropology, the specific field through which I came to think about these issues, the 'crisis of representation' (Marcus & Fischer, 1986), assumed a dual form, forcing a reckoning with both the objectification and marginalization of colonized and racialized women in white feminist scholarship, and the erasure of women and feminist scholarship from the 'new ethnography' championed by post-structuralist-inspired male anthropologists such as Geertz, Clifford, Marcus, Fischer, and Cushman (Behar and Gordon, 1995).

Kamala Visweswaran's classic critique, 'Defining Feminist Ethnography' (1988), explores these two concerns side by side. She argues, on the one hand, that feminist anthropologists who insist on a universal shared experience among women erase the variability of women's experiences and the class, racial and colonial hierarchies that structure relations among them. Thus, any attempt on the part of a woman ethnographer to capture another woman's voice, no matter how sensitively handled, is inevitably caught up in the power dynamics of self and other. On the other hand, Visweswaran suggests, first-person accounts replete with anti-positivist renderings of the disjunctions and misunderstandings central to the fieldwork experience, written by women over many decades prior to the crisis of representation, were being 'consigned to the margins of ethnographic discourse' or dismissed as 'confessional tales' by the men leading the experimental turn. Furthermore, while the experimentalists were advocating for co-authored texts with dispersed authority, they were not prepared to risk 'giving up the (authority) game' (Marcus & Cushman, p. 44), by, for instance, including indigenous anthropologists, or 'self-writing about like selves,' in their work (Visweswaran, 1988).

Visweswaran's essay was just one of a number of devastating critiques that emerged in response to the exclusion of women and feminism from the dominant framing of the crisis of representation (Abu-Lughod, 1993; Behar & Gordon, 1995; Clough, 1998; Mascia-Lees, Sharpe & Cohen, 1989). This work was not simply reactive, but also extended the terrain of the debate. To questions about voice were added related concerns about the myth of objectivity and the situatedness of all knowledge (Abu-Lughod, 1993, p. 6; Haraway, 1988; Hill Collins, 1998). Rather than viewing a lack of objectivity as deleterious to good research, many feminist theorists embraced the lack, making their positionality explicit and undertaking to explore it meanings and effects (Abu-Lughod, 1993). These scholars understood that self-reflexive work could not circumvent its own authority. Haraway took this argument further, claiming that, 'Only partial perspective promises objective vision' and pointing to the value of placing multiple viewpoints in conversation with one another (1988, p. 583). Marcus and Cushman (1982) agreed that authority is hard to shed, but also acknowledged that the ethnographer's 'self-reflection and calculated intrusion' (p. 39) is actually the mechanism through which authority is established in the interpretive paradigm.

Other feminist scholars warned of a different set of dangers emerging from the new ethnography advocated by the likes of Marcus and Cushman. Kathleen Stewart, for example, wrote against the 'rush to contain' representational failures through a 'discipline of correctives and asides that dreams, once again, the old dreams of the perfect text in new textual solutions such as author positionings, formally dialogic presentations, ironic distance, and self-reflection' (1996, p. 23f). She argued instead for a vision akin to what Visweswaran (1994) describes in her book, *Fictions of Feminist Ethnography*, in which ruptured understandings and failure are 'pivotal' to the ethnographic account (Lather, 2001, p. 100).

While reflections on failure have yet to emerge as a central feature of research accounts in sport, exercise and health research, feminist scholars in the field, like their colleagues in anthropology, have been at the forefront of critiques of realism. Susan Birrell's (1990) much-cited essay, 'Women of color, critical autobiography, and sport', drew early attention to the absence of writing about women of colour in the field, while also suggesting that postmodern approaches to identity and experience would enable a much-needed shift away from positivist accounts, in which gender and race appear as variables to be calculated rather than relations of power to be analysed. In a related vein, Katherine Jamieson (2003a, 2003b) has advocated for the potential of Chicana feminism's decolonial and expressly political approach to scholarship for exploring sport as a cultural practice. Jamieson weaves Chicana feminist concepts with a fictional narrative, based on both her own identity and ethnographic research with Latina softball players, in order to highlight the hybridity and ambiguity of researcher and participant subjectivities, the impossibility of 'master narratives', and the need to acknowledge and engage the 'limits of positionality' (2003a, p. 29).

Sharing a feminist epistemology and critique of positivism, Pirkko Markula has been at the forefront of attempts to invigorate sociological scholarship through evocative storytelling, auto-ethnography, and a critical, self-reflexive and embodied approach to research (1998, 2001, 2006; Denison and Markula, 2003). Concomitantly, Jim Denison and Robert Rhinehart's (2000) special issue of the *Sociology of Sport Journal*, 'Imagining Sociological Narratives', marked the arrival of fiction storied represent\ations and autoethnography (see Chapter 23) in one of the leading journals in the sociology of sport. During the same period, scholars such as David Gilbourne (Gilbourne, 2002, 2010; Gilbourne & Andersen, 2011), Brett Smith (Smith & McGannon, 2015; Smith & Sparkes, 2009), Kerry McGannon (McGannon & Smith, 2015) and Andrew Sparkes (Sparkes, 2002; Sparkes & Smith, 2002), have worked across the sociology and psychology literatures to advocate for methodological and epistemological reflexivity, and alternative research and writing practices in the form of autoethnography, ethnodrama (see Chapter 23) and narrative analysis (see Chapter 20). These researchers share in common a repudiation of rigid, standardized and disembodied research methods, and they adhere not to pre-existing methodological frameworks that can be transported, unaltered, from one research problem to the next, but to creative, flexible and tentative exploration and communication. Together such work has helped produce more richly textured, fleshy and deeply felt renderings of bodily experiences, especially in the realm of injury, disability, cancer, ageing and bereavement.

Assessing the present

In 2015, approaches such as autoethnography were more common, if far from standard, in qualitative research in sport, exercise and health (Culver, Gilbert, Sparkes, 2012; Giardina and Laurendeau, 2013). I would submit that underlying much, if not most, literature – including realist tales – is the assumption that knowledge is 'partial, incomplete, and fallible', even if authors do not, as a matter of course, include in their work an elaborate discussion of the nature of truth or whether entities in the world exist outside of the researcher's perception and interpretation of them (Maxwell, 2012, p. 5). Scholars do, however, mark their assumptions about the contingent character of knowledge in various ways: through methodological reflexivity (the extensiveness and explicitness of which fluctuates considerably); through descriptions of their chosen theoretical approach (if an author notes that they work from a 'post-structuralist' or 'postmodernist' perspective their readers might reasonably suppose that the author is working with a notion of multiple and competing truths, even if that is not always the case in practice!); through the subjectivist tone of their writing; or through the presentation of their data or source material as multiple, contested or incomplete. Even when none of these approaches is obviously present in a text, rarely does one get the sense that authors believe in the ability of science to uncover 'the truth', or that impartial knowledge exists 'out there in the world' waiting to be revealed by an omnipotent observer.

This being said, it would be wrong to characterize the field as a hotbed of experimental, self-reflexive, post-realist approaches to communicating research. Back in 1982, Marcus and

Cushman wrote that most current experimental work in anthropology was not 'transcending realist goals', but rather 'bringing them into line with the shift toward a more explicit guiding interest in problems of meaning and the hermeneutic sensitivity this entails' (p. 39). Over three decades later, this stands as an accurate portrayal of research in sport, exercise and health, or at least in the sociocultural field where the critique of realism is more normalized. While qualitative, interpretive, critical and frequently Foucauldian-inspired research dominates the pages of the leading journals in sociocultural studies, and is a growing presence in sport and exercise psychology journals, most scholars in these fields have not fully abandoned the scientific paradigm for communicating results (King, 2009). Whereas plenty of researchers write of multiple, constructed, subjective and situated realities, very few acknowledge or engage in the co-construction of stories with their participants (Smith & Sparkes, 2009). Instead, Trochim (2006)'s definition of the 'post-positivist critical realist' seems like an apt description of the typical scholar in the field. This figure, Trochim says, 'believes that the goal of science is to hold steadfastly to the goal of getting it right about reality, even though we can never achieve that goal!' Part of the problem, as Graham Watson notes, is that it is:

> precisely for news of the world, conveyed by an accredited reporter, that the reader consults an ethnographic text; if he suspects that news brought to him is an effect of the writer's discursive practices, then, as things stand, he will not warrant it as anthropology.
>
> *(Watson, 1987, p. 36)*

The shift away from realism thus depends as much on the willingness of readers – and editorial boards, especially – to 'stop requiring authoritative accounts from writers' (Watson, 1987, p. 36).

Sport, exercise and health research across the realist spectrum

Imprecise but persistent questions about the audience and their changing role in interpreting texts have haunted the writing of this chapter. My questions go something like this: Are critiques of realism so familiar and so naturalized that they have become less crucial (depending on the precise context, of course) for authors to explicitly elaborate and interrogate their location and role in the research process? In other words, do readers read differently today – less innocently, perhaps and with a greater tolerance for ambiguity? (I know I am on dangerous territory here).

The (possible) changing nature of readership, or at least the changing expectations that authors have of readers, loomed particularly large as I reviewed current literature in the field, reflected on its (post)realist underpinnings and figured out what I wanted to say about it. In the end, I chose three recent peer-reviewed journal articles, selected for what they suggest about their assumed readership, as much as their authorial persuasions: 'An Ethnographic Study of Issues Surrounding the Provision of Sport Opportunities to Young Men from a Western Canadian Inner-City', co-authored by a psychologist, Nick Holt, and two sociologists, Jay Scherer and Jordan Koch, and published in *Psychology of Sport and Exercise* (Holt, Scherer & Koch, 2013); 'Civilising Recalcitrant Boys' Bodies: Pursuing Social Fitness Through the Anti-Obesity Offensive', authored by sociologist, Lee Monaghan, and published in *Sport, Education and Society* (Monaghan, 2014); and 'Stop Playing Up!: Racialisation, Physical Education, and Resistance,' authored by critical pedagogue Katie Fitzpatrick, and published in *Ethnography* (Fitzpatrick, 2011). All three essays are ethnographic, critical in their theoretical orientation and broadly concerned with marginalized youth, sport, and physical education.

It goes without saying, given the small sample size, that my purpose is not to offer a comprehensive overview or 'state of the field' summation regarding realism in the sport, exercise and health field. Nor do I want to suggest that these articles are typical of broader patterns that can be simply and straightforwardly 'read off' these examples (for one thing, ethnography is still a highly uncommon methodological choice within the psychology of sport). Rather, I have chosen to focus on these publications because each offers a useful and provocative contribution to the literature, even as they diverge in their relationship to realism. In drawing out their realist orientations (which are only explicitly stated in one instance) and exploring how these might have shaped the research approach, findings and communication, I seek to highlight some key methodological promises, challenges and tensions that emerge in contemporary research concerned with capturing and analysing the complex realities of lived experience in the context of sport, exercise and health. I begin with the article that I find most steeped in realism and work my way along the (short) continuum to conclude with the article that I find least steeped in realism.

Holt, Scherer and Koch's (2013) research took place at a sports programme organized by a local Mental Health Unit for young men living in the inner city of a western Canadian city. Pointing to a dearth of evidence regarding the consequences of sport-for-development approaches, and the precise mechanisms that enable or constrain positive personal, social and structural outcomes, this particular article, which is part of a larger study, explores the experiences and perspectives of twelve youth workers who were responsible for delivering the programme. The researchers found that participation in floor hockey and other activities gave the young men a conduit for relieving their boredom and a fleeting reprieve from the challenging conditions of their daily lives; it also provided opportunities for relationship-building between the youth workers and the young men. Predictably perhaps, the researchers also learned that longstanding and persistent economic and social inequality and a fragmented approach to the delivery of services limited the influence that sport could have in the lives of the participants, thus challenging some of the fundamental assumptions of the sport-for-development paradigm.

Unusually, the ethnographic legwork for this study was performed by only one of the authors (Koch), presumably as part of his doctoral thesis research, though this is not noted explicitly in the article. My sense is that the decision to move away from the classic lone-ethnographer model signifies less a cutting-edge experiment in multi-perspectival authorship than a reflection of the increasing adoption of scientific models of co-authorship and collaboration by the 'softer' social sciences. Differentiating this article from a standard scientific publication, however, is the authors' detailed explanation of their scholarly division of labour (a different researcher, Holt, 'led the writing' of the study [p. 542]), and an explicit discussion both of their shared epistemological perspectives and their disciplinary differences.

Methodologically, I found this paper fascinating and, like all good work, it left me with more questions than answers. The authors appear hyperconscious of the diversity of their possible audiences. And they are clearly juggling a series of competing expectations, including those that arise when conducting relativist, constructivist work for publication in a 'hard' social science journal that either explicitly or implicitly demanded a long justification of the rigour and validity of the research. Moreover, despite an extensive methodological preamble that includes an acknowledgement of the active role that they as researchers played in 'interpreting how the participants made sense of their personal and social world' (p. 540), they ultimately present their work in the form of a realist tale. The modifier – 'tale' – offers a nod to their stated non-foundationalist approach, but the actual presentation of the research is indeed fairly objectivist with the interview participants apparently speaking, unmediated, for themselves, and the authors' critical and interpretive hand largely invisible. This makes for something of a rollercoaster ride, epistemologically, but it also provides an excellent example of the challenges of pulling anti-foundationalist threads through an entire text, and of the impossibility of achieving either a purely realist or a purely non-realist approach.

Monaghan (2014) is also interested in marginalized youth, but in this case the setting is a working-class area of north-east England and the focus a state-sponsored anti-obesity initiative for boys at risk for exclusion from school because of 'behavioural issues'. Monaghan reveals that despite the best intentions of the instructors, the 'Health and Youth' (H&Y) programme he watched unfold provided both the setting and the tools for fat-based bullying and stigma among the boys. A clear paradox, given that in its practical applications, the programme was more focused on social fitness – and instilling middle-class codes of 'civilized' behaviour – than it was on physical fitness.

Monaghan notes that he 'largely adopted an observer role at the college,' though he 'also participated in various ways (e.g., showing the boys how to use weight-training equipment and quelling particularly disruptive classroom interactions)' (p. 692). He gives an example of the latter type of intervention when he mentions trying to 'change the boys' focus' at one particularly fractious moment (p. 695). Later in the same section of the essay, he reveals that he 'breached his usual observer role' by confiscating water flasks that the boys were using to flick and spit water at one another (p. 694). These are significant admissions insofar as Monaghan acknowledges how he actively participated in the programme that he was supposedly largely observing and reveals how he exercised judgement about the boys' behaviour. Although he doesn't frame it this way, or reflect on his actions, the reader might infer from these accounts that Monaghan himself contributed to attempts to encourage bourgeois norms of personal conduct among the boys. Such moments are confined to one section of the text, however – the 'ethnographic glimpse of the H&Y project wherein boys deemed fat were bullied' (p. 693) – and Monaghan is largely absent from the remainder of the article. He provides long descriptions based on field notes, but without acknowledging or interrogating his role in recording and representing events, or discussing how the participants' behaviours might have been shaped by his presence.

Further methodological reflection would surely have been interesting, and useful for researchers who find themselves in similarly challenging ethical contexts, but Monaghan's analysis – especially his descriptions of exchanges (and skirmishes) among and between the instructors and the boys – remains gripping, astute and complex. From my perspective, Monaghan took great care to render his participants – the health educators and the boys – compassionately and complexly, and succeeds in offering a portrait that highlights both their individuality and their implication in broader social structures. Like Holt, Scherer and Koch, he leaves readers with provocative questions and much to ponder. To ask him to ruminate on his role in the programme would be to ask for a different paper, one less concerned with offering either theoretical contributions to the literature on critical obesity and the civilizing process, or political contributions to the movement against fat stigma and oppression – each essential and valuable projects in themselves.

Fitzpatrick (2011) was the only one of the three researchers to conduct her study in a formal school setting. Located in South Auckland, an economically poor yet culturally vibrant suburb of New Zealand's largest city, the secondary school in question serves a population composed predominantly of indigenous Māori and migrant youth from the Pacific Islands. Fitzpatrick's focus is on the fraught place of physical education (PE) in the lives of students. She argues that whereas PE is implicated in the promotion of narrow and oppressive bodily norms, it also offers a space for relationship-building, play and critical resistance – one possible reason for its status as the most popular option subject among students at the school. Based on my reading of the text, the resistive elements are due in no small part to the pedagogical talents of Dan, the teacher featured most prominently in her analysis, but also, on a structural level, to the critical nature of New Zealand's PE curriculum, which is designed to encourage students to study politics, racism, gender and sexuality in relation to sport culture.

Fitzpatrick (2011) is by far the most explicitly self-reflexive of the three authors with her presence and her agency in shaping the narrative acknowledged consistently throughout the text. Fitzpatrick reveals that she taught health and physical education at the school for four years before she returned, four years later, to undertake her study. She offers a detailed discussion of the 'single most important part' of her research project – forming relationships with students – and how she undertook to gain students' trust and 'dismantle her "teacher" self' upon her return to the school (p. 177). Fitzpatrick acknowledges the power dynamics shaping her research and details how she sought to minimize potential negative effects. She also provides substantial context for quotes from participants and the conversational nature of her interviewing technique – the 'back and forth' – is clearly conveyed. Although Fitzpatrick's subjectivity does not dominate the text, I could sense her presence as I read – there is no omnipotent observer in this piece of writing. Even when Fitzpatrick is describing the political, social and economic context of South Auckland, her perspective and location are apparent. I thus got a sense of Fitzpatrick's day-to-day interactions with her participants, her degree of immersion in their school lives and, importantly, their sense of her. Although her writing is less formal, less explicitly theoretical, and less authoritative in tone than the other two pieces, to me it reads most like a first-hand account and thus, somewhat paradoxically, is realist in its effect if not in its structure and design.

On writing well

It should be clear from these examples that a realist approach is not reducible to just one stage of the research process – that is, to the conveying of results or the making of arguments, after the data collection or fieldwork has occurred. Instead, realism reaches far back into the research process, profoundly shaping – and in turn being shaped by – the theoretical assumptions and modes of inquiry at the heart of any project. Moreover, as Watson (1987) argues, 'essential reflexivity' is not simply what one does as a researcher, but is an 'essential and inevitable property of all discourse' (p. 30). One cannot make an intentional choice to be reflexive or not. As academics we are embedded and interested subjects and reflexivity is thus integral to our work, be we bench scientists or literary critics. Indeed, it is the realization on the part of authors and audiences alike that reflexivity is inherent to the research and writing process that produce the proliferation of ways to manage it, ways that include both realism and the search for alternatives to it (Watson, 1987).

I have also tried to make clear throughout the chapter that there is nothing inherently problematic with a realist tale. Surely we can all think of work, including interpretive and apparently reflexive work, which is technically competent but dull to read. Writing in the first person or with acknowledgement of one's social location offers no guarantee of additional layers of insight, creativity or methodological and theoretical courage. We would probably all rather read surprising ideas packaged according to traditional academic conventions, and expressed in clear and felicitous language, than established ideas presented in an experimental or otherwise rhetorically sophisticated format. That said, ideas and the language used to convey them cannot be separated in practice, and new ways of writing will reflect and nurture new ideas, even as the latter is not dependent upon the former. As qualitative research in sport, exercise and health continues to flourish, my hope is that we persist in nurturing tales – provocative, evocative tales – that span the realist spectrum and a rich variety of other conventions of scholarly research and writing.

References

Abu-Lughod, L. (1993). *Writing women's worlds: Bedouin stories.* Berkeley, CA: University of California Press.

Behar, R. & Gordon, D. (Eds.) (1995). *Women writing culture.* Berkeley, CA: University of California Press.

Birrell, S. (1990). Women of color, critical autobiography, and sport. In M.A. Messner & D.F. Sabo (Eds.), *Sport, men, and the gender order: Critical feminist perspectives* (pp. 185–199). Champaign, IL: Human Kinetics Press.

Clifford, J. & Marcus, G.E. (1986). *Writing culture: The poetics and politics of ethnography.* Berkeley, CA: University of California Press.

Clough, P. (1998). *The end(s) of ethnography: From realism to social criticism.* New York: Peter Lang.

Culver, D.M., Gilbert, W. & Sparkes, A.C. (2012). Qualitative research in sport psychology journals: The next decade, 2000–2009 and beyond. *The Sport Psychologist, 26,* 261–281.

Denison, J. & Markula, P. (2003). *Moving writing: Crafting movement for sport research.* New York: Peter Lang.

Denison, J. & Rinehart, R. (2000). Imagining sociological narratives. *Sociology of Sport Journal, 17,* 1–4.

Fitzpatrick, K. (2011). Stop playing up! Racialisation, physical education, and resistance. *Ethnography, 12,* 174–197.

Geertz, C. (1988). *Works and lives: The anthropologist as author.* Stanford, CA: Stanford University Press.

Giardina, M. & Laurendeau, J. (2013). Truth untold? Evidence, knowledge, and research practice(s). *Sociology of Sport Journal, 30,* 237–255.

Gilbourne, D. (2002). Sports participation, sports injury, and altered images of self: An autobiographical narrative of a lifelong legacy. *Reflective Practice, 3,* 71–88.

Gilbourne, D. (2010). 'Edge of Darkness' and 'Just in Time': Two cautionary tales, two styles, one story. *Qualitative Inquiry, 16,* 325–331.

Gilbourne, D. & Andersen, M.B. (2011). *Critical essays in applied sport psychology.* Champaign, IL: Human Kinetics.

Haraway, D. (1988). Situated knowledges: The science question in feminism. *Feminist Studies, 14,* 575–599.

Hill Collins, P. (1998). *Fighting words: Black women and the search for justice.* Minneapolis, MN: University of Minnesota Press.

Holt, N., Scherer, J. & Koch, J. (2013). An ethnographic study of issues surrounding the provision of sport opportunities to young men from a Western Canadian inner-city. *Psychology of Sport and Exercise, 14,* 538–548.

Jamieson, K. M. (2003a). Latina sexualities: What's sport got to do with it? *Avante, 9,* 20–31.

Jamieson, K. M. (2003b). Occupying a middle space: Towards a mestiza sport studies. *Sociology of Sport Journal, 20,* 1–16.

King, S. (2009). Sociocultural sport studies and the scientific paradigm: A response to John Smith. *Qualitative Research in Sport and Exercise, 2,* 101–106.

Lather, P. (2001). Working the ruins of feminist ethnography. *Signs, 27,* 199–227.

Malinowski, B. (1967). *A diary in the strict sense of the term.* Stanford, CA: Stanford University Press.

Marcus, G. E. & Cushman, D. (1982). Ethnographies as texts. *Annual Review of Anthropology, 11,* 25–69.

Marcus, G.E. & Fischer, M. M. J. (1986). *Anthropology as cultural critique: An experimental moment in the human sciences.* Chicago, IL: University of Chicago Press.

Markula, P. (1998). Dancing within postmodernism. *Waikato Journal of Education, 4,* 73–85.

Markula, P. (2001). Bodily dialogues: Writing the self. *International Sports Studies, 23,* 24–29.

Markula, P. (2006). The dancing body without organs: Deleuze, femininity and performing research. *Qualitative Inquiry, 12,* 3–27.

Mascia-Lees, F., Sharpe, P. & Ballerino Cohen, C. (1989). The postmodernist turn in anthropology: Cautions from a feminist perspective. *Signs, 15,* 7–33.

Maxwell, J. A. (2012). *A realist approach for qualitative research.* Thousand Oaks, CA: Sage.

McGannon, K. R. & Smith, B. (2015). Centralizing culture in cultural sport psychology research: The potential of narrative inquiry and discursive psychology. *Psychology of Sport & Exercise, 17,* 79–87.

Mohanty, C. T. (1986). Under Western eyes: Feminist scholarship and colonial discourses. *Boundary, 2(3),* 333–358.

Monaghan, L. (2014). Civilising recalcitrant boys' bodies: Pursuing social fitness through the anti-obesity offensive. *Sport, Education and Society, 19,* 691–711.

Moraga, C. & Anzaldúa, G. (1981). *This bridge called my back: Writings by radical women of color.* Watertown, MA: Persephone Press.

Said, E. (1979). *Orientalism*. New York: Vintage.

Smith, B. & McGannon, K. (2015). Psychology and sociology in sport studies. In R. Giulianotti (Ed.), *Routledge handbook of the sociology of sport* (pp. 194–203). London: Routledge.

Smith, B. & Sparkes, A. C. (2009). Narrative inquiry in sport and exercise psychology: What can it mean, and why might we do it? *Psychology of Sport and Exercise*, *10*, 1–11.

Sparkes, A. C. (1995). Writing people: Reflections on the dual crises of representation and legitimation in qualitative inquiry. *Quest*, *47*, 158-195.

Sparkes, A. C. (2002). *Telling tales in sport and physical activity: A qualitative journey*. Champaign, IL: Human Kinetics.

Sparkes, A. C. & Smith, B. (2002). Sport, spinal cord injuries, embodied masculinities and the dilemmas of narrative identity. *Men and Masculinities*, *4*, 258–285.

Stewart, K. (1996). *A space on the side of the road: Cultural poetics in an 'other' America*. Princeton, NJ: Princeton University Press.

Trochim, W. (2006). Positivism and post-positivism. *Research methods knowledge base*. Available at: http://www.socialresearchmethods.net/kb/positvsm.php.

Van Maanen, J. (2011). *Tales of the field: On writing ethnography* (2nd ed.). Chicago, IL: University of Chicago Press.

Visweswaran, K. (1988). Defining feminist ethnography. *Inscriptions*, *3–4*. Available at: http://culturalstudies.ucsc.edu/PUBS/Inscriptions/vol_3-4/Viveswaran.html.

Visweswaran, K. (1994). *Fictions of feminist ethnography*. Minneapolis, MN: University of Minnesota Press.

Watson, G. (1987). Make me reflexive, but not yet: Strategies for managing essential reflexivity in ethnographic discourse. *Journal of Anthropological Research*, *43*, 29–41.

23

CREATIVE ANALYTICAL PRACTICES

Jenny McMahon

This chapter focuses on creative analytical practices (CAP). It will begin by first describing CAP in broad terms, then outlining the various types of CAP. The second part of the chapter is dedicated to outlining two commonly used written CAP examples: autoethnography and ethnodrama.

What is CAP?

CAP is what Richardson (2000) refers to as an overarching term used to represent the different kinds of writing as well as alterative kinds of arts-based and performance research practices. Qualitative researchers use CAP to ensure the complexity of lived experience is brought to the fore. Most, but not all, kinds of research practices that fall under the CAP umbrella are written, but recently they have extended to include non-written forms.

What are the varying types of CAP?

There are numerous types of research that are considered to be CAP. These include the various kinds of autoethnography such as analytical, evocative, collaborative, meta-autoethnography and auto-phenomenography (see also Chapter 2), as well as poems, autobiography and other types of conversational, multi-vocal, critical and arts-based representations that are both analytical and creative (Richardson, 2000). However, in recent years, CAP has extended to include what has been termed *performance ethnography* (Gergen & Gergen, 2014). Performance ethnography is not just written but also performance-based, that is, the written research is performed by a person or team to an audience. As Gergen and Gergen (2011) state, performance research is defined as the deployment of different forms of artistic performance in the execution of a research project. Examples of performative CAP include performative monologue, performance autoethnography, poetry, dramatic performance and visual art as theory. Other examples are ethnodrama and ethnotheatre. Ethnotheatre differs from ethnodrama in that the dramatic script is performed, whereas ethnodrama is a script or text version of a drama or performance. CAP has also been known to include, visual methodology (see Chapter 11) and music (Richardson, 2000; Sparkes & Smith, 2014). For *how* a CAP might be done, see Chapter 20.

Why use CAP?

There are a number of broad reasons why researchers might choose to use CAP. First, Denzin (2000), Smith and Sparkes (2009), as well as Parry and Johnson (2007), explain how CAP was indeed created in response to the crisis of representation. The crisis of representation relates to the scientific modes of reporting research which are seen to misrepresent human experience, in particular inadequately presenting or describing the lived experiences of those we study. There is no denying that lived experience is not only complex to understand but also difficult to represent; however, CAP enables researchers to recreate lived experiences in ways that represent their personal and social meanings (Parry & Johnson, 2007).

Second, according to Ropers-Huilman (1999), acts of 'witnessing' can occur when the audience or reader engages in the lived experiences of others. Ropers-Huilman (1999) reveals that 'when we participate in knowing and learning about others, engage with constructions of truth, and communicate what we have experienced to others', witnessing occurs (p. 23). In this respect, the lived experiences of others can affect the audience/reader greatly, thus making witnessing powerful. Further, when CAP is done well, it can evoke and represent the complex emotional texture of human experiences and help researchers to hear the heartbeats of other people, thus providing researchers with insights to human lived experience like none other (Richardson, 2004).

Third, Smith and Sparkes (2009) reveal how it can be a complex task for qualitative researchers to ensure the emotionality of the researcher is valued, where the head of the researched is not cut off from their living body, and feeling, hearing, tasting, breathing, smelling and emotionally witnessing an embodied life is brought to the fore. CAP can help to achieve this by bringing the readers' subjectivity to the foreground and lacing their emotions throughout the text or performance.

Fourth, according to Richardson (2004), CAP has the ability to 'enhance and enrich sense making of the topic in question' (p. 923), particularly since CAP is a method of inquiry where you can find out about yourself or the topic. Richardson (2000, p. 930) says that in CAP, 'the writing process and the writing product' are 'deeply intertwined and both are privileged. The product cannot be separated from the producer or the mode of production or the method of knowing'. Thus, CAP enables qualitative researchers to engage with different genres whether it is literary, artistic or scientific to bring clarity to, or crystallize meaning generated from experiences and relationships (Richardson, 2000).

CAP is relevant to all disciplines since it generates thinking about the social world (Denzin, 2000) and is well suited for the broad scope of qualitative scholarship that seeks to contextualize lived experiences and address the complexity of life (Richardson & St. Pierre, 2005).

Risks associated with using CAP

Despite such strengths and benefits, CAP is not without some risks and weaknesses. First, according to Wall (2008), some CAP approaches continue to encounter resistance because they do not adhere to traditional research criteria (see Chapter 25). For instance, Macdougall (2007) revealed how using CAP had implications for her in regard to the acceptability and 'publishability' of such personalised accounts by traditional academic journals, which inherently could come to impact upon research careers.

Second, Holt (2003) warns about the use of 'self' as the primary data, as occurs in autoethnographic and autobiographical research. Research that centres on the self has invited criticisms such as 'self-indulgent' and 'navel-gazing'. However, as Sparkes (2002) makes clear, the universal charge that autoethnographic research is self-indulgent is problematic and should be disputed. This is discussed in greater detail below in the autoethnography section.

Third, according to Richardson (1999) the ethics of representation can be particularly problematic when using CAP. Specifically, Richardson warns about disclosure issues associated with writing about such personalised experiences. Particularly when others (i.e. workmates, family friends) who feature in the stories have not given their informed consent (Richardson, 1999), and may be identified deductively through their physical characteristics, attitudes, actions and relationships with others (Smith, forthcoming). However, as Allen-Collinson (2012), Ellis (2004, 2007), Muncey (2010), and Tolich (2010) argue, none of this means that writing and publishing ethical CAP research is impossible. Smith (forthcoming) explains that this is when it is important to go beyond traditional ethics, such as utilitarianism and principalism, and harness also various aspirational ethical positions (see Sparkes & Smith, 2014). Richardson's (1999) disclosure concern can be addressed through the removal of certain features and details of conversations. While the specific strengths and weaknesses of using autoethnography and ethnodrama are outlined further below, these abovementioned general risks associated with using CAP also extend to other areas of CAP research.

Autotethnography

What is autoethnography?

Autoethnography is a type of CAP which allows the researcher to write in the first person, connecting their own personal experiences to the cultural. In this respect, autoethnographic researchers tell stories that are based on their own lived experiences and interactions with others within social contexts, relating the personal to the cultural in the process and product (Smith, forthcoming). Ellis and Bochner (2000) describe autoethnography as an autobiographical genre of writing and research that captures multiple layers of consciousness, connecting the personal to the cultural.

> Back and forth autoethnographers gaze, first through an ethnographic wide-angle lens, focusing outward on social and cultural aspects of their personal experience; then, they look inward, exposing a vulnerable self that is moved by and may move through, refract, and resist cultural interpretations.
>
> *(Ellis & Bochner, 2000, p. 739)*

More recently, Holman Jones, Adams and Ellis (2013) have built on this earlier definition in a way that assists us further to understand autoethnography as a process and a product, and why it is different from other forms of personal life writing, such as autobiography. For them, while all personal writing could be considered an examination of culture, not all forms of personal writing can be classed as autoethnographic. In order to be classified as the latter, according to Holman Jones *et al.*, the following characteristics need to be present in the work: purposefully commenting on/critiquing of culture practices; making contributions to existing research; embracing vulnerability with a purpose; and creating a reciprocal relationship with audiences in order to compel a response. These characteristics clearly indicate what is required from an autoethnographic piece of work if it is to be worthy of the name and judged as such. Together, the characteristics also highlight that an autoethnography is different from an autobiography.

As Holman Jones *et al.* suggest, if the author writes to tell a story to illustrate an experience, but does not interrogate the nuances of this experience in the light of general cultural phenomena and cultural practices, then the author writes *autobiographically*. Allen-Collinson and Hockey (2008) likewise note the differences.

> Because of the detailed and systematic examination of experiences within the research-er's life that aim to illuminate wider cultural/subcultural aspects, one of the distinctive features of autoethnography as an investigative process lies in its efforts to combine detailed field notes with 'head notes', the researcher's highly reflexive account of engaging with the research process.
>
> *(Allen-Collinson & Hockey, 2008, p. 211)*

Allen-Collinson (2012) further explains how culture is central to autoethnography in the way that autoethnographers write highly readable, insightful and thought-provoking work, 'vividly bringing alive sub/cultural experiences for those unfamiliar with the social terrain under study' (p. 205). She also echoes the crucial point that autoethnography needs to contribute to a schol-arly conversation.

Why use autoethnography?

There are multiple benefits for utilizing autoethnography. First, Sparkes (1999) reveals how autoethnography has benefits for not only the teller but also diverse audiences by assisting them to see 'actual worlds' more clearly. For the audience specifically, it is invited to come into the teller's world, exposing it to alternate ways of knowing by learning from others' experiences with the potential to initiate change.

Second, both Ellis and Bochner (2000) and Sparkes (2002) reveal how autoethnography enables the teller or autoethnographer to display multiple layers of their consciousness. A well-crafted autoethnography is a means of gaining richly textured and nuanced insights into personal lived experience and emotions, and situating these within a wider sociocultural context (Ellis & Bochner, 2000; Sparkes, 2002). Consequently, much can be learned from autoethnographies in relation to the particular sociocultural processes, experiences, emotions and realities involved in the unfolding of physical culture (Sparkes, 2002; Smith, forthcoming).

Third, Smith (forthcoming) explains how autoethnographies, unlike more traditional ways of writing up research, are highly accessible to the general public and to diverse audiences. Because of the storied nature of autoethnography, they can be easily understood and engaged with. In so doing, autoethnography provides the audience with an 'insider' perspective to a culture and access to in-depth and often highly nuanced meanings, knowledge about, and lived experience of the field of study (Smith, forthcoming).

Fourth, McMahon and Penney (2011) as well as Hickey and Austin (2007) reveal how autoethnography opens up possibilities for the teller to be critically reflexive wherein their senses of self and agency are able to be better understood in terms of the social processes that mediate their lived experience. McMahon and Penney (2011) found that those who engaged with autoethnography had an opportunity to organise their lived experiences 'into temporally meaningful episodes' (Polkinghorne, 1988, p. 1), thus bringing about catharsis and emancipa-tion in and through the autoethnographic process.

Fifth, Allen-Collinson (2012) reveals that because the autoethnographic genre is open to a vast range of styles and usages, 'this openness to different forms, and refusal to be pigeonholed, is perhaps one of the great strengths of autoethnographic research' (p. 196).

Given such strengths, it is no surprise that a growing number of qualitative researchers have made use of authoethnography, with notable contributions by Sparkes (1996, 2003a, 2003b) as well as Smith (1999), Gilbourne (2002), Brown, Gilbourne and Claydon (2009), and Caudwell (2011), among others.

Risks of using autoethnography

While the benefits of utilising autoethnography are immense, there are some inherent risks when employing such an approach. First, Smith (forthcoming), as well as Bochner and Ellis (2001), reveal how autoethnographic researchers may be accused of producing self-indulgent research. This may, in some instances, be the case. However, as Sparkes (2002) argues, not all autoethnographies are self-indulgent. The likes of Smith (forthcoming) and Bochner and Ellis (2001) have argued how well-crafted autoethnographies can move beyond the navel-gazing individual to a more in-depth analysis in which lived experience is connected to the surrounding sociocultural structures. Furthermore, Sparkes (2002) argues how autoethnographies extend beyond the self and can initiate empathy and connection, which can in turn contribute to an understanding of a particular culture.

Second, Smith (forthcoming) says that 'doing' autoethnographic research is not easy and can be difficult. This is because autoethnographic research requires high levels of critical awareness, self-discipline and reflexivity from the researcher. He further adds that strong literary writing skills are essential to craft a high quality autoethnography. Likewise, Allen-Collinson says that there is the need for the autoethnographic researcher to possess high levels of critical awareness, reflexivity and self-discipline. She says:

> Of particular interest to autoethnographers in sport and physical culture has been a focus on embodiment and lived sporting experience, together with the emotional dimension of engagement in physical cultures. Autoethnographers seek systematically, rigorously and analytically to portray their own consciousness and emotions, to open up the realm of the interior and the personal.
>
> *(Allen-Collinson, 2012, p. 5)*

Given such strengths and risks, researchers need to consider the balance between these. For example, do the risks outweigh the strengths, and if so, should an autoethnography be then chosen. In other words, as part of making informed choices about how to do research, researchers need to consider both the strengths and weaknesses. As part of making informed choices, a researcher also needs to consider which specific type of CAP are most appropriate and suitable to to utilize.

Different types of autoethnography

There are various ways to communicate autoethnographic research which including written, performed, visually communicated, digitally produced, and so on (Smith, forthcoming). There are also various strands of autoethnography. The autoethnographic genre is open to a vast range of styles and usages (Allen-Collinson, 2012). The different strands and uses of autoethnography that have developed over the years have come to include evocative autoethnography, analytical autoethnography, meta-autoethnography, performance autoethnography and collaborative autoethnography.

Evocative Autoethnography can also be referred to as emotional autoethnography. Ellis and Bochner (2006) describe evocative autoethnography as a literary approach to research that seeks to *show* rather than *tell* through emotionally driven written accounts. Smith (forthcoming) reveals how the objective of evocative autoethnography is *evocation*, where the reader/audience is invited to feel an emotional resonance with the teller, as well as an understanding of the culture central to the story being told. In this respect, evocative autoethnography is a typical representation of CAP research because those who make use of it are committed to a compelling description of subjective emotional lived experience with an intention of creating an emotional resonance and empathy with the reader (Smith, forthcoming; Ellis & Bochner, 2000). Smith (forthcoming) explains how evocative autoethnography has been utilized to detail a broad cross-section of subjects including, illness, health, disability in sport, sports injury, marginalization in sport, and other emotionally charged sport and exercise experiences. It is no surprise that numerous researchers, such as Owton and Sparkes (2015), McMahon and Dinan-Thompson (2011), Smith (2013), and Ellis (2014) to name a few, have made use of evocative autoethnography because of its capacity to impact powerfully upon the reader with the possibility of resulting action.

Despite its significant benefits, evocative autoethnography still encounters some resistance. For example, Anderson (2006) expresses his concerns of 'evocative or emotional autoethnography', saying:

> It may have unintended consequence of eclipsing other visions of what autoethnography can be and of obscuring the ways in which it may fit productively in other traditions of social inquiry. An obvious weakness would be the failure to meet traditional social science research criteria.
>
> *(Anderson, 2006, p. 374)*

However, as Allen-Collinson (2012) aptly points out, those researchers seeking to 'adhere to the traditional triad of evaluation criteria appropriate to the scientific method . . . autoethnographic research would not provide a suitable methodology, and indeed has no concern with fulfilling these criteria' (p. 22). What autoethnographies do instead is call on different criteria, such as evocation, as part of an ongoing list of ways to judge the quality of the research (see Chapter 25).

Analytic autoethnography is not dissimilar to evocative autoethnography in the respect that a key aim of the approach is to deliver evocative stories (Smith, forthcoming). However, a significant difference for analytic autoethnography is that the autoethnographer produces a theoretical analysis of the story, whereas in an emotional autoethnography this is resisted. As Barone (2000) might say, the analytic autoethnographer seeks direct control over the interpretations placed on a story in the act of reading, listening, watching, and so on. In this respect, analytic autoethnography represents a more 'traditional scientific' autoethnographic approach, with a focus both on telling readers what the tale is about and how it should, ideally, be read. Anderson (2006) explains how the purpose of analytic autoethnography is not simply to document personal experience, provide an insider's perspective or evoke emotional resonance with the reader, but rather to 'use empirical data to gain insight into some broader set of social phenomena than those provided by the data themselves' (p. 387). Anderson (2006) says that an obvious strength of analytic autoethnography would be its attempt to conform to traditional social science criteria by placing an emphasis on formalised scientific rhetoric and method. However, Ellis and Bochner (2006) warn that analytic autoethnography is a mere attempt to shift autoethnography away from its more innovative, personally engaged and emotional forms and back towards the more traditional, (neo)realist, ethnographic content and style. For them, then, analytic autoethnographers act as the story analyst which is problematic because:

if you turn a story told into a story analysed . . . you sacrifice the story at the altar of traditional sociological rigor. You transform the story into another language, the language of generalization and analysis, and thus you lose the very qualities that make a story a story.

(Ellis & Bochner, 2006, p. 440)

Despite such criticisms, analytic autoethnography remains a viable option for researchers. Researchers who have made use of analytic autoethnography include McGannon (2012) in her story of her exercise identity and running experiences, Chawansky (2015) in her sport, development and peace research, Fisette (2015) in her tale of injury, illness and a performing identity, and Zehntner and McMahon's (2014) investigation into the relationships of power that Zehntner experienced as a swimming coach.

Meta-Autoethnography is an other type of autoethnography that builds on previous autoethnographic work (Smith, forthcoming). It is a reflexive approach which enables an autoethnographer to re-interpret and reflect upon existing or past autoethnographic representations with the opportunity to re-story them. Thus, Ellis (2009) terms meta-autoethnography as a 'story of the stories where by the autoethnographer uses hindsight or benefit of greater life experience to reflect, expand or build upon previous autoethnographic representations' (p. 12). She explains how in the meta-autoethnographic process, the autoethnographer will revisit original representations 'consider responses, and write an autoethnographic account about autoethnography' (p. 13). Meta-autoethnography is useful for autoethnographers because it provides them with opportunities to alter the frame in which the original story was written by asking questions that were not asked originally. Meta-autoethnography considers others' responses to the original account, as well as vignettes of related experiences that have happened since the original account was constructed, which could have impacted invariably the way the story could be interpreted in the present day (Ellis, 2009). This kind of autoethnography provides researchers, and readers with the opportunity to look back at the original autoethnographic account with the benefit of distance and greater experience of life. Thus, the meta-autoethnographic process is potentially powerful as it enables autoethnographers to 're-examine, and re-vision' (Ellis, 2009, p. 12) previous autoethnographic work making use of alternate reflective lenses that stem from the complexity that is lived experience. Importantly, the process of meta-autoethnography prevents autoethnographers from remaining fixed to the interpretations they have stated or settled on in the past (Ellis, 2009).

Despite its benefits, researchers have made little use of meta- autoethnography. Exceptions include the work of Ellis (2009), and Chatham-Carpenter (2010). For Chatham-Carpenter (2010), meta-auotethnography was utilized to reflect on her ongoing battles with anorexia with positive results. Upon reflection and re-engagement with her original autoethnography, Chatham-Carpenter (2010) revealed that her compulsion to publish became intertwined with the compulsion of her anorexia as she ultimately protected herself as a researcher in the process of publishing an autoethnography about the eating disorder. The meta-autoethnographic approach assisted her to understand how her original autoethnographic accounts were somewhat controlled accounts as she felt she needed to present a certain 'face' as a researcher. Chatham-Carpenter claimed that the meta-autoethnographic process of writing and rewriting helped her to come to terms with her compulsions to control her anorexia and how she expressed it in the original autoethnographic accounts. This invariably led her to rewrite a new plot about her life.

Performance autoethnography is where the autoethnographer/story teller/researcher can be likened to the lead actor in their own story through a theatrical performance. It is about bringing to life or to the stage/theatre transcribed or text-based lived experience. The lead actor enacts the performance in a storied form, particularly in terms of the specific cultural context within the performance. Gergen and Gergen (2001) explain how performance autoethnography enables the teller to expand their mode of expression through the telling which invariably expands the number of people who can join in the 'dance of understanding' (p. 19). Mienczakowski (2001) highlights how performance autoethnography has the potential to make things clearer through a different mode of presentation rather than through a traditional text. Like all other types of autoethnography, performance autoethnography is often a solo endeavour however it is performed.

Collaborative autoethnography, or what is sometimes also termed ***duo autoethnography***, is a dual or multiple autoethnographic collaborations. It can take the form of an evocative autoethnography, analytical autoethnography or meta-autoethnography, but to class it as collaborative, the autoethnography needs to be produced by more than one researcher. Smith (forthcoming) explains how when there is the option for two or more people working together to craft an autography for certain purposes, this is known as a collaborative autoethnography or duo autoethnography. In dual or multiple collaborations, autoethnographers work in tandem to show dialogically the interconnections between the personal and the cultural through the construction of individual stories of experience. Through this collaborative process, the stories are combined resulting in a collective piece. Collaborative autoethnography enables those involved in the process to make sense of their lived experience, both individually and also as a collective.

Collaborative autoethnographers are not restricted to a rigid process of collaboration, but rather adopt various models in the collaboration process. For instance, collaborative encounters can occur at various stages of the writing process, whether it is at the end or occurring continuously throughout the construction of autoethnographic stories (Scarfe & Marlow, 2015). Ngunjiri, Hernandez and Chang (2010) say that whether collaboration is done fully or partially, the cooperative aspect of data collection is the driving force behind collaborative autoethnography. Allen-Collinson and Hockey (2008), who made use of collaborative autoethnography, revealed how for them a 'sense-making at the phenomenological, interactional and analytic levels' occurred, thus providing unique insights into their lived-body experiences (p. 209). As such, the process of collaborative autoethnography had a profound impact on them, as they were both injured runners suffering from long-term knee injuries at the same time and they were able to detail the frustration, pain and suffering associated with being injured. However, serendipitously, through the process of collaboration, emancipatory potential was realised (Allen-Collinson & Hockey, 2008).

Ethnodrama

What is ethnodrama?

An ethnodrama is a word that joins ethnography and drama (Saldana, 2011). Specifically, it is a written playscript consisting of dramatized, significant selections of narrative collected through interview transcripts, participant observation field notes, journals, documents, statistics, and so on (McMahon & McGannon, in press; Smith & Sparkes, 2009). Mienczakowski and Moore (2008) explain how 'ethnodrama is a method and a methodology that combines qualitative research processes with action research, grounded theory and narrative to provide data from which a script can be written' (p. 451). In this respect, an ethnodrama is solely textual and those who make use of it do not force the data to be something that it is not (Smith & Sparkes, 2009). Producers of ethnodramas aim to communicate research in a way that remains genuine to the researched, thus remaining faithful to the veracity of the data or the lived experience (Smith and Sparkes, 2009).

An ethnodrama is not limited to just one teller or actor but may include a number of characters or participants' voices and stories. In this respect, an ethnodrama has the ability to capture language occurring from multiple dimensions along with feelings, thoughts, tensions and inner monologue/s of the participants, with the intention of provoking reader/audience emotion and evocation (McMahon, Penney & Dinan-Thompson, 2012).

Why use ethnodrama?

First, as Smith (forthcoming) suggests, combining photographs, quotes, thoughts, stories and practices into a theatrical script has the capacity to enhance the richness of the data collected and analysed. In this respect, ethnodrama as an approach can be an immensely powerful way of representing real life encounters. Second, Smith and Sparkes (2009), as well as Mason and Davies (2009), state that ethnodrama has the potential to enable the reader to understand the story being told in a different format from that of a traditional written report (e.g. realist tale), further expanding the capacity to reach a greater diversity of audience/readers. Reader impact is thus an inherent benefit of ethnodrama in that the very act of reading, feeling and experiencing through the ethnodrama script has the potential to enable the reader to feel empathy by relating to, and in a sense (re)living, while not enduring, the lived experiences of what is presented (McMahon *et al.*, 2012). It can also communicate complex knowledge in clear, evocative and insightful ways. In so doing, the opportunities to make a difference and generate impact can be enhanced.

Risks associated with using ethnodrama

While the benefits of using ethnodrama are plentiful, Mienczakowski and Moore (2008) reveal the double-edged sword of using ethnodrama. They warn researchers to be mindful of audience impact, in particular how the story might impact upon the audience or the reader particularly, because of its inherent ability to evoke emotion (Mienczakowski & Moore, 2008). Whereas audience impact is also considered a strength of ethnodrama, particularly in terms of how it can evoke audience/reader emotion and a new way of knowing, there is a need to take into account the unwanted, unintended or uncontrollable responses to the performance (Mienczakowski & Moore, 2008). Sparkes and Smith (2014) also reveal another inherent risk in that 'if ethnodrama/theatre is done badly, then none of its potential will be realised. In fact, it might turn people away from engaging with the important issues the data raised' (p. 167).

Despite its significant benefits balanced against the risks, 'ethnodrama' has been made use of by only a handful of scholars in the specific realm of sport and exercise. Cassidy, Kidman and Dudfield (2015), McMahon and McGannon (in press), Sykes, Chapman and Swedberg (2006) and McMahon *et al.* (2012) are researchers who have inadvertently responded to Denzin's (1997) call for performative social sciences. For example, McMahon *et al.* (2012) made use of ethnodrama to specifically present three adolescent swimmers' experiences, the exposure and effect of body practices on the swimmers. The swimmers became the main actors of the theatrical script and their lived experiences were presented as a series of vignettes in a theatrical format, making up two Acts. Each vignette was told through a theatrical and ethnographic lens, with the reader invited into the swimmer's personal story, relating to, but not having to endure their experience (McMahon *et al.*, 2012).

More recently, Cassidy *et al.* (2015) made use of ethnodrama to detail a national sporting organisation [NSO] coaching director's attempt to create a coach development programme that was consistent with the principles of New Zealand's coach development framework. Below is an example of the ethnodrama produced by Cassidy *et al.* (2015).

ACT THREE: Coachpoints

Narrator:	SPARC[1] tried to encourage staff in Regional Sports Trusts (RST) and NSOs to share ideas by financially assisting the collaboration. The following scene occurred in Koru Club (the lounge in New Zealand airports for frequent flyers of Air New Zealand) and documents an informal discussion that occurred between Bob and two other coaching directors, one of whom was located in a RST and the other in a NSO. The discussion focused on potential ways to recognise formal and informal coach learning and development that reflected the philosophy of the new CDF.
Bob:	You know, I always fly Air New Zealand because I get rewarded and recognition through their air points system. Lately I have been thinking . . . what is the rationale behind such a system?
Becky:	I don't really know, but I know I'm enjoying this Sauvignon Blanc.
John:	Umm free drinks in the lounge! No, in all seriousness, it is a brand loyalty scheme, building up affiliation by giving customers rewards. Why do you ask?

(Cassidy, Kidman & Dudfield, 2015, p. 9)

Ethnotheatre

What is ethnotheatre?

Ethnotheatre, a word joining ethnography and theatre, goes beyond research that is presented as text and is research that is actually performed (Saldana, 2011). In this respect, ethnotheatre is a live or mediated performance event which can centre on either research participants' experiences and/or the researchers' interpretations of data. Smith (forthcoming) explains how in ethnotheatre, the researcher employs the traditional craft and artistic techniques of theatre or media production for an audience. McMahon *et al.* (2012) reveal how the staging of data provides researchers with the opportunity to bring to life or to the stage lived experience in the theatrical sense. Ethnotheatre may include a number of characters or actors (participants) that invariably engage with the audience and each other through monologue and dialogue, and scenes that may contain elements of dramatic tension. Despite its dramatic potential, as well as potential to impact the audience, ethnotheatre has not been greatly used with the exception of Spry (2001), as well as Gergen and Gergen (2011, 2014).

Why use ethnotheatre?

First, Bochner and Ellis (2001) explain that through performance, research ultimately becomes more accessible for social action and cultural transformation. Not unlike ethnodrama, ethnotheatre enables the audience to understand the story being told in a different format from that of a traditional written report, thus expanding the capacity to reach a greater diversity of audience

(Smith & Sparkes, 2009). In this respect, Bochner and Ellis (2001) say that through performance, research becomes more accessible for social action and cultural transformation.

Second, according to Gergen and Gergen (2014), performative research such as ethnotheatre enables the entire repertoire of cultural discourses to be represented through the play/ performance, 'including space for otherwise de-legitimated or marginalized discourses to be heard' (p. 214). To achieve this, the researcher can make use of a range of genres, styles, dialects, tropes and forms of communicating (Gergen & Gergen, 2014).

Risks associated with using ethnotheatre

While the dramatic potential of staging 'real-life' experiences is plentiful and may appear straightforward, this can be far from the case. The staging of 'real-life' experiences requires proficiency and practise by the actors or performers so they are acutely aware of the prospective tensions inherent in seeking to retain authenticity and portray the lived encounters as they actually occurred (Spry, 2001; Gergen & Gergen, 2011). As has been seen to occur in traditional research, converting observations of people's actions to numbers is generally no more or less accurate than elaborating on the quality of their experiences (Gergen & Gergen, 2014). Necessarily, a series of communications among the researcher, the researched and the actors may need to be ongoing to overcome such an issue. Acting experience is a necessary requirement in the execution of such performances. Such issues would not be encountered in the construction of an ethnodrama (i.e. theatrical script), where the performance is text-based rather than dependent on the actor's ability to execute a scene. Like Sparkes and Smith (2014) reveal in regard to ethnodrama, if ethnotheatre 'is done badly, then none of its potential will be realised. In fact, it might turn people away from engaging with the important issues the data raised' (p. 167).

Future of CAP

Representing lived experience forms the foundation for the employment of CAP, particularly after the claims of the crisis of representation in qualitative research (Denzin & Lincoln, 2000). This chapter has been dedicated to outlining CAP with the focus being on CAP research that brings to the fore lived experience in unique and creative ways. While Wall (2008) and Macdougall (2007) have highlighted how CAP research has encountered some resistance from those who adhere to traditional research criteria, CAP has come a long way recently in terms of acceptability by a greater number of academics, critics and publication outlets. With many journals now starting to bring in virtual issues, and with digital research now available (see Chapter 27), the possible opportunities for CAP researchers are expanded in that there is potential for performance-based CAP research, such as ethnotheatre or performance autoethnography, to be recorded and considered for scholarly publication to relevant outlets with virtual, digital issues. Audience impact has been recognised by CAP researchers such as Richardson (2004), Sparkes (1999), Smith (forthcoming) and McMahon *et al.* (2012), and the potential of having recorded performance research accessible through virtual issues will only impact a greater number of, and more diverse audiences. The future of CAP therefore appears bright.

I hope this chapter encourages researchers to not only consider more traditional forms of CAP, like autoethnography, but also to creatively expand the repertoire in ways that enrich scholarly dialogues and make a difference in our social worlds. Indeed, CAP can do much more than reveal 'what is' by moving people in spaces that open up vistas of 'what could be'. In so doing, our possibilities for growth, change and different ways of being can be expanded.

Note

1 Sport and Recreation New Zealand (SPARC) was the government agency dedicated to fostering a sport and recreation environment. In 2012 SPARC was replaced by Sport New Zealand.

References

Allen-Collinson, J. (2012). Autoethnography: Situating personal sporting narratives in socio-cultural contexts. In K. Young & M. Atkinson (Eds.), *Qualitative research on sport and physical culture* (pp. 191–212). Bingley, UK: Emerald.

Allen-Collinson, J. & Hockey, J. (2008). Autoethnography as 'valid' methodology? A study of disrupted identity narratives. *The International Journal of Interdisciplinary Social Sciences*, 3(6), 209–217.

Anderson, L. (2006). Analytic autoethnography. *Journal of Contemporary Ethnography*, 35(4), 373–395. doi: 10.1177/0891241605280449.

Barone, T. (2000). *Aesthetics, politics, and educational inquiry.* New York: Peter Lang.

Bochner, A. & Ellis C. (2001). *Ethnographically speaking: Autoethnography, literature, and aesthetics.* New York: Rowman & Littlefield.

Brown, G., Gilbourne, D. & Claydon, J. (2009). When a career ends: A short story. *Reflective Practice*, 10(4), 491–500. doi: 10.1080/14623940903138340.

Cassidy, T., Kidman, L. & Dudfield, O. (2015). Insights into the process of creating a coach development programme: The opportunities and challenges of ethnodrama. *Qualitative Research in Sport, Exercise and Health*, 7, 589–605. doi: 10.1080/2159676X.2015.1012545.

Caudwell, J. (2011). 'Easy, Oar!': Rowing reflections. *Qualitative Research in Sport, Exercise and Health*, 3(2), 117–129. doi: 10.1080/2159676X.2011.572179.

Chatham-Carpenter, A. (2010). Do thyself no harm: Protecting ourselves as autoethnographers. *Journal of Research Practice*, 6(1), Article M1.

Chawansky, M. (2015). You're juicy: Autoethnography as evidence in sport for development and peace (SDP) research. *Qualitative Research in Sport, Exercise and Health*, 7(1), 1–12. doi: 10.1080/2159676X.2014.893900.

Denzin, N. K. (1997). *Interpretive ethnography: Ethnographic practices for the 21st century.* Thousand Oaks, CA: Sage.

Denzin, N. K. (2000). Aesthics and the practices of qualitative inquiry. *Qualitative Inquiry*, 6(2), 256–265. doi: 10.1177/107780040000600208.

Denzin, N. K. & Lincoln, Y. S. (2000). The policies and practices of interpretation. In N. K. Denzin & Y. S. Lincoln (Eds.), *Handbook of qualitative research* (2nd ed., pp. 897–992). Thousand Oaks, CA: Sage.

Ellis, C. (2004). *The ethnographic I.* Walnut Creek, CA: Altamira Press.

Ellis, C. (2007). Telling secrets, revealing lives: Relational ethics in research with intimate others. *Qualitative Inquiry*, 13(1), 3–29.

Ellis, C. (2009). *Revision: Autoethnographic reflections on life and work.* Walnut Creek, CA: Left Coast Press.

Ellis, C. (2014). No longer hip: Losing my balance and adapting to what ails me. *Qualitative Research in Sport, Exercise and Health*, 6(1), 1–19. doi: 10.1080/2159676X.2014.880505.

Ellis, C. & Bochner, A. (2000). Autoethnography, personal narrative, reflexivity: Researcher as subject. In N. K. Denzin & Y. S. Lincoln (Eds.), *Handbook of qualitative research* (pp. 733–768). London: Sage.

Ellis, C. & Bochner, A. (2006). Analysing analytic autoethnography: An autopsy. *Journal of Contemporary Ethnography*, 35(4), 429–449. doi: 10.1177/0891241606286979.

Fisette, J. (2015). The marathon journey of my body-self and performing identity. *Sociology of Sport Journal*, 32(1), 68–88.

Gergen, K. J. & Gergen, M. M. (2001). Ethnographic presentation as relationship. In A. Bochner & C. Ellis (Eds.), *Ethnographically speaking: Autoethnography, literature, and aesthetics* (pp. 11–33). New York: Rowman & Littlefield.

Gergen, K. J. & Gergen, M. M. (2014). Mischief, mystery and moments that matter: Vistas of performative inquiry. *Qualitative Inquiry*, 20(2), 213–221. doi: 10.1177/1077800413519074.

Gergen, M. M. & Gergen, K. J. (2011). Performative social science and psychology. *Qualitative Social Research*, 12(1). Article 11. Retrieved from: http://www.qualitative-research.net/index.php/fqs/article/view/1595/3105.

Gilbourne, D. (2002). Sports participation, sports injury and images of self: An autobiographical narrative of a life-long legacy. *Reflective Practice*, *3*(1), 71–78. doi: 10.1080/14623940220129889.

Hickey, A. & Austin, J. (2007). Pedagogies of self: Conscientising the personal to the social. *International Journal of Pedagogies and Learning*, *3*(1), 21–29. doi: 10.5172/ijpl.3.1.21.

Holman Jones, S., Adams, T. & Ellis, C. (2013). Coming to know autoethnography as more than a method. In S. Holman Jones, T. Adams & C. Ellis (Eds.), *Handbook of autoethnography* (pp. 17–48). Walnut Creek, CA: Left Coast Press.

Holt, N. (2003). Representation, legitimation, and autoethnography: An autoethnographic writing story. *International Journal of Qualitative Methods*, *2*(1), 1–22.

Macdougall, N. (2007). The permeable self: Making connections through personal experience. *The International Journal of Interdisciplinary Social Sciences*, *2*(4), 213–222.

Mason, J. & Davies, K. (2009). Coming to our senses? A critical approach to sensory methodology. *Qualitative Research*, *9*(5), 587–603. doi: 10.1177/1468794109343628.

McGannon, K. R. (2012). Am 'I' a work of art(?): Understanding exercise and the self through critical self-awareness and aesthetic self-stylisation. *Athletic Insight*, *4*(1), 79–95.

McMahon, J. & Dinan-Thompson, M. (2011). Body work – Regulation of a swimmer body: An authoethnography from an Australian elite swimmer. *Sport, Education and Society*, *16*(1), 35–50. doi: 10.1080/13573322.2011.531960.

McMahon, J. & McGannon, K. R. (in press). Slim to win: An ethnodrama of three elite swimmers' 'presentation of self' in relation to a dominant cultural ideology. *Sociology of Sport Journal*. doi: 10.1123/ssj.2015-0166.

McMahon, J. & Penney, D. (2011). Narrative ethnography and autoethnography: Empowering athletes and their bodies in and through research. *Qualitative Research in Sport, Exercise and Health*, *3*(2), 130–151. doi: 10.1080/2159676X.2011.572176.

McMahon, J., Penney, D. & Dinan-Thompson, M. (2012). Body practices: Exposure and effect of a sporting culture? Stories from three Australian swimmers. *Sport, Education and Society*, *17*(2), 181–206. doi: 10.1080/13573322.2011.607949.

Mienczakowski, J. (2001). Ethnodrama: Performed research – limitations and potential. In P. Atkinson, A. Coffey, S. Delamont *et al.* (Eds.), *Handbook of ethnography* (pp. 468–476). London: Sage.

Mienczakowski, J. & Moore, T. (2008). Performing data with notions of responsibility. In J. Knowles & A. Cole (Eds.), *Handbook of the arts in qualitative research* (pp. 451–458). London: Sage.

Muncey, S. (2010). *Creating autoethnographies*. London: Sage.

Ngunjiri, F., Hernandez, K. & Chang, H. (2010). Living autoethnography: Connecting life and research. *Journal of Research Practice*, *6*(1). Article E1.

Owton, H. & Sparkes, A. C. (2015). Sexual abuse and the grooming process in sport: Learning from Bella's story. *Sport, Education and Society*. doi: 10.1080/13573322.2015.1063484.

Parry, D. & Johnson, C. (2007). Contextualising leisure research to encompass complexity in lived leisure experience: The need for creative analytical practice. *Leisure Sciences*, *29*(2), 119–130. doi: 10.1080/01490400601160721.

Polkinghorne, D. (1988). *Narrative knowing and the human sciences*. New York: State University of New York Press.

Richardson, L. (1999). Feathers in our cap. *Journal of Contemporary Ethnography*, *28*(6), 660–668. doi: 10.1177/089124199129023767.

Richardson, L. (2000). Writing: A method of inquiry. In N. Denzin & Y. Lincoln (Eds.), *Handbook of qualitative research* (2nd ed., pp. 923–948). London: Sage.

Richardson, L. (2004). Creative Analytical Practice (CAP) ethnography. In M. Lewis-Beck, A. Bryman & T. Futing Liao (Eds.), *The Sage encyclopaedia of social science research methods* (pp. 212–213). Thousand Oaks, CA: Sage.

Richardson, L. & St. Pierre, E. A. (2005). Writing: A method of inquiry. In N. Denzin & Y. Lincoln (Eds.), *Handbook of qualitative research* (3rd ed., pp. 959–978). Thousand Oaks, CA: Sage.

Ropers-Huilman, B. (1999). Witnessing: Critical inquiry in a poststructural world. *International Journal of Qualitative Studies in Education*, *12*(1), 21–35. doi: 10.1080/095183999236312.

Saldana, J. (2011). *Ethnotheatre: Research from page to stage*. New York: Oxford University Press.

Scarfe, S. & Marlow, C. (2015). Overcoming the fear: An autoethnographic narrative of running with epilepsy. *Qualitative Research in Sport, Exercise and Health*, *7*, 688–697.

Smith, B. (1999). Exploring depression through a narrative of the self. *Qualitative Inquiry*, *5*(2), 264–279. doi: 10.1177/107780049900500206.

Smith, B. (2013). Artificial persons and the academy: A story. In N. Short, L. Turner & A. Grant (Eds.), *Contemporary British autoethnography* (pp. 187–202). Rotterdam: Sense publishers.

Smith, B. (forthcoming). Narrative inquiry and autoethnography. In M. Silk, D. Andrews & H. Thorpe (Eds.), *Handbook of physical cultural studies*. London: Routledge.

Smith, B. & Sparkes, A. C. (2009). Narrative analysis and sport and exercise psychology: Understanding lives in diverse ways. *Psychology of sport and exercise, 10*(2), 279–288.

Sparkes, A. C. (1996). 'The fatal flaw': A narrative of the fragile body-self. *Qualitative Inquiry, 2*(4), 463–495. doi: 10.1177/107780049600200405.

Sparkes, A. C. (1999). Exploring body narratives. *Sport, Education and Society, 4*(1), 17–30. doi: 10.1080/1357332990040102.

Sparkes, A. C. (2002). *Telling tales in sport and physical activity: A qualitative journey.* Champaign, IL: Human Kinetics Press.

Sparkes, A. C. (2003a). Bodies, identities, selves: Autoethnographic fragments and reflections. In J. Denison & P. Markula (Eds.), *Moving writing: Crafting movement in sport and research* (pp. 51–76). New York: Peter Lang.

Sparkes, A. C. (2003b). From performance to impairment: A patchwork of embodied memories. In J. Evans, B. Davies & J. Wright (Eds.), *Body knowledge and control* (pp. 157–172). London: Routledge.

Sparkes, A. C. (2013). Autoethnography at the will of the body: Reflections on a failure to produce on time. In N. Short, L. Turner & A. Grant (Eds.), *Contemporary British autoethnography* (pp. 203–212). Rotterdam: Sense.

Sparkes, A. C. & Smith, B. (2014). *Qualitative research methods in sport, exercise and health: From process to product.* London: Routledge.

Spry, T. (2001). Performing autoethnography: An embodied methodological praxis. *Qualitative Inquiry, 7*(6), 706–732. doi: 10.1177/107780040100700605.

Sykes, H., Chapman, J. & Swedberg, A. (2006). Performed ethnography. In D. Andrews, D. Mason & M. Silk (Eds.), *Qualitative methods in sports studies* (pp. 185–202). Oxford, UK: Berg.

Tolich, M. (2010). A critique of current practice: Ten foundational guidelines for autoethnographers. *Qualitative Health Research, 20*(12), 1599–1610.

Wall, S. (2008). Easier said than done: Writing an autoethnography. *International Journal of Qualitative Methods, 7*(1), 38–53.

Zehntner, C. & McMahon, J. A. (2014). Mentoring in coaching: The means of correct training? An autoethnographic exploration of one Australian swimming coach's experiences. *Qualitative research in Sport, Exercise and Health, 18*(3), 1–21. doi: 10.1080/2159676X.2013.809376.

24

ETHICS IN SPORT AND EXERCISE RESEARCH

From research ethics committees to ethics in the field

Catherine Palmer

Ethical conduct is an essential part of all research. For researchers undertaking qualitative research projects, the processes and practices of ethical conduct are often understood and applied quite differently from those undertaking quantitative research. Taking the idea of an "ethical chain" as its point of departure, this chapter explores some of the ethical considerations that may accompany what Guillemin and Gillam refer to as "procedural ethics"; that is, "the ethical rules and guidelines monitored and approved by ethics committees," as well as "ethics in practice" (2004, p. 263). As part of thinking about ethics as process, the chapter also highlights some of the practical realities and potential pitfalls that qualitative researchers may encounter when undertaking fieldwork (i.e., interviews, participant-observation and ethnographic research) in sport and exercise-based settings.

While the idea of an ethical chain may suggest a linear order to how the procedures and practices of ethics may unfold, the chain metaphor underscores the interlinking and iterative nature of the two in that it alludes to the ways in which links can be lengthened or shortened, or indeed broken, a reflection of the sometimes mercurial and unpredictable nature of qualitative research. Importantly, the ethical chain is underscored at every step by the researcher's own position. That is, we also need to pay attention to our own research *practice*, to be mindful of our own position(s) in our research sites, as well as our own biographies and their potential to impact (positively and negatively) on the situations and interactions we may encounter in the field (see King-White, 2013; Ortiz, 2005; Pavlidis & Olive, 2014; Potroc *et al.*, 2013; Taylor, 2011).

This idea of the ethical chain or "ethics at every step" is a useful guide for thinking about the pinch points in a qualitative research process, where ethical concerns may become more or less apparent. Beginning with "procedural ethics" as the first link in the ethical chain, this encompasses navigating institutional review boards or human research ethics committees, moving through to concerns relating to "ethics in practice," such as entering research sites, doing research with vulnerable people, undertaking covert research and research on illegal behaviors, autoethnography (see Chapter 23), and "insider" research, as well as the ethics of writing about and disseminating our research findings (see Figure 24.1).

Figure 24.1 The ethical chain.

Procedural ethics

The starting point in the chain, albeit one returned to throughout the research process, is the way in which ethics themselves are conceptualized. All human interaction has an ethical dimension to it and, for the most part, "ethics" implies simply "doing the right thing"; that is, acting with respect and concern for those around you. The protection of the rights and interests of research subjects has been recognized internationally in the Nuremberg Code (1947) and the World Medical Assembly's Declaration of Helsinki (first printed 1965; last revised, 2008). This basic assumption that researchers will "do the right thing" by their research participants is the starting point for many of the national statements on ethical conduct in human research (NHMRC, 2007; SRA, 2003). Such statements were also developed in recognition that some research projects such as the Tuskegee Experiment have done irreparable damage to their participants.[1]

The basic assumption here – of "doing the right thing" – also alerts us to the broad category of *traditional ethical positions* in qualitative research that start from a principle of *universal utilitarianism*, or that the research that is undertaken will "produce the greatest good for the greatest number" (Miller *et al.*, 2012; Sparkes & Smith, 2014). This utilitarian approach to research ethics, which emphasizes that the "greatest good for the greatest number" should be a consequence of the research is the principle that guides the decisions of many institutional research boards or human research ethics committees, and many of the mandatory requirements of these boards focus on ensuring that the procedures adopted in the research adequately safeguard the rights of the participants and the outcomes of the research.

Ethical starting points: institutional review boards

For many qualitative researchers, negotiating an institutional review board or human research ethics committee is often the first of the "ethically important moments" (Guillemin & Gillam, 2004) that are encountered in the ethical chain. These boards or committees play a key role in procedural ethics or in setting, monitoring and approving the "rules" of the research that the researcher must follow. The practice of institutional review boards can vary considerably. Kvale and Brinkmann (2009) note that in some countries, qualitative researchers are deemed competent to make an ethical assessment of their own work, whereas in others, the role varies from an advisory one to boards serving as arbitrators of the research process, and as self-appointed guardians and gatekeepers to research sites and subjects.

On the whole, institutional review boards have the responsibility of ensuring that research conforms to national statements on ethical conduct in research, and are charged with approving proposals where the purpose, methods, risks and benefits, and outcomes are outlined to participants, That is, the responsibility of a review board *should* be to review the ethical integrity of a research project across the ethical chain. These "duty ethics of principles" (Miller *et al.*, 2012) have, at one level, a utilitarian concern with the consequences of choosing one action (a method, a choice of research site or subjects, for example) over another, yet at another level, they have a more nuanced concern with the *intent* of that choice; that is, why was that decision made, for what purpose, and to what end? In both cases, however, there is a concern to safeguard the rights of participants in qualitative research, and to regulate how, where, and why the research is used and shared. For ethics in practice this includes researchers being attentive to issues of informed consent, privacy, confidentiality, and monitoring the risks and benefits of participation in the research as they progress along the ethical chain.

The role and remit of review boards, has, however, been brought into question, particularly in relation to qualitative research projects, for several reasons (Hammersley, 2006; Veal & Darcy, 2014). First, review boards often apply a biomedical model to their appraisal of qualitative work, and as a consequence, qualitative research is disadvantaged in the ethics assessment process because biomedical assumptions are imposed on qualitative research (McNamee, 2001). Second, qualitative research embraces an ever-widening range of methods, and thus ethics committees may not always possess the requisite knowledge, either in terms of their practical implementation or, indeed, any ethical questions these new methods may pose (Hesse-Bibber & Leavy, 2010). Third, the mercurial nature of social interaction in qualitative research means that the preplanned, arbitrary rules of ethics approvals don't always work in practice. Indeed, institutional review boards require researchers to anticipate worst-case scenarios, yet unexpected consequences can often be an unexpectedly positive outcome of the research (see Blackman, 2007; Donnelly, 2014). In other words, the criticism is that institutional review boards do not always "get" qualitative research, either methodologically or epistemologically.

Such concerns have been raised with particular reference to research in sport- and exercise-based settings. Olivier and Fishwick (2003) and Brustad (2014) both argue that because research in sports science has been grounded historically in positivist traditions, ethics committees may not be adequately sensitized to the ethical problems posed by qualitative research. Similarly, Hesse-Bibber and Leavy (2010) note that whereas most institutional review boards are relatively up to speed with the ethical tensions implicit in more traditional forms of qualitative research, such as interviews or focus groups, they are less familiar with some of the emergent methods (such as visual [see Chapter 11] and digital techniques [see Chapter 27]), and the ethical dilemmas that these new methods may present for qualitative research undertaken in sport and exercise settings. Working in the field of sport psychology, Krane and Baird argue for greater methodological diversity in this domain and recognize that, accordingly, "new approaches to inquiry require renewed consideration of how to evaluate such research and new responsibilities are placed on readers and evaluators of ethnography and other forms of qualitative inquiry" (2005, p. 101).

Even when readers and evaluators are familiar with the research methods or methodologies being employed, some topics almost inevitably present a particularly challenging set of ethical issues for qualitative researchers to manage and negotiate. A number of researchers have documented their experiences of having their proposals denied by human research ethics committees, or sent back for repeated revisions because their research dealt with illegal or socially deviant behaviors. Sluggett (2007, pp. 25–28), for example, describes how the prospect of interviewing elite athletes about their illegal doping practices and his need to maintain, without exception, confidentiality throughout the project clashed with his review board's ethical values and "rules-based" approach to approving qualitative research with "deviant" research participants.

Along with research that seeks to understand illegal or criminal behaviors in sport and exercise, is covert research; that is, research that is not declared to the research participants and is undertaken without their knowledge or consent, often raises a "red flag" for ethics committees (Calvey, 2008; 2013–2014). Returning to questions of intent, however, covert research is used in qualitative sport and exercise research in situations where it is felt by the researcher that the insights gleaned from the research are deemed to be of such significance that this represents a suitable justification for nondisclosure to participants, and/or where it is felt that there is no other way to gather data (Lugosi, 2006). Covert research is rarely entered into lightly and, when it is, researchers are at pains to stress that adopting covert methods is not a license for cavalier research, rather they recognize as Mitchell (1993) does, that at times "secrecy in research is risky but necessary business" (p. 54).

While questions of intent underpin decisions about the choice of research methods and approaches, they are also informed by the ethical position(s) of the researcher. That is, the choice of methodology is, at one level, a pragmatic decision; at another, it is also shaped by a researcher's own biography and the broader social context within which they, and their research participants, are located.

Ethical positions

Ethical positions in many ways challenge qualitative researchers to move beyond the minimalist, mandatory codes and statements of ethics alluded to earlier, and to reflect on their own values, beliefs, ideological positions, and how these may interact with ethics in practice. In seeking to undertake research that moves beyond concerns with process and outcomes, a number of "aspirational" ethical positions have been espoused, including "virtue ethics," "feminist ethics," and "culturally responsive relational ethics" (Lahman *et al.*, 2011). These will be discussed in terms of their application to qualitative research in sport and exercise settings.

Virtue ethics seek to emphasize the ethical behavior of the researcher over and above the process and pragmatics of research. Such an approach foregrounds the agency of the researcher instead of the acts of research, and asks that researchers conduct themselves with "courage, honesty, resoluteness and humility" (Blee & Currier, 2011, p. 403). Taking its cues from fields like Social Work and Social Care, virtue ethics requires researchers to reflect on their own moral compass and ethical intuitions (Lahman *et al.*, 2011) when interacting with research participants, particularly when researching sensitive topics. In sport and exercise research, Celia Brackenridge's research on sexual abuse in sport is a powerful example of the application of such aspirational ethical positions (Brackenridge, 1999; 2001).

A recognition of historical injustices, epistemological biases, and the accrual of imbalances in power, legitimacy, and authority have given rise to particular ways of framing ethics, such as *culturally responsive relational ethics* and *feminist ethics*. *Culturally responsive relational ethics* stem from the premise that it is not always possible for researchers to fully understand the fine-grained nuances of the various cultures and subcultures that they may wish to engage with, and argument that researchers need to be open to the possibility of understanding ethics through the lens of the participants' perspective. Drawing on the "three 'Rs' of ethics: (i) cultural responsive ethics, (ii) relational ethics and (iii) reflexive ethics" (Lahman *et al.*, 2011, p. 307), culturally responsive relational ethics foregrounds the need for researchers to be sensitive to interactions and imbalances of power between researchers and participants, particularly, but not exclusively when it comes to writing about or representing their research for a broader audience. The relational dimensions of this ethical positional are pivotal and require respectful connections among the researcher, their research participants, and the communities in which they live and work. The unintended consequences of not being attentive to these throughout the research chain can be unimaginably traumatic for research participants.

While it is important to recognize the power differentials implicit in the research endeavor, there is a risk of universalizing vulnerability, and removing agency and choice from the subjects involved. As Lahman *et al.* note, "while we agree sensitivity to vulnerability is vital to ethical research, we believe it is important to remember that someone who is vulnerable in one context might be powerful in another" (2011, p. 308). Nonetheless, researchers working with communities of social and material disadvantage, and/or Indigenous groups (see also Chapters 8, 33 and 34), must be mindful of the historical injustices that have accrued through colonizing practices and ongoing acts of micro violence within these often overresearched communities (Blodgett *et al.*, 2011; Rossi, Steven & Alison, 2013). There is thus a tension between recognizing the dynamics and power differentials in research and acknowledging the risk of perpetuating particular taken-for-granted assumptions about research participants that may, in turn, deny or downplay the agency and the decision-making capacities of people deemed to be vulnerable.

Feminist ethics (see also Chapter 7) respond to the need to acknowledge power differentials, contexts, and social values at all stages of the ethical chain, in particular, the need to challenge oppressive practices that have historically marginalized women. Feminist ethics (Sailors *et al.*, 2012), with its project of highlighting and mitigating imbalances of power for women and other disadvantaged groups in relation to larger social structures (Jaggar, 1994), is centered around questions of power and privilege and attempting to mitigate women's subordination and silencing in research design, delivery and dissemination.

In terms of sport and exercise research, feminist ethics have been applied to a variety of examples, notably that of the female South-African 800-meter runner Caster Semanya being subject to "gender verification testing" following her victory in the 2009 World Championships (Dworkin & Cooky, 2012; Karkazis *et al.*, 2012). An associated approach is that of feminist ethics of care, which advocates acknowledging and responding to conflicts and disparity in relation to gender or other inequities, rather than attempting to fully mitigate them (Edwards & Mauthner, 2012).

The interaction between the ethical position(s) of a researcher and the procedural ethics they adopt influences ethics in practice; that is, the ways in which research sites and subjects are selected and negotiated, data are collected, and then analyzed and disseminated. The realities of ethics in practice in qualitative research often run counter to the notions of universal, utilitarian consequentialism espoused by traditional ethics positions. The following section outlines some of the pragmatic dimensions of ethics in practice both when in the field and writing about the field, drawing on examples from a range of sport- and exercise-based settings to illustrate some of the interactions between procedural ethics, ethical positions, and ethics in practice, as we move along the ethical chain of qualitative research.

Prelude to the field: informed consent

At the risk of implying a lock-step method to the way in which a research project may unfold, having negotiated gatekeepers and gained entry into the field, data are then collected. A key step before (or while) this occurs is gaining "informed consent" from research participants. In essence, informed consent refers to the process by which a research participant is notified of the aims of the research, the methods involved, any risk and benefits, the ways in which data will be presented, and the intended outcomes of the research.

In his ethnography of women's professional golf, Crossett presents a relatively straightforward account of how he obtained consent from his research participants: "I spent considerable time explaining who I was and how I was conducting this study with each interview participant. Each interviewee signed a release form to indicate that they were willing participants and guaranteed their anonymity" (Crossett, 1995, p. 241). Whereas informed consent is mostly required by human ethics research committees as part of their concern for utilitarian consequentialism, gaining informed consent can be a more difficult undertaking, and may require more novel means beyond those employed by Crossett. Researchers using video cameras, for example, can record their participants' consent into the camera frame as part of their filming of the research moment. Equally, and this is a point I will return to, undertaking research with people who are cognitively impaired or under the influence of drugs or alcohol raises a range of concerns relating to duty ethics of principles, and, indeed, definitions and understandings of consent itself. For these reasons, among others, Fleming (2013) and McFee (2006) advance an argument to, in some circumstances, do away with informed consent, arguing that sometimes departing from the need to gain voluntary informed consent enhances the research process and outcomes.

In the field

Assuming consent has been granted, the qualitative researcher now finds themselves in the thick of it, where issues of how to present the research and themselves to their research participants become front of mind. My own research into the social meanings and public health implications of alcohol in Australian Rules football is instructive here, and I offer my research as an extended example. As I have written about elsewhere, being a female researcher conducting research on drinking, with predominantly male research participants, often requires me to negotiate several procedural ethical concerns, as well as reflecting on my own ethical position in the research (see Palmer, 2009, 2015; Palmer & Thompson, 2007).

In terms of procedural ethical concerns, these related mainly to informed consent and the utilitarian consequences of a duty of care to participants when doing research with people consuming alcohol, often to the point of intoxication. In terms of ethics in practice, this related to negotiating my position in the research context, and whether to consume alcohol myself. Whereas individual researchers may reach their own position on what kind of approaches to research are appropriate to their own circumstances, my own visible alcohol consumption was a deliberate research strategy to facilitate my data collection. In many fieldwork situations, how the researcher is perceived and constructed is crucial to the success of the research (Fletcher, 2014; King-White, 2013; Olive & Thorpe, 2011; Richards, 2014), and it was crucial that I was seen to be drinking alcohol, for it offset the perception that I was taking the moral high ground, and then granted me access to them and legitimated my presence in the field.

Informed consent and "duty of care" in practice

Doing research with people who regularly drank to excess opened up a number of ethical concerns to do with informed consent. While I am using the example of inebriation, the issues raised are of concern for research with participants who may be impaired for different reasons, through disability or cognitive function, for example. In my research, on those occasions where I have been unsure of a subject's ability to understand what I am doing, or to appreciate the implications of my notebook, tape recorder and/or camera due to their level of impairment, I did not record data. While I observed and noted the context and ways in which obviously drunk people are drinking, I did not seek personal or individual information in those instances where I was doubtful that informed consent could be given. While it could be argued that because much of what is being observed is already in the public domain, then obtaining informed consent is not necessary, I felt it both invasive and exploitative to observe, photograph, and then record for a wider audience people who were quite clearly incapacitated. Thus, attempts to obtain consent to be interviewed, photographed, or observed were made wherever possible.

Being in environments where heavy drinking is commonplace has also given me pause for thought as to issues of a "duty of care" to those who are drinking. My research teams have on many occasions deliberated about what, if any, our responsibilities are to people who are clearly intoxicated in terms of their own (and others') safety. Our general position has been that our responsibilities to intoxicated people are no more or less than they are in a nonresearch setting (such as having a drink with a friend in a bar where someone was clearly drunk), and it is not in our remit to intervene. Our rationale for this was that the intoxication was not a result of participation in the research, but an integral part of the culture that often orients the research in the first instance. Following Sugden's guiding principle that researchers are not agent provocateurs – "we should not set in motion procedures which otherwise would not have happened in order to unearth interesting material" (1997, p. 243) – we did not initiative action or intervene in events as they unfolded. Even so, the unpredictability of social research was made more so with the unpredictability that alcohol consumption can bring, and called for a particular kind of researcher reflexivity and "sense-checking" before, during, and after the research engagement.

Vulnerable groups

Most national statements on ethical conduct in human research include a list of participants who are considered to be vulnerable or at potential risk of distress through their involvement in qualitative research.[2] If a research project involves people who fall into one or more of these categories, the research is deemed to be "high risk" and requires the researcher to attend to a range of strategies, including identifying counseling, and/or support services should the research cause harm or distress to the participants.

Thinking through the particular methodological responsibilities that may come from sensitive research undoubtedly serves a useful function in that it compels researchers to explicitly consider the dynamics of advantage and disadvantage, and the risk and benefits of the research. In their work on the Homeless World Cup, Magee and Jeanes (2013) recognized the need to prioritize the voices and opinions of the participants. Conducting research with participants experiencing multiple forms of vulnerability, including homelessness, mental illness, drug use and unemployment among others, Magee and Jeanes used a preliminary period of preparing for the Homeless World Cup to gain trust and rapport, and to determine whether the research should be undertaken; a position determined by active discussion with the players training for the tournament and their and social workers. As Magee and Jeanes note:

> [we] emphasized that each player had a right not to partake, could withdraw at any point or could ask for certain instances to not feature in output from the research. In reality the players were enthusiastic about participating in the research and wanted to have their voices 'listened to.' Regular meetings occurred with players to check the research data collected. Whilst the majority were happy to have their discussions/observations included, there were occasions when they asked that the co–author remove particular incidents and such requests were honored.
>
> *(Magee & Jeanes, 2013, p. 9)*

Such an approach of "member checking," both engages a process of iterative consent and speaks to the self-reflexive nature of culturally responsive relational ethics in which, in this case, the value of sport and social development interventions can only be examined when a reflexive analysis of the political-cultural context in which they are embedded is undertaken (see also Phoenix, 2010; Spaaj, 2009).

Returning to the three "Rs" of culturally responsive relational ethics, these dynamics of advantage and disadvantage may look and feel quite different when Indigenous researchers employ Indigenous methodologies and epistemologies in their research (Blodgett *et al.*, 2014; Lavallée, 2008; 2009). Describing her application of an Indigenous framework to her study of the physical, mental and emotional impacts of a tae kwon do program offered at the Native Canadian Centre of Toronto, Lavallée recounts the challenges of bringing together Indigenous ways of knowing and Western ways of qualitative inquiry, arguing that the "rules" of the academy and of research do not always allow an Indigenous research framework to flourish.

Covert research (including illegal behaviors)

I noted earlier that covert research, particularly when it involves illegal or socially deviant practices, often presents a red flag for ethics committees, and covert research is research that is rarely undertaken lightly. So, what might this look like in practice? Walters and Godbold (2014) in their study of "parent rage" at children's sporting events in New Zealand employed covert methods to research the behaviors of the parents. That is, they did not disclose their role as researchers, and observed and surreptitiously filmed the behaviors of parents fighting with each other, and berating their own and others' children for missing key plays such as a shot on goal. The methodological approach speaks to broader debates as to the extent to which the lack of informed consent by the parents and, in some cases deception, in the project justified the means the authors felt were needed to document and record the emerging phenomenon of "parent rage," given that the findings of their research have subsequently been used to inform the design of interventions in New Zealand. Here, the researchers justified their ostensible "deceit" as being both necessary and unavoidable.

Covert research, however, often places researchers in dangerous and compromising situations. Research in the sociology of sport has examined football hooligans and "ultras" using covert methods. Pearson's (2009, 2014) research, for example, raises questions for how the researcher can, if at all, avoid situations where violence or criminal offenses are committed, and what this may mean for their presentation of self in the field and their presentation of data beyond the field.

Autoethnography, friends, and insiders

A considerable body of research on sport and exercise studies employs and examines the use of autoethnography as a particular research strategy. In autoethnography, the researcher is invariably an active participant in or member of the sporting world under study (see also Chapter 23). While autoethnography has been criticized as being little more than a "good story," the methodology raises several questions for ethics in practice, particularly for issues of anonymity and confidentiality, disclosure and informed consent. In autoethnography, the researcher is readily identifiable; they are the main character, laying bare their innermost thoughts, feelings, and experiences of the activity they are undertaking and those around them. Similarly, in small, closed communities such as sporting clubs, organizations, or communities of practice, the club or the individuals within it may be easily identified. As Erben notes, "even when others are anonymized within the account, at least in terms of remaining formally unnamed, they may nevertheless be identifiable via distinctive social or physical characteristics" (1993, p. 16). Once their account is published, it is difficult to retract what has been written, or indeed influence subsequent debates about the accuracy of the description of the field setting and its subjects, or the veracity of autoethnography as robust research method (Muncey, 2010). I return to some of these questions later when discussing writing about the field.

In terms of ethics in practice, in most autoethnographic projects, the researcher is conducting their fieldwork with people that they are likely to encounter regularly – at weekly training sessions, competitions, and events – and who they may regard as friends or acquaintances. For some researchers, this is the most difficult aspect of fieldwork to negotiate, where being a "professional friend" can prove problematic. Taylor (2011) writes of being an "insider researcher," and about some of the strategies she employed for negotiating previously established friendships and intimate relationships in the field, including the need to question more the role that she played in the sporting community, anticipating the possible consequences of "putting your work out there," and "member checking" along the ethical chain.

Certainly, sports-based fieldwork doesn't start or end on the playing field, in the bar or on the bike, as the case may be, which can make for some fluid boundaries at times. In the case of my own doctoral research on the Tour de France, I babysat the children of some of my research participants, I taught English, and I engaged in a whole range of activities that weren't about sport, but were about the wider world of the people I was interested in knowing more about. Drawing on the work of Bauman, Potrac *et al.* (2013) refer to these as "liquid relationships." The importance of maintaining professional friendships, and acknowledging the fluidity of these relationships, is particularly important when the research is done over time, and/or with vulnerable participants, where the need to keep the door open for follow-up studies and/or for researchers who follow (Landale & Roderick, 2013).

What each of these examples attest to is a tension alluded to earlier, namely that sometimes the utilitarian consequentialism of preplanned ethics approval by institutional review boards and the like offers little guidance to researchers in the thick of it; managing personal friendships and professional relationships that may need to continue post-fieldwork; being attuned to the sensitivities of exposing their own vulnerabilities and those of others. There is no easy answer to these dilemmas but a first step in reconciling them is to recognize that these – and other concerns – may emerge as you negotiate the ethical chain.

Writing about the field

So far, I have focused on ethics in qualitative research as relating to the interpersonal dynamics that come from the social interactions necessary for data collection. Ethics, however, don't stop there. There is a need to consider the ethical dimensions of how we write about our fieldwork and present our accounts of those social interactions to a wider audience. Many of the principles in the ethical chain still hold at this stage. As is the case with other stages in the ethical chain, the best of ethical intentions can be impractical in practice.

On this, issues of anonymity and confidentiality provide a useful way into thinking about what is ethically practical and possible.[3] Part of the social contract that qualitative researchers enter into is that the identity of participants will be concealed, unless they have agreed to have their identity disclosed and matched to their responses. In some research settings, holding up our end of the social contract is very difficult. Mellick and Fleming (2010), for example, address the ethics of disclosure in relation to a personal narrative that included the portrayal of a particular rugby player with an identifiable biography, which made him a "unique case study," despite all efforts at anonymization. The specific ethical dilemma confronting the authors was that the biographical information and international reputation of the player were essential to the theoretical framing of the narrative, and removing this information would have greatly weakened the analysis, and rendered it "impotent" in their terms (2010, p. 301).[4]

Some qualitative researchers also face the dilemma of how to write up their fieldwork without being seen to valorize particular behaviors. This is certainly the case for those doing research on overconformity to the sport ethic or in fieldwork in settings where drugs and alcohol are consumed, particularly where a focus is on the pleasure of drug-taking (Joseph & Donnelly, 2012). There is certainly a challenge to representing the experiences of participants authentically, while reflecting on the broader social, political, and ideological contexts that may give rise to such behaviors in the first place.

Conclusion: future directions and do ethics matter?

So far this chapter has focused on the negotiation and management of procedural ethics, and ethics in practice along the ethical chain. It is worth reflecting on why (if at all) ethics are important to qualitative research endeavors.

While my focus in this chapter has been on fieldwork involving interviews (see Chapter 9), observation (see Chapter 10), and ethnography (see Chapter 5), visual methods (see Chapter 11) present ways to push research beyond the conventions of talk and text. Photography, photo-elicitation, and digital video, present innovative methods to excavate the multisensory (see also Chapter 26), and embodied understanding of physical and sporting social worlds, yet raise questions for where and how materials can be used, and the importance of "member checking" about the researcher's interpretation of both the text and the visual images.

Similarly, blog analysis is another research strategy that offers much methodological potential, and therefore ethical considerations. Blogs are a user-generated form of web content where Internet users both produce and consume content at the same time as communicating and interacting with each other. This raises questions for the boundaries of the public and the private, the acquiring of informed consent, maintaining anonymity, and/or confidentiality online, and "deception," both on the part of the researcher and, indeed the research subjects (see Hookway, 2008).

Multisited and transnational research projects such as sport, peace, and development research also raise a series of new considerations for research ethics. Research ethics are very often premised on the assumption of a relatively bounded field site with a single researcher or research team, yet what happens when research takes place in different countries, in different languages, and with several research teams? Fasting *et al.* (1997, 2015) describe the theoretical, methodological, and practical challenges of researching the experiences and meanings of sport in the lives of women in England, Germany, Norway, and Spain. Differing understandings of feminism(s), cross-national comparisons, sampling, language, developing interview guidelines, carrying through the analysis, working and writing across languages and field sites were all exacerbated by the transnational context in which the research was carried out. The transnational dimensions of this research may require the use of interpreters in interviews, sensitivity to local cultural nuances of meaning, interpretations, policy contexts and settings, all of which require the researcher to be especially sensitive to the issues raised by some of the alternative ethical positions discussed earlier.

Considering one's position in the research endeavor, and the need to negotiate boundaries, identities, power, and privilege are key, both in terms of the practical dimensions of qualitative research in sport and exercise settings, but also for its capacity to enable researchers to ask questions of these same dynamics. It is the reflexive capacity of social research to ask questions, not only of the world around us, but also of ourselves, and our place in that social world that makes qualitative research a contentious, challenging, rewarding, and revealing enterprise.

Notes

1 Originally called the "Tuskegee Study of Untreated Syphilis in the Negro Male," the Tuskegee Experiment was undertaken in 1932 by the US Public Health Service and the Tuskegee Institute to record the natural history of syphilis. The study initially involved 600 African-American men: 399 who had syphilis; 201 who did not. Researchers told the men they were being treated for "bad blood," a local term used to describe several ailments, including syphilis, anemia, and fatigue. As such, they did not receive the proper treatment needed to cure their illness. Although originally projected to last 6 months, the study went on for 40 years. It was subsequently found that the men had been misled and had not been given all the information required to provide informed consent. Even when penicillin became available for syphilis in 1947, researchers did not offer it to the subjects. The subjects were never given the choice of quitting the study, even when this new, highly effective treatment became widely used. In 1972, an advisory panel concluded that the study was "ethically unjustified." In 1973, a class-action lawsuit was filed on behalf of the study participants and their families. In 1974, a $10 million out-of-court settlement was reached. As part of the settlement, the US Government promised to give lifetime medical benefits and future burial services to all living participants.

2 In Australia, this list includes pregnant women, minors, people highly dependent on medical care who may be unable to give consent, people with a cognitive impairment, an intellectual disability, or a mental illness, people who may be involved in illegal activities, people in other countries, Aboriginal and Torres Strait Islander peoples, and people who are identifiable by their membership of a cultural, ethnic or minority group (NHMRC, 2007).

3 Anonymity is when a participant provides no personal information about themself, and should not be asked to disclose information that would give their identity away. Confidentiality is when a participant provides information about themself, such as their name, address or birth date, to the researcher that must not be given to anyone who is not directly involved in the research.

4 In some cases, failures or weaknesses in the ethical chain often come to light after the fact. The publication of Nancy Scheper-Hughes's (1977) *Saints, Scholars, and Schizophrenics: Mental Illness in Rural Ireland* is a case in point. Describing the everyday life of a tiny Irish village, residents took offence when the book was published at what they perceived as a breach of trust; the airing of "family secrets" that villagers had confided with Scheper-Hughes in strictest confidence. Scheper-Hughes had attempted to cloak the true name of the village and villagers with pseudonyms, yet the villagers were able to identify each other instantly upon reading the book. The marginal anonymity afforded by pseudonyms might work for fieldwork undertaken in a large city, yet was insufficient for a tiny Irish village.

References

Babbie, E. (2004). Laud Humphreys and research ethics. *International Journal of Sociology and Social Policy*, *24*(3/4/5), 12–19.

Blackman, S. (2007). "Hidden ethnography": Crossing emotional borders in qualitative accounts of young people's lives. *Sociology*, *41*(4), 699–716.

Blee, K. & Currier, A. (2011). Ethics beyond the IRB: An introductory essay. *Qualitative Sociology*, *34*(3), 401–413.

Blodgett, A., Schinke, R., McGannon, K. & Fischer, L. (2014). Cultural sport psychology research: Conceptions, evolutions, and forecasts. *International Review of Sport and Exercise Psychology*, *8*, 24–43.

Blodgett, A. T., Schinke, R.J., Smith, B., Peltier, D. & Pheasant, C. (2011). In Indigenous words: Exploring vignettes as a narrative strategy for presenting the research voices of Aboriginal community members. *Qualitative Inquiry*, *17*(6), 522–533.

Brackenridge, C. (2001). *Spoilsports. Understanding and preventing sexual abuse in sport*. London: Routledge.

Brackeridge, C. (1999). Managing myself: Investigator survival in sensitive research. *International Review for the Sociology of Sport*, 34, 399–410.

Brustad R.J. (2014). Through their eyes: Quantitative researchers' perceptions of qualitative forms of study in sport and exercise psychology. *Qualitative Research in Sport, Exercise & Health*, *3*(3), 404–410.

Calvey, D. (2013–2014). Covert ethnography in criminology: A submerged yet creative tradition. *Current Issues in Criminal Justice*, *25*(1), 540–550.

Calvey. D. (2008). The art and politics of covert research. Doing "situated ethics" in the field. *Sociology*, *42*, 905–918.

Crossett, T. (1995). *Outsiders in the clubhouse: The world of women's professional golf*. Albany, NY: SUNY Press.

Donnelly, M. (2014). Drinking with the derby girls: Exploring the hidden ethnography in research of women's flat track roller derby. *International Review for the Sociology of Sport*, *49*(3–4), 464–484.

Dworkin S. & Cooky C. (2012). Sport, sex segregation, and sex testing: Critical reflections on this unjust marriage. *American Journal of Bioethics*, *12*(7), 1–3.

Edwards. R. & Mauthner, M. (2012). Ethics and feminist research: theory and practice. In T. Miller, M. Birch, M. Mauthner & J. Jessop (Eds.), *Ethics in qualitative research* (2nd ed., pp. 14–29). London: Sage.

Erben, M. (1993). The problem of other lives: Social perspectives on written biographies. *Sociology*, *27*(1), 15–27.

Fasting K., Pfister, G., Scraton, S. & Bunuel, A. (1997). "Cross-national research on women and sport: Some theoretical, methodological and practical challenges. *Women in Sport & Physical Activity Journal*, *1*(6), 85–107.

Fasting, K. & Svela Sand, T. (2015). Narratives of sexual harassment experience in sport. *Qualitative Research in Sport, Exercise & Health*, *7*(5), 573–588.

Fleming, S. (2013). Social research in sport (and beyond): Notes on exceptions to informed consent. *Research Ethics*, *9*, 32–43.

Fletcher, T. (2014). "Does he look like a Paki?" An exploration of "Whiteness," positionality and reflexivity in inter-racial sports research. *Qualitative Research in Sport, Exercise and Health*, *6*(2), 1–17.

Guillemin, M. & Gillam, L. (2004). Ethics, reflexivity and "ethically important moments" in research. *Qualitative Inquiry*, *20*, 261.

Hammersley, M. (2006). Are ethical committees ethical? *Qualitative Researcher*, *2*, 4–8.

Hesse-Bibber, S.N. & Leavy, P. (Eds.) (2010). *Handbook of emergent methods*. New York: Guilford Press.

Hookway, N. (2008). Entering the blogosphere: Some strategies for using blogs in social research. *Qualitative Research*, *8*(1), 91–113.

Hooper, H., Burwitz, L. & Hodkinson, P. (2003). Exploring the benefits of a broader approach to qualitative research in sport psychology: A tale of two, or three, James. *Forum Qualitative Sozialforschung/Forum: Qualitative Social Research*, *4*(1), Article 6.

Humphreys. L. (1970). *Tearoom trade: Impersonal sex in public places*. London: Duckworth.

Jaggar, A. (Ed.) (1994). *Living with contradictions: Controversies in feminist social ethics*. New York: Westview Press.

Joseph, J. & Donnelly, M. (2012). Reflections on ethnography, ethics and inebriation. *Leisure/Loisir*, *36*(3–4), 357–372.

Karkazis, K., Jordan-Young, R., Davis, G. & Camporesi, S. (2012). Out of bounds? A critique of the new policies on hyperandrogenism in elite female athletes. *The American Journal of Bioethics*, *12*(7), 3–16.

King-White, R. (2013). I am not a scientist: Being honest with oneself and the researched in critical interventionist ethnography. *Sociology of Sport Journal*, *30*(3), 296–322.

Krane, V. & Baird, S. (2005). Using ethnography in applied sport psychology. *Journal of Applied Sport Psychology*, *17*(2), 87–107.

Kvale, S. & Brinkmann, S. (2009). *Interviews: Learning the craft of qualitative research interviewing* (2nd ed.). Thousand Oaks, CA: Sage.

Lahman, M., Mendoza, B., Rodriguez, M. & Schwartz, J. (2011). Undocumented research participants: Ethics and protection in a time of fear. *Hispanic Journal of Behavioral Sciences*, *33*(3), 304–322.

Landale, S. & Roderick, M. (2013). Recovery from addiction and the potential role of sport: Using a life-course theory to study change. *International Review for the Sociology of Sport*, *49*(3–4), 468–484.

Lavallée, L. (2009). Practical application of an Indigenous research framework and two qualitative Indigenous research methods: Sharing circles and Anishnaabe symbol-based reflection. *International Journal of Qualitative Methods*, *8*(1), 21–40.

Lavallée, L. (2008). Balancing the medicine wheel through physical activity. *Journal of Aboriginal Health*, *4*(1), 64–71.

Lugosi, P. (2006). Between overt and covert research: Concealment and disclosure in an ethnographic study of commercial hospitality. *Qualitative Inquiry*, *12*(3), 541–561.

Magee, J. & Jeanes, R. (2013). Football's coming home: A critical evaluation of the Homeless World Cup as an intervention to combat social exclusion. *International Review for the Sociology of Sport*, *48*(1), 3–19.

McFee, G. (2006). The epistemology of qualitative research into sport: Ethical and erotetic? *Qualitative Research in Sport and Exercise*, *1*(3), 297–311.

McNamee, M. (2001). Introduction: Whose ethics, which research? *Journal of Philosophy of Education*, *35*(3), 309–327.

Mellick, M. & Fleming, S. (2010). Personal narrative and the ethics of disclosure: A case study from elite sport. *Qualitative Research, 10*(3), 299–314.

Miller, T., Birch, M., Mauthner, M. & Jessop, J. (2012). *Ethics in qualitative research* (2nd ed.). London: Sage.

Mills, C. & Hoeber, L. (2013). Using photo-elicitation to examine artefacts in a sports club. *Qualitative Research in Sport, Exercise & Health, 5*(1), 1–20.

Mitchell, R. (1993). *Secrecy and fieldwork.* London: Sage.

Muncey, T. (2010). *Creating autoethnographies.* London: Sage.

NHMRC. (2007). National Statement on Ethical Conduct in Human Research. Available at: www.nhmrc.gov.au/gudielines-publications/e72.

Olive, R. & Thorpe, H. (2011). Negotiating the "F-Word" in the field: Doing feminist ethnography in action sports cultures. *Sociology of Sport Journal, 28*(4), 421–440.

Olivier, S. & Fishwick, L. (2003). Qualitative research in sports sciences: Is the biomedical ethics model applicable? *Forum: Qualitative Social Research, 4*(1), 201–212.

Ortiz, S. M. (2005). The ethnographic process of gender management: Doing the "right" masculinity with wives of professional athletes. *Qualitative Inquiry, 11,* 265–290.

Palmer, C. (2015). *Rethinking drinking and sport: New approaches to sport and alcohol.* Farnham, UK: Ashgate.

Palmer, C. (2009). "The Grog Squad": An ethnography of beer consumption at Australian Rules football matches. In L. Wenner & S. Jackson (Eds.), *Sport, beer and gender in promotional culture: Explorations of a holy trinity* (pp. 225–241). New York: Peter Lang.

Palmer, C. & Thompson, K. (2010). Everyday risks and professional dilemmas: Fieldwork with alcohol-based (sporting) subcultures. *Qualitative Research, 10*(4), 1–20.

Palmer, C. & Thompson, K. (2007). The paradoxes of football spectatorship: On field and on line expressions of social capital among the "Grog Squad." *Sociology of Sport Journal, 24,* 187–205.

Pavlidis, A. & Olive, R. (2014). On the track/in the bleachers: Authenticity and feminist ethnographic research in sport and physical cultural studies. *Sport in Society, 17*(2), 218–232.

Pearson, G. (2014). Playing on a different pitch: Ethnographic research on football crowds. In M. Hopkins & J. Treadwell (Eds.), *Football hooliganism, fan behavior and crime: Contemporary issues* (pp. 176–200). Hampshire: Palgrave Macmillan.

Pearson, G. (2009). The researcher as hooligan: Where "participant" observation means breaking the law. *International Journal of Social Research Methodology, 12*(3), 243–255.

Phoenix, C. (2010). Seeing the world of physical culture: The potential of visual methods for qualitative research in sport and exercise. *Qualitative Research in Sport and Exercise, 2*(2), 93–108.

Potrac, P., Jones, R.L., Gilbourne, D. & Nelson, L. (2013). Handshakes, BBQs, and bullets: Self-interest, shame and regret in football coaching. *Sports Coaching Review, 1*(2), 79–92.

Richards, J. (2014). Which player do you fancy then? Locating the female ethnographer in the field of the sociology of sport. *Soccer & Society, 1,* 1–12.

Rossi, A., Steven, R. & Alison, N. (2013). Doing Whitefella research in Blackfella communities in Australia: Decolonizing method in sports related research. *Quest, 65*(1), 116–131.

Sailors, P., Teetzel, S. & Weaving, C. (2012). The complexities of sport, gender and drug testing. *American Journal of Bioethics, 12*(7), 23–25.

Scheper-Hughes, N. (2001). *Saints, scholars and schizophrenics: Mental illness in rural Ireland.* Berkeley, CA: University of California Press.

Sluggett, B. (2007). Creating the "pure" athlete: Discourses on steroid use and prohibition in sport. Thesis, Department of Sociology and Anthropology, Simon Fraser University. Available at: http://www.tandfonline.com/doi/abs/10.1080/19398441.2011.547689 (accessed October 14, 2014).

Spaaij, R. (2009). The social impact of sport: Diversities, complexities and contexts. *Sport in Society, 12*(9), 1101–1109.

Sparkes, A. & Smith, B. (2014). *Qualitative research methods in sport, exercise & health. From process to product.* London: Routledge.

SRA (Social Research Association). (2003). Social research guidelines. Available at: http://the-sra.org.uk/wp-content/uploads/ethics03.pdf.

Sugden, J. (1997). Field workers rush in (where theorists fear to tread): The perils of ethnography. In A. Tomlinson & S. Fleming (Eds.), *Ethics, sport and leisure: Crises and critiques* (pp. 223–244). Toronto, ON, Canada: Meyer & Meyer Sport.

Taylor, J. (2011). The intimate insider: Negotiating the ethics of friendship when doing insider research. *Qualitative Research, 11*(1), 3–22.

Thorpe, H., Ryba, T. & Denison, J. (2014). Toward new conversations between sociology and psychology. *Sociology of Sport Journal*, *31*(2), 131–138.

Veal, A.J. & Darcy, S. (2014). *Research methods in sports studies and sports management: A practical guide.* London: Routledge.

Walters, S. & Godbold, R. (2014). Someone is watching you: The ethics of covert observation to explore adult behavior at children's sporting events. *Bioethical Inquiry*, *11*, 531–537.

25

RETHINKING 'VALIDITY' AND 'TRUSTWORTHINESS' IN QUALITATIVE INQUIRY

How might we judge the quality of qualitative research in sport and exercise sciences?

Shaunna Burke

In this chapter I engage with the question 'how might the "quality" of qualitative research in sport and exercise sciences (SES) be judged?' Two overarching positions that can be adopted by researchers in the field are presented. First, I discuss the criteriological approach and provide examples of established criteria that have dominated research in SES. I also highlight the potential problems associated with using the criteriological approach and suggest that universal criteria are, for the most part, inappropriate for judging studies across the landscape of qualitative research. Second, I discuss the relativist approach and explore an alternative and arguably more suitable way of adopting criteria to address the legitimacy of qualitative studies, and recommend that scholars consider adopting self-selected criteria that are contextually situated. It is intended that this chapter will encourage dialogue and critical reflection, and help guide SES scholars when carrying out and judging qualitative research.

The criteriological approach

One position to evaluate qualitative research is what has been termed a 'criteriological approach' (Sparkes & Smith, 2009, 2014). This approach parallels the dominant positivist, postpositivist and neo-realist (see also Chapters 1 and 10) views of what constitutes rigour in quantitative research and advocates the necessity of adopting pre-determined criteria to discern whether a study is of value (Hammersley, 2007). A criteriologist believes that the quality of any study can only be judged against a set of external criteria that are comprehensive enough to assess all aspects of methodological rigour in advance of any study being carried out. In this way, a qualitative criteriologist believes that *all* genres and forms of qualitative inquiry (e.g. phenomenology (see Chapter 2), discourse analysis (see Chapter 18), narrative study (see Chapters 4 and 20), autoethnography (see Chapter 23) can be evaluated using fixed, universal criteria (Gergen, 2014; Smith & Hodkinson, 2005, 2009). Firmly located in what is known as a foundational orientation, determining what constitutes good-and-poor-quality work therefore involves readily identifiable markers of quality via a search for an objective reality and the truth. The majority of qualitative researchers in SES adopt this 'one-size-fits-all' approach to ascertain the quality of their work.

The most widely accepted and cited criteria in sport and exercise qualitative work are those of Lincoln and Guba (1985). On the one hand, Lincoln and Guba believed that the criteria used by quantitative researchers were not appropriate for judging studies using a qualitative approach. On the other hand, however, they sought criteria that paralleled (Sparkes, 1998) the traditional quantitatively oriented criteria of reliability, validity, generalizability and objectivity. New criteria paralleling those within quantitative research were therefore put forward in an attempt to assess all qualitative research. These criteria are as follows:

Credibility: The credibility of a study involves establishing whether findings of a study are credible or believable (Holloway & Wheeler, 2002). Underpinned by the objectivist notion of confidence in the 'truth' of the findings (Vaughn & Daniel, 2012), the concept of credibility is focused on ensuring that the researcher's interpretations of the data accurately represent the constructed realities of the participants (i.e. raw data). In essence, credibility rests on the notions of trust and accuracy (Pitney, 2004), and is commonly used as a substitute for the conventional quantitative criteria of internal validity, which is aimed at ensuring that a study measures or tests what is actually intended. Techniques, as outlined by Lincoln and Guba (1985), for achieving credibility include:

1. Prolonged engagement: Immersing oneself in the field for an extended period of time to understand the multiple features of the social setting or phenomenon under investigation.
2. Persistent observation: Focusing in detail on aspects that are most relevant to the problem or issue being studied.
3. Triangulation: Using multiple perspectives to analyse a research question which may include data source triangulation, multiple analyst triangulation, methodological triangulation, and/or theoretical triangulation.
4. Peer debriefing: Relying on a peer to review and assess transcripts, emerging categories from those transcripts, and/or the final report for feedback.
5. Negative case analysis: Identifying and highlighting parts of the data that do not support or seem to contradict similar themes that are emerging from data analysis.
6. Referential adequacy: Separating and holding off on analysing some of the raw data so that it can be analysed later and compared with similar data analysed previously.
7. Progressive subjectivity: Reflecting on prior and emerging biases and assumptions in relation to the topic of investigation.
8. Member checks: Providing sample participants with the transcripts and/or interpretation of the findings to check the accuracy of the work.

Dependability: Dependability has to do with the stability of data overtime and under different conditions (Guba & Lincoln, 1989). Firmly rooted in the assumptions underpinning the notion of reliability used in quantitative research, dependability is concerned with attaining consistency. It is often achieved by documenting the research process by accounting for changes that occur in the research setting, and describing how these changes may have affected the way in which the researcher approached the study. The major technique used in SES for assessing dependability is what is known as the 'inquiry audit', which involves providing a detailed and accurate description of the steps taken during the research process including decisions made along the way. For a study to be deemed dependable it must be seen as: (1) consistent in that the research process is well established and trackable; and (2) accurate in that the data can be confirmed through the stated research processes.

Transferability: Transferability and fittingness is about making inferences that extend beyond a particular set of findings (Guba & Lincoln, 1994) and is the qualitative analogue to generalizability or external validity used in quantitative work. Informed by non-random and purposeful sampling procedures, qualitative data cannot be directly applied to other settings or population as achieved in quantitative research via statistical sampling procedures and random selection (Sparkes & Smith, 2014). Rather, qualitative researchers tend to establish whether study findings can be transferred to other settings or groups via a technique called 'thick description'. This technique involves the researcher providing sufficient contextual information and a detailed and rich explanation of the assumptions central to the research question (Lincoln & Guba, 1985). The responsibility of transferring the findings to a different context then falls on the shoulder of the reader who makes the judgement of how sensible the transfer is.

Confirmability: Confirmability is the qualitative equivalent to objectivity used in positivist work (Sparkes & Smith, 2014). Here, researchers must take steps to illustrate that interpretations of the findings are clearly derived from the data itself. That is, that study findings mirror the experiences and views of the participants rather than the biases of the researcher. There are a number of strategies for enhancing confirmability. Researchers in SES tend to use a 'critical friend' (e.g. Brewer & Sparkes, 2011) or a reflexive journal to identify/report on the influence of the investigator's own background, perceptions and interests in the research process. They may also incorporate an audit trail, which details decisions made and procedures used so the reader can trace the course of the research step by step. In this way, a detailed methodological description facilitates the reader's ability to determine the extent to which the data may be accepted.

The criteria of Lincoln and Guba (1985), as outlined above, have proven to be very popular in the field of SES. For example, scholars in sport and exercise psychology (e.g. see Hanton, Wagstaff & Fletcher, 2012), sociology of sport (e.g. see Peachey, Cohen, Borland & Lyras, 2013) and sports coaching (e.g. see Falcao, Bloom & Gilbert, 2012) have relied on the neo-realist or foundational position to evaluate their research.

The criteriological approach: a short critique

The ontological and epistemological contradictions associated with Lincoln and Guba's (1985) work specifically, and the foundational position in general, have been carefully examined and exposed by qualitative scholars in SES as problematic (Smith & Caddick, 2012; Sparkes, 1998, 2002, 2009; Sparkes & Smith, 2009, 2014). Applying universal criteria to judge research that is underpinned by an ontological position, wherein reality is considered multiple and subjective is deemed inappropriate (Smith & Deemer, 2000; Smith & Hodkinson, 2005), is akin to trying to fit a square peg into a round hole. For example, using member checking (e.g. giving the transcribed interview back to the participant for verification) to test research findings (i.e. a pathway to the 'truth') contradicts the paradigmatic tenants of qualitative inquiry framed by interpretivism, constructionism or critical approaches, for example, by assuming that participants are possessors of 'truth'. This is not to say that member checks are of no use. They cannot be used to claim trustworthiness, but member checks can provide opportunities for 'reflexive elaboration and an enhanced understanding of how research findings are co-constructed in the creative process of the research' (Sparkes & Smith, 2014, p. 191). Moreover, because qualitative research produces context-dependent knowledge that is fluid and layered, the idea of repeatability and reproducing data is largely inappropriate and diminishes the importance of contextual factors. Judging qualitative research based on the notion that data can be measured twice raises major concerns. Sparkes and Smith expand on the problems associated with the criteriological approach:

> (1) there appears to be no explicit rationale to explain why certain techniques were chosen over others in various studies to establish trustworthiness; (2) the different meanings assigned to given techniques, such as member checking in different studies; (3) some of the actual techniques proposed to achieve aspects of trustworthiness are not appropriate to the logic of qualitative research; (4) the parallel perspective is philosophically contradictory; (5) Lincoln and Guba changed their position toward the end of the 1980s and have continued to do so since then.
>
> *(Sparkes & Smith, 2014, p.190)*

Furthermore, according to Morse (2015), Lincoln and Guba's (1985) work is problematic as many of their strategies recommended for achieving trustworthiness fail to achieve their intended goal of ensuring quality. Moreover, little is actually known about their impact on the process and end product of the research, and therefore when applied arbitrarily their work may in fact be harmful to the practice of qualitative research.

Despite the fundamental problems surrounding Lincoln and Guba's (1985) criteria for assessing qualitative research, and the repeated criticisms of this work for many years (including by Lincoln and Guba themselves), their work has long been used as the 'benchmark' for most qualitative researchers in SES (Krane & Baird, 2005), and continues to dominate the rules for publishing in most sport and exercise journals. Very recently, however, a new 'heir' to the popularity of Lincoln and Guba (1985) – Tracy (2010) – has emerged within sport and exercise psychology. Tracy is now on the verge of becoming the new 'benchmark' for judging all qualitative research within this subdiscipline; that is, her paper is now frequently applied and cited when considering validity.

Yet, Tracy's (2010) position on criteria and *how* these criteria are being applied by researchers in SES raises concerns. First, her position promotes the idea of using universal criteria that are fixed and permanent by advocating the necessity of adopting all eight of her proposed criteria when judging 'quality': worthy topic, rich rigour, sincerity, credibility, resonance, significant contribution, ethical, and meaningful coherence. Universal criteria are, however, problematic. As Sparkes and Smith (2009) note, they are based on very shaky philosophical 'foundations'. Applying universal criteria is also inherently problematic because it calls on a researcher to judge any piece of qualitative research in pre-ordained and set ways. In so doing, new or different ways of doing research that could produce new knowledge or make a difference in society may fail some or all of the criteria, and therefore be deemed 'invalid' from the outset. Much then is lost and the field is not only policed but risks becoming stagnant, insipid and reduced to a technical exercise.

Second, despite advocating universal criteria, sport and exercise psychology researchers rarely use all eight of the 'big tent' criteria (e.g. Carsten, Larsen & Alfermann, 2013; Long, Readdy & Raabe, 2014). As a consequence, they fail to adhere to the universal conceptualization of criteria as set out by Tracy (2010). In other words, they cite Tracy but misuse her ideas. This raises questions not only about the quality of the sport and exercise psychology research produced, but also why researchers continue to misunderstand her paper. Third, scholars are claiming to use 'her' criteria. Yet the criteria put forward by Tracy are not 'hers'. She synthesized this criteria from others' work. Despite this, many in sport and exercise psychology make the false claim that they are applying 'Tracy's criteria'. In short, then, sport and exercise psychology researchers explicitly and readily report on the criteria they have used to judge the quality of their work but often in ways that hold many problems. Interestingly, within the field of sport sociology, scholars tend not to place the same direct emphasis on reporting on criteria. Rather, their methodological writing is covertly directed at such a goal, aimed at giving their readers more general ideas on how they might proceed with their own studies. Perhaps, this lack of including clearly identified criteria in their work is because the traditional criteriological approach does not 'sit well' with sport sociologists in their attempts to establish quality.

The relativist approach

An alternative position to evaluate qualitative research in SES is what has been termed a 'relativist approach'. Like the criteriologst approach, the relativist approach uses criteria to discern 'good' from 'bad' research (and it does not claim that 'anything goes'). A relativist approach differs fundamentally in that criteria are applied in a manner that is contextually situated and flexible (Sparkes & Smith, 2009). Universal criteria are not then proposed. Based on a non-foundational orientation, the relativist approach is closely aligned with the ideas of ontological relativism (i.e. reality is multiple, created and mind-dependent) and epistemological constructionism (i.e. knowledge is constructed and subjective). Unlike a criteriologist approach, it thus fits with the assumptions held by constructionists, interpretivists and critical researchers. Rejecting all notions of realism (see also Chapter 22), a relativist believes that evaluative criteria should be study-specific (i.e. tailored to the study's goals and the researcher's choice of methods), and are only useful under certain conditions and in certain situations (Gergen, 2014; Tobin & Begley, 2004). From this perspective, sport and exercise researchers might reflect on the nuances related to a particular approach to inquiry and offer suggestions for how to evaluate their work. The process of judging research is therefore viewed as a craft skill (Seale, 1999), whereby the relativist must make informed decisions and ongoing judgements about which criteria reflect the inherent properties of a particular study as it develops over time. These judgements are based on a time- and place-contingent list of characteristics (Smith & Caddick, 2012). As Sparkes and Smith note:

> Various criteria, therefore, in list form may act as a starting point for judging a certain kind of inquiry, but these may not apply on all occasions and other criteria can be added to or subtracted from them depending on the circumstances. Importantly, these lists are challenged, changed and modified in their application to actual inquiries and writing practices by the very people involved in the research.
>
> *(Sparkes & Smith, 2009, p. 495)*

For Smith (1993) and Smith and Deemer (2000), once criteria come to be seen as characterizing traits or values that influence our judgements, then any particular traits or values will always be subject to constant reinterpretation as times and conditions change. They have a list-like quality. In saying this, they offered the following warning:

> The use of the term list should not be taken to mean that we are referring to something like an enclosed and precisely specified or specifiable shopping or laundry list. Put differently, to talk of a list in this sense is not at all to talk about, for example, an accumulation of 20 items, scaled 1 to 5, where everyone's presentation proposal is then

numerically scored with a cutoff point for acceptance. Obviously, to think of a list in these terms is to miss the entire point.

(Smith & Deemer, 2000, p. 888)

In contrast, Smith and Deemer (2000) see any list of characteristics as always open-ended, and ever subject to constant reinterpretation so that items can be added to the list or taken away. Against this backdrop, markers of 'quality' are seen as possibilities for assessing knowledge claims, but are not tied to specific paradigmatic practices or epistemic grounds (Smith & Hodkinson, 2005). In this way, 'quality' is internalized within the experiences and background of the researcher/reader, as well as the underlying assumptions of the study, rather than being something to be 'tested' at the completion (foundationalism) of the research (Amis & Silk, 2008).

Those researchers in SES working within the relativist or non-foundational approach tend to 'let go' of the prospect of universal criteria (including the traditional notion of validity/trustworthiness) and apply alternative criteria in situ to judge a piece of work (Sparkes & Smith, 2009). Within this perspective, quality is both *revealed* and *resides* in the research report, placing responsibility for judging quality not only on the researcher but also on the reader (Rolfe, 2006). Bringing together numerous ideas from others, Smith and Caddick (2012, p. 70f) offer the following list of alternative criteria as a starting point for researchers to consider adopting when judging qualitative SES work:

1. Substantive contribution: Does this piece contribute to our understanding of social life? Does the writer demonstrate a deeply grounded (if embedded) social scientific perspective? How has this perspective informed the construction of the text? (Richardson, 2000, p. 937).
2. Impact: Does this affect me? Emotionally? Intellectually? Does it generate new questions? Move me to write? Move me to try new research practices? Move me to action? (Richardson, 2000, p. 937).
3. Width: The comprehensiveness of evidence. This dimension refers to the quality of the interview or observations, as well as to the proposed interpretation or analysis. Numerous quotations in reporting narrative studies, as well as suggestions of alternative explanations, should be provided to support the reader's judgement of the evidence and its interpretation (Lieblich, Tuval-Mashich & Zilber, 1998, p. 73).
4. Coherence: The way different parts of the interpretation create a complete and meaningful picture. Coherence can be evaluated both internally, in terms of how the parts fit together, and externally; namely, against existing theories and previous research (Lieblich *et al.*, 1998, p. 173).
5. Catalytic and tactical authenticity: This refers to the ability of a given inquiry to prompt first, action on the part of the research participants, and second, the involvement of the researcher/evaluator in training participants in specific forms of social and political training if participants desire such training (Lincoln, 1995; Guba & Lincoln, 2005).
6. Personal narrative and storytelling as an obligation to critique: How do narrative and story enact an ethical obligation to critique subject positions, acts and received notions of expertise and justice within and outside of the work? (Holman Jones, 2005, p. 773).
7. Resonance: The research influences, affects or moves particular readers or a variety of readers through aesthetic, evocative representations, naturalistic generalizations and transferable findings (Tracy, 2010).
8. Credibility: Has the researcher spent a significant amount of time with participants? Were participant reflections on the researcher's interpretations of the data sought? Participant

reflections, or what are sometimes known as member checks, can open up dialogue about the fairness, appropriateness and believability of interpretations offered. As participants reflect, fresh light on the study may also be thrown up, providing a spur for richer and deeper analyses. Participant reflections are, therefore, less a test of research findings or a technique to achieve theory-free knowledge than they are an opportunity for dialogue with participants, reflexive elaboration, critique, feedback, affirmation, disagreement and even collaboration (Tracy, 2010).

9. Transparency: Was the research made transparent through, for example, an audit trail? Did another person, acting as a critical friend, scrutinize matters like theoretical preferences, breadth of the interview sample and the process of sorting, choosing, organizing and analysing the data? Did a researcher present their interpretations of the data to critical friends who provided a theoretical sounding board to encourage reflection upon, and exploration of, alternative explanations and interpretations as they emerged in relation to the data? (Tracy, 2010).

Herein, criteria act as suggestions or possibilities for judging a piece of work rather than strict rules that must be always followed in a universal manner and applied to all work (Sparkes & Smith, 2014). At this point then it is worth reflecting back on Tracy (2010). As Tracy did not herself design the criteria outlined in her paper, but instead brings past work from others together (like Smith and Caddick 2012 did above), there is nothing stopping researchers using the various criteria noted in her paper (as Smith and Caddick 2012 did above). The important point, however, is that if a researcher uses the criteria as highlighted by Tracy, the research they do can either be framed by a criteriologst approach, and therefore they must use and apply *all* the criteria, as she laid out, to the work. Or, a researcher can use the various criteria as illuminated by Tracy in a manner that is informed by a relativist approach. In this move, they therefore use and apply certain criteria as part of an ongoing list. Given the continued problems with the application of the work of Tracy in SES, what researchers need to do if they continue to use and cite her is to first state clearly which position they adhere to (e.g. criteriologst approach or relativist approach), and second apply criteria in a manner that fits, not contradicts, the approach stated. As an example of good practice, consider the following description of validity in the work of Smith, Tomasone, Latimer-Cheung and Martin Ginis (2015):

> In terms of validity, the study was guided by a relativist approach. This means that criteria for judging the quality of qualitative research are not applied in a universal manner, but rather are drawn from an ongoing list of characterizing traits (Sparkes & Smith, 2009, 2014). Here, this list included the following criteria: the worthiness of the topic; the significant contribution of the work; rich rigor, that is, developing a sample appropriate for the purpose of the study and generating data that could provide for meaningful and significant claims; and the coherence of the research, which refers to how well the study hangs together in terms of the purpose, methods, and results (Tracy, 2010). As part of a list of characterizing traits for enhancing the quality of our work, the study also used an audit trail (i.e. a colleague independently scrutinized data collection and theoretical matters) and aimed for resonance (e.g. naturalistic generalizations).
>
> (*Smith* et al., *2015, p. 306*)

Accordingly, as highlighted by Smith *et al.* (2015), criteria as illuminated by Tracy can be used. For them though, this use needs to be underpinned by a relativist approach and criteria conceptualized as a list of characterizing traits. Conceptualizing criteria like this also means different traditions and forms of representation can flourish in that they are judged by criteria applicable to them. For example, participation as reciprocity, cultural illumination and reflexivity might be useful when judging autoethnographies (Gergen, 2014; Smith, 2016) whilst verisimilitude, evocation and enlightenment might be better suited to judging ethnodramas (McMahon, Penny & Dinan-Thompson, 2012; see Chapter 23, this volume). In contrast, community researchers might draw on the strategies of localizing research practices, decentralization, and capacity building (Schinke, Smith & McGannon, 2013) as the starting point for judging their work, whereas aesthetic merit, expression of a reality and incitement to action might be used to evaluate creative nonfictions (Smith, McGannon & Williams, 2016). Using criteria in a universal manner to evaluate such diverse forms of qualitative inquiry/representation in SES is akin to judging a 'good' apple by the criteria of a 'good' orange (Northcote, 2012) and would therefore be doomed to failure. Importantly, however, adopting a relativist approach does not mean that anything is acceptable when passing judgement on a piece of work (Sparkes, 2002; Sparkes & Smith, 2009). Rather, the field of SES must reflexively determine the rigour and relevance of its research through emerging and dynamic criteria of evaluation, whilst acknowledging that 'good' studies possess certain characteristics.

Spurred on by pioneers in SES in this area (i.e. Smith, Sparkes & Caddick, 2014; Sparkes, 1998, 2002, 2009; Sparkes & Smith, 2009, 2014), scholars working within different epistemological, philosophical and methodological approaches in SES are adopting the relativist approach, and using criteria they feel are relevant and reflect the inherent characteristics and complexities of their work (e.g. Allen-Collinson, 2012; Carless & Sparkes, 2008; Holt, Scherer & Koch, 2013; Phoenix & Griffin, 2013). The relativist approach offers an alternative way of addressing the quality issue in SES and may appeal especially to those researchers informed by interpretivism, constructionism, critical inquiry and post-structuralism, and/or who use varied genres to represent their research.

Conclusion

This chapter has explored two broad, competing approaches for judging qualitative research and has shown that the qualitative literature in SES contains a diversity of opinions on how to address the issue of quality. As part of this exploration, this chapter has promoted an approach to evaluating qualitative research that takes into consideration the voice of the relativist researcher and attends to different forms of inquiry, thereby emphasizing a paradigm shift within SES research from empiricism to relativism. In this way, the issue of 'quality' in qualitative inquiry is part of a much larger and contested debate about the nature of knowledge produced by qualitative research. Given the diverse forms of inquiry now available to qualitative researchers, a greater acknowledgement of creativity and difference is needed when evaluating such research. By challenging the conventional way researchers have been judging qualitative research, it is hoped that readers are more aware of what makes good qualitative research and are better equipped to make informed decisions.

References

Allen-Collinson, J. (2012). Autoethnography: Situating personal sporting narratives in socio-cultural contexts. In K. Young & M. Atkinson (Eds.), *Qualitative research on sport and physical culture* (pp. 191–212). Bingley, UK: Emerald.

Amis, J. M. & Silk, M. L. (2008). The philosophy and politics of quality in qualitative organizational research. *Organizational Research Methods, 11*(3), 456–480.

Brewer, J. D. & Sparkes, A. C. (2011). Young people living with parental bereavement: Insights from an ethnographic study of a UK childhood bereavement service. *Social Science and Medicine, 72*(2), 283–290.

Carless, D. & Sparkes, A. C. (2008). The physical activity experiences of men with serious mental illness: Three short stories. *Psychology of Sport and Exercise, 9*(2), 191–210.

Carsten H., Larsen, C. H. & Alfermann, D. (2013). Successful talent development in soccer: The characteristics of the environment. *Sport, Exercise, and Performance Psychology, 2*(3), 190–206.

Falcao, W. R., Bloom, G. A. & Gilbert, W. D. (2012). Coaches' perceptions of a coach training program designed to promote youth developmental outcomes. *Journal of Applied Sport Psychology, 24*(4), 429–444.

Gergen, K. J. (2014). Pursuing excellence in qualitative inquiry. *Qualitative Psychology, 1*(1), 49–60.

Guba, E. G. & Lincoln, Y. S. (1989). *Fourth generation evaluation*. London: Sage.

Guba, E. G. & Lincoln, Y. S. (1994). Competing paradigms in qualitative research. In N. K. Denzin & Y. S. Lincoln (Eds.), *Handbook of qualitative research* (pp. 105–117). London: Sage.

Guba, E. G. & Lincoln, Y. S. (2005). Paradigmatic controversies, contradictions, and emerging confluences. In N. K. Denzin & Y. Lincoln (Eds.), *Handbook of qualitative research* (3rd ed., pp. 191–216). London: Sage.

Hammersley, M. (2007). The issue of quality in qualitative research. *International Journal of Research and Method in Education, 30*(3), 287–305.

Hanton, S., Wagstaff, C. R. D. & Fletcher, D. (2012). Cognitive appraisals of stressors encountered in sport organizations. *International Journal of Sport and Exercise Psychology, 10*, 276–289.

Holloway, I. & Wheeler, S. (2002). *Qualitative research in nursing* (2nd ed.). Oxford, UK: Blackwell.

Holman Jones, S. (2005). Autoethnography: Making the personal political. In N. K. Denzin & Y. Lincoln (Eds.), *Handbook of qualitative research* (3rd ed., pp. 763–792). London: Sage.

Holt, N. L., Scherer, J. & Koch, J. (2013). An ethnographic study of issues surrounding the provision of sport opportunities to young men from a western Canadian inner-city. *Psychology of Sport and Exercise, 14*(4), 538–548.

Krane, V. & Baird, S. M. (2005). Using ethnography in applied sport psychology. *Journal of Applied Sport Psychology, 17*, 87–107.

Lieblich, A., Tuval-Mashlach, R. & Zilber, T. (1998). *Narrative research*. London: Sage.

Lincoln, Y. S. (1995). Emerging criteria for quality in qualitative and interpretive research. *Qualitative Inquiry, 1*(3), 275–289.

Lincoln, Y. S. & Guba, E.G. (1985). *Naturalistic inquiry*. Newbury Park, CA: Sage.

Long, N. L., Readdy, J. R. & Raabe, J. (2014). What motivates firefighters to exercise? A mixed-methods investigation of self-determination theory constructs and exercise behavior. *Sport, Exercise, and Performance Psychology, 3*, 203–218.

McMahon, J., Penney, D. & Dinan-Thompson, M. (2012). Body practices – Exposure and effect of a sporting culture? Stories from three Australian swimmers. *Sport, Education and Society, 17*(2), 181–206.

Morse, J. M. (2015). Critical analysis of strategies for determining rigor in qualitative inquiry. *Qualitative Health Research, 25*(9), 1212–1222.

Northcote, M. T. (2012). Selecting criteria to evaluate qualitative research. *Education Papers and Journal Articles*, 99–110. Retrieved from http://research.avondale .edu.au/edu_papers/38.

Peachey, J. W., Cohen, A., Borland, J. & Lyras, A. (2013). Building social capital: Examining the impact of Street Soccer USA on its volunteers. *International Review for the Sociology of Sport, 48*(1), 20–37.

Phoenix, C. & Griffin, M. (2013). Narratives at work: What can stories of older athletes *do*? *Ageing & Society, 33*(2), 243–266.

Pitney, W. A. (2004). Strategies for establishing trustworthiness in qualitative research. *Human Kinetics, 9*(1), 26–28.

Richardson, L. (2000). Writing: A method of inquiry. In N. Denzin & Y. Lincoln (Eds.), *Handbook of qualitative research* (2nd ed., pp. 923–948). London: Sage.

Rolfe, G. (2006). Validity, trustworthiness and rigour: Quality and the idea of qualitative research. *Journal of Advanced Nursing, 53*, 304–10.

Schinke, R., Smith, B. & McGannon, K. R. (2013). Pathways for community research in sport and physical activity: Criteria for consideration. *Qualitative Research in Sport, Exercise and Health, 5*(3), 460–468.

Seale, C. (1999). Quality in qualitative research. *Qualitative Inquiry, 5*, 465–478.

Smith, B. (2016). Narrative inquiry and autoethnography. In M. Silk, D. Andrews & H. Thorpe (Eds.), *Handbook of physical cultural studies*. London: Routledge.

Smith, B. & Caddick, N. (2012). Qualitative methods in sport: A concise overview for guiding social scientific sport research. *Asia Pacific Journal of Sport and Social Science*, *1*, 60–73.

Smith, J. (1993). *After the demise of empiricism: The problem of judging social and educational inquiry*. Norwoods, NJ: Ablex.

Smith, J. & Deemer, D. (2000). The problem of criteria in the age of relativism. In N. Denzin & Y. Lincoln (Eds.), *Handbook of qualitative research* (2nd ed., pp. 877–896). London: Sage.

Smith, J. & Hodkinson, P. (2005). Relativism, criteria and politics. In N. Denzin & Y. Lincoln (Eds.), *Handbook of qualitative research* (3rd ed., pp. 915–932). London: Sage.

Smith, J. & Hodkinson, P. (2009). Challenging neorealism: A response to Hammersley. *Qualitative Inquiry*, *15*(1), 30–39.

Smith, B., McGannon, K. R. & Williams, T. (2016). Ethnographic creative non-fiction: Exploring the whats, whys and hows. In L. Purdy & G. Molner (Eds.), *Ethnographies in sport and exercise*. London: Routledge.

Smith, B., Sparkes, A. C. & Caddick, N. (2014). Passing judgment on qualitative sports coaching research: Validity and goodness criteria. In L. Nelson, R. Groom & P. Potrac (Eds.), *Research methods in sport coaching* (pp. 192–201). London: Routledge.

Smith, B., Tomasone, J., Latimer-Cheung, A. & Martin Ginis, K. (2015). Narrative as a knowledge translation tool for facilitating impact: Translating physical activity knowledge to disabled people and health professionals. *Health Psychology*, *34*, 303–313.

Sparkes, A. C. (1998). Validity in qualitative inquiry and the problem of criteria: Implications for sport psychology. *The Sport Psychologist*, *12*, 363–386.

Sparkes, A. C. (2002). *Telling tales in sport and physical activity: A qualitative journey*. Champaign, IL: Human Kinetics.

Sparkes, A. C. (2009). Novel ethnographic representations and the dilemmas of judgement. *Ethnography and Education*, *4*, 303–321.

Sparkes, A. C. & Smith, B. (2009). Judging the quality of qualitative inquiry: Criteriology and relativism in action. *Psychology of Sport and Exercise*, *10*, 491–497.

Sparkes, A. C. & Smith, B. (2014). *Qualitative research in sport, exercise and health sciences: From process to product*. London: Routledge.

Tobin, G. A. & Begley, C. M. (2004). Methodological rigour within a qualitative framework. *Journal of Advanced Nursing*, *48*, 388–396.

Tracy, S. J. (2010). Qualitative quality: Eight 'Big Tent' criteria for excellent qualitative research. *Qualitative Inquiry*, *16*, 837–851.

Vaughn, B. K. & Daniel, S. R. (2012). Conceptualising validity. In G. Tenenbaum, R. C. Eklund & A. Kamata (Eds.), *Measurement in sport and exercise psychology* (pp. 33–40). Champaign, IL: Human Kinetics.

PART V

Opening up qualitative research practices in sport and exercise

26

RESEARCHING THE SENSES IN SPORT AND EXERCISE

Andrew C. Sparkes

In this chapter, I begin by outlining the contours of the sensory revolution in the social sciences and signal some of the methodological challenges this poses for qualitative researchers. Next, I consider the work of a small but significant group of researchers in sport and exercise, who have taken up these methodological challenges via their explorations of the sensorium in action in various sport and exercise settings. Following this, some suggestions are made as to how we might enhance the sensory intelligence and imagination of researchers so that they are better able to seek the senses, and understand how they operate in dynamic combinations, to shape both their own experiences and the experiences of others they engage with in the field. Finally, I offer some reflections on the dilemmas of representing the senses in sport and exercise and indicate some ways that these might be overcome.

According to Howes (2005) the 'linguistic turn' with its notions of culture as discourse, and the world as constituted by text and signs, dominated much of late twentieth century thought in the social sciences. Work conducted within this framework tended to privilege and produce abstract theories and disembodied accounts of the corporeal realities of daily life. This provoked what Howes calls a *sensual revolution* that demanded attention be focused on what Vannini, Waskul and Gottschalk (2012) describe as 'embodied, multi-sensual, multimodal, pre-objective, and carnal ways of knowing' (p. 15).

Symptomatic of the sensual revolution in the social sciences was the launch in 2006 of a new journal called *Senses & Society*. In their introduction to the first edition Bull, Gilroy, Howes and Kahn (2006) state the following:

> The senses mediate the relationship between self and society, mind and body, idea and object. *The senses are everywhere.* Thus, sensation (as opposed to but inclusive of representations in different media) is fundamental to our experience of reality, and the sociality of sensation cries out for more concerted attention from cultural studies researchers.
>
> *(Bull et al., 2006, p. 5)*

The trajectory of the sensory revolution have been charted elsewhere (e.g., see Howes, 2004, 2006; Paterson, 2008). For the purposes of this chapter, it is worth noting a number of issues that this revolution has raised for scholars seeking the senses. First, as Howes (2004, 2005) points out, besides offering a much needed counterbalance to linguistic paradigms of culture, the sensory revolution has recovered perception from the laboratory and certain strands of psychology that take perception to be private, internal, ahistorical and apolitical. The senses are now taken to be shaped by personal history and are also collectively patterned by cultural ideology and practice.

According to Drobnick (2006), 'no act of perception is a pure an unmediated event; each society inflects and cultivates sensory practices according to its needs and interests' (p. 1f). Supporting this view, Vannini *et al.* (2012) note that the process of sense-making entails minded and embodied social and cultural practices that cannot be explained or reduced to physiological processes alone. For them, the senses 'are skills that we actively employ in interpreting and evaluating the world' (p. 15). Importantly, it is through these sensory experiences and practices that our social roles and interactions are structured on a daily basis as we learn social divisions, along with distinctions of gender, social class, age, (dis)ability, sexual orientation, race/ethnicity and religion, *through our senses*.

The sensual revolution has also raised questions regarding the unequal care and attention afforded to the various senses. There has been an ocular-centric bias that relegates the senses of sound, touch, taste and smell below that of the visual. Thus, Classen (2005) points out that in the academic world touch often passes under the radar. Likewise, Paterson (2007) states, 'within an academic climate that celebrates visual cultures, and the popular media's infatuation with visuality, touch remains largely neglected' (p. 1). Clearly, such relegation ignores the complexities of our *carnal* and thoroughly *embodied* ways of knowing as we both sense and make sense of the world around us. Significantly, it ignores the *somatic work* described by Vannini *et al.*

> Somatic work refers to the range of linguistic and alinguistic reflexive experiences and activities by which individuals interpret create, extinguish, maintain, interrupt, and/or communicate somatic sensations that are congruent with personal, interpersonal, and/or cultural notions of moral, aesthetic, and or logical desirability.
>
> *(Vannini* et al., *2012, p. 19)*

Ignoring the somatic work that people do also means ignoring the negotiated somatic rules that they use to manage their carnal sensation in ways that, as Vannini and colleagues (2012) note, can vary according to personal, interpersonal, contextual, social, cultural, material, geographic and historical circumstances. Likewise, the sensory bias as described deflects analytical attention away from the cultural and ideological dynamics of the senses and the *sensorium* in action. The sensorium, according to Merchant (2011) is the sum of a person's perceptions of their interpretation of an environment. It involves the different 'ratios of sense' that make up the sensuous and perceptual means by which we come to understand and dwell in space and place, and are dependent on shared cultural norms that can vary according to social context and geographical location.

The sensual revolution works against such areas of ignorance by focusing intensely on the dynamics of the senses and the sensorium in action. It challenges Greco-Roman notions of a sensory hierarchy based on Aristotle's fivefold classification of the senses that posits the existence of only a relatively small, specifiable and discrete number of types of senses. These are the exteroceptive senses of sight, hearing, taste, smell and touch that provide information about the world *external* to us. This view is difficult to sustain because there is evidence that more than five senses *actually* exist, that a large number of *possible* sensory modalities are available, and that how these operate varies across cultures. For example, Vannini *et al.* (2012) identify at least three more senses that provide information about the *internal* world of the human body. These interoceptive senses are the senses of pain (nocioception), thirst and hunger.

Vannini *et al.* (2012) also point to our sense of our own internal muscles and organs (proprioception), the sensations that mediate between the external world and the internal body, such as our sense of balance (equilibrioception), movement (kinesthesia), temperature (thermoception), and our sense of time (at least in terms of polychronicity and monochronicity, if not more). Their final list includes thirteen senses and still, they suggest, we experience more that are not accounted for in these categories. Accordingly, Vannini and colleagues argue that to think of the senses as only confined to the five exteroceptive sensory modes 'is grossly to oversimplify human sensual experience, both within and across cultures' (2012, p. 7).

Questions have been raised by the sensual revolution about the common assumption that sensory modalities are perceptual systems isolated from one another and unaffected by the others. Speaking of the sentient body, Blackman (2008) notes that although the senses are often discussed as separate processes, it is now agreed that they work in 'combination and communication with each other rather than as isolated forms of bodily awareness. The term that is used to describe these networked connections and processes is synesthesia' (p. 84). Given this intersensoriality and intercorporeality, researchers are now concerned with the connections and interactions between the sensory modalities in terms of how they generate cross-modal experiences that shape how we come to understand and perform our embodied selves in relation to others as sentient, fleshy, emplaced, permeable beings in various social situations. All this forms part of what Vannini *et al.* (2012) describe as a *sociology of the senses* that attempts 'to rediscover humans' sensuous, erotic, and aesthetic transactions with one another and their environments' (p. 13). We might equally say sport and exercise can attempt to rediscover the sensorial and consider developing a *psychology of the senses*.

Methodological issues

The sensual revolution invokes a number of methodological challenges. For example, normally our bodies are what Leder (1990) calls an absent–presence in our lives as it deals with its 'ceaseless stream of kinaesthesias, cutaneous, and visceral sensations' (p. 23). We are often not aware of our bodies, they just *are*. This is particularly so in settings when rehearsed physical skills, once fully learned, pervade one's corporeality and slip beyond conscious reflection in the actual doing. Accordingly, Merchant (2011) asks, even if the body does announce itself to us in an activity, how then do we get at the sensuous, sometimes 'pre-reflective' almost 'pre-objective' detail of what happened and how people feel during the activity? How do we access fleeting embodied encounters, immanent sensations, practical skills and sensuous dispositions?

The difficulties in communicating what is experienced through the senses to others and how best to access sensory knowledge have been discussed by Orr and Phoenix (2015). Having noted that a number of researchers have used traditional data-collection methods such as semi-structured interviews, they point out, following Merchant (2011), that physical activity is often performed at a pace or place which precludes the use of interviews. Given this dilemma, as Sparkes (2015) points out, many researchers in sport and exercise have chosen to conduct ethnographic studies (see Chapter 5) and immerse themselves for prolonged periods as full participants in the action, as part of a sensual apprenticeship. Speaking of the advantages to this approach he argues that ethnographically 'being there' as a participant observer in the action, calls upon a 'way of being' that involves a form of intentional, reflexive and embodied engagement with a chosen phenomenon over time. For him, by definition, this is multi- and intersensorial in nature. Ethnography (see Chapter 5) as an embodied practice can, therefore, involve intensely sensuous ways of knowing about the mundane and the strange.

Engaging as an ethnographer and serving as a sensual apprenticeship is not a methodologically problem-free process. For example, Merchant (2011) points to the logistical barriers involved when attempting to study the senses in the act of sensing. These include the fact that much of embodied experience is not outwardly expressed. This means, for example, that we cannot just look at a person and know that they are having a visceral reaction to something they have seen or done. Merchant also emphasizes that distinct sporting and exercise spaces and practices are not encountered and played out homogeneously. For her, 'each body is lived through subjectively and brings to the encounter different embodied sociocultural "baggage." Just because the researcher is engaged in the activities being studied does not mean he/she is experiencing them in the same way as others' (p. 55).

Orr and Phoenix (2015) also note that even if the researcher is fully involved in the action, this cannot guarantee a full and accurate description, as they may still have the problem of analysing and verbalizing newly acquired physical skills and bodily practices. Finally, there are many situations in which it is not possible, or desirable, to become a participant observer in the action. Accordingly, Mason and Davies (2009) caution against the assumption that to do sensory research it is 'necessary to literally see, hear, touch, or smell the phenomenon studied' (p. 595). These scholars show how, through a combination of creative interviewing (see also Chapter 9) and visual methods (see also Chapter 11), that it is possible to use and rework existing qualitative methods in order to understand the sensory in everyday lives. Likewise, Harris and Guillemin (2012) make the case for researchers developing a sensory awareness in qualitative interviewing so that this form of engagement can act as a portal to experiences that can be 'too difficult to articulate, too mundane to recount, or too intangible to otherwise access' (p. 692).

These creative possibilities are further explored by Merchant (2011), who adopts an interdisciplinary approach to tackle the challenge of collecting and analysing embodied, sensuous and pre-reflective 'data' by integrating videography into her study of novice scuba divers. The reactions of the divers to a film, produced by Merchant, in which they can see and hear themselves in action underwater suggests that the audio-visual medium can evoke other sensory modalities and appeal to multiple senses. Watching the footage of their dives it evoked physical responses to the sounds and images, which allowed them to 'feel for and in' themselves the sensations instigated by an experience that had taken place in a removed location and at a previous time. The video seems to have provided a means of representing sensory experience in a way that opened more directly onto the sensorium, which encouraged the learner divers to talk through their encounters as shown on the screen in rich sensuous detail. Video elicitation, therefore, appears to offer pathways to other senses and can assist in generating rich and reflective descriptions of events and embodied experiences.

Drawing on Pink's (2009) call for a multisensory approach to visual methods, Orr and Phoenix (2015) use photo-elicitation (see also Chapters 9 and 11) to explore older sporting adults' embodied experiences of physical activity. Initially, they used life-history interviews (see also Chapter 9) and found that these provided rich material on how the participants interacted with other people involved in their physical activity. In contrast, Orr and Phoenix found that the participants' responses to the photographs of themselves being active helped them to reveal their embodied, sensory interactions with objects and the surrounding environment. Their work, with that of Merchant (2011), confirm Pink's (2011) assertion that that photo-elicitation can be 'rethought' and 'reinterpreted' as a 'multisensory artefact' and' the practice of viewing it as 'involving the interconnected senses rather than vision isolation' (p. 608).

Importantly, the methodological challenges raised by the sensory revolution requires researchers to develop a sensory intelligence that, for Vannini *et al.* (2012) involves the ability to understand one's and others' sensations. For them, it is the 'skilled use of sensibility to approach life situations. It is the ability to utilize one's senses as skills to manipulate and adapt to one's environment. It is the combined emotional, visceral, and cognitive ability to engage in somatic work' (p. 67). Likewise, in considering the need for multisensorial and emplaced ways of knowing in ethnography, Pink (2009) talks of developing the 'sensory imagination' and 're-sensing' the process of participant observation. This involves moving from a sensory bias to a sensory subjectivity that entails a reflexive appreciation of one's own sensorium. To cultivate a cross-sensory awareness that other cultures and groups do not necessarily work with the same sensorium or experience as the researcher, in the first instance, the researcher must develop an awareness of their sensory biases in the field.

Developing these forms of sensory intelligence and sensory imagination, whether it be in the form of ethnographic immersion, using more traditional methods such as interviews, or developing these alongside other digital and/or visual technologies, is no easy task. It has major implications for how research in sport and exercise is conceptualised as both a process and a product, in terms of how we access the senses, engage with the sensorium in action and represent our findings to others.

The sensory revolution and research in sport and exercise

To date, the sensory revolution has not had a major impact on research in sport and exercise. As Allen-Collinson and Hockey (2015) comment, 'despite a growing body of ethnographic studies of particular sports, little analytical attention has been devoted to the actual concrete practices of "doing" or "producing" sporting activity, particularly from a sensory ethnographic perspective' (p. 63). This said, the revolution has touched a small but significant group of researchers working within a diverse range of traditions and using different kinds of methods. For example, Hockey and Allen-Collinson (2007) called on researchers to draw on phenomenology, in order to produce accounts grounded in the corporeal realities of the lived sporting body and its sensory activities that include movement and rhythm, the aural and respiration, the visual, the olfactory and the haptic.

This call was reinforced by Sparkes (2009) who, having provided three vignettes to illustrate the senses of smell, touch, sound, taste and vision in action within different sports-related contexts, makes the case for a more balanced consideration with regard to embodiment that includes all the senses rather than a select few. Since then, scholars in sport and exercise have drawn on a range of methodological approaches to answer this call. A selection will now be considered to give a flavour of this emerging work. In making this selection, I am acutely aware of excellent work that I have had to leave out, and to those who have not been mentioned I offer my apologies.

Re-embracing the visual and rethinking how it might be reconstructed within sensory studies of sport and exercise, Merchant (2011) explores the haptic–visual and visceral experiences of novice scuba divers as they watch a video of themselves in action underwater. Likewise, combining ethnography with in-depth analysis of digital visual material gained from a Swedish skateboard park, Backstrom (2014) explores the emplaced and multisensory kinaesthetic experiences of its practitioners in relation to how they express explosiveness though their bodies via the processes of remembrance, enforcement and energy transformation. In so doing, he illustrates that sight is not the most important sense in skateboarding and is subservient to the tactile, the kinaesthetic and the auditory senses working together.

More recently, using photo-elicitation techniques, Orr and Phoenix (2015) illuminated the multisensorial dynamics of the aging body as it engages with physical activity in different environments. For example, under a photograph of one of their participant's named Janice, aged 63, swimming in a pool, they point out that the touch (soft) and temperature (cool) of water, and the sensations of movement (gliding) in water, are important elements in her account of her swimming experience. Orr and Phoenix also suggest that Janice's account illustrates her corporeal awareness in that she is attuned to her ageing body's need to 'warm up', after which 'aches' and 'stiffness' disappear, and her experience of the kinaesthetic sensations of her moving body and limbs in relation to the different swimming strokes. Finally, Janice's corporeal awareness is also taken to encompass her breathing pattern as she listens and evaluates when her breathing is 'right' and 'slows' at the end of her exercise session.

The visual, is also the focus of attention for Hockey and Allen-Collinson (2007) in their collaborative autoethnographic study (see Chapter 23) of how distance runners develop particular ways of seeing and experiencing their training terrain by drawing on specific subcultural stocks of knowledge. Focusing on the same topic and using the same methodology, Allen-Collinson and Hockey (2015) further investigate how, as runners, they visualize their route in terms of hazardous or performance places in relation to feeling time, space and place. Alongside this, Hockey (2006) provides insights into how distance runners use their auditory, olfactory and haptic senses, as well as that of vision, to negotiate their routes. Regarding the olfactory, he notes that, when runners train they produce and engage with immediate smellscapes particular to themselves and their routes. This consists of an amalgam of odours or aromas that change according to activity, space, place and atmospheric/seasonal conditions. For Hockey, those odours relevant to distance runners help individuals substantiate their athletic identity in a number of ways: in an embodied sense; in a biographical sense; and in a space-time sense.

Combining an interview-based study of an experienced diver with autoethnographic data based on their running experiences, the haptic dimensions of temperature and pressure are compared by Allen-Collinson and Hockey (2011) in distance running and scuba diving. They reveal how the texture, movement and temperature of the elements through which they move are central to the embodied experiences of divers and runners. Also using an autoethnographic approach, Allen-Collinson and Owton (2015) further explore the role of the haptic senses in the processes of warming-up and thermoregulation in distance running and boxing. They show how the 'touch' of heat and its corporeal indicators, such as profuse sweating, are central in producing periods of intense pleasurable embodiment in which the senses work together to generate a kind of bodily 'high'.

The sensations of air and water touching the skin are also commented on by Humberstone (2011), who draws on autoethnographic and ethnographic data to explore the interrelationship of space, the elements and the embodied experiences of windsurfing as a water-based physical activity. Her findings illuminate the connections between the flesh, affects, emotions and the senses as the body engages with natural elements. Humberstone's embodied experience as a windsurfer are embedded in nature as she simultaneously sees, smells and feels it through her skin and body as she moves in relation to the changing dynamics of the wind and sea in a given space. Engaging with expressions of spirituality and the speculative notion of kinetic empathy, Humberstone is able to propose the concept of body pedagogics as analytically useful in exploring social and environmental action in local and global spaces.

Similar sensual issues are raised by Fox, Humberstone and Dubnewick (2014) in their autoethnographic, narrative (see Chapters 4 and 20) and comparative exploration of a self-supported long-distance bicycle tour in Hawaii undertaken by Fox. The findings reveal that as her tour proceeded, Fox experienced dramatic shifts in her sensorium as she meandered between conceptual and perceptual space times, between sensory and mystical worldviews and colonial and Eurocentric views, and between the rational autonomous self and the sensory-sensual, self-filled-with-others-self.

The physical form of cycling continued, but everyday life and the production of space-time was altered. Rather than traveling on the road or land, she played with traveling through a vibrant, alive, and sentient world where fragrances, winds, and rains were 'reaching out to her' with information about the location of flowers for leis or teas to soothe an uneasy stomach . . . When she stopped, her hands brushed up among plants to feel their textures and stimulate fragrances; she collected one she now knew for meals; and tasted others to understand how her body responded.

(Fox, Humberstone & Dubnewick, 2014, p. 77)

The aural dimension of sporting embodiment is focused on by Allen-Collinson and Owton (2014). They combine an interview-based study conducted by Owton of a small group of non-elite athletes who had been diagnosed with asthma, with an autophenomenographic (see Chapter 2) study by Allen-Collinson of her own experiences as a runner who suffers from mild asthma that can be exercise-induced. Their findings illuminate how athletes with asthma develop a highly refined auditory attunement, and undertake forms of auditory work by monitoring with attentiveness their environment, the sounds of their asthma and being acutely aware of other proprioceptive indicators. Such auditory work enables them to identify very tiny nuanced changes in the body, and in their body–world relationships, allowing them to make adjustments accordingly.

The development of highly refined sensory attunements is a central feature of the ethnographic study by Hammer (2015) of a tandem-cycling group that pairs blind and sighted riders. Her findings embody vision as an active and somatic sense by revealing how tandem cycling is an intersensory performance, that involves the interplay and integration of visual, sonic, tactile and olfactory experiences, as well as kinesthetic sensations of movement in space.

Blind and visually impaired participants also emphasized the varied use of their senses while riding, describing the physicality of this activity, as well as their experience of nature through a sensory prism. The sense of hearing and the experience of sound, for instance, played a crucial role in this process . . . In addition to hearing, riders mentioned smelling their surroundings (e.g. the smell of flowers), and breathing the 'fresh air' of nature. Alongside hearing and smell, blind and visually impaired riders addressed rich tactile and haptic experiences within cycling, noticing sensations of temperature (riding on a hot/cold day, in the sun/the shade), sense of direction (when turning right or left, descending/ascending), and vibration (the actual movement of the bike), as well as sensations such as 'freedom', feeling 'high', 'good', 'tired', and 'exhausted'.

(Hammer, 2015, p. 7)

By focusing on social dialogue and the sensory body in her study, Hammer (2015) shows the ways in which integrated tandem cycling challenges distinct binary categories, bodily hierarchies and constructions of social otherness. Her study also reveals how the mutual experiences of those involved enriches the meanings of both blindness and sight, and challenges rigid boundaries of and boundaries around the senses, social identities and bodily functions. Here, a fostering of 'togetherness' based on a complex web of physical, emotional, and social interaction, generated an embodiment of reciprocity and interdependency between sight and the other senses, and between sighted and blind people. This challenged their perspectives on disability and the blind other, and allowed blindness to be addressed as a legitimate bodily performance and as an additional medium of experience.

A number of scholars who have conducted ethnographic studies of combat sports and the martial arts have also re-embodied vision as an active and somatic sense as they explore the interplay of the senses within a shifting sensorium. For example, Waquant's (2004) study of boxing reveals the sensuous intoxification that is a core experience for those serving their apprenticeship in this violent sport. Likewise, Downey's (2005) ethnography of capoeira shows the importance of sound and other senses as bodies move in rhythm and kinesthetically *feel* their way through the music and practices involved in this Brazilian martial art in ways that are 'simultaneously cooperative and competitive, aesthetic and antagonistic' (p. 2). Inspired by the work of these scholars, Spencer (2012, 2014) depicts the carnal dimensions of Mixed Martial Arts (MMA) by using his own intersensory, embodied and emplaced experience to introduce us to bodies that touch, see, smell, taste, hear and feel combat.

Spencer (2012) illustrates the temporal and spatial dimensions of his MMA club and the role that sight and sound play in how fighters come to know and act within it. He also focuses on the haptic dimensions of this process that are most evident when fighters are in the clinch, standing or on the floor grappling with each other. As he describes it, 'Combatants must feel when to move, a touch sensitivity that is built up over time and practice. Not only must fighters have a heightened sense of their own bodies, but they must also feel their way through the body of their opponents' (2012, p. 43).

Regarding the olfactory dimension of combat, Spencer (2012) notes that the smelling of a person's body odour is the most intimate perception of them, and that 'our sense of them, their significance to us, and our histories of them are formed in and through smell' (p. 47). The smell of bodies intermingles with other smells that are dependent on place and time.

> The smells of these spaces intensifies according to the accumulation of bodies. In terms of the temporality, intensification of odor corresponds to the time of the classes and the forms of dueling that dominate the experience of MMA. Whereas the mats have the faint smell of cleaning products prior to night classes, odors reach their highest intensity after three hours of grappling or stand-up sparring as bodies shed heat and sweat.
>
> *(Spencer, 2012, p. 48)*

Mingling with the other senses in the MMA club is the taste of the rudiments and products of combat. For example, the taste of the plastic mouth guard can range from sweet fluoride, to neutral, to bitter. Likewise there is the taste of blood that signals the event of battle and characterizes the sensory experience of fighting. Here, 'the breakdown of bodies is reflected in the taste of blood. Its salty-iron flavor reflects the bodies' fissure' (p. 51). To taste one's blood and to bleed in the gym alongside fellow fighters provides a sense of belonging and signifies one's membership amongst the wider MMA community.

The MMA gym, as described by Spencer (2012, 2014) through the corporeal realities of his fighting body is self-evidently multi- and intersensorial in nature. Even though for convenience, he deals with each sense separately, it is clear that MMA fighters rarely experience training in club or combat though a singular sensory modality, but rather in intersensory ways, with two or more senses working together in close harmony. The same can be said for all the other studies that have been considered above in the ways in which they take the reader into the dynamic and shifting sensorium as it operates in 'real time' in various activities. Like Pink (2009), these scholars are acutely aware of the inevitable falsity of separating out the senses for representation and then focusing on one modality. They are well aware that no sense can be totally isolated from others, and in their focus on one or two sensory modalities they often seek to evoke a fuller embodied, multisensory experience for the audience.

Finally, as Sparkes and Smith (2012) argue, the work of the sensory and sensual scholars considered above provide an important corrective to disembodied and distanced perspectives that conceptualise the moving sporting body as nothing but a signifying vehicle of cultural codes. Such perspectives ignore the fleshy, messy, material (biological) and sentient body along with the lived practical experiences of those who inhabit 'real' bodies as members of what Vannini *et al.* (2012) describe as social and cultural *sensory communities* who come to learn and share common ways of using their senses and making sense of sensations.

Brief reflections

Given the work described above perhaps we can begin to think about a mini sensory revolution occurring in sport and exercise research. If this is to develop further in the future then we need to assist young researchers in their quest to seek the senses. Attempting to enhance the sensory intelligence and imagination of researchers, and help them to open up their bodies to the experiential dynamics of corporeal movement through time, space and place, raises pedagogical questions about how 'research methods' courses are taught to students before they conduct fieldwork. In short, how might we begin to develop the features that Harris and Guillemin (2012) believe are required to ensure that researchers are attuned to the sensory? These include researchers acknowledging the importance of the sensory in their research so that they become 'prepared to perceive' before they move on to acquire the skills and strategies that enable them to better tune into the senses.

One way of doing this, Sparkes (2009) suggests, is to assist students to get to know the same location over time, in different ways, using different senses. For example, task one might be to visit a gym and describe it in terms of what is seen via the use of photographs and field notes. Task two, on another day, might be to go in and describe the soundscape of the same gym and how sound works within it. On another occasion, the focus will be on the haptic, the skinscape, and how touch and textures work in the gym to create and sustain meaning. Likewise, the senses of smell (the pan*aroma*) and taste would be the focus of attention on different days.

The purpose of these tasks is to reawaken the senses in the neophyte researcher and to help them realize that all the senses are involved in understanding the life of the gym, or any other place, as a sensescape and sensorium. As part of this reawakening, crucial questions can be raised about how, as people engage in somatic work in various settings according to specific somatic rules, the senses interact in various combinations and hierarchies to shape the experiences and meanings of those involved in terms of various categories, such as gender, ethnicity, (dis)ability, age, social class, sexual orientation and religion.

Another pedagogical challenge, not just to students but to established scholars as well, revolves around the dilemmas of representing the senses and the sensorium. As Spencer (2012) reminds us 'Quotidian and academic descriptions, while hinting at the various ways the senses are registered in sport, fail to adequately engage with the full spectrum of the senses and how sensory dimensions are experienced in concert' (p. 33). Likewise, for Wacquant (2013) there is no point in researchers immersing themselves bodily in the field with a view to producing a carnal sociology (or psychology) if what is 'revealed about the sensorial magnetism of the universe in question ends up disappearing later in the writing' (p. 31). Accordingly, he asks himself the following question: 'How to go from the guts to the intellect, from the comprehension of the flesh to the knowledge of the text?' (p. 31).

In answer to his own question, Wacquant (2013) argues that to capture and convey to the reader 'the taste and ache of action' (p. 30) requires a radical departure from the traditional realist tale described by Sparkes (2002) and Sparkes and Smith (2014), with its characteristic features of experiential author(ity), the participant's point of view and interpretive omnipotence (see also Chapter 22). This involves rejecting the incorporeality of conventional academic writing and embracing more multifaceted forms of experimental writing (see Chapter 23) that mixes styles and genres in order to take us into the fleshy and messy world of the senses.

Others grappling with the challenges of representing the sensuous body in textual form have drawn directly on the work of Stoller (1997) and his calls for *sensual scholarship* in which 'writers tack between the analytical and the sensible, in which embodied form as well as disembodied logic constitute scholarly argument' (p. xv). Developing this notion, Vannini *et al.* (2012) speak of writing sensuously as a way of inviting audiences to a double layer of reflection.

> The first layer is descriptive, not in order to claim that we are portraying reality objectively (writing cannot accomplish this), but in order to evoke and create in our audience sensations that evoke research settings, people, and the phenomena that interest us. The other layer links the ideographic with the nomothetic, private sensations with public discourses, somatic experience with sensory order, somatic careers with sensory histories, private recollections with collective memories.
>
> *(Vannini* et al., *2012, p. 74)*

Such writing, Vannini *et al.* (2010) argue, can take the form of a *somatic layered account* that is proportionately prosaic and poetic, drawing as it does upon multiple forms of consciousness or ways of knowing, such as the embodied, the somatic, the affective, the imaginative, the linguistic and the non-symbolic, and the intellectual and analytical. Having suggested a number of strategies that authors can use to write somatically, Vannini *et al.* (2012) emphasise that producing such accounts and writing sensuously is not an easy or automatic task. For them, it 'requires deploying representation technics and techniques; it demands skill, and constitutes a creative act, a form of poiesis' (p. 80).

For Pink (2009), scholarly writing remains a central, and she believes crucial, medium for the transcription, evocation, argument and theoretical debating of research that attends to the senses. Various forms of writing *can* connect sensory experience and theoretical discussion in instructive ways. This said, she notes the following:

> Yet, conventional scholarly practice is limited in its capacity to communicate about the directness of the sensory and affective elements of emplaced experience. Alternative routes to representing sensory knowing have been developed in arts practice and there are opportunities for these practices to both inform and be developed collaboratively with sensory approaches to ethnographic representation.
>
> *(Pink, 2009, p. 132)*

As part of a growing interest in written creative analytical practices and arts-based performative research methodologies across the social sciences, these alternative routes for representing the senses include autoethnography, poetic representations, ethnographic fiction and non-fiction, ethnodrama and ethnotheatre, dance, musical performance, and installations, to name but a few (see Chapter 23). As Sparkes (2002) and Sparkes and Smith (2014) point out, each of these genres has their strengths and weaknesses when it comes to representing lived experience. They emphasise that any given genre must be chosen with care and used in ways that show respect for the artistic traditions inherent in each if their potential for conveying the senses in sport and exercise is to be achieved. While art can be a powerful tool for communicating research knowledge it can also, as Bartlett (2015) points out, 'overshadow the scholarly to both positive and negative effects. Researchers need to be aware of what art can offer, and what it cannot, when it comes to research communication' (p. 1).

Besides the genres named above, Dicks, Soyinka and Coffey (2006) point out that qualitative researchers have a broad range of media at their disposal for representing their completed work. These include digital media such as photographs, video film, audio-recordings, graphics and others besides (see Chapters 11 and 27). They note how through the computer 'writing space', these media can be integrated together, alongside more conventional written interpretation, into hypermedia environments. While this development offers exciting opportunities, such integration poses a number of potential problems. In particular, Dicks and colleagues argue that different media can be seen to 'afford' different kinds of meaning. Therefore, researchers thinking about using multimodal representations need to give careful consideration to the kinds of meaning afforded by different media, and pay attention to the overlaps among, and distinctiveness of different modes as this alerts us to the ways in which different media can be used for representing multimodality. Importantly, researchers should not assume that 'multimedia automatically gives us multimeaning, satisfactorily reflecting the multimodality of the field' (p. 94).

Clearly, a number of challenges face researchers in sport and exercise in their quest to seek the senses and represent them in vibrant and authentic ways. In this they are not alone, and comfort and sustenance can be found from others working in the social sciences who are facing the same challenges. This sets the scene for some interesting interdisciplinary and transdisciplinary work on the senses to develop in the future, in which researchers in sport and exercise can not only make a major contribution but, in many instances, actually lead the way forward. That such a possibility exists bears testimony to the quality of the work on the senses undertaken by the scholars discussed in this chapter. They should be applauded and thanked for their efforts. Their scholarship has provided a firm foundation on which to build, and it is hoped that many more researchers in sport and exercise will feel motivated to engage more fully with the senses in the coming years.

References

Allen-Collinson, J. & Hockey, J. (2011). Feeling the way: Notes towards a haptic phenomenology of distance running and scuba diving. *International Review for the Sociology of Sport, 46*, 330–345.

Allen-Collinson, J. & Hockey, J. (2015). From a certain point of view: Sensory phenomenological envisionings of running space and place. *Journal of Contemporary Ethnography, 44*, 63–83.

Allen-Collinson, J. & Owton, H. (2014). Take a deep breath: Asthma, sporting embodiment, the senses and 'auditory work'. *International Review for the Sociology of Sport, 49*, 592–608.

Allen-Collinson, J. & Owton, H. (2015). Intense embodiment: Senses of heat in women's running and boxing. *Body & Society, 21*, 245–268.

Backstrom, A. (2014). Knowing and teaching kinaesthetic experience in skateboarding: An example of sensory placement. *Sport, Education and Society, 19*, 752–772.

Bartlett, R. (2015). Visualising dementia: Using the arts to communicate research findings. *Qualitative Research, 15*(6), 755–768.

Blackman, L. (2008). *The body*. Oxford: Berg.

Bull, M., Gilroy, P., Howes, D. & Kahn, D. (2006). Introducing sensory studies. *Senses and Society, 1*, 5–7.

Classen, C. (2005). Fingerprints: Writing about touch. In C. Classen (Ed.), *The book of touch* (pp. 1–9). Oxford: Berg.

Dicks, B., Soyinka, B. & Coffey, A. (2006). Multimodal ethnography. *Qualitative Research, 6*, 77–96.

Downey, G. (2005). *Learning Capoeira: Lessons in cunning from an Afro-Brazilian art*. New York: Oxford University Press.

Drobnick, J. (2006). Introduction: Olfactocentrism. In J. Drobnick (Ed.), *The smell culture reader* (pp. 1–9). Oxford: Berg.

Fox, K., Humberstone, B. & Dubnewick, M. (2014). Cycling into sensoria: Embodiment, leisure, and tourism. *Tourism Review International, 18*, 71–85.

Hammer, G. (2015). Pedalling in pairs toward a 'dialogical performance': Partnerships and the sensory body within a tandem cycling group. *Ethnography, 16*(4), 503–522.

Harris, A. & Guillemin, M. (2012). Developing sensory awareness in qualitative interviewing: A portal to the otherwise unexplored. *Qualitative Health Research, 22*, 689–699.

Hockey, J. (2006). Sensing the run: The senses and distance running. *Senses and Society, 1*, 183–202.

Hockey, J. & Allen-Collinson, J. (2007). Grasping the phenomenology of sporting bodies. *International review for the sociology of sport, 42*, 115–131.

Howes, D. (2004). *Sensual relation: Engaging the senses in culture & social theory.* Michigan: University of Michigan Press.

Howes, D. (2005). Introduction: Empire of the senses. In D. Howes (Ed.), *Empire of the senses: A sensual culture reader* (pp. 1–17). Oxford: Berg.

Howes, D. (2006). Charting the sensorial revolution. *Senses & Society, 1*, 113–118.

Humberstone, B. (2011). Embodiment and social and environmental action in nature-based sport: Spiritual spaces. *Leisure Studies, 30*, 495–512.

Leder, D. (1990). *The absent body.* Chicago, IL: University of Chicago Press.

Mason, J. & Davies, K. (2009). Coming to our senses: A critical approach to sensory methodology. *Qualitative Research, 9*, 587–603.

Merchant, S. (2011). The body and the senses: Visual methods, videography and the submarine sensorium. *Body & Society, 17*, 53–72.

Orr, N. & Phoenix, C. (2015). Photographing physical activity: Using visual methods to 'grasp at' the sensual experience of the aging body. *Qualitative Research, 15*, 454–472.

Paterson, M. (2007). *The sense of touch: Haptics, affects and technologies.* Oxford: Berg.

Paterson, M. (2008). Review essay: Charting the return of the senses. *Environment and Planning, 26*, 563–569.

Pink, S. (2009). *Doing sensory ethnography.* London: Sage.

Pink, S. (2011). A multisensory approach to visual methods: In E. Margolis & L Pauwels (Eds.), *The Sage handbook of visual methods* (pp. 601–614). London: Sage.

Sparkes, A. C. (2002). *Telling tales in sport & physical activity: A qualitative journey.* Champaign, IL: Human Kinetics Press.

Sparkes, A. C. (2009). Ethnography and the senses: Challenges and possibilities. *Qualitative Research in Sport, Exercise & Health, 1*, 21–35.

Sparkes, A. C. (2015). Ethnography as a sensual way of being: Methodological and representational challenges. In G. Molnar & L. Purdy (Eds.), *Ethnographies in sport and exercise research* (pp. 45–58). London: Routledge.

Sparkes, A. C. & Smith, B. (2012). Embodied research methodologies and seeking the senses in sport and physical culture: A fleshing out of problems and possibilities. In K. Young & M. Atkinson (Eds.), *Qualitative research on sport and physical culture* (pp. 167–190). United Kingdom: Emerald.

Sparkes, A. C. & Smith, B. (2014). *Qualitative research methods in sport, exercise and health: From process to product.* London: Routledge.

Spencer, D. (2012). *Ultimate fighting and embodiment: Violence, gender, and mixed martial arts.* London: Routledge.

Spencer, D. (2014). Seeking violence: An ethnography of mixed martial arts. *Ethnography, 15*, 232–254.

Stoller, P. (1997). *Sensuous scholarship.* Philadelphia: University of Pennsylvania Press.

Vannini, P., Ahluwalia-Lopez, G., Waskul, D. & Gottschalk, S. (2010). Performing taste at wine festivals: A somatic layered account of material culture. *Qualitative Inquiry, 16*, 378–396.

Vannini, P., Waskul, D. & Gottschalk, S. (2012). *The senses in self, society, and culture.* London: Routledge.

Wacquant, L. (2004). *Body and soul: Notebooks of an apprentice boxer.* Oxford: Oxford University Press.

Wacquant, L. (2013). Habitus as topic and tool: Reflections on becoming a prizefighter. In R. Garcia & D. Spencer (Eds.), *Fighting scholars: Habitus and ethnographies of martial arts and combat sports* (pp. 19–31). London: Anthem Press.

27

THE WEB AND DIGITAL QUALITATIVE METHODS

Researching online and researching the online in sport and exercise studies

Andrea Bundon

In an era where 'new media' is no longer that 'new' and where digital technologies are integrated into everyday existence, it seems a little stale to ask if we, as qualitative researchers, will use the Internet in our work. The better question is 'how will our use of the Internet inform our work and what will it change?' Will we, as Earl and Kimport (2011) advocate, learn to leverage the technological affordances of the net? Or will we use new technologies to do the same old thing thereby 'backing into the future' (Meikle, 2002, p. 143)? This chapter will address these questions providing first, an overview of how the Internet is currently being used in qualitative sport studies and, second, identifying that research that challenges us to consider what new methods are made possible by new media. Using examples from the fields of sport and exercise, it will explore how the way we talk about the Web has shaped our thinking about the possibilities of the technologies and subsequently informed how digital qualitative methods have been integrated into research practice. It will compare and contrast those digital qualitative methods that extend the reach of projects, enabling researchers to do more with less, to other methods that fundamentally change the type of qualitative research possible and imaginable.

What is the Web?

For most researchers, regardless of the field, the Internet has become embedded in our research processes and integral to how we work. When deciding on our next project, for example, we start by going online. By 'surfing the net' we familiarise ourselves with the field. We visit websites, send email inquiries, read documents and watch videos and, in so doing, we formulate our ideas, identify the gaps in existing knowledge and refine our research questions. Moreover, we do all of this routinely with little conscious reflection on the technologies that make it possible. This in itself is not remarkable. Every day we use technologies with only a minimal understanding of how they work – flip a switch and a light goes on; turn a key and the car starts – why should the Internet be any different?

Because the Internet *is* different. Or, more accurately, the *Web* is different. And contrary to popular usage, the two are not the same thing. The Internet is a global network of computers, or rather, a network of networked computers connected by wired and wireless means through which information is transmitted using standardised communication protocols. The Web, in contrast, is how most of us access the Internet. It is the interface that arranges the information from that network of computers into usable configurations including webpages, email platforms, online forums, apps and more. Not only does this interface enable us to access the information stored on countless networks and servers, but it is also via the Web that we are able to modify it – every message sent and every file uploaded changes the Internet minutely. Even when we are merely following links and making searches, our mouse clicks and key strokes leave traces by calling up and arranging data in new configurations; configurations that then feed back into algorithms and inform the results of our (or someone else's) subsequent searches, this shaping future online forays. To phrase it differently, the Internet is the infrastructure, but the Web is where the Internet happens.

It is that interface between technology and user that interests most of us working in the fields of sociocultural and psychological studies of sport and exercise. While I recognise that there may be individuals who are genuinely interested in understanding the technical aspects of the Internet and the Web, that is not the focus of this chapter and is well outside my expertise. Rather my intent is to explore how people are using the Web and what they are trying to do when they go online. This discussion will span the motives and strategies employed by qualitative researchers when they use the Web as a tool for research, and also the multitude of ways that athletes, sports fans, exercisers, sporting subcultural groups, sport activists and others are integrating the Web into their daily activities. Although this discussion will include specific examples of Web-based platforms and software systems that are being used by qualitative researchers or by the populations they are researching, the swift rate of change when it comes to technologies makes me wary about providing a step-by-step guide of 'how to do digital qualitative methods'. Instead, I take my lead from new media theorist Jodi Dean who wrote in the opening of her book, *Blog Theory* (2010), that it is easy for scholars studying the Web to get caught up in the momentum of rapid changes where we feel we only have time to react and no time to think critically. Despite this challenge, Dean (2010) did not discourage scholars from entering the field – quite the opposite. She stated that it is the responsibility of scholars to slow down and take time to produce work of substance that 'anchors its analyses of technologies, users, and practices in an avowedly political assessment of the present' (Dean, 2010, p. 3). She further pointed out that the studies of Web-based culture that continue to resonate do so precisely because they did not focus on specific technologies, but instead concentrated on the meaning that individuals and groups assigned to their use of these technologies. Thus my aim for this chapter is to encourage qualitative researchers to slow down and reflect upon how, why and where we are currently employing digital methods and, most importantly, to consider how we are positioning the Web in our field. In so doing, I endeavour to produce a chapter that is immediately useful to scholars but that also provides a solid platform for future discussions of digital qualitative methods.

What are digital qualitative methods?

In addition to defining how the Web is conceived of within our field, I want to explain what I mean when I use the term 'digital qualitative methods'. Even though I have been asked to write this chapter, have taught and led workshops on 'how to do digital qualitative research' and regularly employ digital methods in my own work, I am still searching for a satisfying definition that captures the full spectrum of what sport researchers are doing when we say we are using digital qualitative methods. What I can state definitively is that digital qualitative methods include the use of digital tools to collect data and the collection of digital data. In this sense, the term applies equally to online research into sport and also the research of sport online. Those engaged in these tasks draw on different traditions of inquiry including (but not limited to): media studies, youth studies, cultural studies, feminist studies and political sciences and their methods of data collection and analysis are equally eclectic. While I cannot possibly address all the work that might be included in the category of digital qualitative research, I will attempt to highlight the diverse types of digital and online tools that can facilitate research processes, and I will also discuss the new types of digital data available to sport researchers in the digital age.

Sport scholars and the information highway

A series of notes published in 1995 and 1996 by Michael Malec in the *Journal of Sport and Social Issues* explains that though the Internet and Web were technically available to many scholars in the early 1990s, the ability to 'make useful contributions and to absorb useful information' (Malec, 1995a, p. 108: see also Malec 1995b, 1996) were things that academics first needed to learn. In these notes, Malec provided detailed instructions on how to send emails, and find and join listserv discussion groups (including the SPORTSOC listserv started in 1992 by the North-American Society for the Sociology of Sport). While present-day readers will undoubtedly find the bit describing the ability to share out-of-print journal articles with fellow academics as one of the 'greatest virtues' (Malec, 1995, p. 109) of the Internet very dated and a little amusing, I raise this example not to mock but to illustrate that our ability to leverage the Internet in our research is dependent upon the technologies available, *but also upon our knowledge of how to use these technologies and our ability to imagine their possible uses*. Malec's notes remind us that the Web does indeed hold enormous potential but this potential is only realised when we take the time to acquire (and teach) digital literacies.

Technological affordances: leveraging the possibilities of the Web

The Web does genuinely open up new possibilities for research and this will, at times, require new methods or at least a retooling of existing methods. The concept of 'technological affordances' comes from the sociology of science and has been described as the middle road between realist approaches (see Chapters 1 and 22), such as technological determinism (the view that technologies themselves can impact the social world) and constructionist approaches (which refers to the assumption that technologies and the uses to which they are put are socially constructed; see also Chapters 1 and 10). Technological affordances, according to Earl and Kimport (2011), 'have the benefit of simultaneously acknowledging the real material opportunities and constraints that technologies impose on users at a given moment while also acknowledging that without people using a technology in various ways, what it offers is meaningless' (p. 36). In other words, platforms such as online forums, Google, Twitter and Facebook do not in themselves alter the social world, but they do support certain forms of communication and thus make those forms of communication more likely than others. Technological affordances, then, can be defined as '*the actions and uses that a technology makes qualitatively easier or possible when compared to prior like technologies*' (Earl & Kimport, 2011, p. 32; italics in original). Accordingly, scholars who use the Web to do the same type of research that they have always done (albeit more efficiently or with a greater reach) may be failing to take advantage of the affordances of the Web. Conversely, those who explore what new forms of research are now possible because of the technologies available can be said to be leveraging the affordances of the Web.

Web as artefact or Web as place?

Internet theorist Christine Hine (2000) wrote that the Web is simultaneously a cultural artefact and a place where culture occurs. As such, the Web can be the object of one's inquiry (cultural artefact) and/or the research site (place where culture occurs). Reflecting upon how we position the Web in our work – as an artefact, as a place or as both – and the associated affordances is the first step in understanding how to use qualitative digital methods. The first research projects in the field of sport to engage with digital qualitative methods largely viewed Web-based content as an artefact or a text; it was something created or uploaded by an individual, a media network or an organisation that could be subjected to analysis. Furthermore, although Tim Berners-Lee, the man credited with the invention of the Web, described it as a 'communications channel that makes possible a continuous world-wide conversation' (Berners-Lee, 2010, p. 82), the reality is that, in the early days of the Web, there was a clear demarcation between the small group of computer-savvy individuals who produced content and the rest of the population who consumed it. Subsequently, sport scholars studying the Web at that time were largely interested in the 'cybersport media spaces' that were emerging on the Web (McDaniel & Sullivan, 1998). These media spaces included content produced by traditional sport media players as, for example, sport media conglomerates added websites to their existing print and broadcast offerings. But they also included previously unseen media spaces as fans and athletes with the technical skill and resources to engage in online built their own websites and forums. Some of the earliest examples of online research into these nascent media spaces included Mitrano's (1999) study of the use of metaphors by fans in online discussion about the relocation of a sport franchise, and Plymire and Forman's (2000) research into the use of Internet newsgroups devoted to women's basketball, to express support for lesbians in pro-sport. Though some of the groups that formed online were rooted in pre-existing, offline networks (for example, supporters of particular football clubs), in other instances, the digital networks that formed were global, with participants who had never met 'in real life' coalescing around particular interests, common experiences or political and/or embodied identities as was demonstrated, for example, in Wilson's (2002) study of 'anti-jocks'.

Although emerging forms of new media were certainly providing sport scholars with new data sources, the methods used to study this online content were firmly grounded in older methodologies. The scholars researching cybersport media spaces were informed largely by media studies (see Chapter 12) and cultural studies, and they employed methods of analysis that included content analysis, discourse analysis (see Chapter 18) and media framing. Whereas there was a lot of debate in academia about the democratic potential of a Web that would provide 'ordinary citizens' (including sport fans, athletes, sporting subcultural groups and sport advocates/activists) with the opportunity to produce and distribute content of their own making while bypassing the traditional barriers to offline publishing (i.e. prohibitive costs and/or gaining access to and control of distribution channels) (Barton, 2005; Dart, 2009), few were questioning whether the content then published online was qualitatively different from traditional media content. In short, the Web content being digitally mined was considered a digital artefact – something produced by humans and published online that could then provide insight into the cultural context of its creation and its creators.

The other way to think of the Web is as a place and site for social performances: the Web as a cultural space. But learning to think differently about the potential uses of the Web does not happen in isolation and research practices are developed parallel to, and in conjunction with, the Web's employment in broader society. The term 'Web 2.0' was popularised in 2004, and refers to the shift towards digital technologies that privilege user-generated content and support collaborative and social uses of the Web (O'Reilly, 2005). The transition from Web 1.0 (where content was created by a relatively small few for the consumption of many) to Web 2.0 was the result of modifications to how websites were configured, accompanied by changes in how users were using the Web. The most popular example of Web 2.0 is Wikipedia, but the term equally applies to modifications in general Web functionality – modifications that made it increasingly simple for users to upload, download, like, share, repost, edit, mash up or otherwise create, repurpose and transform digital content. Furthermore, changes to the functionality of the Web both influenced and were influenced by an evolution in how people were thinking about the Web's role in society (Hine, 2015). Whereas the terms used to discuss the Web in its earlier iterations (the Information Superhighway and the Electronic Frontier, for example) focused the conversation on who would be the first to access, populate and capitalise on the Internet, the discussion around Web 2.0 centred on the collaborative opportunities the new technologies would support. Web 2.0 was a place where people could form virtual communities, crowd-source (and crowd-fund) ideas, and sow the seeds for collective action leading Rheingold (2014) to claim that Web 2.0 was built on 'platforms of architectural participation' (p. 113).

The progression towards a more collaborative, interactive and user-focused Web also instigated a rethinking of online research frameworks. Evolving understandings of the Web (supported by new technological affordances) meant that the Web was increasingly being thought of as a space that is *co-constructed and contested*. Dart's (2009) study of amateur, independent blogs and professional, commercial blogs during the 2006 FIFA World Cup Finals is emblematic of this shift. Dart (2009) stated that while much had been made of the potential of the Internet in terms of 'allowing fans a greater voice and sense of participation' (p. 109), and the ability to tell their own sport stories rather than relying on the stories created by mainstream media, his empirical evidence indicated that commercially produced sports media still dominated in online environments. The issue, it would appear, is that while anyone can technically publish anything, few independent bloggers can compete with media corporations for online audience shares. Dart (2009) also reported that some fans who attempted to post on established sport media websites had their comments blocked by moderators because they expressed opinions different from those espoused by the networks; an act that seriously undermines the promise of democracy on the Web. Dart's work is a good example of research that marks the shift from thinking about online content as a set of singular texts (or artefacts) that can be downloaded and analysed in isolation, towards thinking about online content as something that is shaped through interactions and exchanges between numerous actors (a site of culture in action).

Included in the body of literature where the Web is conceptualised as a space for cultural performances is MacKay and Dallaire's study of 'skirtboarders' (MacKay & Dallaire, 2013a, 2013b, 2014). In their work, they explored how a group of female skateboarders, originally based in Montreal, Canada, used a website and blog to contest dominant discourses of sportswomen. The skateboarders, in writing blog posts, uploading videos and photographs used their website to 'produce, circulate, and use feminist materials, without professing to be feminists, to expand girls' and women's space in the Internet skateboarding landscape' (MacKay & Dallaire, 2014, p. 549). MacKay and Dallaire drew on multiple sources of data in their analysis, including the content of the skirtboarders' website, comments posted by visitors to the website (both by the skirtboarder crew and non-crew members) and offline group and one-to-one qualitative interviews (once again, with crew members and other non-affiliated blog readers). In addition to being one of the first to provide an in-depth understanding of how collective and individual sporting identities are negotiated in online spaces, MacKay and Dallaire's work also provides an example of research that employed multiple methods to understand online spaces from the perspectives of multiple users, including those involved in creating the content, those involved in the online conversations and those who engage with the online material as readers. The skirtboarder project reaffirms what Wilson (2002) concluded in his study of the 'anti-jock' (cyber) movement – that an individual's engagement with online, global networks is frequently closely entwined with their offline identity and local politics.

However, while MacKay and Dallaire addressed the use of the Web in forming collaborative spaces, Wilson and others focused on the contested nature of cyberspace, and have explored how sports-related activism and advocacy have expanded in the past decade so that online strategies are used to complement, support and extend offline actions. Included in this research are, for example, Millington and Darnell's (2014) investigation of how Olympic stakeholders and Olympic protestors have sought to legitimize competing narratives via online debates, Wilson and Hayhurst's (2009) study of online communication technologies employed by NGOs doing sport for development work, Scherer and Sam's (2010) exploration of the use of new media technologies to publicise local sport stadium debates, and Antunovic and Hardin's (2013) consideration of women's blog networks, and the production of alternative, feminist sports media. Collectively this body of research extends our understanding of the interplay between the online and the offline, demonstrating that the discourses that circulate in the virtual world are both informed by and inform real-world politics.

Getting permission: from lurking to participatory research in cyberspace

To this point I have discussed two different ways of thinking about the Web, as an artefact and as a space, and provided examples of the blurry boundaries between online and offline research. In the next section, I will address how different ways of positioning the Web in research lead to different practical and ethical decisions, particularly around getting access to digital data and obtaining consent for projects undertaken in cyberspace. Although the Web is frequently viewed as a place, there is indeed a crucial distinction between virtual spaces and real-world spaces – namely, that one's physical presence is not required to do digital research. Freed from the logistics of offline travel, the Web has permitted researchers to extend the purview of their research activities and to study populations and cultures that would have previously been barred to them using, for example, Skype to conduct interviews from a distance, or reading online forums to observe 'insider' conversations between members of close-knit, insular groups. However, this particular affordance has some interesting methodological implications because not only are scholars able to study groups that would previously have been inaccessible (or in the case of some online networks and virtual communities, groups that previously did not exist), but they are able to carry out this research discreetly.

'Lurker' is the term used to describe individuals who consume online content (reading messages posted in online forums, for example), but who do not themselves post comments or do anything that would alert other members of the online group of their virtual presence (Baumer, Sueyoshi & Tomlinson, 2011; Baym, 2010). When venturing into online research environments, researchers have to decide *how* they will enter the virtual field and the options include: lurking (observing and collecting data while remaining invisible to those they are researching); partial disclosure (for example, contacting site administrators or forum moderators, asking for consent to study the group); full disclosure (introducing themselves to online participants and/ or seeking consent from each individual); and finally, participatory methods (disclosing their presence and actively engaging with participants in a collaborative fashion).

Qualitative researchers have always had to address how they would enter the research field, who to ask for permission, how much to reveal about the project's purpose to participants and how to navigate the participant/observer role. However, it is only in the digital age that 'staying completely invisible' has become an option. In some instances researchers will choose the view from above (i.e. non-disclosure) for the purpose of collecting naturalistic data; that is, online content and online conversations posted by individuals unaware of the research being undertaken. For example, in their study of men's body projects in the context of weight management, Bennett and Gough (2013) explained that they used data collected discreetly from online forums because they were interested in men's talk 'without the potentially constraining presence of a researcher' (p. 287). Similarly, interested in the role of reality weight-loss television in public discourse of the 'obesity epidemic', Szto and Gray (2015) collected tweets by viewers watching the television programme *The Biggest Loser*, and explained that they used Twitter because it is a publically accessible forum albeit one where individuals frequently place personal information. Yet despite the fact that Twitter states in its privacy agreement that the information shared on the platform is by default public, Szto and Gray chose to present the data anonymously stating that 'out of respect for certain individuals who appear to be grappling with significant body issues, the authors chose to exclude Twitter handles for ethical considerations and because excluding handles did not greatly impact the richness of the data' (Szto & Gray, 2015, p. 327). Other examples of sport- and exercise-related research where scholars have collected data from online forums without seeking consent, or revealing the undergoing research project to forum participants, include Ferriter's (2009) investigation into the co-construction of professional athlete pages on Wikipedia, Hambrick *et al.*'s (2010) content analysis of tweets by major league athletes, Kassing and Sanderson's (2010) research into the use of Twitter during a major stage race by professional cyclists, McGovern's (forthcoming) study of racial discourses in baseball fan forums, and Sanderson's (2013) exploration of Facebook by football fans to elevate group distinctiveness in the face of a crisis within their club. In addition to allowing for data collection without concerns that the researcher's presence will prompt participants to change their behaviours, lurking can also enable scholars to research populations that would be off-limits to them in offline settings, for example, when researching subcultural groups where the researcher's age, gender, ethnicity, (dis)ability or other embodied identities would mark them as an outsider.

That said, researchers are not always outsiders and many conduct research on/with groups with whom they have prior affiliations online or offline. For those with insider status, lurking may not be a viable, desirable or ethical option. An avid blogger, Norman (2014) regularly contributes to hockey blogs and participates in online hockey discussion boards. Thus when he decided to conduct his virtual ethnography (see Chapters 5 and 11) of a fan-produced hockey blog, he was in fact studying an online community (or electronic tribe) of which he had been a part for nearly three years. Norman (2014) noted that the Canadian research council policy on ethical guidelines for using cyber-material did not *require* him to seek any permission to use content from the site, given that it was publically accessible. Yet despite it not being mandatory, he did indeed seek the permission of the blog's three administrators and had ongoing conversations with them throughout the project about how the data collected online was being used. Together they agreed that quotes from the forums could be included but that steps should be taken to maintain the anonymity of individual contributors – usernames were changed and the specific source of the quotes was not given. Norman's decisions were consistent with his positioning of the project in the ethnographic tradition (see Chapter 5) and his dual role of participant/observer. Like many ethnographers before him, Norman sought the permission of a small number of key actors while not disclosing his research to everyone in the immediate area. Similarly, in Pavlidis and Fullagar's (2013) research on 'Derby Grrrls' the authors relied on Pavlidis' insider involvement in derby culture to guide their selection of publically accessible websites, blogs and Facebook groups used in the analysis (with no permission sought), and complemented this online analysis with offline interviews (obtaining consent from participants).

In my own research into disability sport and online social networks, I employed a participatory research framework and worked with five Canadian Paralympians (community co-researchers) to create a blog entitled *AthletesFirst* (Bundon & Hurd Clarke, 2015a, 2015b). The blog team took turns writing posts for the blog and then we all used our existing online social networks (Facebook friends, Twitter, personal blogs and websites, team email lists, etc.) to advertise the posts and generate an online conversation about the topic on the *AthletesFirst* site. When readers clicked the comment box, they were presented with a pop-up box informing them that they could post the comment anonymously, using a pseudonym or 'handle' of their choice, or using their real name (full or partial), along with link to the full description of the project, including how comments would be collected and used, and how to contact the research team for further information. The name/handle under which participants posted their comments was used to identify them in subsequent research outputs (journal articles and conference presentations). Our decision to provide blog readers with a choice in how they were represented was consistent with the participatory research design (which emphasises that community members should have the opportunity to make informed decisions about their participation, and also be publically acknowledged as the authors of their statements should they so choose). It was interesting to note that few people commenting on the blog chose the option of being anonymous – most posted using partial or full names. In follow-up interviews with blog readers, many participants responded that they identified as advocates for disability sport and for people with disabilities more generally, and that engaging publically in online discussions about disability sport was part of being an advocate.

The previously cited examples demonstrate that the decision of how to enter the field – as an anonymous lurker, a participant/observer, or a research partner – is dependent on one's epistemology and methodology. The Web affords us the opportunity to engage with participants in previously impossible ways and that includes the ability to lurk in the background and do research unobserved. But it also enables us to communicate and collaborate with virtual communities that we would never have the opportunity to meet in the real world. Recognising these opportunities, and learning to capitalise on them, while still ensuring that our decisions are premised on rigorous methods and are ethical, is the challenge that qualitative researchers face working in the digital age. Learning to recognise how we are positioning the Web in our work, as a tool for research, as a source of qualitative data or as the field site for community-based participatory research (see Chapter 8) is an essential first step that will enable us to ensure that the decisions made throughout our projects, ethical and practical, are methodologically grounded.

Research on the move: the mobile Web and the evolution of digital qualitative methods

Although I cautioned earlier against focusing too much on the specific technologies because it is easy to get caught up in the hype of new innovations at the expense of trying to understand the more enduring characteristics digital research, there is one final 'shift' in thinking about Web that I need to address: the mobile Web. The mobile Web is the term used to describe the move from fixed-line Internet to wireless services accessed by portable devices. Like the evolution of Web 2.0 before it, this trend, which gained considerable momentum around 2007 (touch-screen smartphones and laptops) and further exploded in 2010 (tablets), has had a tremendous impact on how users think about and use the Web. While I previously discussed the blurred lines between an individual's offline activities and their engagement with online or virtual worlds, mobile technologies have further obliterated the divide. In 2012, I was interviewing an eighteen-year-old university student about his use of blogs and social media to follow Olympic and Paralympic athletes when I asked him the question 'how much time do you spend online?' His immediate response was: 'How would I know if I was offline? Are we offline right now?' His tone and our subsequent discussion confirmed to me that he was being clever, but the point was made; we were sitting in a coffee shop but our phones were on, we were both logged into multiple social-media sites, and our friends were sending us messages and interacting with our online profiles even as the two of us were engaged in a face-to-face conversation. Moreover, throughout the interview we had both used my laptop to 'show' each other what we were talking about – we had visited blogs, online news sources and Twitter, and the online content had stimulated our offline discussion. This is the 'embedded, embodied, and everyday' Internet that Christine Hine (2015) references in the title of her latest book.

Although I have already provided a few examples of Facebook and Twitter-based research, examples of published qualitative research from the fields of sport and exercise are still scarce. Even though individuals frequently (and perhaps increasingly) post to social-media networks via mobile devices, few in our fields have considered how this data might differ from that posted while sitting at a desk. But what could be more enticing to sport and exercise scholars than 'moving data'; data produced by bodies in motion? One scholar doing innovative work in this space is David McGillivray and his participatory research exploring digital citizenship in relation to the hosting of mega sport events and festivals (see, for example, McGillivray, 2014). Other emerging work in this vein includes: a study of solo long-distance runners who diligently upload the files from their GPS running watches to online community pages, and engage in online conversations with other runners while simultaneously rejecting any attempts to meet up for runs in 'real life' (Carlén & Maivorsdotter, 2014); a virtual ethnography of the use of social media by football supporters and football clubs in three European nations that also uses on-the-ground (a.k.a. offline) observations to challenge the discrepancies between how contesting groups portray their actions in mediated environments versus their behaviours in real life (Numerato, 2015); and a project that uses an app to ask questions of spectators in a stadium about the event they are currently watching encouraging them to provide real-time responses (García, Welford & Smith, 2015). These are just a few examples of the research I have encountered recently where mobile methods are being used to open up new research opportunities. I find it particularly interesting how all of these projects encourage us to think of the Web not purely as a space but as a dimension that overlays and provides an additional layer of richness to local environments rather than existing independently in cyberspace.

Conclusion

At the time I write this, the Web is more than a quarter of a century old[1] and few of us need instructions on how to write an email or search a journal article online. But neither are we digital natives. The problem with the concept of digital natives, writes boyd (2014), is that it puts too much emphasis on one's natural or intuitive ability to use Web-based technologies while downplaying the need to continually learn new digital literacies. When we start thinking that we know all we need to know about the Web, it becomes mundane and the risk is that we stop looking for new ways to use it in our research. It is only by being inquisitive and curious about new technologies and their affordances that we can remain open to the possibilities. As discussed, in the early days of its existence, the Web was described as an online media source or a virtual library, and as a result it was used in exactly that manner – people went online to retrieve information and access digital artefacts. Emerging understanding of cyberspace as co-constructed through dialogue and interactions and supported by an 'architecture of participation' (Rheingold, 2014, p. 113), opened the door for new forms of digital qualitative research that drew on the traditions of ethnographic inquiry and participant/observation. The technologies evolve so fast that it would be impossible for anyone to truly be an expert in the field of digital qualitative methods; the best we can do is remain attentive to the transformations that occur in how the Web is being thought of and used in society, so that we can continue to evaluate our methods in light of these changes and recognise when (and if) modifications to our methods are required. Table 27. 1 provides suggestions of things that should be considered before starting your research.

Table 27.1 Practical, ethical and methodological considerations when using digital qualitative methods

The following discussion points and suggested readings provide some examples of how researchers working with digital qualitative methods have addressed these key issues.

Public or private cyberspaces	According to the Canadian Panel on Research Ethics, review by a research ethics board prior to commencing a research project is not required for research that involves the observation of people in public places *provided the individuals targeted have no reasonable expectation of privacy*.
	In the context of Web-based research 'public places' has been interpreted to mean publicly accessible websites, and digital content to which access is unrestricted. There is, however, considerable debate as to what constitutes a 'reasonable expectation of privacy'. Participants in online chat rooms and forums may consider their conversations to be private, or behave as though they are interacting with a closed community even while knowing that access to the site is technically unrestricted. In these instances, the privacy expectation is high and researchers are advised to submit their proposal for research board review. It is, nevertheless, left to the discretion of the researcher to decide whether or not the participants have a reasonable expectation of privacy.
	For examples of different approaches to the issue of public and private cyberspaces, please see:
	Bennett, E. & Gough, B. (2013). In pursuit of leanness: The management of appearance, affect and masculinities within a men's weight-loss forum. *Health, 17*(3), 284–299.
	Brotsky, S. R. & Giles, D. (2007). Inside the 'pro-ana' community: A covert online participant observation. *Eating disorders, 15*(2), 93–109.
	Norman, M. (2014). Online community or electronic tribe? Exploring the social characteristics and spatial production of an Internet hockey fan culture. *Journal of Sport & Social Issues, 38*(5), 395–414.

Authorship or anonymity: Acknowledging online contributors	Within many of our fields there is a long-standing tradition of anonymously quoting participants interviewed for research purposes (a decision explained as being done for their own protection) while citing authors when we quote from published works. Online qualitative methods confound this issue on two levels. Firstly, the Internet has revolutionised what we think of as 'published' work, and many individuals who previously would not have the resources to publish and disseminate their work now self-publish online. Secondly, our interactions with research participants increasingly include written exchanges on blogs and online forums, in addition to or instead of face-to-face interviews. These two factors have blurred the line between participant and author and, increasingly, researchers, particularly those working from participatory research frameworks, are starting to have conversations with participants about whether or not they *want* to be recognised for their online contributions.

For examples of how different researchers have addressed the issue of anonymity versus authorship, particularly in participatory research, please see:

Barratt, M. J. & Lenton, S. (2010). Beyond recruitment? Participatory online research with people who use drugs. *International Journal of Internet Research Ethics*, *3*(1), 69–86.

Bundon, A. & Hurd Clarke, L. (2015a). Honey or vinegar? Athletes with disabilities discuss strategies for advocacy within the Paralympic movement. *Journal of Sport & Social Issues*, *39*(5), 351–370.

Participation and non-participation	In some types of social research, researchers are full participants in the communities in which they are carrying out their work. In other instances, researchers need to keep their participation to a minimum, and limit not only their participations but also what they disclose to participants. When the research spans online and offline spaces, this requires researchers to carefully manage their own online presence and digital profiles.

For examples of two different ways in which academics have managed their online activities and digital profiles while carrying out research with online/offline components, please read:

Numerato, D. (2015). Behind the digital curtain: Ethnography, football fan activism and social change. *Qualitative Research*, doi: 10.1177/1468794115611207.

Olive, R. (2013). 'Making friends with the neighbours': Blogging as a research method. *International Journal of Cultural Studies*, *16*(1), 71–84.

Note

1 The World Wide Web was created in 1990 by Tim Berners-Lee and his colleagues working at CERN, the large particle physics laboratory in Switzerland, and consisted of a single Web site and a single browser located on the same computer (Berners-Lee, 2010).

References

Antunovic, D. & Hardin, M. (2013). Women bloggers: Identity and the conceptualization of sports. *New Media & Society*, *15*(8), 1374–1392.

Barratt, M. J. & Lenton, S. (2010). Beyond recruitment? Participatory online research with people who use drugs. *International Journal of Internet Research Ethics*, *3*(1), 69–86.

Barton, M. D. (2005). The future of rational-critical debate in online public spheres. *Computers and Composition*, *22*(2), 177–190.

Baumer, E. P., Sueyoshi, M. & Tomlinson, B. (2011). Bloggers and readers blogging together: Collaborative co-creation of political blogs. *Computer Supported Cooperative Work*, *20*(1–2), 1–36.

Baym, N. K. (2010). *Personal connections in the digital age.* Malden, MA: Polity.

Bennett, E. & Gough, B. (2013). In pursuit of leanness: The management of appearance, affect and masculinities within a men's weight loss forum. *Health*, *17*(3), 284–299.

Berners-Lee, T. (2010). Long live the Web. *Scientific American*, *303*(6), 80–85.

boyd, d. (2014). *It's complicated: The social lives of networked teens.* New Haven, CN: Yale University Press.

Brotsky, S. R. & Giles, D. (2007). Inside the 'pro-ana' community: A covert online participant observation. *Eating disorders*, *15*(2), 93–109.

Bundon, A. & Hurd Clarke, L. (2015a). Honey or vinegar? Athletes with disabilities discuss strategies for advocacy within the Paralympic movement. *Journal of Sport & Social Issues*, *39*(5), 351–370.

Bundon, A. & Hurd Clarke, L. (2015b). Unless you go online you are on your own: blogging as a bridge in para-sport. *Disability & Society*, *30*(2), 185–198.

Carlén, U. & Maivorsdotter, N. (2015). The meaning of 'running' online. Presented 4 September, 2014, at *The 4th International Conference on Qualitative Research in Sport and Exercise*, Loughborough, UK. Available at: http://nexs.ku.dk/ansatte/?pure=files%2F124838411%2FQRSE2014_conference_programme_FINAL.pdf.

Dart, J. J. (2009). Blogging the 2006 FIFA world cup finals. *Sociology of Sport Journal*, *26*(1), 107–126.

Dean, J. (2010). *Blog theory: Feedback and capture in the circuits of drive.* Cambridge, UK: Cambridge Polity Press.

Earl, J. & Kimport, K. (2011). *Digitally enabled social change: Activism in the internet age.* Cambridge, MA: MIT Press.

Ferriter, M. M. (2009). Arguably the greatest: Sport fans and communities at work on Wikipedia. *Sociology of Sport Journal*, *26*(1), 127–154.

García, B., Welford, J. & Smith, B. (2015). Using a smartphone app in qualitative research: The good, the bad and the ugly. *Qualitative Research*, doi: 10.1177/1468794115593335.

Hambrick, M. E., Simmons, J. M., Greenhalgh, G. P. & Greenwell, T. C. (2010). Understanding professional athletes' use of Twitter: A content analysis of athlete tweets. *International Journal of Sport Communication*, *3*(4), 454–471.

Hine, C. (2000). *Virtual ethnography.* Thousand Oaks, CA: Sage.

Hine, C. (2015). *Ethnography for the Internet: Embedded, embodied and everyday.* London: Bloomsbury.

Kassing, J. W. & Sanderson, J. (2010). Fan–athlete interaction and Twitter tweeting through the Giro: A case study. *International Journal of Sport Communication*, *3*(1), 113–128.

MacKay, S. & Dallaire, C. (2013a). Skirtboarder net-a-narratives: Young women creating their own skateboarding (re)presentations. *International Review for the Sociology of Sport*, *48*(2), 171–195.

MacKay, S. & Dallaire, C. (2013b). Skirtboarders.com: Skateboarding women and self-formation as ethical subjects. *Sociology of Sport Journal*, *30*(2), 173–196.

MacKay, S. & Dallaire, C. (2014). Skateboarding women building collective identity in cyberspace. *Journal of Sport & Social Issues*, *38*(6), 548–566.

Malec, M. A. (1995a). Sports discussion groups on the internet. *Journal of Sport & Social Issues*, *19*(1), 108–114.

Malec, M. A. (1995b). The wonderful 'World Wide Web' of sports: An Internet resource. *Journal of Sport & Social Issues*, *19*(3), 323–326.

Malec, M. A. (1996). Usenet news groups: Another Internet resource. *Journal of Sport & Social Issues*, *20*(1), 106–109.

McDaniel, S. R. & Sullivan, C. B. (1998). Extending the sports experience: Mediations in cyberspace. *MediaSport*, 266–281.

McGillivray, D. (2014). Digital cultures, acceleration and mega sporting event narratives. *Leisure Studies*, *33*(1), 96–109.

McGovern, J. (forthcoming). Does race belong on sports blogs? Solidarity and racial discourse in online baseball fan forums. *Communication & Sport*, doi: 10.1177/2167479515577382.

Meikle, G. (2002). *Future active: Media activism and the Internet.* London: Routledge.

Millington, R. & Darnell, S. C. (2014). Constructing and contesting the Olympics online: The Internet, Rio 2016 and the politics of Brazilian development. *International Review for the Sociology of Sport*, *49*(2), 190–210.

Mitrano, J. R. (1999). The 'sudden death' of hockey in Hartford: Sports fans and franchise relocation. *Sociology of Sport Journal*, *16*, 134–154.

Norman, M. (2014). Online community or electronic tribe? Exploring the social characteristics and spatial production of an Internet hockey fan culture. *Journal of Sport & Social Issues*, *38*(5), 395–414.

Numerato, D. (2015). Behind the digital curtain: Ethnography, football fan activism and social change. *Qualitative Research*, doi: 10.1177/1468794115611207.

Olive, R. (2013). 'Making friends with the neighbours': Blogging as a research method. *International Journal of Cultural Studies*, *16*(1), 71–84.

O'Reilly, T. (2005). What is Web 2.0? Design patterns and business models for the next generation of software. Available at: http://www.oreilly.com/pub/a/web2/archive/what-is-web-20.html [accessed 14 April 2015].

Pavlidis, A. & Fullagar, S. (2013). Becoming roller derby grrrls: Exploring the gendered play of affect in mediated sport cultures. *International Review for the Sociology of Sport*, *48*(6), 673–688.

Plymire, D. C. & Forman, P. J. (2000). Breaking the silence: Lesbian fans, the Internet, and the sexual politics of women's sport. *International Journal of Sexuality and Gender Studies*, *5*(2), 141–153.

Rheingold, H. (2014). *Net smart: How to thrive online*. Cambridge, MA: MIT Press.

Sanderson, J. (2013). From loving the hero to despising the villain: Sports fans, Facebook, and social identity threats. *Mass Communication and Society*, *16*(4), 487–509.

Scherer, J. & Sam, M. P. (2010). Policing the cyber agenda: New media technologies and recycled claims in a local stadium debate. *Sport in Society*, *13*(10), 1469–1485.

Szto, C. & Gray, S. (2015). Forgive me Father for I have thinned: Surveilling the bio-citizen through Twitter. *Qualitative Research in Sport, Exercise and Health*, *7*(3), 321–337.

Wilson, B. (2002). The 'anti-jock' movement: Reconsidering youth resistance, masculinity, and sport culture in the age of the internet. *Sociology of Sport Journal*, *19*(2), 206–233.

Wilson, B. & Hayhurst, L. (2009). Digital activism: Neoliberalism, the Internet, and sport for youth development. *Sociology of Sport Journal*, *26*(1), 155–181.

28

PLURALISTIC DATA ANALYSIS

Theory and practice

Nicola J. Clarke, Nick Caddick and Nollaig Frost

In his provocatively titled book *The Qualitative Manifesto,* Denzin (2010) proposed that in order to effectively advocate the benefits of qualitative work to practitioners, policymakers and stakeholders, social science researchers must find ways of developing meaningful dialogue between and across paradigms. Arguing for "a greater openness to and celebration of the proliferation, intermingling, and confluence of paradigms and interpretative frameworks" (p. 40), Denzin encouraged researchers to creatively embrace the tensions that arise when working with potentially disparate approaches. Methodological pluralism offers a strategy for researchers to engage in this paradigmatic dialogue, by bringing together multiple methods, data collections, theories, analyses, or disciplines within the same research project. Sport and exercise researchers may benefit from using a pluralistic approach as the phenomena we study are often dynamic, complex, and multifaceted; at once physical, personal, social, and cultural. Methodological pluralism can contribute to understanding some of this complexity, by describing and interpreting phenomena from a wide range of perspectives (Chamberlain, Cain, Sheridan & Dupuis, 2011).

Given the variety of ways that pluralism can be applied, to provide a precise definition would be somewhat antithetical to its nature. Instead, there are a number of key features that can be considered characteristic of this approach. Methodological pluralism begins from a position of *openness* toward accommodating a *multiplicity* of perspectives (McLean, 1996), where a perspective can be described as "an optic, a way of seeing" (Kellner, 1995, p. 98). It actively seeks understanding through engaging in *dialogue* across lines of *difference*, or the "spaces between" disciplines, paradigms, theories, methodologies, or methods (Collier, Moffatt & Perry, 2015 p. 398; Johnson & Stefurak, 2014). A common end goal of methodological pluralism is to illuminate new or alternative insights that reflect the *multidimensional nature* of phenomena (Coyle, 2010; Frost & Nolas, 2011).

This chapter focuses specifically on *analytical pluralism*; the application of multiple qualitative analytic methods to the same data set, which has received growing attention in psychology (e.g., Frost & Nolas, 2011; Frost & Shaw, 2014), and responds to calls for greater methodological diversity in sport and exercise research (e.g., Culver, Gilbert & Sparkes, 2012; Giardina & Laurendeau, 2013; Poczwardowski, Barott & Jowett, 2006; Smith & Sparkes, 2005; Sparkes, 2013). This approach shares some similarities with mixed methods research (see Chapter 29), but extends the combination of qualitative and quantitative methods to encompass multiple qualitative perspectives within the same study. It also resonates with interdisciplinary research, as it may involve mixing perspectives creatively and critically to transcend paradigm 'boundaries,' although analytical pluralism can also be applied within the same paradigm. These methodological approaches are compared in Table 28.1.

In this chapter we aim to highlight the potential benefits of bringing multilayered insight to complex phenomena and reflect critically upon the theoretical challenges of mixing multiple analyses within a single study. Using research examples from sport and exercise, and the social sciences more widely, we discuss the practical implications of analyzing qualitative data pluralistically. Finally, we offer some considerations for future research to encourage discussion around how analytical pluralism can be applied creatively within the field of sport and exercise.

Pluralistic data analysis

In practice, pluralistic data analysis involves the application of two or more analytical techniques to qualitative data, in order to represent multiple aspects of the phenomena under investigation. Analyses can be applied in sequence or concurrently, by researchers working alone or as part of a team, and can be underpinned by convergent or divergent philosophical assumptions. For example, a discursive analysis (see Chapter 18) alongside or followed by a phenomenological analysis (see Chapters 16 and 17) could be brought together within the same study, to examine both the lived experience and linguistic construction of an event. Analytical pluralism has the potential to highlight the dynamic and complex nature of sport and exercise phenomena through the comparison of findings produced from different analytic frameworks. Researchers may recognize a similarity here with the methodological approach of *bricolage*, where methods are actively constructed and applied as required to pursue complexity and move beyond reductionist, monological forms of knowledge (Kincheloe, 2005). Analytical pluralism offers a technique for researchers to practice interpretative bricolage (Denzin & Lincoln, 2011), by engaging with a variety of analysis tools within a research study and promoting theoretical eclecticism.

Table 28.1 Characteristics of pluralistic research approaches

Characteristic	Pluralistic Data Analysis	Mixed Methods Research	Interdisciplinary Research
Example uses	– Build complementarity (complex understandings of phenomena) – Produce findings relevant to difference audiences	– Build complementarity (complex understandings of phenomena) – Triangulate findings (identify areas of convergence to enhance credibility)	– Build complementarity (complex understandings of phenomena) – Develop a critical approach to knowledge production
Analysis methods	Mixing of two or more qualitative methods from the same or different disciplines	Mixing of quantitative and qualitative methods	Active construction of methods from more than one discipline
Application of analysis methods	Sequential or concurrent	Typically sequential	Typically concurrent
Representation of findings	Parallel or integrated	Typically parallel	Typically integrated

Analytical pluralism views knowledge produced from multiple analyses as complementary, rather than contradictory, as each can represent a different aspect of the social world (Frost *et al.*, 2011). However, the inclusion of methods from different paradigms within the same study gives rise to tensions concerning the commensurability of findings. That is, if analytic methods are underpinned by fundamentally different assumptions about the world or what can be known about the world, their combination may be deemed incompatible, rendering findings incoherent (Lincoln, Lynham & Guba, 2011). When these tensions are recognized and addressed, analytical pluralism has the potential to produce diverse findings that are sensitive to the variation and subtlety of human expression, and which can speak to different audiences (Frost & Nolas, 2011).

Benefits of pluralistic data analysis

There are several possible advantages that analytical pluralism may offer to sport and exercise researchers. First is its potential to develop richer, nuanced and more complex understandings of phenomena than one analytic technique could offer alone, by accommodating findings produced from multiple methods of analysis that attend to different aspects of data within the same study. In comparison to the relative limitations imposed by the specific focus of a single analytic method, pluralistic analysis enables different interpretive possibilities to be explored. Accordingly, research questions can be tackled concurrently from multiple perspectives. This is demonstrated by Ronkainen, Tikkanen, Littlewood, and Nesti (2014), who combined thematic analysis (see Chapter 15) and narrative analysis (see Chapter 20) with an existential interpretative (see Chapter 2) lens to address the question 'How do athletes bring personal meaning to their careers?' (see Table 28.2). An existential framework enabled the researchers to explore how meaning, spirituality, and authenticity manifested in athletes' lifeworlds, while narrative analysis allowed these themes to be situated within historically and culturally embedded storylines. Similarly, as summarized in Table 28.2, Caddick, Smith, and Phoenix (2015) drew upon phenomenological understandings (see Chapter 2) alongside a narrative analysis to explore the question 'What are the effects of surfing and the natural environment on the well-being of combat veterans experiencing post-traumatic stress disorder (PTSD)?' The authors showed how stories that were influential in shaping the veterans' surfing experiences were also grounded in the visceral qualities of their immersion in the ocean environment. By balancing a narrative focus on broader cultural storylines with a phenomenological emphasis on immediate embodied experience, the findings described how veterans experienced surfing as 'respite' from PTSD, and as an activity constituted through bodily sensations.

As these studies illustrated, the emphasis on lived experience and agency in an existential/phenomenological analysis allowed for participants' personal, embodied experiences to be represented, whereas the focus on language and storytelling in a narrative analysis highlighted the socially and culturally situated nature of these experiences. This suggests that pluralistic research can most effectively represent the multidimensional nature of phenomena when analyses with divergent assumptions about the social world are employed (Clarke *et al.*, 2015). However, pluralistic research does not claim to develop *fuller* understandings of sport and exercise phenomena in a manner that would incorrectly imply that the application of more than one analytical method can help to achieve a more complete representation of reality (Coffey & Atkinson, 1996; Neville, 2013). Neither does it offer a form of triangulation to seek corroboration between findings (see Table 28.1). Rather, analytical pluralism offers an alternative way of representing multiple and potentially contrasting aspects of phenomena.

Table 28.2 Pluralistic data analysis in practice: some examples from sport and exercise research

Study	Research Question	Philosophical Assumptions	Data Collection	Data Analysis	Findings Presented
Caddick et al. (2015)	What effects do surfing and the natural environment have on the well-being of combat veterans experiencing PTSD?	Narrative shapes experience, and experience shapes narrative, recursively (ontological claim).	16 semistructured life-history interviews with veterans and participant observation.	Dialogical narrative analysis (Frank, 2012) with phenomenological analysis (Hockey & Allen-Collinson, 2007).	Surfing as 'respite' from PTSD narrative presented, as constituted through embodied sensations. Effects of surfing on subjective well-being described. How surfing facilitated respite and influenced veterans' well-being discussed.
McGannon & Spence (2010)	What kinds of self-descriptions are available for use in women's conversations in relation to physical activity? Towards what end do women use these ways of speaking to afford and limit their physical activity behavior?	Self-related phenomena are constituted and brought into being in social activity, particularly in discourse (ontological claim).	Five in-depth, open-ended interviews with one female participant.	Discursive psychology (ethnomethodology) with discourse analysis (post-structural).	Three common discourses presented: the body; exercise and physical appearance; and exercise and physiology. Implications of discourses for self-construction and exercise behaviors discussed.
Ronkainen et al. (2014)	How do athletes bring personal meaning to their careers? Do athletes experience authenticity? What are the career concerns of athletes?	Critical realism: realist ontology and constructivist epistemology.	10 high-level athletes produced reflective writing of their sporting practices.	Thematic analysis (Braun & Clarke, 2006) followed by holistic narrative analyses of content and form (Lieblich et al., 1998); narratives then interpreted through an existential lens.	Four storylines presented: struggle for authenticity; sustained love for the performance sport; sport as experiencing and expressing through the body; and sport as a spiritual journey. How existential meaning was brought to athletic lives through storylines discussed.

Alternatively, multiple analyses applied from within the *same* paradigm can also facilitate richer understandings than using one analytic method only. For example, within a narrative framework, Busanich, McGannon, and Schinke (2014) undertook a narrative structural analysis (see Chapter 20) to examine the organization and form of distance-runners' stories of disordered eating, alongside a performative analysis to explore how and why these stories were told. Findings from the structural analysis described how participants' stories were often framed in a performance narrative of winning, results, and achievement. In comparison, the performative analysis highlighted that male and female athletes talked about disordered eating in different and gendered ways; in particular, that male athletes hid or downplayed negative weight-loss thoughts and behaviors, whereas female athletes normalized disordered eating experiences as part of the elite-performance culture. Using multiple analyses in this way enabled both the broader cultural templates that were drawn upon and participants' situated telling of their stories to be illuminated.

A second benefit to researchers is the potential that analytical pluralism offers for enhanced reflexivity; the act of examining and acknowledging how the researcher's background, assumptions and position impacts upon the research process (Finlay & Gough, 2003). Pluralism has the capacity to support researchers toward a deeper appreciation of the role of the researcher in analyzing data and constructing findings through highlighting the "constitutive force of theory" within qualitative analyses (Honan, Knobel, Baker, & Davies, 2000, p. 9). That is, analytic methods are imbued with fundamental philosophical, theoretical, or disciplinary assumptions that guide the analyst toward certain interpretations over others. In his disquisition on sport-coaching practice research, North (2013) commented that the different meta-theoretical positions of psychological scientism or sociological interpretivism encourage researchers to ask different questions, use different concepts and methodologies, and do different types of work. For example, psychological approaches may seek to explain coach behavior using universal models, whereas sociologically informed analyses may focus on the contextual and situational nature of coaching. Working with methods pluralistically can help researchers to recognize and make clear why they have employed particular analytical tools and how these have influenced their findings.

Reflexive awareness is especially called for when different approaches are brought together within the same study. Analysts may find they are required to shift their own perspectives in order to sufficiently attend to their participants' multiple ways of expression, or adjust to analyzing data produced from within an unfamiliar framework (Barnes *et al.*, 2014; Frost *et al.*, 2010). Ronkainen *et al.* (2014) commented that working individually and collaboratively with data allowed a group of researchers to develop a critical reflexivity. Each researcher brought a diverse interpretation of the notions of spirituality and authenticity to the study, which enhanced the analytical dialogue among the group. Pluralism thus provides opportunities for enhanced critical reflexivity regarding analytical practice.

The potential of pluralistic data analysis to achieve multilayered insight into phenomena offers a third benefit to researchers, by producing findings which are relevant to different audiences. Analytical pluralism avoids reducing understandings to one particular interpretive framework, meaning that findings can be accessible to audiences with diverse theoretical, axiological, methodological, or disciplinary allegiances (Frost & Nolas, 2013). Furthermore, by enabling contrasting versions of the social world to be presented with equal significance, pluralism invites researchers to consider not whether one particular interpretation is right or better, but as Honan *et al.* (2000) suggested, "when each one could be useful and for what purpose" (p. 30). In addition to promoting methodological rigor, this has the potential to be of practical benefit. For example, North (2013) advocated that each interpretative lens, be it psychologically or sociologically tilted, can add something new or different to the development of a meaningful and coherent picture of sport-coaching practice. Coaching practitioners can then select the findings most relevant to their own practical experience to guide their action toward a specific goal. Encouraging the synthesis of theoretical and experiential knowledge in pursuit of practical goals can help to generate new ways of understanding reality and transform inquiry from *theoria* into *praxis* (see also Chapter 8).

Illustrating how pluralistic findings can be useful to stakeholders, McGannon and Spence's (2010) analysis of women's exercise adherence integrated ethnomethodology to examine the action-orientated nature of everyday talk, and post-structuralism to focus on discourses, power and subjectivity (see Table 28.2). Findings were produced that reflected both the "*process* and *outcome* of language" (McGannon & Mauw, 2000; McGannon & Spence, 2010 p. 18; italics in original). The authors suggested that increasing women's awareness of how agency is limited by prevailing discourses reproduced by historical and material conditions (the process of language) when choosing whether or not to exercise (the outcome of language), can encourage an expansion of discursive resources. In turn, this can empower women to develop identities that facilitate, rather than restrict, their exercise behavior, and reduce feelings of guilt or self-blame for their lack of exercise.

Challenges of pluralistic data analysis

Ontological assumptions regarding the nature of existence and epistemological assumptions regarding access to and the constitution of knowledge (see Chapter 1) often diverge between different analytical frameworks. Consequently, when analyses imbued with contrasting philosophical assumptions are brought together within the same study, it can be difficult to maintain theoretically coherent understandings and explanations of phenomena, and demonstrate the overall commensurability of findings (Lincoln *et al.*, 2011). For example, mixing a realist or moderate constructionist perspective (which assumes there is a single, objective reality and often underpins a realist thematic analysis (see Chapter 15) and Strausserian versions of grounded theory (see Chapter 3) with a more explicitly social constructionist or postmodern worldview (which foregrounds the existence of multiple, fluid realities, as endorsed by narrative analysis, Bourdieusian informed analysis or, Foucauldian discourse analysis (see Chapter 18) raises tricky questions over how the combined findings are to be interpreted. Are findings considered as representations of personal experience, as culturally situated narratives, or as subject positions created by and located within prevailing structural frameworks?[1] Can underlying paradigmatic differences be reconciled, and if so, how? Or, alternatively, if different philosophical positions are not held to be fundamentally incompatible, how can meaningful dialogue across paradigms be established?

To help sport and exercise researchers grapple with these tensions, there is a useful distinction to be made between *ontological* and *epistemological* pluralism (Clarke *et al.*, 2015). Ontological pluralism assumes that the world itself is multiple and plural. From this stance, different philosophical positions are not held to be foundational and mutually exclusive, but as dialectical and mutually informing. This allows researchers to hold tensions lightly together and interact with multiple paradigms simultaneously (Cooper & McLeod, 2011; Johnson & Stefurak, 2014). In contrast, epistemological pluralism obviates incoherence by using multiple analytic methods that are underpinned by a consistent ontological position to produce diverse, yet complementary forms of knowledge. This reflects the belief that multiple forms of knowledge can be produced without imposing concomitant ontological claims, and enables researchers to use a wide range of perspectives to understand phenomena (Kellner, 1995). Without necessarily seeking to resolve philosophical differences, the challenge for researchers wishing to engage with analytical pluralism is, therefore, to work creatively and reflexively to "hold together interpretations that make sense within their own frames of reference but create epistemological tension when juxtaposed or integrated" (Coyle, 2010, p. 82). Recognizing and addressing paradigmatic tensions within a study is essential to achieving *structural integrity*; "a coherent rationale that considers the question, context, and assumptions that presumably hold the study together" (Walsh & Koelsch, 2012 p. 386).

A further challenge lies in how to judge the quality of pluralistic research. Although universally applicable criteria for evaluating qualitative research are considered problematic (Smith & Deemer, 2000), it is generally accepted that researchers need to demonstrate analytical rigor and maintain meaningful coherence between purpose, theory, methods, analysis and representation (e.g., Sparkes & Smith, 2009; Tracy, 2010; see also Chapter 25, this volume). When multiple analytic methods are used and potentially divergent theoretical perspectives are mixed, the challenges of establishing rigor and maintaining coherence are multiplied. The evaluation of pluralistic research may therefore extend to whether the procedures followed for each analysis were transparent, and whether multiple interpretations were adequately evidenced by data. Assessing whether the commensurability of diverse findings was satisfactorily addressed may also indicate the extent to which interpretations are meaningfully interconnected with the research question, philosophical assumptions, and methods.

As with all high-quality research, studies adopting analytical pluralism should also seek to make a significant contribution to knowledge. In areas where analytical pluralism is relatively untested as a strategy for conducting research in sport and exercise, its capacity to advance the translation of knowledge into practice or deepen theoretical understandings is as yet undetermined. Where studies have been conducted (see examples in Table 28.2), there is evidence to suggest that using multiple analytic techniques can help to develop more complex and multilayered understandings of sport and exercise phenomena. Yet there is also the danger that analytical pluralism could simply become a hollow rhetorical device if researchers fail to communicate a clear rationale for its value in relation to a specific research project (Chamberlain *et al.*, 2011). Indeed, in the absence of a well-crafted rationale and carefully reasoned theoretical position, the danger exists that analytical pluralism could become merely a showcase of the different methods available to us. Rather than pursuing pluralism because it is perceived to be an innovative and useful methodological approach, sport and exercise researchers therefore face the challenge of demonstrating how pluralism might be used creatively within psychology and sociology to advance current knowledge.

Applying pluralistic data analysis in practice

In addition to the philosophical and empirical challenges that analytical pluralism entails, researchers wishing to engage with this approach are presented with a number of methodological decisions and considerations.

Research questions. For some studies in sport and exercise research, the traditional approach of adopting a single analytical tool to interpret data is an entirely suitable strategy for addressing a specific research question. Research questions arise from and are informed by the researcher's epistemological, ontological, and theoretical assumptions. Therefore, research questions that are explicitly designed to understand a phenomenon from multiple perspectives may be better addressed using analytical pluralism. This may include research questions with multiple parts (see examples in Table 28.2). Furthermore, projects can evolve to include pluralistic analysis, as Yanchar, Gantt, and Clay suggest of critical methodology:

[W]ithin any program of research, contextually sensitive research strategies are required, existing questions and strategies must be continually examined and often changed with context and experience, and new questions and strategies must be formulated based on the practical demands of research.

(Yanchar, Gantt & Clay 2005, p. 36)

In our own research, we have experienced the process of adapting our methodologies to encompass more analytical perspectives as we became more immersed in our research settings, and were drawn to find ways of representing additional dimensions of participants' experiences or the structural components that shaped their subjectivity. Although this data-driven rationale may be problematic, as it implies a preliminary reading of data that is inexorably influenced by the researcher (Clarke *et al.*, 2015), this can be anticipated and managed when researchers start out from a position of *openness,* and with a commitment to reflexivity throughout the research process.

Paradigmatic assumptions. Paradigms matter, not least because they underpin and inform a study's research question, purpose, methods, and design (Sparkes & Smith, 2014; see also Chapter 29, this volume). When multiple analyses are employed with differing associated philosophical assumptions, it becomes even more relevant to articulate how and why findings remain comprehensible. The first task for the pluralistic researcher, therefore, is to understand the epistemological and ontological underpinnings of analytical methods, and the relationship between them. Building on this awareness, researchers can then explore strategies to address incommensurability.

Framing findings produced from multiple analyses within the same ontological position (epistemological pluralism) provides one technique to avoid incoherence. For example, Ronkainen *et al.* (2014) combined existential and narrative perspectives within a consistent critical–realist ontological position. This integration was built upon the shared assumptions between existentialism, with its focus on meaning and subjectivity, and a psychosocial approach to narrative, which practices a deep fidelity to the centrality of experience (Smith & Sparkes, 2008). This demonstrated a core thread of theoretical continuity by foregrounding the assumption that authentic being and selfhood is a fundamental feature of existence. From within a more critical framework, McGannon and Spence (2010) held together ethnomethodological and post-structural analyses of women's physical self and exercise behavior, through the shared ontological position that self-related phenomena are socially constituted through discourse.

Alternatively, for researchers engaging in ontological pluralism, strategies have been proposed for interacting with the tensions that may arise when multiple paradigms are brought together within the same study. Approaches including pragmatism (see Giacobbi, Poczwardowski & Hager, 2005, Neville, 2013, and Chapter 29, this volume for discussions in relation to sport and exercise and dialectical pluralism (Johnson & Stefurak, 2014) make sense of findings produced through multiple analyses by uniting interpretations within a shared axiological position – the nature of ethics and values in a study. Emphasizing the role of engaging stakeholders in the research process, knowledge is judged in relation to its value for the specific project. However, whereas pragmatism is unconcerned about the relationship between knowledge and reality, Johnson and Stefurak discuss a respect for "realities that are thoughtfully constructed and revised by multiple paradigms and disciplines" (2014, p. 67), and encourage researchers to actively attend to tensions within and between paradigms in order to extend understanding. It is by engaging with, rather than setting aside, these lines of difference that the full potential of pluralistic understandings can be realized.

Data. In sport and exercise research, analytical pluralism has been applied to different types of data, including interviews texts, participant observation, and participant-created reflective writing (see Table 28.2), illustrating the potential for this approach to be applied to diverse data sets. It is prudent to consider whether data are accessible to multiple analytic techniques, as analyses differ in their requirements from qualitative data. Broadly speaking, phenomenological analyses work with accounts of lived-experience, narrative analyses with stories, discursive analyses with everyday talk, and ethnographic analyses with social-cultural observations. Some analyses have particular transcription requirements; for example, conversation analysis is best performed when transcription includes details of the delivery of talk such as overlap, pitch, and emphasis (see Groom, Cushion & Nelson, 2012, for an example of this transcription). Therefore, researchers may wish to reflect upon the implications of decisions in relation to recruitment, data-collection methods, and transcription procedures when designing pluralistic research studies.

Analytical methods. The choice of which methods of analyses to use together, and how many, is informed by the research question and will inevitably influence the findings that can be produced and the comparisons that can be drawn between them. As noted above, the multidimensional nature of phenomena can be brought into view effectively when analyses with divergent epistemological or ontological underpinnings are employed within the same study. Therefore, pluralistic researchers should seek to present a clear rationale for their selection of analytic methods, explaining the fit with the underpinning philosophical assumptions and the research question. To demonstrate research quality, reporting of the application of methods requires careful consideration. Adequate descriptions of the procedures used to select, transform, and organize data may help to establish rigor, transparency, and meaningful coherence, and enable studies to be judged on their individual merits and limitations (Walsh & Koelsch, 2012).

Decisions regarding the number of analyses to perform may be influenced by the availability of resources. The significant investment of time given the methodological reflexivity this approach demands, the potential training needs of researchers seeking to perform unfamiliar analyses, and the word restrictions of journal publications may shape decisions about the number of analyses (Coyle, 2010; Josselin & Willig, 2014). Moreover, although the capacity of pluralism to illuminate multiple dimensions of phenomena may draw researchers to conclude that more analyses are better, the presentation of multiple findings may risk becoming so complicated that implications for theory or practice are unclear (Clarke *et al.*, 2015; Frost *et al.*, 2010). Thoughtful construction of pluralistic research questions and findings may help researchers to negotiate this balance.

Research design. In practice, analytical pluralism can be undertaken in a variety of ways, by an individual or group of researchers. Researchers can apply multiple analytic frames to a data set on their own (e.g., Aitchison, 2005; Frost, 2009), or can work as part of a group, in which members undertake multiple analyses together (e.g., Ronkainen, Ryba & Nesti, 2013; Ronkainen *et al.*, 2014), or independently analyze a data set each in a different way (e.g., Frost *et al.*, 2010; Honan *et al.*, 2000). For the individual researcher working pluralistically, or for groups performing analytical pluralism together, the sequencing of methods becomes pertinent. Will analyses be applied in a particular order, or undertaken concurrently? In both instances, the interaction between methods (i.e., the influence of prior analyses in shaping subsequent interpretations) invites reflection. McGannon and Spence's (2010) analytical strategy involved using an ethnomethodological analysis to first identify key discourses in their participants' accounts, before applying a post-structural analysis to explore how these discourses were used. The authors acknowledged how the discourses identified in the first analytic stage informed their second analysis. Also using a sequential approach, Ronkainen *et al.* (2013, 2014) performed a thematic analysis to highlight existential aspects of data, followed by a narrative analysis to explore the content and form of stories. Although the authors did not discuss a rationale for this sequencing, this movement from the personal to the cultural aligns with Josselin and Willig's explanation for applying a phenomenological analysis before subsequent narrative and psychosocial analyses; "in an effort to protect potential phenomenological insights from 'contamination' by more constructed, theory-led interpretations." (2014, p. 30). In contrast, Caddick *et al.* (2015) sought to incorporate phenomenological interpretations within a dialogical narrative analysis, by undertaking analyses concurrently. This approach presents additional challenges, such as how to move fluidly between analyses to allow potentially divergent meanings to emerge, and avoid privileging one framework over another.

From our own early experiences of attempting analytical pluralism, we have found that a sequential approach, where one analytical lens is brought to the fore while others are temporarily set aside (in a manner akin to analytical bracketing; see Gubrium & Holstein, 2009; Smith & Sparkes, 2005; Chapter 20, this volume) demanded a great deal of discipline and reflection, as our own proclivities inescapably led us to "see" certain aspects within data. Alternatively, we have found techniques such as *feedback looping* (Kincheloe & Berry, 2004) beneficial in enabling the analyst to move flexibly within and between analyses. Starting with the text, the researcher selects an analysis method to thread through data and back to the text, creating a feedback loop which can expand, modify, or challenge existing interpretations. Feedback loops are used to guide the analyst from one interpretative lens to the next, in a nonlinear fashion (Kincheloe & Berry, 2004). For example, Frost (2009) described how this form of approach allowed for "jumping-off points" to move fluidly between structural, linguistic, and reflexive narrative analyses of an interview transcript, when a focus of interest was recognized in the data. Allowing for jumping off (and on) in response to points in the data, a previous interpretation, or the subjectivity of the researcher, can enable reflexive concurrent analyses, but relies upon the researcher maintaining an awareness of what prompts a shift in focus. Using theoretical and procedural memos to record analytical notes and interpretations can encourage fluid movement between analyses, exploration of their inter-connections, and enhanced reflexivity (Caddick *et al.*, 2015).

Representation and dissemination. A key advantage of analytical pluralism is that rich and nuanced understandings of phenomena can be developed, but this raises the question of how to adequately represent enhanced depth and complexity. The decisions made in relation to how to represent and interpret pluralistic findings are integral to realizing this potential, and to avoid pluralism simply becoming an exercise in illustrating differences between methods. Researchers can choose to present the findings produced from each analysis separately, drawing upon relevant extracts of data to evidence interpretations. This enables the reader to compare findings and appreciate points of convergence and divergence between them (e.g., Frost *et al.*, 2011; Honan *et al.*, 2000), and can allow for multiple possibilities of being to be constructed, rather than 'finalizing' participants to an either/or ontological status (Bakhtin, 1984). For example, Frost *et al.* (2011) suggested that by presenting various dimensions of the experience of second-time motherhood with equal significance, their participant could be recognized as a phenomenological, realist, and post-modern agent, depending on her context.

A different approach to presenting pluralistic findings involves pursuing an integrated synthesis of findings (see examples in Table 28.2). Here, multiple interpretations are woven together, but remain individually identifiable through the choice of language used to construct findings or the theoretical lens used to locate the interpretations. Ronkainen *et al.* (2014)

structured their findings around four narratives of personal and spiritual meaning in sport that were identified in participants' accounts, each incorporating existential themes. Interpretations placed existential meanings (recognizably grounded in the phenomenological philosophy of Heidegger; see Chapter 2) in dialogue with cultural narratives (identifiable through reference to "dominant" and "counter" storylines), to offer an understanding of how participants' meanings were created in and through different stories. A third possible strategy is to present both separate and integrated analyses, such as in King *et al.*'s (2008) exploration of the phenomenon of mistrust. This approach made clear to the reader how each individual analyst constructed their findings, and how these varied depending on their respective epistemological commitments, while also presenting a consensual account of their participant's embodied and relational experience of mistrust.

However researchers choose to represent pluralistic findings, it is perhaps the comparisons drawn between different interpretations that can offer more to sport and exercise than studies which adopt a single analytical technique. Contrasting findings encourages researchers to attend to the *spaces between* analytical frameworks and emphasizes "learning from the juxtaposition of divergent ideas and ways of seeing" (Kincheloe, 2005, p. 344). Aitchison (2005) provides a helpful illustration of this. Exploring gender power relations in sport and leisure management, Aitchison used cultural theory to describe accounts and perceptions of gender inequality in employment settings, combined with structural analysis to explain how and why such practices are constructed, legitimated, and reproduced within the industry. Interconnections between these mutually informing perspectives were explicitly examined, to highlight how gender power relations were shaped globally by patriarchy and capitalism via organizational structures, procedures, and policies, and also locally through social and cultural discourses and processes.

Comparisons of this nature may facilitate findings which are accessible to diverse audiences, including researchers from different academic disciplines, practitioners and policymakers. Research in the sport and exercise domain has begun to demonstrate how analytical pluralism can make a significant contribution to knowledge and practice, through outlining empowerment strategies for women exercisers (McGannon & Spence, 2010), proposing additions to existing theoretical models of career transitions in sport (Ronkainen *et al.*, 2014), and providing implications for the use of surfing in the treatment and support for combat veterans experiencing PTSD (Caddick *et al.*, 2015). Researchers may therefore benefit from reflecting upon how analytical pluralism can contribute to knowledge production, through an exploration of tensions that arise when mixing multiple perspectives within the same study, or production of findings with relevance to different audiences.

Considerations for the future

For researchers wishing to engage with analytical pluralism in informed ways, this chapter has highlighted the importance of attending to the theoretical and practical challenges that seeking multiple understandings of phenomena entails, especially when analyses with different philosophical underpinnings are employed within the same study. Finding ways to recognize and address the paradigmatic tensions this creates is paramount. Analytical pluralism requires researchers to carefully consider how to demonstrate the quality of pluralistic research, make informed decisions about applying multiple analyses in practice, and find ways to adequately represent potentially complex and diverse findings.

These challenges notwithstanding, research within the sport and exercise domain has illustrated the capacity of analytical pluralism to highlight the multidimensional nature of phenomena, enhance researcher reflexivity, and make a meaningful contribution to theory, knowledge, and practice. With these advantages in mind, analytical pluralism may appeal to those research-ers seeking to develop more complex understandings of their data while avoiding the con-straints of "off-the-shelf" prescriptive methodologies (Chamberlain, 2012; Josselin & Willig, 2014). We encourage researchers to creatively consider how the principles of methodological pluralism, an openness toward accommodating a multiplicity of perspectives, engagement with difference through dialogue, and a desire to represent the multidimensional nature of phenom-enon, can be applied within the dynamic field of sport and exercise research.

In particular, studies which apply psychological and sociological analytic lenses to the same data set may glean interesting findings. By contrasting findings produced from multiple ana-lytic frames that vary in the extent to which they privilege agency, the body, and social interaction as some psychological approaches may do, or structure, language, and cultural reproduction, as is often the focus of sociological inquiry, more complex versions of the social world can emerge. Moreover, implications for policy and practice can be grounded in an axi-ological commitment to develop critical and ethical knowledge that is relevant for sport and exercise users, providers, and governing bodies. While we do not wish to suggest that this would be a straightforward or unproblematic endeavor, this type of project resonates with Sparkes' (2013) reflections on the implications of Denzin's (2010) call for a greater openness to paradigmatic dialogue for sport and exercise research. Sparkes broadly supported this posi-tion, although cautioned firmly against dissolving or ignoring tensions when mixing different perspectives. Instead, he suggested that sharing ideas, concepts, and techniques between sport and exercise researchers, and critically exploring points of convergence and divergence across psychological, sociological, philosophical, and pedagogical disciplines may lead to alternative forms of dialogue and heightened understandings of the power relations within the academic community. Therefore, as Sparkes (2013) recognized, this approach may have the potential to galvanize researchers through a common social justice agenda and collective action, and in doing so disrupt the political knowledge hierarchy that currently constrains progressive qualitative research.

Note

1 A subject position describes "a conceptual repertoire and a location for persons within the structure of rights and duties for those who use that repertoire" (Davies & Harré, 1999 p. 35; see also Chapter 18, this volume).

References

Aitchison, C. C. (2005). Feminist and gender research in sport and leisure management: Understanding the social–cultural nexus of gender-power relations. *Journal of Sport Management, 19*(4), 422–441.

Bakhtin, M. (1984). *Problems of Dostoevsky's poetics* (C. Emerson, trans). Minneapolis, MN: University of Minnesota Press. (Original work published 1963).

Barnes, J., Caddick, N., Clarke, N. J., Cromby, J., McDermott, H., Willis, M. E. H. & Wiltshire, G. (2014). Methodological pluralism in qualitative research: Reflections on a meta-study. *Qualitative Methods in Psychology Bulletin, 17*, 35–41.

Braun, V. & Clarke, V. (2006). Using thematic analysis in psychology. *Qualitative research in psychology, 3*(2), 77–101. doi: 10.1191/1478088706qp063oa.

Busanich, R., McGannon, K. R. & Schinke, R. J. (2014). Comparing elite male and female distance runner's experiences of disordered eating through narrative analysis. *Psychology of Sport and Exercise, 15*(6), 705–712. doi: 10.1016/j.psychsport.2013.10.002.

Caddick, N., Smith, B. & Phoenix, C. (2015). The effects of surfing and the natural environment on the well-being of combat veterans. *Qualitative Health Research, 25*(1), 76–86. doi: 10.1177/1049732314549477.

Chamberlain, K. (2012). Do you really need a methodology? *Qualitative Methods in Psychology Bulletin*, *13*, 59–63.

Chamberlain, K., Cain, T., Sheridan, J. & Dupuis, A. (2011). Pluralisms in qualitative research: From multiple methods to integrated methods. *Qualitative Research in Psychology*, *8*(2), 151–169. doi: 10.1080/14780887.2011.572730.

Clarke, N.J., Willis, M.E.H., Barnes, J.S., Caddick, N., Cromby, J., McDermott, H. & Wiltshire, G. (2015). Analytical pluralism in qualitative research: A meta-study. *Qualitative Research in Psychology*, *12*(2), 182–201. doi: 10.1080/14780887.2014.948980.

Coffey, A. & Atkinson, P. (1996). *Making sense of qualitative data: Complementary research strategies*. London: Sage.

Collier, D. R., Moffatt, L. & Perry, M. (2015). Talking, wrestling, and recycling: An investigation of three analytic approaches to qualitative data in education research. *Qualitative Research*, *15*(3), 389–404. doi: 10.1177/1468794114538896.

Cooper, M. & McLeod, J. (2011). *Pluralistic counselling and psychotherapy*. London: Sage.

Coyle, A. (2010). Qualitative research and anomalous experience: A call for interpretative pluralism. *Qualitative Research in Psychology*, *7*(1), 79–83. doi: 10.1080/14780880903304600.

Culver, D. M., Gilbert, W. & Sparkes, A. C. (2012). Qualitative research in sport psychology journals: The next decade 2000–2009 and beyond. *The Sport Psychologist*, *26*(2), 261–281.

Davies, B. & Harré, R. (1999). Positioning and personhood. In R. Harré & L. van Langenhove (Eds.), *Positioning theory* (pp. 32–52). Oxford: Blackwell.

Denzin, N. K. (2010). *The qualitative manifesto: A call to arms*. Walnut Creek, CA: Left Coast Press.

Denzin, N. K. & Lincoln, Y. S. (2011). *The Sage handbook of qualitative research* (4th ed.). London: Sage.

Finlay, L. & Gough, B. (2003). *Reflexivity: A practical guide for researchers in health and the social sciences*. Oxford: Blackwell.

Frank, A. W. (2012). Practicing dialogical narrative analysis. In J. Holstein & J. Gubrium (Eds.), *Varieties of narrative analysis* (pp. 33–52). London: Sage.

Frost, N. (2009). "Do you know what I mean?": The use of a pluralistic narrative analysis approach in the interpretation of an interview. *Qualitative Research*, *9*(1), 9–29. doi: 10.1177/1468794108094867.

Frost, N. A. & Nolas, S. M. (2011). Editorial: Exploring and expanding on pluralism in qualitative research in psychology. *Qualitative Research in Psychology*, *8*(2), 115–119. doi: 10.1080/14780887.2011.572728.

Frost, N. & Nolas, S. M. (2013). The contribution of pluralistic qualitative approaches to mixed methods evaluations. *New Directions for Evaluation, Special issue: Mixed Methods and Credibility of Evidence in Evaluation*, *138*, 75–84. doi: 10.1002/ev.20059.

Frost, N. & Shaw, R. (2014). Editorial: The place of qualitative methods in mixed methods research. *Qualitative Methods in Psychology Bulletin*, *17*, 1–3.

Frost, N., Nolas, S. M., Brooks-Gordon, B., Esin, C., Holt, A., Mehdizadeh, L. & Shinebourne, P. (2010). Pluralism in qualitative research: The impact of different researchers and qualitative approaches on the analysis of qualitative data. *Qualitative Research*, *10*(4), 441–460. doi: 10.1177/1468794110366802.

Giacobbi, P. R., Poczwardowski, A. & Hager, P. (2005). A pragmatic research philosophy for sport and exercise psychology. *The Sport Psychologist*, *19*(1), 18–31.

Giardina, M. D. & Laurendeau, J. (2013). Truth untold? Evidence, knowledge, and research practice(s). *Sociology of Sport Journal*, *30*(3), 237–255.

Groom, R., Cushion, C. J. & Nelson, L. J. (2012). Analysing coach-athlete "talk in interaction" within the delivery of video-based performance feedback in elite youth soccer. *Qualitative Research in Sport, Exercise and Health*, *4*(3), 439–458. doi: 10.1080/2159676X.2012.693525.

Gubrium, J. F. & Holstein, J. A. (2009). *Analyzing narrative reality*. London: Sage.

Hockey, J. & Allen-Collinson, J. (2007). Grasping the phenomenology of sporting bodies. *International Review for the Sociology of Sport*, *42*(2), 115–131. doi: 10.1177/1012690207084747.

Honan, E., Knobel, M., Baker, C. & Davies, B. (2000). Producing possible Hannahs: Theory and the subject of research. *Qualitative Inquiry*, *6*(1), 9–32. doi: 10.1177/107780040000600102.

Johnson, B. & Stefurak, T. (2014). Dialectical pluralism: A metaparadigm and process philosophy for "dynamically combining" important differences. *Qualitative Methods in Psychology Bulletin*, *17*, 63–69.

Josselin, D. & Willig, C. (2014). Layering the wounded self: Using a pluralistic qualitative approach to explore meaning-making around self-injury. *Qualitative Methods in Psychology Bulletin*, *17*, 23–34.

Kellner, D. (1995). *Media culture: Cultural studies, identity and politics*. Abingdon: Routledge.

Kincheloe, J. L. (2005). On to the next level: Continuing the conceptualization of the bricolage. *Qualitative Inquiry*, *11*(3), 323–350. doi: 10.1177/1077800405275056.

Kincheloe, J. L. & Berry, L. S. (2004). *Rigour and complexity in educational research*. Maidenhead, Berkshire: Open University Press.

King, N., Finlay, L., Ashworth, P., Smith, J. A., Langdridge, D. & Butt, T. (2008). "Can't really trust that, so what can I trust?": A polyvocal, qualitative analysis of the psychology of mistrust. *Qualitative Research in Psychology, 5*(2), 80–102. doi: 10.1080/14780880802070559.

Lieblich, A., Tuval-Mashiach, R. & Zilber, T. (1998). *Narrative research: Reading, analysis, and interpretation*. London: Sage.

Lincoln, Y. S., Lynham, S. A. & Guba, E. G. (2011). Paradigmatic controversies, contradictions, and emerging confluences, revisited. In N. K. Denzin & Y. S. Lincoln (Eds.), *The Sage handbook of qualitative research* (4th ed., pp. 97–128). London: Sage.

McGannon, K. R. & Mauw, M. K. (2000). Exploring the exercise adherence problem: An integration of ethnomethodological and poststructuralist perspectives. *Sociology of Sport Journal, 19*(1), 67–89.

McGannon, K. R. & Spence, J. C. (2010). Speaking of the self and understanding physical activity participation: What discursive psychology can tell us about an old problem. *Qualitative Research in Sport and Exercise, 2*(1), 17–38. doi: 10.1080/19398440903510145.

McLean, D. J. (1996). Leisure research and methodological pluralism: A response to Hemingway. *Leisure Studies, 15*(2), 137–141. doi: 10.1080/026143696375675.

Neville, R. D. (2013). The pragmatics of leisure revisited. *Leisure Sciences: An Interdisciplinary Journal, 35*(4), 399–404. doi: 10.1080/01490400.2013.797717.

North, J. (2013). Philosophical underpinnings of coaching practice research. *Quest, 65*(3), 278–299. doi: 10.1080/00336297.2013.773524.

Poczwardowski, A., Barott, J. E. & Jowett, S. (2006). Diversifying approaches to research on athlete–coach relationships. *Psychology of Sport and Exercise, 7*(2), 125–142. doi: 10.1016/j.psychsport.2005.08.002.

Ronkainen, N. J., Ryba, T. V. & Nesti, M. S. (2013). "The engine just started coughing!" – Limits of physical performance, aging and career continuity in elite endurance sports. *Journal of Aging Studies, 27*(4), 387–397. doi: 10.1016/j.jaging.2013.09.001.

Ronkainen, N. J., Tikkanen, O., Littlewood, M. & Nesti, M. S. (2014). An existential perspective on meaning, spirituality and authenticity in athletic careers. *Qualitative Research in Sport, Exercise and Health, 7*(2), 253–270. doi: 10.1080/2159676X.2014.926970.

Smith, J. K. & Deemer, D. (2000). The problem of criteria in the age of relativism. In N. K. Denzin & Y. S. Lincoln (Eds.), *Handbook of qualitative research* (2nd ed., pp. 877–896). London: Sage.

Smith, B. & Sparkes, A. C. (2005). Analyzing talk in qualitative inquiry: Exploring possibilities, problems, and tensions. *Quest, 57*(2), 213–242.

Smith, B. & Sparkes, A. C. (2008). Contrasting perspectives on narrating selves and identities: An invitation to dialogue. *Qualitative Research, 8*(1), 5–35. doi: 10.1177/1468794107085221.

Sparkes, A. C. (2013). Qualitative research in sport, exercise and health in the era of neoliberalism, audit and new public management: Understanding the conditions for the (im)possibilities of a new paradigm dialogue. *Qualitative Research in Sport, Exercise and Health, 5*(3), 440–459. doi: 10.1080/2159676X.2013.796493.

Sparkes, A. C. & Smith, B. (2009). Judging the quality of qualitative inquiry: Criteriology and relativism in action. *Psychology of Sport and Exercise, 10*(5), 491–497. doi: 10.1016/j.psychsport.2009.02.006.

Sparkes, A. C. & Smith, B. (2014). *Qualitative research methods in sport, exercise and health: From product to process*. Abingdon: Routledge.

Tracy, S. J. (2010). Qualitative quality: Eight "big-tent" criteria for excellent qualitative research. *Qualitative Inquiry, 16*(10), 837–851. doi: 10.1177/1077800410383121.

Walsh, R. & Koelsch, L. E. (2012). Building across fault lines in qualitative research. *The Humanistic Psychologist, 40*(4), 380–390. doi: 10.1080/08873267.2012.724260.

Yanchar, S. C., Gantt, E. E. & Clay, S. L. (2005). On the nature of a critical methodology. *Theory and Psychology, 15*(1), 27–50. doi: 10.1177/0959354305049743.

29

MIXED-METHODS RESEARCH IN SPORT AND EXERCISE

Integrating qualitative research

Kass Gibson

Deploying more than one method of data collection and/or analysis in empirical research is certainly not a new phenomenon. Indeed, it is often an intuitive and practical response to the varied demands of understanding the dynamic and multifaceted nature of human practices and the (social) world. To this end, researchers have long been drawing on various traditions, techniques, and tools in order to gain further insight into an array of research problems. Resultantly, we should not view the rise of a specific mixed-methods literature as indicative of a new, or "third" (Johnson & Onwuegbuzie, 2004), way of doing research, but an attempt to encourage and enable researchers to make considered and justified choices for practices they have already been undertaking. Such is the need for careful and considerate examination of mixed-methods research that Denzin notes "we are 30 to 40 years deep into a multiple, mixed-methods discourse, and we still can't define the method or be clear on its benefits" (2012, p. 82). The purpose of this chapter is not to prescribe or proscribe any particular approaches to developing mixed-methods research, nor to make any claim as to what counts as mixed-methods research as related to the type of methods used, location and extent of mixing in the research process. Rather, following Greene, Benjamin, and Goodyear (2001, p. 29) the purpose of this chapter is to encourage and facilitate "thoughtful mixed-method planning" so that any researcher considering using more than one method will make explicit and defensible choices in designing and carrying out their research. In doing so, I hope to encourage quantitative researchers to be more considerate of the complexities of qualitative methodologies, and for qualitative researchers to seek opportunities for deploying quantitative methods.

The aforementioned rise of mixed-methods literature is indicative of a growing popularity within the academy. That said, mixed-methods research does not currently occupy a prominent place within sport and exercise literature, although calls are being made for mixed-methods analyses (McGannon & Schweinbenz, 2011; Moran, Matthews, & Kirby, 2011; Van der Roest, Spaaij & Van Bottenburg, 2015). The complexities of thoughtful mixed-method planning are such that despite voluminous and vibrant literature, qualitative research methodologies are generally recognized as being marginalized in mixed-methods research, arguably more from ignorance than intent. Concomitantly, little consensus has been reached regarding several core "controversies" (Creswell, 2011; Sparkes, 2015; Teddlie & Tashakkori, 2010), including definitional issues ranging from what counts as mixed-methods research to specific concepts and terminology used, (in)commensurability of paradigms, methodological hierarchies, and the overall value of mixed-methods research. These controversies aside, all mixed-methods research proceeds from the assumption that there are multiple valuable and legitimate techniques for developing knowledge of, in this case, sport and exercise. Such assumptions view using more than one method in our research as advantageous. More contentious, however, is whether methods that address, negotiate, and/or reflect fundamentally different assumptions can be mixed in a meaningful manner. As mentioned above, this chapter is not particularly concerned about the specific responses researchers mount to these controversies, instead it promotes that those undertaking mixed-methods research should not only be aware of these controversies but also, and more importantly, take an informed position in relation to them; something that, sadly, too few studies explicitly engage with in mixed-methods research generally, and in sport and exercise specifically.

As Sparkes (2015) rightly points out, debates about mixed methods are characterized by a certain amount of "terminological slippage" regarding integral concepts such as paradigm, methods, and methodology. Similarly, Morgan (2007, p. 50) notes, "it is all too easy for social scientists to talk about 'paradigms' and mean entirely different things." Such slippage is compounded by longstanding tension between qualitative and quantitative research(ers). Within my own research I have seen qualitative researchers present unhelpful, disingenuous, and derisory caricatures of quantitative research and quantitative researchers bewildered, dismissive, and patronizing about how and why qualitative research is conducted. O'Cathain, Murphy, and Nicholl (2008) document how quantitative researchers often feel that qualitative researchers do not respect their expertise and work, contrary to the dominant narratives in qualitative methods literature. Indeed, disappointingly, the most common manner in which you will hear paradigmatic terminology outside of texts like this is pejoratively. I frequently hear in classrooms, seminars, conferences, and corridors interpretivist researchers casually dismissing not only individual studies but also entire disciplines as positivistic. Such smug, apparently self-sufficient yet ill-thought-through dismissal of any research paradigm is superseded in its unhelpfulness only by its spuriousness.

That notwithstanding, Lunde, Heggen, and Strans (2013) present a compelling case study of how interpersonal, as well as interprofessional and interdisciplinary power relations in a mixed-methods study, ultimately reinforced a disciplinary hierarchy within the research team that reflected latent paradigmatic assumptions in the research design. Despite initial enthusiasm and intent for a mixed-methods project that would cross paradigmatic boundaries, in many ways, as Lunde *et al.* (2013) articulate, their study failed to meet their goals and expectations for collaboration and boundary crossing. Correspondingly, the key problems and challenges in mixed-methods research arise not as the result of appropriating different practical means – oftentimes referred to as tools – for gathering and analyzing data (i.e., research *methods*) from the fields in which they originated or developed; researchers should be encouraged to use any and all approaches that will advance insight into their particular research problem. Problems arise when different approaches to framing research problems, ways of asking questions, and processes for evaluating and presenting evidence constructed in dialogue with our disciplinary, and theoretical perspectives (i.e., research *methodologies*) incompatible with central assumptions regarding the goals and purpose of the research, criteria for assessing quality (see Chapter 25), and the role of theory (see chapter 30), values, and the researcher, are not integrated in careful and respectful ways. In short, mixed-methods research is neither a quick fix for paradigmatic shortcomings nor inherently nor necessarily a bridge between paradigms, disciplines, or researchers. As Hesse-Biber reminds us, "jumping on the mixed methods bandwagon without really thinking through the implications of doing so may yield research of dubious quality or research that does not add theoretical value and understanding" (2010, p. 23). Mixed-methods research that adds theoretical value and understanding begins with critical discussion and meaningful reflection on mixed-methods research generally, as well as the integration of qualitative methods specifically. Thus, while researchers in sport and exercise are becoming increasingly interested in mixed-methods research it is important to avoid simply "reproducing a celebratory discourse on mixing methods and, in turn, overlooking critical and complex matters that need to be engaged with to develop our understandings of mixing methods" (Smith, Sparkes, Phoenix, & Kirby, 2012, p. 375).

Paradigmatic beginnings

Debates regarding the nature, purpose, place, and influence of paradigms are a key component of critical reflective literature on mixed-methods research. Following Kuhn (1970), this chapter deploys paradigm to denote, in part, our basic beliefs and fundamental assumptions about the nature of the world, our relationship with the world, as well as the relationship between the world, ourselves, and other subjects, objects, beings, processes, events, and happenings therein (see also Chapter 1). Throughout qualitative research methods literature, including specific sport and exercise literature, paradigms are categorized according to responses to questions about: the nature of reality (ontology); to what extent we can know reality (epistemology); and what the most valuable ways knowledge of that reality can be gained (methodology). Our answers to these questions – that is to say, our paradigmatic perspective – influence how research problems are identified, what kinds of research questions are asked, what evidence is valued in resolving and answering said problems and questions, as well as how methods are both used and evaluated.

Paradigms also refer to the shared beliefs of a research community. Thus, paradigms can, and should, be understood as disciplinary matrices based on a relative consensus among a group of researchers about which questions, both in form and content, are pressing, meaningful, and answerable. Therefore, paradigms are not simply the stuff of abstract philosophical musings; they provide guidelines, systems, and frameworks for conducting research either through philosophical engagement with our underlying assumptions or through socialization into a research community. As Sparkes and Smith note "we conduct inquiry via a particular paradigm because it embodies assumptions about the world that we believe in and supports and values that we hold dear. And, because we hold these assumptions and values we conduct inquiry according to the precepts of that paradigm" (2014, p. 9). Paradigms, then, are normative. And they matter. Paradigms inform and guide our views on the nature of knowledge and evidence, as well as the appropriateness of forms of knowledge and evidence. Below we shall explore both senses and the challenges and opportunities they present for mixed-methods research.

In general and idealized terms, quantitative research is traditionally shaped by realist ontology, objectivist epistemology, and experimentally driven and/or manipulative methodologies; collectively referred to as postpositivism. From such a perspective, there is one regular and predictable reality governed by laws, independent of and external to our experiences and perceptions. Assuming the independence of reality means that the researcher is able to complete their research without unknowingly or unduly influencing, or being influenced by, the objects of their study. Gaining access to the laws governing the mechanisms, actions, and reactions taking place in the world necessitates that researchers minimize and mitigate personal values, perceptions, and biases through the use of, wherever possible, "gold standard" methods in their work. It is often forgotten that there are subtleties and differences within postpositivism, as well as broader differences between and across ontologies, episte-mologies, and methodologies evident within paradigmatic (re)views (Lincoln, Lynham, & Guba, 2011; Sparkes & Smith, 2014; Whaley & Krane, 2011). Quantitative research gener-ally, informed by postpositivism, acknowledges that said laws are not directly apprehended but known imperfectly, probabilistically, and approximately. That being said, the goal is to create as robust as possible approximations through direct manipulation and observation in order to predict and control events, actions, and, certainly in the world of sport and exercise, behaviors. Therefore, postpositivist truth claims are based on excellence in research method. Such excellence requires careful and regimental following of procedure. The regimented and deductive nature of the postpositivist perspective does not mean such work is devoid of creative or critical thinking. However, this thinking usually takes place when defining the research problem and/or developing instrumentation rather than as a central component of research method.

Qualitative research is often been deployed as a label for *any* research that takes place in opposition to postpositivism. In sport and exercise Silk, Andrews, and Mason articulate the basis of this opposition arguing "the critical interrogation of the sporting empirical, by its very nature, cannot treat the dynamism and complexities of the physically active human being as a set of static, isolatable, measurable, mechanical, artificial and observable variables" (2005, p. 5). It is beyond the scope of this chapter to meaningfully review, compare, and contrast the multiple and nuanced ontological, epistemological, and methodological positions in opposition to post-positivism including, but not limited to, critical realism, interpretivism, constructionism (see Chapters 1 and 10), phenomenology (see Chapter 2), critical theory (see Chapters 1, 10 and 30), feminisms (see Chapter 7), participatory action research/critical participatory inquiry (see Chapters 8, 33 and 34), and post–structuralism (see Chapters 10 and 18). In addition to chapters in this handbook, useful guides can be found in Lincoln *et al.* (2011), Smith *et al.* (2012), and Sparkes and Smith (2014). Generally speaking, rejecting postpositivism in favor of developing contextual understandings of meaning and lived experience is based on, to varying degrees, levels of emphasis, and in various combinations, relativist ontologies, subjectivist epistemolo-gies, and hermeneutic methodologies. Such work is generally oriented towards exploring social realities and in doing so ascertaining what participants themselves deem significant and impor-tant. For the sake of succinctness, I will use interpretivist as shorthand for qualitative research opposed to postpositivism throughout this chapter.

For interpretivists, reality is fluid, multiple, and dependent on the meanings given to objects and events, which in turn are influenced by, if not function as, our interpretations. Therefore, we cannot know reality for real, only how it is experienced and made meaningful. It is important to note that the notion of multiple realities does not deny the existence of a mind-independent reality. That is to say the existence of objects, events, processes, out there in the world is not entirely dependent on our sensory experience. To be clear, despite claims to multiple realities, most interpretivists do not reject the existence of the physical and social world outside of them. If they did, they could stay in the library or a comfortable armchair and save themselves the difficult and oftentimes tedious work of empirical investigation. Put simply, assuming multiple (experiences of) realities need not preclude empirically grounded claims. However, if our experi-ences of reality are mind-dependent, as relativist ontologies maintain, then the researcher cannot separate themselves from the researched. Thus, following from relativist ontologies, subjectivist epistemologies hold that values inevitably mediate understandings. Knowledge is coconstructed by researchers and participants. In essence, interpretivist research is about interpretations, which Giddens (1987) famously referred to as the double hermeneutic, where participant meaning-making becomes data for the researcher who engages in further meaning-making, which (may) in turn alter the meaning-making of the participant; thus both participants and researchers actively and dynamically produce and interpret knowledge of, and for, each other. Usually, such research is very careful not to position itself as providing the truth, or even approximations of the truth.

Therefore, while a postpositivist believes that particular tricks of method can "control" for values, biases, and other variables, the interpretivist responds that no method is value-free or objective. At best, objectivity is the result of social and cultural practices and every (supposedly) objective measure is the result of many entirely subjective decisions. Importantly, these assumptions are reflected in assessments of research quality. Good research, according to postpositivists, is valid, reliable, and presented in a dispassionate, objective, and formulaic manner. In essence, these quality judgments reflect knowledge claims as independent of the researcher and reflecting reality, for real. Said differently, for postpositivists the purpose of research is to know the world as it really is, corresponding to a belief that such knowledge is possible. Based on these assumptions, knowing constitutes generalizable causal explanations and, in ideal scenarios, knowledge will be theory-free and timeless. Judging qualitative research is something of a different story. While most accept the need to judge qualitative research to criteria different from quantitative research as self-evident, a range of various criteria have been forwarded, none of which are universally accepted (Bryman, 2012). Judging the quality of any research should be based on criteria consistent with the underlying assumptions and processes of the methodology under question (see Chapter 25). An issue we will return to.

Hopefully this brief review of paradigmatic assumptions demonstrates that while such assumptions are arguably not as obvious or readily testable as other research assumptions, such as assumptions required of statistical data, they are every bit as important. The types of questions we ask, as well as the way we seek to answer them, are strongly influenced by our paradigms, in both senses of the term outlined above, even though many researchers will not reflect on their paradigmatic assumptions. As Mertens (2010, p. 9) points out, failure to recognize or reflect on underlying assumptions does not mean a researcher has none, "it merely means that they are operating with unexamined assumptions." The fundamental task of mixed-methods research is establishing how, or indeed if at all, these differing assumptions can be combined within a research program.

Practical purposes, and pitfalls, for mixing

Some hold that philosophical (and disciplinary) assumptions underpinning research methodologies are incompatible. Such *purists* do not necessarily believe that mixed-methods research is impossible, but rather that philosophical assumptions are of utmost importance and therefore explicit ontological and epistemological positions, manifest in (mixed) methodology, must be recognized, respected, and articulated. In effect, purists maintain that mixing (certain) *methods* is possible, but mixing *methodologies* is highly problematic. Resultantly, some combinations are simply not possible for purists. Contrary to purists, mixed-methods *pragmatists* (this terms does *not* refer to work by John Dewey or others, but means a "what works" approach when used in mixed-methods work) maintain that philosophical posturing does little more than get in the way of research and point to "successfully" completed research that combines qualitative and quantitative methods as evidence for their claims. For pragmatists, the practical needs of finding solutions to research questions and problems should dictate, above all else, the methods to be used and whether mixing methods is desirable or feasible. From the perspective of the pragmatist, purposes for which methods are useful matters far more than any epistemological or ontological differences, and the primary challenge for those considering mixed-methods research is careful delineation of the research problem and purpose of their study. Once this has been developed it is a matter of selecting the most suitable methods; assuming combining certain methods will best enable researchers to achieve their ends of course. Thus, as mentioned above, the rationale for mixed-methods research, according to pragmatists, reflects quality and utility of research manifest in procedural faith and has been the dominant, but by no means only, approach to mixed-methods research. Certain procedures, for the pragmatists, are more useful for certain ends, which enables work to get done. However, it is questionable as to whether this work is as useful as it could, or indeed purports to, be and has the unwelcome side effect of reinforcing particular hierarchies, necessarily disempowering and/or disrespecting certain ways of knowing, as well as research and researchers who identify with epistemologies marginalized in such an approach. As such, it is important to bear in mind that mixed-methods pragmatism is neither a coherent methodological project nor a philosophical perspective (Bergman, 2011; Denzin, 2012). Therefore, consideration of the research problems, questions, and goals are essential, but researchers must guard against the tendency for "methods-centric," problem-focused approaches which sidestep or ignore how paradigmatic assumptions manifest in the research process.

As a result of pragmatic dominance a wide range of "purpose typologies" have been presented for mixed-methods research. Commonly, mixed-methods research purposes relate to improving accuracy, generating a fuller understanding through combining sources of data, mitigating biases or shortcomings in individual methods, developing findings through exploring contrasting data, and/or refining inclusion and exclusion criteria. More specifically, in reviewing mixed-method theoretical literature, as well as empirically evaluating mixed-methods practice, Greene, Caracelli, and Graham (1989) developed a popular and enduring set of five – problem-focused – purposes for mixed-methods research.

Triangulation, taken analogously from surveying, denotes using two (or more) methods in order to check the veracity of results. Most commonly, the purpose of triangulation in mixed-methods research is mitigating inherent biases, shortcomings, and oversights of individual methods as related to a single concept. Thus, triangulation is used to identify areas of convergence, where such areas enhance the credibility of our conceptualizations. Said differently, triangulation is most commonly advocated as a way to compensate for unexplained/irrelevant variance and error as related to methods, hence Hesse-Biber's (2010) description of this as more properly "methods triangulation" (cf. Denzin's (1970) four forms of triangulation: data (using multiple sampling strategies), investigator (using more than one researcher to gather and/or analyze data), methodological (using more than one method), and/or theoretical (using more than one theoretical position). Many questions have been raised about the meaning, possibilities and philosophical positioning of triangulation in mixed-methods literature, most notably in a special edition of the *Journal of Mixed Methods Research* devoted to the topic (see: Mertens & Hesse-Biber, 2012). The relatively simple notion that aggregating analyses through methods triangulation enables more robust knowledge claims belies a range of complicated issues and nuance as to how, when, and if triangulation enables such understanding. Indeed, interpreting agreement or disagreement between data, especially different kinds of data, is not straightforward, unambiguous, or unproblematic. To say otherwise is to advocate, knowingly or otherwise (cf. Mertens, 2010 above), naive realism, which runs roughshod over the possibility of maintaining an epistemologically and ontologically sensitive and coherent position when using different methods (see also Chapter 25). Maintaining epistemological and ontological sensitivity and coherence towards the social world while using different methods, then, is perhaps better approached as methodological bricolage (Denzin & Lincoln, 1994) rather than methodological triangulation. Like triangulation, methodological bricolage enables the appropriation of multiple data–collection and analysis techniques to answer a research question. Unlike triangulation, methodological bricolage does not presuppose any specific methodology and in doing so respects the contextual contingencies of research participants and the sociohistoric conditions of research to determine how the research is conducted in an ongoing, fluid, and emergent way, not formalized procedural best-practice, with predetermined "correct" methods and linear stepwise sequencing.

Generating a more comprehensive understanding of the phenomenon as a whole, rather than a single concept, is mixing methods for the purpose of *complementarity*. Complementarity designs deploy different methods in order to develop a broader understanding of the research problem. To develop this difference we can return to the analogy of triangulation. If surveyors use methods triangulation to generate data on, say, the height of a mountain, then a complementarity method would use a range of approaches to generate an account of other aspects of the mountain such as its geology, ecology, and social and cultural value. A complementary approach does, to some extent, mitigate certain weaknesses and blind spots of method, but the true strength of the approach is aggregation of the strengths of each method. Different methods present different strengths, which are used in order to address different facets and multiple components of the topic of study, rather than mutually reinforce each other regarding a single point. This still raises questions of epistemological and ontological coherence *pace* triangulation. However, complementarity does not make the same assumption that aggregation brings the researcher closer to a single truth. Resultantly, studies display a tendency to be conducted and reported in a parallel rather than integrated fashion, analogous to the differences in collaboration and integration between multi- versus interdisciplinary research.

Methods can be mixed, *developmentally*, to inform sampling, method implementation, and/or construction of instruments. The underlying procedure of developmental designs is the sequential use of methods. Data generated by one method amplifies the strength of each subsequently deployed method by directing and maximizing their focus. In this sense, grounds can be found for questioning whether using one method to inform the deployment of another is actually mixed-methods research. Like triangulation and complementarity, sequential designs are neither novel nor new. For example, quantitative measures have long been used as part of purposeful and/or theoretical sampling procedures by qualitative researchers, and quantitative researchers have used qualitative measures as part of survey construction. Furthermore, developmental designs are not unique to studies deploying qualitative and quantitative methods of data collection and analysis. As such, mixed methods for the purposes of development and triangulation are similar in that they have long operated outside any formal mixed-methods designation. What should be different here is the concatenation of methods within an overall research approach, through specific and explicit attention to areas of convergence and divergence in the underlying assumptions in each method.

Perhaps the most common purpose for mixing methods is to use different methods to expand the study so that each component of the research topic is addressed by the method aligned most intuitively with the problem. *Expansion* studies sit somewhere between triangulation and complementarity; like triangulation, expansion studies focus on the same concept or problem, and like complementarity designs deploy different methods in order to address different facets of the same phenomenon. Expanding your repertoire of methods allows each component of your research problem to be addressed by the most suitable method. Expansion designs, however, tend to determine the best method practically and in isolation from the other methods. That is to say without considering how the different methods can, or should, be integrated. Expansion studies, then, raise particular issues as to how each method can be connected through linking different data and results from the different methods, which while much discussed, seldom yield satisfactory responses. Said differently, questions of ontology, epistemology, and method are not discussed, nor is a position offered.

Finally, *initiation* studies seek disagreement and incongruity, which signal opportunities for further investigation. Contrary to triangulation, complementarity, development, and expansion (albeit to a lesser extent), which view inconsistency between findings as a failure of technique inconsistency is the basis for interesting and valuable exploration in initiation studies. In this sense, initiation designs seek methodological dissonance and as such "a mixed methods study with an initiation intent is likely to be enhanced by identifying methods that are significantly different from one another in stance, form, and perspective" (Greene, 2007 p. 103). Mixing methods for the purpose of initiation is the only purpose that has, as its starting point, an appreciation of paradigmatic differences.

Recall, different approaches to assessing research purpose are informed by epistemological, ontological, methodological positions; in other words, (unacknowledged) paradigmatic assumptions. Therefore, at a general level, pragmatic problem-focused approaches demonstrate that, contrary to the purist position, a range of methods can undoubtedly be mixed in a study. Indeed, Sparkes (2015) proposes when methods are differentiated from methodology, disagreements about the possibility of mixing methods are a nondebate. However, as Sparkes (2015), and others (Denzin, 2012; Lincoln *et al.*, 2011; Hesse-Biber, 2010), also point out, methodological choices concomitantly produce and mutually reinforce paradigmatic assumptions. Thus, mixed-methods pragmatism, where research purpose or question(s) determines research methods, has latched onto philosophical pragmatists' emphasis on inquiry and empiricism, openness to different methods, and insistence on meaning as unknowable in advance of events and their practical consequences. Such a position resonates with dominant (postpositivist) values of scientific inquiry, where results cannot be known ahead of investigation, and is arguably intuitively aligned with research results determined (objectively) by data rather than (subjectively) by values. Unfortunately, there are fundamental discrepancies between philosophical pragmatism and mixed-methods pragmatism, with Bergman (2011, p. 272) describing the latter as "an idiosyncratic and unsatisfactory interpretation" of the former. Specifically, philosophical pragmatism recognizes that meaning is constructed through experience in a social setting and pragmatist experiential empiricism has been developed to argue for an inability to recognize truth outside of the accepted standards of a particular community. Said differently, philosophical pragmatist theories of truth hold that the value of knowledge is determined by the consequences of knowledge claims. Thus, following Hilary Putnam (1994) and Denzin (2012), for philosophical pragmatists "there is no fundamental dichotomy between 'facts' and 'values'" (Putnam, 1994 p. 152), rather they "endorse a thoroughly interpretive, hermeneutic pragmatism that is explicitly antipositivist, antifoundational, and radically contextual. But this is not the pragmatism invoked by mixed-methods research proponents" (Denzin, 2012 p. 83). In short, philosophical pragmatism is not a methodology or problem-solving activity in and of itself. A central problem of mixed-methods research is that not only are justifications for deploying mixed-methods designs often not provided (Bryman, 2006), including in studies of sport and exercise (cf. Van der Roest *et al.*, 2015), but also the most common justification, namely problem-focused pragmatism as outlined above, contradicts the explicitly articulated perspectives of philosophical pragmatists on the experience, truth, and inquiry it claims to advance. Therefore, researchers must be wary of mixed-methods pragmatism, which all too easily manifests in a rather cavalier dismissal of paradigms and a haphazard "everything-is-okay-as-long-as-the-work-gets-done" approach to research.

To be clear, I am not arguing that the goals of research are not integral to methods selection, nor am I policing boundaries of philosophical schools of thought. Ultimately, mixed-methods research should not be defined by which methods are mixed. As Bergman argues "it may be just as interesting and complex to integrate a qualitative thematic analysis with a narrative analysis, or a random controlled trial experiment with a questionnaire" (2011, p. 272), as combining quantitative and qualitative methods. What is of importance, then, is that the goals of the research, the role of the researcher, values, theory, and corresponding judgment criteria all reflect, and respect, paradigmatic differences. Particular challenges are present, for example, when methodologies requiring detached and disinterested observers engage with methodologies that value contingency and nonneutrality of knowledge requiring explicitly politicized positions to be taken by researchers. Further, methods, such as ethnography, for example (see Chapter 5), can be agreed as a qualitative research approach, but can be conducted according to different (combinations of) ontological, epistemological, and methodological assumptions. In short, most methods can cross paradigms relatively untroubled. Resultantly, comparing the "objective" numerical measures obtained through, say, rigorous experimental methods to data collected through, for example, semistructured interviews without discussion of, or attempts to, integrate or connect different philosophical paradigms, only leads to discussions about the difference between the "truth" of the situation, experience, event, process, or happening, and how this is experienced. Such work can be illuminating. More often, though, the lack of thoughtful consideration of paradigmatic issues makes such work more likely to be dull, uninforming, and of poor quality.

Failure to recognize, or perhaps more accurately engage with in conscious and meaningful ways, methodological assumptions in mixed-methods research has reinforced disciplinary hierarchies and continues to privilege particular ways of knowing antithetical to many values and practices of interpretivist researcher, which reveals a troubling postpositivist "methodological orthodoxy" (Hesse-Biber, 2010) in mixed-methods literature. Like Bryman (2006) and Smith *et al.* (2012) I have seen little evidence of mixed-methods research which thoughtfully or sincerely integrates interpretivist sensibilities and values. Therefore, we should, following Sparkes (2015, p. 50) recognize "not *all* research methods are compatible with *all* paradigmatic assumptions and *all* methodologies," and in doing so consider an approach to mixed-methods research that is compatible with values more commonly found in critical, interpretive, qualitative approaches to research. As a starting point, then, mixed-methods research accentuates the need to identify the assumptions that underpin the research endeavor. As such, for purists (and philosophical pragmatists) epistemological and ontological assumptions matter when doing mixed-methods research. On the other hand, mixed-methods pragmatists believe that epistemological and ontological assumptions do not. However, that does not mean that adopting a mixed-methods pragmatism means anything goes. As indicated above, not offering a position does not mean you do not have one. Therefore, decisions made as part of the research process need to be informed and communicated, carefully and with nuance. Considering why and how mixed-methods research will be completed researchers will benefit from:

1. extending the respect and value shown to methodological multiplicity in mixed-methods research to recognizing and appreciating ontological, epistemological, and theoretical diversity;
2. articulating our assumptions and how they prejudice what we see as valuable, desirable, and achievable in research;
3. carefully and considerately identifying where and how crossing boundaries might enable the creation of new knowledge, and acknowledging where differences might be incommensurable.

Interpretively driven mixed-methods research

Throughout both the empirical and theoretical mixed-methods literature much is made of the relative importance and sequencing of methods. Mixed-methods design notation was created specifically to show procedural issues of integration, priority, and sequencing (Teddlie & Tashakkori, 2006). However, the subtleties of qualitative methodologies are not sufficiently or sensitively engaged with, and "position[s] qualitative methods second and quantitative methods as primary with an overall mixed-method design that is in the service of testing out quantitatively generated theories" (Hesse-Biber, 2010, p. 455). Further, Denzin (2012) points out that the most prominent figures in mixed-methods discourse seldom have any meaningful training or recognition of qualitative methods, let alone qualitative methodologies, which I have clumped together as interpretivism. Yet whilst lacking in training, such researchers are determining how and why qualitative research should be conducted in mixed-methods designs. Hopefully by this point anyone considering mixed-methods research has realized that pursuing a research approach that draws on different methodological perspectives and practices is a complex and nuanced endeavor; that methods-centric approaches, including mixed-methods pragmatism, do little to address the methodological complexities of such work. For this reason mixed-methods research and mixed methodologists have been critiqued for inherently reproducing postpositivistic values, which are incommensurate with some qualitative research methods, and for marginalizing or assigning qualitative research to an inferior position within mixed-methods research *despite* "QUAL" studies.

This is not, however, simply a product of philosophes of science. Demand for interdisciplinary and mixed-methods research from funding agencies, coupled with increasing institutional pressure for securing external revenue as part of performance appraisals, has undoubtedly contributed to the growth of mixed-methods research (Teddlie & Tashakkori, 2011). Moreover, even though qualitative methodologists studying sport and exercise oftentimes find themselves in faculties and departments preoccupied with the pursuit of academic legitimacy via replicating practices of hard scientific parent disciplines to study human (in)activity, set against the backdrop of the rise of evidenced-based medicine (replete with explicitly defined methods hierarchies), and in audit cultures that privilege postpositivist ways of knowing, interpretivists should not take the rising interest in mixed-methods research amongst the academy generally and funding agencies specifically as a quick route to demonstrate the versatility and utility of qualitative methodologies, nor as an unproblematic vehicle for asserting the legitimacy and maturation of qualitative methods. Thus, we should take umbrage with arguments of the kind made by Creswell (2011), who believes that in mixed-methods designs "the use of qualitative approaches *whatever their role* in traditional quantitative experiments elevates qualitative research as a legitimate form of inquiry" (p. 227; emphasis in original).

However, by way of response qualitative researchers must not adopt a victim narrative bemoaning a lack of understanding for our practice, nor retrench from debates regarding the purposes, possibilities, and responsibilities of research and academics. As mentioned above, quantitative researchers have grounds for doing the same. Further, qualitative researchers should not become research technicians or engineers in mixed-methods studies, thereby allowing the terms of critical conversations regarding the purpose and value of mixed *and* qualitative methods to be dictated by those who have not been trained as qualitative methodologists, nor should we deploy our paradigmatic backgrounds as reasons or justifications for not being conversant, in *meaningful* and *respectful* ways, of quantitative methodologies. Those who hold that paradigms are commensurable are required to attend explicitly to how commensurability is understood and enacted in their research. Similarly, purists must contribute to discussions to help impress upon researchers the importance of paradigms to enable researchers to undertake research that can borrow from different methodologies while maintaining and respecting the integrity of our methodologies. Qualitative researchers have something truly important to contribute to mixed-methods discourse and research by producing high-quality qualitative research that reflects, explains, and showcases our own epistemological and ontological beliefs, *and* by engaging in critical dialogue about mixed-methods work making fair, critical judgments as to its quality. To this end I propose that the true value of qualitative methodologies and skilled qualitative researchers to mixed-methods research (however defined) is not the technical skills or "perceptive acuity and relational capabilities" specialist qualitative researchers have as the primary instrument of (qualitative) "data generation, analysis, and interpretation," as Greene (2007, p. 39) would have it, but rather as connoisseurs and craftspeople engaged in methodological bricolage. As a starting point, this will require:

1. Explaining legitimacy criteria and concomitantly championing high-quality qualitative research, while refusing to accept narrow-minded or uninformed critiques and/or use of qualitative methodologies;
2. Recognizing that qualitative research is not synonymous with ethically superior research nor empowerment and emancipation;
3. Critical and considerate reading and engagement with research and researchers outside our own disciplinary and paradigmatic areas.

Mixed methods as craft and mixed-method researchers as bricoleurs and connoisseurs

First mooted by Lévi-Strauss (1966) as a metaphor for meaning-making practices and later developed most famously in qualitative research by Norman Denzin and Yvonna Lincoln, as well as Joe Kincheloe (e.g., Kincheloe, 2005), the work of the bricoleur is contrasted to that of the engineer. As mentioned above, the bricoleur uses tools and artifacts reflexively and dynamically to craft knowledge, whereas the engineer follows set procedures with tools designed and used for specific, usually singular and predefined, purposes. Thus, the bricolage metaphor signifies research practice that is open to multiplicity, eclecticism, flexibility, pluralism, and emergent design. I propose that we – that is, self-identified qualitative researchers – should embrace methodological bricolage in the broadest possible sense. As such, we must expand our broad knowledge of interpretive paradigms, political acumen, and reflexive approaches to research as interactive and complex to work towards understanding quantitative methods. Thus, in the spirit of methodological bricolage we should stitch, wherever possible, feasible, and useful quantitative methods into our work. We should expand on Denzin's (2012, p. 85) call to recognize that "the narratives or stories scientists tell are accounts couched and framed within specific storytelling traditions, often defined as paradigms (e.g., positivism, postpositivism, constructivism)," to appreciate that it is not always possible, and seldom easy, to move across certain ontological epistemological, and methodological boundaries in producing and telling these various stories. Yet, we must not be dismissive of opportunities to do so. There is certainly scope for such work. Indeed, the postpositivist predilections in, and quantitative dominance of, mixed methods is well documented and despite continued calls (including this one) to generate interpretively driven analyses drawing from quantitative and qualitative methods we have very few examples on which to draw.

Methodological bricolage and connoisseurship in qualitative research each have a specific and nuanced development, as well as application to research methods discourse, although they share a general emphasis on attentiveness to subtlety, complexity, and nuance. I propose we take the artisanal, craft component of interpretive perspectives and investigate how quantitative methodologies might fit into such work. Not in the cursory manner in which qualitative methodologies have been picked up in mixed methods, but by seeking out opportunities to mix, match, and interrogate philosophical underpinnings, including our own. We will necessarily be required to do so in the knowledge that this is technically difficult and will likely reveal to us our own prejudices, especially paradigmatic prejudices, and shortcomings. Further, the messy and vulnerable work of crafting interpretively driven mixed-methods work may not be well supported by the academy relative to orthodox mixed-methods research, or by some of our interpretivist colleagues. Thus, drawing on fluid, wide-ranging, and deep theoretical and methodological vocabularies we should take on competing and complimentary perspectives and, in the words of C. Wright Mills:

> Avoid any rigid set of procedures. Above all, seek to develop and to use the sociological imagination. Avoid the fetishism of method and technique. Urge the rehabilitation of the unpretentious intellectual craftsman, and try to become such a craftsman yourself. Let every man [sic] be his own methodologist; let every man [sic] be his own theorist; let theory and method again become part of the practice of a craft.
>
> *(Mills, 1959, p. 224)*

To reiterate, practicing unpretentious intellectual interpretivist craft should involve seeking possibilities for incorporating quantitative methods respectful of their limitations *and* power. In the first instance, expansion of qualitative research into mixed-methods research should be based not on the practical piecemeal procedures per expansion purposes outlined above, but rather on reflection of our holistic research endeavor, cognizant of the connections between each individual method and its relationship with our methodology. Developing interpretively driven mixed-methods work will not be a formulaic, orderly, regimented, or straightforward process. Secondly, we must militate against assuming that qualitative research is – inherently, inevitably, always, or unproblematically – superior in "giving voice" to or "empowering" participants. Thoughtful and considerate work is an artisanal craft conducted with excellence in (scientific) method and humility in methodology. Hence, we should gain proficiency in a range of tasks, *especially* those with which we do not normally associate with our paradigmatic or disciplinary backgrounds, and the post-structuralist critical philosophies in which bricolage has been developed even more so, to enable methodological bricolage that is the product of informed choices not ignorance.

Such an approach will require changes in how we evaluate our work. Following Smith *et al's* (2012) advice to physical therapists, mixed-methods research in sport and exercise should be evaluated by methodological connoisseurs appreciative of differences, and cognizant of complex nuances based on discerning and sagacious distinctions of how methods are deployed practically, and the implications of methodological decisions. In the words of Eisner (1991, p. 69) "what is required (or desired) is that our experience be subtle, complex, and informed," so we make fair, ethical, and informed choices in our own research, as well as in our judgment of the research of others, and the utility and effect of other research approaches. As connoisseurs of research we will be required to, above all else, make quality judgments about mixed-methods research generally, and the specific possibilities for and of such work, from our own paradigmatic and disciplinary camps as well as others.

In eschewing an oppressive methodological hierarchy we will necessarily be required to address our own prejudices, and in doing so be committed to the possibility, perhaps inevitability, of engaging in robust exchanges of views, always attentive to what is being expressed, with the recognition that our own views need not be accepted nor do we need to accept the views of others. In short, I hope that in seeking to develop artisanal methodological bricolage informed by connoisseurship we take seriously what kind of research we want to do, and in what ways can that be made possible and effective through careful, considerate, and respectful, but critical, recognition of (as mealy-mouthed as it is) what we are doing when we are doing what we are doing. Simply put, we must place onus on ourselves to:

1. Embrace intellectual curiosity to gain understanding of the broadest possible range of processes, theories, and perspectives used in research.
2. Deploy that knowledge to give critical, but fair, hearings to knowledge and research processes, especially to approaches different from those we normally value, by avoiding trite integration of difference into our own schemas, or out-of-hand, supercilious rejections.
3. Develop relative and fluid criterion for ensuring research rigor and assessing research quality, which will likely entail different judgments both within and between studies.

Future directions

In bringing this chapter to a close I do not wish to end with a conclusion, for it is clear that very little is finished in the world of mixed-methods research. Instead, we should focus on where we want and are able to go from here. Therefore, without wishing to downplay important ontological, epistemological, and methodological debates, political differences between qualitative and quantitative research are not only overstated, but also presented as irrevocably antagonistic. Thus, within an academic environment increasingly subject to business principles, market logics, and impact agendas, a derisive approach to justifying methodological proclivities has redoubled. Following Martin (2011) we can see that while critical, in all meanings of the term, differences exist both within and between research paradigms this should not deter researchers from exploring the potential of combining and transgressing ontological, epistemological, and methodological lines. Hopefully, from the preceding discussion it becomes evident that mixing methods is *potentially* valuable and worthwhile, with the caveat that paradigmatic differences matter, and recognition that "to argue that it is paradigms that are in contention is probably less useful than to probe where and how paradigms exhibit confluence and where and how paradigms exhibit differences, controversies, and contradictions" (Lincoln *et al.*, 2011, p. 97). As such, this chapter does not promote adherence to particularized, exclusive, or limiting understandings of what counts as mixed-methods research, nor promulgate obligations to theoretical positions or methodological precepts except that we are aware of them and engage with them.

In short, too often mixed-methods research deploys qualitative research as a bolt-on or afterthought, to the extent it has been described by Giddings (2006) as positivism dressed in drag. Unsurprisingly, postpositivist modes and methods of knowing remain privileged in the academy broadly, and in mixed-methods research specifically, which serves to compromise not only the potential contributions mixed methods can make, including in studies of sport and exercise, but also to further marginalize methodological diversity. I hope that those from postpositivist positions still left reading this chapter will take the time to carefully consider their paradigmatic assumptions and integrate qualitative methodologies in respectful ways, and implore interpretivist researchers to do the same with quantitative methods in pursuit of producing high-quality research, regardless of whether it fits definitions of mixed-methods orthodoxy.

References

Bergman, M.M. (2011). The good, the bad, and the ugly in mixed methods research and design. *Journal of Mixed Methods Research*, 5(4), 271–275.

Bryman, A. (2006). Integrating quantitative and qualitative research: How is it done? *Qualitative Research*, 6(1), 97–113.

Bryman, A. (2012). *Social research methods* (4th ed.). Oxford: Oxford University Press.

Creswell, J.W. (2011). Controversies in mixed methods research. In N.K. Denzin & Y.S. Lincoln (Eds.), *The Sage handbook of qualitative research* (pp. 269–283). London: Sage.

Denzin, N. (1970). *The research act in sociology*. Chicago, IL: Aldine.

Denzin, N.K. & Lincoln, Y.S. (1994). Introduction: Entering the field of qualitative research. In N.K. Denzin & Y.S. Lincoln. (Eds.), *Handbook of qualitative research* (pp. 1–17). Thousand Oaks, CA: Sage.

Denzin, N. (2012). Triangulation 2.0. *Journal of Mixed Methods Research*, 6(2), 80–88.

Eisner, E. (1991). *The enlightened eye*. New York: MacMillan.

Giddens, A. (1987). *Social theory and modern sociology*. Cambridge: Polity Press.

Giddings, L. (2006). Mixed-methods research: Positivism dressed in drag? *Journal of Research in Nursing*, 11(13), 195–203.

Greene, J.C. (2007). *Mixed methods in social inquiry*. San Francisco, CA: John Wiley.

Greene, J.C., Benjamin, L. & Goodyear, L. (2001). The merits of mixing methods in evaluation. *Evaluation*, 7(1), 25–44.

Greene, J., Caracelli, V. & Graham, W. (1989). Toward a conceptual framework for mixed-method evaluation designs. *Educational Evaluation and Policy Analysis*, 11(3), 255–274.

Hesse-Biber, S.N. (2010). *Mixed methods research: Merging theory with practice*. New York: The Guilford Press.

Johnson, R. & Onwuegbuzie, A. (2004). Mixed methods research: A research paradigm whose time has come. *Educational Researcher*, 33(7), 14–26

Kincheloe, J. (2001). Describing the bricolage: Conceptualizing a new rigor in qualitative research. *Qualitative Inquiry*, 7(6), 679–692.

Kincheloe, J. (2005). On to the next level: Continuing the conceptualization of the bricolage. *Qualitative Inquiry*, 11(3), 323–350.

Kuhn, T. (1970). *The structure of scientific revolutions*. Chicago, IL: University of Chicago Press.

Lévi-Strauss, C. (1966). *The savage mind*. Chicago, IL: University of Chicago Press.

Lincoln, Y., Lynham, S. & Guba, E. (2011). Paradigmatic controversies, contradictions, and emerging confluences, revisited. In N.K. Denzin & Y.S. Lincoln (Eds.), *The Sage handbook of qualitative research* (pp. 97–128). London: Sage.

Lunde, A., Heggen, K. & Strans, R. (2013). Knowledge and power: Exploring unproductive interplay between quantitative and qualitative researchers. *Journal of Mixed Methods Research*, 7(2), 197–210.

Martin, J. (2011). Qualitative research in sport and exercise psychology: Observations of a non–qualitative researcher. *Qualitative Research in Sport, Exercise and Health*, 3(3), 335–348.

McGannon, K. & Schweinbenz A. (2011). Traversing the qualitative–quantitative divide using mixed methods: Some reflections and reconciliations for sport and exercise psychology. *Qualitative Research in Sport, Exercise and Health*, 3(3), 370–384.

Mertens, D. (2010). Philosophy in mixed methods teaching: The transformative paradigm as illustration. *International Journal of Multiple Research Approaches*, 4(1), 9–18.

Mertens, D. & Hesse–Biber, S. (2012). Triangulation and mixed methods research: Provocative positions. *Journal of Mixed Methods Research*, 6(2), 75–79.

Mills, C.W. (1959). *Sociological imagination*. Oxford: Oxford University Press.

Moran, A.P., Matthews, J.J. & Kirby, K. (2011). Whatever happened to the third paradigm? Exploring mixed methods research designs in sport and exercise psychology. *Qualitative Research in Sport, Exercise and Health*, 3(3), 362–369.

Morgan, D.L. (2007). Paradigms lost and pragmatism regained: Methodological implications of combining qualitative and quantitative methods. *Journal of Mixed Methods Research*, 1(1), 48–76.

Putnam, H. (1994). *Words and life*. Cambridge, MA: Harvard University Press.

O'Cathain, A., Murphy, E. & Nicholl, J. (2008). Multidisciplinary, interdisciplinary, or dysfunctional? Team working in mixed-methods research. *Qualitative Health Research*, 18(11), 1574–1585.

Silk, M.L., Andrews, D.L. & Mason, D.S. (2005). Encountering the field: Sports studies and qualitative research. In D.L. Andrews, D.S. Mason & M.L. Silk (Eds.), *Qualitative methods in sports studies* (pp. 1–20). New York: Berg.

Smith, B., Sparkes, A.C., Phoenix, C. & Kirby, J. (2012). Qualitative research in physical therapy: A critical discussion on mixed-method research. *Physical Therapy Reviews*, *17*(6), 374–381.

Sparkes, A.C. (2015). Developing mixed methods research in sport and exercise psychology: Critical reflections on five points of controversy. *Psychology of Sport and Exercise*, *16*(3), 4–59.

Sparkes, A.C. & Smith, B. (2014). *Qualitative research in sport, exercise & health sciences. From process to product.* London: Routledge.

Teddlie, C. & Tashakkori, A. (2006). A general typology of research designs featuring mixed methods in the social and behavioral sciences. *Research in the Schools*, *13*(1), 12–28.

Teddlie, C. & Tashakkori, A. (2010). Major issues and controversies in the use of mixed methods in the social and behavioral sciences. In A. Tashakkori & C. Teddlie (Eds.), *Handbook of mixed methods in social and behavioral research* (2nd ed., pp. 3–50). Thousand Oaks, CA: Sage.

Teddlie, C. & Tashakkori, A. (2011). Mixed methods research. In N.K. Denzin & Y.S. Lincoln (Eds.), *The Sage handbook of qualitative research* (pp. 285–299). Los Angeles, CA: Sage.

Van der Roest, J., Spaaij, R. & Van Bottenburg, M. (2015). Mixed methods in emerging academic subdisciplines: The case of sport management. *Journal of Mixed Methods Research*, *9*(1), 70–90.

Whaley, D. & Krane, V. (2011). Now that we all agree, let's talk epistemology: A commentary on the invited articles. *Qualitative Research in Sport, Exercise and Health*, *3*(3), 394–403.

30

THE ROLE OF THEORY, INTERPRETATION AND CRITICAL THOUGHT WITHIN QUALITATIVE SPORT AND EXERCISE RESEARCH

Tania Cassidy

There is a perception that qualitative research is not informed by theory. To shed light on the relationships that exist between theory and qualitative research I have organized the discussion in this chapter along four broad questions:

1. What is theory?
2. How is theory used?
3. How can qualitative research be interpreted? and
4. What is critical thought?

The chapter concludes with a brief discussion of the potential problems with using theory, specifically focusing on some of the dangers and problems to be avoided.

What is theory?

For decades philosophers of science have debated the question "what is theory?", without reaching a consensus (Savage, 1990). Even scholars working within the same discipline have had difficulty reaching a consensus, as evident in Joas and Knöbl's (2009) observation that despite the input from various theorists, sociologists are no closer to "resolving the issue of the 'nature of theory'" (p. 1). What is more, and pertinent to those working in the sport and exercise fields, is Raab's (2015) claim that "[t]he the interaction between theory and practice has troubled some of the most theoretical thinkers" (p. 12). Given the above it should come as no surprise that sport and exercise researchers, whose collective work draws on the traditions of the natural sciences,[1] social sciences,[2] and humanities,[3] do not have a common understanding of what constitutes theory.

For those whose work is aligned to the natural sciences, any answer to a question about what is theory is influenced by the "scientific method."[4] The composition of the scientific method has been debated for centuries but it is commonly thought to occur along the following lines:

(1) making an observation; (2) asking questions; (3) forming a hypothesis; (4) developing predictions; (5) conducting experiments to gather data; and (6) analyzing data to test predictions. The role of theory in the scientific method is to provide a "systematic view of some phenomenon in order to describe, explain, predict its future occurrences" (Weinberg & Gould, 2011, p. 13). Historically, psychologists have been keen to position psychology as a science. Since sport and exercise psychologists often draw on theories and theorists of the parent discipline, some within this research community assert that:

> [s]port and exercise psychology is above all a science . . . Science is . . . a process or method, of learning about the world through the systematic, controlled, empirical, and critical filtering of knowledge acquired through experience. When we apply science to psychology, the goals are to describe, explain, predict, and allow control of behavior.
>
> *(Weinberg & Gould, 2011, p. 12)*

This assertion reflects a statement made by Kerlinger (1973) that theory, at least in behavioral research, is "a set of interrelated constructs (concepts), definitions, and propositions that present a systematic view of phenomena by specifying relations among variables, with the purpose of explaining and predicting the phenomena" (p. 9).

Sport and exercise researchers whose work is aligned to the social sciences and humanities do not subscribe to the above view of theory. Yet it is a mistake to think that all those working in the humanities and social sciences have a homogenous understanding of theory. This mistaken view arguably arises as a consequence of the conflation of the social sciences and humanities, and sets up a natural/social science binary. An outcome of this binary is that discussions tend to focus on the differences between the natural and social sciences and obscure the various ways theory is understood within, and between, the social science and humanities research communities. Increasingly researchers in sport and exercise psychology are turning their attention to social science and the humanities to help them understand phenomena they are observing, which Weinberg and Gould (2011) described as a "healthy development" (p. 20). Yet it will only be healthy if the differences between the humanities and social sciences are openly acknowledged and understood.

While it is impossible to provide a definitive answer to the question – what is theory? – the aim of this chapter is to make some contribution to the discussion surrounding the question within the sport and exercise research communities. In these communities the question is often initially raised in postgraduate programs. At this point, if the notion of theory is problematized at all, it is done so in relation to what theory means to qualitative and quantitative researchers or science, social science, or humanities researchers. Yet a limitation associated with discussing the question within the confines of these binary categories is that the work categorized as qualitative, quantitative, science, social science, or humanities is not homogenous. What is more, there is evidence that these categories can have a polarizing effect (see Hughson & Tapsell, 2006; Schempp, 1987; Siedentop, 1987), and research being judged "good" or "bad" purely because it is categorized, for example, as qualitative or quantitative rather than because of the quality of the research (Silverman, 2001; see also Chapter 25, this volume).

Despite the challenges associated with categorizing research as either qualitative or quantitative, the focus of this *Handbook* is qualitative research, so much of the following discussion is specific to research that has been categorized as qualitative. Yet, it is not my desire that this chapter be read as an attack on the value of quantitative research. Quality research, regardless of how it is categorized, contributes to our understanding of an issue, albeit different aspects of that issue.

Whereas there is a lack of homogeneity in qualitative research, the assumptions held by qualitative researchers, as is the case with quantitative researchers, influence their understanding of what is theory. In their lecture entitled *What is theory?* Joas and Knöbl (2009) pointed out that when sociologists have attempted to answer that question they have ended up hotly contesting the relationships that exist between theory and empirical research, worldviews, normative or moral questions, and everyday knowledge. In attempting to understand the social world sociologists draw on sociological theories developed, or informed, by sociologists (e.g., Durkheim, Weber, and Parsons). Yet, increasingly, sociologists, in addition to other social scientists and those working in the humanities, draw on social theories. Social theories differ from sociological theories because they are informed by, among others, philosophy and philosophers (e.g., Butler, Derrida, Foucault, Habermas and Kristeva), and have interests in examining, among other things, social problems and power relations within society. Sociologists *and* philosophers make a contribution to our understanding of critical theories, and therefore critical thought; a point I will return to below.

The relationship between social theory and sociology is complex (see Joas and Knöbl, 2009; Turner 2009, for detailed discussions). In introducing the complexities Turner observed that:

> [s]ocial theory provides the necessary analytical and philosophical framework with which the social sciences can develop . . . [Yet any] attempt to offer a generic definition of social theory is confronted immediately by the important differences between various sociological traditions. [Moreover] in considering social theory with a broad international framework, we need to recognize that sociology is inevitably colored by different local, national or civilizational circumstances.
>
> *(Turner, 2009, p. 1)*

Equally, the relationship between social theory and humanities is complex because the theory "changes depending upon how the historian chooses to manipulate and mold it" (Raab, 2015, p. 3). He went onto say that:

> theory in the humanities is rarely presented in formulaic terms . . . For example, historians can borrow from a selection of linguistic theories – whether Foucault on discourse, Derrida on the *hors texte,* Ludwig Wittgenstein on meaning . . . These theories influence, steer, modify, and corrupt interpretation but they do not mechanically process data.
>
> *(Raab, 2015, p. 10)*

The complexities may explain why Wenger (1998) claimed that social theory is a "somewhat ill-defined field of conceptual inquiry at the intersection of philosophy, the social sciences and the humanities" (p. 12). Yet, despite the lack of census concerning what constitutes theory, and the complex relationship between sociology and social theory, it has been suggested that there is some merit in viewing social theory as a meta-theoretical framework. As an advocate of this view Denison (2007) suggested that while it is difficult to have a universal understanding of social theory, a common denominator to many of the understandings is "the importance of context in determining how human beings make sense of their lives" (Denison, 2007, p. 370). Another who sees the potential of social theory as a meta-theoretical framework is Wenger (1998), who said that social theory enables theories "relevant to a number of disciplines, including anthropology, sociology, cognitive and social psychology, philosophy, and organizational and education theory and practice" to be utilized to do different things (p. 12). If a meta-theoretical framework is to be adopted it requires the explicit acknowledgment of the assumptions of the various theories in the social sciences and humanities. This is a challenge, but it provides an opportunity to break up theoretical and disciplinary silos and potentially enrich how we view the complexities associated with sport and exercise. Mindful of the complexities and partial understanding around what constitutes theory, the attention now turns to how theory is used.

How is theory used?

Just as it is impossible to provide a definitive answer to the question, what is theory? it is also impossible to describe a universal process for how theory can be used. A broad goal of qualitative researchers is to use theory to *understand* phenomena. Yet, theory can *inform* researchers' work, and researchers can *apply*, *test*, as well as *develop/build* theory. Researchers who use theory to *inform* their work often use theory as a "lens," through which they interpret observed phenomena, and this is reflected in Silverman's (2001, p. 3) claim that "[w]ithout a theory, such phenomena as 'gender', 'personality', 'talk' or 'space' cannot be understood". Socially critical researchers use theory as a lens through which they to examine data with the aim of gaining insight into issues related to equity and social justice as well as making "a difference to people's lives by exposing and challenging inequities and power relations" (Mallett & Tinning, 2014, p. 14). In the sport and exercise context Purdy, Potrac, and Jones (2008) illustrated this when they used Nyberg's (1981) and Giddens' (1984) theorizing of power and resistance as lenses to inform their understanding of the relationship between a coach and a rowing coxswain. Post-structural researchers also view theory as a "lens" but they use theory as a "disruptive force, a deconstructive tactic, a denaturalizing strategy, to problematize a phenomena, text, or event that is usually taken-for-granted" (Nelson, Potrac, & Groom, 2014, p. 78). Such an approach was adopted by Garratt, Piper, and Taylor (2103), who used the work of Foucault to inform their examination, critique, and discussion of child-welfare policies and the impact they have had on sports-coaching practices and policies.

The application of theory is evident in some narrative research. Here researchers understand theory as *meaning-making* equipment in that it is applied to help *make sense* of phenomena in order to generate meaningful, rich, and complex interpretations. Researchers *apply* theory in the process of exploring "*what* is being said and *how* and *why* a person or group tells and performs the story as they do in certain places (*where*) and under specific conditions at various times (*when*)" (Sparkes & Smith, 2014, p. 131; emphasis in original). For example, life historians locate life stories within a historical context, and as such they are required to "broaden the concern with personal truth" to take into account "the wider socio-historical concerns *even if these are not part of the consciousness of the individual*" (Armour & Chen, 2012, p. 238; emphasis in original). The life historian applies theory when they make connections between theoretical concepts and "specific themes and issues raised by the person telling the story" (Sparkes & Smith, 2014, p. 133). The aims of applying theory are numerous and include, to better understand the life of the person, "to shed light on similar or contrasting lives, and/or to inform an analysis of a particular issue or event" (Armour, 2006, p. 472). In the sport and exercise context Purdy and Aboud (2011) illustrated this when they applied the work of Giddens (1984) in an effort to understand the practices associated with coaching a national rugby team as it prepared to compete in the Rugby World Cup.

Another way to understand and apply theory is via the idea of testing. One way qualitative researchers can *test* theory is by using case studies. There are various interpretations of what constitutes a case study (see Chapter 6). One interpretation is that case studies do not only have to be descriptive or explanatory, rather once phenomena are identified, research questions (or a hypothesis) are generated, it is possible to take a case, which is a small body of data, and examine it and test the hypothesis (Silverman, 2001). The constant comparative method is one way qualitative researchers can test a "provisional hypothesis" (p. 238). What this means for practice is that once researchers have generated "a set of categories" they can test an "emerging hypotheses" by expanding the data set and making comparisons with existing literature (p. 239). In the sport and exercise context, Occhino, Mallett, and Rynne (2013) illustrated this when they hypothesized that high-performance football coaches learn through social networks. They tested this hypothesis by utilizing various conceptualizations of social network, specifically communities of practice (CoP) (Wenger 1998), the associated coach communities of practice (CCoP) (Culver & Trudel, 2006), as well as informal knowledge networks (IKN) (Allee, 2000), networks of practice (NoP) (Nichani & Hung, 2002), and dynamic social networks (DSN) (Mallett, Rossi, & Tinning, 2007). They found that the coaches in the study operated "in an environment that does not display fully functioning CoP, CCoP, NoP, or IKN" (Occhino *et al.*, 2013, p. 101). Consequently they claimed the coaches' interactions were "dynamic," and changed throughout their coaching careers, in part, to the input of many "coaches of influence" they met on their coaching journey (Occhino *et al.*, 2013, p. 101).

Grounded theory researchers do not test theories. Instead they work in the field collecting data "in certain settings, or with a certain population, in order to *develop* a theory based on, and relevant to the participants experiences" (Holt, Knight, & Tamminen, 2012, p. 276; emphasis added; see also Chapter 3, this volume). There are three major interpretations of grounded theory and devotees of each have a slightly different interpretation of theory and how it is to be used. Those using a Glaserian approach attempt to "limit the extent to which their own experiences or knowledge are integrated within the theory" (Holt *et al.*, 2012, p. 279). Researchers using a Straussian approach contend that "researchers' interactions with data leads to the construction of a grounded theory, rather than theory emerging from the data" (p. 279). The third approach, advocated by Charmaz is informed by constructivist theoretical perspectives and claims that "researchers construct a theory through their interactions with the data and, while the theory will be grounded in the participants experiences . . . it is impossible to create a theory entirely separate from the researcher" (Holt *et al.*, 2012, p. 279). In the sport and exercise context, Côté, Lidor, and Hackfort (2009) illustrated a constructivist grounded theory approach when they provided an overview of the empirical and theoretical work that informed the construction of the Developmental Model of Sport Participation.

Another way of thinking about how theory is used is to consider whether it used *inductively* or *deductively*. Qualitative researchers who undertake inductive reasoning, adopt a "bottom-up" approach; in other words, they go from the "specific to the general," and are "concerned with producing descriptions and explanations of particular phenomena, or with developing theories rather than testing existing hypotheses" (Sparkes & Smith, 2014, p. 25). While inductive reasoning is common among qualitative researchers it does not preclude them from also undertaking deductive reasoning, which is when they interpret "working propositions" in light of the existing literature and explanatory frameworks. Often discussions of induction and deduction occur in terms of a binary, and when this is the case, as in all discussions framed by binaries, there are limitations. In most qualitative research there is an element of induction *and* deduction in the construction and enactment of the research process. In an attempt to break down the binaries of induction and deduction, Ryba *et al.* used the term "*abductive reasoning*" to describe researchers who use a mix of deductive and inductive reasoning (see Sparkes & Smith, 2014, p. 27).

Some researchers, especially those who believe that methods drive the research, may consider discussions and debates around what theory is and how can theory be used, as superfluous to the research process. Yet it is important for researchers to understand, and be able to articulate, the theoretical underpinnings and assumptions of their work because these understandings significantly influence research practice. If researchers cannot, or cannot be bothered to, answer questions such as what is theory, and what role does theory play in the research process, then doubts arise as to the rigor and quality of their research.

How can qualitative research be interpreted?

Qualitative research is a set of complex interpretive practices. As a constantly shifting historical formation, it embraces tensions and contradictions, including disputes over its methods and the forms its findings and interpretations take.

(Denzin & Lincoln, 2011, p. 6)

Given the above quote by leaders in qualitative research it should be no surprise that providing a definitive answer to the question in the subheading is impossible. The disciplines that comprise social science and the humanities are varied, with each discipline and research practice informed by their own histories. Despite this, many qualitative researchers working in the social sciences and humanities have a broad goal of using theory to understand phenomena. When that is the case, it is acknowledged that data cannot speak for itself (Schwandt, 2001) and researchers play an important role in the interpretive process. Given their role in the interpretive process qualitative researchers should explicitly acknowledge the theoretical position through which they interpret their observations because "without some conceptual orientation, one would not recognize the 'field' one was studying" (Silverman, 2001, p. 72).

It is important that interpretation of qualitative data is not viewed as a distinctive act, separate from the rest of the research process. Drawing on the work of others, Taylor (2014) stated that qualitative researchers should be "encouraged to view the analysis of material as a recursive and iterative exercise. That is working back and forth between data and theory, the understanding and questioning of the data" (p. 182), with the outcome of each iteration being used as the starting point for the next round of analysis. The recursive and iterative process is a complex procedure because it requires researchers to actively make links to the epistemological, methodological, and theoretical assumptions of the research project, as well as to existing literature. Not only should qualitative researchers be encouraged to view the interpretation of data as a recursive and iterative process, they should also be encouraged to consider it to be a reflexive process, because "[s]ocial life is reflexive" (Carr & Kemmis, 1986, p. 43). They explained this further by contending that social life,

has the capacity to change as our knowledge and thinking changes, thus creating new forms of social life which can, in their turn, be reconstructed. Social and educational theories must cope with this reflexivity: the "truths" they tell must be seen as located in particular historical circumstances and social contexts, and as answers to particular questions asked in the intellectual context of a particular time.

(Carr & Kemmis, 1986, p. 43)

The above discussion highlights what interpretation is not. It is *not* a "cut and paste" exercise where a quote from the data is followed by a paraphrased description of it. This practice does not demonstrate any interpretative aptitude or finesse. Also interpretation does *not* occur just because a researcher has used qualitative analysis software, e.g., NVivo. Software programs, whether they focus on "coding or retrieval" or "theory generating," can assist researchers to organize the data and explore relationships *but* it is the researcher who is the "central agent in

402

any interpretive process of data analysis" (Hastie & Glotova, 2012, p. 315). As mentioned above, the interpretive process is informed explicitly, or implicitly, by theoretical assumptions.

The ways in which the interpretations of qualitative research can be represented are numerous. At times this has resulted in questions being raised about the difference between qualitative research and journalism. In a discussion on interpreting qualitative data, Silverman (2001) claimed that the contribution qualitative research makes, and arguably where it differs from journalism, is that it utilizes "its theoretical resources in the deep analysis of small bodies of publicly shareable data," rather than a simple quantification or description (p. 152).

While the interpretation process of qualitative research is complex, some researchers have provided guidelines that may facilitate the interpretation process (aka tips for qualitative researchers). In his discussion of interpreting qualitative research Silverman (2001, p. 302) proposed eight reminders for social scientists, which arguably would be valuable for those working in the humanities to consider. These were:

1. Take advantage of naturally occurring data.
2. Avoid treating the actor's point of view as an explanation.
3. Study the interrelationships between elements.
4. Attempt theoretically fertile research.
5. Address wider audiences.
6. Begin with "how" questions, then ask "why."
7. Study "hyphenated" phenomena.[5]
8. Treat qualitative research as different from journalism.

Others have shared reflections of their experiences of interpreting qualitative data, in the hope of assisting new researchers and reassuring those with more experience. Nelson, Potrac, and Groom (2014) talked about their "frustrations" of grappling with the "intricacies of a new theoretical framework" (p. 83), which they were attempting to use to frame a research project and subsequently interpret the data. They went on to say that using theory in qualitative research projects is "much messier" than often depicted in the literature. Reflecting on their experiences, the authors confirm suggestions made by others, and described above, that it is important for qualitative researchers to acknowledge that "*we* are the instruments" (p. 83) of analysis, and as such our beliefs, assumptions, and theoretical orientations shape our interpretations. What is more, there is value for researchers in viewing interpretation to be an iterative and reflexive process.

What is critical thought?

The various editions of the *Handbook of Qualitative Research* provide overviews of the many critical theories used in qualitative research (Kincheloe & McLaren, 2000; Kincheloe, McLaren, & Steinberg, 2011). These overviews are useful starting points for gaining insight into, and an awareness of, various theoretical traditions associated with critical thought, even though the authors acknowledge it is "impossible to do justice to all of the critical traditions" (Kincheloe & McLaren, 2000, p. 290). Nonetheless, critical awareness can be an *entrée* into critical practice. Yet Sage (1992) pointed out that "[c]ritical social thought applied to sport is not critical simply in the sense of expressing disapproval of contemporary sport forms and practices" (p. 93). Instead, he argued that the intent of critical social thought is to encourage sport scientists to expand their work "beyond understanding, predicting and controlling to consider the ways in which the social formations of sport can be improved, made more democratic, socially just, and humane" (p. 93). In other words he was calling on the sports scientists to not only think critically but to act (or practice) critically.

To make a difference to practice has been a long-standing challenge for those working with a critical agenda. Lincoln and Denzin (2000) suggested that too much critique can be counterproductive because the exchanges and criticisms generally "operate at a level of abstraction, with opposing sides preaching to the already converted. No dialogue occurs, and the discourse does little to help the people who seek to engage the world empirically" (p. 1050). An additional challenge for some working in the sport and exercise communities is the difficulty of critically thinking about practices they consider "natural" or "normal," because in many cases they have been rewarded by such practices. Despite these challenges, if those working in the sport and exercise communities do not think critically about practice they may suffer the same fate Kirk (1986) suggested what would happen to physical educators if they did not become more reflective and develop a capacity for "informed critical judgement"; that is, they may confirm "their low professional status" and leave "themselves open to political manipulation" (p. 156).

Despite the challenges associated with practicing with a critical agenda, some work does exist which aims to support the development of critical thought infused with action and productive possibilities. For example, work has focused on developing pedagogical tools, such as "critical inquiry" and "critical literacy." While there is value in these pedagogical tools, one of the potential limitations is the lack of recognition of the emotional and embodied aspects of practice. One possible consequence of not acknowledging the importance of the emotional and embodied aspect of practice is a lack of commitment to social critique and social change (Cassidy & Tinning, 2004).

McGannon and Schinke (2015) suggested that an "important pathway toward critical pedagogy and practice is reflexivity" (p. 5). Building on the earlier description of reflexivity, it is worth noting that at the heart of being reflexive is the desire to reflect on power relations. As a consequence of this some qualitative researchers in the sport and exercise community have shifted the gaze inward onto their own practice (e.g., Cassidy, 2010; Crockett, 2015; Denison, 2007; Denison *et al.*, 2015). This shift can be viewed as reflecting the "spirit of the times," which has been described as a "reflexive shift" (Blodgett, Schinke, McGannon, & Fisher, 2015). Being reflexive provides opportunities to recognize "the collaborative and dynamic nature of knowledge production that is at the core of transformative research (or research as praxis)" (Blodgett *et al.*, 2015, p. 15).

Praxis (see also Chapters 8 and 33–35) is reflexive because it assumes that "the fundamental character of the social setting will be reconstructed" (Carr & Kemmis, 1986, p. 34). It is the reflexivity of praxis that marks it as being different from craft or tacit knowledge, because these latter forms of knowledge do not attempt to "change the framework of tradition and expectation through which it operates" (p. 33). The ancient Greeks considered the concept of praxis to be embodied in "the wise man [sic]" who always aimed "to act appropriately, truly and justly in a social-political situation" and "allowed ends as well as means to be problematic, and to be a matter of choice" (Carr & Kemmis, 1986, p. 17). This ancient view of praxis did not position thinking critically as being separate from acting critically. Rather,

> [i]n *praxis*, thought and action (or theory and practice), are dialectically related. They are to be understood as *mutually constitutive* . . . Neither thought nor action is preeminent. . . . In praxis, the ideas which guide action are just as subject to change as action is; the only fixed element is *phronesis*, the disposition to act truly and rightly.
>
> *(Carr & Kemmis, 1986, p. 34)*

The ancient Greeks are not the only ones who have informed our understandings of praxis. *Pedagogy of the Oppressed* written by Brazilian Paulo Freire (1970) influenced educational researchers and practitioners as a consequence of researchers adopting a Freire-inspired methodology known as "Action Research." It is important to recognize that praxis is not a specific behavior. It "can only be understood in terms of the understandings and commitments which inform it" (Carr & Kemmis, 1986, p. 190). Additionally praxis is "risky" because practitioners are required to make "wise and prudent practical judgement[s] about how to act," in ways that is situation specific (p. 190).

Potential problems with using theory: Some dangers and problems to be avoided

One of the aims of writing this chapter was to challenge the perception that qualitative research is not concerned with theory. This was achieved by providing examples of how researchers in the sport and exercise context use theory to *inform* their work, or *apply, test,* and *develop* theory. However, using theory has its own set of potential problems. Researchers working in applied fields have been criticized for focusing too heavily, or exclusively, on theory. In the context of sociology, and a discussion of *Sociological Imagination*, C. Wright Mills (Mills, 2000/1959) argued that researchers who focus too heavily on abstract theory can find it difficult to make links between the theory and problems as experienced in specific structural and historical contexts. When this happens the "value of that theory must be put under rigorous questioning" (Molnar & Kelly, 2013, p. 219). Yet Mills was equally critical of those researchers who privileged the empirical with scant regard to theory. He was clear that empirical data and theoretical constructs should be clearly, efficiently, neatly, and ideally ingeniously, linked (Molnar & Kelly, 2013). Also relevant to the discussions and debates on the role of theory in the fields of sport and exercise are researchers' observations regarding the relationship between theory and practice. When Macdonald *et al.* (2002) discussed theoretical perspectives and their application in contemporary research in physical education, they concluded with five "warnings that relate to research questions and practices regardless of the theoretical perspectives employed" (p. 148).

1. Connect theory to important political, economic, and cultural issues . . .
2. Connect theory to observations and data collection . . .
3. Avoid theory becoming instrumental in academic self-promotion . . .
4. Avoid theoretical fads . . .
5. Retain and develop our collective memory.

(Macdonald et al., 2002, pp. 148–150)

In his discussion of the relationship between theory and practice Thompson (2003) argued against viewing theory solely in terms of academic or formal theory, which he called "theories of practice." He claimed that the informal knowledge and assumptions built up through experience, and often culturally transmitted to new recruits in a field, can also be viewed as theory, which he called "practice theories." Thompson's (2003) framework of "theories of practice" and "practice theories" has been utilized in the field of sport with the aim of understanding coaching practices and athlete learning (Cassidy, 2010).

When using theory researchers should avoid the tendency to select data or chose a case to study that fits the theory. When testing a theory Silverman (2001) suggested that researchers might "seek out negative instances as defined by the theory" since a negative case can provide a critical test of the theory. Another issue for researchers to consider is theoretical fidelity. Some researchers have argued that there is merit in being theoretically faithful because it is difficult to "successfully move between theories with different paradigmatic roots" and "it is necessary to concentrate within a particular theory, in order to be able to exploit its interpretive powers" (Tinning & Fitzpatrick, 2012, p. 64). Yet, other researchers have claimed that being over-reliant on one theory is problematic because it can constrain the interpretation of the data by overlooking or dismissing "inconsistency with the theoretical status quo" (Hastie & Hay, 2012, p. 89). I suspect the issue of theoretical fidelity will increasingly come to the fore as more pressure is placed on researchers to gain external and commercial research grants, and conduct research that is applicable to the communities in which they live. Such pressures may pose problems for researchers, particularly when these pressures clash with the desires of researchers to "use theories they understand, to which they have some emotional connection, and which are aligned to their world-view and political dispositions" (Tinning & Fitzpatrick, 2012, p. 64). While these problems will never be totally resolved, one thing is certain, and that is the debates and discussions regarding the role of theory, interpretation, and critical thought within qualitative research will continue. It is my hope that this chapter contributes to these debates and discussions within the sport and exercise communities.

Notes

1 Academic disciplines concerned with understanding the physical world, e.g., biology, physics and chemistry.
2 Academic disciplines concerned with understanding the social world, e.g., sociology, anthropology, and psychology.
3 Academic disciplines concerned with understanding human culture, e.g., philosophy, history, and literature.
4 A particular view on how science should be conducted.
5 Hyphenated phenomena "take on different meanings in different contexts" (Silverman, 2006, p. 298).

References

Allee, V. (2000). Knowledge networks and communities of practice. *Journal of the Organization Development Network (OD Practitioner)*, *32*(4), 4–13.
Armour, K. (2006). The way to a teacher's heart: Narrative research in physical education. In D. Kirk, D. Macdonald & M. O'Sullivan (Eds.), *Handbook of research in physical education* (pp. 467–485). London: Sage.
Armour, K. & Chen, H. (2012). Narrative research methods. In K. Armour and D. Macdonald (Eds.), *Research methods in physical education and youth sport* (pp. 237–249). London: Routledge.
Blodgett, A., Schinke, R., McGannon, K., & Fisher, L. (2015). Cultural sport psychology research: Conceptions, evolutions, and forecasts. *International Review of Sport and Exercise Psychology*, *8*(1), 24–43.
Carr, W. & Kemmis, S. (1986). *Becoming critical. Education, knowledge and action research*. London: Falmer Press.
Cassidy, T. (2010). Understanding athlete learning and coaching practice: Utilizing "practice theories" and "theories of practice." In J. Lyle & C. Cushion (Eds.), *Sports coaching: Professionalism and practice* (pp. 177–191). London: Elsevier.
Cassidy, T. & Tinning, R. (2004). "Slippage" is not a dirty word: Considering the usefulness of Giddens' notion of knowledgeability in understanding the possibilities for teacher education. *Journal of Teaching Education*, *15*(2), 175–188.
Côté, J., Lidor, R., & Hackfort, D. (2009). ISSP position stand: To sample or specialize? Seven postulates about youth sport activities that lead to continued participation and elite performance. *International Journal of Sport and Exercise Psychology*, *9*, 7–17.
Crockett, H. (2015). Confession of the disc: A Foucauldian analysis of ethics within Ultimate Frisbee. In R. Schinke & K. McGannon (Eds.), *The psychology of sub-culture in sport and physical activity. Critical perspectives* (pp. 184–195). London: Routledge.

Culver, D. & Trudel, P. (2006). Cultivating coaches' communities of practice: Developing the potential for learning through interactions. In R. Jones (Ed.), *The sports coach as educator. Re-conceptualizing sports coaching* (pp. 97–112). London: Routledge.

Denison, J. (2007). Social theory for coaches: A Foucauldian reading of one athlete's poor performance. *International Journal of Sport Science and Coaching*, 2(4), 369–383.

Denison, J., Pringle, R., Cassidy, T., & Hessian, P. (2015). Changing coaches' practices: Towards an application of Foucault's ethics. *International Sport Coaching Journal*, 2(1), 72–76.

Denzin, N. & Lincoln, N. (2011). *The Sage handbook of qualitative research* (4th ed.). Los Angeles, CA: Sage.

Freire, P. (1970). *Pedagogy of the oppressed.* New York: Seabury Press.

Garratt, D., Piper, H., & Taylor, B. (2013). "Safeguarding" sports coaching: Foucault, genealogy and critique. *Sport, Education and Society*, 18(5), 615–629.

Giddens, A. (1984). *The constitution of society: Outline of a theory of structuration.* Berkeley, CA: University of California Press.

Hastie, P. & Glotova, O. (2012). Analyzing qualitative data. In K. Armour & D. Macdonald (Eds.), *Research methods in physical education and youth sport* (pp. 309–320). London: Routledge.

Hastie, P. & Hay, P. (2012). Qualitative approaches. In K. Armour & D. Macdonald (Eds.), *Research methods in physical education and youth sport* (pp. 79–94). London: Routledge.

Holt, N., Knight, C., & Tamminen, K. (2012). Grounded theory. In K. Armour & D. Macdonald (Eds.), *Research methods in physical education and youth sport* (pp. 276–294). London: Routledge.

Hughson, J. & Tapsell, C. (2006). Physical education and the "two cultures" debate: Lessons from Dr Leavis. *Quest*, 58(4), 410–423.

Joas, H. & Knöbl, W. (2009). *Social theory: Twenty introductory lectures.* Cambridge, UK: Cambridge University Press.

Kerlinger, F. (1973). *Foundations of behavioral research* (2nd ed.). New York: Holt, Rinehart and Winston.

Kincheloe, J. & McLaren, P. (2000). Rethinking critical theory and qualitative research. In N. Denzin & Y. Lincoln (Eds.), *Handbook of qualitative research* (2nd ed., pp. 279–314). Thousand Oaks, CA: Sage.

Kincheloe, J., McLaren, P., & Steinberg, S. (2011). Critical pedagogy and qualitative research. Moving to the bricolage. In N. Denzin & Y. Lincoln (Eds.), *The Sage handbook of qualitative research* (4th ed., pp. 163–177). Los Angeles, CA: Sage.

Kirk, D. (1986). Beyond the limits of theoretical discourse in teacher education: Towards a critical pedagogy. *Teaching and Teacher Education*, 2(2), 155–167.

Lincoln, Y. & Denzin, N. (2000). The seventh moment: Out of the past. In N. Denzin & Y. Lincoln (Eds.), *Handbook of qualitative research* (2nd ed.). Thousand Oaks, CA: Sage.

Macdonald, D., Kirk, D. Metzler, M., Nilges, L., Schempp, P., & Wright, J. (2002). It's all very well in theory: Theoretical perspectives and their applications in contemporary pedagogical research. *Quest*, 54(2), 133–156.

Mallett, C. & Tinning, R. (2014). Philosophy of knowledge. In L. Nelson, R. Groom, & P. Potrac (Eds.), *Research methods in sports coaching* (pp. 9–17). London: Routledge.

Mallett, C., Rossi, T., & Tinning, R. (2007). *Report to the AFL: Coaching knowledge, learning and mentoring in the AFL.* St Lucia, Australia: University of Queensland.

McGannon, K. & Schinke, R. (2015). Situating the subculture of sport, physical activity and critical approaches. In R. Schinke & K. McGannon (Eds.), *The psychology of sub-culture in sport and physical activity. Critical perspectives* (pp. 1–13). London: Routledge.

Mills, C. W. (2000/1959). *The sociological imagination.* Oxford: Oxford University Press.

Molnar, G. & Kelly, J. (2013). *Sport, exercise and social theory. An introduction.* London: Routledge.

Nelson, L., Potrac, P., & Groom, R. (2014). The place of theory. In L. Nelson, R. Groom, & P. Potrac (Eds.), *Research methods in sports coaching* (pp. 76–85). London: Routledge.

Nichani, M. & Hung. D. (2002). Can a community of practice exist online? *Educational Technology*, 42(4), 49–54.

Nyberg, D. (1981). *Power over power.* London: Cornell University Press.

Occhino, J., Mallett, C., & Rynne, S. (2013). Dynamic social networks in high performance football coaching. *Physical Education and Sport Pedagogy*, 18(1), 90–102.

Purdy, L. & Aboud, S. (2011). Anthony Giddens: Acknowledging structure and individuality within coaching. In R. Jones, P. Potrac, C. Cushion, & L. T. Ronglan (Eds.), *The sociology of sports coaching* (pp. 67–78). London: Routledge.

Purdy, L., Potrac, P., & Jones, R. (2008). Power, consent and resistance: An autoethnography of competitive rowing. *Sport, Education, and Society*, 13(3), 319–336.

Raab, N. (2015). *The crisis from within: Historians, theory, and the humanities*. Boston, MA: Brill.

Sage, G. (1992). Beyond enhancing performance in sport: Toward empowerment and transformation. In American Academy of Physical Education Papers. No. 25, *Enhancing human performance in sport: New concepts and developments* (pp. 85–95). Champaign, IL: Human Kinetics.

Savage, C. (1990). Preface. In C. Savage (Ed.), *Scientific theories. Minnesota studies in the philosophy of science. Volume 14* (pp. vii–ix). Minneapolis, MN: University of Minnesota Press.

Schempp, P. (1987). Research on teaching in physical education: Beyond the limits of natural science. *Journal of Teaching Physical Education, 6*(2), 111–121.

Schwandt, T. (2001). *The SAGE dictionary of qualitative inquiry*. Thousand Oaks, CA: Sage.

Siedentop, D. (1987). Dialogue or exorcism? A rejoinder to Schempp. *Journal of Teaching in Physical Education, 6*(4), 373–376.

Silverman, D. (2001). *Interpreting qualitative data. Methods for analyzing talk, text and interaction* (2nd ed.). London: Sage.

Sparkes, A. C. & Smith, B. (2014). *Qualitative research methods in sport, exercise and health. From process to product*. London: Routledge.

Taylor, W. (2014). Analysis of qualitative data. In L. Nelson, R. Groom, & P. Potrac (Eds.), *Research methods in sports coaching* (pp. 181–191). London: Routledge.

Thompson, N. (2003). *Theory and practice in human services*. Maidenhead, UK: Open University Press.

Tinning, R. & Fitzpatrick, K. (2012). Thinking about research frameworks. In K. Armour & D. Macdonald (Eds.), *Research methods in physical education and youth sport* (pp. 53–65). London: Routledge.

Turner, B. (2009). *The new Blackwell companion to social theory*. Oxford: Wiley.

Weinberg, R. & Gould, D. (2011). *Foundations of sport and exercise psychology* (5th ed.). Champaign, IL: Human Kinetics.

Wenger, E. (1998). *Communities of practice. Learning, meaning and identity*. Cambridge, UK: Cambridge University Press.

31

TEACHING QUALITATIVE RESEARCH

Camilla J. Knight

Qualitative research has been increasingly accepted within the field of sport and exercise. Such acceptance is evidenced by the publication of excellent texts dedicated exclusively to qualitative research in sport and exercise (e.g., Sparkes & Smith, 2014), the incorporation of more chapters on qualitative inquiry in sport and exercise research methods textbooks (e.g., Atkinson, 2011; Jones, 2014), the substantial growth in qualitative studies featured in leading sport and exercise peer-reviewed journals (Culver, Gilbert, & Sparkes, 2012; Sparkes & Smith, 2014), and an increasing amount of qualitative research being presented at conferences. Although qualitative research in sport and exercise is moving in a positive direction, the speed and quality of future growth will be largely influenced by neophyte researchers' understanding and application of qualitative methodologies. Thus, it is critical that students are taught about the value and contribution of qualitative research to the field, and have sufficient understanding of the philosophical, methodological, and practical components of qualitative research to conduct it appropriately (Terkildsen & Petersen, 2015). Even if students decide not to conduct qualitative research, a thorough understanding and appreciation of different methodologies is required to ensure students can read and evaluate qualitative studies, and apply findings in practice.

Despite the importance of educating students about qualitative research, very few sport and exercise undergraduate degree courses include any teaching on it. If qualitative research is included it is often just one or two lectures, usually on interviewing, within a mostly quantitative research methods module. Such restricted teaching of qualitative research not only results in a misrepresentation of this approach to scientific inquiry, but also prevents students from learning about the beauty and complexity of qualitative work. As educators, we have the opportunity (perhaps even duty) to give students the skills and knowledge to understand and appreciate the breadth of different approaches to research. Unfortunately, there is relatively little guidance available for sport and exercise scholars regarding how to teach qualitative research effectively. The purpose of this chapter is to address this gap and provide a broad overview of some of the philosophical, methodological, and practical considerations associated with teaching qualitative research.

The backdrop to teaching

Although qualitative research has made huge strides within sport and exercise sciences, quantitative research still largely dominates within the field (Sandelowski, 2008). Deductive-hypothesis testing is often equated with science, and other approaches to research are viewed as "lesser" than this (Rossman & Rallis, 2003; Shaw, Dyson, & Peel, 2008). Students and staff have usually been educated in a school system that emphasizes the importance of objective, bias-free, quantifiable research, which is optimized by the "gold-standard" randomized control trial (Gough, Lowton, Madill, & Stratton, 2002; Mason, 2002). The result of such schooling is that "other" forms of science and research are devalued and a hierarchy of research is constructed. Consequently, when (or if) students are introduced to qualitative research during their degree programs it is often perceived as "soft" or "unscientific," resulting in staff having to commit time to overcoming misconceptions about qualitative research before they start to deliver content (Aronson Fontes & Piercy, 2000; Borochowitz, 2005). Additionally, students can experience (at least initially) some hesitation, anxiety, frustration, or resistance as they are introduced to a way of viewing the world and understanding science that almost completely opposes what they have previously been taught (Borochowitz, 2005; Gerstl-Pepin & Patrizio, 2009; Humphreys 2006).

Further, quantitative research still remains the norm within university settings (Gough *et al.*, 2002; Mason, 2002). Academics using qualitative approaches are often greatly outnumbered by colleagues using quantitative approaches (Edwards & Thatcher, 2004; Gough *et al.*, 2002) and it is not uncommon for qualitative researchers to find themselves having to justify their research or educate colleagues regarding the value of their work (Frost & Barry, 2010). Such factors can subsequently influence the support lecturers receive from colleagues when teaching qualitative research methods, the amount of time available for teaching within an undergraduate or graduate timetable, and the resources available to them (Blank, 2004; Edwards & Thatcher, 2004; Frost & Barry, 2010; Shaw *et al.*, 2008). This, in turn, influences the breadth and depth of information that is taught and reinforces the "secondary" status of qualitative research to students.

Notwithstanding such challenges, teaching students about qualitative research is necessary to ensuring the continued growth of our field, and to maximize the impact of our research within society by "humanizing" topics and stimulating changes in perspective and practice. Further, teaching qualitative research provides students with the opportunity to question accepted norms, explore previously inaccessible material, and evaluate their preconceived ideas and assumptions about the world. Consequently, teaching qualitative research can contribute to the production of thoughtful, insightful, and critical graduates, who are able to "look beyond the numbers" and appreciate that research is conducted with people and for people, all of whom have their own experiences, stories, and understanding of the world. As an educator, I personally cannot think of anything more rewarding or powerful than helping to shape students' views of the world and understand the value of each individual's story and experience.

Starting teaching: representing qualitative research

There are differences of opinion regarding how best to introduce the topic of qualitative research and whether it should be presented in contrast to or alongside quantitative approaches. One approach is to draw on students' preexisting knowledge of quantitative research and explain how qualitative research differs to this (Gibson & Sullivan, 2012; Poulin, 2007). Such an approach (the "what it's not" approach) presents qualitative research based on what it is not (e.g., not numbers, not experimental) rather than what it is. Such contrasts can help to illuminate some of the general principles of qualitative inquiry, but given the privileged position of quantitative research in society such comparisons could actually be harmful (Aronson Fontes & Piercy, 2000; Lather, 2006). As Sandelowski explained:

The tendency exists to simplify complex research entities into binaries, to rank order these binaries, and ultimately to present them as antagonists: *this* and *that*, and *this* versus or opposed to *that*. What is less evident, however, is the way in which apparently benign comparisons reproduce dominance. One-way comparisons, especially, make dominant standards the Gold Standard. In the qualitative research/quantitative research binary, qualitative research is, at best, the alternative and, at worst, the deviant entity; it is the *that* standing in stark and strange contrast to the *this,* even when no intention to disparage exists.

(Sandelowski, 2008, p. 194; emphasis in original)

Thus, through such comparisons, the perception of qualitative research as "soft," "unscientific," or "lesser" than quantitative research could be perpetuated, a "them" against "us" mentality can be put into motion, and the fundamental similarities between the two approaches lost.

Recognizing these issues, some academics actively avoid comparisons between qualitative and quantitative research, and instead focus their attention simply upon teaching about qualitative research, usually in separate qualitative and quantitative courses (e.g., Gerstl-Pepin & Patrizio, 2009; Poulin, 2007). Although such an approach can avoid some of the problems outlined above, it too can raise some issues. For example, by avoiding any comparison to quantitative research, students may be prevented from understanding how qualitative and quantitative works can complement each other (cf., Terkildsen & Petersen, 2015). Further, an exclusive focus on teaching qualitative research without reference to quantitative research can reinforce an unhelpful dichotomy between the two approaches (Hopkinson & Hogg, 2004) and result in "unidimensional" researchers, as students align themselves either with qualitative or quantitative research (Onwuegbuzie & Leech, 2005).

To limit the comparison of qualitative and quantitative approaches, while facilitating students' understanding of the positive contribution all (well-planned and executed) research can make to the field, an integrated approach is likely to be beneficial (Terkildsen & Petersen, 2015). By adopting such an approach, educators can work through each step of the research process, ensuring that equal time and emphasis is placed on qualitative and quantitative approaches. The initial weeks in such a course should focus upon philosophical, epistemological, and ethical considerations, given that they are the foundation of all research questions and subsequent methodological decisions. Next, the continuum of research methodologies that can be used to answer different research questions could be explored (Onwuegbuzie & Leech, 2005), followed by the data-collection methods and analysis techniques associated with different methodologies. Finally, the process of writing and presenting results could be discussed to conclude the course (Hurworth, 2008).

Teaching students: integrating experiential learning

Having reflected upon initial key questions, such as how to introduce qualitative research and how to structure a research methods course, the next important step is to consider how and what to teach about qualitative research. As Mason (2002) articulated, the problem for qualitative researchers is deciding "how to teach the tools of an uncertain trade for use on an unknown job" (p.69). Given the plethora of philosophical standpoints, the numerous (and ever-growing) range of methodologies, and the variety of skills required to address different questions, it is difficult to suggest one "correct" approach to teaching qualitative research. However, one consistent message across the qualitative research pedagogy literature is the value of integrating experiential learning into courses, to bring the abstract and complex concepts of qualitative research to life (e.g., Edwards & Thatcher, 2004; Gallagher & Francesconi, 2012; Shaw *et al.*, 2008). Whether it is helping students to understand different epistemologies and ontologies (e.g., Poulin, 2007), or how to collect and analyze data (e.g., Mason, 2002), the utility of providing students with hands-on experience to promote learning, increase engagement with activities, and enhance students' enjoyment, has been consistently identified (Raddon, Nault, & Scott, 2008).

Scholars have distinguished between different approaches to experiential learning in research methods (Wright, 2000). One approach is to take students through a whole research project during a course (e.g., Keen, 1996; Raddon *et al.*, 2008; Stallings, 1995; see Box 31.1 below for examples). Such an approach has consistently been shown to allow students to better understand the links between philosophical, theoretical, and practical components (Machtmes *et al.*, 2009). Further, by working through the entire research process students are pushed to understand their reasons for making each decision (Hopkinson & Hogg, 2004), and demonstrate a greater appreciation for the complexity of qualitative research and the rigorous methodologies (Machtmes *et al.*, 2009). Students also learn how to overcome problems and resolve issues inherent in qualitative research and recall great benefits from such experiences (Raddon *et al.*, 2008).

Box 31.1   Examples of research-project-based qualitative research methods courses

Hopkinson & Hogg (2004). Teaching and learning about qualitative research in the social sciences: An experiential learning approach amongst marketing students. *Journal of Further and Higher Education, 28, 307–320.*

Founded upon Kolb's (1984) experiential learning theory, Hopkinson and Hogg used a combination of integrated classwork- and fieldwork-based experiential techniques to teach students the practical skills and critical thoughts and reflection required to conduct qualitative research. Students' projects were based upon a published study on consumer satisfaction. Students worked through six different stages to complete this assignment.

1. Students worked in groups to plan the research design, drawing on an understanding of different ontological and epistemological assumptions.
2. Students individually went into the field to test their research design and interview format, recruit participants, and interview participants.
3. Students then transcribed their interviews and produced a narrative account of each case.
4. Following transcription, students worked in groups to analyze data and interpret findings. Such analysis led to students generating and refining theories, which were then compared to the article on consumer satisfaction.
5. A group report was produced detailing the findings of the study.
6. Finally, students wrote up individual reports in which they reflected on the effectiveness of the study design and their learning experience.

On reflecting on this task, the authors concluded that conducting a real-world task that aligned with a study published in a high quality journal was beneficial for students. They perceived that the mix

---

of individual and group work was particularly effective in allowing students to experience deeper learning, and students learned about the complexity and ambiguity of research.

Keen, M. F. (1996). Teaching qualitative methods: A face-to-face encounter. *Teaching Sociology, 24*(2), 166–176.

Keen delivered an undergraduate qualitative research course to sociology students. Through this course, students completed an ethnography based on a setting of the instructor's choice. The students worked as a large research team, sharing data and discussing findings to ensure sufficient information was gathered. Students completed the following steps in their course:

1. Students received a general overview of the course and requirements, along with an overview of the research process. Students were required to select one site from the setting category and identify opening hours and activities.
2. Students examined how to evaluate data sites for appropriateness and access. Discussion ensued regarding the relationship of the researcher to the setting, what type of stance and distance to maintain, and the implications of the researchers' characteristics in relation to the persons researched. Ethical considerations were also discussed and ethics board forms were reviewed.
3. Students completed intuitional ethics form to experience the process (ethical approval was gained ahead of time).
4. Students engaged in discussion regarding logging data, mechanics of carrying out field observations, sources of data, writing up field notes, and watching for problems/areas of bias.
5. Students spent six weeks attending their setting once a week for at least 1–2 hours. Students were required to write up at least 2 pages of field notes from each visit. These field notes were handed in and marked and also became part of the collective data pool.
6. Students then moved onto intensive interviewing to obtain information regarding the setting that had not been identifiable through observations.
7. Students spent the final two weeks of the course learning about how to frame their findings and produce a written paper, which was the final assignment for the course.

On reflecting on this course, Keen concluded that for him and his students, this course was one of the most successful and satisfying to teach. He believes the basis for the success was in the experiential learning.

Raddon, M-B, Nault, C., & Scott, A. (2008). Integrating the complete research project into a large qualitative methods course. *Teaching Sociology, 36,* 141–149.

Raddon and colleagues demonstrated how a research project could be integrated into a large (over 100 people) qualitative research class. The course was split between a weekly two-hour lecture and multiple 50-minute seminars. Lectures focused upon teaching about qualitative research and the seminars allowed for discussion of the ongoing research project. The project progressed as follows:

(continued)

(continued)

1. Students were provided with a list of potential research questions from which they could choose or suggest a variation.
2. Students brainstormed questions for a semistructured interview guide and then worked to refine the guide.
3. Application for ethics review was completed. Prior to the course ethical approval had been gained but students submitted a secondary application, including the specific research question and interview guide.
4. While students waited for ethical approval, discussions regarding ethnographic monographs were conducted. Students also practiced mock interviews.
5. Students conducted their interviews with participants (other students in the module) and then transcribed their interviews.
6. All interview transcripts from the course were compiled and students discussed the interview experience.
7. Students received the collated data set and began coding data. Students were required to complete a four-part assignment entailing: (1) coding of three pages of transcripts; (2) identifying a single category pertinent to their research focus; (3) identifying five quotes that illustrate that code; and (4) a one-paragraph memo on how to interpret the code in relation to the data.
8. The students then completed a writing seminar, whereby draft papers were reviewed prior to submission for marking.
9. Finally, students engaged in a reflective discussion regarding the research process.

Overall, reflections from students demonstrated that through this process students' self-reported learning was enhanced, and the learning was satisfying and enjoyable.

However, the process of taking students through an entire research project is not without challenges. One such challenge relates to the feasibility of *supervising* numerous research projects that are being conducted across a range of sites (Hurworth, 2008). To overcome this challenge, students may be asked to conduct their data collection and analysis in groups to reduce the number of projects that must be supervised (Hopkinson & Hogg, 2004). Another approach that has been used successfully is for one site or venue to be chosen for all data collection (e.g., Keen, 1996; Machtmes et al., 2009). In selecting one specific venue, lecturers have more control over the data-collection process and there is a reduction in the range of topics being studied. Additionally, conducting entire research projects can be extremely time-consuming for students and staff, and require extensive planning before the course starts (Hopkinson & Hogg, 2004; Raddon et al., 2008). Even with such preparation, as is the nature of research, there is the potential for plans to change due to access to participants or sites. Consequently, students are likely to require a certain degree of flexibility and an ability to cope with ambiguity in their course, which can be challenging for some (Keen, 1996).

Given the potential challenges and logistical constraints that might prevent students engaging in a complete research project, some lecturers have chosen to teach each component of the research process separately or in small chunks (e.g., DeLyser, 2008; Mason, 2002; Poulin, 2007). Such lecturers have still utilized a range of creative and practical exercises (see Table 31.1 for examples), but, in contrast to a whole research project, these exercises are usually delivered in a more controlled and structured environment, which might be preferable for some students and staff.

Table 31.1 Examples of specific exercises and assignments for teaching components of qualitative research

Authors and Date	Focus of Exercise	Description of Exercise
Mason (2002)	Philosophical Approaches/ The nature of qualitative and quantitative research	A "hegemony" debate whereby students argue the merits and de-merits of both quantitative and qualitative approaches. The debate is supported by the use of large cards that detail key philosophical, scientific, and pragmatic concepts. Integrating an additional staff member whose views differ from those of the lecturer can help to further stimulate discussion.
Poulin (2007)	Philosophical and methodological foundations of research design	Poulin uses five steps to teach the logic of inquiry. The first step is to introduce the philosophical underpinnings of interpretive research by discussing them in relation to the positivistic tradition. Through various methods such as discussion, drawing, reflection, and watching films the students engage in comparison of the two paradigms. Particular examples include the drawing of a scientist to stimulate philosophical discussion and a conversation following viewing the film *Mindwalk* (Cohen & Capra, 1990).
McAllister & Rowe (2003)	Developing a qualitative eye	To help students consider the social world (particularly health) through a qualitative lens, the lecturers present students with images to stimulate conversation relating to health. The images are presented as a slideshow, moving from concrete images to more abstract and artistic representations. Students are asked to comment on what they see and what information is being portrayed in the different images.
Aronson Fontes & Piercy (2000)	Ethics	Students are assigned a number of readings relating to research ethics in their discipline. Students are then presented with a series of 15 scenarios that represent ethical dilemmas. The class is split into small groups, to review two dilemmas and identify what they would do and why.
McAllister & Rowe (2003)	Preparing students to engage in fieldwork	Using an activity termed "scattered pictures," students are provided with a variety of photographs of people engaging in various activities. Students are asked to select and explain why a particular image is meaningful for them as a researcher. Discussions are then centered on understanding how research-ers looking at the same contexts and images might see different things.
Tan & Ko (2004)	Observations	Students watch a feature film and record their observations regarding mundane social interaction. Specifically, students report observations about age and gender relationships, and discuss any patterns they observe. Students complete a written assignment in groups to allow students to compare and contrast their observations.
DeLyser (2008)	Interviewing and transcribing	Each student is asked to record at least a 45-minute (portion of an) interview with a person of their choice on a topic of their choice. Students then transcribe at least 15 minutes of the interview fully. Following this, the students then interview an individual with a limited command of English or conduct an interview in a language of which they have limited command. Detailed notes are produced during these interviews, rather than recording, to allow for students to experience the different approaches to recording interview data.

Some scholars have raised concerns about focusing upon specific components of the research process. For instance, it has been suggested that there could be an overemphasis on the technical tools of qualitative research (i.e., doing qualitative research rather than being a qualitative researcher; McAllister & Rowe, 2003), and that students might not understand how different components are related (cf., Machtmes *et al.*, 2009). Such concerns are likely born out of the agreement between scholars that it is critical for students to learn the philosophical and theoretical underpinnings of a methodology, as well as associated techniques for data collection and analysis, to fully appreciate the purpose and function of qualitative methods (McAllister & Rowe, 2003; Poulin, 2007; Shaw *et al.*, 2008). Fortunately, there are many examples of how to teach underpinning epistemologies and the links to methodologies without the requirements to teach an entire research project (Mason, 2002; Poulin, 2007). By integrating activities such as discussions regarding epistemological considerations and reflecting on readings on these topics, along with carefully selecting assignments (e.g., reflective pieces in addition to transcripts and field notes) and generally embodying the characteristics of a qualitative researcher while teaching, the key components of conducting qualitative research and being a qualitative researcher can and have been delivered.

Optimizing chances of success: anticipating and overcoming challenges

In sharing and reflecting on their teaching experiences not only have academics provided excellent suggestions about how to teach qualitative research and what to teach, they have also highlighted the challenges they and their students encounter when they are completing qualitative research projects and exercises. Such challenges, which are detailed below, range from ethical issues and considerations, to concerns regarding moving from description and interpretation when analyzing data, and obtaining rich responses when interviewing. In planning to teach qualitative research, spending time reviewing teaching reflections can be useful to ensure challenges or issues can be anticipated and strategies developed to overcome these.

Ethical considerations. When introducing students to qualitative research and engaging them in practical exercises, a number of ethical issues arise (see also Chapter 24). For example, when deciding which topics to study lecturers must be cognizant of students' reactions, particularly if the topics being studies are sensitive (Borochowitz, 2005). Similarly, ensuring students are adequately prepared to support participants if they become distressed during interviews is vital (Biggerstaff & Thompson, 2008; George, 2013). If students are trained in certain areas (e.g., counseling), they could find themselves struggling to manage the conflicting roles they face in these situations (George, 2013). Sharing stories from past experiences, providing clear steps to follow if participants become distressed, and limiting students' examination of sensitive topics might be pertinent to help reduce these ethical issues.

When students are collecting data, whether through observations, interviews, or focus groups, it is important to remember these students could have an impact on peoples' lives and academics have a responsibility to ensure that data is collected ethically and appropriately. To limit the potential impact of inexperienced researchers on members of the general public, a number of lecturers use other students on the course for the study (e.g., Chenail, 1997; DeLyser, 2008). However, using other students can raise concerns regarding anonymity, confidentiality, and whether individuals have a choice not to participate (Lincoln, 1998). Ensuring steps are taken to anonymize data that is going to be shared in a group and making it clear that there are no penalties for nonparticipation are critical in these situations. Additionally, restricting or limiting students' access to participants until they are deemed ready is also important (Lincoln, 1998).

Overall, time needs to be spent teaching students about the importance of research ethics so they are aware of the potential issues that might arise. Students need to understand that ethics is a *process/practice,* and different ethical considerations might be encountered during the process. The university ethics committee will likely play an important role in helping academics identify and manage potential ethical issues that could arise when integrating activities within a qualitative research class. Other approaches, such as feminist ethics or virtue ethics (see Chapter 24), may also need to be considered to help guide academics and students through ethical dilemmas.

Obtaining "quality" data. Whether data collection occurs through interviews (see Chapter 9) or observations (see Chapter 10), it appears that students might struggle to obtain data of sufficient depth or quality to enable analysis to be conducted, or insights to be obtained. Specific issues associated with conducting interviews include being unprepared for unresponsive participants or participants who provide limited insights, forgetting how to probe about responses, adhering too closely to interview guides, and students allowing their own perceptions and biases to guide the interview (e.g., Hopkinson & Hogg, 2004; Keen, 1996; Machtmes *et al.*, 2009; Raddon *et al.*, 2008). Providing students with opportunities to observe interviews that are conducted by an experienced interviewer (Chenail, 1997), being observed conducting their own interviews on other students (Hopkinson & Hogg, 2004), reflecting on their data-collection experiences alone or in small groups (Aronson Fontes & Piercy, 2000; DeLyser, 2008), and engaging in discussion regarding strategies to build rapport, reflect on biases, and listen to the participants (Hsiung, 2008) could all help to improve the quality of data students obtain.

Getting it "right." When engaging in data collection, students seem to become preoccupied with a desire to "get it right" (Humphreys, 2006; Poulin, 2007). Specifically, students appear to be concerned with quantifying the process; for example, identifying how many interviews they should conduct, and how long the interviews should be (Borochowitz, 2005). Similarly, when conducting fieldwork or observations, students often worry about knowing exactly what it is they are meant to be looking for (Keen, 1996; Ostrower, 1998; Tan & Ko, 2004). This need for a linear, quantifiable process is likely due to students' previous experiences with quantitative research, their desire for certainty, and need to achieve certain grades and marks on assessments (Poulin, 2007). Providing students with opportunities to practice different techniques, limiting the extent to which they are evaluated on their abilities to carry out skills, embracing and discussing mistakes, and teaching for rather than about qualitative research could help to reduce these concerns (Hurworth, 2008; Poulin, 2007). Further, being prepared to respond to students' questions in informed ways and adapting answers based on, among others, the students' experience, research question, and selected methodology, could help.

Understanding the analysis process. When students are presented with or have obtained data, one of the most consistently discussed issues is students' inability to understand the lack of objectivity in the analysis process (Hopkinson & Hogg, 2004; Stallings, 1995; Wright, 2000). Authors have indicated that students try to fit data into predefined categories and struggle to really understand the different steps in data analysis (Hopkinson & Hogg, 2004; Stallings, 1995). Similarly, students can find it hard to move from descriptive codes and categories to a more abstract or interpretive level of analysis (Keen, 1996). Utilizing some of the exercises provided in Table 31.1, along with group discussion and reflection, could help to enhance students' understanding of analysis more quickly.

Accounting for different backgrounds and experience. When students are learning about qualitative research they often have different perceptions, experiences, and levels of understanding (Borochowitz, 2005; Poulin, 2007). As such, some students will struggle with ideas, while others will not. Subsequently, allowing sufficient time for students to understand the material and pitching the material at the right level can be challenging (Mason, 2002). Providing students with multiple opportunities to receive and gain feedback could be a simple strategy to limit this issue (Mason, 2002). Additionally, providing students with examples of excerpts from your own work can help to illustrate each stage of the research process and make it easier to explain (Biggerstaff & Thompson, 2008).

Conclusion

Through sharing and reflecting on their teaching experiences, academics have highlighted the numerous activities that can be used to enhance student learning. They have also helped to raise awareness of the potential challenges and issues inherent in teaching qualitative research. By drawing on these examples and additional resources (see Box 31.3 for a list of websites and resources) students' learning experiences and consequently their interest in and understanding of qualitative research can (hopefully) be enhanced. Although such resources are increasing and more academics are sharing their experiences relating to teaching qualitative research, there is still a need for scholars within sport and exercise disciplines to share their insights. The qualitative community within sport and exercise is strong and filled with creative and enthusiastic individuals, who are likely to have developed exciting and interesting approaches to teaching. We need students to have positive learning experiences and enjoy the journey of discovering qualitative research to grow our field, and it is by sharing experiences and reflecting upon successes and failures of teaching qualitative research that we can do this.

To start this conversation, insights from a number of scholars who presented at the *4th International Qualitative Research in Sport and Exercise Conference,* at Loughborough University in 2014, or are experienced at teaching qualitative research in sport and exercise, are presented in Box 31.2. In line with the overall aim of this chapter, these tips are provided to initiate conversations and stimulate reflection to enhance teaching and encourage student learning.

Box 31.2   Teaching tips and challenges

Dr. Nollaig Frost, Middlesex University

My tip for teaching qualitative research to students who are new to it and who (usually) have been trained in quantitative techniques is to let them play with qualitative data. I provide a data extract from my own research (so that I am very familiar with it and the different ways in which it can be understood), and ask them to discuss in small groups what it might mean. In large group discussions we then gather the different meanings and consider how these can be understood in terms of different qualitative data-analysis techniques and methods (usually defined on PowerPoint slides that can be perused afterwards). In the discussion I point out where (unfounded) leaps from the data have been made, and try to show through interactive discussion how personal experiences and prior knowledge and training have influenced the interpretations made.

Prof. Brendan Gough, Leeds Beckett University

One exercise I use to highlight how experiences/events/objects can be constructed differently is to get students to compare an article from the *Daily Mail* vs. *The Guardian* (two newspapers in the UK).

To emphasize reflexivity, I ask them to individually come up with a qualitative study design on a given topic [e.g. alcohol] then ask them to compare their designs with another student and to reflect on the [personal] rationale for their study.

Prof. Nicholas Holt, University of Alberta

My three main suggestions for teaching qualitative research are: (1) Conduct a mini-study for the assignment: get a blanket ethics approval for in-class research projects, have students design an interview guide, conduct some interviews, and orally present results. It helps move students from theory to practice, and really helps people understand how they are going to go about their thesis/ dissertation work; (2) I have experimented with teaching philosophy and methodology first, then methods later vs. starting with methods and doing philosophy and methodology later. Although it confuses the students terribly for the first few weeks, I am convinced it is better to do philosophy and methodology components earlier – it just takes patience and eventually students are able to connect the dots; (3) Carry out practical work as much as possible (e.g., role-play interviews in class, or ask students to carry out observations as homework).

Dr. Richard Keegan, University of Canberra

One of the biggest issues I see is trying to present findings once the study is nearing completion. Often people are tempted to offer incomplete or "vanilla" tables and diagrams, when there are better ways of representing the data. I explain the "problem of representation" as follows: Imagine being dropped into a foreign city with only a few days to draw a tourist map before your friends arrive. They can only use that map and you will not be there to help them personally. What overall framework/structure do you use? How much detail is needed, and do you go for exact precision or topographical representations? What are the key navigational features to always return to if lost? What parts can you afford to leave largely alone, versus which bits require extensive detail? And how best can you convey this in the knowledge you will not be there to help them interpret it? I guess the message for me at this point is – we won't know till we get there, but we have some ideas forming!

Prof. Kent Kowalski, University of Saskatchewan

Probably the most effective in-class activity that I use when I teach qualitative research methods is to have students work in small groups to identify qualitative research questions for a range of the qualitative strategies of inquiry in their areas of interest. Through this type of process students learn to develop a wide variety of qualitative research questions of relevance to their chosen fields of study, disentangle how qualitative and quantitative questions differ from one another, and understand how various qualitative strategies of inquiry are both unique and overlapping.

Prof. Kerry McGannon, Laurentian University

If I have a "key" tip it would be that students need to understand "what's behind the research" (i.e., ontology and epistemology informs each methodological choice, which in turn has an impact on the entire research process). Learning what epistemology is and how it informs the theoretical

(continued)

(continued)

perspective, methods, and methodology is difficult for most students to grasp at first if they have never been exposed to it. However, I find that once people grasp these points, they have a better understanding of the research process and they can begin to avoid making "fatal flaws" in how they design, execute and finalize their own research, as well as identify this in other forms of research they read and/or critique. To "teach" or help people grasp the above point, a book by Crotty (1998) called *Foundations of Social Research* is quite useful. Obviously one book does not cover everything, but the first chapter outlines four basic elements of any research process (methods, methodology, theoretical perspective, and epistemology) and each has a very specific meaning and implication associated with it. In order to grasp and apply these concepts, students can be given contrasting pieces of qualitative research in sport or exercise (e.g., postpositivist deductive analysis and narrative analysis grounded in social constructionism) to discuss and deconstruct, based on the above four elements. Students can also be tasked with locating contrasting articles.

Dr. Jennifer McMahon, University of Tasmania

At the University of Tasmania, qualitative research is (currently) taught in the same unit as quantitative research. The course is usually delivered by a quantitative researcher and I am invited to deliver one guest lecture on qualitative research. Consequently, this has resulted in some challenges, including resistance towards qualitative research from students and academics, a perception that qualitative research cannot provide good results from such a small data set and, for those students interested in pursuing qualitative research, there is concern regarding who will mark their dissertations. I have developed numerous strategies to overcome these issues, including: (1). in response to comments regarding the small data set, the following analogy is provided: "If one child was abused by a priest, then action would be taken; why do we need 1,000 kids to be abused before we do anything?" That one voice is valid and should be heard and acted upon; (2) explaining how qualitative research is beneficial for those who are researched; that is, exploring the success in terms of emancipation for participants who are a part of the qualitative research process. The very process enables them to make connections, to reexamine lived experiences, and in that way make sense of what has occurred. It is about giving back to the researched and not just taking.

Prof. Brett Smith, University of Birmingham

My tips revolve around epistemological and ontological familiarity, connoisseurship, complexity and innovation, and storytelling. At the very beginning of each research skills module with new undergraduate or graduate students I have found it useful to begin on familiar territory. Students come with epistemological assumptions – explicit or implicit – about what counts as knowledge and what is the relationship between the knower and known. Most believe that knowledge can be found and discovered in objective ways. In addition, they arrive with ontological assumptions about reality; namely, that a researcher can truly get at the reality independent of them through methods. I start by highlighting such assumptions. I don't critique these. I simply say that there is one group of scientists who hold onto these assumptions and these assumptions are fundamental for how they do research; they underpin and drive their work. I then highlight that there is another group of scientists who have very different assumptions from those noted, and move onto unpacking these. I stress throughout that the assumptions are different; that neither group is better or worse than the other. It is the *informed* scientist that appreciates these differences and that difference among researchers needs to be understood and respected. This art of appreciation is *connoisseurship*. I ask the students who they wish to be – an *informed scientist who is a connoisseur* or an *uninformed scientist who has no appreciation of difference*? All this becomes the backbone for how I then teach research skills and later more advanced qualitative methods modules.

Throughout each qualitative lecture the topic to be covered is discussed first at a fundamental level and then complexity and innovation is introduced. For example, when teaching interviewing the different kinds are introduced (i.e. structured, semistructured, and unstructured) and then some complexity is introduced by highlighting some misunderstanding about interviewing. More novel ways of doing interviewing (e.g. mobile interviews) are also offered. Epistemological and ontological matters are brought in throughout, in order to keep stressing why these assumptions matter so much and how they shape how methods are used and understood.

Also important, for me, is storytelling. Before each class I spend time thinking about how I can illuminate points made through a story about my own research or others. Stories, for me, not only put flesh on the bones of methods, they engage students and help them stay with me, the point, and remember.

Box 31.3   Resources and websites

Book/book chapters

- Eisenhart, M. & Jurow, S. (2011). Teaching qualitative research. In N. K. Denzin & Y. S. Lincoln (Eds.), *The SAGE handbook of qualitative research* (4th ed., pp. 699–714). Thousand Oaks, CA: Sage.
- Hammersley, M. (2004). Teaching qualitative methodology: Craft, profession or bricolage. In C. Seale, G. Gobo, J. F. Gubrium & D. Silverman (Eds.), *Qualitative research practice* (pp. 549–560). Thousand Oaks, CA: Sage.
- Hurworth, R. E (2008). *Teaching qualitative research: Cases and issues.* Rotterdam, The Netherlands: Sense.

Online articles/forums

- Breuer, F. & Schreier, M. (2007). Issues in learning about and teaching qualitative research methods and methodology in the social sciences. *Forum: Qualitative Social Research, 8.* Article 30. Available at: http://www.qualitative-research.net/index.php/fqs/article/view/216/477.
- Paulus, T. M. & Bennet, A. (2014). Teaching qualitative research methods with ATLAS.ti: Beyond data analysis. Available at: https://atlastiblog.wordpress.com/2014/10/31/teaching-qualitative-research-methods-with-atlas-ti-beyond-data-analysis/.

Webinar

- Mayan, M. (2013). Teaching qualitative research well. Webinar available at: https://www.youtube.com/watch?v=p4fbiOY8EiU.

(continued)

(continued)

Websites containing resources or links to resources

- Methodspace
  http://www.methodspace.com/profiles/blogs/teaching-qualitative-research
- Qual Page
  http://www.qualitativeresearch.uga.edu/QualPage/welcome.html
- Qualitative360
  http://www.qual360.com/news-and-blogs/11-editor-s-pick-top-qualitative-research-blogs
- Teaching Qualitative Research Methods at the Undergraduate Level
  http://78.158.56.101/archive/psychology/s.php@p=122.html

References

Aronson Fontes, L., & Piercy, F. P. (2000). Engaging students in qualitative research through experiential class activities. *Teaching of Psychology, 27*, 174–179.

Atkinson, M. (2011). *Key concepts: Research methods in sport, exercise and health science.* London: Sage.

Biggerstaff, D. & Thompson, A. R. (2008). Interpretative Phenomenological Analysis (IPA): A qualitative methodology of choice in healthcare research. *Qualitative Research in Psychology, 5*, 214–224.

Blank, G. (2004). Teaching qualitative data analysis to graduate students. *Social Science Computer Review, 22*, 187–196.

Borochowitz, D. (2005). Teaching a qualitative research seminar on sensitive issues: An autoethnography. *Qualitative Social Work, 4*, 347–362.

Breuer, F. & Schreier, M. (2007). Issues in learning about and teaching qualitative research methods and methodology in the social sciences. *Forum: Qualitative Social Research, 8*. Art 30. Retrieved from http://www.qualitative-research.net/index.php/fqs/article/view/216/477.

Chenail, R. (1997). Interviewing exercises: Lessons from family therapy. *The Qualitative Report, 3*(2). Retrieved from http://www.nova.edu/ssss/QR/QR3-2/chenail.html.

Culver, D., Gilbert, W., & Sparkes, A. C. (2012). Qualitative research in sport psychology journals: The next decade 2000–2009 and beyond. *The Sport Psychologist, 26*, 261–281.

DeLyser, D. (2008). Teaching qualitative research. *Journal of Geography in Higher Education, 32*, 233–244.

Edwards, D. F. & Thatcher, J. (2004). A student-centred tutor-led approach to teaching research methods. *Journal of Further and Higher Education, 28*, 195–206.

Eisenhart, M. & Jurow, A. S. (2011). Teaching qualitative research. In N. K. Denzin & Y. S. Lincoln (Eds.), *The Sage handbook of qualitative research* (4th ed., pp. 699–714). Los Angeles, CA: Sage.

Frost, N. & Barry, R. (2010). Developing a qualitative research culture in university psychology departments. *Qualitative Methods in Psychology Bulletin, 10*, 26–32.

Gallagher, S. & Francesconi, D. (2012). Teaching phenomenology to qualitative researchers, cognitive scientists and phenomenologists. *The Indo-Pacific Journal of Phenomenology, 12*, 1–10.

George, M. (2013). Teaching focus group interviewing: Benefits and challenges. *Teaching Sociology, 41*, 257–270.

Gerstl-Pepin, C. & Patrizio, K. (2009). Learning from Dumbledore's Pensieve: Metaphor as an aid in teaching reflexivity in qualitative research. *Qualitative Research, 9*, 299–308.

Gibson, S. & Sullivan, C. (2012). Teaching qualitative research methods in psychology: An introduction to the special issue. *Psychology Learning and Teaching, 11*, 1–5.

Gough, B., Lowton, R., Madill, A., & Stratton, P. (2002). *Guidelines for the supervision of undergraduate qualitative research in psychology.* Retrieved from http://78.158.101/archive/psychology/s.php@p=256&db=11.html.

Hammersley, M. (2004). Teaching qualitative methodology: Craft, profession or bricolage. In C. Seale, G. Gobo, J. F. Gubrium, & D. Silverman (Eds.), *Qualitative research practice* (pp. 549–560). Thousand Oaks, CA: Sage.

Hopkinson, G. C. & Hogg, M. K. (2004). Teaching and learning about qualitative research in the social sciences: An experiential learning approach amongst marketing students. *Journal of Further and Higher Education, 28*, 307–320.

Hsiung, P. C. (2008). Teaching reflexivity in qualitative interviewing. *Teaching Sociology, 36*, 211–216.

Humphreys, M. (2006). Teaching qualitative research methods: I'm beginning to see the light. *Qualitative Research in Organisations and Management: An International Journal, 1*, 173–188.

Hurworth, R. E. (2008). *Teaching qualitative research: Cases and issues*. Rotterdam, NL: Sense.

Jones, I. (2014). *Research methods for sports studies*. Abingdon, UK: Routledge.

Keen, M. F. (1996). Teaching qualitative methods: A face-to-face encounter. *Teaching Sociology, 24*, 166–176.

Kolb, D. A. (1984). *Experiential learning: Experience as the source of learning and development*. Englewood Cliffs, NJ: Prentice Hall.

Lather, P. (2006). Paradigm proliferation as a good thing to think with: Teaching research in education as a wild profusion. *International Journal of Qualitative Studies in Education, 19*, 35–57.

Lincoln, Y. S. (1998). The ethics of teaching in qualitative research. *Qualitative Inquiry, 4*, 315–327.

Machtmes, K., Johnson, E., Fox, J., Burke, M. S., Harper, J., Arcemont, L., . . . Aguirre, R. T. P. (2009). Teaching qualitative research methods through service-learning. *Qualitative Report, 14*, 155–164.

Mason, O. J. (2002). Teaching qualitative research methods: Some innovations and reflections on practice. *Psychology Teaching Review, 10*, 68–75.

Mayan, M. (2013). *Teaching qualitative research well*. Webinar retrieved from https://www.youtube.com/watch?v=p4fbiOY8EiU.

McAllister, M. & Rowe, J. (2003). Blackbirds singing in the dead of night? Advancing the craft of teaching qualitative research. *Journal of Nursing Education, 42*, 296–303.

Onwuegbuzie, A. J. & Leech, N. L. (2005). Taking the "q" out of research: Teaching research methodology courses without the divide between quantitative and qualitative paradigms. *Quality and Quantity, 39*, 267–296.

Ostrower, F. (1998). Nonparticipant observation as an introduction to qualitative research. *Teaching Sociology, 26*, 57–61.

Paulus, T. M. & Bennet, A. (2014). Teaching qualitative research methods with ATLAS.ti: Beyond data analysis. Retrieved from https://atlastiblog.wordpress.com/2014/10/31/teaching-qualitative-research-methods-with-atlas-ti-beyond-data-analysis/.

Poulin, K. L. (2007). Teaching qualitative research: lessons from practice. *Counseling Psychologist, 35*, 431–458.

Raddon, M. B., Nault, C., & Scott, A. (2008). Integrating the complete research project into a large qualitative methods course. *Teaching Sociology, 36*, 141–149.

Rossman, G. B. & Rallis, R. S. (2003). *Learning in the field: An introduction to qualitative research*. Thousand Oaks, CA: Sage.

Sandelowski, M. J. (2008). Editorial: Justifying qualitative research. *Research in Nursing and Health, 31*, 193–195. doi: 10.1002/nur.20272.

Shaw, R. L., Dyson, P. O., & Peel, E. (2008). Qualitative psychology at M level: A dialogue between learner and teacher. *Qualitative Research in Psychology, 5*(3), 179–191.

Sparkes, A. C. & Smith, B. (2014). *Qualitative research methods in sport, exercise and health: From process to product*. London: Routledge.

Stallings, W. M. (1995). Confessions of a quantitative educational researcher trying to teach qualitative research. *Educational Researcher, 24*, 31–32.

Stalp, M. C. & Grant, L. (2001). Teaching qualitative coding in undergraduate field method classes: An exercise based on personal ads. *Teaching Sociology, 29*, 209–218.

Tan, J. & Ko, Y. C. (2004). Using feature films to teach observation in undergraduate research methods. *Teaching Sociology, 32*, 109–118.

Terkildsen, T. & Petersen, S. (2015). The future of qualitative research in psychology: A student's perspective. *Integrative Psychological and Behavioural Science, 49*, 202–206.

Wright, M. C. (2000). Getting more out of less: The benefits of short-term experiential learning in undergraduate sociology courses. *Teaching Sociology, 28*, 116–126.

32

KNOWLEDGE, NOT NUMBERS

Qualitative research and impact in sport, exercise and health

Tess Kay

Since they first emerged from the positivist swamp, qualitative researchers have been generating impact. In the UK, scholars can look back to the dawn of the modern Welfare State in the 1950s, when the sociologists Peter Willmott and Michael Young established the Institute of Community Studies in East London, to undertake research that would both add to basic knowledge about society and illuminate practical questions of social policy. As seminal post-war texts emerged – on the effects of social policies on working class communities (Young and Wilmott, 1957); the emergence of new family ideologies and practices (Young and Wilmott, 1973); the 'rediscovery' of Britain's prevalent post-Beveridge poverty (Abel-Smith and Townsend, 1965) (accompanied by Townsend's co-founding of the Child Poverty Action Group) – it was the Institute's impacts on social welfare and planning that established its preeminent position among British social research units (Platt, 1971). At the forefront was Young and Wilmott's (1957) own *Family and Kinship in East London*, a study of the effect of post-war rehousing policy on a tight-knit urban working-class community. Acknowledged as one of the most influential sociological studies of the twentieth century, its use of social observation challenged reliance on social statistical evidence and offered new ways for social scientists to explain the workings and injustices of society, and inform the policies and practices that addressed them.

So qualitative research has long been a natural bedfellow of 'impact' and this continues with a modern impact agenda with which its parameters, practices and values also naturally align. These include a closeness of engagement through which impact can be fostered: concern with social issues; the social world as the 'laboratory', and the need to be present within it; a facilitative and inclusive ethos that values interaction with research subjects and includes participatory approaches; and a capacity for collaborative knowledge production, which can allow the research process itself to foster 'impact'. Equipped with methodologies that facilitate these aims, from traditional rich oral accounts from those who are otherwise unheard, to innovative methods that respond to the potentials of the virtual world, qualitative researchers can take their place at the heart of the impact landscape.

Yet on the whole qualitative researchers have found that the promising potential of the impact agenda has not transpired. Far from opening a door for collaboration and influence, it has ushered in a regressive return to scientific rationality. The evidenced-based movement in particular has exerted such influence that the agendas and methods of qualitative inquiry have risked exclusion from resources. The debate has evolved beyond a question of methodology into a more fundamental issue of who controls the definition of evidence, and what evidence is acceptable to whom (Morse, 2006). This narrowness is set to continue, exacerbated by a future shaped by public spending cuts, limited budgets and economic pressure to fund only demonstrably 'useful' research (Lester & O'Reilly, 2015).

Qualitative researchers are not, therefore, concerned about their capacity to generate impact, but about being enabled to do so. While there are dangers in oversimplifying the supposed paradigm 'wars', the uncritical acceptance of scientifically based research establishes a norm with which qualitative research struggles to align. For sport, exercise and health (SEH) researchers working at the interface with public health, the much-vaunted hierarchy of evidence (e.g. Guyatt *et al.*, 1995) is a particularly immediate, tangible illustration of this – a listing in which qualitative research designs are not explicitly recognised at all. Across a wider array of policy agenda, even sport researchers whose expert status derives from career-long qualitative enquiry can find themselves required to abandon these proven forms of knowledge, and comply instead with the prescriptive research designs that produce the 'evidence' that policymakers specify. The alternative is to exclude themselves from these arena.

This chapter examines these tensions. It is not a theoretical consideration of whether qualitative research can generate impact (e.g. Garbarino & Holland, 2009; Garside, 2014; Jabareen & Vilkomerson, 2014), nor is it an extended critique of the evidence-based policy debate, both better covered elsewhere (e.g. Denzin, 2009; Morse, 2006; Otten, Dodson, Fleischhacker, Siddiqi & Quinn, 2015; Shortall, 2012). What it offers is a more *practical* consideration of how sport, exercise and health researchers working within current higher education and funding environments might navigate the systems for doing so. It therefore takes as read the case set out in this introduction – that there is no mismatch or conflict between 'impact' and qualitative research, which from its first origins has pursued and achieved diverse and substantial social, economic and political contributions. In current funding landscapes, in which these forms of research impact are increasingly recognised and valued, qualitative researchers should be positioned front and centre – with SEH researchers among them. That this is only occurring on a limited scale, and that a discourse of irrelevance and rejection prevails, runs counter to a well-established tradition of enquiry. This suggests barriers lie not in the inherent incompatibility of qualitative research and impact, but in the structures and processes through which impact is currently defined and evaluated. In the sections that follow, the chapter therefore first examines the current context in which 'impact' is formally defined and evaluated. It then considers how this plays out for qualitative researchers in SEH, and attempts to distil guidance that can help qualitative researchers overcome barriers to their participation in impact activities, and suggests some strategies for doing this. The overall aim throughout is to provide some practical guidance and assessment.

'Demonstrable impact': the emerging international agenda for research

The increased requirement for researchers to demonstrate the 'impact' of their work is an international trend. At a time of global economic crisis the imposition of austerity across fundamental areas of public service demands that higher education justifies the societal value of research investment (Bornmann, 2012; Lester & O'Reilly, 2015). In Canada, where the key terms of the debate at funding council level tend to be 'knowledge mobilization' and 'knowledge transfer and exchange' (VanEvery, 2011), 'impact' has been high on the social science agenda since the Social Sciences and Humanities Research Council's national transformation consultation in 2004–05; in the UK in 2014, 'impact' was formally evaluated for the first time as one of the three substantive categories in five-yearly national assessment of research, the Research Exercise Framework (REF2014); while in Australia, in December 2015, the government announced its schedule for a national impact and engagement exercise to assess how universities were translating its $3.5 billion annual investment in research into economic, social and environmental impacts 'that benefit Australia' (Australian Government, 2015). The common themes are that research should have impact beyond academia, and that this impact should be 'demonstrable'. These requirements are not confined to research funded directly from public budgets, e.g. through grants from funding councils, but extend to all research within publicly funded institutions.

It is this construction of 'impact' with which qualitative researchers are increasingly required to engage, SEH researchers among them.

At the time of writing the UK is the only country to have developed, implemented and completed a national assessment of research impact. The evaluation took place in 2014, as part of the 'Research Excellence Framework'; the seventh national evaluation of the quality of academic research, covering the period 2008–2013 (HEFCE, 2012). Implemented under the auspices of the Higher Education Funding Councils for the UK nations, 'REF2014' would determine public research funding allocations to universities and other research institutions for 2015–2020. Assessment was based on subject-specific groupings, arranged into 36 'Units of Assessment' (UoAs), to which universities made submissions according to their areas of expertise. The designated UoA for 'sport' was UoA26, a broad multidisciplinary category of Sport and Exercise Sciences, Leisure and Tourism. In each submission, 'research outputs' accounted for 50% of the overall quality rating awarded, 'research environment' for 30%, and 'impact' for 20%, making it the lesser element, but not a minor one.

The inclusion of 'impact' in REF2014 was an innovation globally. In its wake, the UK funding councils commissioned a number of evaluations of the impact element, and a small critical academic literature also began to emerge. The issues raised by these sources are not specific to the UK environment but of broader relevance to the international research community.

The very act of defining research impact is contentious. In the UK the incorporation of impact into the REF elicited strong but very mixed responses, including hostility to the perceived threat to academic freedom; concern that emphasis on 'useable' research would compromise intellectual quality; and relief that high-quality applied work might no longer be disdained as 'unacademic'. Regardless of viewpoint, however, most researchers are likely to be required to engage with the impact agenda, and will be affected by how that is operationalised. The involvement of qualitative researchers is especially required, as there are some early indications that these conditions could be inimical to their work.

Published descriptors of 'impact' appear similar across countries and disciplines. Research Councils UK (RCUK) describe impact as 'the demonstrable contribution that excellent research makes to society and the economy'. For REF2014, impact was as 'an effect on, change or benefit to the economy, society, culture, public policy or services, health, the environment or quality of life, beyond academia'. RCUK distinguishes between academic impact and impact beyond the academy:

Academic impact

The demonstrable contribution that excellent research makes to academic advances, across and within disciplines, including significant advances in understanding, methods, theory and application.

Economic and societal impacts

The demonstrable contribution that excellent research makes to society and the economy. Economic and societal impacts embrace all the extremely diverse ways in which research-related knowledge and skills benefit individuals, organisations and nations.

(http://www.rcuk.ac.uk/innovation/impacts/)

The Economic and Social Research Council (ESRC) provides a further classification of forms of impact as being *instrumental* (influencing the development of policy, practice or service provision, shaping legislation, altering behaviour), *conceptual* (contributing to the understanding of policy issues, reframing debates), and/or *capacity building* (through technical and personal skill development) (http://www.esrc.ac.uk/research/evaluation-and-impact/what-is-impact/).

Impact is thus defined with some lack of precision, but with wide scope for both the form it might take (e.g. influencing policy; enhancing quality of life; developing commercial products) and who or what the potential 'beneficiaries' of the impact might be (e.g. policymakers, the public, organizations). At the conceptual level there is therefore no reason for qualitative research to be disadvantaged; when we look at the outcomes of this system, however, the picture changes somewhat.

Qualitative research and impact: emerging issues from the UK REF

In the week that the results of REF2014 were due to be published, the *Guardian* newspaper claimed that 'the eyes of research evaluators worldwide are on the UK' (Manville, 2014). It was the assessment of the REF impact component that was attracting this international attention. The format had been informed by experienced policy and evidence consultancy RAND Europe, and consisted of an Impact Statement supported by Impact Case Studies. The Statement took the form of a narrative account incorporating both qualitative and quantitative data and described the subject area's infrastructure and activities for maximizing impact. This was supported by four-page impact case studies – examples of impact beyond academia that had occurred during the REF period (2008–2013) – which could be based on research over a longer term (up to 20 years; 1993–2013). The impact case study contained five sections: a summary of the impact, description of the underpinning research, references to the research, details of the impact, and sources to corroborate the impact (Higher Education Funding Council for England (HEFCE), 2012).

The UK REF exercise has so far been subject to two types of analyses: analyses of the substantive data collected through the assessment process (King's College London and Digital Science, 2015); and accounts of the REF process for assessing impact (Greenhalgh & Fahy, 2015; Manville *et al.*, 2015a; 2015b). The former provide a snapshot of the scale and types of impact reported to REF2014, whereas the latter address issues such as the appropriateness of the reporting format for capturing impact; the selectivity of the exercise (only a small number of impact examples reported to the REF, approximately one per 8–10 'eligible' staff); and any wider effect that incorporating impact into the REF may have had on researchers, their institutions and the sector. Together these provide some insight into what forms impact takes and how it is being achieved, but also more importantly, how well – or otherwise – qualitative research fits the impact 'system' as currently shaped.

The HEFCE evaluation of impact in REF2014 was based on 6,975 impact case studies submitted by 154 Higher Education Institutions (HEIs). Analysis of the 6,679 non-redacted case studies provided 'a unique snapshot' of the impact that had emerged from HEI research and knowledge mobilisation activities of the previous 20 years. It found that the societal impact of research from UK Higher Education Institutions was considerable; contributed to the wealth and well-being of all nations globally; was strikingly diverse, occurring across all disciplines; was multidisciplinary, and 'multi-impactful'; and was achieved in multiple ways – 3,709 unique 'pathways to impact' were identified (King's College London and Digital Science, 2015).

The evaluation contained a number of points of more specific relevance to SEH researchers. At the generic level, the evaluators valued the flexibility that the REF case study format gave authors to select the most appropriate data to evidence the exact types of impact that they were claiming. They cautioned against introducing more standardised prescriptive approaches, and warned specifically that the development of robust impact metrics was 'unlikely' to be viable. They also suggested that moving to a more prescriptive framework requiring more structured and standardised information risked discouraging the reporting of diverse and heterogeneous impacts. The HEFCE report is thus broadly reassuring for SEH researchers on issues of how impact is presented, reported and evaluated, favouring formats that are more likely to allow qualitative researchers to do justice to the way their work has impact.

The inclusion of impact in the REF2014 gave a strong stimulus to the wider impact agenda in UK's university research. For qualitative SEH researchers, this brings both benefits and challenges. On the positive side, RAND's assessment of the process of preparing REF impact submissions (Manville, 2015a) identified four benefits: improved ability to identify and understand impact; the stimulation of broader strategic thinking about impact; increased recognition within HEIs of those academics undertaking impact activities; and opportunities to the review and reaffirm relationships with external stakeholders. Three of these – affirming relationships, understanding impact, and recognition – were also identified as benefits in the Excellence in Innovation for Australia (EIA) trial (Morgan Jones, Castle-Clarke, Manville, Gunashekar & Grant, 2013).

At the individual level, some researchers had experienced significant positive shifts. Academic staff commented on the opportunity they had had to reflect on taking a strategic approach to impact, either in relation to their own research, or at a wider institutional level:

> I noticed my perception of research changing slightly and my passion to make an impact with my research enhanced; this was due to constant in-depth thinking about what we (and I) do in the unit and why we do it. I can say that I became totally immersed in the topic of impact and became fascinated by the area.
>
> *(Manville* et al., *2015a, p. 10)*

The impact was not only cultural: the RAND evaluation also identified changes in individual and institutional practices, some directly stimulated by the requirements of the impact element of the REF submission. One key effect was increased recognition that impact needs to be embedded in research from the outset and then throughout its life cycle, in line with the introduction of compulsory impact 'pathways' in research council funding bids. Changes within Higher Education Institutions (HEIs) included the development of institutional strategies and processes to foster a culture of impact, and with some HEIs including impact within their research strategy, or producing a stand-alone strategy to address impact. A number had also begun to include impact as a formal criterion on personnel specifications, using it as an area for consideration in career development at annual appraisals. One academic interviewed for the evaluation gave an insight into the impact on the sector: 'It's been like a shot in the arm for universities, academics will have been trained up, they will understand language and will have proper data collection exercises in place and will start thinking about impact at the outset of projects' (Manville *et al.*, 2015a, p. 13).

Set against these accounts of positive stimulus, were concerns about the structural shift in the research landscape. Attaching greater value to applied research was expected by some to undermine commitment to pure, basic or 'blue skies' research— a suggestion backed by the marked decline in research council and government department expenditure on 'pure basic research' from a peak of 62 per cent in 2005–2006 to 35 per cent in 2011–2012 (Department for Business, Innovation & Skills, 2013, Table 2.6; in King's College London and Digital Science, 2015). Such major rebalancing of research funding emphasises the need for qualitative researchers to be credible and active within applied, impact-generating fields of enquiry. Manville *et al.* (2015a) also reported apprehension about a more specific 'impact' effect in funding:

> A more subtle concern was that the assessment of impact by REF 2014 could direct research funding and activity towards areas that can more easily demonstrate impact, and away from areas where impact is harder to establish . . . For example, because assessing action-based research in the current framing of REF 2014 has proved difficult, it may lead to less of this type of activity.
>
> *(Manville* et al.*, 2015a, p. xiv)*

This point is also a focus in Greenhalgh and Fahy's detailed critique of the 162 impact case studies from the community-based health sciences, submitted to REF2014 UoA02. They noted that the format of reporting adopted for the REF impact case studies 'arguably implied a direct and linear link between a programme of research and its subsequent impact', and that this (implicit) expectation may have accounted for nearly all of the case studies in their sample being presented using a linear, 'logic model' framing (Greenhalgh & Fahy, 2015, p. 7). They reflected on the implications that this has for particular forms of enquiry:

> To some extent, this framing worked . . . But as others have predicted previously, the implicit logic model framing seemed to both invite and reward 'hard', quantitative experimental studies and computational models that had clear, measurable and attributable short-term impacts (most commonly, incorporation into guidelines) . . . Whilst one interpretation of our data is that impact *is* largely linear and best achieved through quantitative empirical studies (hence, such study designs are 'stronger'), another is that the more diffuse impacts from fields such as social science and policy research could not be captured, so institutions made a strategic decision not to submit them as impact case studies . . .
>
> *(Greenhalgh & Fahy, 2015, p. 7)*

They also noted a tendency to present straight linear impact 'pathways', attributing this to the emphasis that the case-study format put on measurable impacts that could be tracked back clearly to studies reported in the 'research' section of the REF submission. Their concern was that this allowed direct but not indirect flows of influence to be demonstrated, and did not favour health services and policy research, where impact is inherently less linear, more complex and multi-stakeholder, and thus harder to demonstrate than the impact of biomedical studies. Looking forward, Greenhalgh and Fahy suggested that impact case studies, using methods such as action research partnerships, should be assessed/judged differently from more conventional study designs such as randomised trials (see also Chapters 8, 25, 33 and 34; Schinke, Smith & McGannon, 2013). They also argued that:

> Research teams should not be penalised for impact activities (such as building relationships with policymakers, professional bodies or citizens) that are worthwhile in the long term but unlikely to map to specific, measurable impact metrics in the timescale of the assessment.
>
> *(Greenhalgh & Fahy, 2015, p. 8)*

In contrast to the broad reassurance from the HEFCE evaluation, the more detailed analyses do reveal issues that could affect SEH researchers adversely. The final section offers some views on what these might be, and how SEH researchers might address them.

The impact environment for qualitative researchers in sport, exercise and health

An impact-oriented research environment has practical implications for those undertaking social science research in sport, health and exercise. If qualitative SEH research is to fulfil its potential as a contributor to impact, four considerations seem important:

1. *Asserting the place of qualitative SEH research in creating impact*: being clear in our own minds of the value and specific contributions that qualitative research can offer, and being able to present this case to others – and counter their resistance.
2. *Creating an impact-oriented research environment and culture* in the area of SEH qualitative research in which impact is valued, legitimate and prized as a research outcome.
3. *'Doing' impact through qualitative SEH research*: undertaking qualitative SEH research that has impact beyond the academy, through the 'pathway' process in which impact is addressed in the planning of research from its earliest conception.
4. *Shaping the machinery of impact evaluation*: ensuring qualitative SEH research is represented in the processes that shape the definition, mechanisms and evaluation of impact, from local faculty discussions within our own institutions, to national and transnational debates.

Of course, not all SEH qualitative research lends itself to impact. Although the impact agenda is universal, it is not applicable to every research study or programme. Funding agencies acknowledge this – RCUK, for example, expects the 'vast majority' of research proposals to include a detailed *Pathways to Impact* statement, but not all. (The 'few exceptions' are, however, required to fully justify the reasons why they have not). The suggestions that follow are not exhorting SEH researchers to wring impact from research where impact does not exist; rather, they aim to foster impact where it might occur, but perhaps has not yet.

Asserting the place of qualitative SEH research in creating impact

To engage effectively in the impact agenda, SEH researchers need to be certain themselves that qualitative research has its place – and be able to advocate this to others. This is especially important in multidisciplinary fields where researchers directly encounter contrasting paradigms, as in SEH research into sport, physical activity and health. This is a fertile area for impact-producing research given the prominence of physical activity in the global health debate. It is also an arena that *requires* a social science sensibility, most obviously to address the social determinants of health – the widely used framework for addressing the social structural processes that underpin health inequalities. Although long-established and globally recognised, the social determinants framework is persistently absent from the plethora of 'evidence-based' national physical activity guidelines (Kay, forthcoming) that have been informed primarily by biomedical research.

Research into physical activity and health does, however, often expose qualitative researchers to resistance rooted in deep paradigmatic differences. The hierarchy of evidence used within health and medical research reflects this (Figure 32.1). The hierarchy positions RCTs (randomised control/led trials) at its pinnacle as the 'gold standard' of research, immediately reducing the status of other forms of enquiry. None of the evidence categories in the hierarchy explicitly accommodate qualitative research; its highest category excludes it, and whether it might be located at 'lower' levels is not assured. This leaves qualitative research arguing 'from the bottom of the pyramid' for its value and inclusion (Lester & O'Reilly, 2015).

This is a difficult position from which to assert a strong case for the value of qualitative research. Veltri, Lim and Miller (2014) list eight 'crucial' contributions it offers:

1. A commitment to viewing (and sometimes explaining) phenomena from the perspective of those being studied; in effect, giving the subjects of research a 'voice'.
2. A reflexive awareness and consideration of the researcher's role and perspective.
3. The absence of methodological orthodoxy and the use of flexible (emergent) research strategies.
4. The use of non-standardised, semi-structured or unstructured methods that are sensitive to the social context of a study.
5. The setting of data collection and analysis into its context.
6. Methods that allow attention to be paid to emerging categories and theories rather than the sole reliance upon a priori concepts and ideas.
7. The development rather than the testing of hypotheses.
8. Explanation offered at the level of meaning or in terms of causality rather than the 'surface workings' of context-less 'laws' (Veltri *at al.*, p. 1).

The first of these crucial points – that qualitative research carries a *commitment* to viewing phenomena from the perspective of those being studied – deserves elaboration. It contrasts with the

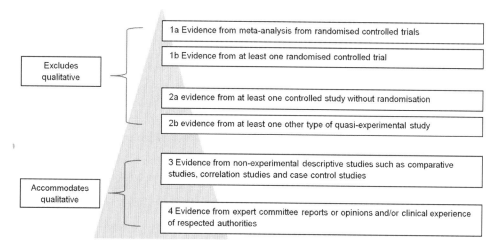

Figure 32.1   Hierarchy of evidence.

Source: Adapted from Lester and O'Reilly (2015).

positioning of biomedical researchers as 'expert' vis-à-vis their research 'subjects'. The current author was recently reminded of this by peer-review comments received on a study design for multidisciplinary physical activity research (Mansfield, Anokye, Fox-Rushby & Kay, 2015), in which a respected health behaviourist cautioned that there would be limited value in obtaining qualitative data about individuals' physical activity as 'people do not always have true insight into the causes of their behaviour, or how it might best be changed (e.g. Nisbett & Wilson, 1977)'. For qualitative researchers this statement is immensely problematic, in every way, for its dismissal of individuals' stories, its suggestion that a 'true' insight is available, and its presumption that this is accessible (only) through 'scientific' research.

To counter such standpoints, it can be useful for SEH researchers to draw on the use of qualitative research in cognate disciplines and areas of research. This may be more expedient than always arguing from first principles, and perhaps more persuasive than only referencing our own field. In health itself, there is growing recognition and demand for qualitative methods, which are now well-established as a component of research-method training in university first and postgraduate degree programmes (e.g. Tod & Hurst, 2014). In psychology, Bhati, Hoyt and Huffman (2014) note that many scholars believe the discipline is taking 'a qualitative turn', and cite diverse examples, from counselling, health, school, clinical, evaluation, sport and exercise and industrial-organisational (Bhati *et al.*, 2014, p. 98). In development studies – pertinent to sport for development and peace (SDP) researchers – responsive, reflexive qualitative methods are frequently in evidence, allowing researchers and evaluators to address cultural specificity, negotiate power relations and engage in coproduction of knowledge (e.g. Mcduie-Ra & Rees, 2010; Savedoff, Levine & Birdsall, 2006). There is also evidence of increased receptivity to qualitative methods in the emergence of resources offering guidance on the value and process of using qualitative data for practitioners, e.g. *How to use qualitative research evidence when making decisions about interventions* (Department of Health, State Government of Victoria, 2010); and *Using qualitative research to assess your impact* (New Philanthropy Capital/CLINKS, 2014; CLINKS is the membership body for charities working in criminal justice in England).

Within sport, qualitative elements are frequently an integral component of commissioned evaluations, which may surprise those not familiar with these evidence-oriented research designs. This applies across a wide swathe of activity, including projects to promote physical activity to children and adults in school (e.g. Hills & Croston, 2012) and community (e.g. Substance, 2009), and engage disaffected youth (Hills & Maitland, 2014). Qualitative components typically include case-study designs, qualitative interviews and focus groups, and in many cases, are a requirement made explicit in Invitation to Tender documents; this often also includes encouragement to use 'innovative' methods, including visual and online technologies (see Chapters 11 and 27). The need to work with 'vulnerable' targets groups has also facilitated the use of inclusive approaches, including in some cases the development of new methods or refinement of established ones (e.g. Fitzgerald, 2005).

Qualitative research is far from fully accepted, but the picture is not one of total exclusion. In health research, Lester and O'Reilly (2015) suggest qualitative researchers are in an 'interesting position, somewhere between acceptance and promotion'. SEH qualitative researchers similarly need to be equipped to advocate their case.

Creating an impact-oriented research environment and culture

The second requirement for fostering qualitative impact-oriented research in SEH is developing an academic environment in this subject area that respects and values it. Resistance to qualitative, impact-oriented research in sport, exercise and health does not only come from external sources; sometimes the enemy is within. SEH researchers would be deluding themselves to think that 'impact' is fully embraced throughout the qualitative community.

Internal critique and lack of support in institutional and subject area communities can be very immediate and constraining experiences. As Kass Gibson (Chapter 29) has noted, when researchers are more dismissive than knowledgeable about each other's work, their interactions can retrench polarised positions. In some cases this can go beyond discourse to translate into tangible effects on formal structures and processes. One simple example is the higher status often accorded peer-reviewed research papers in comparison to policy-related research reports. In the UK, in REF2014, this was addressed through formal guidance that all types of output would be treated equally, judged on content rather than type. The composition of subject-area assessment panels reflected this, with senior research users included in the membership of each. Panels were nonetheless still dominated by senior academics and many of those being assessed doubted that these would really approach 'a report' as potentially comparable to 'a paper'.

Many may, as Burawoy (2004, 2005) notoriously did, disdain 'applied' social science as the 'uncritical sale of knowledge'. But this is itself an uncritical standpoint, ignorant of the much more nuanced and constructive partnership researchers can achieve in such contexts (Shortall, 2012). Burawoy's dismissal also sits uneasily with the social justice orientation of the social sciences which, from their inception, have been committed to making positive social contributions. Academics who engage in work are not naive: undertaking qualitative research 'for impact', especially in partnership, is complex (e.g. Lindsey, Namukanga, Kakone & Grattan, 2012; Thomas & Hollinrake, 2014). Evaluators of sports programmes are only too aware that the inclusion of qualitative components in research designs is often driven by funders' hopes that these will capture human-interest 'stories' that can be used for promotional purposes. Researchers working with research users learn rapidly about the complexities and power relations involved in such endeavours.

Such criticisms also display ignorance about the academic and intellectual opportunities that impact-oriented research can offer. There is no inherent reason why such research should be a-theoretical or methodologically conservative, or compromise either academic freedom or integrity. An impact orientation does not mean that research is theoretically bankrupt; tenders for commissioned evaluations require their theoretical underpinning to be detailed, and larger studies may begin with a systematic or other literature review to distil relevant academic knowledge. Nor does an impact orientation mean abandoning grand theory; rather, it offers the challenge of connecting it more explicitly to the everyday (Golden & Earp, 2012). In the area of health behaviour and health inequalities, for example, many health psychologists wish to embrace the social science offerings pertaining to the structural processes influencing health, but struggle to translate these into meaningful concepts and practical guidance for policy and practice. Impact-oriented research can also offer opportunities to enhance qualitative research in SEH. Undertaking studies that directly engage with complex social issues provides access to samples with which SEH researchers might otherwise be unable to engage.

Lack of peer regard among SEH researchers can undermine work which is ideally suited to the impact agenda. Where this exists it they needs to be identified and addressed.

'Doing' impact through qualitative SEH research

Many academics are experienced in activities that are now classed as impact: e.g. work with policymakers, public engagement, and media activities. The current impact agenda is therefore not new but a shift in emphasis, as VanEvery commented in relation to the approach to impact in the Canadian Social Sciences and Humanities Research Council (SSHRC):

> It seems that the agency's objective is to encourage researchers to broaden their impact while recognising that any wider impact must rest on solid academic research, judged by peers, and developed through the normal channels of academic debate. In other words, they are starting where researchers are and nudging them in the direction being demanded.
>
> *(VanEvery, 2011)*

The direction now being demanded is a universal, deliberate orientation to impact, based on a planned approach.

For research that does have impact potential, the key questions to be addressed are:

1. Who is the impact for: e.g. the public, professionals, policymakers? Funding-council guidance emphasises the need to identify and actively engage relevant users of research and stakeholders at appropriate stages, and consider ways for the proposed research to meet these beneficiaries needs. VanEvery encourages researchers 'to consider appropriate audiences; to make sensible and feasible plans for reaching that audience (preferably based on sound knowledge of how they learn best); and to articulate the difference they think it will make to that specific audience' (VanEvery, 2011). The analysis of the REF2014 case studies identified 36 types of impact beneficiaries, among them the public (children, parents, families, women, consumers, workers, communities, volunteers), professions (engineers, lawyers, teachers, clinicians, curators, farmers), service users (patients, pupils, students, clients), organisations (schools, museums, unions, NHS, charities), business and industry (businesses, manufacturers, banks), knowledge producers (consultants, journalists, writers), political organisations and actors (governments, ministers, policymakers, councils), and animals (King's College London and Digital Science, 2015).

2. What sort of impact is it – e.g. evidence for policymakers; training resources for service deliverers? Greenhalgh and Fahy (2015) identified 14 main impacts in the REF2014 community-based health sciences impact case studies, including: influencing new or revised health guidelines; informing a policy change; changing clinical or public health practice; improving health outcomes (reduced morbidity, mortality, improved quality of life) and/ or economic benefit (to public sector, to industry), informing legal or regulatory change; and promoting vigorous public debate.

3. How is the impact going to occur? Both the HEFCE evaluation report and Greenhalgh and Fahy's more focused analysis of the community health sciences provide useful guidance about the activities and 'impact pathways' through which impact was achieved in the case studies submitted to REF2014. Each comments on the complexity and diversity of these processes, with the HEFCE evaluation pointing to 3,709 unique pathways (across >6,700 cases). As before, it is Greenhalgh and Fahy who raise issues pertinent to qualitative researchers: the danger of underplaying complexity, the long timescale over which impact occurs, and the indirect and unintended ways in which it might do so. The European Research Council's (ERC) EURECIA project captured this in an empirically based conceptualization that emanated from its assessment of the impact of the ERC's own funding schemes on the wider research landscape:

> It is analytically useful to differentiate between four types of impact: *'straight runs'* are intended and expected; *'long shots'* are intended but not expected; *'collateral'*

are the effects that are unintended but expected; and *'accidentals'* are neither intended not expected.

(EURECIA Team, 2012, p. 3)

The available data suggest that there are multiple types of beneficiary available to SEH researchers, and many forms of impact that could be valuable to them. What is less certain is that the type of impact generated would be captured under current systems. It is not enough for SEH researchers to be confident that their research can have impact: they must also ensure that appropriate systems are in place to recognise it.

Shaping the machinery of impact evaluation

Arrangements surrounding 'impact' could offer opportunities to qualitative researchers in SEH, but they also pose some challenges. At the individual level it is important to confront obstacles where and when these occur, and open up dialogue with other paradigms. There are nonetheless limits to what can be achieved through individual effort if the processes for pursuing the impact agenda evaluating it are inimical. Qualitative researchers also need to be part of the policy debate that shapes how impact is defined, recorded and evaluated.

Conclusion

SEH researchers in most countries cannot avoid the impact agenda: international trends in public funding require accountability for public investment. In the UK 'impact' is set to gain in significance, rising from 20% to 25% of the overall rating in the next national research assessment. Researchers engaged in qualitative enquiry into sport, exercise and health will need to demonstrate the impact of their research beyond academia. But not all areas of sport, exercise and health research lend themselves to impact beyond academia, and there is little to be gained in trying to graft impact on to research activity which is not suited to it. Even within 'impact' topics, some activities – work to develop theory or method – will not contribute directly to impact outside academia, but may be part of a wider body of work that does. In contrast, many forms of research that qualitative researchers engage in – e.g. studies that focus on a topical social issue, funded by a policy actor, involving partnership with beneficiaries – have favourable conditions for impact built in. This is where it will be productive to concentrate most effort.

References

Abel-Smith, B. & Townsend, P. (1965). *The poor and the poorest: A new analysis of the Ministry of Labour's family expenditure surveys of 1953–54 and 1960*. London: Bell.

Australian Government. (2015). *Measuring impact and engagement in university research*. National Innovation and Science Agenda Factsheet 16. Retrieved 14 January, 2016, from http://www.innovation.gov.au/page/measuring-impact-and-engagement-university-research.

Bhati, K. S., Hoyt, W. T. & Huffman, K. L. (2014). Integration or assimilation? Locating qualitative research in psychology. *Qualitative Research in Psychology, 11*(1), 98–114. doi: 10.1080/14780887.2013.772684.

Bornmann, L. (2012). Measuring the societal impact of research. *EMBO reports 13*, 673–676. doi: 10.1038/embor.2012.99.

Burawoy, M. (2004). Public sociology: Contradictions, dilemmas and possibilities. *Social Forces, 82*, 1603–18.

Burawoy, M. (2005). 2004 Presidential address: For public sociology. *American Sociological Review, 70*, 4–28.

Denzin, N. K. (2009). The elephant in the living room: Or extending the conversation about the politics of evidence. *Qualitative Research, 9*(2), 139–160.

Department of Health, State Government of Victoria. (2010). How to use qualitative research evidence when making decisions about interventions. Melbourne: State Government of Victoria. Retrieved 24 January, 2016 from: http://www.health.vic.gov.au/health promotion/evidence_evaluation/cdp_tools.htm.

EURECIA Team. (2012). *Understanding and assessing the impact and outcomes of the ERC and its funding schemes final synthesis report.* Brussels: European Research Council Executive Agency.

Fitzgerald, H. (2005). Still feeling like a spare piece of luggage? Embodied experiences of (dis)ability in physical education and school sport. *Physical Education and Sport Pedagogy, 10*(1), 41–59.

Garbarino, S. & Holland, J. (2009). *Quantitative and qualitative methods in impact evaluation and measuring results.* Research Service of the Governance and Social Development Resource Centre (GSDRC). Retrieved 9 January, 2016, from http://www.gsdrc.org/publications/quantitative-and-qualitative-methods-in-impact-evaluation-and-measuring-results-3/.

Garside, R. (2014). Should we appraise the quality of qualitative research reports for systematic reviews, and if so, how? *Innovation: The European Journal of Social Science Research, 27*(1), 67–79. doi: 10.1080/13511610.2013.777270.

Golden, S.D. & Earp, J.A. (2012). Social ecological approaches to individuals and their contexts: Twenty years of health education and behavior health promotion interventions. *Health Education and Behavior, 39*(3), 364–372. doi: 10.1177/1090198111418634.

Greenhalgh, T. & Fahy, N. (2015). Research impact in the community-based health sciences: An analysis of 162 case studies from the 2014 UK Research Excellence Framework. *BMC Medicine, 13*, 232. DOI 10.1186/s12916-015-0467-4.

Guyatt, G.H., Sackett, D.L., Sinclair, J.C., Hayward, R., Cook, D.J. & Cook, R.J. (1995). *Users' guides to the medical literature. IX. A method for grading health care recommendations. JAMA, 274,* 1800–1804.

HEFCE (Higher Education Funding Council for England). (2012). *2014 REF: Assessment framework and guidance on submissions.* London: HEFCE.

Hills, L. & Maitland, A. (2014). Research-based knowledge utilization in a community sport evaluation: A case study. *International Journal of Public Sector Management, 27*(2), 165–172.

Hills, L. A. & Croston, A. (2012). It should be better all together: Exploring strategies for 'undoing' gender in coeducational physical education. *Sport Education and Society, 17*(5), 591–605. doi: 10.1080/13573322.2011.553215.

Jabareen,Y.T. & Vilkomerson, R. (2014). Public policy in divided societies: The role of policy institutes in advancing marginalized groups. *Innovation: The European Journal of Social Science Research, 27*(1), 46–66. doi: 10.1080/13511610.2013.777274.

Kay, T. A. (forthcoming). Bodies of knowledge: Connecting the evidence bases on physical activity and health inequalities. *International Journal of Sport Policy and Sport Politics.*

King's College London and Digital Science. (2015). *The nature, scale and beneficiaries of research impact: An initial analysis of Research Excellence Framework (REF) 2014 impact case studies.* Bristol: HEFCE.

Lester, J. & O'Reilly, M. (2015). Is evidence-based practice a threat to the progress of the qualitative community? Arguments from the bottom of the pyramid. *Qualitative Inquiry, 21*(7), 628–632. doi: 10.1177/1077800414563808.

Lindsey, I., Namukanga, A., Kakone, G. & Grattan, A. (2010). 'Adventures in research': Enabling community impact through sport for development research. *Leisure Studies Association Newsletter, No. 85,* 53–57.

Mansfield, L., Anokye, N., Fox-Rushby, J. & Kay, T. (2015). The Health and Sport Engagement (HASE) Intervention and Evaluation Project: Protocol for the design, outcome, process and economic evaluation of a complex community sport intervention to increase levels of physical activity. *BMJ Open, 5*(10), pp. e009276–e009276. doi: 10.1136/bmjopen-2015-009276.

Manville, C. (2014). Measuring impact: How Australia and the UK are tackling research assessment. *Guardian* online, Sunday, 7 December, 2014. Retrieved 13 January, 2016, from http://www.theguardian.com/higher-education-network/2014/dec/07/research-excellence-framework-2014-measuring-impact-australia-uk-universities-assessment.

Manville, C., Morgan Jones, M., Frearson, M., Castle-Clarke, S., Henham, M.-L., Gunashekar, S. & Grant, J. (2015b). *Evaluation of submission preparation for impact assessment REF 2014: Findings and observations.* Santa Monica, CA: RAND Corporation. RR-727-HEFCE.

Manville, C., Morgan Jones, M., Henham, M.-L., Castle-Clarke, S., Frearson, M., Gunashekar, S. & Grant, J. (2015a). *Evaluation of submission preparation for impact assessment REF 2014: Approach and evidence.* Santa Monica, CA: RAND Corporation. RR-7276-HEFCE.

Mcduie-Ra, D. & Rees, J. (2010). Religious actors, civil society and the development agenda: The dynamics of inclusion and exclusion. *Journal of International Development, 22*, 20–36.

Morgan Jones, M., Castle-Clarke, S., Manville, C., Gunashekar, S. & Grant, J. (2013). *Assessing research impact: An international review of the Excellence in Innovation for Australia Trial.* Santa Monica, CA: RAND Corporation. RR-278-ATN. Available at: http://www.rand.org/pubs/research_reports/RR278.

Morse, J. (2006). The politics of evidence. *Qualitative Health Research, 16*(3), 395–404. doi: 10.1177/1049 732305285482.

Mosse, D. (2001). People's knowledge, participation and patronage: Operations and representations in rural development. In B. Cooke & U. Kothari (Eds.), *Participation: The new tyranny* (pp. 94–113). London: Zed Books.

New Philanthropy Capital/CLINKS. (2014). *Improving evidence: Using qualitative research to assess your impact.* Retrieved on 22 January, 2016 from: http://www.clinks.org/sites/default/files/QualGuidanceFinal.pdf.

Nisbett, R. & Wilson, T. (1977). Telling more than we can know: Verbal reports on mental processes. *Psychological Review, 84*, 231–259.

Otten, J.J., Dodson, E.A., Fleischhacker, S., Siddiqi, S. & Quinn, E.L. (2015). Getting research to the policy table: A qualitative study with public health researchers on engaging with policymakers. *Preventing Chronic Disease, 12*, 140546. doi: http://dx.doi.org/10.5888/pcd12.140546.

Platt, J. (1971). Variations in answers to different questions on perceptions of social class. *The Sociological Review, 19*(3), 409–419.

Savedoff, W., Levine, R., & Birdsall, N. (2006). When will we ever learn? *Improving lives through impact evaluation report of the Evaluation Gap Working Group.* Washington, DC: Center for Global Development.

Schinke, R., Smith, B., & McGannon, K.R. (2013). Pathways for community research in sport and physical activity: Criteria for consideration. *Qualitative Research in Sport, Exercise and Health, 5*, 460–468.

Shortall, S. (2012). *The role of subjectivity and knowledge power struggles in the formation of public policy sociology, 47*(6), 1088–1103. doi: 10.1177/0038038512454950.

Substance. (2009). *Positive Futures: Working for us.* London: Catch 22.

Thomas, W. & Hollinrake, S. (2014). Policy-makers, researchers and service users: Resolving the tensions and dilemmas of working together. *Innovation: The European Journal of Social Science Research, 27*(1), 31–45. doi: 10.1080/13511610.2013.777276.

Tod, A. M. & Hurst, J. (2014). *Health and inequality: Applying public health research to policy and practice.* London: Routledge.

VanEvery, J. (2011). The impact agenda in Canada: How researchers and research councils have found an impact measure they are happy with. Retrieved 19 January, 2016, from http://blogs.lse.ac.uk/impactofsocialsciences/2011/12/07/canada-case-study-research-impact/.

Veltri, G. A., Lim, J. & Miller, R. (2014). More than meets the eye: The contribution of qualitative research to evidence-based policy-making. *Innovation: The European Journal of Social Science Research, 27*(1), 1–4. doi: 10.1080/13511610.2013.806211.

Young, M. & Willmott, P. (1973). *The symmetrical family: A study of work and leisure in the London region.* London: Routledge and Kegan Paul.

Young, M. & Willmott, P. (1957). *Family and kinship in East London.* London: Routledge and Kegan Paul.

33

MOVING BETWEEN WORLDVIEWS

Indigenous physical cultures through Indigenous eyes

Moss E. Norman and Michael A. Hart

By now most readers interested in socially just qualitative research are familiar with Linda Tuhiwai Smith's (1999, p. 1) famous declaration that, from the perspective of the colonized, "'research' is inextricably linked to European imperialism and colonialism." The question remains, however, has anything changed since Smith first wrote these words almost two decades ago? In the Canadian context, the situation appears to have changed little, as Natan Obed, director of the Department of Social and Cultural Development for Nunavut Tunngavik, explains that "health research as it happens in our communities is one of the last vestiges of colonialism" (Vogel, 2015, p. 316). Certainly, it is the case that non-Indigenous researchers continue to be the primary drivers of Indigenous health research in Canada (Vogel, 2015), but perhaps even more troubling than *who* is doing the research is *how* they are doing it. Globally, Indigenous health research – including research on physical activity, exercise, and sport – continues to be rooted in Western research epistemologies, which means that, to put it rather bluntly, Indigenous health and movement continues to be seen through imperial eyes. The remainder of this chapter is going to build a case that, when it comes to Indigenous physical cultures,[1] research-as-usual is insufficient, and potentially deleterious (see also Chapters 8 and 34). We suggest that Indigenous research methodologies offer the potential to not only enrich Western methodologies (Wilson, 2008), but also enable the emergence of different, more relevant, and empowering knowledges for Indigenous peoples, their communities, and their nations. This is because when we limit our understandings of movement to Western frameworks, we foreclose other ways of moving, being moved, and experiencing movement, as well as the other worlds that such movements engender.

Before going further, we would like to address two caveats. First, we are not interested in drawing battle lines between Western and Indigenous frameworks, but rather offer "paradigm proliferation" (Lather, 2006) as a strategy for creatively integrating Western and Indigenous paradigms in producing place-specific constructs, methods, and theories (Chilisa, 2012). Indeed, the authors of this chapter reflect this creative integration of paradigms. Moss is a white settler scholar well versed in Western research paradigms, while Michael is an Indigenous scholar, who has spent his career working to reclaim and integrate Cree knowledge systems into an institutional context that could, at best, be described as "chilly" to such perspectives (see Hart, 2009, 2010). Despite working together on this chapter and other projects, it is crucial to acknowledge that our relationship is not without power imbalances. This is because, as Cordova suggests, too often Indigenous knowledges and experiences are only considered legitimate as far as they are "granted validity by the European researcher" (Moore *et al.*, 2007, p. 164) and, although we do not have space to speak to this more here, this imbalance is important to keep in mind. Second, we use Indigenous as a term that is "inclusive to all first peoples – unique in [their] cultures – but common in . . . experiences of colonialism" (Wilson, 2008, p. 16). Importantly, we want to avoid sweeping pan-Indigenous assumptions by recognizing the tribally specific differences across Indigenous peoples globally, but we also acknowledge that there are some similarities in worldviews (Chilisa, 2012), as we outline below. With these caveats in mind, we now consider why an Indigenous research paradigm is important to Indigenous physical cultural ecologies, as well as briefly overviewing some of the foundational philosophies of such a paradigm.

Why Indigenous methodologies?

According to Paraschak (1998), "Retaining control over one's physical culture, including its representations, is a very important part of cultural survival and self-determination" (p. 121). It is increasingly recognized that physical culture occupies a prominent position in "understandings of Aboriginal history, culture, identity, politics, and health" (Forsyth & Giles, 2013, p. 6). However, within currently dominant health, sport and physical activity research frameworks, Indigenous physical cultures are too often severed from their complex historical, sociocultural and place-specific ecologies and reduced to a Western worldview that positions Indigeneity as "deficit" (Hokowhitu, 2014). Statistics pointing to the Indigenous "lag" in health, economic, social and educational status are determined through comparisons against the non-Indigenous norm (Walter & Andersen, 2013), while the common factors driving poor health outcomes are ignored; namely, the distribution of power that privileges non-Indigenous people, perspectives and practices and the control exercised over Indigenous peoples through Western "solutions" (Hart & Lavallee, 2015). Within the North-American context, this is perhaps most readily apparent in population statistics that position Indigenous peoples – children and youth, in particular – as "at risk" of physical inactivity, obesity, and poor health, especially diabetes. Indeed, almost every research design – regardless of paradigm – on Indigenous health and physical activity uses Indigenous health pathology as justification for intervening into the everyday lives of Indigenous people and their communities (Hokowhitu, 2014). Framing health and physical activity research in terms of deficit not only recuperates a long-standing developmental discourse rooted in the modernist imperative to "close the gap" between Indigenous and non-Indigenous peoples. Even more perniciously such research powerfully influences how Indigenous people come to see and understand themselves generally (Walter & Andersen, 2013), and their physical cultural practices more specifically, by dis-placing culturally specific Indigenous worldviews and replacing them with universal health abstractions.

Given the current research landscape, the question for us is how can Indigenous physical cultures be approached in a manner that fosters and reclaims physical culture as a site of cultural growth and self-determination? Recognizing that Indigenous physical cultures are historically and socially contested cultural engagements, especially so given that Euro-Western sporting practices have been deployed in the service of colonialism (Forsyth & Giles, 2013), research methodologies that incorporate a decolonizing, social-justice oriented agenda are absolutely imperative, but not sufficient (Chilisa, 2012; Smith, 1999). Rather, in order to access the complexity of the physical cultural ecologies of Indigenous peoples, "wholly and inherently Indigenous methodologies" (Kovach, 2009, p. 13) represent the next step.

An Indigenous research paradigm

According to Martin and Mirraboopa (2003), Indigenous research is entering the Indigenist Phase. This phase is characterized by a "radical Indigenism" (Garroutte, 2003) that moves beyond research *on* Indigenous people and their cultural knowledges towards research that is rooted in the restorative and "respectful use of [Indigenous cultural] knowledge systems" (Kovach, 2009, p. 12). This distinction is relevant to sport studies because while there is a burgeoning body of research on Indigenous physical cultures, both in Canada and worldwide, there are relatively few studies that utilize an Indigenous framework (Hokowhitu, 2014). This scarcity is potentially dangerous, as Michael has explained elsewhere:

> When we choose *how* we are going to come to know, meaning when we pick a research methodology, we are privileging particular ways-of-being in the world. When we give this choice little thought, the likelihood is high that we will unconsciously contribute to colonial oppression by bringing non-Indigenous ways-of-being into our relationships with Indigenous peoples and expecting them to at least accommodate our position [which will] likely entrench non-Indigenous perspectives of life.
>
> *(Hart, 2009, p. 168)*

This means that when we fix our conceptualization of movement within a Western frame we foreclose alternative and Indigenous ways of moving and knowing. In the remainder of this chapter we briefly overview three distinct aspects of Indigenous ways of knowing, and suggest that these differences have implications for how we come to know Indigenous physical cultures.

Relationality: Central to an Indigenous research paradigm is that knowledge is relational (Goulet & Goulet, 2014; Hart, 2009, 2010; Wilson, 2008). Crucially, the idea of knowledge emerging relationally moves beyond the self as being *in* relationship with other people and the world, towards an understanding that the self is constituted *in and through* the relationships that we hold (Lambert, 2014; Wilson, 2008). While a relational understanding of knowledge shares similarities with some Western frameworks, where "truth" is understood to be multiple, contextually specific and always in process (Hart, 2009), an Indigenous paradigm differs with respect to which relations matter to the knowledge constructed. For example, many post-structural theories adopt – whether knowingly or not – a human-centric disposition, where human actors are placed at the center of meaning (Grande, 2008), while an Indigenous paradigm approaches knowledge as "shared with all creation," including with "the animals, with the plants, with the earth," and with the "cosmos" (Wilson, 2008, p. 56). Indeed, relationality is the foundation of Indigenous methodologies, where knowledge is rooted in place- and culturally specific contexts, and all relations are equally respected, with no one relation being elevated above another (Hart, 2009, 2010).

Land: Indigenous "methodologies are bound to place" (Kovach, 2009, p. 52), meaning that, as Lambert eloquently explains, "stories and experiences emanate from generations of Indigenous people watching and living in Place" (2014, p. 27). This is not to say Indigenous knowledges are fixed and unchanging, but rather to suggest that knowledge comes from *some place*, and that it evolves in relation to that place. From this perspective, knowledge cannot transcend place and the land from which it emerges, as Kovach (2009, p. 61) explains of her own Plains Cree worldview: "what we know flows through us from the 'echo of generations,' and our knowledges cannot be universalized because they arise from our experience with places." This place-specific, land-based way of knowing has implications for how we come to know Indigenous physical cultures. Therefore, research methodologies that are respectful and relationally accountable to the Indigenous knowledge systems they are working with will acknowledge that movement is always *emplaced*. This means that Indigenous identities and philosophies are *rooted* in the land, which contrasts sharply with contemporary Western social theory, which has an almost fetishistic relationship with metaphors of placelessness and de-territorialization (Grande, 2008). Here, learning and knowing happen through moving across the land and feeling, smelling, tasting, seeing, and hearing the lessons of the Earth, both as an immediate experience, and through intergenerational ancestral knowledges.

Spirituality: Both the empirical and the more-than-empirical are crucial to an Indigenous worldview. For the Mi'kmaq, this balanced perspective on knowledge is described as "two-eyed seeing," where "one eye is strictly human, relating to [the . . . ability of] Indigenous humans to see and think about things rationally" (Lambert, 2014, p. 8). The other eye, however, is "concerned with hearing, seeing, and learning from the Other, whatever that might be" (Lambert, 2014, p. 9). While Western research paradigms are accustomed to empirical ways of knowing, for non-Western paradigms the "extra-intellectual" (Wilson, 2008, p. 111) or the more-than-empirical domains are fundamental to holistic ways of knowing. In keeping with a relational worldview, the spiritual or metaphysical is not separate from the physical or empirical; rather the two are interconnected, meaning that accessing the metaphysical realm is central to knowing the physical. Admittedly, the spiritual aspect of Indigenous methodologies will make researchers trained in the Western academy uncomfortable, if not outright dismissive, as words like "ceremony," "sacred," "spirit" and techniques such as dreaming are typically relegated to the other side of Western rationality. In this way, Indigenous spirituality represents a crucial site of resistance and decolonization:

> Concepts of spirituality . . . are critical sites of resistance for Indigenous peoples. The values, attitudes, concepts and language embedded in beliefs about spirituality represent . . . the clearest contrast and mark of difference between Indigenous peoples and the West. It is one of the few parts of ourselves which the West cannot decipher, cannot understand and cannot control . . . yet.
>
> *(Smith, 1999, p. 13)*

Relationality, connection to the land, and spiritual ways of knowing represent only three, albeit important, aspects of an Indigenous worldview that, while not easily reconciled into Western worldviews, are nonetheless fundamental to radically Indigenous methodologies (Garroutte, 2003).

Discussion

Admittedly, our discussion here has not been exhaustive, nor should it be read as a "how-to-guide" for Indigenous methodologies. Rather, we argued that Western-based, research-as-usual approaches to Indigenous physical cultures, including well-intentioned, social-justice-oriented approaches, are important but not sufficient in and of themselves. Within the Indigenist Phase research on physical cultures needs to be emplaced, meaning that it starts in the community, regardless of whether it is urban or remote, and it needs to move towards using tribally specific knowledge systems. This may make many readers uncomfortable, and such discomfort is certainly true in the case of Moss, but for Michael acknowledging and fostering Indigenous worldviews in the research process not only feels more comfortable, but also feels a little bit more like home. And this may be precisely the point – if we are to take seriously the community-based principle of working *with* as opposed to *for* Indigenous communities, surely this includes accepting the discomfort that comes with working across worldviews, and acknowledging and respecting the distinct tribally specific knowledges of others. By no means is this an easy task, but it is a responsibility that should not fall to Indigenous scholars alone. In paraphrasing Marlene

Brandt-Castellano, Kovach (2009, p. 156) writes that "the challenge and responsibility for Indigenous research lie with us all" and that in order to successfully address this challenge it will require that "Indigenous people . . . suspend their distrust and non-Indigenous people . . . suspend their disbelief." Indeed, if Indigenous and settler scholars can suspend distrust and disbelief, and push back the "oppressive veil" of Western worldviews, allowing Indigenous ways of learning, moving, feeling, and knowing to emerge, than it is possible that the "rivers will sing, ghosts will appear and the earth will move in retaliation" (Hokowhitu, 2014, p. 45).

Note

1 For us, physical culture includes commonly held conceptions of human movement such as sport, exercise and physical activity, as well as community-specific meanings that, for the Cree we are working with, include land-based activities such as fishing, hunting, medicine picking, and gardening.

References

Chilisa, B. (2012). *Indigenous research methodologies*. Los Angeles, CA: Sage.

Forsyth, J. & Giles, A. (2013). *Aboriginal Peoples and sport in Canada: Historical foundations and contemporary issues*. Toronto, ON: UBC Press.

Garroutte, E. M. (2003). *Real Indians: Identity and the survival of Native America*. Berkley, CA: University of California Press.

Goulet, L. M. & Goulet, K. N. (2014). *Teaching each other: Nehinuw concepts and Indigenous pedagogies*. Vancouver, BC: UBC Press.

Grande, S. (2008). Red Pedagogy: The un-methodology. In N. K. Denzin, Y. S. Lincoln, & L. T. Smith (Eds.), *Handbook of critical and Indigenous methodologies* (pp. 233–254). Los Angeles, CA: Sage.

Hart, M. A. (2010). Indigenous worldviews, knowledge, and research: The development of an Indigenous research paradigm. *Journal of Indigenous Voices in Social Work, 1*(1), 1–16.

Hart, M. A. (2009). For Indigenous people, by Indigenous people, with Indigenous people: Towards an Indigenist research paradigm. In R. Sinclair, M. A. Hart, & G. Bruyere (Eds.), *Wicihitowin: Aboriginal social work in Canada* (pp. 153–169). Winnipeg, MB: Fernwood.

Hart, M. A. & Lavallee, B. (2015). Colonization, racism, social exclusion, and Indigenous health. In L. Fernandez, S. MacKinnon, & J. Silver (Eds.), *The social determinants of health in Manitoba* (2nd ed., pp. 145–160). Winnipeg: The Canadian Centre for Policy Alternatives Manitoba Office.

Hokowhitu, B. (2014). If you're not healthy, then what are you? Healthism, colonial disease and body-logic. In K. Fitzpatrick & R. Tinning (Eds.), *Health education: Critical perspectives* (pp. 31–47). New York, NY: Routledge.

Kovach, M. (2009). *Indigenous methodologies: Characteristics, conversations, and contexts*. Toronto, ON: University of Toronto Press.

Lambert, L. (2014). *Research for Indigenous survival: Indigenous research methodologies in the behavioral sciences*. Lincoln, NE: Nebraska University Press.

Lather, P. (2006). Paradigm proliferation as a good thing to think with: Teaching research in education as a wild profusion. *International Journal of Qualitative Studies in Education, 19*(1), 35–57.

Martin, K. & Mirraboopa, B. (2003). Ways of knowing, being and doing: A theoretical framework and methods for Indigenous and Indigenist research. *Journal of Australian Studies, 27*(76), 203–214.

Moore, K. D., Peters, K., Jojola, T., Lacy, A., & Cordova, V. F. (2007). *How it is: The Native American philosophy of V. F. Cordova*. Tuscon, AZ: University of Arizona Press.

Paraschak, V. (1998). "Reasonable amusements": Connecting the stands of physical culture in Native lives. *Sport History Review, 29*, 121–131.

Smith, L. T. (1999). *Decolonizing methodologies: Research and Indigenous Peoples*. New York, NY: Zed Books.

Vogel, L. (2015). The new ethics of Aboriginal health research. *Canadian Medical Association Journal, 187*(5), 316–317.

Walter, M. & Andersen, C. (2013). *Indigenous statistics: A qualitative research methodology*. Walnut Creek, CA: Left Coast Press.

Wilson, S. (2008). *Research is Ceremony: Indigenous research methods*. Winnipeg, MB: Fernwood.

PART VI

Future visions

34

THINKING ABOUT THE FUTURE

Challenges and possibilities

Tara-Leigh McHugh

Research in the area of sport and exercise psychology has seen great advances in the past few decades. Researchers are continuing to push ahead this field of study by challenging traditional or postpositivist research approaches (see Chapters 1 and 10) with qualitative forms of inquiry that incorporate innovate and engaging processes of knowledge generation. Qualitative research in sport and exercise psychology has supported in-depth understandings of complex phenomena by highlighting multiple meanings and the lived experiences of individuals. As such, qualitative inquiry has been recognized, for some time, "as a legitimate area of scholarship within the sport and exercise sciences" (Smith & Gilbourne, 2009, p. 1). Nevertheless, when compared to the plethora of research conducted from a more postpositivist perspective, qualitative inquiry and participatory research approaches in particular are still relatively rare. Participatory research is uniquely situated as a process that can generate unique knowledge, while at the same time resulting in practical outcomes for participants. Nevertheless, participatory research approaches have yet to reach their full potential within sport and exercise psychology. I begin this chapter with a brief description of participatory research approaches and the resistance to such inquiry within sport and exercise psychology. I then outline some of the inherent characteristics of participatory research that position this form of inquiry as a *relevant* and *necessary* approach for furthering understandings in our field.

Participatory research, including community-based participatory research (CBPR) and participatory action research (PAR) (see also Chapters 7, 8, and 33), are collaborative approaches that are committed explicitly to research that will benefit the participants through some form of intervention, or by acting on the results to inform change (Israel, Schulz, Parker, & Becker, 1998; Kemmis & McTaggart, 2008). Through participatory approaches researchers strive to close the gap between knowledge generation and application. Such participatory and community-based research approaches are typically guided by critical and constructionist perspectives that seek to address some of the criticisms related to postpositivist research approaches (Harrison, MacGibbon, & Morton, 2001; Israel *et al.*, 1998). Participatory research approaches emerged, and continue to be used, in response to the inadequacy of postpositivist research to provide insight into the social and cultural issues that are deeply embedded in human experiences. For example, Schinke, McGannon, Watson, and Busanich (2013) provided a detailed overview of the necessary transformation of a sport research project from an "approach steeped in post-positivism" to a CBPR approach. Their research with an Aboriginal community demonstrated that a participatory approach was essential to enhancing understandings and developing a meaningful and enduring sport development project. My personal commitment to CBPR is also founded on the belief that by building on the expertise and strengths within communities we can deepen understandings of complex phenomena and experiences, and also challenge the assumptions that currently limit understandings in sport and exercise psychology. For example, Smith, Findlay, and Crompton (2010) have argued that Westernized definitions of sport have likely limited sport and exercise research that has included Aboriginal peoples. In response to this critical acknowledgment, my research partners and I engaged in a participatory research project to draw upon the experiential knowledge of Aboriginal youth, to provide necessary understandings of the diverse meanings of sport (McHugh, Coppola, & Sinclair, 2013). My commitment to participatory research, and CBPR more specifically, is also driven by the opportunities it presents to cocreate sport programs and research agendas that are relevant to the populations in which sport and exercise psychology researchers work (e.g., McHugh, Kingsley, & Coppola, 2013).

Despite the extraordinary potential for participatory research to transform theory and practice (Kemmis & McTaggart, 2008), my personal experiences as a researcher committed to CBPR provide but a small glimpse into the resistance that has likely slowed down the trajectory of participatory and collaborative approaches as legitimate forms of research within sport and exercise psychology. As a graduate student I gave a presentation at a national sport and exercise psychology conference about the ways in which participatory research, which is typically informed by feminist and other critical research perspectives, could support the advancement of research in our field. I vividly remember being approached by a senior researcher after this presentation and told that I should not "mix sport and exercise with feminism." I am confident that this comment emerged from what was believed to be helpful advice to a novice researcher from a seasoned expert guided by a postpositivist perspective. It is relatively well understood that research in sport and exercise psychology has been dominated by postpositivist research approaches, despite the recognition (e.g., Smith, 2010) that postpositivist research does not typically account for the emotional, contextual, and situational nature of experiences. Unfortunately, such biases towards postpositivist research approaches are not something of the past, nor are they restricted to sport and exercise psychology. Just recently, 76 senior researchers from 11 countries and various disciplines invited the editors of the *British Medical Journal* to reconsider their ongoing tradition and policy of rejecting qualitative research on the grounds that such research lacks "practical value" and is of "low priority" (Greenhalgh *et al.*, 2016). My personal experiences, combined with the unfortunate continued resistance towards qualitative and participatory forms of inquiry, serve as an impetus to my commitment in defining participatory research as a relevant and necessary form of inquiry for advancing research in the field of sport and exercise psychology.

Participatory research approaches have a number of defining features that serve to advance research in sport and exercise sciences, and in this chapter I focus on two specific characteristics. First, the critical and constructionist perspectives that guide many participatory research approaches support a necessary inclusion of underrepresented samples in sport and exercise research. Such perspectives acknowledge that multiple realities are constructed and influenced by social, cultural, ethnic, and gender factors. Through participatory approaches researchers seek to understand the distinct and important experiential knowledge of marginalized populations (Frisby, Reid, Millar, & Hoeber, 2005). It is necessary to include participants from diverse populations if we are to deepen understandings of phenomena and experiences that are studied within sport and exercise psychology. Henrich, Heine, and Norenzayan (2010) argued that behavioral scientists regularly make broad claims about human behavior from research that draws on samples from unrepresentative populations. They described how samples are typically drawn from Western populations even though Westerners emerge as "unusual-frequent global outliers-on several key dimensions" (p. 74), which are often studied by behavioral research-ers. Arguably, research in sport and exercise psychology also has a trend of including Western populations, and has not adequately included or optimized on the experiences of diverse popu-lations. As argued by Messner and Musto (2014), issues of culture and race present a "fascinating blank slate" for sport researchers (p. 114). Researchers (e.g., Balish *et al.*, 2014; McPherson, 1984) have been calling for more studies that examine how culture, race, and ethnicity account for differences that have been observed when studying phenomena within sport and exercise psychology. Such suggestions for future research directions have been occurring for decades, yet research in sport and exercise psychology still has a trend towards including easy-to-access populations.

It is important to note that the populations that have traditionally been underrepresented in sport and exercise psychology research are often at the *forefront* of participatory research approaches. Aboriginal populations in Canada, for example, have generally been overlooked in sport and exercise psychology research. However, participatory research approaches (e.g., McHugh, Coppola, Holt, & Andersen, 2015; Schinke *et al.*, 2013) have provided a mutu-ally beneficial, respectful, and relevant framework for engaging Aboriginal peoples in sport and exercise research. Participatory research has also been used to understand and transform physical activity participation among teenage girls from a disadvantaged urban school (Enright & O'Sullivan, 2012), to explore the physical activity of young Muslim women (Berger & Peerson, 2009), and to improve access to fitness and recreation facilities for people with disabilities (Riley, Rimmer, Wang, & Schiller, 2008). By including populations that represent the diversity of the world in which we live, sport and exercise psychology researchers have an extraordinary oppor-tunity to not only deepen theoretical understandings of complex phenomena, but to inform the development of relevant sport practices for all individuals.

The collaborative process of knowledge generation that is inherent in participatory research is the second characteristic that I propose as necessary for advancing research in sport and exercise psychology. CBPR and various other participatory approaches seek to engage people and communities in all phases of the research process, including the identification of relevant methods of data generation (Israel *et al.*, 1998). Such methods of data generation are often innovative and novel processes, which provide a unique opportunity for highlighting experi-ences and understanding phenomena within sport and exercise psychology. Photovoice – often also called autophotography (see also Chapter 11) – for instance, is a participatory approach that has the potential to generate knowledge through photographs and personal nar-ratives (Wang & Burris, 1997). By drawing upon participatory and visual approaches, research-ers move beyond the assumption that knowledge must be generated and communicated via spoken words. Smith and Caddick (2012) described how visual methods, including the use of photographs, provide participants with the opportunity to "show" rather than just "tell" their experiences. They argued that such visual images support the ability to generate layered mean-ings, subsequently broadening understandings of complex phenomena and experiences within sport and exercise research.

Photovoice has been used to better understand youth experiences and positive youth development in sport (Strachan & Davies, 2015). Strachan and Davies (2015) described how this visual method not only forced them to challenge their own assumptions about high-performance and sport-camp contexts, but also provided an opportunity to support exciting and genuine sport psychology research collaboration with youth. Mills and Hoeber (2013) also used photographs to explore the perceptions of skaters towards artifacts within a figure-skating club.

They described how this participatory approach not only offered an alternative process for participants to share their perspectives, but also addressed power imbalances between the participants and researchers. In addition to photovoice, Phoenix (2010) described the potential of numerous other visual methods to enhance understandings in sport and exercise research. She argued that the use of visual methods, including photographs videos, diagrams, and symbols, has not been well documented within sport and exercise research, and through the use of such alternative methods it is possible to challenge commonly held notions of conducting quality research within sport and exercise. Participatory research approaches are not restricted to the use of visual methods, but can also include other engaging forms of knowledge generation such as talking circles (e.g., Ferguson & Philipenko, 2016) and vignettes (e.g., Blodgett, Schinke, Smith, Peltier, & Pheasant, 2011). Given the variety of methods that can be incorporated into participatory research approaches, it is necessary to consider how the data or knowledge is generated. Research in sport and exercise psychology has traditionally been conducted *on* participants, and participatory approaches support a process of engaging in research *with* participants.

Research in the area of sport and exercise psychology has reached a critical juncture. To continue advancing this field of study it is necessary to broaden the vision of what constitutes legitimate, relevant, and respectful research. The inherent features of participatory research, such as the inclusion of underrepresented populations and the collaborative process of knowledge generation, make this an ideal approach for deepening our understandings of human experiences of complex phenomena. In addition, through participatory approaches researchers can be responsive to the rights and needs of our research partners, who want to see the direct translation and application of research findings into relevant sport and exercise psychology practices or policies.

References

Balish, S. M., McLaren, C., Rainham, D., & Blanchard, C. (2014). Correlates of youth sport attrition: A review and future directions. *Psychology of Sport and Exercise, 15*(4), 429–439.

Berger, G. & Peerson, A. (2009). Giving young Emirati women a voice: Participatory action research on physical activity. *Health & Place, 15*(1), 117–124.

Blodgett, A., Schinke, R., Smith, B., Peltier, D., & Pheasant, C. (2011). Exploring vignettes as a narrative strategy for co-producing the research voices of Aboriginal Community. *Qualitative Inquiry, 17*(6), 522–533.

Enright, E. & O'Sullivan, M. (2012). Physical education "in all sorts of corners." *Research Quarterly for Exercise and Sport, 83*(2), 255–267.

Ferguson, L. & Philipenko, N. (2016). "I would love to blast some pow music and just dance": First Nations students' experiences of physical activity on a university campus. *Qualitative Research in Sport, Exercise and Health, 8*(2), 180–193.

Frisby, W., Reid, C. J., Millar, S., & Hoeber, L. (2005). Putting "participatory" into participatory forms of action research. *Journal of Sport Management, 19*(4), 367–386.

Greenhalgh, T., Annandale, E., Ashcroft, R., Barlow, J., Black, N., Bleakley, A., . . . & Checkland, K. (2016). An open letter to the *BMJ* editors on qualitative research. *British Medical Journal, 352*, i563.

Harrison, J., MacGibbon, L., & Morton, M. (2001). Regimes of trustworthiness in qualitative research: The rigors of reciprocity. *Qualitative Inquiry, 7*(3), 323–345.

Henrich, J., Heine, S. J., & Norenzayan, A. (2010). The weirdest people in the world? *Behavioral and Brain Sciences, 33*(2–3), 61–83.

Israel, B. A., Schulz, A. J., Parker, E. A., & Becker, A. B. (1998). Review of community-based research: Assessing partnership approaches to improve public health. *Annual Review of Public Health, 19*(1), 173–202.

Kemmis, S. & McTaggart, R. (2008). Participatory action research: Communicative action and the public sphere. In N. K. Denzin & Y. S. Lincoln (Eds.), *Strategies of qualitative inquiry* (3rd ed., pp. 271–330). Thousand Oaks, CA: Sage.

McHugh, T-L. F., Coppola, A. M., Holt, N. L., & Andersen, C. (2015). "Sport is Community": An exploration of urban Aboriginal peoples' meanings of community within the context of sport. *Psychology of Sport and Exercise, 18*, 75–84.

McHugh, T. L. F., Coppola, A. M., & Sinclair, S. (2013). An exploration of the meanings of sport to urban Aboriginal youth: A photovoice approach. *Qualitative Research in Sport, Exercise and Health, 5*(3), 291–311.

McHugh, T.-L. F., Kingsley, B., & Coppola, A. M. (2013). Research questions that matter: Engaging Aboriginal youth in the research process. *Pimatisiwin: A Journal of Aboriginal and Indigenous Community Health, 11*(2), 293–305.

McPherson, B. D. (1984). Sport participation across the life cycle: A review of the literature and suggestions for future research. *Sociology of Sport Journal, 1*(3), 213–230.

Messner, M. A. & Musto, M. (2014). Where are the kids? *Sociology of Sport Journal, 31*(1), 102–122.

Mills, C. & Hoeber, L. (2013). Using photo-elicitation to examine artefacts in a sport club: Logistical considerations and strategies throughout the research process. *Qualitative Research in Sport, Exercise and Health, 5*(1), 1–20.

Phoenix, C. (2010). Seeing the world of physical culture: The potential of visual methods for qualitative research in sport and exercise. *Qualitative Research in Sport and Exercise, 2*(2), 93–108.

Riley, B. B., Rimmer, J. H., Wang, E., & Schiller, W. J. (2008). A conceptual framework for improving the accessibility of fitness and recreation facilities for people with disabilities. *Journal of Physical Activity & Health, 5*(1), 158–168.

Schinke, R. J., McGannon, K. R., Watson, J., & Busanich, R. (2013). Moving toward trust and partnership: An example of sport-related community-based participatory action research with Aboriginal people and mainstream academics. *Journal of Aggression, Conflict and Peace Research, 5*(4), 201–210.

Smith, B. (2010). Narrative inquiry: Ongoing conversations and questions for sport and exercise psychology research. *International Review of Sport and Exercise Psychology, 3*(1), 87–107.

Smith, B. & Caddick, N. (2012). Qualitative methods in sport: A concise overview for guiding social scientific sport research. *Asia Pacific Journal of Sport and Social Science, 1*(1), 60–73.

Smith, K., Findlay, L., & Crompton, S. (2010). Participation in sports and cultural activities among Aboriginal children and youth. *Canadian Social Trends, 90*, 51–58.

Smith, B. & Gilbourne, D. (2009). Editorial. *Qualitative Research in Sport and Exercise, 1*(1), 1–2.

Strachan, L. & Davies, K. (2015). Click! Using photo elicitation to explore youth experiences and positive youth development in sport. *Qualitative Research in Sport, Exercise and Health, 7*(2), 170–191.

Wang, C. & Burris, M. A. (1997). Photovoice: Concept, methodology, and use for participatory needs assessment. *Health Education & Behavior, 24*(3), 369–387.

35

A LOOK AT THE FUTURE OF QUALITATIVE METHODOLOGY THROUGH THE PRISM OF ATHLETE CAREER RESEARCH

Natalia B. Stambulova

In our minds the future is embodied by various constructs, including goals, plans, dreams, anticipations, and broader visions that combine anticipation and wishful thinking (where we would like to be) with the reality check (where we are now). In this chapter I take on a challenge to present a future-oriented vision of qualitative research through a prism of the athlete career topic. Being a qualitative, quantitative, and mixed-method researcher of athletes' careers for about 25 years, I have witnessed an increasing contribution of qualitative methodology to this topic, and I think that this growth trend will continue in the future. One of my departure points is that the career topic (although studied a lot quantitatively) has an inherent qualitative "nature," because there are as many careers with various pathways, contexts, and personal meanings of career experiences as there are athletes. Only qualitative research is capable of grasping these diversities, deepening our knowledge about how athletes' identities are constructed and reconstructed, become imbedded into the developmental processes, and also how they influence these processes. Besides being used in research projects, qualitative methodology has an important function in structuring and restructuring research areas through review papers. A number of review papers on athletes' career development and transitions (see references in the next section) have been useful in summarizing our understanding of athletes' careers (where we are) and setting future challenges (where we would like to be). The aim of this chapter is to consider multiple roles of qualitative methodology in enriching and structuring athlete career knowledge in sport psychology. I am also writing with a hope that my reflections might inspire other sport psychology researchers to consider the future of their respective areas in a similar vein.

Increasing role of qualitative methodology in structuring the athlete career topic

As stated by Mellalieu and Hanton, "A review of literature functions as an initial vehicle for a topic organization, reorganization, and defined structure" (2009, p. 1). Authors of review papers usually identify major theoretical frameworks, research directions and applied approaches (i.e., *themes and subthemes*) in the topic, *subordinate or structure* them depending on the perspective taken in the review, *attach significance/meanings* to different *themes/subthemes* and, based on these, *formulate future challenges*. A trained eye would see that these steps are borrowed from the qualitative research methodology, and therefore its particular role in structuring research areas will only grow, given the perpetual expansion in amount of information produced within the social sciences, including sport psychology.

During the last 50 years, the athlete career topic in sport psychology has evolved from a narrow focus on athletic retirement to "a whole career" (i.e., from the beginning to the end), "a whole person" (i.e., including sport and nonsport development), and "a whole environment" (i.e., micro- and macro-environments) research, with the corresponding expansion of applied work on athlete career issues. A number of review papers (e.g., Alfermann & Stambulova, 2007; Park, Lavallee, & Tod, 2013; Stambulova, 2010a; Stambulova, Alfermann, Statler, & Côté, 2009; Stambulova & Ryba, 2013a, 2014; Wylleman, Alfermann, & Lavallee, 2004) and one meta-review (Stambulova, 2012) facilitated negotiations of key definitions, taxonomies of career transitions, classification of theoretical frameworks, and identifying major research and applied directions (see, e.g., Stambulova & Wylleman, 2014). Recently, I attempted to describe the existing structure of the athlete career topic using a metaphor of *edifice* borrowed from Bernard Forscher (1963), with the intention to review and position emerging research trends within it (Stambulova, 2016a). Briefly, the athlete career *"edifice"* consists of *the foundation* (e.g., conceptualization of an athlete as "a whole person" and a transition as a process rather than a single event), *the first floor* of career development research and frameworks (e.g., Wylleman & Lavallee, 2004; Wylleman, Reints, & De Knop, 2013), *the second floor* of career transition research and frameworks (e.g., Samuel & Tenenbaum, 2011; Stambulova, 2003; Taylor & Ogilvie, 1994), and *the third floor* of career assistance, applied frameworks and tools (e.g., Lavallee, 2005; Stambulova, 2010b). All of the *"floors"* are linked by the cultural praxis of the athletes' careers paradigm (Stambulova & Ryba, 2013b, 2014) functioning as *the staircase*. This *edifice* is open for reconstruction as the topic develops. Future review papers might focus not only on systematic analysis and synthesis of research findings on specific transitions (e.g., the-junior-to-senior), but also link the athlete career topic with other topics in sport psychology (e.g., career and performance, career and mental health, career and coach–athlete relationships), and integrate them with career research in, for example, sociology, vocational and counseling psychology. Such reviews might provide researchers with novel ideas for more far-reaching and interdisciplinary projects that would uncover the new facets and meanings in athletes' career development. As I look more broadly across the sport and exercise behavioral sciences, many other topics could benefit from strong reviews that incorporate or focus on qualitative research (see also Chapter 21). This also includes meta-reviews – a review of reviews.

Qualitative athlete career research: accomplishments and gaps

The most heavily investigated research area within the athlete career topic is athletic retirement. Park *et al.* (2013) provided a systematic review of athletic retirement research published in English between 1968 and 2010. Among the 126 papers covered in the review, 44% were quantitative, 44% qualitative, and 12% mixed-method. In contrast, among the 13 papers published in the more recent *Psychology of Sport and Exercise* Special Issue on Dual Career Development and Transitions (Stambulova & Wylleman, 2015), 70% were qualitative, 15% quantitative, and 15% mixed-method. The comparison (although not scientifically rigorous) of the percentage values speaks for the growing contribution of qualitative research in the athlete career topic. I think that this increase in qualitative inquiry derives from researchers' dissatisfaction with a rather superficial view of athlete developmental processes expressed in purely statistical terms. By letting athletes speak and their voices be heard, qualitative studies breathed new life into the athlete career research through revealing diversity, changeability, ambiguity, and nuances in developmental contexts, processes, and meanings. While quantitative career studies are too often context-blind and infused by statistical language, qualitative researchers cannot fully ignore the contexts of athletes' development, and they naturally gravitate toward psychological language when discussing their empirical findings.

For many career scholars who began as quantitative researchers and then made a shift to qualitative research, it was easier to adopt a postpositivist rather than a constructionist perspective. When analyzing the current status of qualitative research in the athlete career topic, it becomes obvious that a majority of studies are postpositivist, with various combinations of inductive and deductive ways of raw-data analysis (see also Chapters 1 and 10). The researchers identify higher- and lower-order themes and either join them into categories, or fit them into categories from existing theoretical framework(s) and structure them inside each category inductively. Much of our knowledge about the junior-to-senior transition (e.g., Morris, Tod, & Oliver, 2015; Pummell, Harwood, & Lavallee, 2008), the transition to the post-athletic career (e.g., Kerr & Dacyshyn, 2000; Lavallee & Robinson, 2007), dual career (in sport and education) transitions (e.g., Aquilina, 2013; Tekavc, Wylleman, & Cecić Erpič, 2015) has been gathered this way. In the future, the postpositivist studies that have made a solid contribution to the career topic should not be abandoned, but complemented by constructionist research (see also Chapters 1 and 10) that can help us "discover" new facets of athletes' development. The problem is that many career researchers with positivist and postpositivist backgrounds are preoccupied with research objectivity and find it difficult to shift to the constructionist type of thinking, with more open and interactive dialogues, the possibility of alternative interpretations, etc. In emerging constructionist research on athletes' careers, narrative, ethnography, case studies, and participatory action inquiries were employed to study perceptions and meanings of career experiences (e.g., Blodgett & Schinke, 2015; Carless and Douglass, 2009; Ryba, Ronkainen, & Selänne, 2015; Ryba, Stambulova, Ronkainen, Bundgaard, & Selänne, 2015; Sandström, Linnér, & Stambulova, 2016; Storm, Henriksen, Larsen, & Christensen, 2014). With this promising beginning we can expect more studies of this type in the future.

At the same time, I don't advocate any particular type of qualitative exploration of athletes' careers. I believe that a variety of qualitative traditions should be used to bridge existing gaps in our understanding of athletes' development. One gap stems from a natural tendency of athletes being interviewed about their athletic careers to focus predominantly on sport issues and skip over the details of their lives outside of sport. Therefore, more studies need to consider how athletic career experiences shape other spheres of athletes' lives and contribute to their life career. Another gap results from too much focus on reasoning about career experiences (i.e., what influenced what), while insufficient attention is given to personal meanings, their internalization from the relevant contexts, and how a change in meaning might change the reasoning and even the whole career path. Therefore, there is a need for more research on personal meanings of career experiences. There is also a gap between the "fixed" theoretical frameworks and the diversity and fluidity of cultural contexts of which the athletes are a part. Therefore, career research has to become more contextualized and culturally competent. As far as I know, the sport and exercise behavioral sciences have been dominated by postpositivist qualitative research. More constructionist informed research that is highly contextualized and culturally oriented is needed in the future. This goes beyond the athlete career topic; other areas of interest could benefit from explicitly grounded constructionist work. I continue this line of thinking in what follows through the prism of athlete career research, but stress that much of what is suggested can be applied to other research areas.

Increasing role of qualitative methodology in contextualizing the athlete career topic

Structuring and contextualizing the athlete career topic are two interrelated processes that characterize its current development (Stambulova, 2016b). The interrelation between these processes had begun with the International Society of Sport Psychology (ISSP) Position Stand on athletes' career development and transitions (Stambulova *et al.*, 2009) that considered athlete career-research foci as being internalized from the sociocultural contexts that the researchers belong to. It continued to develop in the book *Athletes' Careers Across Cultures* (Stambulova & Ryba, 2013a) and the subsequent review of career research through the cultural lens (Stambulova & Ryba, 2014), where the athlete career topic was structured as having three dominant (North-American, European, and Australian) and two emerging (Asian and South-American) cultural discourses, each characterized by specific research foci, theoretical frameworks, and career assistance programs. Further, the major tenets of the *cultural praxis of athletes' careers* paradigm were formulated based on the analysis of contemporary sport attributes (e.g., increased professionalization and transnationalism), and reviews of career research in 19 countries.

Cultural praxis of athletes' careers

The mission of the cultural praxis of athletes' careers is to guide researchers in designing career projects that blend theory, research, practice, and the participants' context(s), to achieve a better fit to the particulars of athletes' careers across cultures (Stambulova & Ryba, 2013b, 2014). It allots a central and integrating role to qualitative methodology in future career research (see also Chapter 8). The transition to the cultural-praxis-type-of-thinking is impeded by the researchers' perception of existing career development and transition models as "fixed" and universal, as well as by their preoccupation with generalizability of research findings (see also Chapter 8). The cultural-praxis-type-of-thinking moves away from developing "something" that is universally applicable toward the idea that the more research findings and practical recommendations are contextualized, the better. More specifically, we encourage researchers to combine the holistic developmental (Wylleman & Lavallee, 2004; Wylleman *et al.*, 2013) and the holistic ecological (Henriksen, Stambulova, & Roessler, 2010a) perspectives, to contextualize all stages of projects' planning and realization (see more in Ryba *et al.*, 2012 and Stambulova & Ryba, 2013b), to focus more on individual career pathways and personal meanings of career experiences, to explore careers of marginalized athletic populations (e.g., Blodgett & Schinke, 2015), and careers of the growing number of transnational athletes (e.g., Ryba, Haapanen, Mosek, & Ng, 2012: Ryba, Stambulova *et al.*, 2015). Interdisciplinary projects, participatory action research, and targeted applications of research findings are also in the spirit of the cultural praxis of athletes' careers. I take a responsibility to say that we need more of these across the sport and exercise behavioral sciences, not just in career work (see also Chapter 8).

From general to empirical career and career transition models

The cultural praxis of athletes' careers has spurred a discussion about how to improve the fit between existing theoretical frameworks and athletes' real career experiences, infused by the contexts they belong to. It is obvious that any model simplifies reality and provides us with a kind of map that is useful for orientation but does not grasp all the richness of the territory. Therefore, existing career frameworks represent general models that are expected to be contextualized or adapted to particular national and/or sport contexts, based on the empirical data.

More specifically, the general career models might guide the initial data collection and then be transformed into empirical models encompassing the nuances of the career or transition process in a specific athletic population and context. This approach is already well accepted within holistic ecological research, where the athletic talent development environment model and the environment success factors model were morphed into empirical models incorporating some shared and also unique features of the various athletic environments under study (Henriksen, Stambulova, & Roessler, 2010 b, 2011; Henriksen, Larsen, & Christensen, 2014). Another example of this approach is a recent case study of the organizational culture of an Australian football club that was recognized as successful in supporting the players' dual careers (Pink, Saunders, & Stynes, 2015). Based on the data from interviews, observation, and analysis of documents, the authors transformed Schein's (1990) model of organizational culture into the empirical model specifying artifacts, exposed values, and basic assumptions of the club's culture that guided the staff and the players in facilitating the players' development on and off the field.

The idea of empirical models has been gaining popularity in the holistic developmental (lifespan) research, through specifying career stages and relevant age markers of the holistic athletic career model (Wylleman *et al.*, 2013), and/or specifying demands, resources, barriers, coping strategies of the athletic career transition model (Stambulova, 2003) in relation to particular career or transition pathways and contexts. We already have some research examples of using general models as a basis for data collection and further transformation into the empirical models (Brown *et al.*, 2015; Debois, Ledon, & Wylleman, 2015). But empirical models can also be created directly from the empirical data within grounded theory (see Chapter 3) or narrative inquiries (see Chapters 4 and 20). The latter was used in developing the empirical career model of Canadian National Hockey League (NHL) players, which was based on the players' narratives, but took account of the relevant general frameworks (Battochio, Stambulova, & Schinke, 2016). To sum up, the empirical models, being more concrete and contextually meaningful than general models, can be helpful in guiding future research of target athletic populations, and developing contextualized and more efficient psychological support services.

Career meaning making

One of the specific features of qualitative research is its focus on meanings of peoples' experiences. During my career as researcher and practitioner, I had the privilege of listening to a number of athletes' career narratives and learned that careers of not just elite, but also non-elite athletes, are dramatic and meaningful life experiences. Even athletes who retied years ago tended to do retrospective meaning making when reflecting about sport. Traditional athlete career research, grounded within existing career development and transition frameworks, deals predominantly with *an objective layer* of career experiences, which is how athletes progress through the career stages or through the transition process and what factors are involved. Emerging career meaning making research shifts the focus to *a subjective layer* of career, which is how athletes perceive and identify themselves through sport, and how they construct and reconstruct their life career paths within the historical, social, cultural, and sport contexts. When analyzing life career meanings, Audrey Collin (2007) used the metaphor of *tapestry,* in which "the multiple career meanings are seen to interweave and overlap; they cannot be separated, indeed they are held simultaneously" (p. 560). This nature of career meanings was supported by a recent narrative (case) study (Ryba, Ronkainen *et al.*, 2015) that examined two athletes' "meanings ascribed to career events and identity" – that is, the subjective career "constructed within the dynamics of social interactions and woven into the historicity contingent cultural scripts available in a society" (p. 48). A performance career, a dual career in sport and education, and a transnational career were the three discourses identified in both athletes' narratives. The cross-case analysis revealed that within each discourse athletes internalized (but also critically evaluated) values and meanings from their particular sport culture, educational experiences, personal/family histories, and cultures of their origin and mobility, and therefore their career paths were perceived and experienced differently.

While meanings are derived from experiences, they also steer experiences one way or another. Therefore, changes in meanings could initiate a career change. For example, a change in the meaning of sport and sport participation might lead an athlete to think about athletic retirement. A corresponding change in the meaning of athletic identity (how much is this part of me now important?) might set off the retirement process. Athletic identity has been studied extensively within the career topic, especially since the Athletic Identity Measurement Scale was developed (Brewer, Van Raalte, & Linder, 1993). This tool was utilized in multiple career studies to demonstrate that high athletic identity works as a barrier for successful adaptation to life after sport (Alfermann & Stambulova, 2007; Park *et al.*, 2013). A traditional recommendation based on the athletic identity research is to help athletes to downgrade their athletic identity as they approach career termination. Based on my athletic, professional, and life experiences I can say that it is true for many, but not for all. Depending on personal meanings of sport, athletes' present situation and perceived future, as well as a broader meaning of life, high athletic identity can either torture or nurture the post-athletic career life. Here is just one example of the latter. In my athletic career as a figure skater, I had the opportunity to meet and occasionally compete with the legends of Russian pair figure skating Ludmila Belousova and Oleg Protopopov (Olympic champions 1964 and 1968). We (younger skaters) saw them as models of full dedication to the world of figure skating, and they often shared in their media interviews and informal talks how all aspects of their life were subordinated to the sport. When they retired from their "objective career" (i.e., stopped competing) at the age of about forty, they wished to establish figure skating show performing classic ballets on the ice. This idea was not supported in the Soviet Union context of the 1970s. They also wanted to summarize their experiences in the form of a doctoral dissertation based on their multiyear athletic diaries, but it was found to not be scientific enough to be awarded a degree in the community of mainly positivist researchers. So, they tried different ways to continue their life through figure skating, but didn't get support. Their solution was immigration to Switzerland, where they practiced figure skating as a pair and performed at exhibition shows for over four decades after their "official" career termination. Of course this case is unique, but it is a real case, and looking at it from a practitioner's eye I would not work with these people on reducing their athletic identity. Instead, I would focus on helping them to develop a proper support system for the life path they had chosen.

Narratives that athletes tell are "data with a soul" (Gallo, 2014, p. 41); that is, with multiple meanings and emotions involved. Some meanings can be hidden and only revealed by the "tensions" between the *"fabula"* (the content of what is told) and *"sjuzet"* (the form, or how it is told) (Hiles & Čermák, 2008). This often happens when athletes are interviewed about their injury or athletic retirement experiences and say things that are "right," but different from what they really feel. Therefore, researchers should be observant of linguistic and nonlinguistic, verbal and nonverbal aspects of communication when collecting narrative data, and prevent or relieve *fabula–sjuzet* tensions by developing a trusting atmosphere during interviews, and asking proper follow-up questions.

Bridging the past and the present of athlete career research

One popular career assistance intervention with athletes is career planning. It is different from simple goal setting and consists of analyzing and structuring the athlete's past, present, and perceived future, followed by bridging the past and the future with the present as an integrative point (Stambulova, 2010b). This bridging process is the most difficult but necessary aspect of career planning, as it helps to balance athletes' dreams and goals with reality. I am going to apply a similar approach to "planning" athlete career research.

In the earlier sections, I briefly reviewed and structured "the past" of athlete career research and outlined some recent new developments within this topic. Bridging the past with the present, I would like to emphasize that the progress achieved over the past five decades (e.g., negotiating the terminology, developing sport-specific frameworks, structuring/restructuring athlete career knowledge, developing career assistance programs and services, attracting more young researchers to the topic, etc.) created a fertile ground for the new ideas and research trends that sprouted during the last five to six years. These new research trends form "the present" of the athlete career research (see more in Stambulova, 2016a).

In the area of career development *research,* new trends are related to studying career pathways of transnational (e.g., Ryba, Stambulova *et al.*, 2015), Indigenous (e.g., Blodgett & Schinke, 2015), and professional (Battochio *et al.*, 2015) athletes, defining the role of significant others in structuring athletes' career paths (Sandström *et al.*, forthcoming; Storm *et al.*, 2014), and exploring career meanings and identity construction through sport (Ryba, Ronkainen *et al.*, 2015). All these studies are qualitative, and a good portion of them take the constructionist angle.

In the area of *career transition research,* new trends are defined by mainly qualitative (both postpositivist and constructionist) and mixed-method studies. First, the researchers have an interest in "zooming" into a transition process and identifying a temporal phase-like structure of athletic retirement and some within-career transitions (Ivarsson, Stambulova, & Johnson, 2015; Reints, 2011; Schinke, Stambulova, Trepanier, & Oghene, 2015). Second, there is a rapidly growing holistic ecological research field, focusing on athletic environments either facilitating or impeding athletes' junior-to-senior transition (Henriksen *et al.*, 2010a, 2010 b, 2011; Henriksen *et al.*, 2014). Third, the *Psychology of Sport and Exercise* Special Issue on athletes' dual careers provided examples of dual career transition studies from the holistic developmental (lifespan) perspective (e.g., Brown *et al.*, 2015; Debois *et al.*, 2015; Stambulova, Engström, Franck, Linnér, & Lindahl, 2015). Fourth, there are new kinds of athletes' transitions that attracted researchers' attention. These are: cultural transitions (e.g., Agergaard & Ryba, 2014; Ryba *et al.*, 2012; Ryba, Stambulova, & Ronkainen, 2016; Schinke, McGanon, Battochio, & Wells, 2013), transitions to elite residential performance centers (e.g., Poczwardowski, Diehl, O'Neil, Cote, & Haberl, 2013), and important competitions (especially Olympic Games) conceptualized as career transitions (e.g., Hollings, Mallett, & Hume, 2014; Samuel, Tenenbaum, & Bar-Mecher, 2016; Schinke *et al.*, 2015; Wylleman, Reints, & Van Aken, 2012). These latter transition studies initiated a discussion about the existing taxonomy of athletes' transitions that is based on their predictability. For decades we operated by *normative* (i.e., predictable for a majority of athletes) and *non-normative* (i.e., fewer or unpredictable) transition terms. Cultural transitions, transitions to residential performance centers, and transitions relevant to important competitions didn't fit into this taxonomy. As a result, the taxonomy has been adjusted by inclusion of *quasi-normative* transitions that are predictable for certain groups of athletes (e.g., transnational, professional, elite), and therefore can be expected, planned, and prepared for (see more in Schinke *et al.*, 2015 and Stambulova, 2016a). All of the aforementioned new research trends led to new directions in *career assistance* to athletes (e.g., dual career support services, "fixing" less successful athletic talent development environments, acculturation interventions). To sum up, these are "the capital" we take with us into the future. Other sport and exercise researchers might learn from us how "to accumulate" their capital and develop their research areas, both deductively (i.e., from existing theoretical frameworks to research findings) and inductively (i.e., from research finding to new terminology and theoretical constructions).

Bridging the future and the present

Based on the analysis of the past and the present of the athlete career research, we can expect the following developments in the future: (1) full adoption of the cultural praxis of athletes' careers, especially in terms of holistic, contextualized, and applied studies; (2) greater diversity but also higher standards of qualitative studies of "old" trends, current trends, and new trends that will be internalized from the future contexts; (3) an increase in mixed-method career research, with qualitative parts being dominant; and (4) addressing the athlete career topic from a multi-interdisciplinary standpoint, in collaboration with researchers from sport sociology, pedagogy, management, vocational psychology, sociology, and counseling psychology. Given this vision of the future, the key question in bridging it to the present reality is: What can we do today to bring about the projected future of our research area?

I think we can start with ourselves as researchers when we plan new projects. We need to reflect on our professional and living backgrounds, the contexts we are part of, and our professional (research) competences, to decide what, how, and why to study. We also need to consider what new knowledge and skills we need to learn in order to realize our research ideas, and what professional network will be useful. Then we should be able to position ourselves within the project, reflecting on how our various backgrounds contributed to the project planning and realization. I think reflexivity is what we need the most to open our research process and our thinking to the readers. As a reviewer and editor, I often read papers in which authors implement an approach with which I am not very familiar, or I think that another approach might be better suited to answer the study objectives. But I am careful to not impose my own agenda, because I think that researchers have a right to decide what approach to use, a right to be creative, and even to invent their own approach, as long as they are really clear about what, how, and why they did. Sometimes the authors think that using solid qualitative method references and the "right" terms in the relevant sections will increase their publication chances, but often their main weakness is a lack of reflexivity, transparency, and clarity.

Except for research on retirement difficulties and situation-related crises (e.g., Lavallee, Gordon, Grove, 1997; Stambulova, 2000), many present studies focus on the more glamorous sides of athletes' careers (e.g., successful athletes, successful environments). However, a wealth of new career knowledge could be gained by studying the darker side of athletes' careers, for example, injuries, drug abuse, burnout, and eating disorders, all of which are imbedded into the career context and capable of instigating undesirable transitions. The two examples of such studies, a case study that compared successful and less successful athletic talent development environments in the Danish context (Henriksen *et al.*, 2014), and a negative case analysis that explored the experiences of the junior-to-senior transition in the UK football context (Gledhill & Harwood, 2015), demonstrate that this "view from an opposite pole" might reveal unexpected nuances in athletes' development and be useful in career assistance.

Along with an increase in qualitative career research, there is also a rise in mixed-method career projects (e.g., Poczwardowski *et al.*, 2013; Stambulova *et al.*, 2015). The mixed-method approach is gaining popularity because it helps to deal with some limitations of both quantitative (wide but not deep) and qualitative (deep but not wide) research (see also Chapter 29). Integration of quantitative and qualitative data requires clear subordination of the data findings in relation to the study objectives. For example, in a study of Swedish athletes' transition to national elite sport schools (Stambulova *et al.*, 2015), we focused on the transition and adaptation during the first year, as well as identity development. Data was collected from surveys with more than 200 participants, as well as in-depth interviews with 10 participants at the beginning and at the end of the educational year. We adopted a pragmatic approach (Yardley & Bishop, 2008) when faced with a question of subordination of quantitative and qualitative research findings. More specifically, in studying the dynamics of the student-athletes' adaptation the quantitative approach was dominant and the qualitative was supportive, whereas in exploring how student-athletes balanced their two roles/identities the qualitative approach was dominant and quantitative was supportive. Measuring the participants' athletic and student identities quantitatively gave us really "selfish" information (i.e., athletic identity was significantly higher than student identity). But the interview (narrative) data gave us a lot more detail in terms of inter- and intra-individual differences in the identity issue. To decide how to structure the mixed-method project and combine insights from both parts in a complementary manner, researchers need to reflect on the nature of each research objective and their subordination in the project.

In response to the need to promote multi-interdisciplinary research, more efforts should go into development of international and interdisciplinary career projects, such as "Gold in education and elite sport" (2015–16), in order to facilitate networking of career researchers and practitioners from different countries and disciplines. Based on my own experience of interdisciplinary collaboration, differences in research cultures between the disciplines are serious barriers that should be reflected upon and negotiated by researchers.

In my parting remarks, I would like to stress that athletes' development, as well as development of the athlete career (or any other) research area, follows the dialectics of a developmental process, with its nonlinear progressions, crises, stagnations, and decays. Although the future is predictable to a limited degree, both athletes and researchers will find it easier to modify existing visions and plans, rather than to start new things from scratch. Qualitative research has a key part to play in this process, just as it has – and will have - in examining many other areas of interest in sport and exercise behavioral sciences.

References

Agergaard, S. & Ryba, T. V. (2014). Migration and career transitions in professional sports: Transnational athletic careers in a psychological and sociological perspective. *Sociology of Sport Journal*, *31*, 228–247.

Alfermann, D. & Stambulova, N. (2007). Career transitions and career termination. In G. Tenenbaum & R. C. Eklund (Eds.), *Handbook of sport psychology* (3rd ed., pp. 712–736). New York: Wiley.

Aquilina, D. (2013). A study of the relationship between elite athletes' educational development and sporting performance. *The International Journal of the History of Sport*, *30*, 374–392.

Battochio, R. C., Stambulova, N., & Schinke, R. J. (2016). Stages and demands in the careers of Canadian National Hockey League players. *Journal of Sport Sciences*, *34*(3), 278–288. doi: 10.1080/0264 0414.2015.1048523.

Blodgett, A. T. & Schinke, R. J. (2015). "When you're coming from the reserve you're not supposed to make it": Stories of Aboriginal athletes pursuing sport and academic careers in "mainstream" cultural contexts. *Psychology of Sport and Exercise*, *21*, 115–124.

Brewer, B. W., Van Raalte, J. L., & Linder, D. E. (1993). Athletic identity: Hercules' muscles or Achilles' heel? *International Journal of Sport Psychology*, *24*, 237–254.

Brown, D. J., Fletcher, D., Henry, I., Borrie, A., Emmett, J., Buzza, A., & Wombwell, S. (2015). A British university case study of the transitional experiences of student-athletes. *Psychology of Sport and Exercise*, *21*, 78–90.

Carless, D. & Douglas, K. (2009). "We haven't got a seat on the bus for you" or "all the seats are mine": Narratives and career transitions in professional golf. *Qualitative Research in Sport and Exercise, 1*(1), 51–66.

Collin, A. (2007). The meanings of career. In H. Gunz & M. Peiperl (Eds.), *Handbook of career studies* (pp. 558–565). Thousand Oaks, CA: Sage.

Debois, N., Ledon, A., & Wylleman, P. (2015). A lifespan perspective on the dual career of elite male athletes. *Psychology of Sport and Exercise, 21*, 15–26.

Forscher, B. K. (1963). Chaos in the brickyard. *Science, 142*, 339.

Gallo, C. (2014). *Talk like TED*. London: Macmillan.

Gledhill, A. & Harwood, C. (2015). A holistic perspective on career development in UK female soccer: A negative case analysis. *Psychology of Sport and Exercise, 21*, 65–77.

Gold in Education and Elite Sport. (2015–16). European Union's Erasmus + Sport Project. Available at: www.gees.eu.

Henriksen, K., Larsen, C. H., & Christensen, M. K. (2014). Looking at success from its opposite pole: The case of a talent development golf environment. *International Journal of Sport and Exercise Psychology, 12*, 134–149.

Henriksen, K., Stambulova, N., & Roessler, K. K. (2010a). Holistic approach to athletic talent development environment: A successful sailing milieu. *Psychology of Sport and Exercise, 11*, 212–222.

Henriksen, K., Stambulova, N., & Roessler, K. K. (2010b). Successful talent development in athletics: Considering the role of environment. *Scandinavian Journal of Medicine and Science in Sports, 20*, 122–132.

Henriksen, K., Stambulova, N., & Roessler, K. (2011). Riding the wave of an expert: A successful talent development environment in kayaking. *The Sport Psychologist, 25*, 341–362.

Hiles, D. & Čermák, I. (2008). Narrative psychology. In C. Willing & W. Stainton-Rogers (Eds.), *The Sage handbook of qualitative research in psychology* (pp. 147–167). London: Sage.

Hollings, S. C., Mallett, C. J., & Hume, P. A. (2014). The World Junior Athletics Championships: New Zealand athletes' lived experiences. *International Journal of Sport Science and Coaching, 9*(6), 1357–1374.

Ivarsson, A., Stambulova, N., & Johnson, U. (2015). Injury as a career transition: Experiences of a Swedish elite handball player. In O. Schmid & R. Seiler (Eds.), *Proceedings of 14th European Congress of Sport Psychology* (pp. 241–242). Bern, Switzerland: University of Bern; FEPSAC.

Kerr, G. & Dacyshyn, A. (2000). The retirement experiences of elite female gymnasts. *Journal of Applied Sport Psychology, 12*, 115–133.

Lavallee, D. (2005). The effect of a life development intervention on sports career transition adjustment. *The Sport Psychologist, 19*, 193–202.

Lavallee, D., Gordon, S., & Grove, R. (1997). Retirement from sport and the loss of athletic identity. *Journal of Personal and Interpersonal Loss, 2*, 129–147.

Lavallee, D. & Robinson, H. K. (2007). In pursuit of an identity: A qualitative exploration of retirement from women's artistic gymnastics. *Psychology of Sport and Exercise, 8*, 119–141.

Mellalieu, S. D. & Hanton, S. (2009). Introduction. In S. D. Mellalieu & S. Hanton (Eds.), *Advances in applied sport psychology. A review* (pp. 1–4). New York: Routledge.

Morris, R., Tod, D., & Oliver, E. (2015). An analysis of organizational structure and transition outcomes in the youth-to-senior professional soccer transition. *Journal of Applied Sport Psychology, 27*(2), 216–234.

Park, S., Lavallee, D., & Tod, D. (2013). Athletes' career transition out of sport: A systematic review. *International Review of Sport and Exercise Psychology, 6*, 22–53.

Pink, M. A., Saunders, J., & Stynes, J. (2015). Reconciling the maintenance of on-field success with off-field player development: A case study of a club within the Australian Football League. *Psychology of Sport and Exercise, 21*, 98–108.

Poczwardowski, A., Diehl, B., O'Neil, A., Côté, T., & Haberl, P. (2013). Successful transitions to the Olympic Training Center, Colorado Springs: A mixed-method exploration with six resident-athletes. *Journal of Applied Sport Psychology, 26*(1), 33–51.

Pummell, B., Harwood, C., & Lavallee, D. (2008). Jumping to the next level: A qualitative examination of within-career transition in adolescent event riders. *Psychology of Sport and Exercise, 9*, 427–447.

Reints, A. (2011). *Validation of the holistic athletic career model and the identification of variables related to athletic retirement*. (Doctoral dissertation). Belgium: Vrije Universiteit Brussel.

Ryba, T. V., Haapanen, S., Mosek, S., & Ng, K. (2012). Towards a conceptual understanding of acute cultural adaptation: A preliminary examination of ACA in female swimming. *Qualitative Research in Sport, Exercise and Health, 4*, 80–97.

Ryba, T. V., Ronkainen, N., & Selänne, H. (2015). Elite athletic career as a context for life design. *Journal of Vocational Behavior, 88*, 47–55.

Ryba, T.V., Stambulova, N., & Ronkainen, N. J. (2016). The work of cultural transition: An emerging model. *Front. Psychol.*, 7, 427. doi: 10.3389/fpsyg.2016.00427.

Ryba, T. V., Stambulova, N., Ronkainen, N., Bundgaard, J., & Selänne, H. (2015). Dual career pathways of transnational athletes. *Psychology of Sport and Exercise, 21*, 125–134.

Samuel, R. D. & Tenenbaum, G. (2011). How do athletes perceive and respond to change-events: An exploratory measurement tool. *Psychology of Sport and Exercise, 12*, 392–406.

Samuel, R. D., Tenenbaum, G., & Bar-Mecher, H. G. (2016). The Olympic Games as a career change-event: Israeli athletes' and coaches' perception of London 2012. *Psychology of Sport and Exercise, 24*, 38–47. doi: 10.1016/j.psychsport.2016.01.003.

Schein, E. G. (1990). Organizational culture. *American Psychologist, 45*, 109–119.

Schinke, R. J., McGannon, K. R., Battochio, R. C., & Wells, G. D. (2013). Acculturation in elite sport: A thematic analysis of immigrant athletes and coaches. *Journal of Sport Sciences, 31*, 1676–1686.

Schinke, R. J., Stambulova, N., Trepanier D., & Oghene, O. (2015). Psychological support for the Canadian Olympic Boxing Team in meta-transitions through the National Team Program. *International Journal of Sport and Exercise Psychology, 13*(1), 74–89.

Sandström, E., Linnér, L., & Stambulova, N. (2016). Career profiles of athlete–coach relationships: Descriptions and interpretations. *International Journal of Sport Science and Coaching*. Advanced on-line publication. doi: 10.1177/1747954116645012.

Stambulova, N. (2000). Athlete's crises: A developmental perspective. *International Journal of Sport Psychology, 31*, 584–601.

Stambulova, N. (2003). Symptoms of a crisis-transition: A grounded theory study. In N. Hassmén (Ed.), *SIPF Yearbook 2003* (pp. 97–109). Örebro: Örebro University Press.

Stambulova, N. (2010a). Professional culture of career assistance to athletes: A look through contrasting lenses of career metaphors. In T. V. Ryba, R. J. Schinke, & G. Tenenbaum (Eds.), *The cultural turn in sport psychology* (pp. 285–314). Morgantown, WV: Fitness Information Technology.

Stambulova, N. (2010b). Counseling athletes in career transitions: The five-step career planning strategy. *Journal of Sport Psychology in Action, 1*, 95–105.

Stambulova, N. (2012). Working with athletes in career transitions. In S. Hanton & S. Mellalieu (Eds.), *Professional practice in sport psychology: A review* (pp. 165–194). London: Routledge.

Stambulova, N. (2016a). Athletes' transitions in sport and life: Positioning new research trends within existing system of athlete career knowledge. In R. Schinke, K. McGannon, & B. Smith (Eds.), *The Routledge international handbook of sport psychology* (pp. 519–535). New York, NY: Routledge.

Stambulova, N. (2016b). Theoretical developments in career transition research: Contributions of European sport psychology. In M. Raab, P. Wylleman, R. Seiler, A-M. Elbe, & A. Hatzigeorgiadis (Eds.), *Sport and exercise psychology research: From theory to practice* (pp. 251–268). London: Elsevier.

Stambulova, N., Alfermann, D., Statler, T., & Côté, J. (2009). ISSP Position Stand: Career development and transitions of athletes. *International Journal of Sport & Exercise Psychology, 7*, 395–412.

Stambulova, N., Engström, C., Franck, A., Linnér, L., & Lindahl, K. (2015). Searching for an optimal balance: Dual career experiences of Swedish adolescent athletes. *Psychology of Sport and Exercise, 21*, 4–14.

Stambulova, N. & Ryba T. V. (Eds.) (2013a). *Athletes' careers across cultures*. New York, NY: Routledge.

Stambulova, N. & Ryba T. V. (2013b). Setting the bar: Towards cultural praxis of athletes' careers. In N. Stambulova & T. V. Ryba (Eds.), *Athletes' careers across cultures* (pp. 235–254). New York, NY: Routledge.

Stambulova, N. & Ryba, T. (2014). A critical review of career research and assistance through the cultural lens: Towards cultural praxis of athletes' careers. *International Review of Sport and Exercise Psychology, 7*, 1–17.

Stambulova, N. & Wylleman, P. (2014). Athletes' career development and transitions. In A. Papaioannou & D. Hackfort (Eds.), *Routledge companion to sport and exercise psychology* (pp. 605–621). London/New York: Routledge.

Stambulova, N. & Wylleman, P. (Eds.) (2015). Dual career development and transitions. [Special Issue]. *Psychology of Sport and Exercise, 21*, 1–139.

Storm, L. K., Henriksen, K., Larsen, C. H., & Christensen, M. K. (2014). Influential relationships as contexts of learning and becoming elite: Athletes' retrospective interpretations. *International Journal of Sport Science and Coaching, 9*(6), 1341–1356.

Taylor, J. & Ogilvie, B. C. (1994). A conceptual model of adaptation to retirement among athletes. *Journal of Applied Sport Psychology, 6*, 1–20.

Tekavc, J., Wylleman, P., & Cecić Erpič, S. (2015). Perceptions of dual career development among elite swimmers and basketball players. *Psychology of Sport and Exercise, 21*, 27–41.

Wylleman, P., Alfermann, D., & Lavallee, D. (2004). Career transitions in sport: European perspectives. *Psychology of Sport and Exercise, 5*, 7–20.

Wylleman, P. & Lavallee, D. (2004). A developmental perspective on transitions faced by athletes. In M. Weiss (Ed.), *Developmental sport and exercise psychology: A lifespan perspective* (pp. 507–527). Morgantown, WV: Fitness Information Technology.

Wylleman, P., Reints, A., & De Knop, P. (2013). A developmental and holistic perspective on athletic career development. In P. Sotiaradou & V. De Bosscher (Eds.), *Managing high performance sport* (pp. 159–182). New York, NY: Routledge.

Wylleman, P., Reints, A., & Van Aken, S. (2012). Athletes' perceptions of multilevel changes related to competing at the 2008 Beijing Olympic Games. *Psychology of Sport and Exercise, 13*, 687–692.

Yardley, L. & Bishop, F. (2008). Mixing qualitative and quantitative methods: A pragmatic approach. In C. Willig & W. Stainton-Rogers (Eds.), *The Sage handbook of qualitative research in psychology* (pp. 352–369). London: Sage.

36

QUALITATIVE RESEARCH IN SEARCH OF 'TRUTH' AND AGENCY

Challenges and opportunities for qualitative research

Cora Burnett

In the field of the sociology of sport and sport (for) development, qualitative research is positioned mainly in the realm of applied research, where thick descriptions and contextual insights underpin exploratory paradigms. Innovative research utilises grounded theoretical approaches and phenomenological modes of inquiry to contribute to a growing body of knowledge in the field. Much of this knowledge is being produced through programme evaluations, dominated by donor-directed research questions and new-Colonial understandings of 'development' (Darnell, 2012). Kay (2012) questions the relevance of such research for local populations earmarked for positive social transformation. She particularly questions the absence of local voices.

In a thought-provoking publication, Coalter (2014) critiqued inadequate and biased research evidence, yet realising that on Gramsci's terms, the 'pessimism of the intellect' needs to be counteracted by the 'optimism of the will' in bringing about a more just and equitable society. These metaphors pitch the scientific scrutiny of finding evidence or 'truths' against the socially constructed or self-professed 'truths' of multiple stakeholders within community settings.

Multiple perspectives represent many 'truths' that are only revealed through a more holistic understanding of the context where experiences are observed and interpreted (Johnston, Harwood and Minniti, 2013). Although contexts are unique, studying them should generate key understandings of similar cases as to be able to forecast cause and effect within comparable settings (Bearman and Dawson, 2013). Qualitative research methods are associated with finding ways of understanding of such settings where research participants construct their understanding of social reality (Crabbe, 2000).

Whose voices are heard?

Ethnography represents explicit phenomenological and interpretivist perspectives of thick descriptions and reflexivity (see Chapter 5). This is evidenced in Monaghan's (2014) study of bodybuilding in search of understanding a 'largely unexplored life-world rather than change the world' (p. 101). It provides unique insights into the particular configurations of masculinity, but does not build a case for potentially marginalised voices, representative of a particular subculture. Such comprehensive descriptions and narratives substantiate emerging and established discourses. Research would select and report the meaningful units derived from reported themes which link to different dimensions of main discourses within, and across disciplinary paradigms (Post and Wrisberg, 2012). The central 'voice', representative of a subculture, is thus understood in the context of the discourse that bears academic validity and value. In the end, the discourse (academic voice) provides a lens which, to a large extent, dictates the selection of narratives and storyline in aid of theory-building.

Simonds and Christopher (2013) demonstrate how theoretical approaches (e.g. social learning theory and social support theory) articulate with thick descriptions (produced by storytelling and non-directive qualitative approaches), to advance knowledge in a particular scientific field. Such research supports theory expansion and allow for reflection, which is inherent in theoretical adaptation and development (see also Chapter 30).

A main challenge for qualitative researchers is to mediate the complexity of social reality expressed in multi-vocality and diverse meaning constructions. Ongunniyi (2015), who researched the process of engendered socialisation of female footballers, captured the 'voices' of players layered with the reflections of family members, coaches and team members. The 'case' (female footballer) describes a social reality within and outside (her) sport participation that not only positions her as player, but also contextualises the 'play' within the greater complexity of a social world. *Stories from the Field* (Burnett, 2012), similarly captures the lifeworlds of players, coaches and/or sport administrators in different African settings as their stories are constructed by multiple actors. The understanding lies in the different 'voices' and relationships, as much as it is influenced by the real-life settings of post-genocide Rwanda, the compound poverty of Zambia or violence-ridden communities of the Cape Flats (Western Cape, South Africa). These 'thick' descriptions with central 'voices' provide insights into the lives of individuals and collectives through intercase comparisons (e.g. coaches as volunteers in contexts of poverty).

No single method or approach can capture all the nuances of diverse 'voices' generated by narratives that could contribute to new ways of knowing within different study fields (Krane, Andersen and Strean, 1997). In a recent study among the Commonwealth Games Associations at the 2014 Commonwealth Games in Glasgow, a sequential qualitative design allowed interviews to generate themes, which could be traced during follow-up focus group sessions for regional input and consensus. In this sense, single 'voices' from country members could be clustered to represent shared realities and perspectives from smaller nations versus first-world power houses, where social realities and needs inform a shared agenda (Burnett and Hollander, 2014).

Such standpoint configurations require consensus among research participants to produce meaningful units for analysis and explanation (Knight and Holt, 2014). A challenge for the researcher is to engage research participants in the participatory process whereby the latter reflect and make sense of their own personal and social worlds. Discourse analysis is not the only level of sense-making, it is also the sense-making (or interpretation) of the research participants that should be recognised as meaningful. The researcher thus interprets semantic units and the reflected meanings of how 'truths' (Indigenous knowledge) are constructed and understood.

The future for 'truth' and agency

The centrality of the researcher's ideological stance and 'voice' constitutes the power of agency of qualitative research. Future debates may increasingly address the ethical obligation of the researcher towards agency, especially those working in the human-justice framework (Kellet, 2009). For researchers in community-development work, the quest for advocacy and social change became omnipresent: taking sides with civic society, especially where some sectors are exploited or marginalised, as in the case of a relatively vulnerable NGO sector; or volunteer administrators and their undervalued contributions to the sport fraternity.

As qualitative research is a tool for deconstructing and explaining the complexity of intersecting social worlds, the researcher may selectively mediate content and manipulate understandings in support of their own stand point (Pawson, Greenhalgh, Havey and Walshe, 2005). Such positionality finds expression in what Mertens (2003) describes as the transformative-emancipatory framework, where the issues of political significance are interpreted as actionable constructs on the agenda of striving for social justice.

Participatory Action Research (PAR) (see also Chapters 8, 33 and 34) places the 'voices' of research participants as affected communities central to the research process (Levermore, 2011). In this way, the research process becomes an empowering experience for researcher and research participants who engage in reciprocal agency, where reflection and dialogue represent a transformative stance. Such an approach allows for community involvement and participant empowerment through a dialectic process.

The 'truths' of qualitative research in the first instance lie in the academic scrutiny and scientific rigour of the research process and the integrity of the researcher. The truthfulness, on the other hand, is endorsed by the meaningful 'voices' that matter where agency is revealed in the activism of the researcher and the mediated vocality of the research community.

References

Bearman, M. and Dawson, P. (2013). Qualitative synthesis and systematic review in health profession education. *Medical Education*, 47: 252–260.

Burnett, C. (2012). *Stories from the Field: GIZ/YDF Footprint in Africa*. Pretoria, South Africa: Van Schaik.

Burnett, C. and Hollander, W.J. (2014). *CGF-CGA Development Programme Research Preliminary Report*. Johannesburg: University of Johannesburg.

Coalter, F. (2014). *Sport for Development. What Game are we playing?* London: Routledge.

Crabbe, T. (2000). A sporting chance? Using sport to tackle drug use and crime. *Drug Education, Prevention and Policy*, 7(4): 381–391.

Darnell, S. (2012). *Sport for Development and Peace: A Critical Sociology*, London: Bloomsbury Academic.

Johnston, J., Harwood, C., and Minniti, A.M. (2013). Positive youth development in swimming: Clarification and consensus of key psychosocial assets. *Journal of Applied Sport Psychology*, 25(4): 392–411.

Kay, T. (2012). Accounting for legacy: Monitoring and evaluation in sport and development relationships. *Sport in Society: Cultures, Commerce, Media, Politics*, 15(6): 888–904.

Kellett, P. (2009). Advocacy in anthropology: Active engagement or passive scholarship? *Durham Anthropology Journal*, 16: 22–31.

Knight, C.J. and Holt, N.L. (2014). Parenting in youth tennis: Understanding and enhancing children's experiences. *Psychology of Sport & Exercise*, 15(2): 155–164.

Krane, V., Andersen, M.B., and Strean, W.B. (1997). Issues of qualitative research methods and presentation. *Journal of Sport Psychology*, 19: 213–218.

Levermore, R. (2011). Evaluating sport-for-development: Approaches and critical issues. *Progress in Development Studies*, 4: 339–353.

Mertens, D.M. (2003). Mixed methods and the politics of human research: The transformative-emancipatory perspective. In A. Tashakkori and C. Teddlie (Eds.), *Handbook of Mixed Methods in Social & Behavioural Research* (pp. 135–164). Thousand Oaks, CA: Sage.

Monaghan, L.E. (2014). Bodybuilding, drugs and risk: Reflections on an ethnographic study. In A. Smith and I. Waddington (Eds.), *Doing Real World Research in Sports Studies* (pp. 93–106). Abingdon: Routledge.

Ogunniyi, C. (2015). The effects of sport participation on gender relations: Case studies of female foot-ballers in Johannesburg and Cape Town, South Africa. *South African Review of Sociology*, 46(1): 25–46.

Pawson, R., Greenhalgh, R., Harvey, G., and Walshe, K. (2005). Realist review: A new method of systematic review designed for complex policy interventions. *Journal Health Serv Res Policy*, 10 (Supplement 1): 21–34.

Post, P.G. and Wrisberg, C.A. (2012). A phenomenological investigation of gymnasts' lived experience of imagery. *The Sport Psychologist*, 26: 98–121.

Simonds, V.W. and Christopher, S. (2013). Adapting western research methods to indigenous ways of knowing. *American Journal of Public Health*, 103(12): 2185–2191.

37

CHALLENGES AND OPPORTUNITIES FOR QUALITATIVE RESEARCH

Future directions

Michael D. Giardina

I have been tasked within this chapter to write on/about the "challenges and opportunities for qualitative research" as related to the broader project of sport, exercise, and physical culture. I surmise that I have been invited to contribute to this chapter for one if not all of the following reasons: 1) I have spent much of my academic career squarely in the midst of debates concerning qualitative inquiry and its practical and political location within the academy at large (see, e.g., Denzin & Giardina, 2015); 2) I have recently written a series of articles seeking to unsettle the ontological and epistemological moorings of our field, especially in relationship to the emerging "physical cultural studies" area (see, e.g., Giardina & Newman, 2011a, 2011b; Newman, Giardina, & McLeod, 2016); and 3) I currently serve as Editor of the *Sociology of Sport Journal* (the flagship journal of the North American Society for the Sociology of Sport) and have recently written an editorial on the state of the field that speaks to some of the questions on offer in this volume (Giardina, 2015).

In my work on qualitative inquiry (see, e.g., Giardina & Laurendeau, 2013; Denzin & Giardina, 2015), I have consistently made the case that we must take seriously questions of *evidence, knowledge,* and *research practice(s)* that we currently face as a community (and to this list I add *ontology* in this chapter). Engaging in such conversations, I have long contended – rather than blithely accepting prescribed, proscribed, and prohibitive ways of conducting research – results in a greater degree of nuance, depth, and reflection about our work than would otherwise be had.

Moreover, I have argued (see Giardina & Newman, 2014) that these above questions turn on the politics of research, of being acutely aware of how and to what extent: (1) the cultural and political priorities of the neoliberal corporate university impact, direct, and/or confound the conduct of research; (2) politics situate methodologies; (3) the research act is impinged on by such particularities as Institutional Review Boards (IRBs), national funding councils like the National Science Foundation (NSF), or National Institutes of Health (NIH), scholarly journals, and the promotion and tenure process; and (4) how and where we as academics fit within this new paradigm (Giardina & Newman, 2014, p. 700).

What all of the above speaks to, I would suggest, is that higher education – especially for those scholars in the humanities and social sciences doing critical, feminist, post-structural, postmodern, and posthuman research – faces a crossroads, one in which: 1) the act of research is an inherently political act; 2) that act is governed by a particular free-market politics of research in the corporate university; 3) (post)positivism still dominates this conversation; and 4) non-foundational approaches to research are often marginalized, or forced to sit alongside foundationalist perspectives in the problematic "mixed-methods" space (see also Chapter 29). As one consequence of this trend, note Michael Silk, Anthony Bush, and David Andrews:

> the training that most doctoral students receive, and in particular the orientation provided in most research design courses, results in the vast majority of students gaining an implicit and explicit understanding of, and comfort with, *foundational* (see Smith & Hodkinson, 2005; Amis & Silk, 2008) beliefs of how to "do" *rigorous* research.
>
> *(Silk, Bush, & Andrews, 2010, p. 111; emphases in original)*

Rather than reproduce arguments against this trend (see Giardina & Newman, 2014, for more on this), I want to use my space in this chapter to consider an alternative way – or direction – of thinking our way forward when it comes to (post)qualitative research: *perhaps we should turn way from "methodology" altogether.*

From methodology to onto-epistemology[1]

What does it mean to turn away from "methodology" (or, in the language of Lather & St. Pierre [2013], to "refuse" humanist qualitative research)? Such a question may seem odd coming in the context of a methods handbook, but indulge me for a moment. Consider what currently passes for method or methodology in the social sciences: surveys, interviews, focus groups, participant-observation, discourse analysis, textual analysis, and so forth. Many qualitative methods handbooks and textbooks go into great detail about how to collect, analyze, and interpret such data (Part II of the book you are reading, in fact, is titled "Collecting qualitative data," and includes excellent chapters on how to conduct interviews, observation, and the like). Moreover, it is the primary means by which graduate students (in the United States, at least, but it is fair to say elsewhere, too) are initially trained in thinking about research methods – as a set of tools to be taken out of the methods toolbox and applied to a particular problem or research question (and in some cases, it is the *only* way they are trained). This much I think we can agree on, and I would submit that having an understanding of the practical or technical operation of such methods is an important aspect of graduate education – an important aspect of developing an understanding of research design and the critical faculties to ask tough questions about a given phenomenon, and the best way to go about conducting one's research into it.

At the same time, however, I find comfort in knowing I am not alone in questioning if there is not a better way to proceed (both pedagogically and in research practice), for I find myself siding with critical education scholar Elizabeth St. Pierre in reacting with despair,

> when doctoral students' response to questions about their dissertation research is something like, "I'm doing a case study" or "I'm doing an autoethnography" or "I'm doing an interview study." In other words, they respond with a "research design." When I ask them what theories they're thinking with in their studies, they seldom respond coherently. It appears they've studied some kind of stripped down methodology (or more accurately, they've learned some methods) but not epistemology or ontology.
>
> *(St. Pierre, 2015, p. 76)*

My despair is not restricted solely to doctoral students, of course. As editor of a major journal in the field, it is increasingly the rule rather than the exception to it that I see a manuscript submitted for publication that identifies itself in a similar fashion, i.e., "This interview study does this . . . ," "This paper is an ethnography that seeks to . . . ," "This paper uses critical discourse analysis to explore . . . ," and so on. This is not to say that such research is "wrong" or "improper," of course. Indeed, many such studies add a critical awareness to a given topic. However, I would contend that we as a field(s) need to push beyond proscriptive or "methods-driven" approaches (i.e. methodolatry) to research (or, at the very least, *to engage in conversations about doing so*), for there are (at least) two concerns at play: the reduction of research to "methods"; and grappling with questions of epistemology and ontology.

Writing in her critical new book *Reconceptualizing Qualitative Research*, Mirka Koro-Ljungberg posits the idea of "methodologies without methodology," which:

> represents methodologies without strict boundaries or normative structures – methodologies that may begin anywhere, anytime, but by doing so can create a sense of uncertainty and loss (or mourning of stable, fixed, preconceptualized, or historical knowledge . . . They can begin anywhere, stay (at least temporarily) lost and uncertain, and still promote change in onto-epistemological practices.
>
> *(Koro-Ljungberg, 2015, p. 1)*

Koro-Ljungberg's argument is grounded squarely in debates over postqualitative research – especially those in relationship to the new empiricisms/new materialisms borne of DeleuzoGuattarian theory. Here she is suggesting not that we should evacuate all methodologies per se from the act of research; rather, she is offering that we might do well to get outside or beyond the idea that an approach to understanding a given topic (e.g., race, class, gender, sexuality, the body, globalization, etc.) should be "formalized, precise, and methods-driven" (St. Pierre, 2015, p. 75). Drawing especially from Deleuze and Guattari, St. Pierre explains this notion further:

> the very idea of method [*ed: within humanist qualitative research*] forces one into a prescribed order of thought and practices that prohibits the experimental nature of transcendental empiricism. Method proscribes and prohibits. It controls and disciplines. Further, method always comes too late, is immediately out-of-date and so inadequate to the task at hand. But method not only can't keep up with events, more seriously, it prevents them from coming into existence. One might say that "method," as we think of it in the methodological individualism of conventional humanist qualitative methodology with its methods of data collection and methods of data analysis, *cannot be thought or done in new empirical inquiry.* [. . .] In fact, the new empiricist might well argue that attempting to follow a given research method will likely foreclose possibilities for the "new." The new empiricist researcher, then, is on her own, inventing inquiry in the doing. Hence, we have methods-driven research that mostly repeats what is recognizable, *what is already known.*
>
> *(St. Pierre, 2015, pp. 79, 81; second emphasis mine)*[2]

It is all well and good to speak of such things in the abstract. And, in truth, more space is required than available here to engage with Deleuze and Guattari's oftentimes-impenetrable work (as well as Barad [2007] and others). But, to be brief, what might a shift from methodology to onto-epistemology look like in practice?

Take the case of interviewing, a classic social scientific method for collecting data (or, as I would prefer to term it, empirical material, but that is for another discussion). Lisa Mazzei (2013) offers that the interview is and has been fundamentally situated within humanist theories of the subject, which "typically equate words spoken by participants in interviews and then transcribed into words in interview transcripts as data . . . in which that voice is produced by a unique, essentialist subject" (p. 732). She counters this view by explaining how, within a post-humanist stance

> interview data, the voices of participants, cannot be thought as emanating from an essentialist subject nor can they be separated from the enactment in which they are produced, an enactment of researcher-data-participants-theory-analysis – what I call here a *Voice without Organs* (VwO).
>
> *(Mazzei, 2013, p. 732)*

As Mazzei argues, understanding the interview in such a differentiated way "requires different conceptions of human agency" (p. 733); from a humanist perspective, "agency is an innate characteristic of the essentialist, intentional free subject" (p. 733); from the post-structural perspective, agency "seems to lie in the subject's ability to decode and record its identity within discursive formations and cultural practices" (p. 733) – a politics of language and representation at work.

But from the posthumanist perspective, "agency is distributed in a way that avoids hanging on to the vestiges of a knowing humanist subject that lingers in some post-structural analysis . . . [such that] intentionality is not attributable to humans" (p. 733) but rather is, after Karen Barad (2007), "understood as attributable to a complex network of human and nonhuman agents, including historically specific sets of material conditions that exceed the traditional notion of the individual" (p. 23; also cited in Mazzei, 2013, p. 734). The implication of thinking ontologically about the interview, then, as St. Pierre (2015) reminds us, is that, "The onto-epistemological formation that celebrates the speech of the humanist human and assigns it pre-eminent value and practice application as scientific discourse is not the onto-epistemological formation of post-qualitative inquiry" (p. 80). For this reason, she continues,

> we should think, and should always have thought, twice before proposing research projects with, for example, an awkward combination of an interview study and a Foucaultian genealogy or a rhizo-analysis of interview data, projects that indicate *onto-logical confusion*.
>
> *(St. Pierre, 2015, p. 80; emphasis mine)*

How "data" is viewed in this context, then, becomes equally important. Koro-Ljungberg (2013) writes that "the 'usual way' of treating such data in the context of qualitative research is as passive objects, waiting to be coded or granted shape and significance through the interpretive work of researchers" (p. 219).[3] This we see both in (post)positivism, as well as post-structural and postmodern approaches that have not shed the lingering remnants of humanist ontology underpinning qualitative inquiry. Against this view, Angelo Benozzo, Huw Bell, and Koro-Ljungberg (2013) suggest that "data" (or, what we have come to *consider* as data) is best conceptualized *not* as something made into being through theory, to then be treated as data, but rather it might best be thought of as "a wave, a flow, as liquid; ever-changing, inconstant, unreliable, noninterpretable; as a dark forest. Data is already there and here, only partially accessible" (p. 309). It is something that "may not need to be collected but may be lived, sensed, and done"

(p. 309). To wit, they implore us to think of data not for "what it produces" or how it is "called into being" but rather for "how it moves and for how it can be lived and sensed by researchers, and how data makes us as people and researchers" (p. 309). On making this ontological turn, then, "something called data" cannot be separate from me, "out there" for "me to 'collect,'" the acknowledgment of which results in "the entire structure of humanist qualitative inquiry fall[ing] apart – its methods, its processes, its research designs, and of, course, its ground, data" (St. Pierre, 2013, p. 224).

In other words, by claiming to call data into being through the process of naming as such, too often do "qualitative researchers sometimes uncritically treat the illusion of the Real data as the Real data" (Koro-Ljungberg, 2013, p. 274). Moreover, "By assigning meanings to objects and signifiers, data is produced, consumed, admired, collected, validated, interpreted, constructed, and destroyed, *but data is not necessarily ontologically related to the Real*" (Koro-Ljungberg, 2013, p. 274; emphases mine). It is this incongruence that we too often see avowed "qualitative researchers," who "continue to use concepts and practices like bias, objectivity, subjectivity statements, triangulation, audit trails, and interrater reliability that signal they are bound to logical positivism/empiricism, objectivism, and realism" (St. Pierre, 2013, p. 2), and who reject outright the performative (see also Chapter 23), the poetic, and/or the moving, embodied, sensual body (see also Chapters 2 and 26) as lacking "evidence" (or, even, an evidentiary narrative). It is in this sense that Norman K. Denzin (2013) argues we should write "data" out of existence, to realize a space in which "neither the material nor the discursive are privileged" (p. 274), for it is more complex than either/or, this or that, but more like both/and/same.[4]

By way of a conclusion

So what do the above discussions mean for the research act, for the future of qualitative research? First, when inquiry is reduced to method and research design – which I am fearful is happening all too often, whether in graduate school courses or in the academy writ large – we "know" the outcome of our (research) acts, such that we are repeating the always already done. As such, conventional methods move beyond the proscriptive to the *prohibitive*, delimiting the boundaries of a study and its results before it even takes place. Second, we should also not, clearly, just make the quick turn to "ontology" and ask, for example, "How can we apply DeleuzoGuattarian concepts to our study?" (or, more specifically perhaps, "How can we use 'entanglement', or 'assemblage', or 'rhizomatics' in our research?"). This is exactly what St. Pierre (and others) caution us about: i.e., just "dropping in" a concept such as "assemblage" without: (1) understanding the ontology in which it is based; and (2) ignoring that it is connected to numerous other specific ideas in DeleuzoGuattarian thought. And third, we should engage in serious conversations over the epistemological and the ontological foundations of our researcher (whether foundational or antifoundational, positivist or constructivist, etc.) (see also Chapters 1 and 29). Doing so can only strengthen our critical faculties and produce more rigorous, nuanced, and emergent (post)qualitative research.

Notes

1 I borrow the term "onto-epistemology" from Karen Barad (2007), who defines it as "the study of the intertwined practices of knowing and being", thus conjoining "ontology" and "epistemology" to mark their "inseparability" (p. 409).
2 Lather and St. Pierre (2013) describe this form of inquiry thus: "This inquiry cannot be tidily described in textbooks or handbooks. There is no methodological instrumentality to be unproblematically learned. In this methodology-to-come, we begin to do it differently wherever we are in our projects" (p. 635).

3 This paragraph, and the one that follows, draws from and updates arguments in Giardina and Laurendeau (2013), especially pp. 240–242.
4 See, for example, the arguments in Sarah Ahmed's (2006) excellent book, *Queer Phenomenology*.

References

Ahmed, S. (2006). *Queer phenomenology: Orientations, objects, others*. Durham, NC: Duke University Press.

Amis, J. M. & Silk, M. L. (2008). The philosophy and politics of inquiry in qualitative organizational research. *Organizational Research Methods, 11*, 456–480.

Barad, K. (2007). *Meeting the universe halfway: Quantum physics and the entanglement of matter and meaning*. Durham, NC: Duke University Press.

Benozzo, A., Bell, H., & Koro-Ljungberg, M. (2013). Moving between nuisance, secrets, and splinters as data. *Cultural Studies <=> Critical Methodologies, 13*(4), 309–315.

Denzin, N. K. (2013). The death of data? *Cultural Studies <=> Critical Methodologies, 13*(4), 353–356.

Denzin, N. K. & Giardina, M. D. (Eds.) (2015). *Qualitative inquiry – past, present, and future: A critical reader*. Walnut Creek, CA: Left Coast Press.

Giardina, M. D. (2015). Editorial. *Sociology of Sport Journal, 32*(1), 1–3.

Giardina, M. D. & Laurendeau, J. (2013). Truth untold? Evidence, knowledge, and research practice(s). *Sociology of Sport Journal, 30*(3), 237–255.

Giardina, M. D. & Newman, J. I. (2011a). Physical cultural studies and embodied research acts. In N. K. Denzin & Y. S. Lincoln (Eds.), *The Sage handbook of qualitative research* (4th ed., pp. 523–534). Thousand Oaks, CA: Sage.

Giardina, M. D. & Newman, J. I. (2011b). What is this "physical" in physical cultural studies? *Sociology of Sport Journal, 28*(1), 36–63.

Giardina, M. D. & Newman, J. I. (2014). The politics of research. In P. Leavy (Ed.), *The Oxford handbook of qualitative research* (pp. 699–723). New York: Oxford University Press.

Koro-Ljungberg, M. (2015). *Reconceptualizing qualitative research: Methodologies without methodology*. Thousand Oaks, CA: Sage.

Koro-Ljungberg, M. (2013). "Data" as vital illusion. *Cultural Studies <=> Critical Methodologies, 13*(4), 274–278.

Lather, P. & St. Pierre, E. A. (2013). Post-qualitative research. *International Journal of Qualitative Studies in Education, 46*(6), 629–633.

Mazzei, L. A. (2013). A voice without organs: Interviewing in posthumanist research. *International Journal of Qualitative Studies in Education, 26*(6), 732–740.

Newman, J. I., Giardina, M. D., & McLeod, C. (2016). Embodiment and reflexive body politics. In D. L. Andrews, M. Silk, & H. Thorpe (Eds.), *The Routledge handbook of physical cultural studies*. London: Routledge.

Silk, M. L., Bush, A., & Andrews, D. L. (2010). Contingent intellectual amateurism, or, the problem with evidence-based research. *Journal of Sport & Social Issues, 34*, 105–128.

Smith, J. K. & Hodkinson, P. (2005). Relativism, criteria, and politics. In N. K. Denzin & Y. S. Lincoln (Eds.), *The Sage handbook of qualitative research* (3rd ed., pp. 915–932). Thousand Oaks, CA: Sage.

St. Pierre, E. A. (2015). Practices for the "new" in the new empiricisms, the new materialisms, and post qualitative inquiry. In N. K. Denzin & M. D. Giardina (Eds.), *Qualitative inquiry and the politics of research* (pp. 75–96). Walnut Creek, CA: Left Coast Press.

St. Pierre, E. A. (2013). The appearance of data. *Cultural Studies <=> Critical Methodologies, 13*(4), 223–227.

EMBRACING THE MESSINESS OF QUALITATIVE RESEARCH

Challenges and opportunities for qualitative researchers in sport and exercise

Vikki Krane

In the past few decades we have seen a steady increase in the use of qualitative research in sport and exercise. With this has come a rise in innovative approaches to our research. Many of us believe that this is a healthy trend for our fields. Diversity in research approaches, methodologies, and methods can only enhance our knowledge base and draw more diverse scholars in to our field. Perhaps paradoxically, as we embrace more diverse epistemologies, methodologies, and methods, we also delve further into Pandora's box, unleashing an array of surreptitious challenges. As Denzin and Lincoln (2005) described, we are in a qualitative moment they termed *fractured future* (2005–present). And a fractured future is a challenging space to inhabit. However, with every challenge comes an opportunity to broaden our perspectives and open the door to creative avenues in our quest to expand the knowledge base. Therefore, in this chapter, I will discuss some challenges and corresponding future opportunities facing qualitative sport researchers, focusing particularly on the analysis and writing phases of our work.

Messy data

Much of what we see in the published literature presents a summary of the predominant themes that emerged from interview (see Chapter 9) and/or observational data (see Chapter 10). When we read finished products of qualitative research, often we are presented with a neat story or a concise series of quotes supporting themes identified by the researcher. The report depicts consistent findings that paint a clear picture of the experiences of the people being observed and/or interviewed. This is what is expected: researchers analyze transcripts and field notes, identify emergent themes, and then communicate the major findings to the readers. However, what this process often glosses over is its messiness in favor of presenting a uniform viewpoint. Such an approach to presenting findings washes away the complexity and contradictions that may appear in our data. Life is messy and so too are our data.

Perhaps we could embrace this messiness and build it into our analysis. This messiness occurs at several junctions in the research process. One of these places lies in the inherent incompleteness of our data. Often, researchers are challenged in their interpretation of the data to make sense of contradictions or missing pieces to the stories we hear. All researchers struggle with such occurrences, yet rarely do the readers learn of these conundrums. Sometimes such things occur in what initially seem to be tangents during interviews (and hence they receive minimal follow-up at the time), yet upon further scrutiny they turn out to be enlightening additions to our data. In an ideal setting, researchers are able to return to the participants and ask for clarification or elaboration. Yet realistically, by the time this level of analysis occurs, we may be far removed from the data collection and no longer have contact with participants.

One way to approach our messy data is to consider what Sermijn, Devieger, and Loots (2008) described as the *monstrous* nature of data. As they explained, monstrous stories "do not fit in a traditional story structure"; have "nonlinearly organized time; e.g., story elements that are difficult to date or that conflict with the separation among past–present–future"; have a "lack of clear, linear cause and effect relationships"; and refer to a "space that is constantly in motion and that lacks a fixed central point" (p. 635). Accepting the monstrousness of data includes recognizing that stories have an inherent vagueness. The metaphor of data as a rhizome also draws attention to this messiness (Masny, 2013; Sermijn *et al.*, 2008). Drawing from the seminal work of Deluze and Guattari (1987), a rhizome is described as a dynamic network of roots emanating from bulbs and tubers that split, branch out, spread unpredictably in all directions, and that does not have a single entryway (Sermijn *et al.*, 2008). Applied to stories, there are no beginning and end; rather, there are ruptures and discontinuities. To employ rhizoanalysis (Masny, 2013) is to embrace this tension in our data. In fact, as Masny suggests, this discomfort and uncertainty in data, and our writing about the data, can lead to greater creativity, new questions, and innovative and novel interpretations. Ruptures, discontinuities, or inconsistencies within a story can be considered as new connections. Beginning a story from different entryways can lead to different conclusions, highlighting varied perspectives and new understandings.

Writing messy data

We can embrace the potentially monstrous and rhizomatic nature of data through diverse writing styles. Often, writing is considered the step *after* completion of the data analysis. We set out to code data consistent with our epistemological and methodological frameworks, meticulously scrutinizing every phrase. This process often follows common textbook descriptions of how to conduct data analysis. Yet the process is never as straightforward and as simplistic as texts make it sound. Richardson and St. Pierre (2005) encourage us to think of writing as analysis: the process of turning our interpretive ideas and connections among data categories into words on a page surreptitiously reengages analysis. Writing a results section infuses another layer of analysis often not acknowledged. "Unexpected things always happen, newly constructed roads turn up and research paths which could not be foreseen surface" (Tanggaard, 2013, p. 410). What seemed to be a logical train of thought, transforms into disjuncted ideas and incomplete quotations attempting to support them. Data shift among coding categories, new themes emerge, and sometimes analytic structures are scrapped in favor of new interpretations or reorganizations. It is not unusual that at this point in the research process the most creative and insightful understandings emerge. This is both the beauty and frustration of qualitative research. Just when we think we have completed our analysis, we begin to question the very essence of it. At the same time, this rebirth of ideas can result in a more compelling analysis.

Perhaps our challenge is acknowledging the evolving nature of qualitative analysis and writing it into our processes. Too often it is swept under the rug and disregarded as an intentional process when describing our analytical procedure. Whereas previously scripted and prescribed analysis strategies (i.e., those we learn about in textbooks) can be important steps, they are not finite and rarely should they be endpoints in interpretive processes. While the degree to which researchers are willing to embrace the messiness of data may vary, it seems germane to encourage continuous engagement with data, and to approach the writing process as the next step in data analysis. Constant reassessment of *final* categorizations will likely deepen theoretical understandings and produce stronger final products.

Employing a narrative approach in our analysis and writing can be one way to address these concerns (see also Chapters 4 and 20). A narrative approach focuses on storytelling, with an emphasis on the stories as told by the participants (Sparkes & Smith, 2014). While stories ideally include the what, how, why, where, and when of the story, they may also have gaps and inconsistencies which should also be revealed. What is important, from a narrative perspective, is to avoid fragmenting or overcoding data, and instead keep stories intact. As Sparkes and Smith (2014) explained, a benefit of this approach is that it can reveal "a great deal about the sociocultural fabric of lives, subjectivity, feelings, agency, and the multilayered human experience" (p. 131). Alternatively, presenting data as vignettes is another way to reveal the messy, rhizomatic nature of data (Masny, 2013). Incomplete, or fragments of, stories (i.e. vignettes) can be revealing and offer genuine insight into a slice of experience. Additionally, Sermijn *et al.* (2008) also offer that a variety of postmodern writing styles may serve this purpose, "such as writing from different 'I' voices, writing in columns, writing multiple storylines, introducing multiple entrances and exits, and so on" (p. 646).

Advances into the future

My call here is to reconsider how we present our monstrous, messy, rhizomatic data. I can remember the first time I read Richardson's words where she described "[Yawning her] way through numerous supposedly exemplary qualitative studies . . . only to find the text boring" (Richardson & St. Pierre, 2005, p. 959). I was stunned: *how could qualitative research be boring?* Yet, at times it may be. Providing clean precise summaries of what we learn via observations and interviews conceals the complexity of human experiences. Telling readers what is important diminishes the potential for rousing empathy, compassion, or understanding from readers (Caulley, 2008). Being creative and developing unique manners to capture the emotion and power of our participants' words can allow us to embrace our messy data and present evocative final products. In this moment of fractured future, there is an emphasis on the narrative turn, featuring storytelling and producing complex and nonlinear texts (Denzin & Lincoln, 2005). Qualitative researchers are provided the opportunity and responsibility to represent someone's life experiences. This tall task is daunting. Yet in this qualitative moment we have more techniques and devices in our writing toolbox than ever before.

References

Caulley, D.N. (2008). Making qualitative research reports less boring: The techniques of writing creative nonfiction. *Qualitative Inquiry, 14*(3), 424–449.

Deleuze, G. & Guattari, F. (1987). *A thousand plateaus: Capitalism and schizofrenia.* Minneapolis, MN: University of Minnesota Press.

Denzin, N.K. & Lincoln, Y.S. (2005). Introduction: The discipline and practice of qualitative research. In N.K. Denzin & Y.S. Lincoln (Eds.), *The Sage handbook of qualitative research* (3rd ed., pp. 1–32). Thousand Oaks, CA: Sage.

Masny, D. (2013). Rhizoanalytic pathways in qualitative research. *Qualitative Inquiry, 19,* 339–348.

Richardson, L. & St. Pierre, E.A. (2005). Writing: A method of inquiry. In N.K. Denzin & Y.S. Lincoln (Eds.), *The Sage handbook of qualitative research* (3rd ed., pp. 959–978). Thousand Oaks, CA: Sage.

Sermijn, J., Devieger, P., & Loots, G. (2008). The narrative construction of the self: Selfhood as a rhizomatic story. *Qualitative Inquiry, 14*, 632–650.

Sparkes, A.C. & Smith, B. (2014). *Qualitative research methods in sport, exercise and health: From process to product.* London: Routledge.

Tanggaard, L. (2013). Troubling methods in qualitative inquiry and beyond. *Europe's Journal of Psychology, 9*, 408–418.

INDEX

Taylor & Francis eBooks

Helping you to choose the right eBooks for your Library

Add Routledge titles to your library's digital collection today. Taylor and Francis ebooks contains over 50,000 titles in the Humanities, Social Sciences, Behavioural Sciences, Built Environment and Law.

Choose from a range of subject packages or create your own!

Benefits for you

» Free MARC records
» COUNTER-compliant usage statistics
» Flexible purchase and pricing options
» All titles DRM-free.

Benefits for your user

» Off-site, anytime access via Athens or referring URL
» Print or copy pages or chapters
» Full content search
» Bookmark, highlight and annotate text
» Access to thousands of pages of quality research at the click of a button.

REQUEST YOUR FREE INSTITUTIONAL TRIAL TODAY

Free Trials Available
We offer free trials to qualifying academic, corporate and government customers.

eCollections – Choose from over 30 subject eCollections, including:

Archaeology	Language Learning
Architecture	Law
Asian Studies	Literature
Business & Management	Media & Communication
Classical Studies	Middle East Studies
Construction	Music
Creative & Media Arts	Philosophy
Criminology & Criminal Justice	Planning
Economics	Politics
Education	Psychology & Mental Health
Energy	Religion
Engineering	Security
English Language & Linguistics	Social Work
Environment & Sustainability	Sociology
Geography	Sport
Health Studies	Theatre & Performance
History	Tourism, Hospitality & Events

For more information, pricing enquiries or to order a free trial, please contact your local sales team: www.tandfebooks.com/page/sales